BROADCASTING IN AMERICA

BROADCASTING IN AMERICA

A Survey of
Television, Radio, and New Technologies
Fourth Edition

Sydney W. Head

with

Christopher H. Sterling

HOUGHTON MIFFLIN COMPANY BOSTON Dallas Geneva, Ill. Hopewell, N.J. Palo Alto London

Grateful acknowledgment is made to the following individuals and publishers for permission to reprint from their works:

From Daniel J. Boorstin, in *Symposium on the Cultural Role of Broadcasting*, Hoso-Bunka Foundation, Tokyo, 1978.

From *Reluctant Regulators: The FCC and the Broadcast Audience* by Barry Cole and Mal Oettinger, copyright © 1978 by Barry Cole and Mal Oettinger, with permission of the publisher, Addison-Wesley Publishing Co., Reading, MA 01867.

From *The Powers That Be*, by David Halberstam. Copyright © 1979 by David Halberstam. Reprinted by permission of Alfred A. Knopf, Inc.

From William S. Paley, *As It Happened: A Memoir* (1979).

From *The New York Times*, © 1972, 1973, 1975, 1977, 1978, 1979, 1980 by The New York Times Company. Reprinted by permission.

From *TV Guide* magazine, Radnor, PA 19088.

Printed in the U.S.A.
Library of Congress Catalog Card Number: 81-83274
ISBN: 0-395-28657-3

Cover photograph by David F. Hughes, *The Picture Cube*.

CONTENTS

Exhibits   x

Preface   xiii

Prologue
The World of Broadcasting   1

Chapter 1
National Contrasts   3

1.1 Broadcasting and National
    Character   3
1.2 Influence of Political Philosophy   4
1.3 Pluralism in Broadcasting   9
1.4 Legal Foundations   12
1.5 Access to Broadcasting   14
1.6 Economic Influences   17
1.7 Influence of Geography and
    History   21
1.8 Programs and Schedules   23
1.9 Broadcasting to Other Countries   26
1.10 Issue: "Free Flow" or "New
    Order"?   31
Summary   33

Part I
Management of Radio Energy   35

Chapter 2
Nature of Radio Energy   37

2.1 Electromagnetic Spectrum   37
2.2 Sound Waves   39
2.3 Radio Waves   41
2.4 Modulation   44
2.5 Wave Propagation   46

2.6 Antennas   48
2.7 Spectrum Management   52
Summary   54

Chapter 3
Broadcast Channels   57

3.1 Basic Concepts   57
3.2 Interference   58
3.3 AM Broadcasting   59
3.4 FM Broadcasting   62
3.5 Short-Wave (HF) Broadcasting   64
3.6 Photographic "Channels"   65
3.7 Electronic Picture Processing   66
3.8 TV Signal Requirements   69
3.9 TV Channel Specifications   71
3.10 TV Transmission and Reception   73
3.11 TV Technical Innovations   76
Summary   78

Chapter 4
Storage, Distribution, and
Delivery Systems   79

4.1 Basic Concepts   79
4.2 Sound Recording Technology   80
4.3 Picture Recording   81
4.4 Digital Signal Processing   82
4.5 Terrestrial Relays in Networking   87
4.6 Space Relays   88
4.7 Relay/Delivery Hybrids: Radio   91
4.8 Relay/Delivery Hybrids: Cable   92
Summary   96

Part II
Origin and Growth of
Broadcasting 97

Chapter 5
Preconditions: The Stage Is Set 99

5.1 Development of Mass Media
    Consumption 99
5.2 Wire Communication 101
5.3 Invention of Wireless 103
5.4 Technological Progress: 1896–1915 106
5.5 Business Developments 110
5.6 Development of Wireless Services 113
5.7 Experiments with Radiotelephony 116
5.8 Wireless and World War I (1914–
    1918) 117
Summary 120

Chapter 6
Emergence of Broadcasting:
1919–1927 121

6.1 The Broadcasting Concept 121
6.2 Government Monopoly: The Road
    Not Taken 122
6.3 The "First" Broadcast Station 125
6.4 Radio Broadcasting vs.
    Radiotelephony 129
6.5 National Networks Begin 133
6.6 Evolution of Radio Advertising 136
6.7 Government Regulation 138
Summary 141

Chapter 7
Radio After 1928 143

7.1 Radio in the Great Depression
    (1929–1937) 143
7.2 From World War II to the Present 147
7.3 The Fall and Rise of FM Radio 151
7.4 The Parsimony Principle 154

7.5 Radio Network Development 156
7.6 Radio News and Public Affairs 160
7.7 Broadcast Music 164
7.8 Radio's Response to TV
    Competition 169
7.9 Specialty Radio Formulas 172
7.10 Fate of Network Radio 175
Summary 176

Chapter 8
Development of Commercial
Television 179

8.1 Overview: The Contrast with Radio 179
8.2 Quest for High Resolution 181
8.3 TV Freeze: 1948–1952 187
8.4 Implementation of Post-Freeze
    Allotment Plan 188
8.5 TV Network Rivalries 192
8.6 Changeover from Live to Recorded
    Entertainment 201
8.7 Program Syndication 204
8.8 Ethical Crises 209
Summary 215

Chapter 9
Commercial Television
Programming 217

9.1 Scheduling Strategies 217
9.2 Prime-Time Network
    Entertainment 220
9.3 Non Prime-Time Network
    Entertainment 225
9.4 Television News 228
9.5 Public Affairs Programming 236
9.6 Sports Programming 239
9.7 The Electronic Church 240
9.8 Children's Programming 244
9.9 Appraising the TV Program Service 246
Summary 247

Part III
Noncommercial and Nonbroadcast Systems — 251

Chapter 10
The Noncommercial Alternative — 253

10.1 Why "Public" Broadcasting?	253
10.2 Rise of Educational Broadcasting	254
10.3 National Organization	259
10.4 Types of Public Stations	266
10.5 The Search for Funding	269
10.6 Programming	278
10.7 Children and Classrooms	286
10.8 Impact of Public Broadcasting	289
10.9 The Outlook	291
Summary	293

Chapter 11
Cable and Newer Technologies — 295

11.1 Evolution of Cable	295
11.2 Cable Economics	302
11.3 Interactive Cable	305
11.4 Satellite Interconnection	307
11.5 Pay Cable	315
11.6 Subscription Television (STV)	317
11.7 Home Video	322
Summary	323

Part IV
The Business of Broadcasting — 325

Chapter 12
Administrative and Financial Organization — 327

12.1 The Station	327
12.2 Networks and Affiliates	333
12.3 Network-Affiliate Relations	335
12.4 Regulation of Network/Affiliate Contracts	338
12.5 Program Economics	339
12.6 Financial Framework of Broadcasting	341
12.7 Employment in Broadcasting	343
Summary	348

Chapter 13
Broadcast Advertising — 351

13.1 Psychological Advantages	351
13.2 Flexibility of Coverage	352
13.3 Integration of Commercials in Programming	356
13.4 Time and Taste Standards	358
13.5 Deceptive Advertising	364
13.6 Advertising Rates	366
13.7 Selling Broadcast Advertising	371
13.8 Unethical Business Practices	374
Summary	376

Chapter 14
Audience Measurement and Testing — 377

14.1 Feedback in Broadcasting	377
14.2 The Ratings Business	378
14.3 Ratings Concepts	380
14.4 Collecting Set-Use Data	384
14.5 Sampling	386
14.6 Broadcast Audiences	390
14.7 Issues: Use and Abuse of Ratings	392
14.8 Nonrating Research	396
Summary	398

Part V
Social Control of Broadcasting   401

Chapter 15
Law of Broadcasting   403

15.1 National Communications Policy   403
15.2 Constitutional Context   405
15.3 Communications Act Basics   408
15.4 Licensing   413
15.5 Control over Programs   416
15.6 Communications Act Issues   419
15.7 Other Laws Affecting
        Broadcasting   421
Summary   425

Chapter 16
**Administration of the Law: FCC
at Work**   427

16.1 FCC Basics   427
16.2 License Application   432
16.3 Basic Licensee Qualifications   434
16.4 Applicant Program Plans   436
16.5 Operating Under License:
        Contingent Requirements   439
16.6 Appraisal of Licensee
        Performance   445
16.7 License Renewal   447
16.8 License Deletion   452
16.9 FCC Issues   455
16.10 Deregulation   459
Summary   461

Chapter 17
**Freedom and Fairness in
Broadcasting**   463

17.1 First Amendment Basics   463
17.2 Unprotected Speech   466

17.3 Uniqueness of Broadcast Speech   473
17.4 Regulated Fairness   474
17.5 Fairness and News   478
17.6 Fairness in Advertising   481
17.7 Antimonopoly Regulation   484
17.8 First Amendment Issues   486
Summary   490

Chapter 18
**Beyond the FCC: Nonregulatory
Influences**   493

18.1 Informal Government Controls   493
18.2 Direct Citizen Action   495
18.3 Consumer Standing to Challenge
        Renewals   499
18.4 Negotiated Settlements   503
18.5 Consumerism Issues   506
18.6 Industry Self-Regulation   507
18.7 Other Influences   510
Summary   512

Part VI
Effects of Broadcasting   513

Chapter 19
Inventory of Effects   515

19.1 Pervasiveness of Effects   515
19.2 Effects of Advertising   518
19.3 News and Pseudonews   521
19.4 Entertainment Programming   525
19.5 Effects of Violence   527
19.6 Effects on Political Life   531
19.7 Broadcasting and ''Performance of
        Leisure''   539
Summary   541

Chapter 20
Research on Effects   543

20.1 Uses of Research   543
20.2 Development of Behavioral
      Research Concepts   544
20.3 Communication Process   549
20.4 Methods of Studying Effects   552
20.5 Status of Effects Research   559
Summary   561

Epilogue
Future of Broadcasting   563

Chapter 21
Challenge and Change   565

21.1 Two Views of the Future   565
21.2 Technological Challenges   566
21.3 Challenge to Massification   568
21.4 Economic Challenges   571
21.5 Regulatory Challenges   573
21.6 Conclusion   577
Summary   578

Further Reading: A Selective Guide to
   the Literature of Broadcasting
   Christopher H. Sterling   581

Bibliography   603

Index   627

EXHIBITS

AND BOXED FEATURES

1.2.1	Lord Reith	6
1.2.2	Broadcasting House, London	7
1.3.2	Ownership of world broadcasting transmission facilities	9
1.6	U.S. share of world population and broadcasting facilities	18
1.9	The ten leading external broadcasters	26
2.1	How the electromagnetic spectrum is used	38
2.2.1	Wave motion concepts	40
2.2.2	Complex wave	42
2.3	Subdivisions of radio frequency spectrum	43
2.4	Modulation of carrier waves	45
2.5.1	Direct and ground wave propagation	47
2.5.2	Sky wave propagation	49
2.5.3	Frequency bands and their characteristics	50
2.6.1	AM radio antennas	51
2.6.2	TV antenna	52
2.7.1	Radio station licences by type of service	53
2.7.2	Broadcast station authorizations by type	54
3.3.1	Areas dependent on clear channel service	61
3.3.2	Classification of AM channels and stations	62
3.5.1	Short-wave (high-frequency) broadcast bands	64
3.5.2	Voice of America short-wave antennas	65
3.7	TV pickup tubes	68
3.8	TV pickup tube output	70
3.9.1	How the TV channel is used	71
3.9.2	World TV standards	72
3.9.3	Summary of broadcast channel specifications	73
3.10.1	TV system components and signals	74
3.10.2	Color kinescope tube	76
4.3.1	Videotape recorder formats	83
4.3.2	Home videodisc systems	84
4.5	Microwave relay station	88
4.6.1	Satellite global coverage	89
4.6.2	Orbital positions of U.S. domsats	90
4.8.1	The many channels of cable TV	93
4.8.2	Cable TV system plan	95
4.8.3	Cable TV's wideband channel	96
5.3.1	How Hertz measured wavelength	105
5.3.2	Guglielmo Marconi	107
Box	The department store and the *Titanic* disaster	114
5.7.1	Reginald Fessenden	116
5.7.2	Lee de Forest	118
6.2	The RCA ''family'' in 1926	124
6.3.1	Conrad's 8XK and its successor, KDKA	126
6.3.2	KDKA's studio in 1922	128
6.4	RCA opens its Washington, D.C., station	132
6.5	Sarnoff and Paley early in radio era	135
7.1	Growth of radio stations	144
Box	Broadcasting nostalgia	149
7.3	Edwin Armstrong	152
7.6	Murrow in London during World War II	163
7.8	Radio program automation	173

8.1.1	*See it Now* joins Atlantic & Pacific	180
8.1.2	Growth of television stations	182
8.2.1	Vladimir Zworykin	184
8.2.2	First U.S. TV star	185
8.2.3	Sarnoff Introduces TV at World's Fair, 1939	186
8.3	TV channel allotment plan	189
8.4	TV channel utilization	191
8.5.1	*Today*, yesterday and today	195
8.5.2	TV network affiliates	198
8.5.3	Network owned and operated stations	199
Box	PTAR fallacies, exceptions, and exemptions	207
9.1.1	TV station day parts	218
9.1.2	Amount of TV network programming by day part	219
9.2	Decline in diversity of prime-time network programming	222
9.4.1	Local and nonentertainment TV programming	230
9.4.2	"The most trusted man in America"	232
9.4.3	Electronic newsgathering (ENG)	234
Box	Inside the electronic church	243
10.2	Growth of educational stations	257
10.3	PBS satellite distribution system	265
10.5.1	Public TV funding flow	271
10.5.2	Comparison of public and commercial TV economics	272
10.5.3	Public broadcasting revenue by source	274
Box	How the piper called the tune	275
10.6.1	Public TV program production & distribution flow	280
10.6.2	Public TV program types	281
10.6.3	Public radio program types	285
11.1	Indicators of cable TV growth	296
11.2	Types of cable TV system owners	303
11.4.1	TVRO earth station	309
11.4.2	Satellite distribution of superstation programming to cable TV systems	310–311
11.4.3	Examples of satellite-distributed video program services	313
11.4.4	A direct broadcast satellite system	314
11.6.1	Growth of pay TV subscribers	319
11.6.2	Teletext and closed captioning	321
11.7	Costs of home video center inputs	323
12.1	Station functional organization	328
12.6.1	Broadcast income and market size	342
12.6.2	Tangible investment of broadcasting industry	343
12.6.3	Broadcast pre-tax income	344
12.7	Employment in commercial broadcasting	345
Box	Advice for job seekers	346
13.1	Advertising volume of major media	352
13.2	National, spot, and local station revenues	353
13.4	NAB membership and code subscribership	360
Box	Decoding the code	361
13.6.1	Sample SRDS radio station rate listing	368
13.6.2	Influence of market size on TV rates	370
13.7.1	How top advertisers spread their budgets	372
13.7.2	Top advertising agencies and broadcast billings	373
13.7.3	Broadcast advertising sales flow	375

14.2   Excerpts from Nielsen net-
        work ratings report   381
14.3   Ratings concepts   383
15.1   Spectrum management   404
15.2   Chain of legal authority
        over broadcasting   406
16.1.1 FCC organizational plan   428
16.1.2 Rule-making process   430
16.5   Fairness doctrine and equal
        time law compared   442
16.6   Public complaints received
        by FCC   446
16.7   License renewal routes   449

16.8   Reasons for license deletions 452
16.9   Representative FCC mem-
        bers   457
Box   Indian derogatories   497
19.5   Trends in television violence 529
19.6   The Great Debates   534
20.2   Information theory commu-
        nication model   548
20.3   Evolution of research on ef-
        fects of mass media   553
20.4   Characteristics of main re-
        search strategies   555

PREFACE

Like its predecessors, this edition of *Broadcasting in America* is more than a revision. Much of it is entirely new and what remains from previous editions has been extensively rewritten. Improvements have been sought particularly in the following areas:

■ Organization has been tightened and clarified. A new system of subheadings, designed to call the reader's attention to each new topic as it is introduced, has helped greatly to discipline the logic and flow of the exposition.

■ A number of steps have been taken to make the text easier and more interesting both to read and to study. The improved organization has enabled reducing the number of chapters and flagging each important topic with its own eye-catching headline. Tables, charts, displays, photographs, and side bars have been increased by 50 percent and made more relevant and informative. Finally, the prose style of the book has been made leaner and more direct, without (one hopes) either talking down to the reader or sacrificing stylistic quality.

■ Programs and programming strategies are treated much more fully in this edition, with balanced attention to radio, broadcast television, and cable television.

■ Materials on public broadcasting, previously interspersed throughout the book, have been pulled together to form a single, comprehensive chapter.

■ New media and delivery systems are examined in depth, both as to their technologies and their competitive demands on audience attention and investment.

■ Material on foreign broadcasting is treated more systematically on a true comparative rather than simply a descriptive basis.

■ The extensive deregulatory actions of the courts and the FCC over the past few years are accorded thorough and up-to-date coverage.

■ The text has been given an epilogue: a new chapter discussing the likely future of broadcasting in an era of more competition and new technologies.

■ A new student study guide, written by Roger D. Wimmer of the University of Georgia, provides exercises, self-test items, and projects that reinforce concepts, terms, and relationships discussed in the text. Its organization parallels that of the text.

Despite these and many other changes the book retains its basic goal: to treat broadcasting as a bona fide academic subject, emphasizing its linkages with the more traditional disciplines such as physical science, history, economics, political science, psychology, and sociology. This approach is rooted in the belief that for purposes of both general and professional education, broadcasting should be studied as a product of social forces and as a social force itself. The book deals not only with the question "What makes broadcasting in America the way it is?" but also with its reciprocal, "What part does broadcasting play in making America the way it is?" I hope that in the end the book will also help readers to form their own ideas about how to answer yet another question: "What should we as consumers and concerned citizens expect of broadcasting in the future?"

An important feature of previous editions, retained in this one, is the liberal use of quotations so that readers can experience the authentic voices of acknowledged authorities in the many aspects of broadcasting. These quotations range over a wide spectrum of diverse styles, from the colloquial comments of radio disc jockeys to the magisterial dicta of Supreme Court justices. A second purpose for their use is to stimulate an interest in further reading. To this end, easily available news and periodical sources are often cited as well as scholarly books and public documents.

In the preface to the previous edition I mentioned the recruitment of Christopher H. Sterling to contribute a guide to the literature of broadcasting. He has done the same service for the present edition, but, more important, he has taken on the role of full-scale collaborator. In this edition he had primary responsibility for Chapter 10, on public broadcasting, and for Chapter 11, on the evolution of the new communication technologies. Although the underlying concept and organization of the book remain mine, Sterling collaborated to the fullest extent in the planning and preparation of the entire manuscript. He read every word of every chapter more than once and suggested innumerable improvements.

As it happened, during the writing Sterling took a leave of absence as professor of communications at Temple University to serve as assistant to FCC Commissioner Anne P. Jones. His presence in Washington helped immensely in the final work on this edition, keeping us abreast of the latest developments in communications at a time of unprecedented change in all aspects of the communications field.

We wish to mention a number of individuals who read parts of the manuscript and offered expert advice in special areas: Bernard Bumpus of the BBC, foreign systems; Bruce Cook of the David C. Cook Foundation, and William Fiore of the National Council of the Churches of Christ, religious broadcasting; Melvin DeFleur of University of Miami, communications research and theory;

Susan Tyler Eastman of Indiana University, ratings systems and communications research and theory; Erwin Krasnow of the National Association of Broadcasters, law and regulation; Ralph Renick of WTVJ-Miami, local television news; John Roberts of Voice of America, VOA broadcasts; and Elliot Sivowitch of the Smithsonian Institution, the physics of radio and history of technology. They all spoke for themselves, of course, not their organizations, and have no responsibility for the uses we made of their advice. Nor, we must add, does the fact that Sterling worked at the FCC during part of the book's gestation period imply any official endorsement of his contributions. We appreciate the constructive suggestions for improving the text made by the following persons: Charles Bantz, University of Minnesota; David Champoux, Herkimer County Community College; Kenneth Kyoon Hur, University of Texas at Austin; Herbert Meinert, University of Northern Iowa; Deanna M. (Campbell) Robinson, University of Oregon; and Gay Russell, Grossmont College.

On the technical side of book preparation, we are grateful to Dean Robert Smith of the Temple University School of Communications and Theater and Gordon Gray, chairman of its Radio-Television-Film Department, for allowing us to use the resources of the school and department; to Bob Roberts, librarian of the school's communications collection, for bibliographical assistance; to Dorothy Head, for undergoing for the fourth time the labor of manuscript and index preparation; to Ellen Sterling for assuming a share of this exacting task; and to Donna Travis for library research assistance.

Finally, our thanks to students and teachers who have made useful suggestions and corrections that we have incorporated in this edition.

Sydney W. Head
Coral Gables, Florida

PROLOGUE

The World of Broadcasting

CHAPTER 1

National Contrasts

Broadcasting is a global enterprise. Its physical basis is universal, so that radio waves behave in California, Kenya, or Denmark according to the same natural laws that govern them in Maine, Singapore, or France. The technology, equipment, programming concepts, and many of the programs themselves are interchanged on a worldwide basis.

Yet each national broadcasting system has developed its own unique character. "Every society," wrote the English broadcasting scholar Anthony Smith, "has to reinvent broadcasting in its own image, as a means of containing or suppressing the geographical, political, spiritual and social dilemmas which broadcasting entails" (1973: 50). Smith speaks of "containing" and "suppressing" because broadcasting can be a very dangerous force, especially to governments that want to control what their citizens hear and see.

Comparison of broadcasting in America with broadcasting in other countries at the very outset of this survey serves to emphasize the fact that the American way is not the only way — indeed not necessarily in all respects the best way. This realization is an essential first step in making a fair and informed appraisal of broadcasting in America. In comparing the American system with others, we shall pay particular attention to the British system. The historical and cultural links between the two countries make the contrasts between their systems all the more striking as evidence of the need to "reinvent" broadcasting to suit each national image.

1.1 Broadcasting and National Character

Each country, as we have said, started with identical broadcasting potentialities, yet each capitalized on these potentialities differently in order to make broadcasting serve the nation's needs, circumstances, and limitations.

National broadcasting systems are bound to reflect national character because of the very nature of the medium itself. It has three attributes that especially promote this mirrorlike relationship. *First*, broadcasting uses public property — the "airwaves" (actually electromagnetic radiations) that make communication without wires possible. *Second*, these radiations are subject to self-interference, which can be prevented only by regulation of physical aspects of transmission such as wavelength, power, and types of emission. *Third*, broadcasting has political and social power because of its unique ability to communicate instantly with an entire nation and even with the entire world.

3

Airwaves as Public Property Because the electromagnetic frequencies used in broadcasting and all other forms of radio communication are regarded as public property, each government regulates their use according to its concept of what is best for its own people. The public character of the electromagnetic spectrum sets broadcasting apart from other communication media. No other medium depends for its very existence on the use of a public resource that cannot be manufactured or privately owned. This dependence imposes a duty on each government to administer the use of the radio frequencies in its national interest. Interpretations of the nature of this duty vary, of course, from one nation to another, according to the political philosophy of each. That is one reason we find a diversity of national broadcasting systems in the world.

Prevention of Interference Without regulation, stations operating on the same channel in the same general area will inevitably interfere with each other, and often also with others on adjacent channels. Because only a limited number of channels are physically available, interference can turn the entire radio communication system into a hopeless jumble of competing signals. In fact this actually began to happen to broadcasting in America during the early 1920s, creating a babel that led to enactment of the Radio Act of 1927, the law upon which present U.S. regulation is based.

Electromagnetic waves do not, of course, stop at international boundaries; prevention of interference therefore requires international as well as national regulation:

One clearly cannot communicate by radio with another country without its cooperation as to frequency, time, power, and place of communication. In some cases one cannot even use radio within one's own boundaries without the forbearance of

other nations. These and other limits on national discretion could be said to make the spectrum an international resource comparable in theory to airspace over the high seas, to international waterways, or even to migratory fisheries. (Levin, 1971: 37)

Political Control One of the first targets of a revolutionary group attempting to overthrow a government is the country's broadcasting facilities. Even the most stable and democratic countries take care to prevent any one political party from gaining undue control over broadcasting. In unstable and authoritarian countries much greater care is taken to prevent opposing factions from gaining access to the airwaves. In short, no nation, whatever its politics, can afford to leave so powerful and persuasive an avenue of communication unregulated.

These are the three most urgent reasons why national differences in broadcasting systems reflect differences in political philosophy. A country's economics, history, geography, and culture also have great influence, but always with political overtones. As Anthony Smith put it, to the outside observer the way a country organizes its broadcasting system reveals "a strange coded version of that country's entire political culture" (1973: 257).

1.2 Influence of Political Philosophy

One way a national political philosophy expresses itself is in the attitude assumed by a country's leadership toward its own people. When we look in broad perspective at the world of broadcasting from this viewpoint, three basic orientations emerge: the permissive, the paternalistic, and the authoritarian.

Permissive Orientation: U.S.A.

Broadcasting in America is the major example of a permissive broadcasting system. Government operation was considered only briefly before the decision was made to turn U.S. broadcasting over to private enterprise. Private operators took a little more time to decide on a method of financing the new medium, but soon settled on advertising as the source of funds. These decisions automatically made the primary criterion of programming whatever seems most popular to the most people. The profit incentive, minimally hampered by government regulation, results in catering to the widest possible audience.

Operating within the permissive framework of the free-enterprise system, American commercial broadcasting has all the pragmatism, aggressiveness, materialism, improvisation, expansionism, and free-swinging competitiveness of American marketing. Whatever its critics may say, the overall result has been a more lively, inventive, and varied broadcasting system than can be found elsewhere in the world. Nevertheless, most governments disagree with the extreme permissiveness of the American commercial system, with its emphasis on what people "want" rather than what they "need." They feel that programming cannot be left entirely to the uncontrolled interaction of popular supply and demand. Each country feels a need to preserve its language and its national cultural traditions, as well as an obligation to decide on what it considers to be the proper balance among programs of information, education, and entertainment.

Paternal Orientation: Great Britain

The paternalistic attitude aims to maintain a healthily balanced program diet, with neither too much spinach nor too much ice cream for social and psychological well-being. Paternalism holds that popular tastes tend to be frivolous. Leaders have an obligation to gratify such tastes; but they also have a duty to balance them with programming of a more cultivated nature.

Most noncommunist industrialized countries practice varying degrees of paternalism in their broadcasting systems. Pretelevision broadcasting in Great Britain is an apt example, for it was originally designed to avoid the "mistakes" the British felt had been made in America (Briggs, 1961: 67). The British Broadcasting Corporation (BBC), founded in 1927 to replace a short-lived private commercial company, is a public, chartered, nonprofit corporation. It derives its funds from annual fees paid by the public for receiving-set licenses. The British government appoints the BBC board of governors but leaves the board free to do its job without interference. It is true that the Home Secretary, who grants the licenses in Britain to use designated channels, has certain "reserve" powers that could be used to justify interference. For example, the secretary could veto the broadcasting of any program or class of programs — a power that is constitutionally forbidden to government officials in the United States. In Britain, which has no written constitution, only long-standing traditions of governmental restraint protect the BBC's freedom.

From its earliest days, the BBC adhered to a philosophy of conscientious public service. Its aim was to "give a lead" by programming at least part of the time somewhat above the level of prevailing popular taste. Not only the paternalism but also the firm independence and the high sense of mission of the BBC bore the personal imprint of its remarkable first director general, or chief executive, John Reith (later Lord Reith). A dour, deeply religious Scot, Reith was first introduced to broadcasting in 1922 as the general manager of the predecessor private company from which the BBC was fashioned five years later.

Reith had a powerful physical presence (Exhibit 1.2.1) and a visionary dedication to public service broadcasting:

The responsibility as at the outset conceived, and despite all discouragements pursued, was to carry into the greatest number of homes everything that was best in every department of human knowl-

Exhibit 1.2.1
Lord Reith (1899–1971)

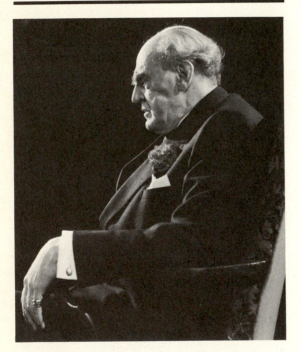

John Reith was a 34-year-old engineer at the time of his introduction to broadcasting in 1922 as general manager of the British Broadcasting Company, the private concern that four years later became the public corporation now known as the BBC. He left the BBC in 1938, still a comparatively young man, to take over the faltering British government airline, Imperial Airways. This picture was taken many years later when Reith returned to Broadcasting House to participate in a program.

Source: BBC copyright.

edge, endeavour and achievements; and to avoid whatever was or might be hurtful. In the earliest years accused of setting out to give the public not what it wanted but what the BBC thought it should have, [our] answer was that few knew what they wanted, fewer what they needed. (Reith, 1949: 101)

He ran the BBC for its first sixteen years, leaving an indelible mark on it, and indeed on the entire world of broadcasting. His concept of the medium spread worldwide, following the British Empire's far-flung influence to every continent and to the islands of every ocean. Many hundreds of broadcasters from scores of countries came to the BBC's famous Broadcasting House in London for training and indoctrination (Exhibit 1.2.2). It is no exaggeration to say that Reith was the world's most influential figure in the pretelevision phase of broadcasting history.

Symptomatic of the BBC's paternalistic approach was the fact that, in the earlier years, its officials refused to acknowledge that their personal programming judgments needed guidance from systematic audience research. Not until it was discovered that a large fraction of the BBC's supposedly loyal audience was actually listening to Radio Luxembourg, a European commercial station (§1.6), was listener research taken seriously at the BBC. As late as 1960 a BBC official could still write:

The real degradation of the BBC started with the invention of the hellish department which is called "Listener Research." That Abominable Statistic is supposed to show "what the listeners like" — and, of course, what they like is the red-nosed comedian and the Wurlitzer organ. (Quoted in Briggs, 1965: 261)

Television and the turbulent political and social changes of the 1960s did much to dispel the "Reithein" tradition but the BBC remains the outstanding example of enlightened paternalism in broadcasting.

Authoritarian Orientation: USSR The authoritarian approach characterizes the broadcasting of the Soviet Union, other communist countries, and most of the Third World. In the USSR the state itself finances and operates broadcasting, harnessing it directly to the implementation of government policies. Broadcasting is run by a committee directly responsible to the Council of Ministers. The guiding philosophy ordains that all programming must serve an ideological purpose. When questioned about government controls, Soviet broadcasters are prone to reply, "We are not controlled by the government. We *are* the government."

Exhibit 1.2.2
Broadcasting House, London

The famous art deco building in the heart of London was the mecca of radio broadcasters from all over the world during the pretelevision era. The BBC moved here from its original quarters on the banks of the Thames in 1932. Though planned to triple the corporation's previous space, the new building was already too small to accommodate all the BBC's activities by the time construction was completed. The sculpture over the entrance, by Eric Gill, represents Prospero, the wise magician of Shakespeare's *The Tempest,* with Ariel, the sprite who could move with lightning speed, symbolic of radio. BBC's television center is located in a London suburb.

Source: BBC copyright.

Because communist ideology stresses the importance of using the media to further the political education of the masses, the Soviets embraced radio broadcasting early and developed it extensively. The Russian masses, however, failed to invest heavily in home radio receivers as early as did Western audiences. This reluctance was not entirely due to lack of purchasing power. The government itself was not anxious to encourage the sale of receivers that could be used to pick up broadcasts from the outside. But perhaps the main reason was the fact that communist programming simply lacked sufficient mass appeal to motivate the general public to invest in receivers.

In any event, communist countries tended to rely heavily on subsidizing listening by means of *wired radio*. This is a system of government-controlled, centralized reception of radio broadcast signals, with delivery by telephone wire to speaker boxes in individual homes and public places. People rent the speakers for a nominal fee, or listen without cost in public squares, factories, and other gathering places. About 14 percent of the world's radio receivers are actually wired boxes of this kind. Half the total receivers in the USSR and nearly three-quarters of those in mainland China are wired (BBC, 1980). State-subsidization of reception thus compensated to some extent for the fact that radio programming failed to motivate universal public investment in over-the-air receivers.

Gradually over the decades the inflexibly didactic tone of Soviet radio softened. Worldwide success of Western models of production and programming, as well as their own research, eventually persuaded the Soviets that in broadcasting you can lead an audience to radio but you can't make it listen.

Russian television, developed belatedly in the 1960s, started with the same heavy-handed didacticism of early radio. Again, the Western example gave Moscow an apprecia-

tion of what American broadcasters call "production values" — even in programs devoted to extolling the achievements of workers in tractor factories.

In recent years Americans have seen examples of Soviet programming on U.S. public television. It compares favorably in technical quality and uses the formats familiar on the U.S. networks. The emphasis is on serious programming: documentaries, political commentary, classical music, ballet, theater. Even "pure" entertainment formats, however, serve ideological goals:

The quiz show, a popular item, is an example. One, called "Let's Go, Girls" ("A nu-ka, devushki"), is telecast once a month for an hour and a half. Everyone wins something, a small prize of flowers or books, and the object is not to get rich, but rather to popularize occupations and encourage good work. Recently, a group of policewomen performed on the show, marching and drilling to music with their nightsticks. They were asked ("quizzed") how to improve traffic rules, and they offered such suggestions as redesigning traffic signs. (Mickiewicz, 1981: 20)

Commercials are the least well-developed aspect of content in Russian television. They address a captive audience and advertise monopoly products. Lacking brand names and competitive incentives, they make no attempt to *sell* products but simply inform the audience of their availability and of their more obvious intrinsic values.

Third World Authoritarianism   Third World countries started with broadcasting systems modeled on those of the colonial powers. When independence approached, the British reorganized their colonial systems in the hope of insulating them somewhat from direct control by the new governments. In every instance, however, the moment a colony won independence it began dismantling this structure and adapting the system to its changed status. The authors of a comprehensive survey of such broadcasting systems concluded that "the most striking fact to emerge from our study is the virtual abandonment, throughout the developing world, of Western patterns of broadcasting in which, however defined, the broadcasting system has some element of autonomy from the government of the day" (Katz & Wedell, 1977: 212). The writers go on to point out that the leaders of such countries seem more concerned with broadcasting as a "potentially disruptive factor" than with its potentiality for assisting positively in the tasks of nation building.

Not surprisingly, then, Third World broadcasting tends to be authoritarian. In most developing countries control of broadcasting is vested in ministries of information or "national guidance." Even seemingly routine programming decisions often have to be held up while awaiting approval from the top political authorities. Leaders feel they dare not trust broadcasting professionals, much less the illiterate and unsophisticated masses, to deal with disturbing new ideas or politically controversial subjects. They therefore prescribe a spoon-fed diet. Authoritarianism of this type is usually more pragmatic than ideological, but the net effect on programming is similar to the effect of dogmatic Marxism. The similarity of communist and Third World systems means that government ownership is by far the most common type of broadcast setup in the world today, as shown in Exhibit 1.2.3.

1.3 Pluralism in Broadcasting

The three prototype systems — permissive, paternalistic, and authoritarian — exist nowhere in pure form. American permissivism

Exhibit 1.2.3
Ownership of world broadcast transmission facilities

| | Percentage of countries (N = 184) | |
	Radio	Television
Government	46	41
Public corporation (nonprofit)	17	20
Commercial proprietor	8	10
More than one of above	29	29

Comment: Government ownership of broadcast facilities is even more widespread than the table suggests. Governments also own facilities in many of the countries with more than one type of ownership.

Source: Based on 1976/1977 data in UNESCO, *Statistical Yearbook, 1978–79.* UNESCO, Paris, 1980.

is tinged with a sense of social responsibility, the BBC's paternalism increasingly defers to mass public tastes, and even the USSR's authoritarianism finds it helpful to do a little paternalistic head-patting.

Role of Motives   In the West, at least, the conviction has developed that a *monolithic* broadcasting system inevitably cramps the potentialities of the medium. In the light of over half a century of broadcasting experience, *pluralistic* systems seem best able to assure optimum development. Pluralism in this context means putting more than one motivating force to work, normally the motives of commercial profit and of public service, operating side by side.

Commercial motives alone, no matter how carefully restrained by regulation, tend to constrict the range of programming, for example by avoiding controversy, imitating success, and concentrating on segments of the audience with the most buying power. By the same token, if a noncommercial, public-service system has a monopoly, it tends toward bureaucratic complacency and excessive deference to the politicians who vote the operating funds. Competition between the two, on the other hand, stimulates creativity and innovation, giving audiences a wider range of choices as a result.

American Pluralism   American broadcasting began with a weak, but nevertheless recognizable, pluralistic tendency. Educational and religious institutions were among the first to obtain radio licenses. But not until specific television channels were set aside *exclusively for noncommercial use* in 1952 was pluralism given the potentiality for succeeding. Only relatively recently have some of the potentialities of noncommercial broadcasting as a true alternative begun to be realized, but the commercial stations and networks in America still attract the great majority of lis-

teners and viewers. Noncommercial broadcasting has yet to attain the level of financial security it needs in order to offer full-scale competition.

In the meantime, cable television and other alternative ways of delivering and financing programs have added to the diversity of commercially motivated program services. But the pluralistic principle applies equally to them: the need remains for alternative motives, not merely alternative technologies.

Pluralism in Britain   For nearly a quarter-century the noncommercial BBC had a broadcasting monopoly in Britain. In 1954, however, the government authorized a commercially supported television service, followed in 1972 by a few commercial *local* radio stations (the BBC retains a monopoly on network radio).

British commercial broadcasting is regulated and supervised by a second nonprofit, chartered corporation, the Independent Broadcasting Authority (IBA). The BBC's *royal* charter confers somewhat more autonomy than the IBA's *parliamentary* charter, but the two have similar legal status. Like the BBC, the IBA owns and operates its own national network of television transmitters; unlike the BBC, it has *no programming function*. Instead, private television program companies bid for regional commercial franchises issued by the IBA. The authority has the power to withdraw franchises without having to go through a long process of appeals. In 1981, for example, the IBA declined to renew franchises of two of the 15 companies then in operation and awarded their regions to competing applicants. At the same time the authority authorized a separate company to launch a new morning program, *TV-AM* (prior to that the only morning programs were the Open University's courses, seen on the BBC).

Franchised commercial companies produce their own programs, sell advertising, and lease time on the IBA-owned network of transmitters. The IBA not only enforces the programming and advertising policies laid down in its charter, it both owns and operates the transmission facilities used by the program companies. This division of operational control between a public authority and private companies restrains the influence of commercial interests. The IBA gets no income from advertisers and therefore has no reason for deferring to advertising pressures.

Limiting the independent program companies to regional coverage prevents one or more companies from dominating the field. This principle is carried out to the extent of dividing the right to cover London (by far the most lucrative market) between two companies — Thames Television, responsible for weekday programming for the London area, and London Weekend, responsible only for Saturday and Sunday programming. Another aim of the regional franchising scheme is to prevent neglect of regional interests in the pursuit of profit in the national market. Regionalization was a deliberate strategy adopted to avoid duplicating the American pattern, which allows three national commercial television networks to dominate the entire television industry with nationally oriented programs and advertising.

Nevertheless, the ideal of pluralism requires that the commercial and noncommercial services have an opportunity to compete on approximately equal terms. Therefore the commercial companies are allowed to combine their resources part of the time to form a *cooperative national network.* The larger companies contribute varying amounts of programming to the national schedule. All companies combine forces to support an independent news organization to produce national news programs for the network. Thus the independent companies are able to offer national as well as regional competition to the BBC.

Until the 1980s the BBC retained the advantage of two networks (BBC-1 and BBC-2) against the IBA's single network. British viewers had a maximum of only three programs available at any one time. But these could be received in every city and town in the nation. The marked inequalities of U.S. television, with eight or ten stations available in metropolitan areas but only one or two (or even none) in small towns, does not exist in Britain.

Under international and regional agreements, sufficient television channels remained unused in Britain to enable authorizing a fourth network. Who should be allowed to operate the "fourth channel," as it is called, was a hotly contended question. Proposals included not only a third network for the BBC and a second network for IBA, but also an entirely new and highly innovative network devoted to formal education, public access programs, and experimentation. The prize was finally awarded to the IBA for franchising to private companies.

Pluralism in Britain has been a success. Some die-hards still argue that things were better in the good old days of the BBC noncommercial monopoly. They point out that when the IBA companies began competing they soon captured 75 percent of the television audience, forcing the BBC to resort to mass-appeal programming to meet the competition. It is true that the BBC abandoned its image of a rather strait-laced old auntie, but time would have forced change, with or without an IBA. In any event, the BBC still offers viewers some genuine alternatives.

The BBC retains its monopoly on *national and regional* radio, operating four national networks plus regional services in Northern

Ireland, Scotland, and Wales. The radio networks took on their present character in 1970, when a break was made with the Reith tradition. Reith had insisted that each network offer a comprehensive program service. The new style, known as *generic programming*, allots specialized types of programs to each service. Radio 1 stresses pop music, Radio 2 middle-of-the-road music, Radio 3 more serious music and fine arts, and Radio 4 the spoken word.

Local radio (in the sense of stations designed to service individual towns and cities), stressed in the United States from the very beginning, is a relatively new development in Britain. Commercial local radio is even more recent. The BBC started its first local stations in the 1960s, but by 1980 still had only 20 stations in operation. The IBA was allowed to award local commercial radio franchises in 19 localities, starting in 1974. Plans exist for increasing the number of local radio stations under both IBA and BBC auspices, but in Britain radio remains much more nationally oriented than in the United States.

1.4 Legal Foundations

American Broadcasting Law   The American method of legally controlling its thousands of mostly private licensees is exceedingly complex, involving a large bureaucracy and mountains of paperwork. Under the Constitution, broadcasting is classed as a form of interstate commerce. It therefore comes under central regulation by the federal government. In terms of both ownership and operation, however, the law favors *local* control. Decentralized operational control reflects the ideal of the First Amendment to the Constitution, which calls for the maximum possible *diversity* in the information sources available to the public. This principle ac-

counts in part for the extraordinarily large number of stations licensed in the United States as compared to the rest of the world (Exhibit 1.6).

Regulation of American broadcasting also reflects the Constitution's concern for individual freedom and due process of law. An elaborate machinery for review and appeal can be invoked to preserve broadcasters' freedom of expression or to prevent arbitrary government action. Appeals can take years to settle. Meanwhile the documents keep piling up.

As a result, American broadcasting has spawned a legal library of amazing proportions. The Communications Act of 1934, the basic federal law, runs to only about a hundred pages, but the Federal Communications Commission rules and regulations based on the act fill four volumes. The FCC's published decisions ran to some 120 volumes by the end of 1980. Federal courts of appeal and the Supreme Court have written hundreds of opinions on broadcasting cases.

Foreign Systems   In most countries broadcasting law is relatively brief and simple. Operational control of stations is usually highly centralized, if not actually in the hands of the government. Administrative decisions are usually final, with no avenues of appeal as in American broadcasting.

For example, in Britain the BBC and IBA charters are short documents that rest on a few brief statutes governing finances, control of frequency allocations, and transmitter deployment. Documentation for the entire legal machinery of British broadcasting could be bound in a single volume. Moreover, Britain has no written constitution with a First Amendment to serve as the basis for court challenges to alleged curtailments of licensee freedoms. Instead the two chartered authorities carry out their jobs without benefit of public hearings, reviews of decisions, or appeals to the court. In fact autonomous licensees as private individuals controlling both programming and transmission functions of individual stations scarcely exist in Britain as they do in the United States.

While the United States relies on a government regulatory commission (the FCC) to ensure the accountability of broadcasters and to see that they operate in the public interest, Britain puts its faith in the less formal machinery of citizens' advisory councils. The two broadcasting authorities in Britain appoint their own councils. Over fifty citizens' groups advise the BBC on such varied subjects as archives, programs for immigrant Asians, agriculture, education, music, religion, science, and the social effects of broadcasting.

The authorities also set up their own complaint commissions. In 1979–1980 the BBC's three-member complaint board heard only four complaints — a remarkable record compared to the FCC's many hundreds of complaining letters, hearings on complaints, and lawsuits about decisions on complaints. Plans were afoot in 1981 for creation of a single commission to respond jointly to complaints against either the BBC or the IBA.

International Broadcasting Law Because radio waves have no respect for national boundaries, regulation of broadcasting on an international scale is essential. The International Telecommunication Union (ITU), an agency of the United Nations with headquarters in Geneva, Switzerland, regulates both radio and international telephone and telegraph communication. Over 150 nations belong to the ITU. Membership does not involve any surrender of national sovereignty, but most countries follow ITU regulations as a matter of self-interest. Wholesale violations would be disastrous, not only to international communication but to domestic communica-

tion as well. When self-interest dictates violation, however, the ITU is powerless to force compliance.

The ITU has four main functions: (1) *rule making* to govern the international conduct of telecommunications; (2) *regulating* the uses made by member countries of the frequency spectrum; (3) *standardizing* technical aspects of telecommunications; and (4) *assisting* the less developed countries in improving their telecommunications facilities and training their personnel. Of special concern to all members is ITU regulation of frequency spectrum uses. Not enough frequencies exist to meet the demands of every country and every communications service, so a certain amount of compromise is essential. The ITU's International Frequency Registration Board (IFRB) keeps track of frequency use throughout the world and reports violations of established rules.

Three separate functions are involved in putting the frequency spectrum to use: allocation, allotment, and assignment. *Bands* of frequencies are *allocated* to each radio service (for example, separate bands have been designated for standard, FM, television, and short-wave broadcasting). Frequencies within these bands are *allotted* to specific ITU member countries. And specific groups of frequencies are *assigned* to individual stations. Most assignments are made by individual countries from their respective ITU allotments.

WARC 1979 Periodically the ITU holds World Administrative Radio Conferences (WARCs) at which member nations meet to hammer out international agreements covering specific telecommunications subjects. A WARC of great importance for broadcasting occurred in 1979, for the purpose of revising the radio regulations adopted in 1949.

During the intervening thirty years over

70 new countries had won independence. This was an opportunity to claim their share of the frequency pie. At the time of WARC 1979 it was estimated that the less developed countries used only 7 percent of the spectrum, yet represented 75 percent of the world's population. Of course these countries were not yet ready to expand their use of the spectrum dramatically, but they approached WARC 1979 with the expectation of obtaining guarantees that their future needs would be met as their telecommunications systems expanded.

Prior to the meeting, commentators predicted that it might degenerate into a fruitless wrangle between the haves and the have-nots of the world. However, true to the traditions of the ITU (which is sometimes cited as the most successful case of world cooperation in the interests of common goals), the conferees managed to reach compromise agreements on most points of dispute. This was no mean accomplishment, considering that the conference debated 15,000 separate proposals, 900 of them from the United States alone.

Most of the WARC 1979 agreements were scheduled to be implemented only after further regional meetings to be held throughout the 1980s. The following examples highlight some of the WARC 1979 decisions that will affect the future of broadcasting:

■ The standard (AM) radio frequency band was nearly doubled in size, though most of the additional frequencies are to be shared with other services.
■ Parts of the high-frequency (HF) band used both for international short-wave broadcasting and for many nonbroadcast services were increased by 60 percent.
■ The portion of the ultra-high-frequency (UHF) band used by television was retained for television, subject to sharing with other services.

■ Broadcast satellites were assigned their own special frequencies.

One eventual effect of these and other changes will be to enable an increase in the number of broadcasting stations that many individual countries can license within their borders.

1.5 Access to Broadcasting

The power of broadcasting to inform, persuade, and cultivate values has always made access to the airwaves a jealously guarded prerogative. Traditionally, access has been reserved for professional performers, for experts on subjects of public interest, for people currently in the news, and for politicians.

Candidates and Office Holders   In any political system that allows free elections, broadcasting plays a vital and constructive role. But it also poses a threat to such systems. The party in power will always be tempted to use the advantages of incumbency to monopolize access to broadcasting, turning it into a medium of political control rather than a medium of information. One of the critically important tasks of regulation in a democracy, therefore, is to devise ways to preserve fairness in the political uses of broadcasting.

Broadcasting law in the United States deals with this problem in terms of "equal time" (actually the law speaks of "equal opportunities"). Stations are free to make unlimited time available to candidates but, once a candidate is granted time, all other candidates for the same office automatically have the right to demand the same opportunities. The weakest candidates and parties are entitled to the same opportunities to air their views as the strongest.

In few other countries are candidates and parties able to exploit broadcasting to the extent they can in the United States. In Great Britain election broadcasting is severely restricted, with the emphasis on party rather than on individual candidates. The two broadcasting authorities, the BBC and the IBA, come to an annual agreement with representatives of the political parties. In the recent past, only parties with fifty or more parliamentary candidates in the field have been granted access, each getting from one to five broadcasts of only five to ten minutes' duration. Individual candidates for Parliament are governed by a law that forbids any broadcast appearance "in which any other rival candidate neither takes part nor consents to its going forward without his taking part." Thus the interminable merchandising of candidates, so wearisome to American voters, is unknown in Britain.

When the BBC and the IBA agree on standards for political campaigns they also set up standards for "ministerial broadcasts." If the Prime Minister obtains broadcast time to talk to the nation, the party officially in opposition has an automatic right to reply. That reply in turn mandates a third program, a discussion in which *all* parties may participate. On other occasions, when Members of Parliament are involved in news programs, for example, the two broadcasting authorities have a responsibility to take their own measures to ensure fairness.

Proporz System   West Germany and some of the other European countries seek to maintain the political impartiality of broadcasting by what the Germans call *proporz*. The word means "proportion," referring to the fact that the governments of the West German states appoint governing boards and broadcasting executives in such a way as to give proportional representation to the main political parties in the current legislatures.

(The chief officer of a broadcasting organization must have a deputy of the opposing party.) According to one analyst, the proporz system is "widely criticized as leading to party control of broadcasting, and as being a denial of the principles of neutrality and accessibility" that underlie the states' broadcasting laws (Sandford, 1976: 79).

Of course neither proporz nor the U.S. equal opportunities law has any relevance in most countries of the world. Allotting time for political use of broadcasting creates no problem in nations that have no opposition parties. There broadcasting is run by the government and speaks only for those in power. In Third World countries especially, broadcasting systems tend to become personal mouthpieces for the chief of state, who has unlimited access. According to news reports, in one small country when the premier became exasperated at the unreliability of the telephone system he turned to the broadcasting system. Interrupting whatever programs might be on at the moment, he would go on the air personally with messages to his ministers and staff.

Access Seekers   During the restless 1960s people began to question the traditional restrictions on access to the airwaves. Are professionals and politicians the only ones with anything worthwhile to say? If the electromagnetic frequencies are a common resource of mankind, why cannot more of mankind make use of them? The access movement became a worldwide phenomenon — so much so that UNESCO commissioned a study of the people in various countries who were seeking a chance to air their views.

The UNESCO study identified five classes of access seekers, in addition to minority politicians: (1) advocates of social reform who demand an opportunity to influence public opinion; (2) creative artists who demand an opportunity to use broadcasting as a medium of self-expression; (3) educators who want to use broadcasting as a medium of instruction; (4) entrepreneurs who want to capitalize on the medium for personal gain; and (5) futurists who see the medium as a part of a brave new world of innovative communication technology. All these access seekers share, said the editor of the UNESCO study, "a common mood and tone, at once romantic, radical, and missionary" (Berrigan, 1977: 15).

One reason broadcasting access is withheld from nonprofessionals is that many broadcasting systems are highly centralized. In the United States localism is a basic goal of regulation. Nevertheless network and centrally produced recorded programming dominates. But at least part of the time network stations function as local outlets, and some types of radio stations, such as telephone talk shows, operate largely without the benefit of prerecorded material produced at distant production centers.

In Third World countries, however, stations outside the capital city are likely to function simply as relay outlets for national programs. Lack of trained personnel and fear of subversion make it both simpler and safer to keep all program control at the center. Even in most Western democracies, though for different reasons, programming tends to be national or regional rather than local. Local programming in Britain was not introduced until 1967, and then as a separate class of stations, distinct from those carrying the network programs (§1.3).

Access in Holland The Dutch have gone to greater lengths than any other country in restructuring their national broadcasting system to assure maximum access to nearly all types of people. In the mid-1960s Holland became one of the targets of offshore pirate stations offering commercially sponsored pop music (§1.6). This infusion of mass-appeal material, so different from the stodgy programming of official Dutch radio, caused a political upheaval. The new government gave broadcasting a thorough overhaul, rejecting the monolithic type of national broadcasting organization originally favored in Europe. The new system, as described by Anthony Smith,

enshrines the grass-roots political aspirations of its time in a way which gives them a status in national life in Holland which they do not yet possess elsewhere. It enabled every group of discontented or inspired individuals to propagate its beliefs on its own terms. In providing this facility as of right (a right unrecognized in any other broadcasting system) it tried to bring by implication all the movements of the time out of the shadows . . . It tried to make broadcasting as flexible and available as printing. (1973: 273)

Control of programming in Holland is divided among the various sociopolitical and religious groups of the country. Each group that wants to participate sets up a nonprofit corporation, which is granted air time (both radio and television) according to its size. The government makes available the national transmission facilities and centrally organized studios to all groups, each being allotted an amount of time proportionate to its size. Broadcasting associations obtain funds by the sale of program guides for their segments of the schedule. Class A associations have 500,000 or more members. Groups as small as 40,000 are classed as "candidate broadcasters." One of the groups in this category was organized by "Veronica," formerly a pirate station. Small ethnic groups such as immigrant workers and people from the former Dutch colonies in the Far East get some air time, even if it is only a few minutes a week.

As one might guess, such diffusion of control and specialization of content does not necessarily result in the best possible overall program service. As Smith puts it, the Dutch take more pride in their system than in their programming: "An air of earnest dullness surrounds the entire output. It lacks dynamism" (1973: 276). In order to attract mass audiences capable in turn of attracting advertisers, the Dutch continue, as do virtually all small countries, to fill part of their schedule with popular foreign imports.

Access in Italy   Access has been obtained in Italy by more colorful means. The national service, RAI (Radio-televisione Italiana), has a legal monopoly on national network broadcasting. Its programming, strongly influenced by partisan politics, fails to win the popular support of Italian audiences, who tune to neighboring countries whenever possible.

In 1975 a loophole was discovered in the broadcasting statute that authorizes the RAI monopoly. It granted exclusive rights over *national* broadcasting to the government-appointed organization, but did not actually forbid others from engaging in *local* broadcasting. Hundreds of local radio and television stations took to the air all over Italy, representing an incredible variety of interests. There may have been a thousand or more of these "alternative" stations — no official count was made. Some were run commercially by merchants, some by hobbyists, some by political parties and radical groups. Homosexuals, the unemployed, counterculture groups, feminists, and off-duty members of the army and police all had their say on the air.

1.6 Economic Influences

World Distribution of Facilities   The extent to which a nation can exploit broadcasting depends, of course, on how much it can afford to invest in the hardware of the medium. The nations of the world vary widely in the numbers of transmitters and receivers they have relative to their populations. For example, a UNESCO tabulation made in the 1970s comparing developed with developing countries showed the following contrasts:

Developed countries: 693 radio receivers, 301 TV receivers per thousand population

Developing countries: 83 radio receivers, 22 TV receivers per thousand population

Even more startling is the difference between the U.S. share of facilities compared to the rest of the world (Exhibit 1.6). Relative to its population, in the mid-1970s the United States alone had several times as many broadcast receivers and transmitters as all the rest of the countries in the world put together.

Such massive investment in broadcasting hardware can be ascribed to three principal causes: (1) Of course, high *living standards* allow virtually the entire U.S. population to buy receivers. (2) *Programming* is of a type that strongly motivates people to invest in receivers. (3) National policy favors erecting as many *local stations* as possible (far fewer stations could cover the country, but at the cost of allowing each community to have its own local outlets).

In countries where the mass of the population cannot afford to buy sets, investment in transmission and production facilities is extremely uneconomic. It costs just as much to reach a tiny fraction of the population in a transmitter's coverage area as to reach the total population within that area. Broadcasting can also be hamstrung in poorer countries by lack of *communications infrastructure* — the basic wire and radio relay grid needed to interconnect broadcasting networks and to gather news and other program materials efficiently.

Economics and Politics Economic influences in broadcasting are never without political overtones. In the less developed countries, decisions about investments in broadcasting facilities involve such questions as: Will such-and-such a provincial location for a transmitter be politically secure? Will placing a transmitter in one section of the country win more important local loyalty for

Exhibit 1.6
U.S. share of world population and broadcasting facilities

Basis of comparison	U.S. percentage of world total
Population	5
Radio transmitters	30
Radio receivers	42
TV transmitters	15
TV receivers	32

Comment: The U.S. share of facilities was from three to six times that of all the rest of the world, relative to the U.S. population. These data are only rough approximations. The rest of the world has been catching up since UNESCO drew up this tabulation (the last in which the yearbook gave world totals), and China, North Korea, and North Vietnam were not included. Even if cut in half, however, the U.S. share would still be amazingly high.

Source: Based on 1975/1976 data in UNESCO, *Statistical Yearbook, 1977.* UNESCO, Paris, 1978.

the government than it would in another section of the country?

Among the industrialized countries economic chauvinism has resulted in such absurdities as three incompatible color television systems in use throughout the world. Which system a country chooses depends not so much on the intrinsic merits of the color picture it produces as on political affiliations. American NTSC color is used in most of Latin America, Japan, and the Philippines. Germany's PAL system is used in most of Europe — except for France, whose SECAM system is also used in the USSR. Ex-French colonies use SECAM, while ex-British colonies use PAL, and so on.

How a country decides to finance broadcasting depends pretty much on its political philosophy. The three basic sources of funding are general tax revenues, receiver license fees, and advertising. Many systems combine two or more of these sources, but broadly speaking the three funding methods match the three political orientations previously described (§1.2). Authoritarian systems receive their support from *tax revenues* as an allocation from the central treasury, paternalistic systems from *license fees,* and permissive systems from *advertising.* The current trend is toward supplementing either government or license-fee funding with advertising income, though many countries cannot generate enough advertising revenue to defray a major part of the cost of their national broadcasting systems. The pluralistic ideal calls for two or more services supported by two or more different funding sources.

Government Funding Authoritarian socialist governments that regard broadcasting as an arm of the state accept government support of broadcasting as a normal expense of government (the Soviet Union originally charged license fees, but discontinued them in 1962). The developing countries have no choice. Even if they preferred to rely on license fees or advertising they cannot get anywhere near enough revenue from these sources. Democracies avoid government funding because of the inevitable probability that, having paid the piper, the government in power will want to call the tune, undermining the credibility of the entire broadcasting service.

License Fees The Annan Committee, latest of the advisory groups that periodically make recommendations for the future of British broadcasting, put the arguments in favor of license fees in the form of an analogy:

Economists regard broadcasting as "a public good" — of which the classic example is the lighthouse. Once the light is shining for the benefit of some ships, it is impossible to prevent other ships using the light. Moreover, society does not incur any additional costs if the crews of these other ships do look at the light. (Great Britain, 1977: 132)

The committee went on to point out that even though broadcasting is a public good, it is not *essential* in the same sense as a police force and therefore should not be supported by taxation.

The BBC, which depends entirely on license fees to pay for its domestic services (aside from the small fraction of its income derived from the sale of programs and publications), regards the fee system as ideal. It makes set-owners feel they have a direct stake in the system, and at the same time gives the broadcasting organization a strong sense of public responsibility. Most important, though, it insulates the system from political or advertiser influence.

Nevertheless, the license-fee system of support has its drawbacks. Evasion of fees is a constant problem, especially in countries where tax evasion is commonplace or where no efficient machinery for collection exists. Collection in any event is an expensive business. In Britain, where the post office serves as a relatively efficient collecting agency, about 8 percent of the fees goes toward collection and enforcement expenses. In many countries fee collection costs a great deal more. By 1980, annual license fees for black-and-white television in Britain had reached £12 (over $25) and for color £34 (over $70). Fees for radio-only licenses were dropped in 1971. Most other European license fees are substantially higher than the British rates.

A more serious problem for broadcasters dependent on license fees is the fact that the population can absorb just so many receivers. After that, the number of licenses increases only as the population increases. Income levels off, but operating and capital replacement costs continue to rise. The public resents and politicians oppose continual increases in fees without corresponding increases in service. Moreover, it takes time to obtain government approval of fee increases. The BBC, like all services dependent on license-fee income, began having difficulty in living within its means in the 1970s. One proposed solution is an "indexed" fee scale that would automatically rise or fall with the level of inflation.

Advertising Support All the major European broadcasting systems once depended entirely on license fees for funding. Now only Belgium, Denmark, Norway, and Sweden still bar advertising. Some of these holdouts have had to curtail services to keep within their incomes. Advertising as a funding source has in its favor the fact that it is a relatively painless and nondiscriminatory way of exacting payments for broadcasting services. It spreads the cost over the entire population, making it relatively low for each individual; and it avoids rewarding the chiselers who otherwise get a free ride at the expense of law-abiding citizens.

Decisions as to whether to rely on advertising income to support broadcasting systems involve social and political as well as economic questions. Early radio systems often looked toward America as the prime example of the adverse social consequences of advertising support. They abhorred the permissiveness of the American system and what they considered to be its advertising excesses. Moves toward commercialism were also powerfully opposed by newspapers, which feared competition for advertising revenue. In Great Britain the Conservative party favored commercialism while the Labor party opposed it. Some observers claimed that Britain capitulated to narrow commercial interests as a result of maneuvers by a few influential politicians when the Conservatives won the election that led to establishment of the commercial television service in 1954 (Wilson, 1961).

International Commercial Stations

Broadcasting abhors a vacuum. Whenever a national system fails to provide what people want, sources outside the country spring up to remedy the lack. In the days when the BBC and the other European noncommercial national systems were still too paternalistic to respond to popular tastes, commercial stations located abroad made inroads on their audiences. Among these Radio Luxembourg is a notable example. The Grand Duchy of Luxembourg, located at the intersection of Belgium, France, and Germany, gets most of its national income from commercial broadcasting revenue. It aims the programs at other European countries, including Britain. A local service on FM reaches its own people in the Luxembourgian language, but powerful AM radio transmitters cover the surrounding countries with programs in French, German, Dutch, English, and Italian. Ironically, during the period when France refused to allow its own stations to accept commercials, the French government owned substantial shares in the commercial stations broadcasting into France from Andorra, Luxembourg, and Monte Carlo (the last even has transmitters located on French soil).

Commercial Pirates Even more striking evidence of the "broadcasting-abhors-a-vacuum" principle was the success of illegal commercial radio stations located on ships and abandoned World War II forts in the English Channel and the North Sea. The first such *pirate* station started in 1958 on a ship anchored between Sweden and Denmark. Frankly imitative of American popular-music formats and capitalizing on American advertising techniques (in fact many of the investors were American), the pirates quickly captured huge audiences. They heightened national appetites for pop-music programming to such an extent that the official broadcasting systems could no longer evade the issue. In Holland the coalition in power, which opposed commercialism, was voted out of office as a direct result of the influence of the pirate stations. In Britain the BBC reorganized its national radio networks, adding a fourth service to preempt the pop-music appeal of the pirates. Some of the offshore DJs, who reaped enormous dividends in publicity from their risky ventures on the pirate ships, ended up working for the despised establishment on BBC's Radio-1 network.

Cost Sharing No matter what combination of funding sources they employ, small countries have serious difficulties in financing their television programming. Television consumes expensive program materials at such a rate that to maintain a reasonably full schedule with exclusively home-grown productions is literally impossible in small countries, even those that have the most advanced industrial economies. The easiest solution to this dilemma is to import programs from foreign countries. Imports, rented at a small fraction of what it would cost to produce programs of similar quality locally, usually come from Britain and the United States. Politics as well as economics are involved in making such purchases. No country wants to allow its own culture to be swamped by imported programming; nor does it want to depress its own production capacity by dissipating its program budget abroad, or to spend limited hard currency reserves on nonessentials. For these reasons there are strong incentives for developing other, less damaging ways of paying for programs.

A partial solution is international cost-sharing. An example is mutual program exchanges by means of *broadcasting unions.* This term refers not to trade unions, but to associations of national broadcasting organizations. The European Broadcasting Union operates *Eurovision*, an international network for the exchange of nationally produced programs among the countries of Western Europe. East Europe has a similar union, the International Radio and Television Organization. Program exchanges of ideologically neutral programs between the two European unions have become commonplace. Asia, Africa, the Caribbean, the Arab Middle East each has its own broadcasting union, although only the two European organizations have so far succeeded in mounting effective program exchanges.

Another cost-sharing expedient is *co-production*. Producing organizations of two or more countries agree to share in the cost of joint production ventures. Co-production has been common in Europe for many years but American producers have entered the field only relatively recently, largely as a result of the success of British programs imported by U.S. public broadcasting.

1.7 Influence of Geography and History

A country's size, its shape, its neighbors, and its history all affect its broadcasting system. One has only to think of a country like Israel to realize the importance of these factors.

Coverage   Sheer size and shape of a nation determine the cost and the effectiveness of national broadcasting coverage. Aside from its outlying states and territories, the United States consists of a compact, unified land-mass surrounded mostly by large bodies of water — highly favorable geographic factors from the broadcasting point of view. American broadcasting has relatively little problem with intrusion by signals from foreign countries and can cover its own territory efficiently. Treaty agreements with Canada, Mexico, and the Caribbean islands deal with problems of transnational interference. In recent years, however, Cuba has put 500-kilowatt AM stations on the air (ten times the maximum power allowed under the treaty) in defiance of international agreements. These high-power stations interfere with U.S. stations in Florida during the day and at night can be heard across the entire country.

The U.S. situation contrasts with that of European nations, all of which suffer interference from neighboring countries. Many standard AM radio stations in the United States gain extra coverage at night because reflected sky waves send their signals far and wide, beyond their local daytime service areas. In Europe, however, nighttime sky-wave reception is virtually impossible. So many stations crowd the broadcast band that service areas shrink at night because of sky-wave interference.

Spillover   American listeners and viewers do not generally pick up foreign broadcast stations unless they live near the Canadian or Mexican borders or within reach of Cuba's AM stations. More distant stations can easily be heard on short waves, but only a small percentage of U.S. homes are equipped with short-wave receivers (surveys have estimated between 7 and 11 percent). However, sales of short-wave receivers began to increase in the late 1970s as more and more Americans discovered that it was relatively inexpensive to listen to foreign countries, most of which broadcast at least part of the time in English.

In most parts of the world, audiences receive many *spillover signals* from neighboring countries on ordinary receivers. Several years before television started in Israel, thousands of Israelis had already bought receivers in order to pick up the signals of neighboring Arab countries. Spillover between West Berlin and East Germany creates a somewhat paradoxical situation. Citizens on each side of the Berlin Wall, though political enemies, enjoy each other's programs. The need to buy converters to compensate for differing color systems does not deter the East Germans, most of whom tune in to the two West German networks (Kiester, 1977). Similar East-West spillover situations occur at other points along the perimeter of the communist bloc countries of Europe.

Canadians get a great deal of their radio and television as spillover from stations in the United States. In addition, Canadian cable companies pick up American stations for their subscribers. Ninety percent of the Canadian population is concentrated along the U.S. border; thus American broadcasting tends to overwhelm Canada's own culture. Although not all spillover services are deliberate, the Canadians are understandably resentful of American dominance. In many cases, however, spillover coverage is deliberately contrived. Americans invest in certain high-powered stations in Mexico, located near the United States border, for example.

These stations broadcast commercial programming designed for the American market, exempt from American program and commercial regulatory controls.

Impact of History   Events of history had a major influence on the broadcasting systems of the defeated nations of World War II. Hitler used radio as an effective political weapon, both at home and abroad. The world's first television service started in Berlin in 1935, shortly before the war (because its pictures were of low quality, Britain could claim priority as the first regular high-definition television service in 1936). Hitler failed to encourage television, however, because he believed his special charisma came across better on radio (Sandford, 1976: 97). After Hitler's defeat, the Allies broke up the highly centralized German system. Each of the four occupying powers, Britain, France, Russia, and the United States, installed a broadcasting service in its own sector, each imposing its own philosophy of broadcasting. Of the three Western systems, the British had the most lasting effect (the USSR, of course, had a lasting effect on its sector, which became East Germany). According to a broadcast historian, in West Germany

the stamp of the BBC is still clearly recognizeable . . . indeed it is often the BBC of twenty years ago that seems to inform program presentation: the all-pervasive air of dignity and decency of ''Auntie BBC'' has changed less across the channel than it has in Britain. (Sandford, 1976: 88)

The West Germany of today is a federal republic, with each of nine states in the federation retaining cultural autonomy and its own distinctive character. The states vary greatly in size, one of them being the city of West Berlin. The West German federal constitution places matters of culture so firmly under state rather than federal control that the only way Germany can have national television networks is by the joint action of the nine state broadcasting systems (somewhat like the case of the regional companies under the IBA in Britain, which cooperate to offer a national network service). Radio is almost exclusively regional, but television's high cost made it essential for the states to get together to share in establishing the two German networks.

West Germany's unique system . . . has proved resistant to change. Whilst its apologists see it as a guarantee of diversity and independence, and fully in keeping with the spirit of West German federalism, others, pointing to the fact that it is a haphazard result of uncoordinated Allied policies during the Occupation, call for a more rational use of broadcasting resources. (Sandford, 1976: 74)

Thus can history influence the fundamental organization of a nation's broadcasting system.

1.8 Programs and Schedules

Program formats are universal, used throughout the world of broadcasting. News, commentary, music, drama, children's programs, education, studio games, play-by-play sports events — all represent logical responses to the intrinsic nature of the medium. Marked national differences emerge, however, when one examines the details within basic formats. Schedules also vary. Few services stay on the air 18 or more hours a day as do most U.S. commercial stations other than daytime-only radio stations.

News and Public Affairs The most marked national differences emerge in the treatment of news and public affairs formats. In virtually every country the main news presentation of the day, whether it occurs early or late in the evening or at midday, is one of the most universally popular program segments. If one could hear and see the news on a single day from different broadcasters throughout the world, however, one would get the impression that they lived in many different worlds. Parochialism, chauvinism, and ideological biases affect what is reported as well as when and how.

TV Guide once compared a single week's television news in six widely scattered countries. The first fact to emerge was, not unexpectedly, that each country stressed its own national news events, few of which had the slightest interest for the rest of the world. The second was that even when treating the same story, each saw it in a different light. The U.S. networks reported on vigorous debates within government about a summit meeting on the controversial SALT II (arms limitation) treaty between the two superpowers. Viewers in the USSR heard quotations from the head of the American Communist Party to the effect that there was no U.S. opposition to the treaty at all. Chinese television ignored the whole subject during the monitoring week, but showed the opening of the meeting a week later. On the night Israeli television showed its team defeating the USSR in a championship basketball game in Italy, Soviet television chose to show an earlier contest between two East European teams. As for domestic news events

U.S. television news covered in depth America's energy crunch. Egyptian TV news pursued the runoff elections for the Egyptian parliament. Israeli TV news focused on a member of the Nigerian mission to the United Nations caught smuggling arms into Israel on behalf of the Palestine Liberation Organization. On Japanese TV, the major domestic news story was the payoff scandal rocking the Japanese parliament. . . . Soviet TV news was fascinated by the marathon ordeal of Russian cosmonauts orbiting in the Salyut 6 space lab. Even China had a story to cover: the Second Session of the Fifth National People's Congress.

Yet no one — including the U.S. TV news — devoted anything but minimal coverage to the major domestic stories of any of the other five nations that week. (Kowet, 1979)

Third World nations complain bitterly about domination of Western organizations in the worldwide gathering and distribution of news. For example, a billion people each day are said to hear, see, or read stories distributed by the Associated Press, one of the two U.S. news agencies with worldwide scope. Third World critics complain that Western reporters look mainly for negative stories in their countries — the bizarre antics of an Idi Amin in Uganda or famine in Mali hold more interest for Western reporters and editors than sober stories about new factories, dams, educational advancement, hospitals, and agricultural projects.

For this reason the Third World tends to agree with the communists' approach to news. Broadcasters in communist countries have no need to compete with alternative domestic sources. Timeliness, human interest, and what Western journalists consider "news values" take second place to political correctness and educational value. Stories about murders, accidents, riots, natural disasters are downplayed or avoided entirely—unless used to illustrate the decadence of capitalistic societies.

In the Third World, concentration on Western-style reporting would usually result in depressingly downbeat newscasts, loaded with stories of food shortages, industrial mismanagement, crop failures, corruption, and other horrendous problems that face the less developed nations. Governments in those countries instruct broadcasters to downplay such negative events. Instead, journalists must use the news constructively, supporting the government and its leaders, heralding the nation's accomplishments, and urging listeners and viewers to work hard at nation building.

Entertainment American travelers in foreign countries are often surprised to discover that the rest of the world's popular mass entertainment can be even more inane than the sitcoms they see at home. But they are also often impressed by the number of high-quality, serious programs they see on services such as BBC-2, the British television network that features cultural programming. But what impresses travelers most is the fact that almost wherever they go they see reruns of *I Love Lucy, Mission: Impossible, Gunsmoke,* and other familiar American network series.

Broadcasting is perceived as a major vehicle of national cultural expression. Traditions of literature, music, and the visual arts all contribute to broadcast programming, which in turn plays an important role in passing on these traditions to new generations. Most countries are therefore concerned about the impact of broadcasting on their cultures. Imported programming can be seen as a threat to cultural survival. Not only do imports impose images, values, and concepts from an alien culture on television audiences, they also drastically reduce opportunities for employment for national artists and crafts people. Even highly developed nations with their own flourishing production resources such as Canada and Britain feel it necessary to impose ceilings on the amount of foreign programming that may be imported. Third World countries feel much more vulnerable. In addition to being less able to produce their own programming, their cultures differ totally from that represented by *Dallas* or *Three's Company*. Many developing nations see broadcasting as part of a deliberate campaign of cultural-economic exploitation — a modern substitute for the old-fashioned colonialism that relied on force of arms. They call it *cultural imperialism*.

Schedules Twenty-four-hour broadcast schedules are unknown in most countries. Many radio systems go on the air for a short time in the morning, take a midmorning break before midday programming, another midafternoon break before evening programming. Television schedules are likely to be limited to only a few hours in the late afternoon and evening. Even in such a highly developed system as that of Britain, 24-hour network radio broadcasting by the BBC did not begin until 1979, when Radio-2 filled in the previously blank hours of 2:00 A.M. to 5:00 A.M. And as noted previously, early morning television was not authorized in Britain until the 1980s.

Scheduling of commercials also differs in many countries from the U.S. practice. Often they are limited to one or two time-periods each day, with all commercials run consecutively within the designated time-blocks. It is not uncommon for commercials to be barred completely on Sundays and religious holidays.

Audience Research All broadcasting systems agree in principle on the importance of audience research. Not all systems, however, can afford the cost of continuous, systematic studies, such as the rating services familiar in the United States. Commercially supported systems are naturally more highly motivated to spend money on measurement than others.

U.S. broadcasters, extremely research conscious, spend large sums on studying audiences. Their emphasis has been more on measuring audience size and composition than on assessing audience opinions and reactions. This American preoccupation with *quantitative* measurement is not shared by most foreign systems.

In Britain, for example, the charters of both the BBC and the commercial broadcasters require them to conduct research on audience likes and dislikes as well as on audience size. The BBC has long used listener and viewer *panels* (meaning groups of individuals whose views are sought repeatedly). Panel members fill out questionnaires indicating their reactions to programs. The man who developed the BBC research department explained the reasoning in favor of *qualitative* research as follows:

in a properly balanced audience research service the continuous measurement of the quantity of listening — the estimation of the size of each programme's audience — should be supplemented by a continuous assessment of audience reaction — what listeners felt about the programmes they were listening to. So long as quantitative data alone was pouring out from Audience Research day after day there was real danger that the bigger-necessarily-means-better heresy would gain adherents by default. (Silvey, 1974: 113)

In Russia, social research (of which audience measurement is an example) was at one time frowned on by the government. It was taken for granted that if something was put on the air it was certain to be heard or seen and understood (Mickiewicz, 1981: 6). During the 1970s, however, Soviet broadcasting authorities increased both the amount and the quality of their audience research. Improvements in the attractiveness of their programming seem to have followed, striking evidence of the role audience research can play in shaping broadcasting, even in an authoritarian system.

1.9 Broadcasting to Other Countries

Broadcasting introduced a potent new factor in the relations among the countries of the world. Never before had it been so easy to cross international boundaries to talk directly to the citizens of foreign countries. Using mostly short-wave radio (because of its long range), *external broadcasting* has become a powerful new weapon in both warfare and times of peace.

Dimensions of External Broadcasting

Russia and the United States lead the more than 80 countries that engage in external broadcasting operations. With over 2,000 hours on the air each week, the USSR leads the pack (Exhibit 1.9). However, even some very small countries such as Albania and Cuba rank among the top ten international broadcasters. This came about because China and the Soviet Union respectively financed their external services as a way of getting access to strategically placed transmission sites beyond their own borders. The United States and other Western countries obtain

Exhibit 1.9
The ten leading external broadcasters

Country		Estimated hours on the air per week
1. USSR		2,020
2. U.S.A.		
VOA	828	
Radio Free Europe	555	
Radio Liberty	462	
Total U.S.A.		1,845
3. People's Republic of China		1,390
4. West Germany		798
5. Great Britain		712
6. North Korea		597
7. Albania		557
8. Egypt		389
9. Cuba		382
10. East Germany		371

Comment: In the years immediately following World War II, Britain was the leading international broadcaster in hours on the air. At that time the countries ranked sixth through tenth in the table had not yet even begun their external services.

Source: Based on 1979 data in *BBC Annual Report and Handbook, 1981*, British Broadcasting Corporation, London, 1980, p. 58.

transmitter locations abroad by entering into treaties to lease sites where they erect their own facilities. The U.S. external service, the Voice of America, has leased sites for relay stations in Africa (Liberia and Morocco), Germany, Great Britain, Greece (on the mainland and on the island of Rhodes), the Philippines, Sri Lanka, and Thailand.

Origins of External Services

Britain's world-girdling empire still existed when broadcasting began in the 1920s. The implications of broadcasting for the empire were immediately recognized by the BBC. It began experimenting with overseas transmissions in 1928. Britain officially launched the Empire Service in 1932. This pioneer external service, entirely in English, was aimed at both British expatriates in the colonies and residents of the dominions (independent nations like Canada and Australia), to maintain their ties with the "home country." Earlier external services, also prompted by colonial interests abroad, had been started by the Dutch and Germans (1929) and the French (1931).

The BBC launched its first foreign language external broadcasts in 1938, on the eve of World War II. They were in Arabic, aimed at counteracting Italian radio propaganda directed toward the Near East. Soon Germany and Britain began a deadly "war of words."

The United States added its voice to the word war when President Franklin D. Roosevelt appointed Elmer Davis, a popular radio newscaster, to head the Office of War Information (OWI). An important component of the OWI was the Voice of America, which went on the air in February 1942. Congress was wary of creating a government propaganda agency, fearing it might in the future be turned against Americans themselves by a political party in power. In fact, after the OWI was set up, conservative congressmen accused it of covertly campaigning for President Roosevelt's reelection and pro-

moting his controversial New Deal policies (Winkler, 1977: 66). To this day U.S. law forbids release within the United States of government radio, television, and film programs designed for overseas use.

Voice of America

After the war the OWI was disbanded, but the VOA continued operation, shunted about from one federal agency to another over the years. The latest change came in 1978, when the International Communications Agency (ICA) was created to take over functions previously carried out by both the United States Information Agency and the State Department's Bureau of Educational and Cultural Affairs. In brief, the ICA is responsible for international exchange of information and persons. In announcing the ICA's formation, President Jimmy Carter said, "The Agency will undertake no activities which are covert, manipulative or propagandistic."

This mandate was in keeping with the original spirit of the VOA, expressed in its first broadcast to foreign countries in 1942: "Daily at this time we shall speak to you about America and the war. The news may be good or bad. We shall tell you the truth." Despite some lapses for expediency's sake, truth-telling has continued as the policy of the VOA. Its news staff has a keen sense of professionalism and vigorously resists occasional efforts by government officials at higher levels to get the VOA to bend the truth to suit momentary political objectives.

The Voice of America originates its programs from studios in Washington, D.C., using, in addition to English, some 40 foreign languages, ranging from Albanian to Vietnamese. Choice of languages is influenced by current events and changing international relationships. For example, when the Iranians seized the U.S. embassy in Teheran in 1979, the Voice soon resumed broadcasts in the language of that country, Farsi, after a lapse of twenty years. Previously the BBC and Moscow had been the leading external sources of programs heard in Iran.

Programs go from the Washington studios to short-wave transmitters located in North Carolina, Florida, Ohio, and California (Exhibit 3.5.2). Signals from these transmitters are picked up by relay facilities located overseas in target regions, which then beam them on toward specific target countries. Satellite relays are also used to send programs overseas. However, satellite transmissions can be interrupted. The earth stations that receive the signals from satellites are under control of the countries in which they are located. For this reason, U.S.-based short-wave transmitters are still essential to the VOA's mission.

VOA programs consist of news, commentary, popular music, and features about American culture. Services directed to specific regions also carry material about those regions. The VOA does not broadcast television programs, but the overseas field offices of the ICA, the parent agency, supply U.S. material on film and tape to foreign television stations.

RFE/RL In addition to the more conventional external services of the VOA, the United States supports two specialized overseas services aimed exclusively at the USSR and Soviet-dominated Eastern Europe. Radio Liberty (RL) broadcasts to the USSR itself, Radio Free Europe (RFE) to Poland, Hungary, and the other buffer states. They both have studios in Munich, with transmitters in Germany and Spain. These unusual operations originated after World War II as covert Central Intelligence Agency operations. Annual fund drives were conducted in the United States to make it appear that the operations were supported by voluntary public subscription. In 1973, after the CIA connec-

tion was made public (though it never was a well-kept secret), Congress created a special agency to supervise the combined RFE/RL operations, the Board for International Broadcasting, with funding directly by Congress.

RFE/RL programming differs from the usual external propaganda fare such as the VOA's broadcasts to the USSR and Eastern Europe. The aim is to program just the way *internal* domestic stations would in the target countries — if they were free of government censorship. News about what is going on in the USSR and her satellites, rather than news of the United States, is their stock in trade. RFE/RL obtain background for their broadcasts from extensive research libraries of publications and transcriptions of broadcasts originating in the target countries. They also collect material from contacts with travelers and defectors from behind the Iron Curtain. One of their most effective resources are the clandestine publications known as *samizdat*. These are literary and informational materials informally duplicated and circulated secretly by Russians within their own country.

The United States bears the entire expense of the RFE/RL operation except for provision of space for production and transmission facilities on foreign soil. Congress has been of two minds about RFE/RL. Some legislators think they represent a hangover from the Cold War of the 1950s, a counterproductive irritant in U.S. relations with the communists. Others argue that it is in the interest of the West to use such means to help keep alive the spirit of resistance among citizens of communist countries and to counteract their domestic anti-U.S. propaganda.

AFRTS Broadcasting Although not intended for foreign consumption, U.S. military broadcasting has a certain amount of impact on foreign audiences. The American

Forces Radio and Television Service (AFRTS)* operates low-power radio and television stations at bases overseas and closed-circuit systems on many U.S. Navy ships. Some AFRTS programming is selected from regular offerings of the U.S. commercial and public service networks; the rest comes from its own local and stateside staff personnel and military reporters. Public service announcements are substituted for commercials in the network material. Timely radio materials (news and live play-by-play sports) are relayed directly to overseas AFRTS stations by VOA transmitters and via leased circuits on commercial satellites. Television and less timely radio material are sent on tape or film.

Because of the inevitable spillover into neighboring civilian areas, the AFRTS stations reach many host-country citizens. The programs differ considerably in tone from VOA services, giving foreigners a more realistic and informal glimpse of American lifestyles. According to a British commentator,

There is little doubt that British soldiers and civilians alike [during World War II] thoroughly enjoyed the more relaxed, informal atmosphere of American-style broadcasting and found the entertainment more sprightly than that of the pre-war BBC. To some extent, at least, the dreaded "Americanization" of British tastes by Hollywood and "pop" records was given additional impetus by the American Forces Network. (Wilson, 1961: 23)

AFRTS impact on postwar Germany was especially significant. One observer estimated that the local residents rather than GIs constituted the majority of AFRTS listeners. He speaks of "the tantalizing glimpses of an affluent and swaggeringly self-confident life style that the presentation and contents of [AFRTS] programs provided, attracted for it

*Originally the "A" stood for "armed," but the less aggressive-sounding title was adopted in 1969.

a wide and enthusiastic audience in the broken Europe of the post-war years . . . Its listeners totalled tens of millions in both Western and Eastern Europe" (Sandford, 1976: 94).

BBC External Service In foreign countries, the Voice of America is generally regarded as a relatively objective source of news. The BBC, however, undoubtedly remains the leading international broadcaster in terms of credibility and perhaps in popularity. This is partly because many people around the world feel more comfortable with the British speech pattern, but primarily because the BBC has a longer tradition and greater insulation from government. The VOA is clearly understood by most listeners to be a government agency, staffed by federal government employees. The BBC is just as clearly understood to be independent of government. True, the BBC External Service relies on government funds allocated by the Foreign Office rather than on the license fees that support the BBC domestic services. However, the Foreign Office controls only the choice of languages to be used.

Throughout the world listeners tune automatically to the BBC when in doubt about the authenticity of local versions of the news. It is not uncommon for foreign government officials, in times of local disorders, to depend on the BBC for vital information about the state of affairs in their own countries. However, the British no longer lead the world in the quantity of their external broadcasts as they once did, now ranking only fifth (Exhibit 1.9).

Soviet External Broadcasting Communist nations have always placed much faith in the power of propaganda. In fact one of the early propaganda uses of external radio (in prebroadcasting days) was the radiotelegraphic transmission of Lenin's 1917 message to dissidents in other countries announcing the communist revolution (Hale, 1975: 16). During the 1970s the Soviet Union forged ahead of the United States as the leading international broadcaster in terms of hours on the air (Exhibit 1.9).

Communist external services tend to be relentlessly propagandistic in tone. One commentator described Russian broadcasting as suffering from "ponderousness, parochialism, and partiality" (Hale, 1975: 20). He explained that the Soviets' seeming disregard for credibility resulted from a policy of "preaching to the saved." Most of their messages were apparently designed to reinforce confirmed believers, rather than to win converts.

With the increase in output during the 1970s, however, the Soviets began to lighten the ponderous tone of their broadcasts. Radio Moscow recently began a 24-hour daily service in English, using the BBC's long-established title, "World Service." It departs markedly from the traditional tone of Soviet broadcasting, even going so far as to make jokes about itself.

Jamming   Ideally, the truth should be the best rebuttal for propaganda. But sometimes the truth hurts, and nations resort to *jamming* of foreign broadcasts. A form of electronic interference, jamming consists of making an offending signal unintelligible by broadcasting sheer noise on the same or an adjacent channel. The most persistent and massive jamming occurs in communist countries, though most countries that can afford the high cost have resorted to jamming on occasion.

Jamming is an extremely expensive, yet uncertain, business. Western sources estimated that in the early 1970s Russia devoted 3,000 transmitters to jamming operations, at

an annual cost of $185 million. It is a measure of the Soviets' anxiety that they were willing to spend so much on a defense of such doubtful value:

The effectiveness of jamming varies: at times it can block a signal in a city and fail to do so a few miles away in the countryside; the use of high-power transmitters and several frequencies can overcome some jamming; and there are limited periods during the day when propagation conditions give a properly sited broadcaster virtual immunity. (President's Study Commission, 1973: 19)

The amount of jamming carried on by the USSR and its allies serves as a barometer of the state of East-West relations. For a time during the détente of the late 1970s jamming almost ceased, only to erupt again later because of the tension caused by the 1980 Soviet invasion of Afghanistan and the confrontation between Polish trade unionists and their communist government. The Polish crisis provided RFE/RL with the kind of opportunity those services especially prize. RFE/RL have always been more deeply resented than the VOA, and therefore more subject to jamming. The 1980 political turmoil in Poland, however, triggered jamming of the VOA, BBC, and German external services.

Clandestine Broadcasting   Dissident political elements, exiled by choice or force from their own countries, often set up *clandestine stations* in neighboring territories to beam propaganda back home. In times of civil unrest such stations even operate within the home country. Clandestine stations operate in violation of both national and international law, though usually with the connivance of the host countries. They spring up along the borders of unrest almost anywhere in the world except Latin America, where it is easy for guerrillas to capture local commercial stations for temporary use (Hale, 1975: 105). Prior to the fall of the Shah of Iran, dissidents operated at least three clandestine stations against his regime. Immediately after his fall clandestine stations opposing the new regime went on the air.

A variant of clandestine operations is the open use of facilities loaned by countries friendly toward dissident groups. For example, under Prime Minister Gamal Abdel Nasser in the 1950s, Egypt gave many radical opponents of African and Middle Eastern regimes free use of Egypt's powerful international transmitters.

Wherever rules exist there will be people to challenge them. Clandestine stations constantly spring up in the United States, motivated by the sheer exhilaration of being able to broadcast in defiance of the law.

1.10 Issue: "Free Flow" or "New Order"?

Media Imperialism Thesis In the preceding sections we indicated some of the ways in which U.S. broadcasting affects other systems in the world:

■ In the early days of radio, some countries avoided using American commercial broadcasting as a model because of what they perceived as its detrimental social effects.
■ The sale of American programs throughout most of the developing world has led to the charge of cultural imperialism.
■ The intrusive nature of Radio Liberty and Radio Free Europe exacerbates relations between the United States and the USSR, which regards these stations as going beyond the bounds of normal external services.

Other influences could be added, such as U.S. aid programs that supply broadcast equipment, advisers, and training to foreign systems.

All this buttresses the charge that American broadcasting exercises undue influence on other countries, contributing to *media imperialism*. The leading American supporter of this thesis, Herbert I. Schiller, expressed his view of the process in strong words:

Messages "made in America" radiate across the globe and serve as the ganglia of national power and expansionism. The ideological images of "have-not" states are increasingly in the custody of American information media. . . . The facilities and hardware of international information control are being grasped by a highly centralized communications complex, resident in the United States and largely unaccountable to its own population. (Schiller, 1971: 147)

Free Flow Controversy The media imperialism thesis leads, among other things, to the claim that curbs should be imposed on the *free flow* of information. American opposition to such curbs is based on the doctrine that the interests of all nations, great and small, are best served by a climate that encourages unimpeded flow of information, both within and between nations. Freedom of expression, a fundamental article of faith in American political philosophy, was at one time fully accepted by the world community. The UN Declaration of Human Rights, for example, states that "everyone has the right . . . to seek, receive and impart information and ideas *through any media regardless of frontiers."*

Since the UN voted to adopt that principle, however, the world has changed drastically. Some 70 new states have joined the United Nations. Most are underdeveloped and extremely conscious of their prior history as colonial territories of the Western powers. Known as the Third World bloc in the UN, they are intensely preoccupied with *neocolonialism*, which they see as threatening to drag them back into their former dependent status. What is the value of free flow to us, they ask, when it runs almost entirely in one direction — from the United States and a few other industrial countries to the Third World? Free flow, they assert, stacks the cards in favor of the Western powers. Nor is this one-sidedness just a matter of television programs and news reports. As an American observer, formerly an officer of the VOA, summarized the Third World view in his book, *America's Mass Media Merchants*, one-way flow means that

Citizens of the less developed countries must depend on foreigners to a significant extent for the books they read, the television programs and films they watch, and the news stories they read. They rely on foreign foundations for scholarly research grants, depend on universities abroad for better-quality higher education, and, indeed, must even learn a foreign language, most often English, in order to avail themselves of desired information. (Read, 1976: 163)

UNESCO's "New Information Order"
In 1972 the UN Educational, Scientific and Cultural Organization (UNESCO) took up the free-flow debate at its biennial general meeting. Third World members sponsored a resolution aimed at giving governments the right to impose certain controls over both the domestic and the international flow of news. Opponents of the motion managed to postpone votes on the motion at the next two meetings, but in 1978 UNESCO adopted a "Declaration on the Free Flow of World News."

Despite opposition from the United States and some of its allies, UNESCO set up a commission to investigate a *new world information order* — UNESCOese for a revised way of organizing and controlling world communications. In 1980 the commission, called the MacBride Commission in honor of its chairman, a distinguished Irish statesman, delivered its report. It proposed a number of checks on the unimpeded flow of news. It could be likened to a global "affirmative action" plan, aimed at redressing past discrimination against Third World countries.

The United States could not oppose affirmative action, of course. Both government and private organizations said they were ready to give both equipment and training to help developing countries improve their communication systems. But U.S. representatives and media commentators continued to oppose any impediments to the free flow of information. Such recommendations in the MacBride report as machinery for assuring "socially responsible reporting" and an international code of ethics for reporters sound innocent enough, but they are regarded in the West as endorsements of government censorship of the media.

Typical was the reaction of the editors of *Broadcasting* magazine. Commenting on the fact that the UN had passed a unanimous resolution recommending that member nations refer to the MacBride report when setting up national communications policies, they wrote that the report

is heavy with recommendations that go against the grain of press freedom. It advocates free access to news sources and professes to oppose censorship, but at the same time it urges news media to support — not merely report on, but support — social, cultural, economic and political goals set by governments. (Broadcasting 12 Jan. 1981)

Appraisal of Imperialism Thesis
At the root of the opposition to the free flow of information is a profound and fundamental conflict between two ideologies, broadly identifiable as East vs. West. The Third World has joined hands with communist ideologues on this issue — though not necessarily because of doctrinaire Marxist con-

victions. As we pointed out earlier (§1.8), to developing countries the communist view of media seems better suited to their needs. They see the Western model as endangering their struggle to attain and preserve nationhood. The USSR, for its part, is happy to encourage Third World countries in cultivating anti-Western doctrines.

The media imperialism thesis gained ground in the 1960s at a time when television was just beginning to take hold in most of the smaller countries. Evidence of Western dominance gathered during that formative period, though dramatic, reflected a temporary, transitional situation. Many new television systems that at first depended entirely on foreign equipment, training, know-how, and program materials have since become reasonably self-sufficient.

But there are practical limits as to how much autonomy small, underfinanced broadcasting systems can achieve. It is not a realistic answer to say, as do some critics, that Third World broadcasters should make their already short schedules still shorter to avoid having to import programs from abroad. That is tantamount to saying, if you cannot staff the hospital without importing doctors, shut down the hospital part of the day. A certain amount of program importation will always be necessary and may often even be desirable. Indeed, sad to say, not all the cultures allegedly being overwhelmed by imported television are capable of surviving intact outside of museums. Once their shell of isolation was broken, they were doomed, television or no television.

A British media scholar, Jeremy Tunstall, wrote a book on this subject, *The Media are American*. Though sharply critical of some Anglo-American broadcasting influences, Tunstall rejects the media imperialism thesis. He writes this of Herbert Schiller, the American scholar who argues that thesis most vehemently:

[He] attributes too many of the world's ills to television. He also has an unrealistic view of returning to traditional cultures, many of which although authentic are also dead. In my view a non-American way out of the media box is difficult to discover because it is an American, or Anglo-American, built box. The only way out is to construct a new box, and this, with the possible exception of the Chinese, no nation seems keen to do. (Tunstall, 1977, 63)

Subsequent events have shown that even the Chinese are not keen on constructing a new box in isolation from the West but plan to exchange programs like everyone else.

Summary

Broadcasting in America, like every other broadcasting system, tends to reflect national character. Comparing the U.S. system with systems of other countries leads to a better understanding of broadcasting in America than can be gained by examining it in isolation. Some of the major points of difference among systems are the following:

1. American broadcasting reflects a generally permissive political philosophy, as contrasted with the paternalism of most Western countries and the authoritarianism of the communist and most Third World countries.

2. American broadcasting is pluralistic, combining both commercial and noncommercial motivations. Such combinations of motives represent the general trend in the most advanced democratic systems, some of which have been more successful than the United States in attaining pluralism.

3. American broadcasting is governed by elaborate legal machinery, with ample opportunity for long-drawn-out appeals from regulatory decisions. Most other countries are more peremptory in their control.

4. Access to broadcasting in America is facilitated by equal time and fairness rules, as well as by a policy of favoring local ownership of stations. Elsewhere ownership control is usually more centralized and access generally more restricted, though some countries have developed novel methods for broadening access.

5. The U.S. population has sufficient buying power to make commercial operation highly successful. Successful mass-appeal programming motivates set-buying and localism encourages growth in the number of stations. For these reasons, the United States has been able to support the highest number of stations and receivers of any country in the world, relative to the size of its population. Systems that depend on set-use license fees for financial support are experiencing difficulties because of inflation and the fact that they have approached the saturation point in the sale of licenses. Most systems, however, depend on direct government support, either because of policy or economic inability to rely on license fees and advertising income.

6. The contiguous states of the United States present a large, compact land-mass surrounded mostly by water, making broadcast coverage less complicated than it is in smaller countries that are crowded together.

7. Historically, the United States system has escaped the disruption and transformation by war that have affected the German system, for example.

8. Program formats are universal, but each country tends to fulfill formats differently. Treatment of news varies markedly as between the democracies and authoritarian states, but treatment of entertainment formats also differs.

9. The United States exports more programming than any other country. This one-way flow of program materials has led to charges of cultural imperialism by some critics, who allege that the cultures of small countries are overwhelmed by U.S. programs.

10. Few countries schedule programs 24 hours a day as is common in the United States.

11. In addition to its regular external service, the Voice of America, U.S. broadcasting to other countries includes the focused efforts of Radio Free Europe and Radio Liberty in Eastern Europe, and the incidental coverage of American Forces Radio and Television Service stations at military bases located on foreign soil. In terms of quantity, however, the USSR has the largest external service. The British Broadcasting Corporation, at one time the largest, has fallen behind in quantity but still retains high credibility because of its long history and separation from direct government control.

12. The principle of free flow of information advocated by the United States is opposed by most communist and Third World nations, which advocate a "new world information order" that allegedly would redress what they perceive as past injustices resulting from the free-flow philosophy.

PART I

Management of Radio Energy

As we saw in the prologue, each country adapts broadcasting to suit its own political, economic, and social characters. Though countries can make their own laws about the use of broadcasting, they cannot repeal the laws of nature. Stubborn physical facts are at the root of most important and universal questions about broadcasting. They limit where and how far broadcast signals travel and how much information each can carry. Physical limitations govern the distribution of transmitters, putting a ceiling on the number that can operate in any one locality. They commit nations to standardizing of systems and equipment, demanding a high degree of international cooperation. They make it necessary to regulate broadcasting in ways not common to other mass media of communication.

These are the types of activity that are involved in the management of radio energy. In the three chapters of this part of our survey we look first at the underlying nature of that energy, then at how it is managed so as to create a great variety of communication channels, and finally at the physical means of distributing and storing program materials to enable filling those broadcast channels with an endless supply of entertainment and information.

CHAPTER 2

Nature of Radio Energy

The property of broadcasting that stands out most clearly as unique is its wirelessness. The ability to radiate through empty space, to travel in all directions without benefit of any vehicle, gives broadcasting its most dramatic advantage over all other ways of communicating. Radio* waves can leap over oceans, span continents, penetrate buildings, pass through people, go to the moon and back, reach the earth from the farthest star in outer space. A satellite transmitter, hovering some 22,000 miles above the equator, can cover nearly a third of the earth with radio signals.

2.1 Electromagnetic Spectrum

Nature of Electromagnetic Energy

Radio is first of all a form of *energy*. As such it belongs in the same class as light, X-rays, and the cosmic rays that come from outer space. Collectively they constitute *electromagnetic energy*. All forms of electromagnetic energy share three fundamental characteristics:

*As used in this chapter the word "radio" refers not to sound broadcasting alone, but to the wireless *method* of communicating. In this physical sense, "radio" transmits not only sounds and pictures, but also Morse code dots and dashes, streams of coded data, and even sheer noise.

they are all *radiant* energy, have the same *velocity*, and travel with a *wavelike* motion.

Radiation is best understood in terms of light. Turn on a light bulb and light *radiates* through the surrounding space; light "rays" are basically the same thing as radio "waves." Velocity refers to speed or rate of travel, like 55 miles per hour in an automobile. The velocity of electromagnetic waves, however, is measured in miles or meters *per second* — about 186,000 miles, or 300,000,000 meters, per second.

Wave motion refers to the fact that all electromagnetic energy is characterized by an *oscillating* (vibrating, alternating) motion that can be depicted as a wave. The number of separate wavelike motions produced in a second is the measure of a wave's *frequency*, an important concept because the varied forms that electromagnetic energy assumes (radio, light, etc.) depend on frequency.

Electromagnetic Spectrum A large number of frequencies visualized in their numerical order constitutes a *spectrum*. The keyboard of a piano represents a spectrum of sound frequencies, starting with the low frequencies at the left and ending with high frequencies at the right. A visible spectrum can be observed when a prism or a rainbow breaks up sunlight into its component colors

— for "colorless" light is actually a combination of "all the colors of the rainbow." We see the lower frequencies of light as red and as we ascend in frequency we see yellow, green, blue, and finally violet. _Ultraviolet_ light is electromagnetic energy just _above_ visible light frequencies and _infrared_ light is just _below_ visible light frequencies.

Exhibit 2.1 represents the entire electromagnetic spectrum, showing where the various types of energy occur in terms of frequency or wavelength. As Exhibit 2.1 shows, usable radio waves occupy only the lower end of the spectrum. As frequency increases the practical difficulties of using the spectrum for communication also increase. Historically, the upper usable limit has been pushed higher and higher. Eventually, no doubt, the present limit of about 300 GHz will be surpassed.

Exhibit 2.1
How the electromagnetic spectrum is used

Electromagnetic phenomenon	Examples of uses	Approximate frequency range	Typical wavelength
Cosmic rays	Physics, astronomy	10^{14} GHz and above	Diameter of an electron
Gamma rays	Cancer therapy	10^{10}–10^{13} GHz	Diameter of smallest atom
X rays	X-ray examination	10^8–10^9 GHz	Diameter of largest atom
Ultraviolet radiation	Sterilization	10^6–10^8 GHz	1 hundred millionth of a meter
Visible light	Human vision	10^5–10^6 GHz	1 millionth of a meter
Infrared radiation	Photography	1,000 GHz–10^4 GHz	1 ten thousandth of a meter
Microwave radio waves	Radar, microwave relays, satellite communication	1–300 GHz	1 centimeter
Radio waves	UHF television	470–806 MHz	1/2 meter
Radio waves	VHF television, FM radio	54–216 MHz	3 meters
Radio waves	Short-wave radio	3–26 MHz	30 meters
Radio waves	AM radio	535–1,605 KHz	3,000 meters

Comment: Note that as frequency increases (reading from the bottom of the table upwards), the manifestations of electromagnetic energy become both more powerful and more dangerous to man (though not necessarily less useful). Not mentioned in connection with radio wave uses are the numerous _nonbroadcast_ and _auxiliary broadcast_ uses, which occur throughout radio wave portions of the spectrum. Not shown are the lowest frequencies, which we perceive as radiant heat and electric power.

2.2 Sound Waves

In order to examine the frequency, length, and other characteristics of waves in more detail, it is convenient to use the example of sound, which also depends on vibratory motion.

Sound Wave Motion   Using the example of a conversation between two people in a room, we can analyze what happens physically in terms of waves and wave motion as follows: a speaker's vocal cords vibrate, producing word sounds; the vocal cord vibrations set molecules of air in wavelike motion; the energy travels through the air in waves to the eardrum of the listener; the eardrum responds by vibrating in step with the wave motion of air molecules; the vibration of the eardrum stimulates nerve fibers leading to the listener's brain, which somehow makes sense of them. Because the eardrum cannot "tune out" other voices, competing sounds may interfere with comprehension. The speaker may increase volume (amplitude) in order to overcome the interference.

The chief wave-motion concepts can be deduced from this sequence of events. Clearly at each step in the process, vibration (alternation, oscillation) is involved. Equally obvious, the vibratory energy in one form caused similar vibrations in other objects or mediums — vocal cords, air, eardrum, nerves. Finally, *communication* through a medium (vibrating air molecules) carried *meaning* from one point to another (speaker to listener).

Wave-Motion Concepts   We need next to analyze vibratory motion in more detail in order to assign the appropriate terms to its various aspects. One way to observe slow-motion vibration is to look at the swinging of the pendulum in Exhibit 2.2.1. At rest the pendulum hangs straight down at the point of zero motion. Given a charge of energy by means of a push, it begins to swing back and forth. The extent of the swing, its *amplitude*, depends on how much energy is given to the pendulum by the first push. In sound, we perceive this aspect of vibration as *loudness.*

A single complete *cycle* of motion by a pendulum includes a swing in each direction. The number of cycles occurring in a given time period defines the frequency of the vibratory movement. We perceive sound frequency as *pitch.* For example, large, heavy musical instruments vibrate with low frequencies and so have low pitches. Small, light instruments vibrate with high frequencies and so have high pitches.

In order to simulate the pendulum's vibratory motion traveling *through space,* imagine a pen attached to its tip so that it can trace its own movements on a roll of paper. If we move the paper downward past the pen point at a constant speed, the pen will trace out a line that depicts a *wave train* — a series of waves of the same frequency traveling through space (look at Exhibit 2.2.1 again, but turn it sideways). We have now given the components of time and distance to the pendulum's movement. They enable us to measure *wavelength* (how far a wave travels to complete a single cycle) and velocity (how far a wave train travels in a given unit of time).

In terms of sound we perceive wavelength — just as we did frequency — as pitch. Large vibrating objects have long wavelength (the long strings at the left end of the piano keyboard), small vibrating objects have short wavelength (the short strings at the other end of the keyboard). We become aware of the velocity of sound whenever we notice that a sound (a thunderclap, the report of a gun) reaches us later than its corresponding visual impression (a lightning or muzzle flash).

The wave train of Exhibit 2.2.1 illustrates one further basic principle of wave propagation; as radiated energy travels away from its source it gradually loses strength. This is *attenuation,* represented by the running

down of the pendulum. We perceive acoustic attenuation as the fading of a sound as we move farther away from the source.

Phase Engineers visualize wave motion in terms of the movement of a point on the rim of a traveling wheel. After the point goes

Exhibit 2.2.1
Wave motion concepts illustrated by pendulum

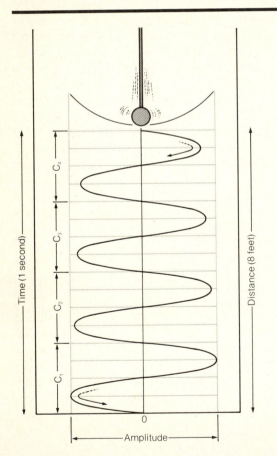

First view the pendulum from this perspective. Picture it swinging back and forth. As it does so, a pen at the tip draws a continuous line on a moving roll of paper. Now turn the figure sideways to study the resulting wavetrain diagram.

Viewed from this perspective, the pendulum's motion becomes a series of waves. Each complete cycle of movement consists of two phases, one above and one below the zero line, representing the right and the left swings of the pendulum. Four cycles have been depicted (C_1, C_2, C_3, C_4). The four cycles reached a distance of 8 feet; hence the wavelength is $8 \div 4$, or 2 feet. It took one second for the pendulum to complete four complete swings, i.e., to produce four cycles; hence the frequency is 4 cycles per second. Since the waves (actually the paper) traveled 8 feet in one second, the velocity is 8 feet per second. Finally, note that the amplitude decreases as the pendulum's energy attenuates.

through half a circle (180°) it reverses its direction to go through the rest of the circle. Each half of the complete cycle of motion is called a *phase*. This means that a complete wave consists of two 180° phases, moving in opposite directions.

These opposite phases of a cycle may be regarded as positive (plus) and negative (minus) aspects of the wave. If the positive aspects of two waves coincide, their energies will combine to make a larger total amplitude at that point. If, however, a negative and a positive aspect of two waves coincide, the smaller will subtract from the larger, making a smaller total amplitude at that point. When two waves of the same frequency exactly coincide they are "in phase."

Phase considerations play important roles in many practical applications throughout electrical and electronic systems. Two or more microphones fed to the same amplifier must be phased correctly; color television makes important use of phase differences; directional antennas use phase reinforcement and cancellation to strengthen radiation in one direction and weaken it in another.

Overtones   Phase has an important bearing on sound *quality.* A perfectly smooth, symmetrical wave represents a pure tone. To the ear it would sound like a dull drone. Pleasing musical tones and natural sounds consist of many different frequencies, all produced at the same time. When frequencies combine, their phase differences create *complex* waves with irregular patterns (Exhibit 2.2.2).

One of the sources of complexity in sounds is the presence of *overtones* or *harmonics*. They are multiples of the fundamental pitch. Thus the 264-cycles-per-second sound of middle C may have overtones at 528 cycles, 792 cycles, 1056 cycles, and so on. Differences in the distribution and amplitudes of the overtones account for the qual-

itative difference between sounds of the same fundamental pitch (Exhibit 2.2.2). Since overtones are, by definition, high in pitch (that is, frequency), it follows that high-quality sound reproduction requires equipment capable of reproducing relatively high frequencies.

Acoustic Environments   Sound waves, once they have been launched into a given environment, begin to *attenuate*. Drapes, human bodies, and other soft objects tend to *absorb* wave energy, especially the higher frequencies. Hard, flat surfaces *reflect* sound waves, causing reverberation or echoes (reverberations are echoes so closely spaced in time they are not heard as separate sounds). The combination of absorptive and reflective surfaces creates an acoustic environment. Sound absorption gives a room a "dead," flat sound; hard, flat surfaces produce a "live," bright sound. Studio and auditorium designers plan room size and shape and treat reflective surfaces so as to create an optimum acoustic environment, neither too dead nor too live.

2.3 Radio Waves

Comparison of Sound and Radio Waves   The sound wave characteristics and behaviors mentioned in the preceding section also apply to radio waves. They have velocity, frequency, length, and phase characteristics. They attenuate, can be absorbed and reflected, and can have echoes. The "ghosts" seen as double images in television pictures are actually visual echoes caused by wave reflection.

One must keep in mind, however, the fundamental differences between sound and radio waves as to frequency, velocity, and the need for a physical vehicle. As to frequency, limitations of the human ear confine audible sound frequencies to a range from about 50 up to about 15,000 cycles per second (people's hearing abilities vary). The frequency range of the electromagnetic spectrum is vast by comparison, running as high as 300 *billion* cycles per second. As to velocity, radio waves travel with the speed of light, about 900,000 times the speed of sound in air. Furthermore, radio waves need no intervening medium such as air. Indeed, they travel best in a vacuum. Air merely impedes them.

Finally, sound and radio waves differ in the direction of their vibratory motion rela-

tive to the paths they travel. Sound-wave motion is called *longitudinal*, meaning that the waves vibrate in the same plane as the sound's direction of travel — what might be described as a push-pull motion. Radio waves are called *transverse* waves because they vibrate back and forth, *across* the direction in which the waves travel. This fact has an important bearing on the design of radio antennas, as we shall see later (§2.6).

Relation of Frequency to Wavelength

The phrase "cycles per second" has been simplified by international agreement to the term "hertz," meaning a frequency of one cycle per second. Because the higher radio

**Exhibit 2.2.2
Complex wave**

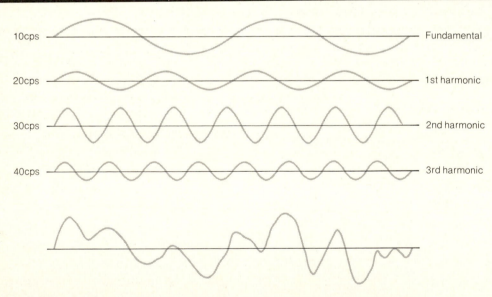

10cps	Fundamental
20cps	1st harmonic
30cps	2nd harmonic
40cps	3rd harmonic

Reading from top to bottom, the drawings depict a fundamental wave and three of its harmonic (overtone) waves. Each is regular in shape. When the four combine, however, phase differences result in an irregularly shaped, complex wave, as shown in the bottom drawing.

Source: Diagram adapted from Paul Davidowitz, *Communication*, Holt, Rinehart & Winston, New York, 1972, p. 129, Fig. 11-1.

frequency numbers get unwieldy, the standard metric prefixes *kilo-* (for thousand), *mega-* (for million), and *giga-* (for billion) are added to hertz (which is spelled the same in both singular and plural). Exhibit 2.3 shows the use of these terms in the division of the radio spectrum into frequency bands.

The position of any wave in the electromagnetic spectrum can be stated either in terms of its frequency or its wavelength, as shown in Exhibit 2.1. When we speak of "microwaves" we are identifying waves by their length, but when we speak of "UHF" we are identifying them by their frequency. If either frequency or wavelength is known, we can easily find the other simply by dividing it into 300 million meters (about 185,000 miles), the per-second velocity of radio

waves in a vacuum. Example: a wave is known to have a frequency of 1 MHz (1 million hertz). What is its length? Dividing the frequency of 1 million into velocity of 300 million gives wavelength as 300 meters. Velocity is in fact the *product* of frequency times wavelength.

The positions of broadcasting stations within their respective frequency bands can thus be identified either by the frequency or the length of their carrier waves. Frequency is commonly used in the United States, but wavelength is sometimes preferred in Europe. In U.S. radio, an AM station's dial number refers to kilohertz ("60" means 600 kHz) and an FM station's dial number refers to megahertz ("98.9" means 98.9 MHz). Television stations, however, are

Exhibit 2.3
Subdivisions of radio frequency spectrum

Name of subdivision	Frequency range expressed in		
	Kilohertz (thousands of cycles per second)	Megahertz (millions of cycles per second)	Gigahertz (billions of cycles per second)
Very low frequency (VLF)	Below 30	——	——
Low frequency (LF)	30–300	——	——
Medium frequency (MF)	300–3,000	——	——
High frequency (HF)	3,000–30,000	3–30	——
Very high frequency (VHF)	30,000–300,000	30–300	——
Ultra high frequency (UHF)	300,000–3,000,000	300–3,000	——
Super high frequency (SHF)	3,000,000–30,000,000	3,000–30,000	3–30
Extremely high frequency (EHF)	30,000,000–300,000,000	30,000–300,000	30–300

Comment: Each band simply adds another zero to the limits of the next lower band, making it easy to reconstruct the table from memory. Note how unwieldy numbers become when expressed as kilohertz at UHF and above, demonstrating the need to switch to the terms megahertz and gigahertz.

identified by arbitrarily assigned channel numbers (for example the video carrier frequency of channel 6 is 83.25 MHz).

Generation of Carrier Waves   Sound, it will be recalled, is generated when some physical object (vocal cords, drum head, saxophone reed, guitar string) is made to *vibrate*. Radio waves, too, are generated by causing vibration (oscillation), but vibration of an electrical current rather than of a physical object. The oscillation of an electrical current can be envisioned as a surging back and forth of energy, rising to a maximum in one direction (one phase) then to a maximum in the other direction (the other phase).

Current alternating in any electrical system releases electromagnetic energy into the surrounding space. This tendency of alternating current to radiate electromagnetic energy depends on its frequency. The higher the frequency of alternation, the more radiation takes place.

Thus the most fundamental job of a radio transmitter is to generate alternating energy that will radiate into space. This basic emission is a transmitter's *carrier wave*, which alternates at a designated frequency. A transmitter radiates energy at that frequency as long as it is turned on, even though no actual sound or picture may be going out at the moment.

2.4 Modulation

Energy Patterns   Imposing information (pictures, sounds, or any other material to be transmitted) on a carrier wave is called *modulation*. We can modulate a flashlight beam merely by turning it on or off. A distant observer can decode the modulated light beam according to agreed meanings — a pattern or code of four short flashes means "all OK,"

perhaps, while a combination of short-long-short flashes might mean "having trouble — bring help." Thus modulation is used to produce a *signal*. Any physical variation that conveys information is a signal — a light changing from red to green, a head nodding up and down, or in the case of the flashlight, on-off variations in light output.

On a more complex level, sound also consists of patterns — patterns of amplitudes (loudness variations) and of frequencies (pitch variations) — traveling through the atmosphere by means of air-molecule movements. A microphone, responding to variations in air pressure caused by these movements, transfers the sound pattern into a signal — in this case a corresponding pattern of electrical variations. Next the electrical signal, or pattern, *modulates* the transmitter's carrier, causing its oscillations to assume the same pattern, but now at a much higher frequency. At last we have a radio signal — physical variations in the carrier wave that convey information (Exhibit 2.4). All we need to complete the communication process is a decoding device at the receiving end to *demodulate* the carrier. A receiver reverses the process, finally causing a loudspeaker to set air in motion with a pattern of vibratory movements, reproducing something like the original sound. Notice that the sound is only *reproduced*. Sound itself — or a picture or any other original material — is *not* transmitted, only patterns. It is like making a paper pattern of an article of clothing and mailing the pattern to a tailor in a distant city. One mails the pattern, not the clothing. But in the distant city the tailor uses the pattern to construct an article of clothing much like the original item. In sum, modulation involves transferring a pattern from one form of energy to another.

Transduction   At each point where the crucial transfer of energy patterns takes place an instrument is needed to do the job. The general term for such instruments is *transducer* (literally, "leader across"). A microphone as a transducer changes sound patterns to electrical patterns. A television camera as a transducer changes light patterns to electrical patterns. A transmitter as a transducer shifts electrical frequency patterns into a higher frequency domain, that of *radio frequency* (RF) energy.

Sidebands The single frequency that identifies a carrier wave can carry only a single "bit" of information each second. For a signal any more complicated than simply "off" vs. "on" (for example), more frequencies are needed. Modulation by a complex signal involves using radio frequencies *adjacent* to the carrier, both above and below its particular frequency. These additional frequencies are referred to as *sidebands*. The number of frequencies in a sideband determines the *bandwidth* of the channel, which in turn affects the amount of information it is able to carry.

Either the upper or the lower sideband (with reference to the carrier frequency) suffices to convey all the information imposed on the carrier. Because spectrum space is always in short supply, some radio services

Exhibit 2.4
Modulation of carrier waves

An *unmodulated* carrier wave emitted by a transmitter has an unchanging frequency and amplitude pattern:

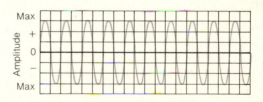

An AM carrier wave, modulated by a pattern of *amplitude* changes representing a signal:

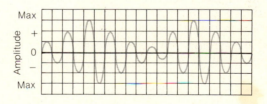

An FM carrier wave, modulated by a pattern of *frequency* changes representing the same signal:

In AM, frequency remains constant, amplitude varies; in FM, amplitude remains constant, frequency varies. The patterns of change, whether of amplitude or frequency, represent the energy patterns of the transmitted signal.

Source: Federal Communications Commission.

conserve frequencies by using *single sideband* (SSB) or *vestigial sideband* (VSB) transmission.

Channels   The fact that modulation of a carrier wave generates sidebands means that each station must be allotted not just one but a group of frequencies. Such a group is referred to as a *channel.* The concept of channel is central to an understanding of radio communication systems.

A channel might be visualized as a water pipe. A very thin pipe could eventually fill a big reservoir with its trickle of water, but if it is important to fill the reservoir quickly, a gush of water from a large-diameter pipe is essential. In radio communication we are usually interested in large pipes, or channels, because we want immediate results. Sometimes, however, we are willing to make a trade-off — to exchange economies in channel width or in equipment costs for slow delivery. The pioneer Mariner satellite that sent back pictures of Mars in 1965 carried a tiny black-and-white television camera that took 48 seconds to build up one complete picture. The picture information was converted into coded form and stored by a tape recorder on board the satellite. It then took nearly *nine hours* to transmit to earth the string of coded digits representing the 40,000 elements in a single picture.

Types of Modulation   The chief methods of modulation used in broadcasting are amplitude modulation (AM) and frequency modulation (FM). As the names imply, in the one case information is encoded by varying the amplitude, or strength, of the carrier wave; in the other case, encoding varies its frequency (Exhibit 2.4).

Imagine a transmitter being fed a sound having a pitch of middle C, which is an acoustic vibration of 264 cycles per second. Amplitude modulation would produce 264 alterations per second in the amplitude of the carrier. The loudness of the sound would be encoded in terms of the *amount* rather than the frequency (rate) of amplitude change in the carrier. If the sound doubled in volume, the carrier would double in average amplitude.

Because amplitude modulation depends on *amount* of energy, AM signals are vulnerable to electrical interference. Radio receivers pick up random pulses of electrical energy in the atmosphere, such as those caused by lightning and electrical machinery. These random bits of energy interact with the transmitted radio energy and are heard as *static.*

FM keeps carrier wave amplitude constant, modulating its *frequency* (Exhibit 2.4). This method avoids the static interference that bedevils AM. In FM reception, variations in amplitude caused by static can be clipped off the peaks of the waves without disturbing the information pattern.

2.5 Wave Propagation

Modulation is imposed on the carrier wave by the transmitter, which feeds the signal to the *antenna,* the physical element from which the signal radiates into the surrounding space. The traveling of the wave energy outward from the antenna is referred to as *propagation.* As the energy travels it *attenuates* (gets weaker). This necessarily happens because the energy is being distributed over a progressively larger area. The greater the distance it travels the more thinly it is dispersed.

Coverage Contours   If all conditions were ideal, the geographical coverage pattern of a transmitter would be circular. Its energy would radiate evenly in all directions, assuming the absence of any deliberate effort to control propagation direction. However, in the course of propagation the wave energy is affected unevenly by a variety of conditions it meets along the way. Conditions that influence propagation patterns include such variables as weather, physical obstructions, and seasonal changes in radiations from the sun. Waves are susceptible to *refraction* (bending of waves into a new direction), *reflection, absorption, interference,* and *ducting* (unusually long-distance propagation of FM radio and television signals). As a result of these and many other variables, actual coverage patterns are usually irregular in shape.

How much and in what way a given signal will be affected by specific conditions in its wave path depends upon which frequency band it occupies. Just as waves in different parts of the electromagnetic spectrum, taken as a whole, behave differently in accordance with their frequency (light occurs in one band of frequencies but not in others, for example), so the waves in different parts of the radio frequency band vary in their behavior. The differences in propagation behavior that depend on frequency can be summarized by dividing waves into three types — direct, ground, and sky waves.

Direct Waves Line-of-sight waves that follow a nearly straight path from transmitting antenna to receiver antenna are called *direct waves.* Their useful coverage area reaches only to about the horizon; beyond that point they fly off into space, as shown in Exhibit 2.5.1. Line-of-sight distance to the horizon depends, of course, on the height of the antenna — the higher an antenna the farther it can see before reaching the horizon.

Direct waves use the higher radio frequency bands — VHF, UHF, SHF, and EHF (Exhibit 2.5.3). They are subject to being blocked by objects in their path that are one wavelength wide or larger. At the highest usable frequencies even objects as small as

the leaves of trees and raindrops cause blockage. These higher-frequency waves are called "quasi-optical" because they behave like light. In fact one can make the generalization that the higher the frequency of radio energy the more it resembles light in its behavior. Television and FM use direct waves exclusively.

Ground Waves Because ground waves are propagated through the surface of the earth, they can travel beyond the horizon (Exhibit 2.5.1). They therefore have the po-

Exhibit 2.5.1
Direct and ground wave propagation

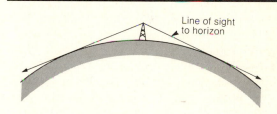

Direct waves travel, like light rays, straight out from small radiating elements atop the antenna structure. The line-of-sight angle to the horizon limits their radius of coverage. TV antennas have directional characteristics to prevent energy radiating at an angle above the horizon so that it will not be wasted by flying off into space.

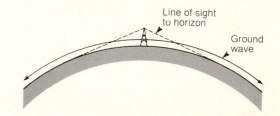

Ground waves follow the curvature of the earth. If sufficiently powerful and aided by sufficiently conductive soil, they travel beyond the horizon. The entire antenna structure radiates energy, but the radiation is symbolized by a single ray in the drawing.

tentiality for covering a wider area than direct waves. In practice, however, the distance ground waves travel depends on several variables, notably power and soil *conductivity*, the ability of electromagnetic energy to pass through the earth surrounding the antenna site. Dry, sandy soil is a poor conductor.* Ground waves occur at low and medium frequencies (Exhibit 2.5.3). AM (standard) broadcasting depends primarily on ground waves and, to a lesser extent, on the third type, sky waves.

Sky Waves   Most radio waves, when allowed to radiate upward toward the sky, lose much of their energy by atmospheric absorption. Any remaining energy escapes into space. Waves in the medium-frequency (MF) and high-frequency (HF) parts of the spectrum, however, tend to bend back toward the earth, forming *sky waves*. This bending effect is caused by the *ionosphere,* a series of high-altitude layers of atmosphere (Exhibit 2.5.2). Because of bombardment by high-energy radiations from the sun, the ionosphere takes on special electrical properties that cause the refraction (bending back) of sky waves. These refracted waves, bouncing back and forth between earth and ionosphere, are not affected by the curvature of the earth and so can travel vast distances.

As shown in Exhibit 2.5.2, the ionosphere occurs in several layers, each with differing characteristics. During the daytime MF waves are absorbed, but at night they bounce off the ionosphere, providing distant nighttime service. HF waves, however, can utilize the ionosphere day and night. Sky waves are thus very important to broadcasting because they afford the *only* method of obtaining

*The FCC publishes a map showing the variations of soil conductivity throughout the United States (47 CFR 73.190). The best soils are about 15 times as conductive as the worst. Salt water is an ideal conductor, being 2,500 times as effective as the least conductive soil.

long-distance radio transmission (in the hundreds and even thousands of miles) by land-based stations. Some standard (AM) broadcast stations are designed to provide only ground-wave coverage; others, more powerful, are designed to provide additional coverage by sky wave at night. International short-wave (HF) stations depend on sky waves both day and night.

Frequency and Propagation Range
Exhibit 2.5.3 summarizes the effects of frequency on the range of radio waves, along with corresponding modes of propagation. Ground waves are most useful at the lowest frequencies, sky waves at the middle frequencies, and direct waves at the higher frequencies. The lower frequencies are more subject to atmospheric noise, the highest to electron noise. In general, the higher the frequency the more power it takes to generate a usable signal. Thus from the user's point of view a channel located at a lower point in the frequency spectrum is always preferable (other things being equal) to one at a higher point.

2.6 Antennas

Antenna Length   All types of waves depend on antennas as the means of launching electromagnetic energy into the surrounding space. Antennas vary greatly in size because in order for them to work efficiently the size of the radiating elements must correspond to the length of the waves they are designed to radiate. Usually the radiating elements are one-half or one-quarter the length of the carrier wave. The length of the waves at the lower end of the standard AM broadcasting dial (540 kHz) is about 1,823 feet. At the upper end of the dial (1,600 kHz) the waves are 593 feet long. The length of the waves used

**Exhibit 2.5.2
Skywave propagation**

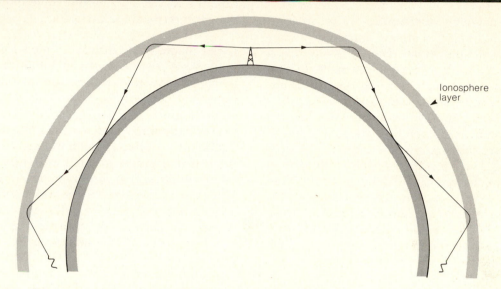

Skywaves radiate outward above the horizon into space. However, when they encounter the ionosphere, waves of certain frequencies are refracted back toward the earth. The return wave may bounce off the earth back to the ionosphere, then back to earth and so on, in a series of skips.

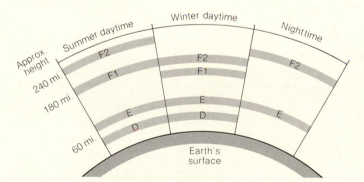

The ionosphere consists of several layers, identified by the symbols D, E, F-1, and F-2. Each layer refracts radio waves of only certain frequencies. Influenced by the sun, the layers move up and down with day/night and summer/winter changes.

by UHF television channel 48 (for example) is under two feet.

Ground-Wave Antennas   The antenna structure of an AM station is usually a quarter-wavelength long. The structure as a whole acts as the radiating element (Exhibit 2.6.1). In choosing a location for an AM antenna, engineers look for good soil conductivity and freedom from surrounding sources of man-made interference. They also have to avoid creating hazards for aircraft approaching and leaving airports. Height above surrounding terrain has no importance as it does for FM and television antenna sites. In fact a low-level site is preferable to a mountain top for AM antennas. Because their signal is propagated through the earth's crust, AM

antennas must be extremely well grounded, with many heavy copper cables radiating out from the base of the antenna tower buried in the ground (Exhibit 2.6.1).

Direct-Wave Antennas   Engineers seek the highest possible locations for FM and TV antennas so as to obtain maximum coverage from their line-of-sight radiations. In this case the antenna tower functions simply to raise the antenna proper as high as possible (Exhibit 2.6.2). Both transmitting and receiving antenna elements for direct waves are relatively small and are positioned horizontally with reference to the ground below. This is because the United States has adopted *horizontal polarization* as the standard for broadcast FM and television antennas.

Exhibit 2.5.3
Frequency bands and their characteristics

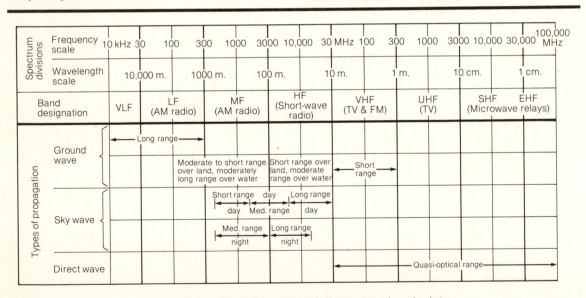

Rough approximations of the distances reached are as follows: *quasi-optical*, to horizon (the waves behave like light, so that their range depends on the height of their point of origin with reference to the horizon); *short*, up to 50 miles; *medium*, 50 to 500 miles; *long*, above 500 miles.

Polarization of Waves   As they are propagated, radio waves oscillate back and forth *across* their propagation path. The orientation of the antenna determines the orientation of the oscillations. The horizontal *polarization* of FM broadcast signals is disadvantageous when it comes to automobile radios because auto antennas are usually oriented vertically.

In recent years television stations have begun to install antennas so constructed as to radiate *circularly polarized* waves (Exhibit 2.6.2). The waves from these antennas travel with a corkscrew motion. Although circular polarization requires higher transmitter power, it has the advantage of eliminating ghosts. The system works something like polarized sunglasses that reject glare because the polarity of reflected sunlight tends to be the reverse of direct sunlight. When a circularly polarized signal is reflected, its direction of rotation is reversed and the receiving antenna will reject it, eliminating the possibility of its being received as a ghost signal.

Directional Antennas   Radio waves can be controlled, much as light is controlled, by

Exhibit 2.6.1
AM radio antenna

The entire steel tower of an AM radio antenna serves as its radiating element. Efficient propagation depends on soil conductivity, which in turn necessitates an exceedingly good ground system for the tower. The photo shows an array of several antennas (for obtaining directional propagation). Heavy copper ground cables are buried in the trenches that radiate out from the bases of the towers.

Source: Courtesy of Stainless, Inc., North Wales, PA.

blocking off radiations in some directions and reinforcing them in others. Directional antennas that achieve these effects are used to prevent interference with other stations, to match coverage contours to population distribution patterns, to avoid sending energy upward into space, and for other purposes. Concentrating radiations increases their effective strength. This increase is called *antenna gain.*[*]

Television antennas are designed to keep their angle of radiation low enough to direct the waves toward the surrounding terrain, preventing the loss that would occur if part of the radiations were aimed above the horizon. Their resulting beefed-up signal strength is expressed as ERP (effective radiated power). AM radio directional antennas work on the principle of phase interference and reinforcement (§2.2). Several AM antenna towers, erected in a line, simultaneously radiate the signal. They are spaced in such a way as to produce the desired phase relationships, reinforcing the radiations in one direction, attenuating them in another.

**Exhibit 2.6.2
TV antenna**

Because height is important to maximize direct-wave coverage, Boston's WQTV (TV) chose the 55-story Prudential Center's roof as its antenna site. A helicopter had to be used to lift the antenna assembly into place. The circularly polarized antenna's radiating elements are mounted in a spiral pattern around the supporting column.

Source: CETEC Antenna Corporation.

2.7 Spectrum Management

Efficient use of the radio spectrum is the objective of spectrum management. The huge and ever-growing number of radio transmitters of many different kinds (over 17 million in the United States alone in 1979) must share the limited frequency spectrum. The constant threat of interference between stations and the international political complications all this involves make spectrum management extremely important to the future development of broadcasting.

Frequency Allocation National telecommunication authorities agree, through the

---

[*]An extreme case of antenna gain is the microwave relay antenna, which uses a reflector to concentrate the energy into a powerful narrow beam, just as a searchlight concentrates light. Such an antenna can achieve a gain of 100,000 times the effective radiated power of an omni-directional antenna.

International Telecommunication Union, on ways of dividing up the available electromagnetic spectrum among the various types of radio services. This process, called *allocation,* means designating specific segments (bands) of the spectrum for the use of specific services.

Allocation involves matching the needs of a service to a part of the spectrum with the appropriate propagation characteristics. Thus a service that needs to communicate over very long distances has to be allocated to HF or lower bands so that sky waves can be employed. On the other hand, a service needing to make only short-range line-of-sight transmissions could best use the quasi-optical bands of frequencies. Some services require continuous, around-the-clock communication, others only occasional contacts. Some require radiotelephony, others radiotelegraphy. There are never enough frequencies to satisfy all needs. New services constantly emerge and old services expand.

Multiplexing Because of shortage of spectrum space, an important aspect of commu-

Exhibit 2.7.1
Radio station licenses, by type of service

Type (with examples of uses)	Number of authorizations[a]
Personal services (citizens band, radio controlled devices)	15,000,323
Private land mobile (police, fire, ambulance, news gathering)	617,304
Industrial services (business, power, petroleum exploration)	462,096
Amateur and disaster services	375,528
Marine services	371,223
Aviation services	226,957
Public safety services (police, fire, local government, highway maintenance)	128,959
Common carriers (microwave relays, radiotelephone, satellites)	58,988
Broadcasting (radio, television, auxiliary services)	35,973
Land transportation services (railroads, taxicabs, auto emergency)	26,249
Operational fixed services	16,066
Total radio transmitting stations	17,319,666

Comment: Eleven nongovernment services, each covering several different uses, share the frequency spectrum. They are divided into three groups: common carriers, private services, and broadcasting. Note that broadcasting is one of the smallest classes of service. For details of the broadcasting group see Exhibit 2.7.2.

[a]Authorizations include both fully licensed stations and those with preliminary construction permits.
Source: Based on 1979 data in FCC, *45th Annual Report, Fiscal Year 1979,* Government Printing Office, Washington, D.C., 1980, pp. 90, 115, 116.

Not the same as simulcast

nication technology today is *multiplexing.* Two or more independent signals transmitted simultaneously in the same channel are said to be multiplexed. Multiplexing is used to increase the efficiency of both wire and radio channels. Multiplexing is used routinely in broadcasting to obtain stereophonic and quadraphonic sound, to convey black-and-white as well as the three primary color signals in the television channel, to encode transmitter meter readings in the broadcast channel, and in many other ways.

Types of Radio Service Exhibit 2.7.1 shows the number of *nongovernment* radio transmitters authorized in the United States (government users occupy over half of all the available frequencies). Broadcasting represents only a fraction of one percent of all radio transmitter authorizations.

The low number of broadcasting transmitter authorizations compared to other services must be seen in the light of broadcasting's special requirements: it needs wide channels and it needs to be able to use them continuously, up to 24 hours a day. Many other services can share frequencies because they need to transmit only intermittently or during only parts of the day. Thus broadcasting makes greater demands on the spectrum than other services.

Broadcasting also differs from most other services in employing an average of 2.5 *auxiliary transmitters* for every main transmitter (Exhibit 2.7.2). Auxiliary transmitters serve many purposes such as providing radio links between main transmitters and studios, between remote mobile units and main studios, and between portable cameras and control room. Another large category of auxiliary transmitters, *translators,* serves to extend television coverage to areas not accessible to main transmitters because of signal blockage by terrain features.

Summary

It is important to start with an understanding of the physical basis of broadcasting because so many of its attributes and problems arise out of its physical nature and because new technology is changing the medium so drastically.

**Exhibit 2.7.2
Broadcast station authorizations by type**

Type of station	Number of authorizations[a]	
Primary stations		
AM radio	4,634	*9,000*
FM radio	4,412	
Total radio		9,046
VHF television	635	
UHF television	447	
Total television		1,082
Auxiliary stations		
Remote pickup	13,522	
Translators	4,238[b]	
Other	8,085	
Total auxiliary		25,845
Total broadcast		35,973

Comment: Note that for every regular broadcast station there is an average of about 2.5 auxiliary stations, adding to the demands broadcasting makes on the spectrum.

[a]Authorizations include both fully licensed stations and those with preliminary construction permits. Both commercial and noncommercial stations are included.
[b]Translators are low-power repeater stations that fill in areas not covered by a main station's signal.
Source: Based on 1979 data in FCC, *45th Annual Report, Fiscal Year 1979,* Government Printing Office, Washington, D.C., 1980, p. 90.

Radio (including sound, picture, and all other types of transmission by radio waves) is a form of electromagnetic energy, which also accounts for visible light. Like sound, radio energy has a vibrating or oscillating characteristic that can be described in terms of waves that have length, frequency, velocity, and phase. They are subject to attenuation, reflection, refraction, and absorption. The radio frequencies occupy only part of the electromagnetic spectrum. Within that part, the frequencies are grouped into bands designated low (LF), medium (MF), high (HF), very high (VHF), ultra high (UHF), super high (SHF), and extremely high (EHF). Each band has its own modes of behavior.

The basic emission of a broadcasting station is its carrier wave. It may be propagated as a ground wave (reaching beyond the horizon), direct wave (line-of-sight), or sky wave (long-distance). Sky waves occur because of ionosphere refraction. Modulation imposes information on a carrier wave, creating sidebands, which occupy a group of frequencies called a channel. The more information a channel must deliver simultaneously, the wider it must be. The types of modulation familiar in broadcasting are amplitude and frequency modulation. The modulated carrier wave is fed to an antenna, which radiates electromagnetic energy. Antennas differ in size according to the length of the waves they are designed to radiate. Directional antennas control the spread of signals outward so as to increase their intensity in desired directions.

Demand for radio frequencies exceeds supply. Spectrum management, the efficient allocation of frequencies, relies on matching the needs of each radio service to the characteristic behavior of waves at varying frequencies. Multiplexing assists in conserving the use of frequencies. Broadcasting has relatively few transmitters compared to other major types of services but it occupies a disproportionate share of the spectrum because it needs relatively wide channels and continuous use of its channels. Broadcasting uses additional spectrum space for a variety of auxiliary transmitters employed to assist in program production and distribution.

CHAPTER 3

Broadcast Channels

This chapter describes the physical basis of the several kinds of broadcast services — standard radio, FM radio, short-wave radio, VHF television, and UHF television. We title the chapter "broadcast channels" because the act of dividing the electromagnetic spectrum into the groups of frequencies called *channels* is the most fundamental step in defining a particular service. The intrinsic physical capabilities of a service are determined both by the number of frequencies in its channels and by the position of its channels in the frequency spectrum.

3.1. Basic Concepts

Allocation Certain blocks of frequencies are *allocated,* in accordance with international agreements, to specific radio communication services. National allocation plans allot these frequencies in more detail to the various domestic and external services. Broadcasting in America uses allocations in the MW, VHF, and UHF bands for domestic broadcasting and in the HF band for international broadcasting. In some other countries the LF and HF bands are also used domestically.

The large blocks of frequencies allocated to services are in turn broken down into smaller blocks, designated as *channels.* These are groups of frequencies used by individual stations within a service. Channel sizes are not standardized internationally, but vary from country to country. For example, all U.S. television channels are 6 MHz wide, but in other countries they vary in width from 5 to 15 MHz.

Allotment and Licensing Again in accordance with national allocation plans, governments *allot* channels to particular geographical locations. National allotment tables designate one or more FM and television channels to each U.S. community of sufficient size to warrant allotments. AM channels, however, are allotted only upon individual applications from would-be users who make an engineering study to find an unused channel that could be activated without causing interference.

The final regulatory step in the activation of channels is to *license* particular users. A license confers upon a user the right to activate a designated channel in a designated locality under specific conditions as to time, power, and other requirements.

Among other things, the licensing process enables governments to maintain equipment *compatibility.* For any given service, all receivers that are sold should work with any transmitters. Radio and television sets purchased in Maine must work equally well in California. Compatibility among nations, however, is often sacrificed for political and economic reasons. In general, radio receivers will work anywhere in the world where signals in the bands they are designed to tune in are available, but television receivers do not always work when transferred from one country to another.

Channel Capacity   In designing any communication service, planners must decide how much *information capacity* its channels really need for the service to fulfill its purpose. The maximum amount of information desired must be balanced against the cost of communicating it — not only the cost of providing the necessary physical apparatus but also the expense in frequencies. No service should be allowed to use more than the minimum number of frequencies required to perform its essential functions.

The telephone's band width of about 300 to 2,700 Hz suffices for intelligibility. Radio broadcasting, however, needs more than simple intelligibility; it is concerned with aesthetic aspects of sounds as well — the beauty of music, song, and speech and the realistic rendering of actual sound events. Ideally this would mean a bandwidth equal to the maximum range of sound frequencies detectable by the keenest human ear — on the order of 20 to 20,000 Hz. In practice, however, each radio service makes a compromise between the ideal and the tolerable.

Not all the frequencies in a channel are necessarily available for use. It will be recalled that modulation involves *sidebands* above and below the carrier frequency (§2.4). Each sideband carries the same information, so that the effective capacity of a channel is only one-half its total width.

3.2 Interference

We know from §2.5 that the frequency band to which a station is assigned determines the type of propagation path or paths its signals will follow. This in turn determines its potential area of coverage. In practice, other factors also influence coverage, in particular the factor of *interference* among stations in the same frequency band. This type of interference can come from other stations on the same channel and also from nearby stations on adjacent channels.

Co-channel Interference   The fact that two stations assigned to the same channel can interfere with each other limits the number of stations that can be assigned to each channel. This *co-channel interference* can be avoided by spacing stations far enough apart geographically to prevent their signal contours from overlapping. This problem is complicated by the fact that in some frequency bands a station's coverage area is unstable. Coverage varies with propagation conditions, which are affected by time of day, season of the year, and weather. A station's *interference zone* may extend far beyond its service zone. Signals too weak or erratic to render satisfactory service will still be strong enough to interfere with other signals.

The simplest way to prevent co-channel interference would be to license only one station in the whole country to each available channel. Since each broadcasting service has been allotted only about a hundred channels, this solution would place too drastic a limitation on the number of stations that could be licensed. In the United States the goal is to allow as many stations as possible to operate; therefore other ways of minimizing the effects of co-channel interference have to be employed. The chief methods are: (1) limiting transmitter power and antenna elevation; (2) requiring the use of directional antennas and the lowering of power at night; (3) limiting some stations to daytime operation only; and (4) making two stations in the same area share time on the same channel. Which of these strategies are needed depends on the types of waves involved. AM broadcasting has a special need because its MF radiations produce sky waves. It will be recalled (§2.5) that MF waves generate long-distance sky waves *only* at night. Because of these sky waves, AM co-channel stations that operate at night have to be widely spaced.

Adjacent Channel Interference

In the near vicinity of a transmitter, where the power level of signals is still extremely high, sidebands spread beyond the limits of the station's designated channel into *adjacent* channels. Rapid initial attenuation of signals limits adjacent channel interference to the immediate vicinity of transmitters. Nevertheless, to avoid adjacent channel interference within a given community, several unoccupied channels must be left between occupied channels. This imposes an upper limit on the number of stations that can be licensed to any single locality.

3.3 AM Broadcasting

Terminology   Because it was the first of the broadcasting services to develop, AM broadcasting has been officially designated "standard broadcasting" in U.S. regulations. FM broadcasters object to this designation because it suggests that their service, which now attracts about as many listeners as AM, is not quite in the same league. We will use the term "AM," but with the reminder that in the generic sense AM simply refers to a method of modulation.

AM Channels   By international agreement, AM channels occupy a segment of the MF (300–3,000 kHz) band. In the United States it runs from 535 to 1,605 kHz, providing a total band width of 1,070 kHz; the AM channel spacing has been set at 10 kHz, thus allowing for 107 AM channels (1,070 divided by 10). The channels are identified by the frequencies of their carrier waves, expressed in kilohertz — 540, 550, 560, and so on up to 1,600 kHz.*

Because all the information in a channel is contained in each of its two sidebands, only half the total channel width is usefully employed. Thus the nominal 10 kHz AM channel has the capacity for frequencies up to 5 kHz — much less than the 15 kHz range of sound frequencies that many people can actually hear. However, the 10 kHz limit refers to AM channel *spacing* rather than to maximum channel width. Stations can, and many do, modulate beyond 5 kHz on either side of the carrier frequency. Nevertheless, AM broadcasting is limited by the fact that inexpensive AM receivers usually have low-fidelity loudspeakers, incapable of handling an audible range beyond 5 kHz.

Coverage Variables   MF propagation entails both ground waves and sky waves. AM ground waves cover a radius of roughly 10 to 75 miles from the antenna location. In each case actual coverage depends on transmitter power, frequency of the channel, conductivity of the soil, amount of interference present, and other factors.

*A World Administrative Radio Conference (WARC) called by the International Telecommunication Union in 1979 extended the upper limit of the AM band to 1,705 kHz. In the same year the U.S. government proposed reducing the spacing of AM channels to 9 kHz instead of 10 kHz, the standard already in effect in Europe. Adoption of the narrower AM channels depends upon agreement by ITU countries in the Western Hemisphere. If finally adopted these two changes would increase the number of AM channels available in the United States.

Frequency and soil conductivity account for surprisingly large differences in AM coverage. Power becomes progressively less effective as channel frequency increases. A 5,000-watt station near the lower end of the AM band at 550 kHz can have as much coverage as a station with ten times as much power located in the same city but on a channel near the upper end of the band at 1,200 kHz. A minimum-power station (250 watts) can have as much ground-wave coverage as a maximum-power (50,000 watts) station because of differences in soil conductivity in their respective coverage areas.

The ground wave defines an AM broadcasting station's *primary* coverage area, the area in which the signal is reliable at most receiver locations most of the time. Sky waves of AM stations reach far beyond the primary coverage area to receivers located from about 100 to as much as 1,500 miles from the transmitter. This sky-wave zone constitutes the *secondary* coverage area. Because it depends on the ionosphere (§2.5), secondary coverage can be counted on only at night. Even then, sky waves are so subject to fading and interference that they provide only a second-best form of coverage, though they are still of great importance to places where no other nighttime coverage is available.

AM Channel Classification   A system of channel and station classification has been adopted to ensure, to the extent possible, that everyone who wants to has a chance to pick up an AM signal. The 107 channels have been divided into three categories — *local, regional,* and *clear.* Local and regional channels are for stations of limited power intended to cover small and medium-size areas. Clear channels are for powerful stations intended to cover large areas, including the more remote parts of the country, far from population centers. These channels

have been "cleared" of interfering nighttime signals, so that stations assigned to them can cover distant areas with a usable sky-wave service.*

AM Station Classification   Stations licensed as "dominant" on clear channels are called Class I. Secondary stations on a clear channel, called Class II, must avoid interfering with the Class I station on their channel. Avoidance is accomplished primarily by means of wide geographical separation. But the Class II stations must also accept a variety of restrictions such as directional antennas (sometimes with different patterns for day and night), reduced power at night, and in many cases going off the air at night altogether. Exhibit 3.3.1 shows the parts of the country that still depend on clear channel service at night.

Class III stations occupy regional channels and Class IV stations occupy local channels. Only six of the 107 AM channels are classified as local, but the Class IV stations assigned to them constitute about a quarter of all the stations (Exhibit 3.3.2). This discrepancy is due to the fact that Class IV stations have such low power (and hence such short range) that many can be assigned to the same channel without causing co-channel interference.

By treaty agreements, the United States and its neighbors honor each other's clear channels. The Bahamas, Canada, Cuba, and Mexico each has dominance on certain clear channels to which the United States may assign only secondary stations.

---

*When first so named, clear channels actually were clear of any co-channel competition at night anywhere in the nation. The demand for more stations, however, caused gradual abandonment of this principle. Since 1980 all primary stations on clear channels have been subject to sharing their channels with other primary stations in distant parts of the country.

Power Limitations   Power has great significance for AM stations. It has a direct bearing on the efficiency of both ground-wave and sky-wave propagation and hence on station coverage. Power is also important in overcoming interference and static. Moreover, high power is regarded as psychologically useful in persuading advertisers that a station has strong audience impact.

Power authorizations, varied to match the coverage needs of each station classification, run from 250 watts to a maximum of 50,000 watts (see Exhibit 3.3.2 for details). AM transmitters of a million watts are not uncommon in some countries, but in the United States a power ceiling of 50,000 watts (50 kw) has been adopted so that Class I stations will not have too much competitive edge over less favored classes.

Carrier Current Services   When an extremely low power AM radio signal is fed to

Exhibit 3.3.1
Areas dependent on clear channel service

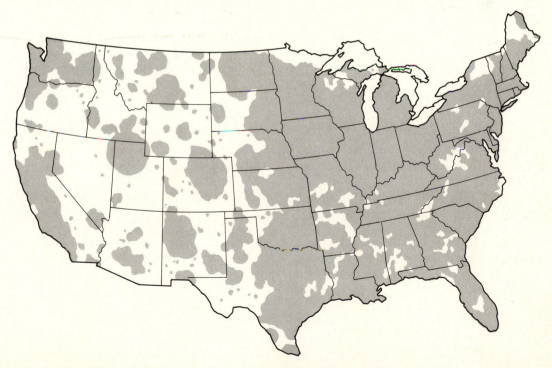

The white areas of the map represent places where neither AM groundwave service nor FM direct wave services can be heard at a satisfactory level at night. People living in these areas depend on skywave service from distant Class I stations on clear channels.

Source: Reprinted with permission from *Broadcast Communications Magazine* (copyright 1979).

a metallic network, such as the steam pipes or power lines of a building, the metal conductors will radiate the signal for a short distance into the surrounding space. This is a *carrier current* system, combining elements of both wire and wireless propagation. The most familiar applications of the method are carrier current stations that serve dormitories and other buildings on college campuses. As long as their radiations do not interfere with licensed users of the spectrum, such stations are considered *nonbroadcast* uses and do not require licensing.

There is also a licensed service, Traveller's Information Service (TIS). It uses carrier current radiation to supply information to motorists on the approaches to airports and in similar congested traffic areas (Turnage, 1979).

3.4 FM Broadcasting

FM Channels   Frequency modulation broadcasting occupies a block of frequencies running from 88 to 108 MHz in the VHF band (30–300 MHz). The channel width is set at 200 kHz (.2 MHz), allowing for 100 channels in the 88–108 MHz FM band. Channels are identified by the numbers 201 to 300 in the regulations, but stations identify themselves by the dial positions of their carrier waves — 88.1 for Channel 201, and so on. The first 20 channels (numbers 201 to 220) are reserved exclusively for noncommercial educational (public) broadcasting use.

FM Coverage   In the VHF region of the spectrum, as indicated in Exhibit 2.5.3, the propagation path is *direct*; therefore FM has no interference problems arising from night-time sky waves. An FM broadcast transmitter

Exhibit 3.3.2
Classification of AM channels and stations

Station class	Channel class	Power (in watts)	Number of channels	Percentage of stations
I	Clear	10,000–50,000 ⎫	60	{ 1
II	Clear	250– 5,000 ⎭		{ 28
III	Regional	500– 5,000	41	48
IV	Local	250– 1,000	6	23

Comment: The smaller the coverage the fewer the channels but the greater number of stations on each channel. More co-channel allotments of low-power stations can be made without causing interference than of high-power stations, whose signals cause interference over wider areas.

Source: Station percentages for 1975 from Christopher H. Sterling and Timothy R. Haight, *The Mass Media: Aspen Institute Guide to Communication Industry Trends,* New York, Praeger, 1978, p. 45.

has a stable coverage pattern, its shape and size depending on power, height of transmitting antenna above the surroundings, and obtrusive terrain features or buildings that block wave paths. Maximum coverage reaches approximately to the horizon. For the interference planner FM has still another advantage, the fact that the FM signal blanks out allotment from other stations more effectively than does the AM signal. An FM signal need be only twice as strong as a competing signal to override it, whereas an AM signal needs to be twenty times as strong.

FM Station Classes Because of the relative stability and uniformity of their coverage areas, FM stations have no need for such an elaborate system of channel and station classifications as does AM. FM stations are divided into three main classes, designated A, B, and C. Antenna elevation as well as power enters into a formula that defines the classes, but the maximum power/height combination is 100,000 watts and 2,000 feet. Class A stations are authorized power/height combinations enabling a coverage radius of about 15 miles, Class B about 30 miles, and Class C about 60 miles.*

FM Quality From the listener's standpoint, the most important advantage of FM over AM is its superior sound quality. For one thing, FM is almost completely free of static. This advantage comes from the fact that the VHF band is inherently less contaminated with atmospheric noise than AM's MF band, as well as the fact that amplitude is inherently subject to distortion from static (§2.4). FM

can provide undistorted reception in areas where, and at times when, satisfactory AM reception is impossible. A third advantage is FM's ability to reproduce sounds up to 15,000 cycles per second, a pitch so high that not everyone's ears are sufficiently sharp even to hear it. Nevertheless, such high frequencies play an important role in high-fidelity sound reproduction, which relies on overtones.

FM scores over AM in still another way, its greater *dynamic range* — the range in degrees of loudness between the faintest reproducible sound and the loudest. The human ear has an amazing capacity to adjust to extremes of loudness and softness, but sound-reproducing systems have much less flexibility. Very faint sounds tend to become lost in the noise of the system itself, whereas very loud sounds tend to overload the system and cause distortion. AM broadcasting even sacrifices some of its already limited dynamic range by artificially compressing the signal in order to maximize average power output.

FM Multiplexed Services FM's 200-kHz channel has twenty times the width of an AM channel. In addition to enabling increased sound fidelity compared to most AM stations, this generous channel width allows FM stations to *multiplex* stereophonic sound in their channels. Stereophonic FM requires picking up two separate ("left" and "right") versions of the original sound with two separate sets of microphones and amplifiers. The added signal modulates a *subcarrier* and the two signals go out as one. The stereophonic receiver separates the signals for delivery to separate sets of amplifiers and speakers.†

---

*A special noncommercial group, Class D, is authorized to operate on very low power (10 watts or less) to enable educational institutions to take advantage of radio with minimum investment. Class D stations, having only secondary status, are allowed to operate only if they can find a vacant channel that will not interfere with other classes of stations.

†AM stations are experimenting with several competing methods of stereophonic broadcasting, while FM stations are experimenting with quadraphonic, or double stereo, sound.

FM's wide channel also allows for multiplexing *Subsidiary Communications Authorization* services. These added signals cannot be picked up on ordinary home receivers because they are intended for subscribers who pay a fee to receive the transmissions on a special, fixed-tuned set. Typical SCA services are background music for stores and offices, readings for the blind, refresher information for physicians. Even slow-scan video still-pictures can be transmitted via SCA.

3.5 Short-Wave (HF) Broadcasting

Propagation Factors International radio services designed to cover very long distances use short-wave AM broadcasting. Parts of the HF band, located between the band used by standard AM and the band used by FM/TV, have been set aside for this type of use (Exhibit 3.5.1). In this frequency range, it will be recalled, long-range sky waves can be used *both day and night* (§2.5). However, the ionosphere layers constantly change, so that a frequency that works well over a given wavepath at ten in the morning may not work at all at four in the afternoon. Such changes can be predicted in advance on the basis of experience and propagation theory. Short-wave transmitters are therefore usually equipped to switch their outputs to several different antennas, each constructed to radiate a different frequency. Antennas are also designed to be directional so that they can beam transmissions to specific target areas. The antennas themselves are constructed differently from either AM or FM antennas, as indicated in the Voice of America installation shown in Exhibit 3.5.2.

U.S. Short-Wave Stations Only a half dozen privately operated international short-wave stations exist in the United States, all devoted to noncommercial, evangelistic broadcasting. Recently, however, consideration has been given to starting commercially operated short-wave stations.

The Voice of America employs over 30 short-wave transmitters at four U.S. sites to send its programs to overseas listeners either directly or via VOA relay transmitters located in eight foreign countries. The latter pick up signals from the U.S.-based stations and pass

Exhibit 3.5.1
Short-wave (high frequency) broadcast bands

Band designation in		Band limits in
Meters	**Megahertz**	**Kilohertz**
49	6	5,950–6,200
41	7	7,100–7,300
31	9	9,500–9,775
25	11	11,700–11,975
19	15	15,100–15,450
16	17	17,700–17,900
13	21	21,450–21,750
11	25	25,600–26,100

Comment: These bands are used by international broadcasters to reach distant targets by means of skywaves. Additional HF broadcast bands have been allocated in the 2 to 5 MHz range especially for local use in the tropical zone, where MF propagation is subject to heavy atmospheric interference. Only about 10 percent of the entire HF region of the spectrum is allocated to broadcasting; the rest is used by marine, air, land mobile, amateur, and other services.

them on to nearby target areas. VOA transmitters operate on much higher power than U.S. domestic AM stations, running as high as a million watts.

3.6 Photographic "Channels"

Picture Definition The varying abilities of photographic picture-making systems to

Exhibit 3.5.2
Voice of America short-wave antennas

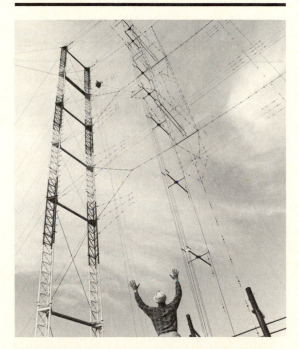

HF antennas for external broadcasting differ from both television and domestic broadcasting antennas. The radiating elements are hung between the steel towers. Each VOA transmitter site has many antennas to enable using several different frequencies. Antennas are also variously positioned to beam signals toward selected target areas.

Source: Courtesy Voice of America, Washington, D.C.

convey information can be likened to the varying capacities of radio channels. Most photographic systems break down the pictured scene into separate bits of information, or *picture elements*. The size of these bits governs picture *resolution*, or *definition*. Resolution refers to the ability to distinguish two small adjacent objects as separate objects. "Graininess" in photographic reproduction indicates lack of fine detail, meaning that the picture elements are too large to *resolve* such details.

Motion Pictures Several factors combine to determine the information capacity of motion picture systems: the inherent resolving ability of a given film stock, the picture area available in the film strip, and the speed at which the film moves through the camera (the number of frames per second). Three standards of quality have emerged, designated in terms of film-stock width: 35 mm, 16 mm, and 8 mm. The professional theatrical standard is 35 mm, along with some wider formats. The intermediate standard, 16 mm, was originally intended for amateur use. With the coming of television and its great appetite for film, 16 mm developed into a professional medium, but when highest quality is desired 35 mm remains the standard. It is much preferable to reduce original 35 mm to 16 mm for television use than to enlarge original 16 mm to 35 mm for theatrical exhibition. Eight mm, along with an improved small format, Super 8, is the amateur, home-movie standard. Super 8 is used to a limited extent for television news, but most technicians regard it as below broadcasting quality.

In all the film formats, some picture area must be sacrificed to leave room for sprocket holes, for between-frames space, and for the soundtrack. This sharing of channel capacity

70mm in cinema now popular

between *picture information* and *auxiliary information* has its parallel in television, as we shall see in the next section.

Motion as Information   Imparting motion to pictures adds another requirement to channel capacity. The motion aspect of cinema itself constitutes information that has to be carried in the channel. Multiplying the capacity of each individual picture frame by the number of frames exposed (or projected) per second gives a measure of the necessary total "channel" width required.

In cinema, what appears to be motion consists of still pictures (frames) projected in rapid succession. Each frame freezes the action at a slightly later moment than the preceding frame. *Persistence of vision*, a useful tendency of the eye to retain the image of an object for a brief moment after the actual object has been removed, blends the successive frames together. The "motion" of motion pictures is merely an *illusion* of motion.

The frequency with which frames are presented to the eye is vital to this illusion. At 16 frames per second (fps), persistence of vision gives the illusion of smooth motion; therefore this *frame frequency* was adopted as the standard for silent film. But a film sound-track passing over the sound pickup head in a projector at 16 fps does not allow for adequate quality of reproduction. A higher frame frequency, 24 fps, was therefore adopted for sound motion pictures. This is the reason for the comical apparent speeding-up of the action that occurs when old silent films are screened on a modern projector. The original projection rate of 16 fps has been increased by 50 percent.

Flicker Problem   Although at 24 fps the eye seems to see continuous action, it still detects intermittency of the light falling on the screen. After each frame flashes on the screen, a moment of blackout must follow while the projector pulls the next frame into position. The eye reacts more sensitively to these gross changes from complete illumination to complete blackout of the screen than it does to the smaller changes in the position of objects within frames. We perceive these gross alternations of light and dark as *flicker*. In fact, early movies were called "flicks" because of their low frame frequency.

The flicker sensation can be eliminated by increasing frame frequency, but economy requires the use of as few frames of film as possible. Since the 24-fps rate gives all the visual and sound information required, it would be wasteful to use a higher frame rate just to avoid flicker. The problem was solved by projecting each frame *twice*. In other words, when a given frame is pulled into place it is flashed on the screen once, remains in place while the screen is blacked out momentarily, and then is flashed on the screen a second time. During the next momentary blackout the next frame is pulled into place and the process repeated. Although only 24 different frames are projected per second, the screen is *illuminated* by a picture 48 times per second. This is frequent enough to deceive the eye into accepting the illusion of continuous illumination. Thus motion pictures require *two* projection frequency standards: *frame frequency* for continuity of motion and *field frequency* for continuity of illumination. Television uses a similar trick to increase field frequency without increasing information.

3.7 Electronic Picture Processing

Comparison with Photography   Consideration of the photographic method of

T.V.
30 FPS

motion picture making suggests that an electronic version must be able to do four things: (1) convert picture elements into electrical equivalents; (2) generate enough frames per second to give the illusion of movement; (3) generate enough screen illuminations per second to give the illusion of continuous illumination; and (4) have channel capacity sufficient to carry all this plus sound information and auxiliary signals in "real time."

closed captions + crawls

When light from a scene falls on the film in a motion picture camera, all the thousands of light-sensitive particles in each film frame respond *simultaneously*. After being developed, the film "remembers," retaining a permanent record of the images the camera "saw." The television camera, however, delivers a stream of individual, transient bits of information. It puts out some 200,000 of these bits each second, one bit at a time — an operation requiring fantastic speed and exquisite precision. The television receiver, in turn, must reassemble the image, positioning each bit in its proper place on the screen. At no time does a complete video picture exist as does the complete photographic image on film. Instead of being a remembering medium, then, television is a forgetting medium. As soon as a bit at a given location in the frame has been released, another bit takes its place. One must use a storage device such as film or magnetic tape to make a permanent record of what the television camera sees.

TV Pickup Tube The heart of the television system is the pickup tube, the electronic device that breaks the image up into its thousands of separate elements and converts each bit of light energy into electrical energy. The live or filmed scene to be televised is focused on the face of the pickup tube by a conventional photographic lens system. Thereafter electrons take over. Without the speed and precision of electrons, high-definition television of today would not be possible.

A pickup tube is just that — a tubular glass object, aimed at a scene to be televised in order to pick up the information the scene contains (Exhibit 3.7). The vidicon, the most commonly used type of television pickup tube, works as follows: visual information, in the form of light patterns, passes through the glass face of the tube and falls on a *target plate* covered with specks of *photoconductive* material. This substance has the property of converting light energy into electrical energy. Each of the thousands of specks on the target plate takes on an electrical charge proportional to the amount of light that falls on that speck. Next, each of these charges stored on the target plate must be released one at a time. This released energy is the output of the pickup tube — an amplitude-modulated electrical current, the amplitude variations representing variations in light intensity.

Scanning Pattern Electrons come into play as the releasing agent. At the opposite end of the tube an *electron gun* shoots out a stream of electrons toward the front of the tube, where they strike the back of the *target plate*, on which the picture information is momentarily stored. As the electron gun shoots its stream of electrons down the length of the tube they pass through magnetic fields generated by *deflection coils* surrounding the tube. Magnetic forces attract and repel (deflect) the electron stream, making it move systematically in a *scanning* (reading) *motion*, left to right, line by line. As the electron stream strikes picture elements stored on the target plate it discharges each of them in sequence. The electron gun may be said to "read" the information on the target plate, much as the human eye reads the information stored on a printed page. However, the electron gun's role is merely to *release the information*, not to interpret it.

A pickup tube has no moving parts. The

electron gun does not actually move its muzzle back and forth but stays rigidly fixed in place. The magnetic fields that control the scanning movements of the beam are themselves controlled by electrical messages sent to the deflection coils. A film camera must have a revolving shutter to interrupt light from the scene each time a new film frame is pulled into place. The pickup tube needs no such shutter, for the video picture never exists as a complete frame, only as a sequence of individual picture elements. Complete pictures occur only as illusions, in the brain of the observer.

Exhibit 3.7
TV pickup tubes

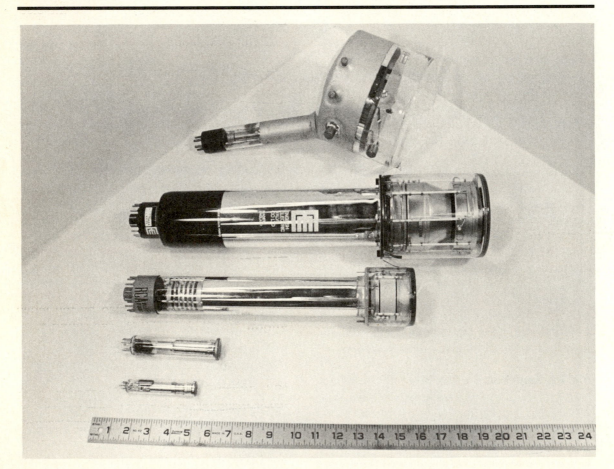

The odd-shaped tube at the top is an *iconoscope*, the type first used in commercial broadcasting. It was replaced by the *image orthicons* with 3-inch and 4.5-inch diameter faces. These in turn have been replaced by smaller *vidicon* and *plumbicon* tubes, varying from 1¼-inch to ⅔-inch sizes.

Source: Photo by Frank Sauerwald, Temple University.

Scanning Frequency Standards   It will be recalled from §3.6 that pictures in motion require two frequency standards, one for continuity of motion, one for continuity of illumination. The scanning frequency standard used in U.S. television is 30 frames per second (fps) instead of the 24-fps rate of motion picture film. The choice of 30 fps was dictated by the fact that a precise, universal timing standard is available throughout the country, the 60 Hz of ordinary house current.* The 60-Hz rate governs *field* frequency, the higher rate of screen illumination needed to prevent flicker. The television solution of the flicker problem is to split the frame into two fields by scanning first the odd-numbered lines, then the even-numbered lines. This ensures that the screen will be illuminated 60 times a second, even though each illumination involves only half the information of a complete frame. This method, known as *offset* or *interlace* scanning, calls for the electron beam to scan line 1, line 3, line 5, and so on to the bottom of the frame, then to fly back to the top to pick up line 2, line 4, line 6, etc.†

3.8 TV Signal Requirements

TV Picture Definition   The television picture, then, is constructed of *elements* arranged in *lines*, lines arranged in *fields,* and fields combined into *frames.* All four factors affect resolution, but the number of lines per frame is taken as a convenient index to a system's resolution capacity. Lines determine *vertical resolution.* The U.S. standard is 525 lines per frame, but this standard is only nominal because some of the channel must be used for accessory signals. In actual practice, only about 340 lines per frame are effectively involved in conveying black-and-white picture information.‡

Accessory Signals   One of the sources of line loss is the time spent while the electron beam flies back from the ends of lines and from the ends of fields to start anew. Special signals are needed to cut off picture-pickup during these *blanking* (or *retrace*) intervals so that the retrace path will not destroy the orderly scanning of lines. During the blanking intervals, therefore, no picture information can be transmitted.

Other accessory signals are needed to *synchronize* the scanning in the camera with the scanning in the receiver. If, for example, the tenth line in the pickup tube were laid down as the first line on the receiver tube, the top of the picture would be cut off.

TV Sound   Sound has its own portion of the channel, 25 kHz wide. The sound carrier frequency is located higher in the channel than the frequencies occupied by the video information (Exhibit 3.9.1). The sound component is *frequency modulated*, the video component amplitude modulated.§ No synchro-

---

*One reason for international differences in television frequency standards is the fact that in many parts of the world house current is 50 Hz instead of 60 Hz. In 50-Hz areas television uses 25 fps. At this slower rate flicker becomes evident when picture brightness is turned up.
†The discrepancy between film and television standards creates a mismatch problem. Television stations use special film projectors to televise films. This video-film machine projects every fourth frame an extra time, thus adding 12 projections per second to film's normal 48 fields to bring it up to the 60-field television standard.

‡Color television uses even fewer lines — about 280. By way of comparison, a 35-mm color film frame has the equivalent detail of 1,000 lines, a 16-mm color film frame 490 lines, and an 8-mm color film frame 230 lines.
§Amplitude modulation was chosen for the video signal so that amplitude could be artificially increased beyond the amplitude level representing "picture black" to the "blacker-than-black level" at which accessory signals are transmitted. See Exhibit 3.8 for details. Some national systems use AM for television sound, but most chose FM for its quality advantages.

nizing signals are needed to keep sound in step with picture; however, if the sound carrier is not tuned in correctly, intermodulation between sound and video signals takes place, introducing visible disturbances in the picture.

Color and Luminance

The color aspect of the television signal relies on the fact that mixing three primary colors in various proportions can produce all other colors. Color filters separate the primary color information (red, blue, green) before it reaches the camera tube. Any color has, in addition to actual color (*hue*), an attribute of brightness (*luminance*). The sum of the luminance components of the three primary colors supplies the fine detail of the television picture. A monochrome receiver interprets a color picture in terms of the luminance signal alone. Thus the color television system is *compatible* — a black-and-white receiver can interpret a color signal in monochrome terms.

Multiplexing Color

Color information is multiplexed by means of a subcarrier (Exhibit 3.9.1 shows its location in relation to the main carrier). A special "color burst" synchronizing signal controls the multiplexing, which depends on *phase* differences. Some overlap of signal energy between the two carriers occurs; however, the carriers do not conflict appreciably because the color information is *interleaved* with the luminance information. This is possible because the monochrome (luminance) signal is distributed unevenly among the frequencies of the video channel, leaving room for interleaving the color infor-

Exhibit 3.8
Television pickup tube output

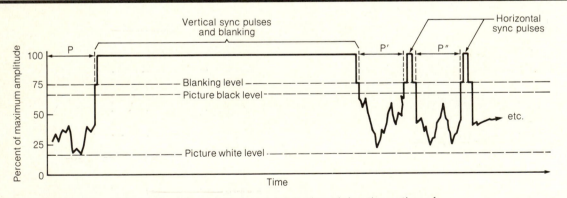

This represents the voltage output from a pickup tube and explains the notion of "blacker than black." The interval "P" represents the information picked up when the last line of a field is scanned. It is followed by the auxiliary information sent out while the scanning beam is returning to the top of the picture (vertical retrace) to start the next line. This auxiliary information is sent at a voltage level higher than the voltage that represents black in the picture — hence the term "blacker than black." At the end of the vertical retrace time the first line in the next field is scanned (P'), followed by another shorter blanking period while the scanning beam flies back to the start of the next line (P").

mation between the occupied frequencies. If the teeth of a hair comb can be imagined as the frequencies occupied by the monochrome information, the spaces between the teeth can be visualized as available for interleaving color information. The highest-quality cameras use a separate tube for picking up each color, but some smaller, light-weight cameras use only one or two.

3.9 TV Channel Specifications

Channel Width   Recalling that channel width defines channel capacity, we can conclude from the preceding description that the television channel's heavy information load requires a very wide channel. A single U.S.

television channel is 600 times the width of a standard AM broadcast channel. In fact *all* the AM and FM channels together occupy less spectrum space than only four television channels.

In the United States, each television channel (whether VHF or UHF) occupies a band width of 6 million hertz — six megahertz (6 MHz). Exhibit 3.9.1 shows how the channel is utilized. A net bandwidth of only 4 MHz is available for picture information, including accessory signals. The rest of the channel is occupied by *guard bands* (to keep side-by-side signals from interfering with each other), sound information, and vestiges of the suppressed lower sideband.

Fidelity Standards   The standard of picture fidelity possible within the information capacity of the 6-MHz channel is not high in

Exhibit 3.9.1
How the TV channel is used

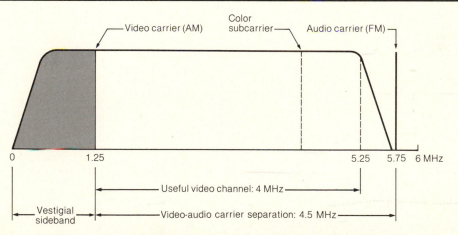

If it were not for the suppression of one sideband, the TV channel would have to be almost twice its present 6 MHz width. As it is, 1.25 MHz are lost because of the vestigial lower sideband, which serves as a buffer between this channel and the adjacent channel below. The audio portion of the signal uses part of the upper end of the channel, where another buffer zone occurs. Only 4 MHz of the total 6 MHz channel width is available for video information.

terms of photographic reproduction. In practice, the average home receiver produces about 150,000 picture elements, or dots, per frame. The best quality 16-mm film produces some 250,000 elements per frame, and 35-mm film, when projected, has the equivalent of about 1 million. A good 8 × 10-inch photoengraving has about 2 million dots. Magnifying the received television picture by use of large-screen projection adds no detail; a larger picture area simply makes it possible to sit farther away from the screen.

Television standards are the result of compromises and arbitrary choices; so it is not surprising that different compromises and choices have been made elsewhere in the world. Exhibit 3.9.2 summarizes the chief characteristics of world broadcast-television systems. Great Britain started with a 405-line system, but finding its quality not up to later world standards, Britain is gradually replacing it with a 625-line system. Since Britain's frame frequency is only 25 per second (because of 50-cycle house current), its 625 lines convey about the same net amount of information (15,625 lines per second) as the U.S. 525-line, 30-fps system (15,750 lines per second). These frame and line frequency standards, along with their corresponding channel width requirements, reflect the need of home television to deliver tolerably detailed pictures in *real time*. In situations where more time can be spent in transmitting picture elements, a much narrower channel can be

Exhibit 3.9.2
World TV standards

System desig-nation	Lines per frame	Channel width (MHz)	Sound modu-lation	Frames per second	Examples of users
A	405	5	AM	25	Great Britain (being phased out)
B(CCIR)	625	7	FM	25	Most of Western Europe
D	625	8	FM	25	China, Eastern Europe, USSR
E	819	14	AM	25	France
M	525	6	FM	30	Canada, Japan, Latin America, United States

Comment: Counting minor variations, there are 14 different basic (black-and-white) standards, plus three different color systems. Outside the American sphere of influence, the most widely used is System B, also known as the CCIR System (referring to a committee of the International Telecommunication Union). To find out which system each country uses, consult the annual *World Radio-TV Handbook*, edited by J. M. Frost.

used, as in the case of slow-scan television multiplexed on FM channels (§3.4).

Location in Spectrum   When the time came to allocate frequencies for television, the lower bands in the frequency spectrum had long since been tied up by earlier services. The search for sufficient space for television's huge 6-MHz channels ended with their being allocated in four different blocks. Channels 2 to 4 in one VHF block, 5 and 6 in a higher VHF block, 7 to 13 in a much higher VHF block, and 14 to 69 in a UHF block. Exhibit 3.9.3 shows this checkerboard allocation pattern, which means that the adjacent channel pairs 4/5, 6/7, and 13/14 can be assigned to the same community without causing interference because they are adjacent in name only.

3.10 TV Transmission and Reception

Studio   As indicated in Exhibit 3.10.1, a synchronizing generator, separate from the camera, originates the drive pulses for the scanning action as well as for blanking and synchronizing information. Video sources include studio cameras, remote cameras, film, slides, videotape, or network feeds. An operator at a control console combines video signals from the various sources to produce the flow of pictorial program material.

Transmitter   At the video and audio transmitters, picture and sound signals modulate their respective carrier waves (AM for video, FM for audio), which are then fed to a common antenna. The video transmitter

Exhibit 3.9.3
Summary of broadcast channel specifications

Broadcast service	Channel width	Number of channels	Band	Allocated frequencies	Channel identification numbers
AM (standard) radio	10 kHz[a]	107[a]	MF	535–1605 kHz[a]	[b]
FM radio	200 kHz	100	VHF	88–108 MHz	201–300
TV	6 MHz	3	VHF	54–72 MHz	2–4[c]
		2	VHF	76–88 MHz	5–6
		7	VHF	174–216 MHz	7–13
		56[d]	UHF	470–806 MHz	14–69

[a]The number of channels available will be increased by the planned extension of the frequency allocation upward to 1705 kHz.

[b]AM channels are identified by their midpoint frequency; the lowest channel is referred to as 540, the next as 550, etc.

[c]A TV channel 1 was originally allocated at 82–86 MHz but because of interference from existing services the frequencies were reallocated in 1948 to nonbroadcast uses.

[d]In practice not all 56 UHF channels are used by TV; channel 37 is allotted to radio astronomy, and in some areas channels 14–20 are allotted to land mobile services.

has 5 to 20 times as much power as the audio transmitter because of the much greater load of information the video transmitter has to process. Also the AM video signal is more susceptible to interference than is the FM audio signal. Television transmitter power is usually stated in terms of effective radiated power (ERP) of the *video* signal.

Transmitting Antenna As explained in §2.6, television uses directional antennas to concentrate the signal toward the terrain between the antenna and the horizon. The antenna tower (often mounted on a tall building or atop a mountain) supports the antenna proper, which consists of radiating elements mounted on a *pylon*. The antenna illustrated

Exhibit 3.10.1
TV system components and signals

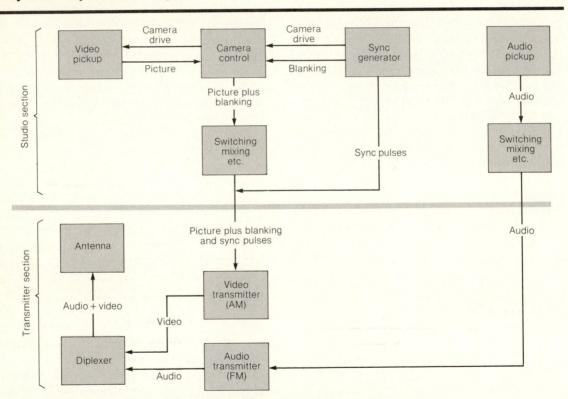

The upper half of the diagram represents the basic items found in the studio side of the operation, the lower half the ones found in the transmission side. Each block stands for a function that in practice may involve many different pieces of equipment. Note that the audio portion of the signal is handled separately until the output of its transmitter is combined with the video transmitter output for delivery to the antenna as a composite signal.

Source: Harold E. Ennes, *Principles and Practices of Telecasting Operations*, Howard W. Sams, Indianapolis, 1953.

earlier (Exhibit 2.6.2) shows a modern circularly polarized antenna. It sends out waves in a corkscrew pattern, making them virtually immune from the reflections that cause ghosts in the received picture.

Signal Propagation The fact that television uses both VHF and UHF frequencies has unfortunate consequences because of the differing behaviors of waves in the two bands. UHF signals are more subject to being cut off by buildings and other obstructions in their path. Such objects cast radio "shadows," just as they would in the path of a light beam. On the other hand, UHF waves have an advantage in being more directional than VHF waves, so that UHF receiving antennas are better able to reject reflections that cause ghosts. More important, however, is the fact that UHF signals *attenuate* more rapidly than VHF signals because of their inherently greater susceptibility to absorption by the atmosphere. The rules permit UHF stations to use much higher power than VHF stations (up to 5 million watts) to compensate for this difference, but VHF retains a fundamental coverage advantage.

Receiving Antennas Television coverage depends not only on transmitter channel frequency, antenna height, and terrain features, but also on receiving antenna efficiency and height. Within about 20 miles of a strong transmitter, indoor antennas often suffice. At about 30 miles outdoor antennas become essential.

Transmitting antennas are optimally adjusted to radiate the frequencies of just one channel. Receiving antennas, on the other hand, must be designed to pick up either all channels or all channels in one of the bands (VHF or UHF). They are highly directional and so must be oriented correctly.

TV Receivers Just as in the transmitter, in the receiver video and audio information are handled separately. The video information goes to the picture tube, called a cathode ray tube or *kinescope*. Its face is coated on the inside with phosphorescent material that glows when bombarded with electrons. An electron gun, comparable to the one in the pickup tube but usually much larger, shoots electrons toward the inner face of the tube. Guided by magnetic fields, the electron stream delivers picture information, element by element, line by line, field by field, and frame by frame. Synchronizing signals (as described in §3.8) keep the scanning sequence of the pickup tube and the kinescope tube in step with each other.

Color kinescope tubes are coated with phosphors that glow in three primary colors (red, green, and blue), arranged in lines consisting either of thin stripes or rows of triads of dots. Receiver circuits sort out (decode) the signals for each color and deliver them to one or more electron guns (Exhibit 3.10.2). The eye blends the simultaneous glow of the three primaries (each varying in intensity, according to the "mix" of a particular hue) to re-create the original hues. Examination of the face of an activated kinescope tube with a simple magnifying glass resolves the apparent hues into the three primary elements.

In principle, the kinescope displays only one element ("bit") of the picture at a time; in practice a series of elements glow simultaneously because it takes a while for the activated phosphor dots to stop glowing. Nevertheless, television relies on an optical illusion even more remarkable than the illusion of motion pictures. In television the eye must blend together not only separate elements, lines, fields, and frames into an illusion of continuity, it must also combine the three primary colors into an illusion of all the hues of the rainbow — plus some that no rainbow ever had.

3.11 TV Technical Innovations

Miniaturization   The changeover in electronics from dependence on vacuum tubes to solid state devices enabled miniaturization of equipment, with important consequences for production methods. Vacuum tubes are so

**Exhibit 3.10.2
Color kinescope tube**

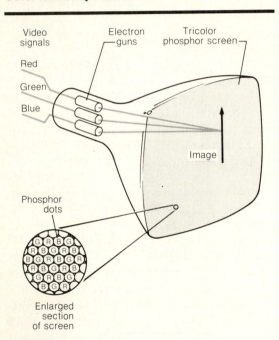

Enlarged
section
of screen

The drawing indicates the operation of a receiver tube that uses three electronic guns and tricolor phosphor dots. Varying amplitudes in the modulated current fed to the electron guns provide varying intensities of red, green, and blue to obtain the range of hues seen on the screen. Using a small magnifying glass you can easily see the dot-structure on the face of the screen when the receiver is turned on. Some tubes use red-green-blue phosphor stripes instead of dots.

Source: Paul Davidowitz, *Communication*, Holt, Rinehart & Winston, New York, 1972, p. 114.

called because they supply enclosed spaces at a near-vacuum within which to manipulate electrons. Both the television pickup and receiver tubes are types of vacuum tubes and there are hundreds of other types. A rack of electronic equipment containing scores of tubes takes up a great deal of space and generates so much heat it has to be artificially cooled.

Solid state devices eliminate both of these problems. The first type to develop, *transistors*, deals with electrons in a solid instead of in a vacuum. Transistors are much smaller and more rugged, require less power, create less heat, and last longer. These advantages are even more marked in the next generation of solid state devices, *silicon chips*. Assembled into complex *integrated circuits* no larger than the head of a pin they enable subminiaturization of electronic equipment. This made possible a wide range of recent innovations in computers, satellites, and other forms of electronic communication. The latest version of this technology, large-scale integrated circuit, enables making *microprocessors* to handle information. A single chip, no larger than an eighth of an inch in diameter, can do the work of several thousand separate transistors.

ENG Equipment   An example of the benefits of miniaturization is "ENG" (Electronic News Gathering). Formerly, when covering events outside the studio, television stations used cumbersome *remote vehicles*, loaded with heavy equipment. Miniaturization enables the same coverage with portable equipment easily carried by one or two persons. The key to the technology of ENG is the *time-base corrector*. This device supplies synchronizing pulses that free portable equipment of time-base errors, which show up as jittery pictures, skewing, and color breakup. Digital time-base correctors, which are in effect microcomputers, overcome this problem.

Receiver Improvements Solid state devices have made receivers much lighter, cooler, and less expensive to operate than they were in the vacuum tube era. The next major breakthrough expected in receiver design is an entirely new method of displaying the picture, eliminating the one remaining vacuum tube, the bulky kinescope. The new design will be a solid state flat picture device, offering a much larger display than kinescopes can possibly attain. The larger size will necessitate doubling the present resolution standard, which will probably involve some new scanning method capable of overcoming the time lost during electron beam retrace movements. This development, which has been anticipated almost since television itself began, will take still more years to materialize. In the meantime public interest has been shown in receivers that *project* oversize pictures onto a screen. This does not involve new technology, however, for large-screen projected television has been used in theaters and classrooms for decades.

Ancillary Signals Several possibilities exist for adding additional signals to the existing television channel without interfering with its normal operation. They include inserting, by means of multiplex techniques, *ancillary* (additional) information at points in the video portion of the channel that are not fully occupied by video information. Multiplexing uses time (expressed in terms of lines) otherwise wasted when the electron beam in the pickup tubes flies back at the ends of lines and fields to start new lines and fields. For example, each field takes one-sixtieth of a second, of which the vertical blanking interval (the end-of-field electron beam blackout time) takes about 8 percent. That is the equivalent of 21 lines not actually used for picture information. Some of this line-time is already devoted to synchronizing and other auxiliary information, but other unused lines are available for ancillary signals.

Among the uses of ancillary signals are improving television sound, monitoring program content (needed by advertisers to verify fulfillment of contracts), captioning (used by the deaf to follow the audio aspect of programs), and teletext (pages of text or graphic material displayed on the home television receiver). Development of these uses was one of the most active areas of television technical progress during the 1970s (Spongberg, 1975).

■ An example of improved television sound is *DATE (Digital Audio for Television)*. As the name implies, DATE converts sound into digital equivalents (a process described in §4.4). Samples are taken in rapid succession from four different sound sources. The stream of digital information representing the four sound components is multiplexed in a part of the video channel not heavily used by the modulated video information. DATE can be used in many ways, for example to accompany a program with narrative in a choice of four different languages. Like most digital devices, DATE is too expensive to incorporate in home receivers, but could be useful in television network interconnection.

■ *Closed captioning* for the deaf, on the other hand, is available to home viewers, although it requires an adapter attached to the home receiver (hence the term "closed"). Brief printed captions are inserted during line 21 of the vertical blanking interval. They appear at the bottom of the television screen like English subtitles in foreign movies.

■ The most versatile of the ancillary signal developments is *teletext*, a general term for several different methods of transmitting whole pages of textual matter (including maps, drawings, and other types of displays) during vertical blanking. In one version the transmitting station stores in microcomputers up to several hundred pages of information in digital form. Pages are transmitted in the vertical blanking interval in rapid succession. At the receiver a smaller computer stores a requested page, decodes the digital information, and feeds the text to the receiver screen, where it can either temporarily displace or be superimposed over the regular television picture.

■ Teletext displays only one page at a time, and only on the television screen. *Home facsimile* provides a "hard-copy" version by making a permanent copy on paper. This, of course, requires yet another add-on device attached to the already much-used home receiver.

Summary

Each broadcasting service is allocated certain bands within which each station is licensed to use a specific channel. Interference among stations arises from those on the same channel and, at lesser distances, from those on adjacent channels. The U.S. AM (standard) broadcasting channels are 10 kHz apart. A system of AM channel and station classifications facilitates allowing the maximum possible number of stations to operate without causing objectionable interference. AM uses medium frequencies that cause sky waves at night. Power, one of the most important factors influencing AM radio's area of coverage, is limited to a relatively low maximum level of 50 kilowatts.

Because FM uses VHF frequencies that do not generate sky waves, FM coverage patterns are stable, simplifying the interference problem. The 200-kHz width of FM channels enables transmitting both stereophonic sound and special auxiliary services such as background music. FM has other advantages in terms of fidelity and freedom from static and co-channel interference. Short-wave radio broadcasting, a third service, is used in the United States only for international broadcasting, but some countries use it domestically.

Motion pictures set a precedent for television by developing the basic concepts of resolution, picture elements, and frame and field frequency standards. Electronic pictures are picked up one element at a time by an electronic scanning process. Television picture elements are transmitted in the form of varying signal amplitudes. Color information, in terms of three primary colors, is multiplexed so that no increase in channel capacity is required. In addition the 6-MHz television channel carries auxiliary video information such as synchronizing signals to keep pickup and receiver scanning in step, as well as sound information. Sound is frequency-modulated on its own carrier in the upper portion of the channel.

Television channels are located in both the VHF and UHF bands. Television signals reach at a maximum approximately to the horizon. UHF waves, because of their inherent tendency to attenuate rapidly, cover smaller areas than VHF waves. The received video signal is displayed on a kinescope tube, which repeats the scanning sequence of the camera pickup tube. Although pictures are presented on the kinescope face only one element at a time, persistence of vision causes the viewer to perceive them as complete pictures in motion. The 525-line, 30-frames-per-second standard of U.S. television results in a satisfactory picture, although it is well below the quality of high-quality 16-mm film.

Current technological innovations include miniaturization of production equipment, improvements in receivers, and the use of ancillary signals for such services as closed captioning and teletext. Probable future developments include flat picture display devices of unlimited size, home facsimile, and multichannel television sound.

CHAPTER 4

Storage, Distribution, and Delivery Systems

4.1 Basic Concepts

Storage By "storage" we mean the warehousing of program materials for release and rerelease after production. Means of storage include disc and tape recordings, still and motion picture films, and (increasingly important in recent times) the several types of memories used by computers.

Except for news and live sports events, virtually all broadcast materials are prerecorded. Moreover, to compensate for differences in time zones, national networks feed *delayed broadcasts* from the East Coast so that stations in other time zones can release network programs at the same local time in all zones. Affiliates also sometimes record network feeds for later broadcast. Most program material thus goes through one or more recording steps before reaching its ultimate destination.

Nevertheless, the distinctive character of broadcasting networks remains their ability to provide for simultaneous broadcast of identical programs in *real time* throughout the nation, and, in the case of great public events, throughout the world. Only broadcasting, by means of networks, could furnish to an audience of over half a billion people on six continents the sight of Neil Armstrong placing the first foot on the moon.

Networks A broadcasting network, defined in its simplest terms, consists of two or more broadcasting stations *connected* to each other so that they can put identical programs on the air *simultaneously*.

The interconnecting links of a network are referred to as *relays*. A relay station passes on an electronic signal just as a relay runner at a track meet passes on a baton. Relays in this sense are *point-to-point* communications, not broadcast communications. Relay systems and the firms that run them are often referred to as *common carriers*. Such firms sell the use of their facilities to all comers on a first-come, first-served basis at fixed rates. The telephone is the most familiar example of a common carrier in the communication field. Common carriers are *neutral* toward programming, merely passing it on from one place to another without having any voice in its selection or production. Broadcasters, on the other hand, are crucially concerned with content (that is, programming) because they are legally responsible for it.

Stations as Delivery Systems To appreciate the importance of the distribution and storage functions in broadcasting, one need only imagine what it would be like if relay and recording technologies did not exist. Each station would be limited to the live programs that it could produce locally. Few if any stations would be able to attract and hold large audiences. There would be no national programming, no great star performers, no coverage of wide-flung live news and sports events. *All* stations are, by their very nature, essentially *local* stations; only the existence of networks and recordings enables their programming to rise above the local level. The primary role of the station can thus be viewed as *delivery,* not production.

Syndication Technology All mass media enterprises depend crucially on means of recording and of rapid distribution. The technoeconomic device for doing this job is *syndication.* In the present chapter, we are concerned with the technological aspects of syndication, the physical means whereby very expensive communications materials are centrally produced and then distributed among many users who share in the costs. Economic aspects of syndication are discussed in §8.7. Without syndication we could not afford to buy recordings of top musical artists, to attend movies, to receive today's news from every corner of the globe, to enjoy prime-time television, or to witness a presidential news conference. All such achievements become possible because of syndication.

Broadcasting networks, as a system of distribution, introduced a novel form of syndication, different from the news, motion picture, and music syndication methods that were already familiar when broadcasting began. Networks can bind an unlimited number of individual, local outlets into a single, unified national outlet. One of the unique features of broadcasting is the fact that stations can function in this way without giving up their ability to function at other times as local outlets. The ability to operate locally, regionally, and nationally — indeed, even internationally — and to switch from one type of coverage to another on a moment's notice, gives broadcasting a flexibility shared by no other medium.

To understand broadcasting, then, it is not enough to understand the attribute of "wirelessness" discussed in the preceding chapters. Distribution and storage play vital roles in extending and diversifying the potentialities of radio and television. Without benefit of these technologies, broadcasting would not only be very different; it would also be far less successful, probably not a medium of mass communication at all.

4.2 Sound Recording Technology

Discs In disc recording the recording *stylus* (needle) modulates the sides of a spiral groove in the recording master. A transducer (§2.4) activates the stylus, translating the voltages generated by microphones into stylus motion. The movements of the stylus cut variations of appropriate amplitudes and frequencies in the sides of the groove. In playback, vibrations of the pickup stylus riding in the groove activate another transducer (the pickup head) that converts motion back into modulated electrical current. These voltage variations in turn activate transducers in the form of loudspeakers to complete the cycle of transductions back to sound energy. The information storage capacity of a disc sound recording depends on a number of variables, such as the sensitivity of the recording and pickup styli, the accuracy with which the styli track the variations in the sides of the groove, and the speed with which the disc revolves.

Tape In magnetic tape recording, the storage medium consists of magnetized particles of an iron compound that coat a plastic tape. The smallness of the particles and the number available per second — as determined by the tape's width and the speed at which it passes the record head — define storage capacity. For master sound recordings on quarter-inch tape a speed of 15 inches per second is used. The standard for broadcasting and other professional playback uses is 7½ ips. Much lower speeds are used for ordinary home recording, office dictation, and monitoring.

Information to be tape-recorded is fed to the record head in the form of a modulated electric current that varies a magnetic field in the head. The pattern of these variations is transferred to the tape in the form of a corresponding magnetic pattern that is induced in the molecules of the ferrous particles. On playback, the tape passes over a similar electromagnet causing the playback head to generate a modulated electric current that goes to the loudspeaker after amplification. Running the tape over a third electromagnet, the erase head, rearranges all the molecules, neutralizing the stored magnetic pattern so that the same tape can be used repeatedly.

A *reel-to-reel* tape configuration is used when editing is required, but for many professional and most amateur uses, cassettes and cartridges are more convenient. *Cassettes* incorporate double hubs for feed and takeup reels in a single housing and must be either rewound after play or flipped over to play a second side. A *cartridge*, usually called a "cart," has a single hub and contains an endless tape loop that repeats

itself. Carts are especially useful in automated equipment, each cart containing a single program item; inaudible cues recorded on the tape tell the playback unit to stop at the end of a recorded item.

4.3 Picture Recording

Kinescopes The only surviving recorded versions of the earliest television shows are *kinescope recordings.* A film camera took pictures of television images as they appeared on the face of a black-and-white picture (kinescope) tube. The recording camera was especially designed so as to produce a 24-frames-per-second motion picture from the 30-frames-per-second kinescope picture. Kinescopes were far from satisfactory. Broadcast-quality television picture recording had to await the introduction of magnetic tape for television in 1956.

Videotape Recording (VTR) Picture recording on magnetic tape relies on the same principle as magnetic sound recording. The several thousand-fold increase of information in the picture channel posed problems that delayed successful application of the principle for decades. Recalling that among the chief variables affecting the information capacity of a magnetic tape system is the speed at which tape passes over the recording head, one can visualize the problem — tape would have to run at such a high speed it would wear out recording heads in minutes and require reels of impractical size.

Scientists at Ampex Corporation solved this problem ingeniously by imparting motion to the recording head as well as to the tape. In fact Ampex mounted *four* recording heads on a revolving drum (hence the name *quadraplex* or *quad* format). The drum rotates at high speed *transversely* (across the width of the tape) while the tape itself moves *longitudinally*. The combined movements of heads and tape produce an effective head-to-tape speed of 1,500 inches per second, yet the tape itself moves at only moderate speed. The two-inch-width tape is held by suction against the curvature of the revolving drum to maintain head contact (Exhibit 4.3.1).

Subsequently less expensive tape recorders were developed using one-inch and smaller tape. These retain the Ampex principle of combining head-plus-tape movement, but use only one or two heads, laying down a *slanted* track instead of a transverse track. The change in track angle makes possible a longer sweep for the head than would be possible if it swept the narrow tape transversely (Exhibit 4.3.1). This type of recorder is called *helical* because the tape wraps around a stationary drum or capstan in a spiral (helical) path while a spinning disc inside the drum brings each head in contact with the tape as it passes by. The professional one-inch VTR most widely used in the United States conforms to a standard known as Type C. It has two heads, one of which records all but a few lines in each television field. The second head handles the remaining lines and all the accessory signals, including three audio tracks and a control track.

Home Video Recorders Several different formats of *videocassette tape recorders* (VCRs) compete in the "home video" market. They use one-half-inch magnetic tape in cassettes about the size of a paperback book. They depend on the buyer's own television receiver to display the recorded pictures. The buyer does the recording, either off the air or with a video camera. The recorder contains its own tuner so that it can record programs on one channel while the owner views programs on another channel. Of the several competing formats the leader is known as VHS, originated by the Japanese firm Mat-

sushita and distributed by several U.S. firms. The runner-up format, called Beta, was originated by Sony, also a Japanese firm.

Video also has its equivalent of the audio disc designed for home use. For consumers, *videodisc recording* (VDR) has several advantages: (1) discs store more information per square inch of recording surface than tape; (2) they are much cheaper to reproduce than tape because they can be stamped out on an assembly line, whereas tape has to be copied foot by foot; (3) it is easier to search back and forth on a disc to find a wanted portion; and (4) discs wear better than tapes.

Two home-use versions have been put forward. The Philips-MCA version uses a laser beam to "lift" information off the surface of the disc. RCA's "Selectavision" uses a stylus riding in a track, but without the lateral motion of audio recordings; instead the stylus, passing over microscopically small "slots" in the grooves, senses stored electrical values in terms of capacitance changes. More details of these systems are shown in Exhibit 4.3.2. Both systems rely on the buyer's own television set to display the recorded pictures. They cannot be used for home recording as can VTRs, nor are discs interchangeable between the two VTR types.

4.4 Digital Signal Processing

Analog vs. Digital Signal Processing Conventional recording methods use the *analog* method of signal processing, not basically different in principle from the system used by Edison when he invented the phonograph in the nineteenth century. That system reproduces signals by means of *continuous* patterns of change, corresponding to (that is,

Exhibit 4.3.1
Videotape recorder (VTR) formats

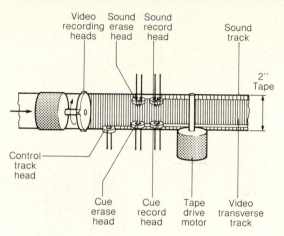

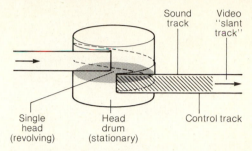

Transverse Quadruplex Format. Four video recording heads mounted on a rapidly spinning wheel, shown at the left, lay down transverse tracks across the width of the two-inch tape. Sound is recorded longitudinally along one edge, auxiliary information along the other edge.

Helical Format. The tape spirals around a large, *stationary* drum. Within the drum, the video-recording head spins on a revolving disc, making contact with the tape as it slips over the drum's smooth surface. Because of the spiral wrap the tape moves slightly downward as well as lengthwise, so that the combined movements of tape and recording head produce a *slanting* track, as shown. Some helical recorders use two heads, some use different wraparound configurations.

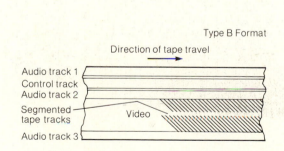

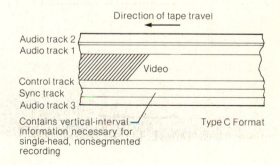

Type B and Type C Formats. These drawings show the ways information is laid down on the one-inch tape now in general use. Type C is the one most widely employed in broadcasting.

Source: AMPEX Corporation.

Exhibit 4.3.2
Home videodisc systems

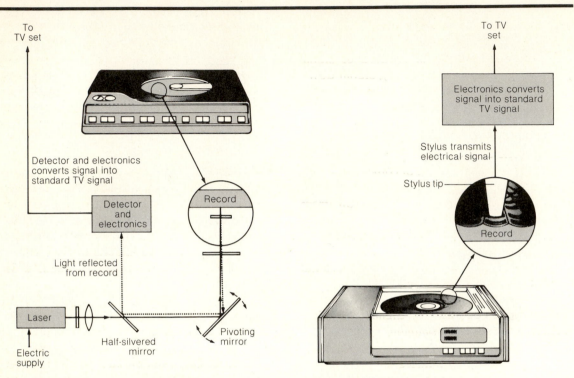

A professional tape recorder using 2-inch-wide magnetic tape needs the equivalent of 200 square feet of tape surface on which to store a half-hour program. Home videodiscs pack the same amount of information onto a disc surface less than a square foot in area. Some of the characteristics of the two competing videodisc systems diagrammed above are:

■ *Encoding method:* RCA (shown at right) stores electrical information in slots etched by an electron beam in pre-cut grooves on the disc surface; Philips uses a laser beam to etch pits on a smooth disc surface.

■ *Pickup scanning device:* RCA uses an electron beam, Philips a laser beam.

■ *Stylus used?* RCA yes, but the stylus picks up information from the slots in the disc electronically, not by means of vibrations as in an audio disc; Philips no — in fact its disc is sealed in a clear plastic protective coating through which the laser beam passes.

■ *Revolutions per minute:* RCA 450, Philips 1,800 (RCA can use slower speed because of the smaller diameter of the electron beam compared to a laser beam).

■ *Revolutions per picture:* RCA 4, Philips 1.

Source: © 1975 by The New York Times Company. Reprinted by permission.

analogous to) the continuous flow of sounds or images that impinge upon a microphone or a television camera pickup tube. This continuous pattern is inherently susceptible to distortion.

In contrast, the *digital* method of signal processing breaks the incoming signal down into a stream of separate, individual pulses of energy, which are inherently resistant to distortion. This breakdown is accomplished by a rapid *sampling* of the original continuous signal, done at such high speed that the observer has the impression of continuousness. The method is called "digital" because the individual energy pulses that result from sampling are codified so that each can be represented by a number. The signal consists of a string of separate, individual numbers instead of a continuously varying electrical current.

Encoding Process   A digital processor consists basically of a *sampling* device and a *digitizing* device. Signals (for example, sounds picked up by a microphone) arrive at the sampler as an electric current of continuously varying amplitudes. The sampler rapidly reports amplitude levels at successive moments, sending these samples to the encoder. The encoder *quantizes* each momentary energy level by assigning it a number. Usually encoders employ the *binary code*. This is the familiar number system used in computers, based entirely on the two digits, 0 and 1. Every quantity that can be expressed in the conventional decimal system (based on the numbers 0 to 9) can be expressed in binary code.

For processing purposes, this simplification of the signal has a great advantage because, no matter how complex the incoming signal may be, it can be reduced to a sequence of coded "zero" and "one" combinations. Information handled in this way is therefore immune from the many sources of interference and distortion that adversely affect the quality of analog signals. For example, repeated recording and relaying of analog information inevitably causes loss of quality, and the loss increases as the number of steps increases. Streams of digitized information, however, can readily be stored in computer memory banks and shunted from one place to another, going through any number of complicated processes without losing any of their subtle nuances.

Bit Speed   The minimum item of information conveyed by the difference between "zero" and "one" is called a *bit*. Digital channel capacity is measured in terms of *bit speed*, the number of bits a channel can handle per second, expressed as kilobits or megabits. A telephone circuit, for example, needs a 64-kilobit capacity.

The penalty paid for the simplicity of the binary system is that it requires very high bit capacity to handle complex information. That is why digital methods were long used in data processing, telephone, and experimental satellite communications before being applied to broadcasting. The high demand on channel capacity makes it impracticable, with present technology, to use digital methods for over-the-air broadcasting to homes. Not only would it require much wider channels than the present analog methods; it would also require excessively costly receivers.

For these reasons, digital processing has been confined to prebroadcast phases of program processing. These include a variety of animation, graphic, and editing applications that increase enormously the range of creative tools available to the director and video artist. Digital techniques are undoubtedly the most significant areas of broadcasting technological developments to be expected in the 1980s.

Digital Audio   Conventional sound recording exists within a constricted environment, bound by a fixed ceiling and a fixed floor. The ceiling is imposed by the fact that at a certain point audio overloads cause distortion, the floor by the fact that at a certain point the noise inherent in all electrical systems begins to overcome the signal. Digital recording spreads the upper and lower limits farther apart than is possible in analog recording. Digitally processed discs are already available on the consumer market, though home reproduction equipment still operates on the analog principle (despite a few digital accessories, such as a memory that will select the desired bands from a multiband disc).

Application of digital techniques to television sound has been successful in the DATE experiments mentioned earlier (§3.11).

Digital Video   The author of a recent television production handbook points out that "the full impact and potential of digital technology and its application to production can be fully appreciated" in the field of video processing in the studio (Wurtzel, 1979: 422). Video processing capitalizes on the availability of microcomputers that store and manipulate video information with fantastic speed and flexibility. Among the current applications are the following:

■ *Time-base correctors* that enable the use of lightweight portable equipment for "electronic news gathering" (§3.11).
■ *Tape-editing* equipment that uses digitally generated numbers to visually identify each frame, enabling the editor to identify the exact points at which to make cuts or begin fades.
■ *Digitally controlled video cameras* that automatically adjust themselves, "remembering" the settings on their electronic controls from one day to the next.

■ *Digital character generators* that enable directors to incorporate an unlimited variety of type faces and graphic resources into programs, simply by typing up the desired titles, legends, messages, diagrams, etc., on a keyboard.
■ Devices such as CBS's *electronic palette* that enable artists to use electronic brushes and pigments to create the video equivalent of water colors, oils, and other types of paintings on the television screen.
■ *Electronic animation* that eliminates time-consuming and costly film techniques.
■ *Effects* of almost unlimited variety such as *action track,* a digital frame-storing device that remembers motion and can reproduce the actual path that a golf ball just took across the putting green.

Collectively these and other digital resources give television the means of becoming a new art medium whose potentialities artists are only beginning to explore.

Digital TV Recording (DVR)   The applications just mentioned concern short-term effects that exploit limited frame-storage capabilities. They are grafted on to pictures that basically still depend for their existence on analog techniques. More difficult to achieve will be a complete digital system from original production to distribution by networks or syndication channels to broadcast stations or cable systems for delivery to home terminals. The first major step in this direction, *digital video recording (DVR),* is expected to be taken by the mid-1980s. DVR would probably have developed even more rapidly had it not begun to appear at the same time as improved conventional recorders in the one-inch Type C format, in which broadcasters and production firms had just invested heavily. By 1979, British, American, and Japanese manufacturers had all shown demonstration models of digital video recorders to the industry.

4.5 Terrestrial Relays in Networking

The second type of technological resources essential for syndication consists of the interconnection facilities that make networks possible.

Interconnection The "net" of network broadcasting is the matrix of connecting links — private (that is, nonbroadcast) point-to-point *relay* circuits that carry network programs from their origination point to each station affiliated with the network. This is what we referred to earlier as the distribution function, as contrasted to the delivery function that stations perform when they send the programs on to their audiences. Some organizations call themselves networks even though they have no such simultaneous interconnection facilities. These must be regarded, in both the legal and the practical sense, as only *pseudonetworks*. A true broadcast network must have connecting links between the point of origin and the affiliated stations, enabling *simultaneous* delivery of programs by all affiliated stations.

Any wire or radio link that intervenes between the original source and the delivery system can be regarded as a relay. Considerations of channel capacity determine which types of relays can be used for which purposes. Ordinary telephone circuits (usually especially *equalized* to compensate for the fact that higher frequencies attenuate over distance sooner than lower) suffice for radio programs, but not for television.

Coaxial Cable When wide bands of frequencies are pushed through a wire conduc-

tor (as happens when the broad 6-MHz channel of television is involved) their energy tends to fly off into space in the form of radiation. *Coaxial cable* traps this energy and conducts it within an artificially controlled space. The cable is actually two conductors — a hollow tube with a wire running down its middle, the two insulated from each other, so that the tube encloses a free space that may be occupied by air or any nonconducting material (Exhibit 4.8.3). Such a cable can conduct a broad band of frequencies in the millions of hertz. Attenuation does occur, of course, but it can be corrected by amplifiers inserted at intervals of about every third of a mile.

Coaxial cable used for intercity relays is buried underground. Installation costs add to the heavy expense for the rights of way and for the cable itself. In rugged mountainous terrain cable installation can become prohibitively expensive. Nevertheless, U.S. network television originally depended on the coaxial cable network (supplemented by some short microwave links) of the American Telephone and Telegraph Company (AT&T), which since 1926 has also supplied the long-distance telephone circuits for radio networks. Now, except for local short-run links, AT&T uses microwave relays for network interconnection.

Microwave Relays Waves used for relaying signals in the UHF, SHF, and EHF bands are referrrd to as *microwaves*. They range in length from a meter down to a millimeter. Waves this short attenuate so rapidly in the atmosphere that they were not at first thought to be usable for communication. When concentrated into a narrow beam, however, microwave power can be increased by a factor of 100,000. This gives microwaves the strength to punch through the atmosphere for a distance of up to about 30 miles. Because the waves are so short, relatively small sending and receiving reflector-concentrators suffice.

Exhibit 4.5 shows a typical AT&T microwave installation, with horn-type reflecting antennas mounted on a high tower. Such towers must be spaced within sight of each other. Each relay station receives, reamplifies, and retransmits signals to the next link in the chain. It takes over 100 such repeaters to span the continental United States landmass.

Microwave relay networks have an advantage over coaxial cable in not requiring continuous right-of-way easements. Moreover, microwaves actually benefit from rough terrain, which usually throws up high points that help in laying out line-of-sight transmission paths. Neither system, however, can span large bodies of water.

Exhibit 4.5
Microwave relay station

This repeater station on the summit of Wolf Creek Pass in the Colorado Rocky Mountains is nearly 12,000 feet above sea level, part of an AT&T transcontinental microwave radio relay route connecting New York with Oakland, California. The horn-shaped antennas have replaced the circular, dish-shaped type originally used for microwave relays.

Source: Photo courtesy of AT&T Long Lines Department.

4.6 Space Relays

Advantages of Satellites The answer to the problems of long-distance relaying is the *communication satellite*. This is essentially a relay station located in space, far beyond the earth's atmosphere, able to "see" almost a third of the globe's surface before encountering the horizon (Exhibit 4.6.1).

Satellites have been likened to microwave repeater towers thousands of miles high. This analogy can be misleading, however, because a microwave repeater links only one specific location to two other specific locations — the next sending and receiving points in the relay network. A satellite repeater links a single sending station (the satellite) to *any number* of receiving earth stations at *any distance* within its coverage area. Adding more receiving locations adds nothing to transmission costs as it does with microwave links.

Satellites have still other advantages. Unlike HF sky waves, their direct microwaves are relatively free from sunspot disruptions. Microwave relay signals become degraded in the course of dozens or scores of reamplifi-

Exhibit 4.6.1
Satellite global coverage

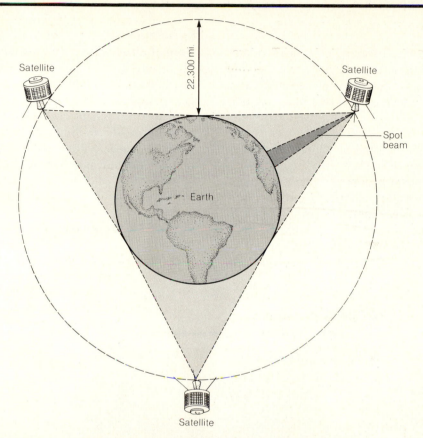

Hypothetically, three communication satellites positioned at equidistant points
on a circle above the earth's equator, 22,300 miles in space, would be able to relay
signals to the entire globe. In practice the outer edges of the coverage areas would
experience too much signal attenuation as the angle of the satellite waves caused
them to pass through more and more atmosphere before reaching the earth's
surface. Each satellite carries several transmitters and directional antennas,
enabling simultaneous delivery of several signals from a single satellite by means
of spot beams aimed at particular regions.

cations by successive repeater stations, but satellites put signals through only one intervening processor, the satellite *transponder* itself.

Geostationary Orbit   When positioned at a precise height (about 22,300 miles) above the equator, a satellite becomes *geostationary*, meaning that it remains in one place relative to the earth. Actually, of course, it travels, like the moon, in an orbit about the earth. At the stipulated height, however, the orbit is geosynchronous ("in step with the earth") so that the satellite appears to hover in one place above the equator. Small propulsion jets aboard the craft enable ground-control to make minor adjustments to keep it from drifting out of the prescribed orbit. Each geo-

synchronous satellite is assigned a specific orbital location, expressed in degrees of a circle, as shown in Exhibit 4.6.2.

Spectrum Allocations   More than a score of different types of satellite service exist, of which broadcasting is only one. Each makes its own demands for spectrum space. Competition for allocations is thus just as keen in the higher reaches of the spectrum used by most satellites as in the lower frequencies used by the older types of radio services. Broadcast satellite frequency allocations go as high as 86 GHz, but most allocations are in the 3–23 GHz range.

Signal Propagation   The terrestrial sources and destinations of relay satellite sig-

**Exhibit 4.6.2
Orbital positions of U.S. domsats**

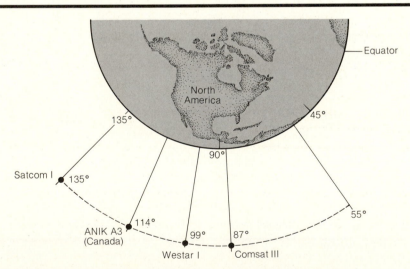

Geostationary satellites are assigned to fixed positions on an imaginary projection of the earth's equator, 22,300 miles high. Only the segment of the arc from 55° to 136° will allow U.S. domsats to cover the entire continental United States. Shown in the sketch are the positions of four of the many domsats now in orbit and projected for the future in this region.

nals are called *earth stations*. Their most conspicuous feature is a large bowl-shaped antenna, up to a hundred feet in diameter. The use of such large antennas, despite the fact that satellites make use of waves that are very short, reflects a deliberate design strategy. Because of limitations on launchable weight, satellites must be relatively light and hence must make do with low power. The larger the ground antenna, however, the more energy it can collect. Thus a trade-off was made — small, lightweight satellites in exchange for massive ground stations.

As launch capabilities improved and heavier satellites were lofted, ground antennas grew smaller. At present, single-channel receive-only antennas on the order of 15 feet in diameter are in regular use. Eventually, the minimum diameter will be reduced to three feet or less, enabling convenient direct satellite-to-home reception.

The relay transmitters on board a satellite, limited to solar power stored in batteries, must operate on only a few watts of power. However, their signals are propagated without attenuation through an almost complete vacuum until they reach the thin blanket of air surrounding the earth. Because the satellite looks virtually straight down, its signals suffer atmospheric attenuation for only a short distance. Terrestrial radio relays, on the other hand, operate close to the ground and are therefore subject to atmospheric absorption over their entire route. Even so, the satellite signal that arrives at the receiving earth station is extremely weak. A special *low-noise amplifier* (LNA) magnifies the signal some 100,000 times before feeding it to the receiver. The same antenna, appropriately equipped, can be used both as an *uplink* (transmitter) and as a *downlink* (receiver).

Satellite Construction   Communication satellites of the type used for relaying broadcast programs are equipped with several *tran-*sponders* (combination receiver-transmitters). The payload also includes steerable antennas, batteries, solar panels to collect energy, propellant for maneuvering the craft, and facilities for receiving and putting into effect commands from a control center on earth. Transmitting antennas are, of course, directional and can be adjusted to beam signals toward desired areas on the earth's surface.

4.7 Relay/Delivery Hybrids: Radio

Terminology   In some cases the distinction we have drawn between the two functions of *relaying* (private, nonbroadcast, point-to-point distribution) and *delivery* (broadcast release directly to listeners and viewers) becomes blurred. Broadcasting in fact increasingly finds itself involved in, or affected by, nonbroadcasting or quasi-broadcasting kinds of operations.

The technologies for producing, recording, and delivering programs can be regarded as building blocks that can be assembled in various ways to serve a variety of purposes. We refer to some combinations as *hybrids* not to imply inferiority, but to call attention to the process of cross-fertilization that is highly characteristic of contemporary applications of communication technology.

Rebroadcasting   Why could not networks save money by asking their affiliates to pass on the *broadcast* signal from station to station — B picks up A's signal off the air and *rebroadcasts* it, C picks up B's signal, sends it on to D, and so on all across the country? Some regional FM networks do in fact depend on rebroadcasting for interconnection instead of hiring nonbroadcast types of wire or microwave relays. Although rebroadcasting as a method of relay works, it has many disadvantages. Chief among them are: (1) Each time a signal goes through the broadcast-receive-rebroadcast cycle, it loses some of its original quality; after a series of such losses, signal quality becomes seriously impaired. (2) Broadcasting stations are not ideally spaced geographically for network coverage — many gaps occur where stations are too far apart for successful rebroadcasting. (3) Rebroadcasting offers no option for delayed delivery to enable identical clocktime release in time zones remote from the originating station.

Translators Rebroadcasting is routinely used to extend the coverage of individual television stations in mountainous areas where the terrain causes dead spots, or in sparsely settled areas beyond the coverage of regular television transmitters. For example, KREX in Grand Junction, Colorado, is on 51 such rebroadcasting stations. Altogether, some 4,000 *translators* have been authorized. These specialized rebroadcast stations or *satellites* (in the terrestrial rather than space sense) are called translators because they pick up the originating station's signal and "translate" its carrier to the frequency of a different channel so as to avoid co-channel interference with the originating station. Translators beyond the range of the parent station's signal may pick up the signal by means of satellite relay, in which case they are sometimes called *satellators.*

Instructional Television Fixed Services (ITFS) A short-range microwave relay service is authorized specifically for educational use. The rules allocate 28 television channels in the SHF band for ITFS. Most

users are public schools, but university graduate schools employ them too. Stanford University, for example, operates a released-time training program for employees of companies located within line-of-sight range of the campus. Over 5,000 employees receive instruction relayed directly to their company premises by ITFS, saving money and time by eliminating the need to travel to the campus for instruction (Curtis & Blatecky, 1978).

Multipoint Distribution Service (MDS) A commercial counterpart of the ITFS service allocates SHF frequencies for two television channels adjacent to the ITFS channels for short-range relay/delivery of data, facsimile, and programming. Commercial MDS operators charge subscribers an installation fee for a special rooftop antenna and *down-frequency converter* (from the MDS frequency to that of an unused channel on the customer's television set) as well as a monthly subscription fee.

MDS is especially well adapted to serving office or apartment buildings where many subscribers can be found in close proximity, able to use a single down-converter. The service has also been sold to individual homes in situations where cable television is not available, relaying to subscribers types of programming they would otherwise expect to get by cable.

4.8 Relay/Delivery Hybrids: Cable

Terminology Dependence of the just-discussed hybrid systems on over-the-air delivery subjects them to all the problems inherent in spectrum crowding and resulting mutual interference. Cable, however, creates in effect an artificial, interference-free environment in which to exploit the frequency spectrum, completely independent of the natural limitations imposed by open-space use of the spectrum. Thirty television channels can be fed simultaneously through a single coaxial cable without mutual interference, all from a single point of origination — the equivalent of having 30 different television stations operating in the same market. More advanced types of coaxial cable can even accommodate 52 channels. If still more channels are needed two or more cables can be used.

Simultaneous conduction of 30 channels in a single cable is achieved by *frequency division multiplex* — meaning that the total channel capacity of the cable (usually 300 MHz) is divided into subchannels. Each television carrier frequency is located within a subchannel. Exhibit 4.8.1 shows how the frequency band may be divided in a 300 MHz system.

Cable TV Coaxial cable technology was originally used for *distribution* of signals to stations, not for delivery to homes. The radical innovation introduced by *cable television* (originally called community antenna television or CATV) was the use of cable to feed programs directly into the home, *combining the relay and delivery functions in a single operation*. This new use for cable came about because of a demand created by the frustration of would-be television viewers who could pick up over-the-air either no stations at all or less than the desired number. Translators (§4.7) are only a partial solution because each one rebroadcasts only a single station. Cable, with its many channels, gives access to any number of stations and other sources of programs as well.

Exhibit 4.8.1
The many channels of cable TV

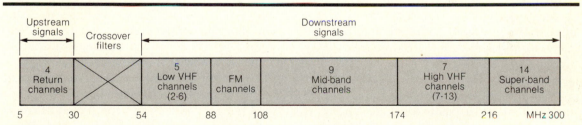

Most cable TV systems use coaxial conductors capable of handling a band width of 300 MHz. This example shows how such a band can be divided by frequency division multiplex into many separate TV channels. It assumes a system using four response (return) channels, which are located at the lower end of the band. After a space to prevent the "upstream" and "downstream" signals from interfering with each other, the rest of the band width allows for 35 TV channels and 100 FM channels. The normal frequencies of the TV over-the-air VHF channels are retained; other TV channels (either UHF stations or programs from sources other than stations such as pay cable and local origination channels) occupy the "mid-band" and "superband" segments. If UHF stations are picked up, their signals are downconverted from the UHF (above 300 MHz) band to the "superband" VHF channels of the cable system.

Source: Cable Television Information Center.

How Cable Delivery Works Cable television systems use several antennas, one for each of the stations a cable company wants to pick up directly off the air. Each antenna is cut especially for its station's wavelength and feeds a separate receiver at the cable system's *headend*. Stations too far away to be picked up directly may be fed to the headend by microwave or satellite relays (Exhibit 4.8.2).

Programs received at the cable system headend are forwarded to subscriber homes by means of coaxial wires of the type shown in Exhibit 4.8.3. *Trunk cables* carry the signal from the headend to dividing points in the cable network where *feeder cables* take off to carry the signals past subscriber locations. At each location a *drop cable* leads to the home receiver.

Differing types of cable are needed for trunk, feeder, and drop-off functions in order to deal with cable's biggest enemy, *rapid attenuation*. As noted in §4.5, radio frequency energy attenuates in cable much more rapidly than it does in the atmosphere; the higher the frequency, the more rapid the attenuation. In the midrange of frequencies used by cable, signals lose half their strength in traversing a mere 200 feet of cable. Booster amplifiers and equalizers must be inserted at frequent intervals to keep all channels up to strength and at the same level. A major part of a cable system's capital costs, therefore, must be devoted to the fight against attenuation. Obtaining rights of way and making the installation are also major cost items. Wherever possible, cable operators mount cables on existing utility poles, but within cities they must usually go underground in conduits and tunnels.

Cable systems that deliver 12 channels or less to their subscribers are directly connected to home receiver antenna terminals, relying on the VHF tuners in subscribers' sets to select channels. Systems that deliver more than 12 channels need an adapter unit (provided by the cable company on a rental basis) that acts in effect as an expanded VHF tuner. In this way, cable can avoid having to use the UHF broadcast channels, which would attenuate too rapidly to be practicable in coaxial cable systems. It should be recalled that cable is not tied to the over-the-air system of channel frequency allocations. The cable operator is free to convert the received frequencies to more convenient channels for distribution over the coaxial cable system.

Optical Fiber Cable Although conventional coaxial cable passes a wide band of frequencies, it nevertheless has its limits. Frequencies beyond 300 MHz attenuate too rapidly for practical use; when a cable distribution network needs the capacity to carry 50 or 60 television channels, a second cable has to be strung at great additional expense.

Cables made up of bundles of hair-thin strands of glass overcome this band width problem. Such *optical fibers* must be made of a very special, expensive glass. The signal is conveyed by a special type of light, traveling through the optical fibers. Usually the light source is a *laser*, which produces a concentrated beam at a single frequency — a pure color within the rainbow of colors that make up white light.

A single laser beam conducted through optical fibers has the channel capacity of hundreds, even thousands, of conventional coaxial cables. Optical fiber cables have other advantages as well. (1) They cause less signal attenuation than coaxial cable, requiring only about a quarter as many repeater amplifiers; (2) they are lighter in weight, more flexible, and smaller in diameter; and (3) they are impervious to electrical interference. Optical fiber cables are already used for short, critical runs in cable distribution systems in satellite earth station installations. As their cost

**Exhibit 4.8.2
Cable television system plan**

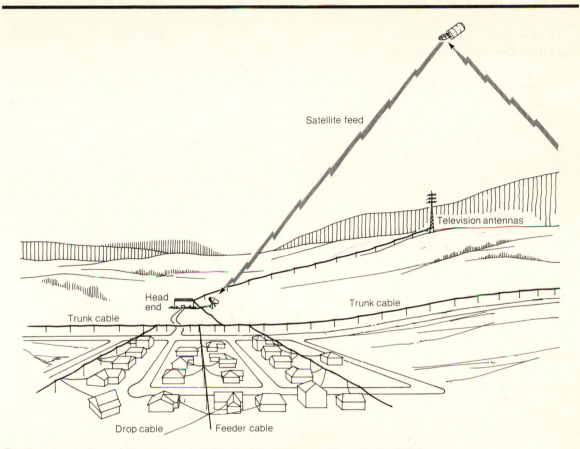

The headend of a cable system contains the amplifiers and local origination facilities of the system (if any). Feeding the headend are off-the-air TV station signals picked up by special antennas and possibly also signals from more distant stations fed by microwave relay. In recent years the most important input adjunct, however, has become a small earth-station receiving antenna for picking up satellite signals relayed from a variety of program sources. Trunk and feeder distribution cables, shown mounted on poles in the sketch, would be run underground within cities.

comes down they will doubtless replace coaxial cable for installations that require extremely wide-band capacity.

Summary

Broadcasting stations can be viewed as being primarily delivery systems, highly dependent for program material on syndication. The technological aspects of syndication include storage of program material (in the form of tapes, discs, films, and computers) and distribution by means of networks using common carriers — terrestrial and space relays — and by cable.

Sound storage technology includes disc recordings, magnetic tape, and optical sound on film. Television picture storage includes kinescopes, videotape recording, and video-

Exhibit 4.8.3
Cable TV's wideband channel

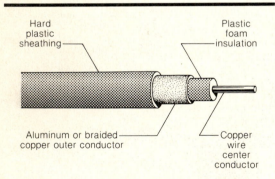

Cable TV gets its name from coaxial electrical conductors like this. There are many types of coaxial cable, but all have the basic structure shown here — a wire suspended within a tube, creating a protected, artificial, wideband channel for electromagnetic energy.

Source: Adapted from illustration in Walter S. Baer, *Cable Television: A Handbook for Decision Making*, The Rand Corporation, Santa Monica, California, 1973:4.

disc recording. The newest technology involves digital instead of analog recording. This method rapidly samples the sound or video signal, assigns a quantitative value to each sample, and transmits the values in binary code. Digital video storage and processing enables producers to obtain a wide variety of special effects with minimum effort. Digital methods are confined mainly to the studio, not yet having been applied to the mass market.

Relaying, the second aspect of syndication technology, refers to the distribution of programs from central sources to delivery systems. Terrestrial relays use either wire (usually coaxial cable) or radio (microwave) transmission. Both require frequent reamplification of the signal and therefore cannot span large bodies of water.

Reliable long distance relaying is accomplished by communication satellites, which have important advantages in cost and convenience over other methods. Relay satellites are placed in geostationary orbit above the equator, such that three satellites spaced out evenly around the earth can cover nearly the entire globe. Satellites function somewhat like enormously high microwave relay repeaters, but unlike microwave relays are distance-insensitive.

Hybrid relay/delivery systems blur the distinction between the relay function and the delivery function. These can be classified as either radio or cable hybrids. In the radio category are rebroadcasting, translator stations, instructional fixed services, and multipoint delivery systems. In the cable category are community antenna television (or cable) systems, with various links to program sources. The basic service of cable television is to relay/deliver television programs to subscribers by means of coaxial cable. This method of transmission offers many more local channels than over-the-air transmission. Still more channels can be delivered by optical fiber cables.

PART III

Origin and Growth of Broadcasting

In the preceding chapters we summarized the physical bases of broadcasting as they are now understood. It took time, of course, for that understanding to evolve, and we turn now to the story of that evolution. We consider the inventors who made broadcasting possible and the business innovators who made it a universal reality. We trace the growth of programs and networks from the first tentative radio show and radio station hook-ups of the crystal-set era in the 1920s to the cornucopia of broadcast services available in the 1980s.

CHAPTER 5

Preconditions: The Stage Is Set

Not the least of the many amazing facts about broadcasting is the speed with which it spread from a series of tentative local ventures to a recognized national service, more universal than bathtubs and refrigerators. To introduce photography into general use took a century, the telephone half a century; radio in general took 35 years, but broadcasting specifically only about 8 years. Broadcasting's popular acceptance and rapid growth did not come about by chance. The preconditions for its emergence had been evolving for at least a century.

In this chapter we look at some of these historical preconditions, the events that set the stage for broadcasting, giving it almost immediate star billing when it stepped before the public. Several strands of development intertwine: (1) the emergence of social conditions favorable to the development of mass communication, leading to the habit of media consumption; (2) the corresponding growth of the appropriate industrial and business institutions able to provide consumer goods in quantity (including entertaining and informative media content); and (3) the progress of scientific know-how that made possible new ways of communicating that content.

5.1 Development of Mass Media Consumption

Long before broadcasting began, the habit of mass media consumption had already been cultivated by the popular press, the phonograph, and the motion picture. These older media stemmed from the mechanical inventive tradition that was typical of the nineteenth century. Radio, on the other hand, stemmed from the electronic inventive tradition that, though born in the nineteenth century, flowered in the twentieth. Nevertheless, these differing traditions converged in complex and interesting ways as newspapers, recordings, and movies felt the competition of broadcasting and the impact of its technology.

Social Preconditions The Industrial Revolution (roughly 1750–1850) helped bring about fundamental changes in the daily life of the masses of people living in Western countries. For centuries the primary occupations of common people had been agricultural; then industrial occupations began to draw people away from the land. Eventually, most people lived and worked in cities. Along with this urbanization came the spread of education and the growth of leisure time. The concentrations of people in cities became the target of what we now call the "mass media" — those means of communication that use technology to reach large parts of the total population almost simultaneously with the kinds of news and entertainment that ordinary people find attractive and at a price that ordinary people can afford to pay.*

The Penny Press Urban concentration, education, and leisure all contributed to changing the medium of print from a special amenity primarily for the elite to a commonplace product for the masses. The penny press was the most visible example of this transformation. Previously, newspapers had been sold to subscribers in small editions numbering no more than a few hundred copies. In the 1830s, however, the *New York Sun* led a new trend toward mass-oriented papers that were sold on the streets for a mere penny a copy. They sold in the thousands and eventually in the millions of copies.

Until that time newspapers had concentrated on news of commerce, party politics, and other such "serious" subjects. The popular press broadened the coverage exploiting news of everyday events, sensational crimes, gossip, human interest stories, and sports — all presented in a breezy, colloquial style in contrast to the flowery essay style of the past. Popular newspapers also broadened their appeal, cutting across the dividing lines of party, class, sex, age, and cherished beliefs. Along with these changes in content and style came improvements in marketing to increase readership still more, and in

printing technology to enable faster, cheaper production. By the 1890s some mass-oriented newspapers had circulations of over a million. All this helped to create the habit of mass media consumption by which broadcasting would profit in the 1920s.

The Phonograph A later nineteenth-century invention, the phonograph, was even more directly influential than newspapers in preparing the public to be receptive to broadcasting. The phonograph accustomed people to the idea of investing in a piece of furniture that brought entertainment into the home. It was encased in a beautiful cabinet and given a place of honor in the living room.

Curiously enough, Thomas A. Edison, who patented the phonograph in 1878, intended it as an office dictation machine and strongly resented the idea of turning it into a mere "toy." However, public appetite for this entertaining novelty was so great that by the time of World War I a flourishing phonograph manufacturing and recording industry had emerged. In 1919, just after the war and on the eve of the introduction of radio broadcasting, some two hundred phonograph manufacturers were turning out over two million machines a year. The already mature phonograph industry, looking with disdain on the upstart radio and its entirely different technology, carelessly neglected to protect its future by taking the precaution to invest in electronic research. When radio broadcasting began in the 1920s, phonograph recording was still dependent on acoustic methods not fundamentally different from those originally used by Edison in 1878. The industry's shortsightedness became painfully clear in 1929, when the Radio Corporation of America (RCA) bought out the famous Victor ("His Master's Voice") phonograph plant in Cam-

---

*It is worth remembering that the word *media* is a plural noun (the media *are*), in spite of the fact that many writers use it as a singular. This is more than a petty usage error, for it implies that all the media — broadcasting, print, film, and the rest — are identical, obscuring the important fact that each medium has its own separate identity and unique characteristics. One of the goals of this book is to delineate the uniqueness of broadcasting as a medium among media.

den, New Jersey. RCA promptly discontinued phonograph production and began putting the despised radios in the handsome wood cabinets for which Camden was famous.

The combination of radio competition and the impact of the 1929 stock market crash devastated the phonograph industry. By 1933 "the record business in America was practically extinct" (Gelatt, 1977: 265). Ironically, not long after putting many phonograph companies out of business, broadcasting began reviving them. This revival was caused partly by the increased mass appetite for music that radio created and partly by the dramatic improvements in recordings made possible by the belated application of radio's technology to the phonograph. RCA eventually began producing RCA Victor records and developed its own electronic recording/playback process (§7.7). In many other ways the broadcasting and phonograph industries have continued linkages ever since.

Motion Pictures Closely paralleling the phonograph in its evolution was the motion picture. Edison's name is linked with both. His 1889 invention, the *kinetoscope*, was the first commercially usable motion picture camera (though some contend he merely placed his marketable name on the work of others). With slight modification it served also as a projection device that enabled one viewer at a time to see a brief film sequence as a peepshow in the 1890s. The earliest movie theaters for films projected on screens began in 1896 and were often called *nickelodeons* (combining the price of admission with a Greek word for theater).

Like the phonograph industry, motion pictures had achieved the status of a well-established industry by the time radio began in 1920. The movies created a mass audience for information and entertainment (newsreels were an important part of movie theater presentations before television phased them out). Far more people could attend the local "Odeon" or "Bijou" movie house than ever had a chance to attend the "legitimate" theater. Even the smallest movie house in the most remote town could show on the silent screen much of the best talent the world of theater had to offer.

Again, as in the case of the phonograph, the motion picture had something to learn from radio technology — the ability to talk. Although Edison had experimented in the 1890s with combining sound and pictures, progress toward "talkies" was stymied by the need for *synchronized* sound (precise matching of sound and picture). The self-satisfied Hollywood producers remained indifferent to the possibility of sound pictures, even after the problem of synchronization had been solved. Talkies finally began in earnest in 1928, with several rival sound systems competing for acceptance. One of these had been developed by RCA, an example of the many links between broadcasting and motion pictures that began in the 1920s, long before the advent of television.

5.2 Wire Communication

Though broadcasting benefited from the prior arts of sound recording and the motion picture, its direct technical and industrial descent was from the telegraph and the telephone — from point-to-point rather than from mass-oriented communications media. This means that electrical technology, rather than the mechanical technology of the early phonograph and the movies, led to the invention of radio and, eventually, to its application to public rather than private communication purposes.

The Land Telegraph   Most people did not feel any urgent need for instant communication beyond the horizon in times of peace until the era of the steam railroad. Then some means of signaling to distant stations became essential for safe and efficient rail operations. To meet this need, the British developed a form of *electrical telegraphy* in the 1820s.* Electrical impulses sent along a wire caused deflections of a pointer in a detecting device at the receiving end. An operator "read" the message by interpreting the movements of the pointer.

Crucial improvements were made by an American, Samuel F. B. Morse, after extensive experiments in the 1830s. His telegraph receiver had the great advantage of automatically making a permanent record of messages on strips of paper. We still use the term "Morse code" for the system that he and a partner developed for translating the letters of the alphabet into patterns of electrical impulses. The code consists of short and long impulses ("dots" and "dashes"), with simpler combinations for the more frequently used letters (the letter *e,* for example, is a simple "dot"; the less frequently occurring *q* is "dash-dash-dot-dash").

With the help of federal money, Morse installed the first operational telegraph line using his system in 1844 between Washington, D.C., and Baltimore. The first message over the forty-mile line suggests the awe with which the achievement was regarded — "What hath God wrought!" In most parts of the world governments still retain responsibility for operating national telegraphic systems. Congress, however, fearing the federal Post Office would lose money if the government competed with itself by running the telegraph as well, sold its interest in Morse's

line to private investors, retaining only the right of government regulation. By the 1860s and the Civil War, a single company, Western Union, had emerged as the dominant force in the telegraph field.

Submarine Cable   Laying telegraph lines underwater offered a more difficult challenge than overland telegraphy. The first short submarine link ran under the English Channel between Dover and Calais, about twenty-five miles. This cable was laid in 1851, but it took fifteen more years of repeated trials (including a six-month success in 1858) before a permanent cable was finally laid on the floor of the Atlantic between Europe and America. This feat, accomplished in 1866, was the work of the Anglo-American Telegraph Company, headed by a persistent American, Cyrus W. Field.

Regular transatlantic cable communication began in 1868, and soon all the major centers of the earth could exchange information in minutes instead of weeks or months. This meant a profound change in the nature of the world. The first breach had been made in the walls of international isolation, with far-reaching effects on trade, politics, diplomacy, and war. The submarine cable has been aptly called "the grand Victorian technology."

Telegraphy had an early and lasting association with news. Even before the electric telegraph became available, newspapers had begun to share the costs of newsgathering, which was, in effect, the first form of media syndication (§8.7). In the 1840s Paul J. Reuter started a carrier-pigeon service in Europe to supply financial news. He switched to telegraphy in 1851 when the Dover-Calais submarine cable became available. Thereafter, Reuter "followed the cable" wherever it led throughout the globe, establishing what is today one of the five worldwide *news agen-*

---

*The word *telegraphy* ("distant writing") was already in use, referring to relaying semaphore (visual) messages by means of a series of line-of-sight signaling stations.

cies or *news wire services*. The others are Associated Press and United Press International (the two U.S. agencies), Agence France Presse (French), and Tass (Russian).

Bell's Telephone The next goal of inventors was to transmit speech itself, eliminating the tedious business of encoding and decoding telegraph messages. Sound, of course, is a much more complex form of modulation than the simple "on-off" of the telegraph. The problem of the telephone centered on finding a sensitive *transducer*, a modulating device able to convert complex sound-energy from one medium (air) to another medium (electrical current). Many investigators were struggling with this problem and were approaching a solution when Alexander Graham Bell filed the key telephone patent in 1876.

Because he was by profession a teacher of the deaf, Bell had made a profound study of human hearing. However, his discovery of the telephone principle came about as a by-product of attempts to invent an improved form of the telegraph. In fact his basic patent of 1876 (said to have been the most valuable single patent ever issued) was titled "Improvements in Telegraphy." It described two ways of converting the vibrations of a membrane (a tightly stretched sheet of material, comparable to the eardrum) into electrical current of varying amplitudes (Brooks, 1976: 47).

Bell's 1876 patent, together with a second one obtained the following year, formed the basis for the company which we know today as the American Telephone and Telegraph Company (AT&T). Bell himself had little involvement with the business after the 1880s, but AT&T is still familiarly known as "The Bell System."

5.3 Invention of Wireless

Remarkable though the telegraph and telephone were, they could not reach out to ships at sea. Moreover, the installation and maintenance of wires and cables cost immense amounts of money. The notion that it should somehow be possible to do the job of the telegraph and the telephone without using costly and confining wire connections stimulated the inventive juices of many scientists and tinkerers in the last quarter of the nineteenth century. Their goal was *wireless* communication — what we now call *radio*.

Conflicting Claims Many inventors in many countries claimed to have been the first to solve the problem of wireless transmission. Mahlon Loomis, an American, patented a wireless system as early as 1872. The French date radio's invention from 1891, when Edouard Branly demonstrated a radio detection device called the *coherer*. Russia celebrates Radio Day on May 7, commemorating a demonstration made by Alexander Popoff in 1895. The British scientist Oliver Lodge experimented with wireless at about the same time. "Stupidly enough," as Lodge himself wrote, he failed to grasp its value, thinking that the telegraph and telephone were good enough.

Most of those who claimed the invention had common access to critically important scientific knowledge about electromagnetic energy that had recently been published by two physicists: (1) a theoretical paper by James Clerk Maxwell, predicting the existence of invisible radiant energy similar to light; and (2) the report of a laboratory experiment by Heinrich Hertz, in which he proved Maxwell's theory by generating and detecting radio energy and measuring its wavelength.

Maxwell, a Scot, published his paper, *A Treatise on Electricity and Magnetism*, in 1873

— a routine-sounding title that gave no hint of the far-reaching consequences it would have. In it Maxwell hypothesized that electromagnetic wave energy must exist. Using mathematical proofs and drawing upon observable facts about the behavior of light waves, he constructed a theory about electromagnetic energy, hypothesizing that this energy existed not only as light, but also in forms invisible to the eye. More than a dozen years went by before Hertz, a German, succeeded in a laboratory demonstration that detected the invisible waves that Maxwell had predicted. His experiment gave conclusive proof of Maxwell's theory. His 1888 paper, *Electromagnetic Waves and Their Reflection,* led directly to the invention of radio within a few years after publication. In recognition of the importance of his contribution, other scientists at first called radio waves "Hertzian waves." Later his name, abbreviated *Hz,* was adopted internationally as the standard way to express the frequency of radio waves, with the meaning "one cycle per second."

Hertz sought to verify a scientific theory, not to invent a method of communication. Like Lodge, he failed to realize the practical implications of his experiments. Indeed, when asked if Hertzian waves might be used to send messages, he said that wireless communication would never work. He may have been deceived by the fact that his experiments were conducted with tenuous short (HF) waves; the first successful wireless communication efforts used the longer, more rugged LF waves.

Marconi's "Releasing Touch"   It remained for Guglielmo Marconi — more an inventor than a scientist — to supply the "right releasing touch," as a Supreme Court justice put it in an opinion on a patent case many years later. "The invention was, so to speak, hovering in the general climate of science, momentarily awaiting birth. But just the right releasing touch had not been found. Marconi added it" (320 US 65, 1942).

Stimulated by Hertz's paper, Marconi as a young man of twenty-one experimented with equipment similar to Hertz's, first indoors and then on the grounds of his father's estate in Italy. Fortunately, Marconi had the leisure for experimentation and the money for equipment. Equally important, he had access through his family to high official and business circles.

For some of his earliest crude experiments in the outdoors, Marconi suspended a sheet of metal in the air to act as a transmitting antenna, connecting it to a battery and a spark gap. Sparks induced electromagnetic energy in the metal sheet. He picked up the radiated energy at a distance of a few hundred feet with another suspended sheet of metal, which caused answering sparks. Endless experiments with different shapes, sizes, and types of antennas, ground systems, and other components gradually improved the performance.

As soon as Marconi had convinced himself that wireless was more than a laboratory toy, he offered it to the Italian government, only to be rebuffed. His mother, who came from a well-known family of British whiskey distillers, was able to arrange matters with English postal and military officials, the most likely customers in Britain for the invention. Marconi went to London and registered his patent there in 1896. He was twenty-two.

The British were definitely interested in obtaining a license to use Marconi's patent, but bureaucratic delay held up an official offer. Impatient at the delay, Marconi launched his own company with the help of his mother's family in 1897. Its object was to manufacture wireless equipment and to offer wireless telegraphic services to the public. The Marconi Company's first sale occurred

Exhibit 5.3.1
How Hertz measured wavelength

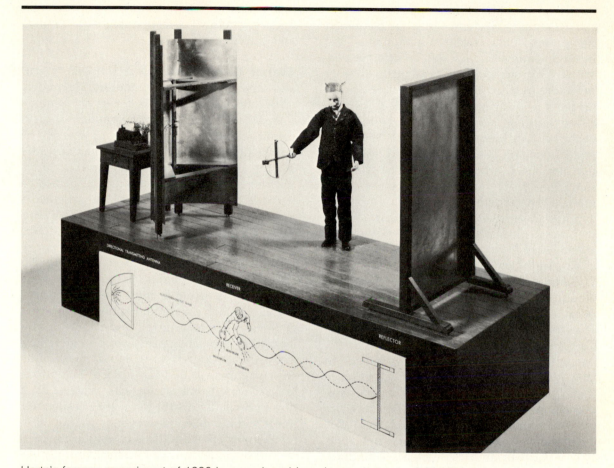

Hertz's famous experiment of 1886 is reproduced in a demonstrator model built by the Smithsonian Institution in Washington, D.C. The transmitting antenna at the left sent radio waves down the length of Hertz's laboratory. The structure at the right served to prove that the waves could be reflected. The inventor changed the position of the sparking detector, held in his hand, to determine the length of the waves. Measuring the distance between the points of maximum and minimum energy, he found the length of half a complete wave-cycle.

Source: Courtesy Smithsonian Institution, Washington, D.C.

the following year when the British War Office bought wireless equipment for use in the Boer War in South Africa.

To a remarkable degree Marconi combined the genius of the inventor with that of the business innovator. As an inventor he persisted tirelessly, never discouraged, even by hundreds of failed attempts at solving a problem. As a businessman he had a flair for effective public relations. In the early years of the century he constantly staged dramatic and convincing demonstrations to prove the usefulness of wireless. In 1909 Marconi shared the Nobel prize in physics with Germany's Ferdinand Braun for achievements in wireless telegraphy. He continued experimentation throughout his life, using his steam yacht *Elettra* as a floating laboratory.

Among Marconi's business ventures, the U.S. branch of his company, known as American Marconi, is of particular interest because it had decisive influence on the development of broadcasting in America. Founded in 1899, American Marconi finally began to realize substantial profits in 1913. In that year Marconi acquired the assets of an American firm, Lee de Forest's United Wireless Company, which had gone bankrupt after Marconi won a patent infringement suit. The takeover gave American Marconi a virtual monopoly on U.S. wireless communication, with ownership of 17 land stations and 400 ship's stations. All these Marconi facilities were devoted to extensions of the telegraph principle — point-to-point communications between ships and shore stations, between ships at sea, and between countries (Exhibit 5.3.2).

5.4 Technological Progress: 1896–1915

Progress in the evolution of wireless to the point where it would be usable for broadcasting awaited essential improvements in technology. Improved methods were needed for generating and modulating radio frequency energy, detecting signals, tuning, and amplifying.

Signal Generation   Marconi, like Hertz and other pioneer experimenters, depended at first on electrical *sparks* for signal generation. When sufficient voltage builds up in a circuit, electricity in the form of a series of sparks jumps across a small air-gap separating the ends of two metal rods or rods fitted with small spheres. Sparks create bursts of *alternating* current, essential for generating *radio frequency oscillations* capable of radiating into space. Spark-induced Morse signals thus consisted of a rapid series of isolated energy pulses (Marconi spoke of their sounding like "whipcracks"). A *continuous wave*, uniform in amplitude, was much more desirable — essential, in fact, for radiotelephony.

Several improvements were made on the spark-gap type of signal generator, including the *Poulsen arc*, whose rapid continuous sparking approached the ideal of a continuous wave generator. It was widely used throughout the world after 1911, especially for maritime traffic. However, it did not work well above 250 kHz (thus confining radio to the VLF band), nor was it effective for intelligible radiotelephony.

The search for a more versatile radio frequency generator continued. A natural candidate was the ordinary alternating-current electrical generator, but it was difficult to build generators capable of producing the high frequencies needed by radio (house current uses a frequency of only 60 Hz). In 1906 General Electric built a high-frequency generator for the pioneer radiotelephone experiments of Reginald Fessenden (§5.7). Such

Exhibit 5.3.2
Guglielmo Marconi (1874–1937)

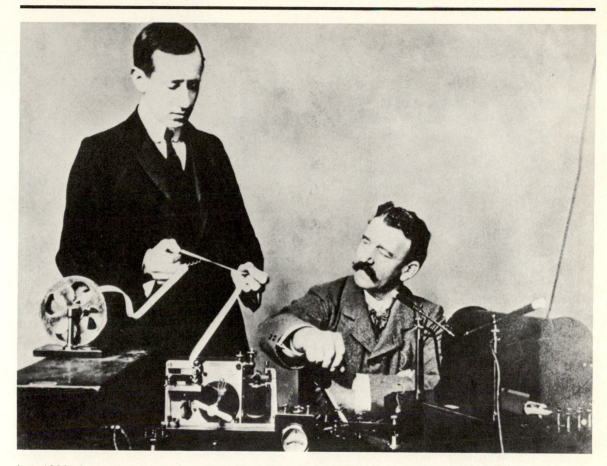

In a 1902 photo, the inventor examines the paper tape on which a radiotelegraphic
message is inscribed in Morse code. At that time radio equipment was still very
crude, but the already well-developed equipment of wire telegraphy was readily
adaptable to the task of recording wireless messages. Seated: George Kemp,
Marconi's most trusted engineering assistant.

Source: Courtesy Smithsonian Institution, Washington, D.C.

generators became known as *Alexanderson alternators,* named for a General Electric engineer, Ernst Alexanderson.

Later another type of signal generator, the *vacuum tube oscillator,* was introduced. This type of generator eventually became standard in all radio transmitters. It enabled effective transmission of speech by radio and allowed the use of higher frequencies than the cumbersome Alexanderson generator could ever hope to attain.

Detection   Another key problem of early wireless was providing adequate *detection* — the method of sensing an incoming signal. The spark-gap, originally used as a detector by Marconi, was impractical. A variety of other devices were tried, among them the Branly *coherer,* a glass tube of metal filings that "cohered" when influenced by an incoming radio frequency current. Coherence caused the filings to conduct electricity and thus to produce an electrical analog of the radio frequency Morse signals. It had a serious drawback, however. After each pulse of energy was received the filings had to be "decohered," which was done rather primitively by tapping the glass tube with a little hammer.

A much more effective device, the *crystal detector,* was discovered in 1903 and introduced generally in 1906. It consisted of a small lump of crystalline metal (several different types were used) that had the effect of converting radio-frequency, alternating-current energy into audible-frequency, direct-current energy, thus removing modulation information from the radio frequency carrier.

The most widely sold type of crystal detector had to be probed for a sensitive spot on a fragment of crystal with a piece of stiff, fine wire known as a "cat's whisker." Thou-

sands of amateurs could afford to build simple crystal sets, and they continued to do so on into the 1920s. Many of broadcasting's original radio fans picked up their first programs on homemade crystal sets — an unforgettable experience. As in the case of radio frequency generators, however, really efficient detection had to await development of the vacuum tube.

When Marconi tried to cover the America's Cup yacht races in 1901, in one of his typical public-relations stunts, a boat carrying the rival de Forest wireless system was also on hand, and the two signals interfered with one another. "The result was a complete fiasco. Neither the de Forest nor the Marconi boats were able to send any information to their shore stations, which were reduced to the ultimate journalistic recourse of fabricating race reports out of whole cloth" (Aitken, 1976: 246).

This dilemma arose because early transmitters were *untuned.* Spark-induced pulses of energy spread all over the wave band, so that any one transmitter interfered with all others. In 1904, however, Marconi obtained a U.S. *tuner* patent, enabling his transmitters to restrict their radiations to a limited group of frequencies. Receivers could then select ("tune to") the desired frequencies, excluding simultaneous signals present in other parts of the band.

Amplification   Another drawback of the early equipment was amplifying signals, whether at the sending or receiving end. This problem was shared by wire communication. It will be recalled that attenuation in wires makes it essential to use repeater amplifiers at frequent intervals (§4.5). In the early 1900s only an inefficient mechanical amplifier was available. The electronic device that eventually solved this problem, the Audion, also solved detection and radio frequency generation problems, making possible radio as we know it today. For that reason the Audion's inventor, Lee de Forest, felt justified in titling his autobiography *Father of Radio* (1950).

De Forest's Audion   After receiving a Ph.D. from Yale in 1899, de Forest worked first as an engineer with the Bell telephone company's subsidiary, Western Electric. However, he found routine engineering research dull and soon began devoting full time to developing his own inventions. In 1903 he experimented with an open gas flame as a radio detector. Because a flame has practical disadvantages, he turned to the idea of using gas heated within a glass enclosure by a glowing filament. He had such a device fabricated by a commercial electric lamp maker in 1905.

De Forest was following up leads left by Edison in 1883 and Ambrose Fleming, a Marconi researcher, in 1904. Each had patented devices based upon the then-unexplained fact that an electric current would flow between the hot filament of an electric lamp and a nearby metal plate sealed inside the lamp. Because such lamps (or tubes) had two elements, the filament and the plate, they were called *diodes*. Fleming patented a diode detector, but it was not a practical success, soon giving way to the more effective crystal detector.

De Forest took the crucial next step by adding a third element to the tube, making it a *triode*. He positioned the new element, called a *grid*, between the filament and the plate. The heater filament throws off clouds of *electrons*. Being negatively charged, electrons are attracted to the positively charged plate. But in order to get to the plate, the electrons have to pass through the grid. A small voltage applied to the grid can control with great precision the flow of electrons from filament to plate. Weak incoming radio signals were fed to the grid. The amplitude variations (that is, the modulation) of the in-

coming signals caused corresponding variations in the powerful current flowing between filament and plate. Thus the weak became strong — amplification took place. De Forest first used the triode in 1906 and was granted a patent in January 1907. An associate of de Forest made up a trade name for the new device — *Audion.* We now speak of the offspring of de Forest's great invention as the *electronic* (vacuum, thermionic) *tube* or, in British usage, valve.

Development of the Audion   De Forest started with the notion that the heated gas in the tube was the important feature of the device. Had he realized, as became clear later, that the gas trapped in the tube was a hindrance rather than a help, ensuing patent suits might have been avoided. The electron tube did not become really efficient until it could be made to enclose a near-perfect *vacuum*. Irving Langmuir at General Electric and Harold D. Arnold at AT&T recognized the theoretical basis of the electron tube and secured the high degree of vacuum needed.

Development of the Audion and the new circuits to go with it took more than a dozen years. Its first practical application in commerce was not to radio at all but to telephony. The Bell Telephone company desperately needed an efficient amplifier for long-distance telephony. Coast-to-coast telephone service was still impossible in the early 1900s because of signal attenuation. In 1913 the Bell company bought from de Forest seven basic Audion rights, limited to telephonic applications. The company paid the inventor only $50,000, though it was prepared (de Forest later claimed) to pay as much as $500,000 if necessary. By 1915 Bell was able to open the first coast-to-coast telephone circuits, using vacuum-tube repeaters.

As de Forest put it, the Audion gave mankind the power to command "electricity itself, not just its manifestations." It freed technology from dependence on mechanical moving parts. Ability to manipulate the electron made possible operations of a complexity, delicacy, and precision undreamed of in the age of gears, levers, belts, and pulleys. The thousands of electronic marvels, ranging from automatic door openers to space probes, so commonplace today, were made possible by the vacuum tube breakthrough. In the last quarter-century the tube has been largely replaced by solid state devices — first the transistor, then the silicon chip (§3.11). But they simply represent more efficient ways of doing the same jobs of electron manipulation originally done by the vacuum tube.

5.5 Business Developments

Role of Patents Frequent references to patents and patent suits in the preceding sections suggest their importance. They formed, in fact, both the building blocks and the stumbling blocks of great business empires. Patent litigation reached its heyday in the marathon struggles over control of basic radio patents in the first half of this century.

To be defensible a patent must describe a "novel" invention — it must introduce something genuinely new, not merely improve on a previous invention. One of the reasons de Forest had so much difficulty defending his Audion patent was the fact that it built upon the previously patented diode. Such interdependence was characteristic of improvements in the radio field; as a result, the history of wireless invention in the first half of this century was marked by constant patent litigation.

The grand objective of wireless inventors was to carve out a self-sufficient system, independent of the need to get licenses from rival patent holders. The more the wireless art progressed the more impossible that goal became. Literally thousands of patents were on the books and no one patent holder was safe from suit.

Constitutional Basis Article I, Section 8, of the U.S. Constitution provides that "Congress shall have the power . . . to promote the progress of science and useful arts, by securing for limited times to authors and inventors the exclusive right to their respective writings and discoveries." This provision lays the constitutional foundation for laws of copyrights and patents. Copyrights are still the source of a major economic burden to the broadcasting industry (§7.7), and patents have been the pivotal factors in the struggles for industrial control.

A patent gives an inventor an exclusive property right to an invention for a period of seventeen years. During that time the inventor has a legal monopoly. The inventor can manufacture and sell the product himself or can license others to do so. The early purpose of the patent was to offer economic incentives to native inventors at a time when the country depended wholly on Europe for scientific knowledge. The Constitution emphasized not so much the *private* gain of inventors as the *public* interest in encouraging invention. In creating private patent rights the authors of the Constitution could hardly have foreseen that, after the Industrial Revolution, patents would become the cornerstones of great monopolies that sometimes benefited neither inventors nor the public.

AT&T (the Bell System) The preeminent case of skillful patent manipulation in the interest of big business enterprise was that of the telephone (§5.2). Alexander Graham Bell organized his original firm in Massachusetts in 1877, the year in which he secured his second basic patent. But the inventor and his friends could not raise enough capital to develop the company. Control over the patents soon passed to others. Nevertheless, Bell's name has been associated with the company ever since, though it ceased to be his own company almost as soon as it was founded.

The company went through changes in organization and name as it expanded and brought in new investors. It now consists of a parent holding company — the American Telephone and Telegraph Company (AT&T) — and over a score of subsidiary telephone firms that constitute the "Bell System." That system provides most of the local and nearly all of the long-distance telephone services in the United States.

While its original 17-year patent monopoly lasted, the telephone company's strategy centered on keeping its patent position impregnable by vigorously suppressing infringements. During this period the Bell company brought six hundred suits against competing firms.

Rather than spread to ungainly proportions by attempting to supply service throughout the country, the Bell company adopted a policy of franchising independent regional operators. The franchised companies received the exclusive and permanent right to use the Bell patents. They in turn gave the Bell company substantial stock holdings. By the time the patents came to an end, the Bell company had attained controlling interests in these franchised companies. Expiration of the patents in 1893–1894 brought an upsurge of competition, but in the long run the Bell company held a trump card: it had installed the *long lines* connecting the central offices of telephone companies in one area with the centrals in other areas. Supremacy

in the long-distance field was assured in 1914 by AT&T's acquisition of the right to use de Forest's Audion (§5.4). For the first time coast-to-coast long-distance telephone service became practicable.

Even after the original Bell patents expired, the company continued a policy of not selling telephone equipment outright. It purchased Western Electric in 1881 as its manufacturing arm, thus making it possible to keep the whole process of manufacture, installation, and servicing within the Bell family. Patents continued to play a major role in the strategy of the AT&T business empire in the wireless era, enabling the telephone company to dominate the infant broadcasting industry (§6.4). Although the company gave up its broadcast stations in 1926, to this day it still profits from the broadcast industry through its near monopoly of the long-distance terrestrial relay facilities used for network interconnection.

AT&T's control over long-distance telephony was made possible because of its status as a *regulated monopoly*. In exchange for its privileged position the company accepted a degree of government regulation (through the Federal Communications Commission) of its rates and other aspects of its business. In 1968, however, a small data transmission company won the right to attach its own equipment to Bell telephone lines. This invasion of Bell's equipment monopoly was the first in a series of far-reaching changes that began to revolutionize the communications industry in the 1970s.

The revolution was triggered by the emergence of new technology linking conventional telephone facilities with microwave and satellite networks, enabling computers as well as people to talk to each other. One of the prices of AT&T's telephone monopoly was that the company was barred from entering the field of computerized communications. However, in 1980, as compensation for having to give up exclusive control over use of its long-distance network, AT&T was given the right to set up an independent computer communications subsidiary. The emergence of Baby Bell, as the projected new subsidiary has been called, is expected during the 1980s as part of a massive restructuring that will affect every aspect of the telecommunications industry, including broadcasting.

AT&T's manufacturing monopoly is also under attack. The Justice Department started a suit in 1974 to force AT&T to divest itself of its manufacturing arm, Western Electric. It is known as a "one-owner, one-client" company because it is wholly owned by AT&T and sells its entire output to the parent company. Though Western Electric is only a subsidiary of AT&T, its task of fabricating billions of feet of telephone wire and tens of thousands of other products each year for AT&T has made it the fifteenth U.S. corporation in size.

General Electric   Another communications giant, the General Electric Company, goes back to a watershed invention — Edison's incandescent electric light. The present company was born of a merger in 1892 between the Edison Electric Light Company and another manufacturing concern. GE took an immediate interest in that key wireless device, the vacuum tube. It became one of the chief investors in early radio broadcasting and to this day owns a group of pioneer stations, headed by outlets in its headquarters town, Schenectady, New York — WGY(AM), 1922; WGRV(TV), 1939; and WGFM(FM), 1940.

Westinghouse   Railroad air-brake patents formed the basis for the Westinghouse Man-

ufacturing Company. In the late 1800s, Westinghouse became embroiled in an epic battle with Edison over whether alternating or direct current should be adopted as the standard for the nation's electric power systems. Westinghouse installed the first alternating-current system in 1886, in competition with the earlier direct-current system advocated by Edison (later GE). The ten-year AC-DC battle became so heated that when New York state began using AC current for the newly invented electric chair, Edison publicists argued that AC's fatal effect on criminals proved it was unsafe in the home. The contest ended when the two companies agreed to standardize on AC power and to pool their patents for their mutual benefit. Even so, some parts of New York City were still served by DC power until the 1920s.

Westinghouse pioneered in broadcasting even earlier than GE. Its original station, KDKA, still operating in Pittsburgh, dates back to the very beginning of broadcasting in 1920. It is now part of Group W, which comprises seven AM, two FM, and five television stations under Westinghouse ownership.

The increase in the importance of electric power after the turn of the century made both Westinghouse and GE extremely rich. Together with AT&T (including its subsidiary, Western Electric) they formed an invincible triumvirate in the fields of electrical manufacturing and communication. Their patents, their power, and their know-how were all to have a crucially important effect on the emergence of broadcasting.

De Forest and the Feedback Circuit
All the inventors of the wireless era engaged in constant patent litigation, but de Forest seemingly more than most. He filed over thirty patents in the pioneer years 1902–1906, and in all was granted over a hundred. His

most bitterly fought suit had to do with the *feedback*, or regenerative, circuit — the subject of "the most controversial litigation in radio history" (Maclaurin, 1949: 78). This design feeds back part of a received signal on itself, greatly increasing signal strength. The circuit was of vital importance because it increased tremendously the sensitivity of radio receivers. In fact, it has been called "as historic as the first Bell telephone patent and as clearly decisive in the development of the modern world" (Lessing, 1956: 78).

Four powerful companies claimed to hold the controlling patent on this improvement: AT&T, with the de Forest patent; General Electric, with the Langmuir patent; American Marconi with a patent granted to Edwin Armstrong; and the Telefunken Company, with the German Meissner patent. This four-way battle moved in and out of the courts for twenty years. In 1934, after the contenders had spent millions of dollars in legal fees, the Supreme Court finally decided in favor of de Forest.

Even the final court decision did not completely clear the atmosphere. Armstrong still claimed priority. He seems to have understood the principle underlying the feedback circuit better than de Forest, who arrived at the invention by largely empirical methods (Maclaurin, 1949: 78). Engineers today generally recognize Armstrong's claim, despite the court's award to de Forest.

This case shows how the growing complications of the wireless patent situation during the early twentieth century made inevitable substantial control of the new industry by the great corporations. They alone had the resources to build up patent strength, to withstand frequent court battles, and to undertake the developmental work that patents always need.

5.6 Development of Wireless Services

During its first two decades wireless as a business made its money from supplying *communications services*. Wireless manufacturing was not yet a big industry because the market for the equipment was limited to the specialized needs of the few communications service companies. The mass market for millions of broadcast receivers and thousands of broadcast transmitters lay in the future. The main demand was for services that wire could not duplicate; therefore, overland wireless services were not important at first. The efficient network of existing telephone and telegraph lines already did the job.

Maritime Service Ships at sea were the first commercial customers for radio communication. For thousands of years ships leaving port on long voyages had sailed off into utter silence. Now for the first time they could communicate with each other and with coastal stations far beyond the horizon. The natural efficiency of over-the-water propagation made the maritime service workable even with the crude equipment available in the earliest days of radiotelegraphy. Moreover, the service had dramatic impact because of its value in times of emergency. As early as 1898 wireless had been used in a maritime disaster. In 1909, when the S.S. *Republic* foundered off New York, all passengers were saved by wireless-alerted rescue ships. In that same year wireless came to the rescue in twenty other emergencies at sea, and each year the number increased.

The most dramatic disaster at sea occurred in 1912 when the *Titanic*, a luxury liner advertised as unsinkable, struck an iceberg and sank in the Atlantic on her maiden voyage from Britain to the United States (see Box). A heroic Marconi operator stayed at his post and went down with the ship. Nevertheless,

The Department Store and the *Titanic* Disaster

Overland telegraphy was used mainly as a source of publicity at first. For example, in 1910, Wanamaker's Department Stores contracted with American Marconi to install wireless stations in its outlets in Philadelphia and New York. The Wanamaker stations exchanged messages between the two stores and with ships at sea.

In a 1913 promotional book the company claimed that "the two stations in the Wanamaker Stores are next to the most powerful stations in the country, second only to that at South Wellfleet, on Cape Cod. The Philadelphia Station has sent messages as far as Colon, Panama, a distance of 2,000 miles, and incoming steamers report that they can copy Wanamaker messages 1,000 miles at sea" (Wanamaker, 1913: 183).

By chance the station at Wanamaker's New York store played a bit-part in radio history, for it was the first station to make contact with the rescue ships involved in the *Titanic* disaster.

The young operator who ran the New York Wanamaker station was David Sarnoff, later to become the preeminent industrial leader in the broadcasting field

Sources: *Titanic* courtesy United Press International; Sarnoff courtesy RCA.

fifteen hundred people died — among them some of the most famous names in the worlds of art, science, finance, and diplomacy — making the *Titanic* disaster the most unforgettable tragedy of its kind in history.

The fact that for days radiotelegraphy maintained the world's only thread of contact with the survivors aboard a rescue liner brought the new medium of wireless to public attention as nothing else had done (see Box). Subsequently, inquiries revealed that a more sensible use of wireless (such as a 24-hour radio watch) could have prevented the accident, or at least decreased the loss of life. Because of these findings, the *Titanic* disaster had an important influence on the worldwide adoption of stringent laws governing shipboard wireless stations. It also set a precedent for regarding the radio business as having a special public responsibility above and beyond the obligations of ordinary businesses. This concept carried over into broadcasting legislation a quarter of a century later.

Naval Wireless Naturally, the naval powers of the world took an immediate interest in military applications of wireless. Carrier pigeons had been the only means of communication with ships beyond the range of sight. Both the British and American navies began experimenting with ship installations in 1899. Germany followed the next year. The first naval use of radio in actual war occurred in the Russo-Japanese War in 1904–1905. The Japanese victory is ascribed at least in part to the superiority of their Marconi equipment over that used by the Russian Navy.

Transoceanic Wireless Long-distance radio communication across oceans held commercial promise as an alternative to telegraph cable, but because of technical limitations this radio service did not become strongly competitive until the 1920s. In the meantime, the Marconi company, which dominated the transatlantic wireless business, built several high-power coastal spark-transmitter stations in the United States and Canada prior to the outbreak of World War I in 1914.

In 1917 GE installed a 200-kilowatt Alexanderson alternator in New Brunswick, New Jersey. The alternator, a huge and costly machine, put out a powerful very low frequency (VLF) signal of about 20 kHz. It represented a major improvement in long-distance radio communication.

During the 1920s the alternator was displaced by vacuum tube transmitters. They enabled development of the short-wave (high-frequency) portion of the spectrum, which turned out to be much more efficient than the lower frequencies previously used for long-distance communication. A dramatic rise in transatlantic radio traffic followed.

Amateur Service During these pioneer years amateur operators, who built their own transmitters, played a significant role. When forced to move into the HF band so that they would not interfere with commercial traffic at lower frequencies, amateurs first developed the techniques for successfully employing these supposedly undesirable frequencies.

Radio amateurs, or "hams," are not to be confused with modern CB operators, whom amateurs disdain. Amateurs identify with a long and proud tradition as serious hobbyists, technically qualified and licensed by the government only after passing tests of skill. In the early days their ranks included the leading wireless inventors and engineers. By 1912, licensed amateur stations numbered 1,224, at a time when commercial stations numbered only 528 — 405 on ships and 123 on land.

5.7 Experiments with Radiotelephony

All these wireless services used *radiotelegraphy*, not voice transmissions. Throughout this period, however, eager experimenters sought the key to *radiotelephony*, the essential precursor of broadcasting.

Fessenden's 1906 "Broadcast" The first known wireless transmission using radiotelephony and resembling what we would now call a broadcast took place in 1906. It was made by Reginald Fessenden, "the first important American inventor to experiment with wireless" (Maclaurin, 1949: 59). Using his Alexanderson alternator to generate radio energy (§5.4) and an ordinary telephone microphone, Fesenden made his historic 1906 transmission on Christmas Eve from Brant Rock, a site on the coast of Massachusetts south of Boston (Exhibit 5.7.1). Fessenden himself played a violin, sang, and read from the Bible. He also transmitted the sound of

Exhibit 5.7.1
Reginald Fessenden (1866–1932) at Brant Rock

Fessenden (center) stands with his associates in front of the building where he made the historic 1906 broadcast. The column in the background is the base of his antenna.

Source: Courtesy Smithsonian Institution, Washington, D.C.

a phonograph recording. Ships' operators heard the transmission far out at sea. They were utterly amazed to hear actual voices and musical tones in earphones that up to then had reproduced only static and the harsh *dits* and *dahs* of Morse code. In a sense this event marked the start of broadcasting, though of course it lacked the essential attribute of continuousness of service. Fessenden's historic transmission was merely the first in a long string of demonstrations that would culminate in the start of regular broadcasting services in 1920.

De Forest's Experiments   The prolific inventor who patented the Audion (§5.4) also felt the challenge of radiotelephony. Lee de Forest, as a lover of fine music, naturally turned toward the idea of using radiotelephony to communicate sound. In 1907, hard on the heels of Fessenden, de Forest made experimental radiotelephone transmissions from a building in downtown New York City. Intended listeners were fellow engineers in nearby buildings, but the U.S. Navy supplied an unexpected additional audience on ships in the Brooklyn Navy Yard (Exhibit 5.7.2). In 1908 de Forest transmitted phonograph music from the Eiffel Tower in Paris. Two years later he staged the first transmission of live opera. It came from the Metropolitan Opera House in New York City and featured the famous tenor Enrico Caruso. Listeners to the wireless transmission, however, said the voices were hardly recognizable.

In 1916 de Forest began using his Audion as an oscillator to generate radio frequency energy. In doing so he opted for electronic means, rather than the mechanical means of Fessenden's alternator. He set up an experimental transmitter that year in his Bronx home and began to transmit phonograph records and announcements. In his autobiography he described his personal announcements — in which he credited the Columbia

Gramophone Company for the recordings and mentioned the wireless equipment sold by his own firm — as the first radio commercials. He even transmitted election returns in the fall of 1916, anticipating by four years a similar program on KDKA, now considered to have been the first regular broadcasting station.

During the United States' participation in World War I (1917–1918), de Forest had to dismantle his station, but after the radio ban was lifted he resumed his experimental transmissions. By then, however, the war experience had led to more formalized government regulation of radio transmitters. A government radio inspector told de Forest that there was "no room in the ether for entertainment" and forced him to close down (de Forest, 1950: 351).

The Fessenden and de Forest radiotelephone transmissions are examples of the many experiments conducted at university laboratories and in private research facilities throughout the United States and elsewhere in the world during the early years of the century. The most important influence in bringing these scattered efforts into focus was World War I.

5.8 Wireless and World War I (1914–1918)

Military Wireless   When U.S. direct participation in the war began in April 1917, the Navy took over all U.S. stations, commercial and amateur alike, and either dismantled them or ran them as part of the Navy's own facilities, which included 35 shore stations.

Among the commandeered stations was the American Marconi facility at New Brunswick, New Jersey. There the Navy used a late

Exhibit 5.7.2
Lee de Forest (1873–1961)

It was by sort of this equipment and through these two headphones that the voice of Madame Farrar was heard at Brooklyn Navy Yard in October 1907 — She being the first woman to Sing over the Wireless Telephone

Frank E. Butler

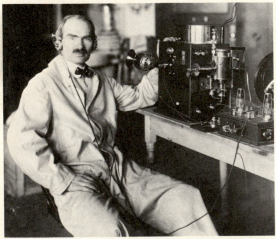

The inventor is shown in 1907 with a transmitter of the type used in his famous 1907 voicecast, along with a shipboard receiver of the type that picked up the transmission.

Source: Courtesy Smithsonian Institution, Washington, D.C.

model of the Alexanderson alternator (§5.6) to maintain reliable radio contact with Europe. In 1918 General Electric made an alternator with the unprecedented power of 200,000 watts available. President Woodrow Wilson used this monster to keep in touch with Washington by radiotelephone as he sailed to the Paris Peace Conference in December 1918.

The Army Signal Corps also used radio, as did the Air Service. However, U.S. combat participation was so brief, and the trench warfare in Europe so static, that radio's ground and air uses were limited. The Navy, however, having the most urgent need for wireless, had been developing its use since the turn of the century. Some ten thousand soldiers and sailors received wartime training in wireless. After the war they helped popularize the new medium. They formed part of the cadre of amateur enthusiasts, laboratory technicians, and electronics manufacturing employees that constituted the ready-made first audience for broadcasting.

Patent Pooling   In order to mobilize the total wireless resources of the country for war, the Navy decreed a moratorium on patent suits. Manufacturers agreed to pool their patents, making them available to each other without risk of suits for infringement. Such extraordinary measures were necessary because by that time the tangled web of conflicting patent rights had begun to strangle the progress of wireless manufacturing.

The wartime patent pool broke this stalemate. After the war, the radio industry profited from its wartime experience by voluntarily entering into patent-pooling agreements. These, as we shall see, had important implications for broadcasting in the 1920s.

Industrial Development   Military purchases and the moratorium on patent suits greatly increased the quantity and sophistication of wartime wireless manufacturing. The armed forces needed

mobile "trench transmitters" (using barbed wire for antennas), "pack transmitters," and compact receivers. They wanted submarine detectors, radio direction finders, and equipment for the recording and study of code transmissions. All of these used electronic vacuum tubes; assembly lines that had produced electric light bulbs before the war were now turning out vacuum tubes by the hundreds of thousands. (Barnouw, 1978: 10)

The war served as a transitional period. In prewar days the wireless industry had been dominated mainly by inventor-entrepreneurs, struggling to market their discoveries while at the same time feverishly experimenting on new ones. After the war, big business took over. AT&T had added wireless rights to its original purchase in 1914 of telephonic rights from de Forest. General Electric was in the forefront with the powerful Alexanderson alternator and the ability to mass-produce vacuum tubes. Westinghouse, also a producer of vacuum tubes, was casting about for new ways of capitalizing on wireless.

Prospects for Radiotelephony   Despite the technological and manufacturing progress stimulated by the war, the future prospects for nonmilitary radiotelephony were by no means clear at the war's end in 1918. Wartime developments had built up a great corporate head of steam for the production of wireless telephone equipment for which there was no civilian market.

De Forest suggested that radiotelephony might be used on small ships to save the expense of skilled Morse operators. David Sarnoff, then still associated with American Marconi, predicted that radiotelephones would eventually replace the wired telephones in homes and offices. But the Navy still clung to radio's original role as basically a seagoing communication system. Navy witnesses at a congressional hearing said radio had no business competing with the telephone and telegraph on shore.

Thus the time was ripe for a business and social innovation. Some practical moneymaking use for radiotelephony was needed, one that would have a good growth potential without competing head on with existing wire or wireless services. In a word — there was a crying need for *broadcasting*.

Summary

Preconditions for the emergence of broadcasting included social, industrial, and scientific developments of the nineteenth century and the first two decades of the twentieth century. The Industrial Revolution created the social conditions that led to the habit of mass media consumption. Development of the penny-press newspaper, the phonograph, and the motion picture gave rise to mass media production, distribution, and consumption. The technology of these media was rooted in an older, mechanical inventive tradition rather than in electronics, from which telecommunications sprang. Eventually, however, all of the mass media came to benefit from the innovations of electronic technology.

In the direct line of descent, the immediate precursors of radio broadcasting were the wire telecommunications systems — first the telegraph and underwater cable, then the telephone. The telegraph enabled the growth of worldwide newsgathering organizations that greatly influenced all news media. Wire communications enterprises in general built up a collective fund of expertise and business experience that would later strongly affect broadcasting.

James Clerk Maxwell's theories about the nature of electromagnetic energy and Heinrich Hertz's subsequent laboratory proofs led to the invention of wireless, or radio, by Guglielmo Marconi in 1896. Marconi applied the invention first to maritime and transoceanic communication, in the point-to-point tradition of the telegraph. These early uses of radio were confined to radiotelegraphy.

From 1906 on, experiments in radiotelephony were carried out by such inventors as Reginald Fessenden and Lee de Forest. But only after the development of the vacuum tube did practical radiotelephony, and hence broadcasting, become possible. The vacuum tube opened the door to the electronic age and hence to all the subsequent developments in broadcasting and other modern media of telecommunication.

Patents such as those of Samuel Morse (the telegraph), Alexander Graham Bell (the telephone), Thomas Edison (the phonograph and motion picture projector), and de Forest (the vacuum tube) served as the bases for building huge business empires, among them the American Telephone and Telegraph Company (descendant of Bell's original telephone company), now the largest private corporation in the world. AT&T, along with such industrial giants as General Electric and Westinghouse, already had a major stake in the developing radio industry when broadcasting came into being.

World War I accelerated the development of radio in terms of technology (improvements in equipment for military use), utilization of resources (patent pooling), industrial development (stimulated by large military orders), and personnel development (training of people to understand and use radio). By the end of World War I (1918), the stage was set. Within two years broadcasting was to emerge.

CHAPTER 6

Emergence of Broadcasting: 1919–1927

6.1 The Broadcasting Concept

Tunnel Vision Before broadcasting began, all radio messages were intended for *specific addressees*. Even SOS emergency signals are intended specifically for those who can be of help, not merely for the entertainment of casual listeners. Communication executives found it hard to see how profit could be made from transmitting indiscriminately to anyone and everyone. Moreover, both wire and wireless communication businesses had so far dealt with *private* messages and had concentrated on the interests of senders rather than receivers of messages. It was easy to collect fees from the sender of a telegram or the maker of a telephone call, but how could one collect fees from an unknown, uncounted mass of "listeners-in"?

The visionaries of radiotelephony, on the other hand, thought less about making money than about the adventure of creating a new art. Concerning his 1907 experiments with radiotelephony, de Forest wrote, "I cannot, of course, claim that I originated the term 'broadcast,' but I think that I was the first one to apply so descriptive a term to this new art which I was then beginning to cre-

ate" (1950: 226).* When broadcasting finally did become a profitable business, de Forest grew bitter about the effect of commercialism on the quality of programs.

Sarnoff's "Music Box" One of the visionaries, however, had a foot in both worlds. David Sarnoff had followed up the favorable notice he had won in connection with the 1912 *Titanic* disaster (§5.6) by becoming assistant traffic manager of American Marconi's radiotelegraphic business. In 1916 he wrote a memorandum to his chief proposing that the company branch out into a new form of radiotelephony:

I have in mind a plan of development which would make radio a "household utility" in the same sense as the piano or phonograph. The idea is to bring music into the house by wireless. . . . The receiver can be designed in the form of a simple

---

*Others lay claim to the term as well. For example, Fessenden's wife, in her biography of the inventor, wrote, "On Christmas Eve and New Year's Eve of 1906 the first *Broadcasting occurred*," referring to her husband's famous Brant Rock radiotelephone transmissions (Fessenden, 1940: 153, italics in original).

"Radio Music Box" and arranged for several different wave lengths. . . . The main revenue to be derived will be from the sale of the "Radio Music Boxes" which if manufactured in lots of one hundred thousand or so could yield a handsome profit . . . . The Company would have to undertake the arrangements, I am sure, for music recitals, lectures, etc. . . . Aside from the profit to be derived from this proposition, the possibilities for advertising for the Company are tremendous; for its name would ultimately be brought into the household and wireless would receive national and universal attention. (Quoted in Archer, 1938: 112)

In retrospect, this "Music Box Memo," as it came to be called, may not seem remarkable, but we must bear in mind that Sarnoff had won attention first as an exceptionally skillful *telegrapher*; at the time he wrote the memo, he was a relatively minor official of a company whose business was devoted entirely to radiotelegraphy. The best evidence of the radical nature of Sarnoff's proposal is the fact that the higher-ups at American Marconi did nothing whatever about it.

Four years later A. N. Goldsmith, a Marconi engineer, showed Sarnoff the first "unicontrolled" radio receiver — a set with a single knob for tuning, another for volume, and a built-in speaker. Previously most vacuum tube sets came with a horn speaker and an array of knobs that had to be adjusted with some finesse — a formidable barrier to the ordinary consumer. When Sarnoff saw the simple unicontrolled receiver he exclaimed, "This is the radio music box of which I've dreamed!" (Bitting, 1965: 1016).

In those four years Sarnoff had been steadily moving up the executive ladder. Soon he would be in a position to act on his hunch without having to defer to unimaginative superiors. First, however, radio needed to break free of wartime controls.

6.2 Government Monopoly: The Road Not Taken

The Navy's Claims   Governments monopolize the great majority of the world's broadcasting systems (§1.2). For a time it was touch-and-go as to whether American broadcasting too might turn out to be U.S. government broadcasting.

World War I ended in November 1918; yet the Navy did not relinquish control of radio properties until early in 1920. The critical decisions made during this delay of over a year affected the whole future of radio in the United States, including the not-yet-born service of broadcasting. The war had demonstrated the vital importance of wireless to national security. Before the United States entered the war, for example, a German high-power station in Sayville, New York, violated United States neutrality by sending intelligence to German ships at sea. Later, a single message interception netted the U.S. alien property custodian ten million dollars worth of enemy goods.

Was radio too vital to entrust to private hands? The U.S. Navy thought so. In fact, the Navy had always asserted jurisdiction over radio as a natural right, assuming that it was destined to remain primarily a marine service. The Navy supported a bill, introduced into Congress late in 1918, proposing in effect to make radio a permanent government monopoly. Despite strong arguments from Navy brass at the congressional hearings, the bill failed to get out of committee. Its wartime powers over civilian radio having thereby lapsed, the Navy reluctantly turned the stations it had seized back to private ownership early the next year.

Issue of the Alternator   Restoration of private ownership meant, however, turning over most commercial wireless communication facilities in the United States to a foreign company, American Marconi. Moreover, that company seemed about to capture exclusive rights to use a most important American invention — the Alexanderson alternator that had greatly improved transoceanic radiotelegraphy during the war (§5.8). Marconi himself had instantly grasped the significance of the original alternator three years earlier and had started negotiations with GE for exclusive rights to its use. The talks had been interrupted by the U.S. entry into the war, but now, in March 1919, the negotiations were reopened. The Navy was deeply disturbed at the prospect of American Marconi consolidating its U.S. monopoly by capturing exclusive rights to the Alexanderson alternator. Just the year before the Navy had spent a million dollars to block American Marconi from securing rights to the Poulsen arc, the next-best radio energy generator to the Alexanderson alternator.

American Marconi Bows Out President Woodrow Wilson himself took an interest in the situation, even in the midst of the Paris Peace Conference. He considered that communication, oil, and shipping represented the keys to the balance of power in international affairs (Archer, 1938: 164). In 1919 Great Britain led the world in maritime strength, and the United States led in petroleum production. Britain already had a long lead in the field of worldwide cable facilities and was now on the verge of obtaining a world monopoly on international wireless communication.

British Marconi found itself caught in a squeeze play. The U.S. government made no actual overt move to expropriate British Marconi's American holdings. But with tacit government approval negotiations were carried out on a private level by Owen D. Young, board chairman of General Electric (Exhibit 6.2). The Marconi company's position in the United States was plainly untenable. As the

president of American Marconi told his stockholders in 1919, "We have found that there exists on the part of the officials of the Government a very strong and irremovable objection to [American Marconi] because of the stock interest held therein by the British Company" (quoted in Archer, 1938: 178).

RCA Founded Under such pressures British Marconi agreed to sell its stock in its American subsidiary to General Electric, on condition that it be allowed to buy Alexanderson alternators for its own use outside the United States. GE thereupon created a new subsidiary in the fall of 1919 to carry on American Marconi's extensive wireless telegraphy business — the Radio Corporation of America (RCA). Under RCA's charter all its officers had to be Americans and 80 percent of its stock had to be in American hands.

RCA took over the operation of American Marconi's assets on November 20, 1919. Eventually RCA's name became closely linked with broadcasting, but in 1919 the first broadcasting station was still a year away, and its founders had no plans to enter that field. RCA Board President Owen D. Young told a Senate committee a few years later, "We had no broadcasting in our minds in 1919 and 1920."

Westinghouse and AT&T joined General Electric as investors in the new corporation. In 1922 the stock distribution was approximately as follows: General Electric, 25 percent; Westinghouse, 20 percent; AT&T, 4 percent; former American Marconi stockholders and others, 51 percent (FTC, 1924: 20). Eighteen hundred small U.S. investors had held shares of American Marconi stock. AT&T sold its RCA interest in 1923. RCA remained under the control of General Electric and Westinghouse until, in order to settle an antitrust suit, they sold their stock in 1932, leaving RCA as an independent corporation, as it is to this day.

Sarnoff's Role   We first met David Sarnoff as the young Marconi radiotelegraph operator who stayed at his key in the New York Wanamaker store for 72 hours, keeping in contact with survivors of the 1912 *Titanic* disaster (§5.6). His name cropped up again in 1916 when, as assistant traffic manager of the Marconi company, he submitted his prophetic "music box" memo. In 1919, when American Marconi became RCA, he stayed on with the new company, promoted now to the job of commercial manager.

His role was to convert the company from

Exhibit 6.2
The RCA "family," 1926

Back row: David Sarnoff, RCA vice president and general manager, and Martin H. Aylesworth, president of the newly created National Broadcasting Company. Seated: Charles G. Dawes, Vice President of the United States; Owen D. Young, chairman of the board of both RCA and General Electric; and General J. C. Harbord, president of RCA.

Source: Courtesy Smithsonian Institution, Washington, D.C.

a collection of small radiotelegraph firms into a major corporation, presiding over numerous subsidiary companies. It has been said that it took less than a year for Young to create RCA on paper, but it took Sarnoff twenty years to make it into a completely integrated operating concern (Maclaurin, 1949: 248). In 1930 he became president of the company, in 1947 chairman of the board, finally retiring in 1969. As *Time* said in its obituary in 1971, his was "one of the last great autocracies in U.S. industry." His sixty-three-year career spanned the entire evolution of broadcasting from the first experiments with spark transmitters to international television relayed by space satellites.

Cross-Licensing: Phase 1 RCA's mission was more than to take over the half-dozen American Marconi wireless communication businesses. Each of its parent companies held important patents, yet each found itself blocked by patents held by the others. As GE's (and RCA's) board chairman, Owen D. Young, testified to a Senate committee. "It was utterly impossible for anybody to do anything in radio, any one person or group or company at that time [1919]. . . . Nobody had patents enough to make a system. And so there was a complete stalemate" (Senate CIC, 1930: 1116). Young proposed that in RCA the major patent rivals could find common meeting ground. Accordingly, in the period 1919 to 1923 the contenders worked out a series of *cross-licensing agreements*, modeled after the World War I patent pool (§5.8). Despite its subsidiary status RCA participated fully, having inherited an important group of patent rights of its own from American Marconi.

In addition to resolving the patent stalemate, the cross-licensing agreements divided up the communications pie, giving each company exclusive rights in its special area of interest. General Electric and Westinghouse used the pooled patents to manufacture electronic goods while RCA acted as their sales agent. AT&T's exclusive right to manufacture, sell, and lease transmitters for commercial use was intended to ensure the telephone company's control over telephonic communication, whether by wire or wireless means. GE and Westinghouse were allowed to make transmitters for their own use but not for sale to others. Within a few years, however, these carefully worked out plans were thrown into utter confusion by the astonishingly rapid growth of a brand-new use for radiotelephony — radio broadcasting.

6.3 The "First" Broadcast Station

Amateur Beginnings In 1920 Dr. Frank Conrad, an engineer with Westinghouse in Pittsburgh, operated an amateur radiotelephone station, 8XK, in connection with experimental work at the factory (Exhibit 6.3.1). Conrad fell into the habit of transmitting recorded music, sports results, and the like in response to requests from other amateurs. These informal programs built up so much interest that they began to get mentioned in the newspapers. None of this was particularly unusual; similar amateur transmissions had been made by other experimenters, in other parts of the world as well as elsewhere in the United States. What made Conrad's 8XK transmissions unique was the chain of events they set in motion.

Horne's department store in Pittsburgh, noting the growing public interest in wireless, sensed an opportunity to develop a hitherto untried commercial sideline. Previously, wireless had been primarily the domain of engineers and earnest amateurs.

Exhibit 6.3.1
Conrad's 8XK and its successor, KDKA

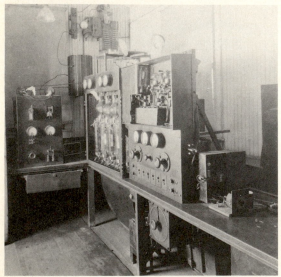

Frank Conrad's transmitter (top) is typical of the improvised setups used by wireless inventors and experimenters. It contrasts with the spit-and-polish of the KDKA professional broadcasting facilities, from which the Harding-Cox election returns were broadcast on November 2, 1920.

Source: Courtesy Group W (Westinghouse Broadcasting Co.), Pittsburgh, PA.

Now it seemed the general public might be willing to buy ready-built receiving sets. Horne's installed a demonstration receiver in the store and ran a box in their regular newspaper display advertisement of September 22, 1920. It was headlined "Air Concert 'Picked Up' by Radio Here," and concluded: "Amateur Wireless Sets made by the maker of the Set which is in operation in our store, are on sale here $10.00 up."

Opening of KDKA Westinghouse executives had been looking for a profitable entry into the consumer communications field — in fact they had already explored several possible new types of radio service. For this reason they were alert to the implications of Horne's modest advertisement. They saw the possibility of a novel merchandising tie-up: Westinghouse could manufacture home radiotelephone receivers and at the same time create a demand for the new product by transmitting programs for the general public. Accordingly, Westinghouse Vice President H. P. Davis ordered conversion of a radiotelegraph transmitter for radiotelephony. It went on the air as KDKA from an improvised studio on the roof of the Westinghouse factory in East Pittsburgh on November 2, 1920 (Exhibit 6.3.1).

KDKA's opening was scheduled to coincide with the presidential election of 1920 so that the maiden broadcast could take advantage of public interest in the voting results. This first KDKA program consisted of news about the Harding-Cox presidential election, fed to the station by telephone from a newspaper office, interspersed with phonograph music and live banjo music.

The Listeners Broadcasting would have developed much more slowly than it did had it not been for a ready-made audience — the thousands of amateur set-builders who created a demand for a type of radio service

never before supplied commercially — entertainment.

In order to appreciate the fascination of the 8XK and early KDKA transmissions for listeners of the day, we have to remember that, with rare exceptions, previously the only signals on the air had been in code. To hear music and the human voice instead of the monotonous drone of Morse was a startling and thrilling experience for listeners. Moreover, amateur set-builders felt a unique satisfaction in realizing that here were programs sent out especially for themselves. Always before they had merely eavesdropped on messages intended for other people.

The audience quickly expanded beyond the original nucleus of amateurs. Ready-made crystal sets were cheap, as the Horne ad indicates, and could be built at home even more cheaply. A homemade set consisted at the minimum of a hand-wound coil (a round Quaker Oats box was a favorite form on which to wind the coil) with a slide to make contact at various points along the coil as a means of tuning, a crystal, and a pair of earphones. A simple length of wire strung outdoors acted as an antenna.

The tiny scratching sounds as one first began to probe the crystal with a cat's whisker created unbearable suspense. The thrill was unforgettable when the cat's whisker found a sensitive spot and the distant sounds came floating out of space and into the earphones. Moreover, the experience of listening-in created an insatiable appetite for bigger and better receiving equipment — first (after 1922) a detector vacuum tube, then another tube for an amplifier, then more tubes for a superheterodyne circuit, then a loudspeaker. Manufacturers could not keep up with the demand.

KDKA's Success Because there was as yet no crowding of the broadcast channels, station interference did not yet exist. KDKA's sky wave could be picked up at great distances. Newspapers all over the country and even in Canada printed the station's program logs. To assist DX (long-distance) listeners, stations later observed a local "silent night" each week when they went off the air so as not to interfere with incoming signals from distant stations (Barnouw, 1966: 93).

In its first year of operation, KDKA pioneered in broadcasting many types of programs that later became standard radio fare — orchestra music, church services, public service announcements, political addresses, sports events, dramas, and market reports (Exhibit 6.3.2). But one now-familiar type of broadcast material was conspicuously absent — *commercials*. Westinghouse did not sell advertising but rather bore the entire expense of operation as a means of promoting sales of its own products. It was taken for granted that each firm that wanted to promote its

Exhibit 6.3.2
KDKA's studio in 1922

Before development of the modern acoustic wall treatments, heavy drapes were used to dampen reverberation. The producer Robert Saudek visited this studio as a boy, remembering it as "very much like the inside of a burlap-lined casket. Burnt orange, a favorite decorator color in 1922, was chosen for the draped silk meringues that billowed from the ceiling" (Saudek, 1965: 25).

Source: KDKA Radio Photo, Pittsburgh, PA.

wares over the air would open its own station and do likewise.

Who Was First? KDKA's 1920 Harding-Cox election program is usually cited as the historic beginning of regular broadcasting in America. Nevertheless, a number of other stations claim the honor, including some in other countries. For example, KQW (San Jose, California) first transmitted programs in 1909 and even ran a regular schedule in 1912; a Detroit amateur station, 8MK (later WWJ), began regular transmissions two months before KDKA's maiden broadcast. In addition, inventors like Fessenden and de Forest made many test transmissions starting as early as 1906 (§5.7).

Nevertheless, KDKA meets five criteria that qualify it as the *oldest U.S. station still in operation*, despite earlier experiments, demonstrations, and temporary operations: KDKA (1) used radio waves, (2) to send out noncoded signals, (3) in a continuous, organized program service, (4) which was intended for the general public, and (5) was licensed by the government to provide such a service (Baudino & Kittross, 1977).*

Competition Begins Westinghouse did not, in any event, have the field to itself very long. Broadcast station operation had strong appeal for department stores, newspapers, educational institutions, churches, and electrical equipment supply dealers. The number of stations increased slowly in 1920, with only 30 licenses issued by the end of the year. In the spring of 1922, however, the new industry began to gather momentum. In that year alone 100,000 sets were sold. By May over 200 stations had been licensed, and the

upward trend continued during the next twelve-month period, reaching 576 early in 1923.

Among these early stations, however, mortality was high. Would-be broadcasters hastened to get in on the ground floor of — they knew not quite what. Inadequately backed stations soon fell by the wayside. Educational stations were particularly heavy losers in this process of elimination.

GROUP A. Question

6.4 Radio Broadcasting vs. Radiotelephony

No such problems of money or managerial support bothered the two leading New York stations, representing major groupings in the patent-pooling consortium — WJZ, flagship station of the Radio Group (General Electric, Westinghouse, and RCA), and WEAF, flagship of the Telephone Group (AT&T and Western Electric). They represented two opposing philosophies of broadcasting, the one stressing radio as such, the other stressing radio as an aspect of telephony.

Radio Group Station Westinghouse opened WJZ in October 1921. That station, like KDKA, started in a Westinghouse factory, this one in Newark, New Jersey. Westinghouse transferred ownership of WJZ to RCA, which moved it across the river to Manhattan as the flagship station of the Radio Group. As manufacturing companies (in contrast to AT&T as a service company), the Radio Group at first saw WJZ as a sales-promotion device, a way to stimulate interest in their own products. Attractive programming was needed to motivate people to buy receivers. WJZ therefore accepted from the start the responsibility for producing its own programs.

*There was of course no *broadcasting* license as such in 1920. KDKA received a license equivalent to the ones issued to commercial shore stations that exchanged messages with ships under the Radio Act of 1912 (§6.7).

Telephone Group Station   AT&T's WEAF went on the air August 16, 1922. A company official told a congressional committee that AT&T spent over a quarter of a million dollars on its first year of operation. The company spared no expense because WEAF served both as an AT&T showcase and as a laboratory for experimenting with ways of making a profit out of the new medium. As the country's leading communication firm, AT&T gave WEAF every technical advantage.

Programming was a different matter. In announcing plans for WEAF earlier in the year at a Washington radio conference, AT&T explained that it would "furnish *no programs whatsoever* over that station" (Dept. of Commerce, 1922:7, italics supplied). In other words, telephone company officials thought of broadcasting as a *common carrier,* as a new form of telephony. In a 1922 press release about WEAF, AT&T emphasized the point:

Just as the company leases its long distance wire facilities for the use of newspapers, banks, and other concerns, so it will lease its radio telephone facilities and will not provide the matter which is sent out from this station. (Quoted in Banning, 1946: 68)

It soon became clear, however, that the idea of filling the schedule entirely with leased time simply would not work. Not only were there not enough customers at first, but more important, advertisers were not prepared to fill their leased time with program material capable of attracting listeners. The telephone company therefore found itself forced into show business after all — a decidedly uncomfortable role for a regulated monopoly extremely sensitive about maintaining a serious and dignified public image.

Rival Theories   Thus the two groups started with opposing theories about the way

broadcasting should work. In the end it turned out that each group was partly right, partly wrong. The idea of the Radio Group that each advertiser would own a separate station devoted exclusively to promoting that advertiser's goods was not practicable. The Telephone Group correctly foresaw that the number of stations would have to be limited, and that each station would be used by many different advertisers. It miscalculated, however, in placing the primary emphasis on message *senders* rather than on the interest of the general public, whose good will had to be earned. In this matter the Radio Group's concept — to accept responsibility for providing a service to the receiving public, emphasizing the public's own needs and wishes — prevailed. It took about four years for these conflicting ideas to sort themselves out.

"Toll" Broadcasting   WEAF called advertiser-leased time "toll" broadcasting. Its first lease of facilities for a toll broadcast occurred on August 28, 1922. A Long Island real-estate firm paid a $50 toll for ten minutes of time, during which it explained the advantages of living in Hawthorne Court, an apartment complex in the Jackson Heights section of New York.

True to the telephone company concept, WEAF at first allowed advertisers to fill entire segments of leased time with promotional talk. The idea that advertising messages would occupy only occasional one-minute-or-less announcements in programs consisting mostly of entertainment came later.

AT&T thought in terms of *institutional* advertising, the type it used itself. Nothing so crass as price could be mentioned. The next year the first weekly advertiser appeared on WEAF, sponsoring a musical group it called "The Browning King Orchestra" — a handy way to ensure frequent mention of the sponsor's name. The fact that Browning King sold clothing, however, was never disclosed.

AT&T Monopoly on Radio Advertising

Even had it wished to, WJZ was not in a position to sell time to advertisers, as did WEAF. A clause in the patent cross-licensing agreements (§6.2) gave AT&T the exclusive right to sell transmitters that used the patents in the pool. AT&T refused to sell to stations that planned to offer broadcast time for sale.

AT&T foresaw that if every firm that wanted to advertise bought its own station, co-channel interference would become intolerable. It had already received no less than sixty requests for delivery of transmitters from would-be broadcasters in the New York area alone. Shared use of facilities by advertisers, therefore, seemed essential. At the same time, AT&T saw wireless telephony as a natural outgrowth of wire telephony, in which it had a monopoly position. In an AT&T meeting, the firm's radio administrator explained:

We have been very careful, up to the present time [1923], not to state to the public in any way, through the press or in any of our talks, the idea that the Bell System desires to monopolize broadcasting; but the fact remains that it is a telephone job, that we are telephone people, that we can do it better than anybody else, and it seems to me that the clear, logical conclusion that must be reached is that, sooner or later, in one form or another, we have got to do the job. (Quoted in Danielian, 1939: 123–124)

The effect of AT&T's policy on commercial operation was soon reflected in the relative economic positions of WJZ and WEAF. Within a few years, WJZ was costing the Radio Group $100,000 a year to operate without realizing any direct income whatever, while WEAF was grossing $750,000 in advertising revenue annually.

AT&T was not so successful in preventing other stations from infringing on its patent rights. By early 1923, 93 percent of the 576 stations on the air were selling time in violation of AT&T restrictions (Banning, 1946: 134). Worried about the charges of monopoly, the telephone company was reluctant to take aggressive action against the infringers. Rather than let its rights go by the board completely, AT&T reluctantly issued licenses to the transmitter owners permitting them to operate commercially.

"Chain" Broadcasting

AT&T also interpreted the cross-licensing agreements as giving it the right to prevent other broadcasters from connecting broadcast equipment to its telephone lines. WEAF soon began to capitalize on this advantage.

In 1923 WEAF fed a one-time program by wire to WNAC for simultaneous broadcast in New York and Boston. Later that year the first permanent interconnection was set up between WEAF and WMAF (South Dartmouth, Massachusetts), the latter owned by a rich eccentric who operated WMAF for his own amusement but who had no means for programming the station. He persuaded WEAF to feed him both toll (commercial) and nontoll (sustaining) programs, paying a fee for the latter and broadcasting the commercial programs without additional cost to the advertisers.

AT&T gradually added to its "chain" (network) of stations. By October 1924 it was able to set up a temporary coast-to-coast chain of 22 stations to carry a speech by President Calvin Coolidge. The regular WEAF network at this time, however, consisted of only six stations, to which WEAF fed three hours of programming a day. Interconnection was by regular AT&T telephone lines, temporarily *equalized* (to compensate for the tendency of higher frequencies to attenuate with distance more than the lower frequencies). By 1926, however, the telephone company began setting aside permanently equalized circuits for the exclusive use of its radio network.

Meanwhile WJZ, already debarred by the cross-licensing agreements from selling advertising, was also refused network interconnection by AT&T. The Radio Group's station turned to the telegraph lines of Western Union, but telegraph wires pass such a narrow band of frequencies that these lines were far less satisfactory for broadcast programs than AT&T's telephone lines. The Radio Group even explored the use of radio-relay interconnection, but microwave relays were still twenty years in the future. Despite these difficulties WJZ persisted. In 1923 it opened a station in Washington, D.C., and by 1925 it had succeeded in organizing a network of 14 stations.

New Cross-Licensing Agreements

The rivalry between WEAF and WJZ was not the only source of irritation among the companies that signed the patent-pooling agreements of 1919–1923 (§6.2). The market for broadcasting equipment, and in particular the mass market for receivers, upset the delicate balance of commercial interests that cross-licensing had devised. The unexpectedness of the new medium's rapid growth is suggested by a comment of Herbert Hoover (then Secretary of Commerce) at the first of four annual radio conferences he organized in the 1920s:

We have witnessed in the last four or five months one of the most astounding things that has come under my observation of American life. [The Department of Commerce] estimates that today over 600,000 (one estimate being 1,000,000) persons possess wireless telephone receiving sets, whereas there were less than 50,000 such sets a year ago. (Dept. of Commerce, 1922: 2)

Exhibit 6.4
RCA opens its Washington, D.C., station

Listen in
To-night to
WRC

New Radio Broadcasting Station in Washington, D. C.
Open August 1st

The Radio Corporation of America announces a new broadcasting station of the very latest type. On top of the Riggs National Bank Building—one of the highest points in Washington. With a transmitter of great power, range and clearness, the equal of any station now in operation. From coast to coast, Washington may be heard with fine programs of music, lectures and fun; with important Governmental news, and vital information. To residents of Washington this new "Voice of the Capital" means a home station surpassed by none. Listen in tonight! See daily radio programs in your favorite newspaper.

Wavelength, 469 Meters.

Radiograms via R C A to Europe and Asia	R C A Marine Radio	R C A Radiolas for Every Home

Radio Corporation of America
233 Broadway, New York.

WRC, opened by RCA August 1, 1923, remains an NBC owned-and-operated station to this day. Note how RCA took advantage of the occasion to advertise its radio communications and receiver manufacturing businesses. The claim that WRC would be heard "from coast to coast" was no exaggeration in that interference-free period.

Source: RCA.

The fad that Horne's department store anticipated in 1920 had really caught on: "The public appetite for sets was insatiable and not to be filled for years. Queues formed before stores that had any sets or parts. Dealers were a year catching up on orders" (Lessing, 1969: 111). RCA put the Radio Group's first set, the Radiola I, on the market in 1922. Thereafter sales skyrocketed. In the first eight years of broadcasting, the value of receiver sales went from $5 million to $650 million.

Between 1923 and 1926 continual behind-the-scenes negotiations went on aimed at settling the differences among the cross-licensees. A federal suit, alleging that the pool violated antitrust laws, added urgency to the need for action. By 1926 the telephone company was ready to admit that it had been mistaken in its original concept of broadcasting as just another branch of telephony. WEAF had served its purpose, proving that broadcasting was going to develop into a business far afield from AT&T's primary business of telephony. But the telephone company's direct involvement in broadcasting had begun to create bad public relations for AT&T, something a regulated monopoly industry cannot afford. For AT&T, "as an experiment, broadcasting had been necessary; as a business, it was almost certain to be a liability" (Banning, 1946: 272).

Accordingly, the signatories of the cross-licensing agreements finally arrived at a revised set of three agreements in July 1926.

The new agreements redistributed and redefined the rights of the parties to use their commonly owned patents and to engage in the various aspects of the business that grew out of the patents. Briefly summarized, the following terms directly affected broadcasting:

1. AT&T was granted exclusive control over wire telephony and *two-way wireless* telephony (that is, nonbroadcast radiotelephony).

2. Telephony was defined in a way that left AT&T in control of both wire and future wireless *relays* used for broadcasting.

3. RCA agreed to lease *network relay facilities* from AT&T.

4. Western Electric was barred from competing with the Radio Group in the *manufacture* of radio receivers.

5. AT&T surrendered its exclusive right to use the pool patents to control the manufacture of broadcast *transmitters*.

6. AT&T agreed to *sell WEAF* and all its other broadcasting assets to the Radio Group for a million dollars.

7. AT&T agreed *not to reenter* the broadcasting field. RCA received the right to carry on *commercial broadcasting*.

RCA had come a long way in its six years of corporate life. Originally a mere sales outlet for other Radio Group manufacturers, it was now, thanks to the revised agreement, a manufacturer in its own right and the dominant force in broadcasting, with two networks (both the WJZ and the WEAF chains) under its control.

It would be difficult to overestimate the significance of the 1926 cross-licensing revisions to the future of broadcasting in America. As long as the two groups of major communications companies disagreed about fundamental policies, broadcasting's economic future remained uncertain. The 1926 agreements removed this uncertainty.

6.5 National Networks Begin

Sarnoff's Foresight RCA's David Sarnoff had long since recognized what had not been apparent to the officials of AT&T: broadcasting was a genuine innovation that would require its own special organization, business methods, and personnel. It could not continue indefinitely as an incidental sideline to some other kind of business.

Sarnoff had renewed his "music box" memo of 1916 immediately after the transformation of American Marconi into RCA in 1919. As early as 1922 he predicted the direction broadcasting would take as it matured:

When the novelty of radio will have worn off and the public [is] no longer interested in the means by which it is able to receive but rather, in the substance and quality of the material received, I think that the task of reasonably meeting the public's expectations and desires will be greater than any so far tackled by any newspaper, theater, opera, or any public information or entertainment agency. . . . Let us organize a separate and distinct company, to be known as Public Service Broadcasting Company, or National Radio Broadcasting Company, or American Radio Broadcasting Company, or some similar name. (Quoted in Archer, 1938: 30)

NBC Organized   A few months after the 1926 settlement, the Radio Group, under Sarnoff's leadership, created a new subsidiary, the National Broadcasting Company (NBC), owned initially 30 percent by RCA, 50 percent by GE, and 20 percent by Westinghouse.

NBC was the first company organized solely and specifically to operate a broadcasting *network*. In its four-and-a-half-hour coast-to-coast inaugural broadcast on November 15, 1926, Walter Damrosch conducted the New York Symphony Orchestra, with cut-ins from opera singer Mary Garden in Chicago and humorist Will Rogers in Independence, Kansas. The 25 stations in the network reached an estimated 5 million listeners on that occasion. Not until 1928, however, did coast-to-coast network operations begin on a regular basis (Exhibit 6.4).

Starting with the new year in 1927, RCA organized NBC as two semiautonomous networks, the Blue and the Red. WJZ (later to become WABC) and the old Radio Group network formed the nucleus of the Blue; WEAF (later to become WNBC) and the old Telephone Group Network formed the nucleus of the Red. This dual network arrangement arose because NBC now had duplicate outlets in New York and other major cities. There would have been no point in merely broadcasting the same programs on two stations in the same service area. As competitive networks developed, however, the dual-network operation took on more significance: by tying up not one but two of the best stations in major cities, and by playing one network off against the other, NBC gained a significant advantage over rival networks.

Paley and CBS   The second network followed soon after NBC, in 1927. It began as United Independent Broadcasters (UIB), launched by an important talent-booking agent who wanted an alternative to NBC as an outlet for his performers. Off to a rocky start, the UIB network went through rapid changes in ownership, picking up along the way the name Columbia Phonograph Broadcasting System as a result of an investment by a record company. The latter soon withdrew but UIB retained the right to use the Columbia name.

The network's future remained uncertain until early in September 1928, when William S. Paley purchased the "patchwork, money-losing little company," as he later described it. At that point it had only 22 affiliates. Paley quickly turned the failing network around with a new affiliation contract. In his autobiography a half-century later he recalled:

I proposed the concept of free sustaining service . . . I would guarantee not ten but twenty *hours of programming per week, pay the stations $50 an hour for the commercial hours used, but with a new proviso. The network would not pay the stations for the first five hours of commercial programming time . . . to allow for the possibility of more business to come, the network was to receive an option on additional time.*

And for the first time, we were to have exclusive rights for network broadcasting through the affiliate. That meant the local station could not use its facilities for any other broadcasting network. I added one more innovation which helped our cause: local stations would have to identify our programs with the CBS name. (Paley, 1979: 42, emphasis added)

Paley innovations (emphasized in the above passages) became standard practice in network contracts, though some of the more restrictive terms were later banned by the Federal Communications Commission (§7.5).

Paley also simplified the firm's name, calling it Columbia Broadcasting System (the corporate name was later further simplified to CBS, Incorporated), and bought a New York outlet as the network flagship station (now WCBS). From that point on CBS never faltered, and Paley eventually rivaled Sarnoff as the leading executive in the history of broadcasting in America (Exhibit 6.5).

Exhibit 6.5
Sarnoff and Paley early in the radio era

The two leading network executives are shown in portraits taken in the early 1930s.

Sources: Sarnoff, courtesy RCA. Paley, courtesy CBS.

A Contrast in Leaders   Both these pioneers of network broadcasting came from immigrant Russian families, but there the similarity ceases. Sarnoff rose from the direst poverty, a self-educated and self-made man. In sharp contrast, Paley had every advantage of money and social position. After earning a degree from the Wharton School of Business at the University of Pennsylvania in 1922, he joined his father's prosperous cigar company.

The differences between Sarnoff and Paley extended to their personalities and special skills. Sarnoff was "an engineer turned businessman, ill at ease with the hucksterism that he had wrought, and he did not condescend to sell, but Bill Paley loved to sell. CBS was Paley, and he sold it as he sold himself" (Halberstam, 1979: 27).

Sarnoff had been introduced to radio by way of hard work at the telegraph key, Paley by way of leisurely DX listening: "As a radio fan in Philadelphia, I often sat up all night, glued to my set, listening and marveling at the voices and music which came into my ears from distant places," he recalled (Paley, 1979: 32).

Paley's introduction to the business of radio came by way of sponsored programming. After becoming advertising manager of his father's cigar company in 1925, he experimented with a program on WCAU (Philadelphia). Impressed with the results, he explored radio further. The rest is history.

6.6 Evolution of Radio Advertising

Doubts About Commercialism   Paley's enthusiasm for the exploitation of radio as an advertising medium was not universally shared in the 1920s. At the First Radio Conference, called by Secretary of Commerce Hoover in Washington in 1922, the sentiment against advertising had been almost universal. In the same year, when Sarnoff proposed that RCA set up a radio network company, he made no claim that the network would profit from advertising: "I feel that with suitable publicity activities, such a company will ultimately be regarded as a public institution of great value in the same sense that a library, for example, is regarded today" (quoted in Archer, 1930: 33).

This institutional approach to broadcasting reflected the older generation's outlook, essentially rooted in the Victorian ideal of the privacy and inviolability of family life. The idea of introducing advertising into the intimacy of the home, mingling it with information and entertainment, seemed to violate that ideal.

At the Fourth Radio Conference, in 1925, the broadcasters' Committee on Advertising and Publicity still considered direct advertising objectionable, recommending good-will announcements only. Two years later the author of a book titled *Using Radio in Sales Promotion* could write, "the broadcast listener regards any attempt at radio advertising as an affront" (Felix, 1927: 211). As the book's title implies, the author saw radio only as a *supplement* to direct advertising: "clearly it is not an advertising medium, useful in disseminating sales arguments and selling points"(8). This same concept had governed WEAF's early experiments with toll broadcasting, described in §6.4.

Advertising Agencies Take Over   Contrary to Sarnoff's high-minded conception, a dignified broadcasting service reflecting the hush of a great public library would have been an anachronism in the jazzy atmosphere of the 1920s. William Paley, an archetypical "gilded youth" of the twenties, recognized this inherent contradiction. So did the advertising agencies, hitherto concerned with the print media. They brought to broadcasting their own ideas about how advertising should be conducted and — more important — about how programs could be designed as vehicles for advertising.

Because stations themselves had not yet developed the production and programming skills needed for mass appeal entertainment, the agencies moved in and took over the programming role, introducing the idea of *sponsorship*. Sponsors did more than just advertise: they also brought to the networks the shows that served as vehicles for their advertising messages. Advertising agencies thus became program producers, and during the height of network radio's popularity most major entertainment shows were controlled by agencies on behalf of their advertiser clients.

The agencies evaded early network rules against frequent mention of sponsor by tacking trade names to performers' names. Audiences of the 1920s heard "The Cliquot Club Eskimos," "The A&P Gypsies," "The Ipana Troubadours," and so on.

Here is an example of an opening "billboard" from this period that manages to add four indirect product mentions to the permissible single direct mention of sponsor name and product name:

Relax and smile, for Goldy and Dusty, the Gold Dust Twins, are here to send their songs there, and "brighten the corner where you are." The Gold Dust Corporation, manufacturer of Gold Dust Powder, engages the facilities of station WEAF, New York, WJAR, Providence, WCAE, Pittsburgh, WGR, Buffalo, WEEI, Boston, WFI, Philadelphia, and WEAR, Cleveland, so that listeners-in may have the opportunity to chuckle and laugh with Goldy and Dusty. Let those Gold Dust Twins into your hearts and homes tonight, and you'll never regret it, for they do brighten the dull spots. (Quoted in Banning, 1946: 262)

Anyone not already aware of the product could hardly guess that the commercial refers to laundry soap powder.

N. W. Ayer and Son, an established advertising agency in print media, claims to have been the first major agency to take radio seriously as an advertising medium (Hower, 1949: 132). Ayer handled advertising for an optical company on WEAF in 1922 and in 1923 introduced one of the earliest sponsored network programs, the National Carbon Company (batteries) *Eveready Hour*.

Another pioneer agency in radio was Lord and Thomas, whose Albert Lasker was one of the legendary figures of media advertising history. Lasker placed nearly half of NBC's national advertising for the 1927–1928 season, overcoming NBC's reluctance to use direct advertising (Gunther, 1960: 194). Lasker fought against the institutional concept of radio advertising, insisting on using commercials closely modeled on the copywriting style used in the print media.

In the 1926–1927 broadcast season the NBC Red and Blue networks had 34 programs on the air, 24 of which were sponsored. Most commercial programs were musical variety shows, sponsored by advertisers of batteries, radios, soft drinks, bread, and candy. The next season CBS joined in and the number of sponsored programs nearly doubled. Even though such down-to-earth details as price-mentions were still banned, advertising was already well on its way to becoming the dominant factor in broadcasting in America.

A Still Small Voice Despite the triumph of commercialism, some people continued to oppose the trend. The pioneer inventor Lee de Forest, for example, remained a bitter opponent of radio advertising to the end of his life:

Throughout my long career I have lost no opportunity to cry out in earnest protest against the crass commercialism, the etheric vandalism of the vulgar hucksters, agencies, advertisers, station owners — all who, lacking awareness of their grand opportunities and moral responsibilities to make of radio an uplifting influence, continue to enslave and sell for quick cash the grandest medium which has yet been given to man to help upward his struggling spirit. (De Forest, 1950: 422)

Many of the earliest broadcasting stations had in fact been licensed to universities, outgrowths of experiments in their science and engineering laboratories. Though usually operated noncommercially, educational AM stations held the same kind of licenses as commercial stations — the Radio Act of 1927 made no provisions for a separate noncommercial service. As channel allotments increased in commercial value, most of these early educational stations lost their channels to commercial interests. Only a score survived — representing a still, small voice crying out for broadcast pluralism in the ever-growing commercial wilderness. Had it not been for the stubborn devotion of this handful of AM noncommercial pioneers, broadcasting in America might never have achieved the flourishing public radio and television services of today, which we discuss in Chapter 10.

6.7 Government Regulation

There remains one final foundation block to put in place before the story of broadcasting's emergence is complete — the passage of legislation capable of imposing order on the new medium.

Regulation of Wire The government's decision to return radio to private operation after World War I (§6.2) did not mean abandonment of government oversight. Since the beginning of telegraphy, governments throughout the world had recognized that both national and international regulation were essential to fair and efficient operation of telecommunication systems. In 1865, 25 European countries drew up the International Telegraphic Convention, precursor of the International Telecommunication Union that now regulates all forms of wire and wireless communication (§1.4). Thus prior experience in the regulation of the wire services set a pattern for radio regulation when it came on the scene.

Maritime Wireless Regulation The first international conference specifically concerned with wireless communication took place in Berlin in 1903, only six years after Marconi's first patent. Its main object, in fact, was to deal with the Marconi Company's refusal to exchange messages with rival maritime wireless systems. This situation recalled the chauvinistic practice that at first inhibited telegraphic communication in Europe, when national companies demanded that telegraph messages be decoded and passed across international boundaries by hand, only to be reencoded for transmission on the next country's national system.

At the Berlin wireless conference it was agreed that humanitarian considerations had to take precedence over commercial rivalries when human lives were at stake in maritime emergencies. Three years later, at the Berlin Convention of 1906, the nations agreed to require ships to be equipped with suitable wireless gear and to exchange SOS messages freely among different commercial systems.*

The United States withheld its signature from the Berlin agreement for six years. Finally, prodded by the terrible lesson of the *Titanic* disaster (§5.6), Congress confirmed the 1906 convention rules by passing the Radio Act of 1912. This was the first comprehensive U.S. *radio* (not broadcasting) legislation, replacing earlier piecemeal enactments. The 1912 act remained in force during the period of broadcasting's emergent years of 1920–1926.

Failure of the 1912 Act   The new law worked well enough for point-to-point services. Broadcasting, however, introduced unprecedented demands on the spectrum never imagined when the 1912 act was written. That act directed the Secretary of Commerce and Labor to grant licenses to U.S. citizens "upon application therefor." It gave no grounds on which the secretary could *reject* applications. In 1912 the demand for channels was so limited that Congress had no reason to anticipate the need to reject applicants. Presumably all who had a good reason to operate radio stations could be allowed to do so.

Secretary of Commerce Herbert Hoover at first made all broadcast stations share time on the same channel. Then in 1921 he allocated the carrier frequency 833 kHz for "news and entertainment" stations and 618 kHz for "crop and weather report" stations. The practice of time-sharing worked well for ships' stations, which need to make only oc-

casional exchanges of specific messages and can wait in line to get access to a shared channel. Broadcast stations, with their need to transmit uninterrupted program services, demand continuous access to their channels.

The rapid growth in the number of stations soon created intolerable interference. Adding more channels helped not at all, for stations multiplied faster than ever. Some station owners took matters into their own hands and began to change frequency, power, times of operation and location at will — all in violation of their licenses. These changes created even worse interference, of course, so that intelligible reception became impossible.

An example of the bizarre problems faced by the Secretary of Commerce was the station owned by Aimée Semple McPherson, a popular evangelist of the 1920s. She operated a pioneer broadcast station from her "temple" in Los Angeles. The station "wandered all over the wave band." After delivering repeated warnings, a government inspector ordered the station closed down. The Secretary of Commerce thereupon received the following telegram from the evangelist:

PLEASE ORDER YOUR MINIONS OF SATAN TO LEAVE MY STATION ALONE. YOU CANNOT EXPECT THE ALMIGHTY TO ABIDE BY YOUR WAVELENGTH NONSENSE. WHEN I OFFER MY PRAYERS TO HIM I MUST FIT INTO HIS WAVE RECEPTION. OPEN THIS STATION AT ONCE. *(Hoover, 1952: II-142)*

Evangelist McPherson, after being persuaded to engage a competent engineer, was allowed to reopen her station.

National Radio Conferences   Herbert Hoover, a Republican and an ardent believer in free enterprise, hoped that the industry would be able to discipline itself without government regulation. To that end he called a series of four national radio conferences in

---

*The international distress, or SOS, frequency was set at 500 kHz. This decision had a bearing on the eventual allocation of the broadcasting band. It would have been more efficient to start the AM band lower in the spectrum, but this was prevented by the need to avoid interference with the 500-kHz distress frequency.

Washington. At the first, in 1922, only 22 broadcasters attended; by 1925 the number had risen to 400. Speaking at the 1925 conference, Hoover said, "Four years ago we were dealing with a scientific toy; today we are dealing with a vital force in American life" (Dept. of Commerce, 1926: 1).

Hoover optimistically called the national radio conferences "experiments in industrial self-government" (Dept. of Commerce, 1924: 2), but even at that time he must have suspected the hopelessness of the experiment. He commented repeatedly on the fact that here was an industry that actually *wanted* government regulation. For example, at the very first national conference in 1922 he said, "This is one of the few instances that I know of in this country where the public — all of the people interested — are unanimously for an extension of regulatory powers on the part of the Government" (Dept. of Commerce, 1922: 1). From year to year the radio conferences grew more explicit in their suggestions for government regulation.

Zenith Decision   Finally, a 1926 court decision completely undermined the secretary's power of enforcement. A Zenith Radio Corporation station, WJAZ (Chicago), had operated at times and on frequencies different from those authorized in its license. The Secretary of Commerce brought suit under the Radio Act of 1912 to enforce compliance but the court found in favor of the station, stating:

If section 2 [of the Radio Act of 1912] is construed to give the Secretary of Commerce power to restrict the operation of a station as [the secretary] contends is done by this license, what is the test or standard established by Congress, by which the discretion of the Secretary is to be controlled? . . . *Administrative rulings cannot add*

to the terms of an act of Congress and make conduct criminal which such laws leave untouched. (12 F 2d 618, 1926, emphasis added)

The Zenith case illuminates a fundamental concept of the American system of "government by laws, not men." No government official, whether the president or the municipal dogcatcher, is granted unlimited authority. Paradoxically, by failing to limit the secretary's discretionary powers to enforce the radio act, Congress left him with unconstitutionally broad powers and so he became powerless.

In less than a year, 200 new broadcast stations took advantage of the government's inability to enforce licensing rules. By this time meaningful reception had become impossible in most places. "Co-channel interference became so bad at many points on the radio dial," reported the Federal Radio Commission later, "that the listener might suppose instead of a receiving set he had a peanut roaster with assorted whistles" (FRC, 1927: 11). Thirty-eight stations created bedlam in the New York area as did 40 in the Chicago area. Sales of radio sets declined noticeably. In his message to Congress in December 1926, President Calvin Coolidge said, "The whole service of this most important public function has drifted into such chaos as seems likely, if not remedied, to destroy its great value. I most urgently recommend that this legislation should be speedily enacted" (Coolidge, 1926: 32).

Radio Act of 1927   Coolidge was referring to the proposed new radio law, which Congress finally passed on February 23, 1927. The Radio Act of 1927 embodied the recommendations of Hoover's Fourth Radio Conference and so can be said to represent what most of the broadcasters themselves wanted.

The act provided for a *temporary* Federal Radio Commission (FRC) to put things in order. After two years, though, it became clear that broadcasting and other radio services would in fact need continuing and detailed attention and so Congress made the FRC a permanent body.

The FRC was not in a position to wipe the slate clean by canceling existing licenses and assigning channels from scratch, but it did take immediate steps to reduce interference. It limited license periods temporarily to only 60 days (the law allowed a maximum of three years), continuing an earlier edict of Congress. The commission defined the broadcast band, standardized channel designation by frequency instead of by wavelength, closed down portable broadcast stations, and cut back on the number of stations allowed to operate at night. At last investors in broadcasting could move ahead with assurance that signals would not be ruined by uncontrollable mavericks of the airwaves. The passage of the Radio Act of 1927 and the start of year-round supervision by the FRC meant that the final foundation stone of broadcasting as a new communication service was in place. The period of emergence was over and the period of stable growth could now begin.

Summary

In the period 1919–1927 the foundation stones of broadcasting in America were laid: (1) the very concept of broadcasting was clarified; (2) financial support from advertising proved feasible; (3) competitive national networks began; and (4) Congress passed a statute setting up effective regulation of the new medium.

The vital first step was the return of non-military radio services to private ownership in 1920, following the Navy's takeover during World War I. The next step was the sale of American Marconi to the leading U.S. communications concerns, which led to the creation of RCA to run the Marconi radiotelegraphic business. The major companies entered into cross-licensing agreements in the period 1919–1923, pooling their accumulated patents and sharing the wireless market, which consisted of both radio services and radio manufacturing. The balance among competing commercial interests that these agreements sought to ensure was soon upset by the growth of broadcasting, with its new mass market for receivers.

Among the cross-licensees, Westinghouse ventured into broadcasting first with KDKA (1920). It was followed by WJZ representing the Radio Group (1921) and WEAF representing the Telephone Group (1922). In the ensuing business rivalry, WEAF had the advantage because its owner, AT&T, claimed exclusive rights to use the pooled transmitter patents to broadcast commercially (that is, to sell advertising); furthermore, AT&T would not allow other stations to use Bell System telephone lines for network interconnection. Nevertheless WJZ built a small network using telegraph-line interconnection. The groups differed in their approach to how broadcasting should develop; eventually, the growing industry adopted concepts from each approach.

In 1926 dissatisfaction with the earlier cross-licensing division of the spoils came to a head and the companies struck a new agreement. AT&T agreed to withdraw from broadcasting altogether except for supplying network interconnection. It sold WEAF and its network contracts to the Radio Group. Both networks came under the control of RCA, which was also allowed to enter into the radio manufacturing field. RCA, now headed by David Sarnoff, thereupon set up a new subsidiary, the National Broadcasting

Company (1926), the first network company. The second company, later called the Columbia Broadcasting System and headed by William Paley, followed in 1927.

In the meantime, the original wireless law, the Radio Act of 1912, had proved unable to control the development of broadcasting. In 1926 regulation broke down altogether and broadcasting fell into a chaotic state. Congress passed new legislation the next year, the Radio Act of 1927, the first to address broadcasting as such. With this act the final step was taken in building the foundation of broadcasting in America.

CHAPTER 7

Radio after 1928

7.1 Radio in the Great Depression (1929–1937)

During the early 1930s, for the first and only time in broadcasting history, the number of stations on the air actually decreased (Exhibit 7.1). This decline occurred both because of the efforts of the Federal Radio Commission to clear up interference among stations and because of the shortage of investment funds during the Depression years. By the end of the 1929–1937 period, however, three-quarters of all U.S. homes had radios and the number of stations had again begun an upward climb that has continued ever since.

Stock Market Crash of 1929 Radio broadcasting's formative years of 1920 to 1928 had been years of national prosperity and devil-may-care gaiety. This was the Jazz Age, hauntingly depicted in F. Scott Fitzgerald's novels — the era of the roadster, the Charleston, and speakeasies (the Eighteenth Amendment had banned liquor in 1919).

But the laughter abruptly died away in October 1929 when the bottom fell out of the New York stock market, signaling the onset of the Great Depression, a worldwide economic slump of unprecedented severity.

During these years a third of U.S. workers lost their jobs and national productivity fell by half. Suffering was intense, for none of the welfare programs that now cushion unemployment and poverty were then in place. In this time of great trial, radio entertainment came as a godsend, the one widely available distraction from the grim realities of the daily struggle to survive. As little as $15 could buy a vacuum tube receiver. Listener loyalty was so intense it became "almost irrational," according to historian Erik Barnouw:

destitute families, forced to give up an icebox or furniture or bedding, clung to the radio as to a last link to humanity. In consequence radio, though briefly jolted by the Depression, was soon prospering from it. Motion picture business was suffering, the theater was collapsing, vaudeville was dying, but many of their major talents flocked to radio — along with audiences and sponsors. Some companies were beginning to make a comeback through radio sponsorship. In the process, the tone of radio changed rapidly. (Barnouw, 1978: 27)

Roosevelt's New Deal The lowest point of the Depression came in 1932–1933. Herbert Hoover, the Republican former Secretary of Commerce who had nurtured broadcasting developments in the twenties, had become president. In 1932 he shocked the conscience of the nation when he ordered the military to use armed force to disperse the "Bonus Marchers," some 15,000 World War I veterans who encamped in Washington to press for payment of veterans' benefits.

Hoover went down to defeat later that year at the hands of the Democratic candidate, Franklin D. Roosevelt, whose New Deal measures eventually eased the worst effects of the Depression. Thus began the massive federal intervention in financial and social matters that we now take for granted. At the same time, radio was entering into the cultural life of the masses in its own unique way. Never before in human history had so

Exhibit 7.1
Growth of radio stations, 1920–1980

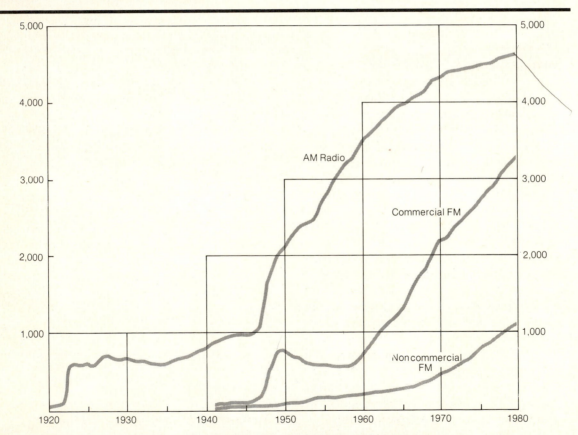

Note that the only down-trends in the growth curves occurred in 1930s AM (when the FRC was imposing order on the pre-radio act chaos) and in 1950s FM (when its initial promise seemed not to be paying off). The sharp upward trend in the AM growth curve in the late 1940s occurred after removal of World War II's restraints on consumer goods.

Sources: Adapted from *Stay Tuned: A Concise History of Broadcasting*, by Christopher H. Sterling and John M. Kittross. Copyright 1978 by Wadsworth Publishing Co., Inc. Reprinted by permission of Wadsworth Publishing Company, Belmont, CA.

much attention been lavished on entertaining and informing a nation's total population regardless of social or financial status or place of residence.

Roosevelt proved to be a master broadcaster, the first (and some still think the most skillful) national politician to exploit the new medium to its full potential in presidential politics. The nation's spirit was lifted during his inaugural address by the ringing phrase "The only thing we have to fear is fear itself," broadcast throughout the country by both the CBS and NBC networks (still the only national networks on the air in 1933).

Soon Roosevelt's distinctive, patrician voice became familiar to every listener who tuned in to his "fireside chats," the term used to suggest the informality, warmth, and directness of these presidential radio reports to the people — a brand-new phenomenon in American politics. "It was in the most direct sense," wrote David Halberstam, "the government reaching out and touching the citizen . . . Roosevelt was the first professional of the art" (1979: 15).

Broadcast Conservatism   Major stations and networks of the 1930s maintained standards of deportment that today would seem absurdly formal. Network announcers were expected to wear dinner jackets in the evening and to speak literate English with perfect diction. It was taken for granted that radio set the correct standard for spoken English for the entire country. Moreover, both broadcasters and advertisers were sensitive to radio's status as a guest in the home. In 1934 CBS refused to carry a speech by the Surgeon General of the United States because he planned to allude to venereal disease. A public furor erupted in 1937 over some lines read by Mae West in a comedy dialogue with Charlie McCarthy, the late Edgar Bergen's ventriloquist dummy (now in the Smithsonian Institution):

West: *Why don't you come home with me? I'll let you play in my woodpile. . . . You're all wood and a yard long. You weren't so nervous and backward when you came to see me at my apartment. In fact, you didn't need much encouragement to kiss me.*
Charlie: *Did I do that?*
West: *You certainly did, and I got marks to prove it, and splinters, too. (Quoted in* Broadcasting, *1970: 119)*

The Federal Communications Commission responded to outraged complaints by lecturing NBC on its obligation to maintain proper standards of taste and propriety.

Another aspect of broadcast conservatism was its refusal to permit all-out advertising. This austerity continued into the 1930s even though the 1928–1929 season is regarded as the first full-scale network advertising year (Spalding, 1964). In December 1928 for the first time regular coast-to-coast networking became possible, and some 65 national sponsors bought time on the two NBC networks and CBS. Nevertheless, in 1929 the National Association of Broadcasters (then already six years old) adopted an advertising code saying: "Time before 6 pm is included in the business day and therefore may be devoted in part, at least, to broadcasting programs of a business nature; while time after 6 pm is for recreation and relaxation, and commercial programs should be of a good will type." The networks continued their ban on mentioning prices until 1932.

A prime mover in overcoming radio's reticence about direct advertising was William Benton, who cofounded the Benton and Bowles advertising agency in 1929. A remarkable innovator who pioneered in many different fields, Benton realized that to be effective on radio, advertising had to make two adaptations: it had to break away from the print-media style of copywriting and to compensate for radio's lack of visual cues. When Benton started writing advertising copy for radio, a commercial simply stopped the show while someone read an announcement — "as though he were reading from a magazine," Benton later recalled. "I *staged* commercials, you could hear the spoons, people clinking cups of coffee, everything acted out" (quoted in Whitman, 1973, emphasis added). Besides helping to revolutionize the writing and production of commercials, Benton developed consumer research techniques, launched some of the most successful radio network shows of the period, introduced live studio audiences as an acoustic setting (using audience reaction cue cards), and popularized the singing commercial.

Programming Excesses Side by side with the self-conscious correctness and the conservatism of network radio, however, there existed another, quite different standard of broadcasting. All across the country radio proved irresistibly attractive to a variety of raffish, offbeat individualists who exploited it as a personal mouthpiece. As pioneer radio critic Ben Gross recalled it:

Tailors, preachers, loan sharks, swamis, and physical-culture men, merchants, nostrum dispensers and frenzied advocates of odd ideas, such as Colonel Henderson of Shreveport, Louisiana, who combined primitive theology with hatred of chain stores, indulged in a saturnalia of "free speech." . . . In a steady procession, there came before the microphones newscasters who merely read word-for-word items from the daily papers, owners of diploma mills, crystal-gazing fortune-tellers, installment furniture men, conductors of matrimonial bureaus, fakers, nuts and dreamers making merry carnival. (Gross, 1954: 68)

In most cases the Federal Radio Commission (FRC) was able to correct abuses without withdrawing licenses (which at first had to be renewed at six-month intervals). But in two notorious instances of the early 1930s the commission did administer the ultimate penalty. In one case the FRC objected to the broadcasting of medical advice by a "Dr." J. R. Brinkley, on his station, KFKB, in Milford, Kansas. Brinkley was not a qualified physician and yet he prescribed drugs that he packaged himself and sold by number, rather than by name. The FRC refused to renew KFKB's license, saying Brinkley conducted the station only in his personal interest, not in the interest of the public.

The second case involved a religious crusader alleging municipal corruption. The Reverend Dr. Shuler of the Trinity Methodist Church (South) broadcast in Los Angeles over KGEF, a small shared-time religious station. His fire-and-brimstone personal attacks drew the biggest audience in Los Angeles when he was on the air. When KGEF's license came up for renewal in 1931 some ninety witnesses appeared in opposition. The FRC turned down the renewal application.

Both the KFKB and the KGEF renewal denials withstood court appeals, establishing in the early 1930s the commission's legal right to review a station's past programming in deciding whether license renewal would be in the public interest.

The fact that Brinkley and Shuler were *broadcast licensees* made them vulnerable. Most personal exploiters of radio, however, simply bought time on the air. Notable among this group during the 1930s was the Reverend Charles E. Coughlin, a Catholic priest with a charismatic radio appeal. From the unlikely base of a small parish church, the Shrine of the Little Flower, in a suburb of Detroit, Father Coughlin built up a fanatically loyal national radio following. His vitriolic sermons against communism, Wall

Street, Jews, labor unions, and other targets generated millions of dollars in small donations from his devoted followers. Because of his pro-Nazi sympathies his opponents called his church "the Shrine of the Little Führer." He was finally silenced in 1940, not by his political opponents directly or his church superiors, but by the refusal of networks and most larger stations to continue selling him time (Brown, 1980). With U.S. entry into World War II imminent, his tirades had become an embarrassment to the broadcasting industry.

Brinkley, Shuler, and Coughlin were examples of the more extreme consequences of radio's innate susceptibility to misuse. Their downfall did not put other exploiters out of business; it merely caused most of them to lower their profile. Spellbinders, quacks, cultists, zealots, and get-rich-quick schemers have always been part of the broadcasting scene. They cannot be completely suppressed without violating the First Amendment's guarantees of freedom of expression and of religion and the constitutional separation of church and state.

7.2 From World War II to the Present

For a bird's-eye view of radio's evolution after the testing period of the Great Depression, it is convenient to divide the intervening years into four periods: World War II and its aftermath, the postwar phase, the decade of the 1960s, and the 1970s.

World War II Period (1938–1946) The country shook off the last shackles of the Great Depression when it began to increase production in response to the threat of war. Radio brought vivid on-the-spot news of the dark events in Europe that led up to U.S.

entry into the war, relayed by short wave directly from the scene — Hitler's annexation of Austria in 1938, the invasion of Poland, followed by the British and French declarations of war in 1939. Finally, with Pearl Harbor on December 7, 1941, came the U.S. declaration of war on Japan, reciprocated immediately by German and Italian war declarations.

Broadcast news came of age in these tense years. First it played an important role in arousing the country to the necessity for military preparation, despite isolationist opposition. Later it contributed to maintaining civilian and military morale alike (§7.6).

During World War II, radio escaped direct military censorship by complying voluntarily with common-sense rules. For example, man-on-the-street and other live interviews were avoided and weather reports were discontinued.* In 1942 President Roosevelt appointed a well-known CBS radio newscaster, Elmer Davis, to head the newly created Office of War Information. The OWI coordinated the mobilization of domestic broadcasting and initiated the external broadcasting service that eventually became the Voice of America.

By 1944, even though broadcasting had been declared an essential industry and therefore exempt from the draft, half the broadcast employees of the country had

---

*During World War I private radio stations had been closed down (though this was before the broadcasting era). During World War II the president refrained from using his right, under §606 of the Communications Act of 1934, to assume sweeping controls over all federally regulated wire and radio communications. Currently, broadcasting stations voluntarily participate in the Emergency Broadcasting System, a set of standby procedures that can be put into immediate effect in case of national emergency.

joined the armed forces. The two leading radio broadcasting executives, David Sarnoff and William Paley, became respectively a brigadier general and a colonel on the staff of General Dwight D. Eisenhower in Europe.

Sarnoff served as a communications trouble-shooter and organizer and was responsible for setting up radio and press coverage of the D-day landing in France, masterminding what a colleague of that time called "the largest hookup of communications ever put together, comprising radio telegraph and telephone, cable and voice broadcasting" (Dreher, 1977: 155).

Paley served in the Psychological Warfare Branch in North Africa and Europe and was given the responsibility for preparing a manual of instructions on how the Allies would reconstitute German information services following the surrender. After VE Day Paley went to Germany to begin implementation of the manual. He was offered a brigadier general's star to stay on and supervise the gradual turnback of the media to German control, but he was anxious to get back to CBS and another battle — his struggle with NBC for dominance in American broadcasting.

Although wartime restrictions on civilian manufacturing, imposed in 1942, cut back on station construction and set production, during this period the number of stations on the air more than doubled, reaching just over a thousand by the end of 1946. Moreover, the lack of civilian goods actually worked to radio's advantage. The government allowed manufacturers to write off advertising costs as a business expense, even though they had nothing to advertise. This stimulated manufacturers to spend freely to keep their names before the public. They were willing at times to invest in first-rate programming, because they were not under competitive pressures

to maximize audiences with sure-fire, mass appeal material.

The networks, too, invested in creative programming, particularly drama. The most sensational radio play from this period, "The War of the Worlds," was a production of *The Mercury Theater on the Air*, a series directed by Orson Welles and John Houseman. The play presented an imaginary invasion from Mars, in the form of a series of radio news reports. It caused widespread panic among listeners, many of whom began to flee the imaginary Martians even though the play had been clearly identified as a Halloween prank.* One reason for the extraordinary impact of the play may have been that it was broadcast on October 30, 1938, only a month after the Munich Crisis (§7.6). Today it is one of the most often requested programs at the Museum of Broadcasting in New York (see Box).

Less sensational but more significant from an artistic point of view were the achievements of the *Columbia Workshop* (1937–1942), a drama series supported by CBS as a purely noncommercial venture. Its contributors included established distinguished literary figures such as W. H. Auden, Dorothy Parker, and Stephen Vincent Benét.

But radio also developed its own playwrights, notably Norman Corwin and Arch Oboler, who won their chief literary fame in broadcasting. CBS commissioned Corwin to celebrate the great moment of Allied victory in Europe with an hour-long radio play, "On a Note of Triumph."

"On a Note of Triumph" climaxed an extraordinary flowering of radio art — original writing of high merit, produced with con-

---

*A legacy of the "invasion" panic is a present-day program standard in the National Association of Broadcasters' Radio Code: "Sound effects and expressions characteristically associated with news broadcasts . . . shall be reserved for announcement of news, and the use of any deceptive techniques in connection with fictional events and non-news programs shall not be employed."

Broadcasting Nostalgia

In the late 1960s a cult of nostalgia began to form around the artifacts, programs, and personalities of old broadcasting. Collectors restored old sets, hobbyists exchanged tapes of programs dubbed off surviving electrical transcriptions (ETs), enthusiasts subscribed to fan magazines devoted to old radio. Modern radio stations have even begun playing some of the historic programs and reviving such classic formats as the radio mystery drama.

Some early radio sets have achieved the status of antiques. They were encased in an amazing variety of exotic designs — cabinets "resembling toolboxes, Gothic cathedrals, Aztec temples and streamlined trains . . . embel-lished with Moorish fretwork, Bakelite amber, coral or malachite cases, chromed radiator detailing or blue mirror frames . . ." (Reif, 1975).

The Museum of Broadcasting, founded in 1976 by William Paley at 1 East 53d Street in New York, proved so popular that within two years it had to acquire more space. In 1980 it had nearly 10,000 radio and television programs on file; they can be heard or seen by visitors for a small fee at the consoles shown below. Every eight months the museum acquires a complete day's programming of a single station as a historical benchmark. The collection includes a growing complement of programs from foreign broadcasters as well.

Source: Photo courtesy Museum of Broadcasting.

summate skill and always live, for the networks still banned recordings. With the end of the war years and the artificial support for culture, competitive selling resumed and this brief, luminous period of radio creativity came to an end.

Postwar Phase (1947–1959) The hostilities of World War II came to an end with the surrender of Japan in September 1945, but the postwar radio era dates from 1947 because it took some time for the country to return to routine civilian life. The upward trend in radio licensing continued throughout this period, despite the growth of television, which started in earnest in 1948. The radio networks felt the first effects of the new competition in the early 1950s, when television first began to erode prime-time radio audiences and to lure major advertisers away from network radio. In 1948 the radio networks grossed more revenue than ever before or since (excluding profits from their owned-and-operated stations).

Outside the major markets (where television first established a beachhead) the smaller independent radio stations felt the impact only later. Moreover, wartime restrictions had created a tremendous backlog of would-be broadcasters, giving radio a momentum that carried over into the postwar years. By the end of the 1947–1959 period, 1,500 more AM radio stations had gone on the air, for a total of nearly 3,500.

Providentially for radio, the *transistor* (§3.11) arrived in the nick of time to help the adjustment to television competition. Introduced by the Bell Telephone Laboratories in 1948, the transistor took several years to evolve, but by 1957 "pocket radios" were being marketed by Sony. This development had a profound effect on radio broadcasting because it made the receiver truly portable.

In fact the very word *transistor* gained international currency as a synonym for "portable, battery-operated radio receiver." Radio has become largely a portable and bedside medium, leaving television to take over as that big piece of entertaining furniture in the living room.

The Turbulent Sixties At first overwhelmed by television, radio faltered in the 1950s but began to find a new equilibrium during the turbulent sixties — the era of the Vietnam war, the Beatles, hippies, protests, civil rights marches, urban riots, and the drug culture. The music of the period reflected these violent social crosscurrents, and radio found a unique role as the disseminator of that music. Freed of the hopeless task of trying to please everyone on small budgets, the new radio risked its future on *segmenting* its audience, selecting specific audiences, and sacrificing potential listeners who did not fit the mold. By 1965 the proportion of U.S. homes with radio had leveled off at 98 percent, the saturation level that has remained essentially the same ever since. Nevertheless, average listening had declined to a new low as the decade began.

The Selfish Seventies Despite inflation and an energy crisis, radio found renewed vigor in the 1970s. By the end of the decade, average radio listening had climbed back to 3.5 hours a day. Over a thousand new stations went on the air during the decade, 84 percent of them FM.

Once again in this decade, as in the 1930s, radio succeeded because it was uniquely in tune with the times, though now for very different reasons. Journalist Tom Wolfe called the 1970s "The Me Decade," a period characterized by a wild proliferation of self-centered cults, individualistic lifestyles, how-to-do-it advice, back-to-nature movements, and ethnic separatism.

Radio's segmentation of the audience aptly suited this mood, encouraging single-constituency programming appeals and personal self-absorption. Phone-in talk shows flourished, giving every caller a chance to play secretary of state, judge, mayor, or fire chief. President Jimmy Carter exploited the trend, using radio more intimately than any president since Roosevelt. Consumer advocates told people how to "put on the gorilla suit" to assert themselves against government bureaucracy and computerized business. Radio astrologers, health faddists, and religious revivalists profited from listeners' preoccupation with self.

Radio became a reflecting pool in which listeners could constantly enjoy narcissistic images of their very own liberated selves. No personal problem was too bizarre or intimate for therapists to discuss on the air with their listeners. Commercial radio achieved an openness and candor that would have been unthinkable on even the most avant-garde free-form FM stations of the 1960s.

1980s Trends   As the decade began, the most profound influence on radio of the 1980s was the swing of the pendulum away from regulatory control toward market control through more free-wheeling competition. Entering the broadcasting field was to be made easier, especially for members of minority groups. Stations are now expected to set their own standards for programming and commercials, with minimum interference from the FCC.

Increase in the number of stations was also in prospect. The 1979 World Administrative Radio Conference (WARC) agreed to enlarge the AM band and to authorize subsequent ITU regional conferences to consider adopting 9-kHz AM radio channel separation in place of 10 kHz. These spectrum-use changes, if adopted by the Western Hemisphere regional conference in the 1980s, could enable licensing hundreds of new U.S. stations (estimates vary from 200 to 1,400) to compete for ever more fragmented audiences.

AM radio broadcasters put high priority on development of stereophonic capability in the 1980s. They see this improvement as essential to enable AM to compete with the runaway growth of FM radio. Fidelity of the AM medium has always been limited by the low quality of built-in loudspeakers, and engineers count on stereo to force manufacturers to improve the sound quality of AM receivers. Under study since 1959, AM stereophonic radio finally seems on the road to reality in the 1980s. As the decade began, the immediate problem was to agree on one of the five different technical systems that competed for acceptance.

7.3 The Fall and Rise of FM Radio

FM's Origins   For its first quarter-century, "broadcasting" meant only one thing — amplitude-modulated radio. Edwin Armstrong invented a much improved alternative system using frequency modulation in 1933, but for almost thirty years it languished as a poor relation of the established AM system.

Initially, Armstrong delayed making a public announcement of his invention because of his friendship with David Sarnoff, to whose RCA he gave a first option. Unknown to Armstrong, Sarnoff was about to commit RCA to a multimillion-dollar investment in the development of electronic television. Moreover, FM threatened the continued high profitability of the AM system and its networks. RCA did collaborate with Armstrong for two years in carrying out tests, using antennas mounted atop New York's Empire State Building, then still the world's tallest skyscraper (antenna height being a vital factor in FM coverage). In the end, however, RCA turned down the chance to pioneer FM development, replacing Armstrong's antenna installation with its own experimental television antennas. Deeply mortified by RCA's indifference, the inventor became convinced that the broadcasting establishment was bent on suppressing FM.

The Anti-FM "Conspiracy"   Determined to fight on, Armstrong built his own experimental FM station, W2XMN, which went on the air in 1937 from Alpine, New Jersey, on the heights above the Hudson River near New York (Exhibit 7.3). One of Armstrong's early FM demonstrations originated from the New York World's Fair of 1939 — by no coincidence also the occasion for the first public display of RCA's new electronic television system (§8.2).

"The historic significance of Station W2XMN was never widely realized," wrote the inventor's biographer. "Armstrong lavished on it all the care and attention to detail of which he was prodigiously capable. With this station, the first full-scale one of its kind, many basic contributions were made to ultra-shortwave communications" (Lessing, 1969: 193).

RCA's failure to take up the cause of FM increased Armstrong's bitterness at having lost the long court battle over paternity of the regenerative radio circuit to de Forest in 1934 (§5.5). Now he started another frustrating suit, this time against RCA for patent infringements. It was not that Armstrong lacked money — he had become a millionaire from his inventions as a comparatively young man. But he saw himself as the victim of a

conspiracy to kill FM, to frustrate his second chance at fame.

Costly changes in spectrum allocations, favoring television over FM, seemed to Armstrong still more evidence of conspiracy. First, in 1939 the FCC allocated 19 VHF channels to experimental television, only 13 to FM. The next year the FCC authorized commercial FM operation in the VHF band, 42 to 50 MHz, but only 30 stations had gone on

**Exhibit 7.3
Edwin Armstrong (1890–1954)**

The inventor is shown on the catwalk of his 400-foot experimental FM antenna, built in 1938 on the Palisades high above the Hudson River at Alpine, N.J. He opened station W2XMN at this site in 1939, the first high-powered FM station, the only previous one having been a low-power amateur station used for demonstration purposes.

Source: Courtesy Armstrong Foundation, Columbia University.

the air when further development was frozen in 1942 by World War II. At the close of the war, on the basis of controversial engineering advice, the FCC took away FM's prewar channels and awarded the space to television, moving FM up to its present location at 88–108 MHz. This 1945 move made obsolete the half million FM receivers that had been built up to that time.

Most major AM station owners nevertheless obtained FM licenses, simply as insurance against the possibility that FM might catch on and make AM obsolete. They made no attempt to take advantage of FM's superior quality or even to program it as a separate service. Instead they merely "simulcast" their AM programs on FM transmitters. In the absence of high-fidelity programming, listeners had little incentive to buy, and manufacturers had little incentive to develop, high-fidelity receivers.

The interest in FM stations, mostly planned as minor partners in AM/FM combinations, peaked in 1948, when over a thousand were authorized. But in that year television began its rapid climb to power, and FM was pushed into the background. In 1949 alone, 212 commercial FM stations went off the air, and total authorizations continued to decline until 1958 (Exhibit 7.1). Then at last FM stations began to multiply rapidly.

The long-delayed vindication came too late for Armstrong, however. One night in January 1954, the inventor left his New York apartment for the last time.

He was completely and neatly dressed, in hat, overcoat, scarf and gloves. He did not walk out of the door, however, but out of the window, thirteen stories above the street, falling from the last high place to which he would ever climb. His body was found by a building maintenance worker the next morning, lying on a third-floor extension overlooking the river. . . . Around him stood Manhattan's once shining towers, from which all

magic had fled, drab and gray in the light of mid-century. (Lessing, 1969: 248)

Thus ended the life of one of radio's most brilliant inventors. Later that year his estate settled Armstrong's patent infringement suit against RCA for a million dollars — the same amount that RCA had offered to pay the inventor fourteen years before when Armstrong began the suit.

FM's Triumph   The resurgence of FM that began in 1958 has continued at an accelerated pace to the present day. This success is attributable not only to the inherent physical advantages of FM in terms of sound quality, versatility, and stability of coverage; it was also stimulated by the drying up of AM channel availabilities and by a deliberate FCC policy of encouraging FM licensees. In the earlier years, when FM stations had difficulty in persuading advertisers to use their facilities, their financial survival was helped by the sale of Subsidiary Communications Authorization (SCA) services (§3.4). Muzak, a company that supplies background music for offices and stores, became a major customer for SCA. The subsequent development of digital signal processing opens up many further possibilities for the use of SCAs in new types of data delivery by FM stations, including slow-scan still pictures and textual information.

In 1964 the FCC's *nonduplication rule*, requiring AM/FM owners in major markets to program their FM stations independently of AM sister stations at least 50 percent of the time, gave an important stimulus to independent FM programming. The FCC stiffened this rule in 1979, requiring nonduplication 75 percent of the time in markets as small as 25,000. By then, however, FM had already turned the corner and needed little further incentive for programming independently of AM sister stations. A sign of this change was a trend toward adoption of separate call letters for FM sister stations, rather than relying on hyphenated call signs using AM call letters.

FM's final triumph came, however, only after it cleared one more hurdle — the ingrained belief of advertising agencies that FM was not a viable commercial medium. For years AM/FM combinations had thrown in the FM component of coverage without extra charge to AM advertisers. This giveaway had created an enduring image of FM as an ineffectual commercial medium.

Jerry Lee, president of WVDR (FM) in Philadelphia, was the first FM operator to gross a million dollars in annual advertising revenues. He recalls that in 1969, even after his station climbed from twenty-second to third place in its market, he still had to go to extraordinary lengths to get advertising agency executives to take FM seriously. They relied more on their prejudices than on the factual evidence that FM had finally arrived. By 1973, however, the trade journal *Broadcasting* could headline its annual report on FM "The Rites of Passage Are All Over for FM Radio: It's Out on its Own" (24 Sept.: 31). And by 1976 the FCC reported that commercial FM as a whole could at last say that it had begun to make a profit.

Today three-quarters of all radio receivers sold incorporate FM. The FM audience equals and in some markets even surpasses that of AM, despite the fact that over half the commercial radio stations on the air are AM. FM still has one drawback — relatively poor coverage of the important "drive-time" audience, still dominated by AM in 1980. Not all autos are equipped with FM, partly because AM/FM installations cost more, partly because vertical auto antennas are not ideal for picking up FM's horizontally polarized signal

(§2.6). The FM industry has lobbied Congress for an all-channel radio law similar to the one requiring television receivers to incorporate both UHF and VHF tuning.

7.4 The Parsimony Principle

Voracity of the Medium   In the 1920s most broadcast schedules were on-again, off-again affairs because all stations were at first licensed to operate only part time. Most programming was catch-as-catch-can, with singers and pianists dropping by the studio to perform free. One early New York announcer recalled that on an occasion when a scheduled performer failed to show up he became so desperate that he announced a program on "the sounds of New York" and simply hung the microphone outside a studio window. It soon became apparent, however, that one of radio's main advantages as a public medium was its ability to be *continuously* available. Moreover, once the continuous use of a channel had been acquired and the investment made in transmission facilities, cost-effectiveness dictated that a station should stay on the air as long as possible with as few interruptions as possible.

Continuous operation created an incredible appetite for programming. To cope with this voracity, programmers resorted to a variety of strategies based upon what might be called "the parsimony principle." This basic rule of broadcasting dictates that program material must be used up as *sparingly* as possible, *repeated* as often as possible, and *shared* as widely as possible.

Sharing is achieved by means of recording and networking. Without these ways of rising above local limitations, broadcasting could never have developed to anywhere near its present dimensions. Purely local programming resources would soon be exhausted and continuous operation would be impossible.

At both local and national levels, scheduling and formatting strategies ensure sparing and repeated use of materials. A regularly scheduled daily or weekly entertainment program series uses standardized openings, closings, and transitions; it presents ready-made personalities or characters building upon established situations or plot lines. Primary examples of the parsimony principle at work in early radio program formulas were soap operas, game shows, and disc jockey programs.

Soap Operas Among serialized radio drama formats, the soap opera (so called because soap companies often owned and sponsored them) is the classic case of frugal expenditure of program resources. Notorious for the snail-like pace of their plots, these daytime serials used every tactic of delay to drag out the action of each episode. Irna Phillips, who wrote *The Guiding Light* for 21 years, estimated that in her 41-year writing career she turned out the equivalent in length of 2,500 novels — striking evidence of broadcasting's voracity (Gelman, 1971: 48). Her career started at WGN-Chicago in 1930, when she began writing a serial story in which she and one other actress played all the parts — economy in production expenses as well as frugality in expenditure of program materials being another advantage of the serial format. At their high-water mark in the early 1940s nearly 50 daytime radio serials could be heard on the networks each week. Not until 1960 did NBC and CBS drop the last few survivors. In the meantime, the format had made a successful transition to television.

Game Shows Audience-participation or game shows, another parsimonious format, became a major ingredient of network radio programming in the late 1930s, although game shows can be traced back to 1924 (Fabe, 1979: 293). The first to get wide attention was *Professor Quiz,* a much-imitated show started in 1937 on CBS. *Information Please,* launched by NBC Blue in 1938 and featuring such well-known literary figures of the period as Clifton Fadiman and John Kieran, has been called "one of the most intelligent, erudite, and entertaining programs ever on radio" (Fabe, 1979: 104). In 1949, their peak year, game shows occupied 11 percent of the radio prime-time network schedules, surpassed in quantity only by musical variety shows, dramas, and news programs (Sterling and Kittross, 1978: 521).

Game shows had the advantage over soap operas (as they still have in television) that the main talent expense was limited to the salaries for an MC plus fees for a panel of a few show-business personalities who usually worked for minimum union scale for the sake of the exposure the shows gave them. The format capitalized on the inexhaustible supply of amateurs willing to show off their abilities — or simply to make fools of themselves.

Disc Jockey Format Most parsimonious of all formats, the disc jockey (DJ) show exploits to the full the availability of recorded music and reduces production costs to the lowest possible level. Unlike the formats previously discussed, it still survives in radio and suits even the smallest station's local programming needs. At first DJs had low status in the talent hierarchy because of the prejudice against the use of recorded material (§7.7). As the quality of recordings improved, however, so did the status of DJs.

The DJ format came to represent a form of expression unique to radio, with no equivalent in other media. It gives scope for the exploitation of personal idiosyncrasies and for their interaction with the rapidly changing popular music scene.* Radio history is full of strange and wonderful stories of the bizarre antics and amazing achievements of the great DJs. No one has yet done full justice to this colorful strand of broadcasting history. The biggest star of the DJ format in the 1930s was Martin Block, who started his *Make Believe Ballroom* on WNEW-New York in 1935 at a salary of $25 a week. Eventually *Ballroom* was earning WNEW half a million a year and Block's annual salary reached $200,000. The *Ballroom* format was simplicity itself — Block asked the audience to picture a giant turntable stage that revolved on his command. As each imagined segment brought a different well-known popular band to the front of the stage, Block would introduce the orchestra and its best-known tunes, interspersing them with commercials. More than the format, however, accounted for his phenomenal success; he was an exceptionally compelling pitchman, with a sexy voice and uninhibited invention (Gelman, 1971: 30).

7.5 Radio Network Development

The Network as Syndicator Another evidence of the parsimony principle at work was the rapid rise of national networks to the dominant position in the broadcasting industry. By enabling instant sharing of programs, networks constitute a form of syndication, technological aspects of which (relay distribution) were discussed in §4.1. As a trade term in the broadcasting industry, however, the term "syndication" refers more narrowly to

program materials distributed on a nonnetwork basis by firms specializing in that business. But it should be understood that networks themselves are *functionally* just another form of syndication — that is, a means of producing or procuring high-cost program materials centrally and distributing them to many separate users at moderate average cost to each.* In this sense, network is a form of syndication uniquely adapted to the broadcasting medium.

Network Benefits A broadcasting network offers three basic services to affiliated stations: it provides (1) a structured *program* service; (2) a means of program *distribution* so that the service can be instantly received by all affiliates at the same time; and (3) a *sales* organization that finds national advertisers to purchase part of the affiliates' commercial time.

Affiliated radio stations in the 1940s (like television stations today) benefited from top-quality programming and the sale of their time to network advertisers. Equally important, stations also benefited from the enhanced value to local and nonnetwork national advertisers of their nonnetwork time. Network advertisers, in turn, benefited from getting access to the best stations in the nation's major markets in a single transaction. An incidental public benefit is the fact that networks create an instantaneous means of reaching the entire nation with news and information.

---

*The word *syndicate* was first used as a media term in the nineteenth century, referring to the distribution of special features to subscribing newspapers. Today there are several hundred such press syndicates, distributing comic strips, opinion columns, and other specialized material. In the generic sense news agencies, which originated in the 1840s, were the original syndicators of press material.

---

*It also gave rise to "payola," the practice of bribing DJs and others responsible for selecting new recordings for air-play to give favorable consideration to particular releases (see §13.6).

Chain Broadcasting Investigation In 1938, radio stations representing 98 percent of the total nighttime wattage were affiliated with either NBC or CBS. This amounted to only 40 percent of the 660 stations on the air, but included virtually all of the major stations in the country. Then as now, the great majority of affiliated stations were tied to their networks not by ownership but by contract. Originally, NBC's affiliate contracts had been rather loose and informal, but William Paley, struggling to catch up with NBC's lead, evolved more binding contracts for CBS affiliates (§6.5). NBC followed suit.

It will be recalled that NBC had the advantage of deploying a double network, NBC Red and NBC Blue, against CBS. This meant that NBC tied up the two best stations in many markets and could afford to use the weaker of its line-ups, NBC Blue, as a kind of loss leader to undercut CBS.

In 1934 a third network, the Mutual Broadcasting System (MBS), began to emerge in the Midwest. Frustrated in its attempts to expand from a regional into a national network, MBS complained to the Federal Communications Commission that the older chains unfairly dominated the network field. The FCC initiated a major inquiry, based on the fact that the Communications Act of 1934 empowered it to "make special regulations applicable to radio stations engaged in chain [i.e., network] broadcasting." After more than three years of investigation, the FCC issued a set of "Chain Broadcasting Regulations" aimed at relaxing the hold of the older networks over affiliates and talent. Among other things, the new rules forbade dual networks covering the same markets and forced both CBS and NBC to give up the talent-booking agencies they had developed as sidelines. The rules also forbade the networks to force stations to carry programs they did not wish to accept, or to infringe in other ways on the autonomy of affiliates.

CBS and NBC were outraged at these intrusions into their business affairs. Predicting total collapse of the network system if the regulations went into effect, they fought the case all the way to the Supreme Court, but in 1943 the Court finally settled the argument in favor of the FCC (319 U.S. 190).* The most tangible immediate outcome was the end of NBC's dual network operation, with the sale in 1943 of its Blue network, which became the American Broadcasting Company (ABC). The predicted collapse of network broadcasting failed to materialize and Mutual began to expand rapidly. Thus emerged radio's four-network pattern, which endured until the 1960s.

National Broadcasting Company
NBC continued as the leading radio chain. By 1930, as a result of antimonopoly suits, two of the original part-owners of NBC, Westinghouse and Western Electric, had sold off their interests to RCA. Two years later RCA itself became independent of its original co-owners in the patent pool (§6.2). NBC remained a wholly owned RCA subsidiary while RCA itself developed into a giant diversified corporation with worldwide interests in communication services and manufacturing. NBC, reflecting the parent company's high corporate status, tended to assume the role of a dignified elder among the networks. Its image was further enhanced in 1933 when NBC moved into its new headquarters in the 70-story art-deco style RCA building, part of New York's famed Rockefeller Center.†

*The Chain Broadcasting Regulations were later extended in 1946 to television networks. In 1977, after radio networks had ceased to play a dominant role, most of the original chain regulations were lifted for radio. (For details see §12.4.)
†CBS did not achieve its own architectural monument until 1965, when it moved into splendid new headquarters at the corner of 52d Street and Avenue of the Americas, two blocks from NBC. Sheathed in elegant dark granite, the CBS building came to be known as "Black Rock."

Columbia Broadcasting System   William Paley's upstart rival network, CBS, struggled for years to overcome its image as the number-two chain, laboring in the wake of NBC. Big advertisers and star performers automatically preferred NBC to CBS whenever they had a choice, regardless of CBS's growing popularity. "We were at the mercy of the sponsors and the ad agencies," wrote Paley. "They could always take a successful show away from us and put it on NBC" (1979: 174).

CBS enhanced its reputation during World War II by its outstanding news operation (§7.6). Following the war Paley launched an all-out attack on NBC's leadership. "I would grant NBC its greater reputation, prestige, finances, and facilities," said Paley, "but CBS had and would continue to have the edge in creative programming" (1979: 174). By 1948 CBS was packaging 29 sponsored radio programs, two of which were in the top ten — *My Friend Irma* and *Arthur Godfrey's Talent Scouts.* Paley's next target was the biggest prize of all — NBC's superstars.

The ensuing CBS "talent raid" used a secret weapon — the discovery that star performers could increase their income by incorporating themselves, then selling their corporations to a network instead of taking salaries. Profits on corporate sales were taxed as capital gains at only 25 percent, whereas the tax on a correspondingly high salary was 77 percent (Paley, 1979: 193).

With this leverage, Paley went after Jack Benny in 1948. The star was willing, but the sponsor to which he was tied by contract, the American Tobacco Company, remained doubtful. Taking a tremendous risk, Paley offered to compensate the tobacco company for every rating point it lost by shifting from NBC to CBS for the weeks remaining in the Benny contract. As Paley put it, "there was nothing left for them to argue about," and Benny moved over to CBS (Paley, 1979: 198). Within a short time Bing Crosby, Red Skelton, Edgar Bergen, George Burns and Gracie Allen, Ed Wynn, Fred Waring, Al Jolson, Groucho Marx, and Frank Sinatra all deserted NBC for greener fields at CBS.

By the fall of 1949 Paley finally achieved his dream of taking the lead away from NBC, a lead which CBS held for the short remaining life of big-time network radio.

Mutual Broadcasting System   The network whose complaints against CBS and NBC had precipitated the chain broadcasting investigation, MBS, started on a different premise from the older networks. Only two major-market radio stations on clear channels had remained in the early 1930s without affiliation with CBS or NBC — WGN-Chicago and WOR-New York. They arranged in 1934 to form a network organization to sell time jointly with WXYZ-Detroit and WLW-Cincinnati. The four stations started the network by exchanging programs on a regional network basis. Their chief program asset at the start was *The Lone Ranger,* a series that WXYZ had introduced in 1933.

Mutual signed up several of the regional networks and, in the post-World War II period, offered a haven for the newly emerging small stations that began to go on the air in great numbers. By 1948 MBS affiliations had passed the 500 mark and it was advertising itself as "the world's largest network." The significance of the number of affiliates in a network has to be judged in terms of their power, however, and most of MBS's affiliates were in the lower power classes. Many were located outside the major urban centers, and

Mutual took on a somewhat conservative political tone. Lacking the prestige and the corporate resources of the older networks, MBS had to scramble to stay alive. It tended to be less choosy about both its programs and their sponsors than the older networks and over the years carried many paid religious and politically right-wing programs that would have had difficulty finding time on the more prestigious networks.

Under the pressure to survive, MBS introduced innovative business practices, such as network *cooperative advertising*. This is a means of using local advertisers to support network programming, originally the exclusive domain of national advertisers. For example, Mutual's baseball *Game of the Day* was supported in 1954 by over 4,000 local sponsors. CBS or NBC would have expected such a program to be supported by a single national sponsor.

Such expedients never succeeded in making Mutual stable financially, however, and its whole history has been marked by frequent changes in ownership. During a four-year period in the 1950s its ownership changed six times. The latest owner is Amway Corporation, which bought the network for $18 million in 1977. The next year, abandoning the original MBS concept of not owning stations, Mutual bought its first owned-and-operated station, paying $12 million for WCFL(AM) in Chicago.

American Broadcasting Company

When NBC was forced to sell one of its two networks in 1943 as a result of the chain broadcasting investigation, it naturally chose to sacrifice the weaker of the two, NBC Blue, which had descended from the old WJZ-Radio Group network of the 1920s (§6.4). NBC had used the Blue primarily as a loss leader to protect the Red network and had not done much to strengthen it in the intervening years. Thus the new owner of the Blue network (who renamed it American Broadcasting Company in 1945 and dropped the historic WJZ call letters in favor of WABC) faced a difficult competitive situation, running well behind both NBC and CBS.

A second government-decreed corporate breakup came to ABC's rescue in 1953. Earlier the Justice Department had forced "divorcement" on the Big Five motion picture companies. This meant that the major Hollywood production studios had to sell off their extensive theater chains. One of the spin-off companies, Paramount Theaters (once the largest movie theater chain in the world), merged with ABC, injecting not only much-needed funds into the radio network, but also establishing a link with Hollywood that eventually paid off handsomely when ABC went into television. But these developments came after the period of network radio dominance; during it, ABC ran third to NBC and CBS, with MBS trailing even further behind.

Network Programming During their heyday the radio networks supplied a full schedule of programs much as television networks do today.

In those days network advertisers *sponsored* entire radio programs, rather than buying scattered spot announcements as they do now in television. This close identification of advertisers with the most popular programs and star performers gave network advertising added value. By the same token, sponsorship gave performers added value. Bing Crosby, already a top star, received $1,500 a week when his program was sustaining, double that when CBS found a sponsor for him.

The first network radio entertainment program to achieve addictive popularity was a prime-time, five-days-a-week situation comedy, *Amos 'n' Andy*. Charles Correll ("Andy") and Freeman Godsen ("Amos") came to radio as a "song-and-patter" team, a format much esteemed in early radio. At a station manager's suggestion they tried their luck at a comedy series. The two white performers developed a black dialect show in fractured ghetto English, featuring the ups and downs of the "Fresh Air Taxicab Company of America, Incorpulated."

Amos 'n' Andy became the top network show in the early 1930s. Traffic would stop on the main streets of towns across the country and movies would be halted in midreel at 7 P.M. so that people would not miss their nightly fifteen minutes of chuckles over the antics of Amos, Andy, the Kingfish, Lightnin', Madam Queen, and a host of minor characters, most of whom Correll and Godsen played themselves.

Today the impersonation of blacks by white actors using exaggerated dialect and comedy situations based on ghetto poverty could not be seriously proposed. A Pittsburgh newspaper asked the FCC to ban the series in 1931, alleging racism, but its defenders had a convincing argument: most blacks seemed to enjoy the program just as much as whites. Opposition became more general in the 1950s. CBS ran a television version of *Amos 'n' Andy* (with black actors) from 1951 to 1953, but dropped it because of opposition from the National Association for the Advancement of Colored People. Syndicated showings continued until 1966, but the syndicator finally agreed to withdraw the series from both national and international syndication (Brown, 1977: 16).

7.6 Radio News and Public Affairs

By assuming a serious function as distributors of news and public affairs information, responsible broadcasters cast themselves in a far more important role than that of mere entertainers. They became, in effect, sharers with the printed news media in the Western world's great tradition of press freedom. But this role was not won easily. There were (and are) plenty of broadcasters who care not at all about being part of a great press tradition if it interferes with that other great American tradition — making money through free enterprise. Nor was the traditional press eager to welcome into its ranks a new and possibly dangerously competitive rival for public attention.

Press-Radio "War" News no less than broadcast entertainment depends on syndication. Newspapers share material by means of *press associations* — or *wire services* as they were called traditionally, referring to the fact that they flourished with the telegraph (§5.2).

Just as radio upset the world of music, so it disturbed the vested interests of the news agencies and their customary clients, the newspapers. Radio, in bypassing the written word, seemed to threaten the very future of news publications. Who would want to buy a paper to read news already heard on the radio? Who would want to buy advertising space in papers whose news was already stale? The newspapers recognized that the key to suppressing radio competition was control over broadcasters' access to the output of the major established news agencies. At the time these were the Associated Press (AP) (owned cooperatively by newspapers themselves), International News Service (INS), and the United Press (UP).

NBC's Blue Network inaugurated regular

15-minute nightly newscasts by Lowell Thomas in 1930, a sign that radio was about to assume a serious competitive role. In response to threats that news agency services would soon be cut off, CBS began forming its own newsgathering organization. To defuse a possible press-radio war, the publishers proposed a truce in 1933. The result, known as the Biltmore Agreement, set up a Press-Radio Bureau designed to protect the papers' interests.*

CBS suspended its own newsgathering, and the two networks agreed to confine themselves to two five-minute press-wire news summaries a day from the Press-Radio Bureau. These could be aired only after the morning and evening papers had appeared, could be used only on a sustaining (non-sponsored) basis, and had to be followed by the admonition, "For further details consult your local newspaper(s)." The bureau agreed to issue additional special bulletins on events "of transcendent importance," but they had to be written "in such a manner as to stimulate public interest in the reading of newspapers" (quoted in Kahn, 1978: 81).

In practice, however, the Press-Radio Bureau never worked effectively. Only about a third of the existing stations subscribed to it, and several independent radio news services sprang up to fill the gap. Broadcasters also took advantage of escape clauses in the agreement that exempted news commentaries. In consequence a great many radio newscasters became instant commentators.

United Press broke the embargo in 1935, soon to be joined by International News Service. The Press-Radio Bureau finally expired, unmourned, in 1940 when the Asso-

ciated Press began to accept radio stations as members of the association.

As broadcast news matured it became evident that, contrary to the expectations of the newspaper publishers, radio coverage actually stimulated newspaper reading instead of discouraging it. The press services eventually acquired even more broadcasters than publishers as customers and began to offer services especially tailored for broadcast stations, including audio feeds ready to go directly on the air. Today broadcasting in America has at its disposal over sixty news services, including those of the radio and television networks and the U.S. international agencies, now reduced to two, AP and UPI (the latter a combination made in 1958 of the old UP and INS of the Press-Radio Bureau days). In 1979, radio paid about $35 million for news services.

Radio News in World War II Still another reason for the breakdown of the Press-Radio Bureau was the mounting public demand for up-to-the-minute news from Europe as the tense pre-World War II drama unfolded. Radio was ideally qualified to do this job.

At first, however, U.S. network representatives in Europe had to pass up hard news. Because of the networks' agreement with the news agencies they were confined to personality interviews and feature stories. César Saerchinger originated European feeds for CBS in the early 1930s, making a deal to use BBC facilities — an important precedent for extensive cooperation between American and British broadcasting during the war. Edward R. Murrow, destined to be broadcasting's most revered news figure, went to Europe for CBS in 1937 not as a newsman but as "an arranger of 'talks' and a supervisor of 'events'" (Kendrick, 1969: 139). At the very moment in 1938 when Austria was succumbing to the Nazis, Murrow was in Warsaw

---

*CBS and NBC were parties to the agreement, but not the nonaffiliated stations. The relevant parts of the document are reprinted by Kahn (1978: 80).

organizing a feature about Polish children for a CBS educational series.

Anxious to outdo NBC's developing European news operation, CBS decided on a bold stroke, a full half-hour devoted to a CBS foreign news "roundup" on the Nazi invasion of Austria, originating live from key points — London, Paris, Rome, Berlin, Vienna. No one had ever tried such an ambitious news production. The problems of coordination and precise timing were tremendous, for in 1938 the networks did not allow the use of recordings. In that historic half-hour, which was anchored by Robert Trout and featured reports by William Shirer, Ed Murrow, and others, "radio came into its own as a full-fledged news medium" (Kendrick, 1969: 158).

Later in 1938 came the Munich Crisis, appeasement of Hitler, and British Prime Minister Chamberlain's memorable claim of "peace in our time" — a peace shattered only a year later by the outbreak of World War II. The Munich Pact, by which the Allies abandoned Czechoslovakia to Hitler, climaxed eighteen days of feverish diplomatic negotiations among the great powers. During these tense days and nights, a pioneer news commentator, H. V. Kaltenborn, achieved fame and fortune by extemporizing a remarkable string of 85 live broadcasts from New York, reporting and analyzing news of each diplomatic move as it came in by wire and wireless. News staffers at CBS would shake Kaltenborn awake (he slept on a cot in a studio), hand him the latest bulletin; he would go on the air immediately, first reading the bulletin, then ad-libbing his own lucid, informed commentary. "Even as I talked," wrote Kaltenborn, "I was under constant bombardment of fresh news dispatches, carried to my desk from the ticker room. I read and digested them as I talked" (Kaltenborn, 1938: 9).

The other radio networks were also extremely active. During the Munich Crisis, for example, NBC originated 147 European pick-ups to CBS's 157 (Barnouw, 1968: 83). But Paley was determined to take the lead from NBC in at least one field, and the war gave him the opportunity. "From the ad hoc organization of stringers and the permanent staff of four foreign correspondents on September 1, 1939," recalled Paley, "we jumped to fourteen regular foreign correspondents by the end of the year, to thirty-nine in 1940, and to more than sixty in 1941" (1979: 138). The appetite for news was insatiable, with the number of network newscasts nearly doubling during the war years to 135 a week in 1945.

Thanks to CBS's early start, Paley's enthusiastic support, and his good luck in assembling a superlative staff of news specialists, CBS set a high standard for broadcast journalism during the war years, establishing a tradition of excellence that has lasted to this day.

Edward R. Murrow   Of all the stars in CBS's news crown, none shone so brightly as Edward R. Murrow. Unlike the others, Murrow did not come to radio from a newspaper or wire service background. He had earned a degree in speech from Washington State College. There he was strongly influenced by a remarkable teacher, Ida Lou Anderson, who taught speech and supervised the campus carrier current station. After his graduation in 1930, Murrow gained initial overseas experience working for the Institute of International Education before joining CBS in 1935.

During the war Murrow first came to the notice of the wider public through his memorable live reports from bomb-ravaged London and from even more dangerous vantage points at the war front (Exhibit 7.6). The

Exhibit 7.6
Murrow in London during World War II

Murrow is walking not far from the BBC's Broadcasting House, a major target for German bombing raids that was hit more than once. Murrow and other American correspondents originated programs from a tiny studio located in a subbasement. On one occasion when the building took a hit, Murrow continued broadcasting as stretcher bearers carried dead and injured past the studio to a first aid station (Kendrick, 1969: 212).

Source: CBS News.

British appreciated the way he brought realistic and moving word-and-sound pictures of the war to Americans; at home, listeners appreciated him because, as William Paley wrote, "he radiated truth and concern" (1979: 151). Few people were so universally admired and respected during and just after the war. He was, wrote David Halberstam, "one of those rare legendary figures who was as good as his myth." When the war was over, Murrow "was in his own way as much a hero and a personage of that epic era as Eisenhower himself" (1979: 38, 39). Les Brown called him "broadcasting's supreme journalist" (1977: 288), and his boss, William Paley, described him as "the soul of integrity . . . fearless, strong-willed, and honor-bound by his convictions" (1979: 151).

CBS benefited from Murrow not only as an on-the-air personality; equally important was his ability to attract to CBS News a superb supporting staff. In 1947 Murrow resigned as CBS news vice president to resume personal daily newscasting. As an on-the-air personality, he survived the transition to television better than some of the other famous wartime journalists, moving on to still greater achievements in the video age (§9.5).

News Commentary   One of the early discoveries about the use of news-related material in broadcasting was that the medium was ideally suited to editorial commentary as well as to straight news reporting. H. V. Kaltenborn had started a series of commentaries on WEAF in 1923. To his surprise, he found that the same comments he wrote for his paper, the *Brooklyn Eagle*, without causing a ripple of concern sometimes provoked sharp public reactions when spoken on the radio (Clark, 1965).

He learned also how sensitive the executives of a company like AT&T, the WEAF licensee, could be to such reactions. After only a few months WEAF abruptly discontinued Kaltenborn's popular news commentary program because of the controversies it inspired. Nevertheless, news commentary became a radio fixture by the late 1930s, when world events called urgently not only for fast reporting but also for interpretation.

Editorializing   Broadcasters distinguish between commentaries made by qualified individuals such as Kaltenborn, in their own names, and station editorials aired in the name of licensees. An editorial, according to newspaper tradition, represents the *publisher's* point of view. By contrast, both station licensees (the equivalent of publishers) and the regulatory agency questioned the propriety of editorializing by licensees. Moreover, licensees (as in the case of AT&T and the Kaltenborn commentaries) were not always ready to face the adverse reactions that controversial opinions inevitably provoke.

Broadcast editorials were not generally offered and in fact were banned by the Federal Communications Commission in 1941, but it reversed this stand in 1949 (§17.4). Despite positive encouragement from the FCC thereafter, editorializing never caught on with the networks; after all, they are hardly in a position to speak out on controversial issues on behalf of all their affiliates. Individual stations began editorializing in 1949, but this type of public affairs programming has never loomed large in radio schedules, and today editorializing on radio is relatively uncommon.

Radio Documentaries   Radio excelled, however, in a news-related program format, the *news documentary*. Perhaps because of the difficulties the press at first put in the way of radio news reporting, broadcasters early turned to an unconventional format — dramatized re-creations of news events, with

actors impersonating the public figures of the day. *The March of Time*, inaugurated by CBS and *Time* magazine in 1932, was extraordinarily successful in spite of its questionable mixture of fictional form and factual content. *The March of Time* pioneered in documentary journalism, a form that became a characteristic and praiseworthy element of broadcast programming. Later, when the *Time* series was transferred to film, it linked the established documentary tradition of radio to the emerging one in television.

Hear It Now, an hour-long radio documentary series broadcast by CBS in 1950–1951, with Ed Murrow as narrator, consisted of extracts from past news broadcasts (parsimony at work!), featuring the voices of newsmakers, edited together into a coherent review of recent events. It marked the start of the broadcast collaboration between Murrow as performer and Fred Friendly as producer, a successful team that became even more famous for *See It Now* (1951–1958) and other documentary series in television (§9.5).*

7.7 Broadcast Music

Live Music Era   Both networks and the larger stations relied heavily on music from the very beginning of radio. In the mid-1930s over half of all radio programming was music, and three-quarters of it was carried on a sustaining (nonsponsored) basis. Most large stations had their own musical groups and the networks even had their own symphony orchestras.

---

*The two had actually collaborated earlier, outside CBS, in producing a popular series of record albums using the same format, *I Can Hear It Now*.

In its early years, a quarter of the entire CBS schedule was devoted to music. NBC began regular broadcasts of the Metropolitan Opera in 1931, carrying it mostly on a sustaining basis until 1940. Thereafter Texaco, Inc. underwrote the Met broadcasts and has continued to do so ever since — "the longest continuous commercial underwriting of the same program by the same sponsor in the history of radio" (McDowell, 1979). Texaco, which now organizes a special ad hoc 300-station radio network to carry the programs, abstains from commercial interruptions, inserting only sponsor identifications at intermissions.

In 1937 David Sarnoff dispatched an emissary to Italy to sign up Arturo Toscanini, the greatest symphony conductor of the day, to lead the NBC Symphony Orchestra. Toscanini made musical history at NBC for a decade. After his departure in 1946 the orchestra continued independently as the Symphony of the Air, finally disbanding in 1965.

All this had tremendous impact on the musical world, creating vast new public appetites for all sorts of music, old and new, classical and popular. While expanding the market for music, however, radio also created novel copyright and union rights problems never before faced by the creators and performers of musical works.

Music Performing Rights: ASCAP and BMI Under the copyright law* the playing of a recording in public for profit is regarded as a performance. As such it obligates the user (in this case the radio station) to pay for the *performing right* to the copyright holders, who may include composers of the music, lyricists, and music publishers.

*The present law, the Copyright Act of 1976 (17 U.S. Code), replaced the 1909 law that was in effect when radio broadcasting began. (Details of the 1976 Act are discussed in §15.7.)

Music copyright holders cannot possibly monitor personally all the tens of thousands of commercial establishments where music is performed, including concert halls, hotels, nightclubs, and other such public places as well as broadcasting stations. Instead they rely on *music licensing* organizations to act on their behalf in collecting copyright fees for performances of both live and recorded music. The first U.S. organization of this type, the American Society of Composers, Authors and Publishers (ASCAP), was founded in 1914. It checks on the public performances of music copyrighted by its members, collects royalty fees, and distributes the net income to the copyright owners.

When radio began, no one could be sure what impact this new way of performing music would have. Would repeated radio performances quickly kill off interest in new musical works, or would they enhance the market for sheet music, recordings, and in-person performances? As early as 1922 ASCAP began making substantial demands for payments by broadcasters for the use of musical works in its catalog, whether broadcast live or from recordings. These demands imposed a new and unexpected financial burden on radio stations. In 1923 station owners formed the National Association of Broadcasters (NAB) to deal with ASCAP's demands on an industry-wide basis. Nevertheless, as radio grew the fees collected by ASCAP also grew and soon broadcasting was contributing the major share of the association's royalty collections. Effective resistance to ASCAP's demands was impossible because it was the sole U.S. licensing organization and controlled virtually all contemporary American music, along with contemporary arrangements of older compositions on which original copyrights had expired. Radio stations found it impossible to produce listenable music programs without infringing on ASCAP copyrights.

Finally the broadcasters moved to break the ASCAP monopoly. When ASCAP proposed yet another substantial fee increase in 1937 the broadcasters rebelled, forming their own cooperative music-licensing organization, Broadcast Music, Inc. (BMI). The new organization started business in 1940. Its first "affiliates," as the copyright owners are called, were composers of country, western, and "race" music (black popular music), most of whom had never registered with AS-CAP. Eventually BMI built up a comprehensive library representing over a million musical works owned by some 55,000 publishers and writers. BMI also has reciprocal agreements with 38 foreign music-licensing organizations. Nowadays the networks and most radio and television stations pay for both AS-CAP and BMI licenses. In 1979 radio stations paid over $60 million for music licenses.

A long-drawn-out controversy continues as to the legality of the methods of licensing used by both ASCAP and BMI. The most practicable system, now in general use, provides for a "blanket" license fee, figured as a percentage of a station's gross income and permitting unlimited use of the licensing society's catalog. The networks oppose blanket licensing and CBS is attempting to have it ruled illegal under the antitrust laws (620 F 2d 930, 1980).

To calculate the amount due each copyright holder from blanket fees, the music-licensing organization obtains detailed per-use logs from a cross-section sample of all stations in the country. The logs establish frequency-of-performance levels for each composition used. These levels are then multiplied by a payment rate agreed upon by the individual composers in their contracts with ASCAP or BMI.*

Union Battle Against Recordings A second special interest group was concerned with the new way of performing music in public, the musicians' union. Although broadcasting created many new jobs for musicians, they saw its increasing reliance on recorded music (especially the electrical transcriptions then used for syndicated programs) as a threat. In 1922 an implacable opponent of radio's use of recordings, James Caesar Petrillo, became president of the Chicago chapter of the American Federation of Musicians (AFM).

"Little Caesar," as he was called, first built a strong political base locally in Chicago, then went on to become national AFM president in 1940. He embarked on a series of outrageous demands. First he prevented broadcast of the Interlochen Music Camp, a well-loved annual Michigan music festival featuring young amateur symphonic artists. Next he threatened to close down transcription makers, forcing syndication firms to pay substantial extra fees for every broadcast transcription made, the money going to a union slush fund that Petrillo alone controlled. He succeeded in forcing broadcasters to hire professional musicians as "platter turners" in the control rooms and as librarians in the station record libraries of his hometown, Chicago. He demanded that stations increase musicians' pay as much as fivefold. With unprecedented bravado, Petrillo defied the National War Labor Board, President Roosevelt, the Supreme Court, and the Congress of the United States.

*The Copyright Act of 1976 makes a special provision for compulsory licensing of public broadcasting stations and their networks. They obtain licenses either by paying a voluntary, mutually agreed fee or one set by the Copyright Royalty Tribunal, a federal body established by the copyright act.

Congress finally passed a bill known as the Lea Act in 1946, amending the Communications Act of 1934 specifically to bring Petrillo under control. The Lea Act forbade stations to hire unneeded personnel to satisfy union demands, banned union restrictions on the use of transcriptions, and forbade unions from preventing broadcasts by amateur musicians. It took another two years of litigation before the courts finally upheld the Lea Act, at last relieving broadcasters of the constant musicians' strikes that had embroiled them for nearly a decade. Petrillo's antics hastened the demise of live studio orchestras, an end that doubtless would have been eventually brought about by the changing economics of the industry. Nevertheless, organized labor interests still chafe at the constraints imposed by the Lea amendment and a bill to repeal it was passed by the House of Representatives in 1980.

Network Recording Ban When radio began, phonograph recordings were still relatively primitive. In fact Edison cylinders were still in use, along with discs. The latter were made of shellac, a heavy, brittle material easily damaged or shattered. They ran at 78 revolutions per minute, allowing time for only three or four minutes to a side. Sixteen-inch ETs (electrical transcriptions), running 15 minutes to a side at 33 1/3 rpm, were introduced in 1929 specifically for radio program syndication and for subscription music libraries. The latter provided stations with a basic library of music on ETs, supplemented at regular intervals by additional recordings.

The radio networks, however, scorned recorded programs. They regarded their ability to distribute *live* programming to their affiliates as a major asset. Even if more convenient and better-quality methods of recording had been available, the chains would have resisted the suggestion that they should program "secondhand" material. The radio commission, too, looked down on recorded programs, requiring in the early years that each recording be conspicuously announced as such. This was to assure listeners that the broadcaster had no intention of fooling them into accepting canned material as the real thing.

ABC was the first network to do away with the recording ban completely. It did so in order to lure Bing Crosby away from NBC in 1946. The singer hated the tension and risks of real-time broadcasting, which were compounded by the need to repeat each live program in New York a second time for the West Coast to compensate for time-zone differences. Crosby himself financed a company to make tape recorders, based on magnetic tape recording technology developed by the Germans during World War II. As soon as broadcast-quality audio tape recorders became available Crosby insisted on recording his weekly prime time program. CBS and NBC soon followed the ABC lead.

Development of LP Recording Meanwhile, in the mid-1940s CBS had assigned Peter Goldmark, head of the network's research laboratories, to explore ways of improving the technology of disc recording. In his autobiography, Goldmark says he was amazed to discover that the old-fashioned phonograph technology had never been subjected to modern, systematic scientific analysis (1973: 134).

Goldmark took the entire process apart, piece by piece, from the recording microphone to the playback speaker, analyzing each component and the relationships of one to another. In the experimental recording studio he used actual gunshots (particularly difficult sounds to record), fired into a mattress, as a test sound. The first recorded shot "sounded like a baked potato falling on the floor" (Goldmark, 1973: 136). He had a long way to go, but by 1948 CBS was able to announce its new long-playing (LP) 33 1/3-rpm records and new playback equipment to go with them.

CBS's arch-rival, RCA, countered with the 45-rpm "extended play" recording, but soon had to accept the longer-play CBS system as well. Both systems use vinyl — light, flexible, and durable, a great improvement over the old 78-rpm shellac. More grooves per inch and slower turntable speeds enable dramatic increases in playing time. For the first time music lovers could hear long pieces played back without interruption. Well-designed electronic components greatly improved quality and reduced noise. These improvements soon started a boom in high-fidelity music, which in turn increased public interest in the "hi-fi" capabilities of FM broadcasting.

The Role of Rock   If music had been important to radio during the pretelevision era, after television began it became all-important. With the loss of network dramas, variety shows, quiz games, and documentaries, radio programming fell back essentially to music and news/talk, with music occupying by far the majority of time on most stations. Providentially for radio, this programming transition came at a time when a new musical culture was arising, one that was to find in radio an ideally hospitable medium.

Early in the 1950s, a Cleveland DJ named Alan Freed gained national recognition. Freed

began playing a strange new sound. A sound that combined elements of gospel, harmony, rhythm, blues, and country. He called it "rock and roll." And people everywhere began to listen. . . . It transcended borders and race. It was enjoyed down South as well as in the North. The music was no longer segmented. Both blacks and whites were

able to listen. . . . Rock and roll sang to the teenager; it charted his habits, his hobbies, his hangups. (Drake-Chenault, 1978: 1)

Rock became the vehicle for expressing feelings about the expanding generation gap. Music spoke the language of the counter-establishment and took up its movements, one by one — civil rights, sexual freedom, drugs, opposition to the Vietnam war, and general rebelliousness. "Before the advent of rock, the arts had never attempted to deal with such passions in quite so direct and democratic a way" (Rockwell, 1979).

Radio proved to be the ideal outlet for this new form of expression. Rock lyrics spread the slogans of the disenchanted and the disestablished in a coded language, in defiance of the stuffy standards that broadcasting had previously sought to maintain. In fact, with prompting from the Nixon White House, the FCC caused an uproar in 1971 when it warned licensees that it was their duty to know what the lyrics were saying about drugs. Commissioner Nicholas Johnson, an outspoken supporter of the youth culture, strongly dissented, but a court appeal against the FCC failed (478 F2d 594, 1973).

Elvis Presley made his first television appearance in 1956 (from the waist up), but television lagged behind radio as a medium for rock music. From the youthful audience's point of view, television was the establishment medium, identified with big advertising and committed to broad mass appeal programming. From the rock stars' point of view, television networks were too easily shocked by their radical styles. Moreover, the technical inferiority of television sound failed to do justice to their music, while the ordinary live-audience television studio created a depressing, stuffy atmosphere (Gunther, 1978). Radio therefore became the primary medium of the new musical culture, working hand in glove with the recording industry and responding instantly to every nuance of change in musical fashions.

7.8 Radio's Response to TV Competition

Decline of Networks   First to suffer from television inroads were the radio networks. Television swiftly captured the mass audience, luring away the major advertisers and with them the major performers. Declining income told the story in a nutshell. In 1948, the year that television began its phenomenal growth, the radio networks and their few owned-and-operated stations earned $18 million. By 1958 their income had dropped to zero. Total income of the rest of the stations dropped in the same period from $46 million to $41 million, but by 1958 twice as many stations claimed a slice of the pie. On an average, each station earned only half as much in 1958 as it had in 1948.

Radio's Identity Crisis   As radio stations continued to expand in number and shrink in revenue, they faced a growing problem of *anonymity*. Cast adrift from their network program moorings, stations floundered in a sea of sameness. Networks had given their affiliates ready-made personalities and unaffiliated stations were few enough in number to have relatively little difficulty in creating recognizable independent public images. With the loss of star talent to television and the cutback in network program schedules, all stations became very much alike. In metropolitan areas it was possible to tune in to scores of different radio stations, all sounding pretty much the same.

The answer to radio's identity crisis came with *formula* programming. It was first em-

ployed with striking success in the late 1950s in the form of "Top-40" programming. The name referred to the practice of rigidly limiting DJs to a prescribed *playlist* of currently best-selling popular recordings. Gordon McLendon, a colorful sportscaster and station owner, is one of those credited with launching the format.

Another pioneer, Todd Storz, applied the Top-40 formula to group-owned stations. Such innovators frequently moved bottom-ranked stations to the first rank in their markets in a matter of months.

Top-40 Radio   The prescribed playlist removed the DJ from the position as sole arbiter of musical programming. Designing the all-important playlist soon came to involve a great deal more than simply looking up the latest popularity charts in *Billboard* or some other trade publication. Much ingenuity and research went into deciding which and how many tunes should be considered the current hits, which versions of them to feature, how frequently each should be played in the program "mix," when an established tune should be dropped, when a new one picked up, how often and when to insert a "golden oldie."

In addition to prescribing a playlist, Top-40 stations mandated a hard-driving announcing style and the suppression of DJ improvisation, liberal use of such production gimmicks as echo and filter, station identifications wrapped up in tricky jingles, frequent repetition of catch-phrases and slogans, and constant hammering on identity by means of attention-grabbing promotional contests.

An hour's monitoring of a Storz Top-40 station in the late 1950s yielded the following statistics: 125 program items in the single hour; 73 time, weather, promotional, and other brief announcements; 58 repetitions of call letters; a three-and-a-half minute news-cast featuring accidents and assaults, each item averaging two sentences in length. The overall effect was loud, brash, fast, hypnotic — and memorable. The station acquired an instantly recognizable "sound." No other station on the dial in a Storz market sounded anything like the newly programmed Storz station.

The dramatic success of the Top-40 formula came as much from its ruthlessness in repelling listeners as in its skillfulness in attracting them — a seeming paradox to programmers who still thought in old-fashioned, pretelevision, family-audience terms. They could not conceive of deliberately offending listeners. Formula programmers, however, had learned that consistency was the secret of success. They defined a specific audience *segment* (in terms of age and musical taste), programmed relentlessly for that segment no matter how many other segments took offense, and fulfilled the formula with unwavering consistency. Formula programmers cheerfully scrapped beloved old programs that had been attracting loyal audiences for decades but which struck false notes in the station's new sound.

The second ingredient in Top-40 success came from equally single-minded dedication to ceaseless promotion and advertising. Everything possible was done to imprint call letters and dial position indelibly on the listener's mind. Tens of thousands of dollars were spent on prizes to the winners of "treasure hunts" and other promotional contests. Such efforts were redoubled during "sweeps" — the intermittent periods during which national and audience measurement firms collect listening data (§14.2).

Many stations have been penalized for using contests (some of them syndicated) that violated the federal antilottery law (§15.7). Moreover promotional contests sometimes encouraged such unruly conduct by frenzied

contestants that the FCC issued a warning against causing public alarm, infringing on property and privacy rights, and creating traffic jams and other hazards requiring police intervention (2 FCC 2d, 464, 1966).

Extension of the Top-40 Principle

Top-40 was not, of course, the only possible formula. Let several stations in a market convert to Top-40 and soon all begin to sound about the same. But the larger lesson of the Top-40 formula or format* was to show program strategists that highly disciplined programming aimed at well-defined audience segments could overcome anonymity and create a loyal, if limited, following. Dozens of different music formats and subformats as well as talk formats have since emerged. Modern radio programming demands constant improvisation and experimentation as music fads come and go and as youthful audiences grow up and shift their loyalties.

Defining target segments of the audience is made easier by the fact that *demographics* — age, sex, and rural vs. urban residence in particular — have a strong statistical relationship to program tastes. Twice as many people in the 64-and-up group prefer MOR (middle-of-the-road) stations as do people in the 18–24 age group, for example. Three times as many rural as urban listeners prefer "country" stations. On the other hand, the trendiness of musical fads makes it impossible for a station to rest on its oars once it develops a successful formula. Stations constantly change formulas as fads come and go. Disco

---

*The terms "formula" and "format" are used interchangeably, though "formula" tends to focus attention on program *ingredients* (in the sense of "recipe"), while "format" tends to focus on program *structure* (in the sense of "layout").

music was a striking example in the late 1970s. Many stations scrapped their existing formulas to get on the disco bandwagon, only to find its popularity wilting, sometimes within months of its adoption.

Format Syndicators So exacting has the art of program formula design and execution become that many stations now employ the services of firms known as *format syndicators.* They provide what amounts to a new form of syndication,* in which the syndicator supplies not only actual program material but also a wide range of advisory services. Syndicators guide stations in every nuance of programming, program promotion, and research, charging each subscribing station fees ranging from several hundred to several thousand dollars a month.

About a dozen major companies operate in the format syndication field. Bill Drake of Drake-Chenault Enterprises, believed to be the most influential programmer in the field of radio today, led the reaction to the excesses of the original Top-40 formula. A 1971 *Broadcasting* special report, called "On the Leading Edge of Broadcasting," credited Drake with "cleaning up" radio:

He did it by first believing that the radio listener was being insulted as well as assaulted by the top-40 sounds as broadcast [in the 1950s], then by proving that the broadcaster stood to gain by catering to these sensibilities rather than offending them. The first station given the Drake treatment

(KGB [AM] San Diego) went from last to first position in 63 days. (West, 1971: 44)

Drake-Chenault, founded in 1963, is the oldest and probably the biggest format syndicator. Its eight formats aimed at specific demographic segments, include for example "Contempo-300," appealing to the 18–44 group, and the "XT-40," appealing to the 18–34 group. Drake-Chenault also syndicates music packages such as its 48-hour *History of Rock 'n' Roll*.

Another popular format syndication firm, Schulke Radio Productions (SRP), offers a service designed especially for stereo FM stations. The basic SRP library consists of 130 tapes, each holding four quarter-hour segments (minus time for local insertions). Two days of production effort go into the preparation of each one-hour tape to achieve a quality that SRP calls "matched flow." In the course of a year at least 80 new tapes are added. Each quarter-hour is programmed individually to fit into a particular hour of the 24-hour broadcast day, carefully calculated to match audiences available in each of eight different day parts. In addition, the formula reflects changes between spring/summer ("happier, more up-tempo") and fall/winter ("more romantic"). The client station gets a manual of instructions along with the tapes, additional services such as a promotional kit, and ongoing advice based on monitoring of station output. SRP's "beautiful music," bland and unobtrusive, is aimed primarily at the 18–49 female audience on the theory that women "dominate" male listening in this age category.

Station Automation Over a third of the radio stations on the air use some degree of automation, most commonly to handle routine logging of program details and billing of

---

*Conventional radio program syndication also occurs, with packaged features varying in length from a few minutes to many hours available as ready-made program items. A popular example is *American Top-40*, a weekly four-hour package of music, interviews, and comments heard in over 500 markets. The syndication of entire formats seems to have been inspired by a practice that arose in the 1950s, when successful DJs such as Martin Block (§7.4) began selling their programs to more than one station.

advertisers.* Much of the work in program, production, and business departments is highly repetitive and so lends itself readily to automation. The daily program log, for example, normally requires only minor updating from day to day. Most of the items such as commercial, public service, promotional, and station identification announcements, remain in place over a period of time. Automated systems provide for deleting old and adding new material without altering the rest.

More sophisticated automation systems can carry out most programming, production, traffic, and engineering functions. They make an ideal marriage with syndicated music formats, which demand precise controls over content and timing. Sophisticated automation uses microprocessors and digital memories, keyboards on which instructions can be typed out in plain English, video-screens that give the keyboard operator instructions and information on the status of the system, and "hard copy" printers that deliver information for the record, such as program logs (Exhibit 7.8).

7.9 Specialty Radio Formulas

Although the great majority of radio stations employ music formulas, among the 8,000-plus commercial stations on the air every conceivable variation occurs. Some try to broaden their appeal by "dayparting" — alternating formats to suit different parts of the day. For example, some use an all-news for-

mat during drive-times, shifting to MOR music at other times. Some build up DJ personalities, others suppress them. Some abide by rigid formulas, some favor free-form programming. Even the old-fashioned general interest program philosophy still claims some followers. The variety of programming available is truly prodigious, despite the essential sameness of the typical music formulas.

All-News Format   A particularly striking example of the parsimony principle at work, the all-news station, began to emerge in the 1960s. In a sense the name is a misnomer because there is nowhere near enough fresh, relevant news available to fill every single hour of programming. So-called all-news stations actually devote only a quarter or less of their time to news, and even that small news budget is repeated frequently. The rest of the time is occupied by many kinds of non-news informational and service features. All-news stations count on holding the attention of listeners only for about twenty minutes at a time, long enough for them to arm themselves with the time of day, the latest news headlines, weather tips, and information about driving conditions.

This "revolving door" programming principle demands a large audience reservoir to draw upon. Moreover, all-news stations are expensive to program. In the top 500 stations (the 10 leading stations in the top 50 markets) only 15 claim to be all-news stations (*Broadcasting,* 25 Aug. 1980).

Talk Formats   More widespread, though still representing a minority of only about three percent of the formats in use, are the talk and information stations. Typically these combine in-studio and telephone interviews with listener two-way telephone talk.

The commercial viability of the two-way

---

*Automated transmitter systems (ATS) are another option. First authorized by the FCC in 1977, ATS provides for automatic adjustment of power and modulation levels. If, despite the adjustments, authorized levels are exceeded or malfunctions develop, the system shuts itself down and sends an alarm signal to an engineer.

telephone format is affected by the fact that it attracts an older and generally conservative class of listeners — people who have both the time and the inclination to engage in polemics with talk-show hosts. Program directors must take care lest a small but highly vocal group of repeat callers, often advocates of extremist causes, dominate the talk, killing advertiser interest.

Religious Formats Broadcasting has always attracted religious organizations and charismatic figures. Over fifty religious organizations held station licenses in the 1920s,

**Exhibit 7.8
Radio program automation**

This example of an installation at KYYX(FM) in Seattle shows three modes of tape playback — conventional reel-to-reel machines (left), banks of individual cartridge players called Instacarts (center), and oval lazy-susans called Gocarts that revolve to move cartridges into position for playback (right). The three different playback modes allow efficient integration of varied program elements such as music, commercials, promos, PSAs, and IDs, which are automatically switched on and off in sequence according to the program log.

Source: IGM Communications.

but, like the educational licensees, most of them later gave up their grants. Only a dozen of these pioneer AM stations survive, but more recently FM encouraged a resurgence of religious radio stations. According to the president of the National Religious Broadcasters (NRB), which had over 800 members in 1979, some 600 radio stations "broadcast religious content virtually fulltime and are owned by evangelical believers" (Armstrong, 1978: 56). Other estimates suggest that the number of radio stations identified at least in part with religious programming runs as high as 1,400.

The practice of selling time to promoters of religious programming, one of the most striking features of modern radio, has always been controversial, and many stations still oppose it.* Nevertheless, such sales amount to a multimillion-dollar business that even nurtures its own specialized advertising agencies. Paid religious radio programming is in fact so widespread that a world directory of stations that accept such business has been published (ICB, 1973). Much of this programming consists of old-fashioned back-to-the-Bible fundamentalist preaching, but there are also recognized religious musical formulas — traditional "gospel," "contemporary Christian," and "Christian rock" (Routt et al., 1978: 211).

Free-Form Radio   In the 1960s, as a reaction to rigidly formatted radio and as an expression of dissent from established values, some small stations began what was called "underground" or "free-form" radio. They were mostly FM stations, willing and able to risk experimentation. "Some great things were done," recalls one observer.

*The Radio Code of the National Association of Broadcasters is silent on the subject, but the Television Code states: "A charge for television time to churches and religious bodies is not recommended."

"Tough, creative, unpolished, kinky scenes, but great. FM radio was a world full of surprises, like the world of early television" (Pichaske, 1979: 151).

Particularly influential in this movement was a small group of stations called by their leading champion, Lorenzo Milam, "free-form noninstitutional radio." The original inspiration came from Lew Hill, an idealist who initiated the movement when he founded KFPA (FM) in Berkeley, California, in 1949, under the umbrella of the Pacifica Foundation, so named because of Hill's lifelong devotion to pacifism (Trufelman, 1979). Four more stations have since been added to the group, in Houston, Los Angeles, New York City, and Washington, D.C. Pacifica stations operate noncommercially, depending on listeners and foundations for financial support, supplemented by income from a news bureau and a tape syndication service.

The Pacifica stations have been constantly embroiled in legal challenges, internal disputes, and outrageous programming experiments. The Pacifica name is attached to the most significant Supreme Court broadcasting obscenity decision, the "seven dirty words" case (§17.2). Pacifica stations have scheduled such unusual features as the news read in Mandarin Chinese, a reading of all the Nixon tapes that have been released, letters from the kidnappers of Patty Hearst during their standoff with authorities, recitations of lengthy novels such as Tolstoy's *War and Peace* and Joyce's *Ulysses* in their entirety, and a two-hour opera improvised on the air by phone-in singers. Absurd though many Pacifica programs have been, limited though their audiences have remained, they have played a useful role in shaking up established radio. Hundreds of stations have benefited, if only indirectly, from Pacifica's challenge to the safe, the conventional, and the routine (Post, 1974).

According to Lorenzo Milam's idealistic theory of noninstitutional radio:

A radio station should be a place in the community for concerned and talented and plain-home-folk individuals to have a chance to express themselves. In the place you live right now, there are hundreds of secret talents: there is someone who collects (and loves) old jazz; there are politically aware people — who can speak to reality, and raise so many consciousnesses in the process. . . . There are individuals, walking down the street right now, right there: live, living people who can play the guitar or the kazoo or the harp — people who would be delighted to know that there is one door to the ether which is open and free to them: a door to all the hungry minds and souls of so many people who will, at last, know (through your station) that they are not alone. (1972: 43)

7.10 Fate of Network Radio

By the mid-1950s the complacent radio network way of life of pretelevision days was rapidly fading away. As William Paley recalled it:

Although [CBS's] daytime schedule was more than 90 percent sponsored, our prime-time evening shows were more than 80 percent sustaining. Even our greatest stars could not stop the rush to television. Jack Benny left radio in 1958; Bing Crosby left nighttime radio in 1957 and quit his daytime program in 1962. It was sad to see them and other old-timers go. Amos 'n' Andy, which had been on radio since 1926 and on a network since 1929, left the air in 1960. (1979: 227)

The ultimate blow came when radio stations actually began refusing to renew network contracts — a startling change, considering that previously a network affiliation

had always been regarded as a precious asset. But rigid network commitments interfered with the freedom that stations needed to put their new tailor-made, post-television program formulas into effect. Only a third of the stations had network affiliations by the early 1960s. Networks scaled down their service to brief hourly news bulletins, short information features, a few public affairs programs, and occasional on-the-spot sports events.

Revival Although slower to revive than the stations, radio networks climbed back somewhat from their low ebb of the 1960s. In 1979 they still accounted for only about four percent of radio's total advertising revenue. Nevertheless, new networks are emerging, with a dozen already in business and still more promised. One reason for the increase is that in 1977 the FCC revised its definition of what constitutes a radio network, broadening it to include the audio services supplied by the national news agencies.

Compared to the stability of television affiliations, those of radio stations seem somewhat casual. It is not unusual for one station to appear in the affiliation lists of two or three networks, and affiliates often carry only a small part of the offerings of their networks. For these reasons the numbers of affiliates claimed by each network are meaningful only in general terms. In 1980 the leading radio networks in terms of affiliates, expressed in round numbers, were: ABC 1,700 (divided among four subnetworks); UPI Audio, 1,000; Mutual, 950; AP Audio, 700; CBS, 350; NBC, 300. Smaller chains included the National Black Network, RKO, and Sheridan.

Adaptation One of the more imaginative network responses to the new demands of formula radio was that of ABC in 1968. Recognizing the central role played by audience segmentation in station programming, ABC designed four different network services, each with a different type of audience in mind. Selection of network news and features and the styles of presentation were adjusted to suit specific audience age ranges and to blend smoothly into local program formulas. ABC adopted the following alternatives (affiliates as of 1980 in round numbers):

■ *American Contemporary Radio* tries to complement the style of rock stations, targeting the 18–24 age group (about 400 affiliates).
■ *American FM Radio* matches the needs of FM stereophonic stations with appeals to teens and young adults (about 200 affiliates).
■ *American Entertainment Radio* appeals to "up-tempo" middle-of-the-road music stations, aiming at the big midrange audience segments aged 18–49 (about 500 affiliates).
■ *American Information Radio* seeks to please the followers of MOR music and all-talk formulas aimed at the older audience group (about 600 affiliates).

ABC spaces out its short news feeds to the four sets of affiliates throughout each hour, using the intervening time to feed sports, features, and commentaries on a closed-circuit basis for later playback by the stations. This scheduling plan gets maximum use out of its single network of interconnecting relay circuits. The subnetwork plan also enables ABC to have more than one affiliate in a single market, something that had been forbidden by the old chain broadcasting rules adopted during the heyday of network radio.

Another interesting network adaptation is that of the Mutual Broadcasting System's *Larry King Show*, which capitalizes on the example of the local all-talk format. Reversing the accepted wisdom that network radio segments must be short and punchy, MBS offers an all-night talk show, lasting from midnight to 5:30 A.M. Listeners find the blend of interviews, two-way telephone talk, and badinage by talk host King so fascinating they are willing to pay for long-distance calls from all over the nation and from Canada as well, sometimes waiting for hours to get through to the MBS studio in Arlington, near Washington, D.C. Guests are fascinated by the experience of receiving calls in quick succession from knowledgeable listeners scattered across dozens of different states.

Program adaptations such as the ABC and Mutual examples represent a comedown from the palmy days when stars like Bing Crosby, Bob Hope, Fred Allen, and Jack Benny dominated the airways. But these adaptations helped give network radio a new lease on life as a minor but seemingly permanent feature of the radio scene.

Summary

The post-1928 period for radio began with the Great Depression, a time when the new medium helped relieve the universal gloom. Broadcasting at the network level was generally conservative and cautious during this period, but there was also a less decorous aspect of radio — stations that served as personal mouthpieces. Two such stations lost their licenses in the early 1930s because of irresponsible programming.

After the Depression years came World War II, during which radio news came of age. In the postwar period television undermined traditional radio network programming. During the 1960s radio stations found new roles to play, emphasizing musical formats. By 1980 some 8,000 commercial radio stations were on the air, yet the medium prospered. There was even a resurgence of interest in network radio.

Introduced during the 1930s, FM radio was held back by the simultaneous emergence of more attention-compelling television and by the reluctance of AM stations to give FM free reign to develop. Not until the 1960s did FM begin its major growth. The FCC's nonduplication rule in 1964 gave it a big boost. Now the audiences for FM and AM are about equal.

Radio programming development was affected by the medium's voraciousness, which made necessary the sparing, repeated, and shared use of program materials. Soap operas, game shows, and DJ programs were early examples of parsimonious use of resources. Networks exemplify shared use of materials. The original two national networks, NBC (Red and Blue) and CBS, expanded to four in the 1940s with the emergence of MBS and the sale of NBC Blue, which became ABC. CBS originally played second fiddle to NBC, but climbed to first place by developing a superlative news operation and by raiding NBC's talent pool. ABC assumed the third position, MBS the fourth.

At first the traditional press associations and news organs resisted radio's intrusion into the news field, but during World War II radio news assumed great importance. During this period Edward R. Murrow, broadcasting's most distinguished journalist, emerged as a key radio personality and executive.

Recorded music had great importance in radio station programming from the outset because it enabled repeated use of program materials. But radio's use of recorded music was impeded at first by high costs imposed by music licensing organizations and the musicians' union. Later, after these problems receded, the advent of rock and roll and the political overtones that music took on during the 1960s contributed to radio's revival. Recording technology, much improved by the introduction of LP and ET recordings, stimulated interest in music and hence eventually also the growth of FM.

Radio's decline as a result of television and its subsequent recovery hinged on the realization that radio was no longer a family medium. Basically this meant adopting highly structured and readily recognizable program formats aimed at small audience segments. Starting with the Top-40 format, this trend spread and accelerated rapidly in the 1960s. Syndicated format companies sprang up to assist in the process, which was also aided by automation of production and programming functions. Radio networks survived, and today are even growing in numbers, by adapting their programming to fit the needs of stations using program formulas.

CHAPTER 8

Development of Commercial Television

8.1 Overview: The Contrast with Radio

Development of Technical Standards

The idea of wireless transmission of pictures occurred to inventors quite as early as the idea of wireless sound transmission. However, even after sound broadcasting became a reality, television still remained in the experimental stage.

This delay was partly because of the more sophisticated technology that television requires, but even more because of the need for *compatibility*, the need to adopt a single national standard specifying the details of the television signal. The act of standardizing such technical details as frame- and line-frequency freezes development at a particular level. If it turned out later that standards should have been set at a higher level, tremendous waste would occur because millions of receivers and much studio and transmitter equipment would be outmoded.

Setting television standards involved finding a compromise among the conflicting interests of patent holders, manufacturers, and government bureaucracies, all with their own economic and political concerns. For these reasons, in the years before 1948 television moved forward in fits and starts as standards were improved bit by bit and FCC permission was won to try the improvements out on the public.

This technological evolution went through two phases: that of mechanical scanning and that of electronic scanning. The latter began to take the lead in the early 1930s and had just begun to reach a satisfactory level when World War II interrupted further development. Accordingly, widespread introduction of modern television occurred only after the conclusion of the war.

The watershed year in the United States was 1948, when a series of technical, legal, economic, and organizational developments converged. Thus television as a functioning mass medium lagged some twenty years behind radio.

Radio Precedents

The very fact that radio broadcasting had already had two decades of growth as a mass medium gave television a different start. Networks immediately assumed a leading role in television because they furnished ready-made organizations and operational patterns for the new medium. Moreover, the very nature of television programming favored the network approach. The type of shoestring operation based on a turntable and a stack of recordings that served to get many small radio stations on the air was out of the question in television.

On the other hand, radio had come on the scene with the essential facility that the networks needed already in place — the nationwide web of long-distance telephone lines. Television had to await the development and installation of special coaxial cable and microwave relay links by AT&T. The first regular intercity relay circuit, running between New York and Washington, D.C., became available as early as 1946, the first transcontinental link five years later. A few months after the opening of the east-west link, Edward R. Murrow celebrated the occasion in a famous *See It Now* program on November 18, 1951 (Exhibit 8.1.1). Murrow showed both the Atlantic and the Pacific oceans, both the Brooklyn and the San Francisco Bay bridges, simultaneously on monitors in the control

Exhibit 8.1.1
See *It Now* joins Atlantic and Pacific

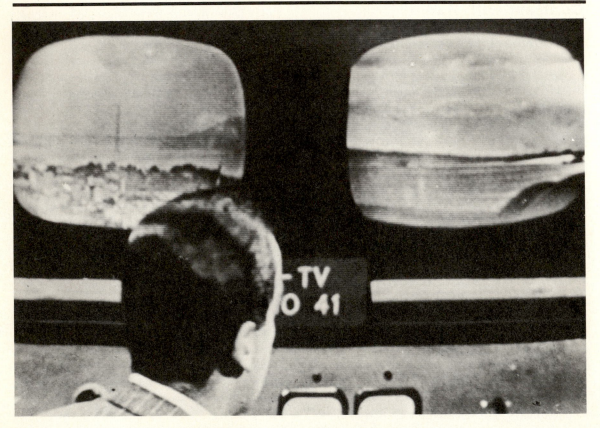

The famous scene on the first *See It Now* program in 1951, a shot of Ed Murrow in the control room looking at monitors showing simultaneous views of the Pacific and Atlantic oceans, symbolizing attainment of coast-to-coast television.

Source: CBS News.

room (he was the first to use the control room as a studio). Murrow's biographer called it "perhaps the most significant television half-hour presented on the home screen until then. . . . For the first time the continental sweep, dramatic power and sheer magic of television were displayed in the simplest and most striking way" (Kendrick, 1969: 335).

During these developmental years, however, full network competition was still not possible because on most routes AT&T could supply only a single relay channel. Taking turns using the cable, the networks could not offer affiliates a continuous sequence of programs.

The recorded alternative to a direct network feed was the *kinescope,* a filmed version of the television picture as it appeared on the face of a receiver tube (§4.3). These filmed "recordings" of network programs were available by 1948 but looked so flat and unrealistic that they did little to encourage people to buy receivers. Nearly a decade went by before videotape solved the problem of television recording.

Growth of Stations Television station growth patterns differ markedly from those of radio, as a comparison of Exhibits 7.1 and 8.1.2 shows. Despite competition from television, the upward curve of radio growth has continued throughout its history. When usable AM channels began to dry up, FM took over and continued the trend. The VHF television growth curve began to level off by 1965; after an irregular growth pattern in the 1950s, UHF growth leveled off by 1970. Since then the number of commercial television stations has risen only slightly.

These differences between the two broadcast media reflect differences in costs and in channel availabilities. More commercial television stations would go on the air if it were possible for small markets to support the expense and if more channels became available in the larger markets.

8.2 Quest for High Resolution

Experimental television existed for decades before it became a mass medium. Early systems worked, but the pictures were far too crude to be regarded as anything but curiosities. The problem was basically one of obtaining sufficient resolution. A standard equal to that of home movies was needed for general public acceptance.

Nipkow's Scanning Wheel Mechanical television systems used the *scanning wheel* or disc, invented in 1884 by a German, Paul Nipkow. It was a large, flat metal disc, perforated with a series of small holes. Starting near the rim of the disc, the holes were regularly spaced in a spiral pattern. As the disc spun in front of an aperture, each hole scanned one line of the scene to be televised. Thus the number of holes in the disc determined the number of lines in each frame. A wheel on the order of two feet in diameter was needed to scan an area about the size of a postage stamp.

Two pioneers, Charles Jenkins in the United States and John Logie Baird in Britain, demonstrated mechanical systems in the 1920s. Jenkins's interest in television arose from the fact that he had developed several important motion picture projection patents. In 1928 he began regular transmissions of what he called "radiomovies." He used a 48-hole Nipkow disc, spinning at 15 revolutions per second — line and frame frequencies sufficient to yield only an exceedingly crude picture. Amateurs could build a simple receiving

device capable of displaying a one-inch sil-
houetted picture. Despite their crudity, the
Jenkins telecasts from an experimental station in Washington, D.C., enjoyed considerable popularity. Because he conducted his
experiments in the low-frequency band instead of the VHF and UHF bands we now
use, his transmissions could travel long distances — up to 2,000 miles when sky-wave

propagation conditions were favorable (Lachenbruch, 1971).

Baird, working in Great Britain, set up the
world's first television company in 1925 to
exploit a 30-line mechanically scanned television system. The next year the British government authorized experimental transmissions and the sale of receivers. Baird's
persistent efforts, along with the competing

**Exhibit 8.1.2
Growth of television stations, 1948–1980**

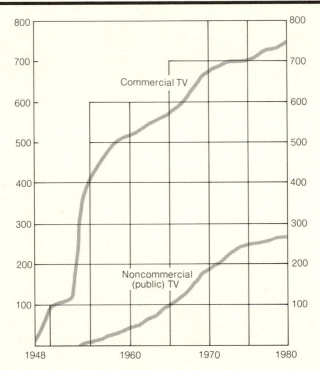

The modern TV era started in 1948, with 16 stations on the air. A few more than a
hundred stations had been authorized when the 1948–1952 freeze imposed a
temporary ceiling. After the thaw the number shot up remarkably until about 400
was reached in 1955. Growth began to slow down at that point, but has never
actually stopped. Noncommercial stations grew more slowly, starting with the first
two in 1954.

Source: Adapted from *Stay Tuned: A Concise History of Broadcasting*, by Christopher H.
Sterling and John M. Kittross. Copyright 1978 by Wadsworth Publishing Company, Inc.
Reprinted by permission of Wadsworth Publishing Company, Belmont, CA.

efforts of the British Electric and Musical Industries, Ltd. (EMI), culminated in 1936 with the first high-definition television to be offered on a regular basis to the public, the British Broadcasting Corporation's television service.*

Baird had won the battle, but was soon to lose the war, for the BBC hedged its bets. It alternated two competing systems — Baird's 240-line mechanical system and the rival all-electronic 405-line EMI system. Within less than a year the BBC discontinued Baird's operation, marking the end of the long campaign to win acceptance for mechanically scanned television. "Baird occupies an important but curious position in history," concluded Asa Briggs, the British broadcasting historian. "He publicized television more effectively than any other individual, but eventually when television established itself it was not on the lines he had so long envisaged" (1965: 523).

The BBC closed down its pioneer television service at the outbreak of World War II in 1939. Just a few months earlier an American version of electronic television had made its public debut at the New York World's Fair.

Farnsworth and Zworykin The names most prominent in U.S. television developments after Baird's mechanical system was abandoned were two inventors of widely different backgrounds, Philo T. Farnsworth and Vladimir Zworykin. Farnsworth, an American genius who was virtually self-taught, developed an electronic (non-mechanical) scanning system he called "image dissection." He

*Who was "first" depends on what constitutes "high-definition." In the early 1930s even 180-line pictures were considered high-definition, and by this standard Germany began regular television broadcasts in Berlin in March 1933.

is credited with the invention of the basic methods still used for suppressing retrace path and for inserting synchronizing pulses.

In the early 1900s Zworykin had been a brilliant student of the great Russian experimental physicist Boris Rosing. He emigrated to the United States after World War I in 1919 and worked as an engineer for Westinghouse. In 1923 he applied for patents covering the basic all-electronic television system, but he immediately found himself embroiled in a seven-party patent interference suit. One of the seven parties was Farnsworth, who finally won a key decision on his electron optics patent in 1934. RCA acknowledged Farnsworth's victory by paying him a million dollars for the rights to use his discoveries. In the interim Zworykin had won lasting fame as the inventor of the *iconoscope,* the electronic camera pickup tube, for which he was granted a patent in 1928 (Exhibit 8.2.1).

In 1930, Zworykin became head of a celebrated research group of over 40 engineers at the RCA laboratories in Camden, New Jersey. Formed from a merger of the television research programs of General Electric and Westinghouse as well as that of RCA, the Camden team mounted a systematic investigation of all aspects of television development, aimed at solving not only technological problems but also the subjective problem of setting the specific standards of picture quality that would be needed to win full public acceptance. No one knew for sure how good television had to be to persuade the mass public to invest in receivers. The RCA studies made it clear that much higher resolution than had been obtained in the early 1930s was essential for mass acceptance.

During the 1930s the Camden team tackled and solved all the outstanding problems. They progressed to higher and higher line frequencies, year by year, from the 60-line standard of 1930 (Exhibit 8.2.2) to 120 in 1931, 240 in 1933, 343 in 1936, and 441 in 1939.

They increased image size and brightness, introduced interlace scanning, adapted equipment to use the newly opened VHF band, and introduced sets into homes on an experimental basis.

NTSC Standards Adopted   By 1939 the Camden group felt ready for a major public demonstration. RCA chose the 1939 New York World's Fair with its "World of Tomorrow" theme, as a suitably prestigious and

**Exhibit 8.2.1
Vladimir Zworykin**

The inventor holds the 1923 invention for which he is most famous, the iconoscope camera tube. RCA made Zworykin an honorary vice president of the company upon his official retirement in 1962, but he was still active in his late 80s at the company's Princeton, N.J., research laboratories.

Source: Brown Brothers.

symbolic launching pad. David Sarnoff personally introduced the 441-line RCA television demonstration, and President Franklin D. Roosevelt was among those televised at the fair (Exhibit 8.2.3). For the first time the U.S. general public had a chance to see (and to be seen on) modern television.

Nevertheless, these 1939 telecasts were still experimental. The Federal Communications Commission withheld permission for full-scale commercial operations pending industry-wide agreement on engineering standards. This came with the recommendations of the National Television Systems Committee (NTSC), representing the 15 major electronics manufacturers. In 1941 the FCC adopted the NTSC standards for black-and-white television, including the 525-lines per-frame and the 30-frames-per-second standards still in effect.

Within the year the FCC authorized construction of the first 18 commercial stations; but on December 7 the Japanese bombed Pearl Harbor and the United States was at war. Five months later production on civilian consumer electronics came to a halt and television development had to be shelved for the duration.

World War II (1941–1945) and Its Aftermath   During the war six experimental stations remained on the air, located in New York (two stations), Schenectady, Philadelphia, Chicago, and Los Angeles. They devoted their brief schedules (they were required to be on the air only four hours a week) primarily to civilian defense programs. About 10,000 sets were in use, half of them in New York City.

The end of the war in 1945 did not, as some expected, bring an upsurge in television activity, despite a backlog of 158 pending station applications. Investors held back

**Exhibit 8.2.2
First U.S. television star**

A 12-inch model of Felix the Cat (a popular cartoon movie character of the 1920s), posed on a revolving turntable, was used at the RCA laboratories as a moving subject to televise during the development of electronic television.

The image at left shows how Felix looked on television in 1929 when picture definition was still only 60 lines per frame.

Source: Photos courtesy of the National Broadcasting Company, Inc.

for several reasons. The 1941 decision on standards had left the issue of color television unresolved, and many experts believed that all-out development should await adoption of a color system. Hence there were doubts as to the permanence of the 1941 standards. Moreover, potential investors wondered whether the high costs of sets would repel buyers who were accustomed to inexpensive radios, and whether the major advertisers would be willing to pay the higher cost of television programming. Owners of successful radio stations, accustomed to making money with the greatest of ease, were reluctant to take on the formidable complexities of an unknown new medium. On March 18,

Exhibit 8.2.3
Sarnoff introduces TV at the World's Fair, 1939

David Sarnoff presided at an historic occasion on April 20, 1939, when he stood before television cameras and dedicated RCA's pavilion at the 1939 World's Fair in New York. The dedication marked the first time that television covered a news event. Sarnoff delivered a speech, entitled "Birth of an Industry," that predicted television's future as a major entertainment and information medium.

Source: RCA News, New York.

1947, however, the FCC encouraged applicants by reaffirming the NTSC black-and-white standards and announcing that it had no intention of adopting color standards in the near future.

Two other favorable developments had occurred shortly before the FCC's decision: (1) the *image orthicon* camera tube, introduced in 1945, had improved camera sensitivity, eliminating the need for the uncomfortably high levels of studio light that the iconoscope had required; and (2) AT&T had begun to install intercity coaxial cable links to enable network interconnection, starting with the New York–Washington, D.C., link in 1946. In the summer and fall of 1947, the long-predicted rush into television finally began.

8.3 TV Freeze: 1948–1952

1948: Start of TV Era   Thus 1948 became a pivotal year in American television history — the turning point when the medium, after several false starts, finally began its explosive growth as a mass medium. For the first time the industry could move ahead on a firm footing.

During 1948 the number of stations on the air increased from 17 to 48. The FCC reported an "unprecedented surge in the number of applications for new television stations." The number of cities served by television went from 8 to 23. Set sales increased more than 500 percent over the 1947 level and by 1951 had already surpassed radio set sales. Increased opportunities for viewing in 1948 multiplied the audience in one year by an astonishing 4,000 percent.

In 1948 coaxial cables for network relays became available in the Midwest as well as on the East Coast, and regular network service began. Important advertisers started experimenting with the new medium. Large-scale programming emerged — the national political conventions, Milton Berle's *Texaco Star Theater*, Ed Sullivan's *Toast of the Town*, a telecast of the Metropolitan Opera production of Verdi's *Otello*. Between 1947 and 1948 the number of network prime-time television programs on the air per week jumped from 24 to 135.

Freeze Imposed (1948)   Television's growing pains were not yet over, however. The FCC's go-ahead for commercial television had made only 12 VHF channels available to serve the entire United States.* As more and more stations began to go on the air it became obvious that (1) the demand for stations would soon exceed the supply of channels, and (2) the FCC had not required enough geographical separation between stations on the same channel to prevent serious co-channel interference.

To forestall a potentially chaotic situation, on September 29, 1948, the FCC abruptly imposed a freeze on processing of further applications. The freeze did not affect applicants whose permits had already been approved; thus they were able to go ahead with construction of stations. As a result, for the nearly four years of the freeze, 108 "pre-freeze" stations had an enviable monopoly.

Enough stations were on the air throughout the freeze years to constitute a "critical mass," so that television's forward surge was not seriously inhibited. During the freeze the number of sets in use rose from a quarter-million to over 17 million. After heavy losses at the outset, by 1951 stations began to earn back their investment. The coaxial cable and

*Originally there were 13 channels, but channel 1 experienced too much interference from adjacent frequencies. It was reassigned in 1948 to land mobile communication. The rest were the same VHF channels, numbered 2 through 13, still in use today.

microwave networks joined the East Coast to the West Coast in 1951, inaugurating national network television, which soon reached 60 percent of American homes.

Sixth Report and Order (1952) Meanwhile, the FCC had been holding a series of hearings to settle the engineering and policy questions that had brought on the freeze. The long-awaited decision, the charter of present-day U.S. television, came on April 14, 1952, in the FCC historic *Sixth Report and Order* (41 FCC 148).* The new rules expanded the number of channels by supplementing the 12 existing VHF channels with 70 new channels in the UHF band (the feasibility of using this higher range of frequencies had been proved during World War II).

A table of 2,053 allotments awarded the use of one or more channels to each of 1,291 communities — a sharp contrast with the prefreeze plan, which had allotted channels to only 345 cities. Over 66 percent of the allotments were UHF. About 10 percent of the total were reserved for noncommercial educational use, mostly in the UHF band. Exhibit 8.3 shows how co-channel allotments are spread around the country to avoid interference and also gives an example of individual city allotments. The table of allotments has been amended many times, one of the more significant changes being an increase in educational reservations to about 35 percent of the total.†

*When faced with complex decisions the FCC often issues preliminary "reports and orders" for public comment before arriving at a final version. The fact that it took six such reports to decide on the television allotment plan is evidence of the complexity of the problem.
†Other major changes include reallocating Channel 37 to radio astronomy and Channels 70–83 to land-mobile use. In 1980 the FCC proposed over a hundred additional VHF channel allotments, to be made available as "drop-ins." These would be shoehorned into the allotment plan by reducing co-channel mileage separations and using directional antennas.

8.4 Implementation of Post-Freeze Allotment Plan

Tremendous pressures for new stations had built up during the freeze. In less than a year after the thaw, all outstanding uncontested applications had been granted. Then began the long-drawn-out process of deciding among competing applicants for the few, immensely valuable remaining channels in the most desirable markets. The number of stations more than tripled in the first post-freeze year (Exhibit 8.1.2).

Channel Distribution However, the new channel allotment plan had serious defects. For one thing, there still were not enough channels to give viewers in every market an equal number of choices. Ideally, every viewer would eventually have the choice of being able to tune in at least five *local* stations — an affiliate of each of the three commercial networks, a noncommercial station, and at least one independent station.

In practice 90 percent of the television *households* in the country can receive five or more stations. But only 8 percent of the *markets* in the country have five or more local stations. The entire state of New Jersey, for example, has no VHF station and only four or five UHF commercial stations. Yet New Jersey is flooded with signals from two major neighboring markets, New York and Philadelphia.

This inequitable distribution makes sense in commercial terms, but New Jerseyites resent the implied inferiority of being unworthy of a single VHF station. Originally the FCC allotted Channel 13 to Newark, New Jersey, just across the river from New York. This station proved commercially unviable, and after several changes of ownership it was

Exhibit 8.3
TV channel allotment plan

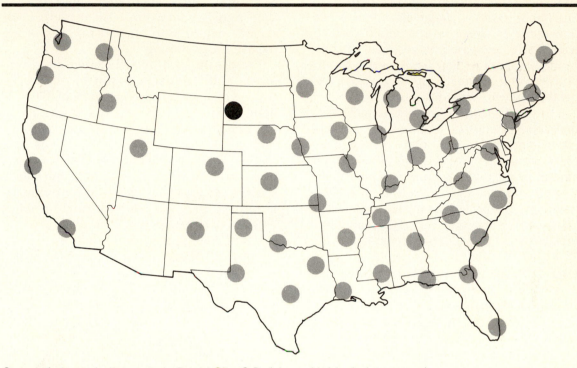

Status of channel allotments in Rapid City, S.D. (shown by black dot on map)
3 — Occupied by KOTA (NBC/CBS affiliate)
7 — Occupied by KEVN (ABC affiliate)
9 — Occupied by KBHE (noncommercial,
licensed to state ETV system)
15 — Not occupied
21 — Not occupied

The map shows the *occupied* Channel 7 allotments. They are scattered relatively
evenly throughout the country, separated from each other by a minimum of 170
miles. The list of all channels available in one of cities to which Channel 7 has
been allotted is shown above. Rapid City's UHF channels have not been activated,
but it gets service from translators that bring in signals of several stations allotted to
other cities in that region.

finally sold to New York's noncommercial (public) television interests in 1961 for over $6 million. It became WNET, one of the leading public stations. Later New Jersey petitioned the FCC for restitution. In 1980 the commission proposed to reallot Channel 9 from New York to New Jersey, subject to the outcome of a pending decision to take Channel 9 away from its current licensee.

The purchase by WNET of Channel 13 was indicative of another weakness of the allotment plan: in several of the biggest cities, New York, Los Angeles, and Philadelphia among them, the maximum feasible number of VHF channels had already been licensed before the freeze, so that it was impossible to designate noncommercial VHF channels in those cities in the allotment table.

UHF Dilemma   The inequities of channel distribution were increased by the FCC's decision to allocate television to both VHF and UHF channels, and, moreover, to *intermix* the two in many localities. The commission had tried originally to ensure equal coverage potentials for both VHF and UHF allotments by authorizing UHF to use much higher power, hoping in this way to overcome the inherent propagation weakness of UHF waves as compared to VHF waves. Even if added power could have had the desired effect, however, years went by before maximum-power UHF transmitters became available.* UHF transmitters cost more than VHF to install and operate, and at first there were no UHF receivers on the market. To pick up UHF stations, set-owners had to buy converters. Long after UHF was introduced, manufacturers continued to build VHF-only receivers

because of the low demand for all-channel sets. Viewers had no incentive to buy UHF receivers in areas where they could pick up VHF signals because in such markets UHF stations had little to offer in the way of attractive programming.

Faced with such overwhelming disadvantages, UHF television began to slip backward. From an initial high point of 120 stations in 1954 soon after the freeze was lifted, the number of UHF licenses steadily declined until the low point of only 75 stations was reached in 1960. (Exhibit 8.4) The FCC tried a variety of measures to encourage the failing stations. In Fresno, California, for example, it deleted the one VHF channel, making Fresno a five-station all-UHF market. But this *deintermixture* option could not be widely adopted without making a shambles of the entire allotment table.

In 1961 and 1962 the FCC financed a model station in New York to demonstrate the viability of a well-engineered UHF operation. The most useful step, however, was to compel manufacturers to equip all receivers with UHF tuning. This rule became effective in 1964, mandated by an amendment to Section 303 of the Communications Act of 1934. Television receiver manufacturers at first undermined the rule by installing continuous tuners, which the public found difficult to use. Not until the late 1970s was this problem resolved by the introduction of "click-stop" tuners. In 1980 the FCC was still struggling with the problem. In that year it released a special study on how to improve UHF reception (Free et al., 1980). It stressed the importance of upgrading receiving antennas.

In practice it appears that at present UHF stations can achieve only 80 to 85 percent of the coverage enjoyed by competing VHF stations, though UHF proponents still have

---

*The pioneer commercial UHF station, KPTV (Portland, Oregon), went on the air in September 1952, using an RCA experimental transmitter. The first maximum-power (5 million watts) UHF transmitter did not go on the air until 1974.

hope that improved receivers and antennas will some day equalize coverage with VHF except in areas of rough terrain and in cities with many tall buildings.

UHF's Growth By 1965 some of the FCC's efforts took effect and UHF began a steady, though not spectacular, growth. FCC financial reports indicate that until 1974 UHF stations as a group continued to lose money. Thereafter their profit margin increased each year.

Only 36 percent of the commercial UHF stations have network affiliations, as against 94 percent of the VHF stations. Uninhibited by fixed network program commitments, independent UHF stations have the freedom to counter their VHF competitors with alternative program offerings. For example, independents often schedule popular off-network syndicated series against network news, capitalizing on the fact that many viewers prefer entertainment to serious program fare. UHF stations are also freer to carry numerous live sports events that occur during the week. Programs cost too much to allow UHF stations to specialize narrowly as do formula radio stations, but Spanish and religious programming specializations have proved to be commercially viable in some cases. Another

Exhibit 8.4
TV channel utilization

Type of channel	Channels allotted	Channels in use[a]	Percentage in use
Commercial			
VHF	579	520	90
UHF	652	409	63
Public (noncommercial)			
VHF	136	114	83
UHF	567	193	34
Total, all types	1,934	1,236	64

Comment: This table refers to the FCC's allotment of specific channels for use, upon application, in specific communities. That a third of these allotments are unused appears to indicate a scandalous waste of spectrum space, but it must be borne in mind that the unused channels are assigned to small towns, or to cities that have several other channels in use. For example, none of the five channel allotments to communities in Delaware has been activated because that small state gets service from stations in nearby large cities such as Philadelphia.

[a]"In use" category includes stations licensed, those with construction permits, and those merely applied for.

Source: Based on 1980 data in FCC, *Television Channel Utilization.* FCC Mimeo 35899, 30 Oct. 1980, Table 1.

option is over-the-air subscription television, which so far has been offered only on UHF stations (§11.6).

Channel Utilization The decision as to whether to make use of available commercial channels depends entirely upon their economic viability; consequently in densely populated areas more could be used, while many channels lie idle in thinly populated areas. Overall, only 60 percent of the available channels have been activated, and percentages of UHF channels in use are much lower (Exhibit 8.4).

Low-Power TV Geographical coverage of television stations can be extended by low-power rebroadcast stations called *translators* (§4.7). They provide local community coverage, operating unattended on either UHF or VHF channels. Most are licensed to community groups that build them as cooperative ventures in order to get television service from regular stations too distant to be received directly. Community groups must secure special translator licenses and are not allowed to originate their own programs, with the exception of short emergency and fund-raising announcements. In sparsely settled areas of the West it is not uncommon for regular television stations to be rebroadcast by scores of translators.

One of the novel combinations of resources typical of the new technology is the possibility of feeding translators by satellite relays instead of confining them to the rebroadcasting of earth-bound television stations. This link-up would open the possibility of entire networks of translator stations.

In 1980 the FCC proposed a radical liberalization of rules for low-power television (LPTV). The proposal envisioned highly localized, personalized television stations, almost as free-wheeling as Citizens Band (CB) radio. They would have very low power (from a low of 10-watt VHF, up to 1,000-watt UHF) and would use any of the regular television channels, subject to their not interfering with full-power stations. They are thus comparable to Class II AM stations, which operate on the same clear channels as Class I stations, but only if they avoid causing interference. Licensing requirements would be simplified and operating and programming procedures would be virtually free of all regulation. Stations could combine at will the rebroadcast function of translators with unrestrained local origination of programs.

The proposal to introduce this new class of free-form television station generated a great deal of interest from would-be licensees. Their enthusiasm was not shared by existing commercial licensees, especially UHF owners, who feared that this new source of competition for audience attention might cancel the gains UHF has recently made. The FCC hoped to start licensing LPTV stations with minimum delay, dispensing with some of the time-consuming formalities usually attendant on licensing procedures. But the commission was inundated with an avalanche of applications, most of them mutually exclusive (that is, requiring hearings because of conflicting plans to cover the same areas). Rapid clearing of the backlog seemed unlikely when the FCC began sorting out the applications in 1981.

8.5 TV Network Rivalries

Color Rivalry RCA's leadership in the original development of television gave NBC a head start over the other networks. But television started in black and white, and CBS thought it saw an opportunity to counter NBC's advantage by capturing the lead in color. Peter Goldmark, head of CBS Laboratories, had developed a workable color system based on the old scanning wheel principle for its color component. The CBS system was *incompatible*, meaning that viewers would have to buy separate receivers to pick up color programs. Because its color system needed a wider channel than the NTSC black-and-white system, CBS urged the FCC to allocate channel space for color in the UHF band (this was before the freeze and the subsequent decision to add the present UHF channels).

Meanwhile, RCA continued working on its own compatible all-electronic color system. Round one went to RCA in 1946, when the FCC turned down CBS color. Round two went to CBS in 1950, when the FCC reversed itself and accepted the scanning wheel system after CBS staged a convincing demonstration of its workability. RCA countered with a lawsuit to overrule the FCC decision. In 1951 RCA lost the suit — round three to CBS. CBS alone began manufacturing color sets, while RCA continued doggedly to work on its compatible system. "I must admit a certain admiration for the cockiness of General Sarnoff," confessed CBS's Goldmark. "He was plucky, no doubt about it. Before he was through with the color war, he was to pour 150 million dollars into color-television research and development — the highest investment up to that time on a strictly private industrial gamble" (Goldmark and Edson, 1973: 117). Before CBS could gear up for full production, the Korean War (1950–1953) intervened, delaying further development. Finally, with the end of the Korean War came the end of the color war. Tired of wrangling, all parties accepted new standards proposed by the NTSC for an electronic color system, based primarily on

RCA's research and completely compatible with the existing black-and-white system already in use. This meant that black-and-white receivers already on the market could pick up color signals in black and white.

Eighteen cities saw the Pasadena Tournament of Roses in color on New Year's Day, 1954. This breakthrough did not, however, cause an immediate rush into color production by the networks. Nor was the public in a hurry to turn in its old monochrome sets. Five years after adoption of the NTSC color standards, only NBC was producing any programs in color. Full network color production in prime time did not come until 1966. Color may be said to have arrived by 1972, when about half the U.S. television homes had color sets. At that point *TV Guide* stopped tagging color program listings with a special symbol and began instead tagging black-and-white shows. Aside from small portables, virtually all receivers manufactured today are color sets.

Weaver's Innovations at NBC Most of NBC's early programming strategies sprang from the fertile imagination of Sylvester "Pat" Weaver, "a 6-foot, 4-inch, jug-eared redhead with a smiling open face," a Phi Beta Kappa key, and a magna cum laude degree from Princeton (Metz, 1977: 19). Weaver resigned his job as the broadcasting chief of a major advertising agency in 1949 to become NBC's vice president for television. He left NBC only six years later as chairman of the board, but in those few formative years made a permanent mark on television programming. Though assuredly an intellectual, Weaver had the common touch in mass entertainment without being common. Most presumed television "experts" at that time simply tried to adapt radio or the theater to television. Weaver's special talent was the ability to free himself of preconceived media habits and to look at television with a fresh vision. He foresaw, for example, that the single-sponsor show, the hallmark of big-time network radio, simply could not last in television.* Program costs would eventually become far too high for any but a few rich, highly prestigious corporations to bear, and even they would be able to afford full sponsorship only occasionally. Instead, Weaver introduced *segmented sponsorship,* which enabled a number of different advertisers to share the spotlight in a single program, and the *magazine format,* which combined a number of separate features within the framework of a single program. Disregarding conventional wisdom about the inviolability of established viewing habits, he disrupted regular schedules to run occasional one-time "spectaculars," 90 minutes long. The other networks refused to take such risks at first, but eventually, under the name "specials," Weaver's spectaculars became common practice on all networks.

William Paley at CBS shared Weaver's urge to recapture control of commercial entertainment from the advertising agencies, who had taken command during radio days (§6.6). They both recognized that advertiser control meant conservative, no-risk programming. Only the networks, Weaver said, could "gamble on shows, on talent, on projects; and we will lose in doing this all too often. But only a great network can afford the risk, and that is essentially why the great network service is so important to this country" (1955). As production costs rose, fewer advertisers could afford to supply programs. A study of prime-time program sources in the period 1957 to 1968 showed that advertisers declined as a source from 33 percent of the

total to 3 percent. Networks also declined, from producing 29 percent of their output to 16 percent. Packagers increased during the same period, producing 81 percent of all regularly scheduled prime-time programs by 1968 (Little, 1969: 1).

Two of Weaver's innovations are still on the air — *Today* (1952–) and *Tonight,* (1954–) "the perfect formats for live television from which all the other desk and sofa talk shows descend" (Brown, 1971: 235). Such extensions of network television into hitherto unprogrammed early morning and late evening hours were considered extremely radical. "Morning television was available here and there," wrote a chronicler of the *Today* program, "but watching it was a taboo . . . It was acceptable to listen to morning radio, but like sex and alcohol, television was deemed proper only after sundown" (Metz, 1977: 33).

Weaver staged *Today* for maximum attention, in full public view of passersby on New York's 49th Street, in a window-front RCA exhibition hall at Radio City. One of the features of the show was the hand-lettered signs people in the crowd on the street would hold up for the cameras, greeting the folks back home in Iowa. *Today* showcased a series of memorable television personalities such as Dave Garroway, Hugh Downs, Barbara Walters, Gene Shalit — and J. Fred Muggs (Exhibit 8.5.1). The last was an intelligent and mischievous chimpanzee whose antics captured popular attention, rocketing the show to the top — "the biggest one-year grosser" in broadcasting history in the 1950s (Metz, 1977: 95).

As a *Fortune* magazine writer put it at the time, Weaver had been "looked upon by many in the industry as a sort of personification of TV's potential scope, dynamism, and audacity" (Smith, 1958: 161). Despite Weaver's success with specific innovations,

*Following the radio precedent, early network television programs were single-sponsor shows, often featuring the names of their sponsors — *Texaco Star Theater* (1948–1956), *The Kraft Television Theater* (1947–1958), *The Philco TV Playhouse* (1948–1955), and so on.

Exhibit 8.5.1
Today, yesterday and today

The 1981 *Today* show stars (l. to r.) are Gene Shalit, critic; Jane Pauley, co-anchor with Tom Brokaw; and Willard Scott, weatherman, whose folksy humor helped considerably in establishing the program's contemporary easy-going image.

Dave Garroway, the original host of *Today* (1952–1961), is shown with J. Fred Muggs, the chimpanzee whose antics first brought success to the program. Muggs lasted over four years before becoming too rough for the rest of the cast to tolerate. The visiting chimp in the picture is Phoebe B. Beebe.

Source: Photo courtesy of the National Broadcasting Company, Inc.

CBS steadily gained in the *overall* ratings race with NBC during Weaver's tenure. In consequence, NBC let Weaver go. With his premature departure, said *Fortune*, "an entire programming philosophy was abandoned."

CBS Leadership   William Paley's struggle to prevail over prestigious NBC started to pay off in 1953 when CBS Television first became profitable — after a start-up investment of $60 million. By 1955 CBS achieved number-one place in the ratings, holding undisputed leadership for twenty-one years.

Paley had become chairman of the board of CBS in 1946, but he continued to act as the master programmer. On CBS's fiftieth anniversary, when Paley was seventy-six, it was reported that he still saw every program pilot, read many new scripts, and expected to have a say in the details of program decision making and scheduling. His instincts must have been right, for "no corporation can trace as long and unbroken an ascent to prosperity under the unquestioned control of a leader on active duty" (*Broadcasting*, 19 Sept. 1977).*

Another legendary programmer had a powerful impact on CBS in the early 1970s — Fred Silverman, recruited in 1963 as director of daytime programming and elevated to head of all CBS programming in 1970. In sharp contrast to that earlier innovator, Sylvester Weaver, Silverman comes from a lower middle-class background, son of a New York City television repairman. He earned a master's degree in broadcasting from Ohio State University, writing a thesis on ABC's television programming.

Studying such a novel subject — the emergence of a new television programming

philosophy — Silverman could not rely on books and scholarly journals for his sources. He had to interview the executives who made the programming decisions and study the results of their decisions as they unfolded on the television screen. He sent the completed study to network program executives — hardly the normal readers for MA theses, but they were impressed. "Reading the thesis," said one executive, "I could see the kid had an instinct that was unbelievable" (quoted in *Time* 5 Sept. 1977). Silverman's jobs at CBS served as steppingstones to his success later at ABC and his eventual elevation to the presidency of NBC in 1978. There his skills as a master programmer proved of no avail. After three years of frantic maneuvering to revive NBC's lagging ratings, he resigned in 1981.

To return to his CBS phase, while at that network Silverman participated, under the direction of network president Robert Wood, in a historic undertaking, described by Paley as "the most drastic overhaul in CBS history" (1979: 267). In 1970 CBS scrapped 14 prime-time program series, introduced eight new ones, and rescheduled 11 others — all to change the network's demographics. Since the early 1960s CBS's prime-time lead had been based on rural comedies such as *The Andy Griffith Show* (1960–1968) and *The Beverly Hillbillies* (1962–1971). Such programs, though popular, tended to appeal to the lower and upper age brackets more than to the mid-range, "upscale" segment of the audience that is responsible for the bulk of consumer spending. CBS's new programming strategy called for ruthless cancellation of shows with the wrong demographic appeals, no matter how high their ratings, in favor of more contemporary shows that appealed to the active, urban, high-consumption audience segments.

*Paley reached sixty-five, the normal retirement age at CBS, in 1966, but his contract guarantees him his present office suite in "Black Rock" until 1987, by which time he would be eighty-six.

The replacements were innovative programs like *All in the Family* (1971–1979) and the *Sonny and Cher Comedy Hour* (1971–1974). Such emphasis on demographics in programming philosophy had already been presaged at ABC, but with CBS's conversion to that philosophy a new era of television programming began — an era in which both demographic considerations and intricate scheduling strategies were to play more significant roles than ever before.

ABC Seizes the Lead   As the networks entered the television age in 1948, ABC Television found itself in somewhat the same position that CBS had occupied in the early days of network radio. Top television advertisers and performers automatically turned first to CBS or NBC, regarding ABC only as the last resort. This humiliating role forced ABC into offbeat strategies — what one commentator aptly called "expedient moves and the exploitation of fads" (Brown, 1977: 2). In 1958, for example, ABC cut its daytime prices to advertisers in half in a dramatic bid to attract business. At about this time it began to pay more attention to demographics, tailoring prime-time shows to the young, urban, adult segments of the audience. In practice, this policy meant emphasizing action, violence, and sex, and abandoning any serious attempt to offer the more balanced range of programming that the older networks had always thought essential to their national image.

ABC was aided by its link with the motion picture industry, an association that had begun with the ABC-Paramount Theaters merger in 1953 (§7.5). In 1954 Walt Disney, first of the major studio leaders to make a deal with television, agreed to produce a series of programs for ABC called *Disneyland*

(1954–1957; then under various titles on NBC until finally dropped in 1981). The ABC deal was an exceptionally good one for Disney, who got free advertising for his theme park (also called Disneyland and just then opening), and for Disney feature films. The entire television program often served as an elaborate promotion for the Disney feature film that was about to open in the movie theaters. In the following year came Disney's *The Mickey Mouse Club* (1955–1959), which had an impact on popular culture out of all proportion to its relatively short run on the ABC network.

An ABC contract with Warner Brothers first brought a major Hollywood studio into the production of routine prime-time entertainment, with series such as *Cheyenne* (1955–1962), an example of the "adult cowboy" shows that had a vogue in the 1960s. ABC was the first network to gain access to a major library of feature films when it obtained the rights in 1955 to a hundred J. Arthur Rank (British) features, which it programmed as *Afternoon Film Festival.* Later ABC led the networks in the trend toward "blockbuster" features in prime time when it paid $2 million for the right to telecast two showings of *The Bridge on the River Kwai* (1966).

Another stratagem in ABC's search for identity was an all-out emphasis on sports, a trend it initiated during the 1960s. Roone Arledge, the network's hard-driving and innovative sports chief, introduced such novelties as instant replay, the controversial commentary of Howard Cosell, *Monday Night Football* (1969–), and the first of the weekend sports "anthologies," *Wide World of Sports* (1961–). It was typical of ABC's daring that it eventually promoted Arledge to head its news division as well as its sports programming.

As part of a programming revolution rivaling CBS's wholesale changes of 1970, ABC lured Fred Silverman away from CBS in 1975.

The revolution paid off, because in the 1975–1976 season the unthinkable happened: ABC, after decades of playing third fiddle, moved into the network lead. The next season ABC had seven of the top prime-time programs, including such phenomenal youth-appeal shows as *Happy Days* (1974), its spin-off, *Laverne and Shirley* (1976), and *Charlie's Angels* (1976). ABC was not winning any prizes for profound quality, but it was walking away with all the popularity ratings. Now, for the first time in television history, large-scale defections of CBS and NBC affiliations began to occur. Between 1976 and 1979, ABC picked up 35 new stations, finally achieving "affiliate parity" (Exhibit 8.5.2).

Corporate Character of Networks

Despite ABC's blossoming as number-one in the ratings in the late 1970s, it remained number-three among the networks in terms of corporate size. A move to put ABC into the corporate bigtime in 1965 by merging it with a multinational conglomerate, International Telephone and Telegraph (ITT), fell through after three years of suspense. The FCC approved the merger, but the Justice Department opposed it, insisting "that the integrity of ABC news would be affected because of ITT's foreign interests, which involved it in close and confidential relations with foreign governments" (Sampson, 1973: 92).

American Broadcasting Companies, Inc. (as ABC's parent company is called) ranks eighteenth in size among U.S. communications firms, compared to the number-three rank of RCA (parent company of NBC), and the number-ten rank of CBS, Inc. By the same token, ABC depends on broadcasting for over three-quarters of its income, compared to RCA's 19 percent and CBS's 43 percent (Sterling, 1979: 85). All three networks derive substantial profits from owned and operated stations apart from their network operations (Exhibit 8.5.3).

American Broadcasting Companies, Inc., has interests in recordings, magazines, such theme attractions as Silver Springs (Florida), videocassette production, and cable pro-

Exhibit 8.5.2
TV network affiliates, 1979

Network	Number of affiliated stations	Percentage of U.S. households reachable
ABC	203	98.1
CBS	198	96.5
NBC	212	96.9

Comment: The affiliate counts include network O&O stations. Each network also has a few secondary affiliates that add between 1 and 2 percent more potential households.

Source: Households data from FCC Network Inquiry Special Staff, *New Television Networks: Entry, Jurisdiction, Ownership and Regulation,* Final Report, Government Printing Office, Washington, DC, 1980, p. 65.

grams. CBS, after failing in a major effort in the 1950s to challenge RCA in the manufacturing field, diversified widely in entertainment instead. It has 16 divisions that produce high-quality musical instruments, toys, publications, recordings, feature films, videocassette programs, videodiscs, and other such products. One of CBS's most lucrative ventures was an investment of a third of a million dollars in the 1956 stage musical *My Fair Lady*. By 1979 the company had earned over $33 million from live performances, recordings, and motion picture rights from that one show. RCA qualifies as a true conglomerate,

Exhibit 8.5.3
Network owned and operated stations, 1980

Market (Rank)	Radio			Television		
	ABC	**CBS**	**NBC**	**ABC**	**CBS**	**NBC**
New York (1st)	WABC(AM) WPLJ(FM)	WCBS(AM) WCBS-FM	WNBC(AM) WYNY(FM)	WABC-TV Ch. 7	WCBS-TV Ch. 2	WNBC-TV Ch. 4
Los Angeles (2d)	KABC(AM) KLOS(FM)	KNX(AM) KNX-FM	——	KABC-TV Ch. 7	KNXT-TV Ch. 2	KNBC-TV Ch. 4
Chicago (3d)	WLS(AM) WDAI(FM)	WBBM(AM) WBBM-FM	WMAQ(AM) WKQX(FM)	WLS-TV Ch. 7	WBBM-TV Ch. 2	WMAQ-TV Ch. 5
Philadelphia (4th)	——	WCAU(AM) WCAU-FM	——	——	WCAU-TV Ch. 10	——
San Francisco (5th)	KGO(AM) KSFX(FM)	KCBS(AM) KCBS-FM	KNBR(AM) KYUU(FM)	KGO-TV Ch. 7	——	——
Boston (6th)	——	WEEI(AM) WEEI-FM	——	——	——	——
Detroit (7th)	WXYZ(AM) WRIF(FM)	——	——	WXYZ-TV Ch. 7	——	——
Washington (8th)	WMAL(AM) WRQX(FM)	——	WRC(AM) WKYS(FM)	——	——	WRC-TV Ch. 4
Cleveland (9th)	——	——	——	——	——	WKYC-TV Ch. 3
Houston (12th)	KXYZ(AM) KAUM(FM)	——	——	——	——	——
St. Louis (14th)	——	KMOX(AM) KMOX-FM	——	——	KMOX-TV Ch. 4	——

Comment: Only in New York and Chicago do the three major networks have complete parity in station ownership (Chicago having been the number two market until recently). Only ABC succeeded in the minor triumph of obtaining the same channel number for each of its O&O TV stations.

with interests in such diverse fields as auto rentals, global communications, money lending, satellites, electronic manufacturing, consumer electronics, and recordings.

A "Fourth Network"? The three national networks so far discussed — ABC, CBS, and NBC — are *full-service* networks. This means that they operate every day of the year, providing a substantial percentage of their affiliates' programming; they reach the entire country and offer a wide range of programming — prime-time and nonprime-time entertainment, news and public affairs, sports, and special live coverage of great public events. All this requires a huge investment in studios and other facilities, worldwide newsgathering organizations, elaborate engineering and program research resources, as well as programming and time-sales expertise.

A combination of factors has limited the field to three such commercial networks — limitations on the availability of suitable program materials, on advertiser support, on hours available on affiliated stations, and (most crucial of all) on the number of channels available. To be competitive, a full-service commercial network must have access to affiliates of approximately equal coverage potential in all the major markets of the country. If all the independent commercial stations in the country were to combine forces in a fourth network, they would still be able to cover only about 60 percent of the population.

Nevertheless, there have always been candidates for a "fourth network," or at least for some alternative between the extremes of complete independence and affiliation with a full-service network.*

When television networking began, the fourth radio network, MBS, was too weak to consider competing in the television field. As we have seen, even the third network, ABC, had an extremely difficult period before it became fully competitive with CBS and NBC. One reason for ABC's difficulty was the fact that from 1946 to 1955 a fourth chain did in fact exist, the Dumont Television Network. Founded by Allen B. Dumont, developer and manufacturer of cathode ray tubes (of which kinescopes or picture tubes are just one of many types) and a pioneer maker of television receivers, the Dumont network succeeded only while the lack of interconnection facilities kept network television somewhat localized. Once networking on a true national scale became possible, Dumont could not keep up the pace. In 1955 it dropped out, leaving only three full-service networks. ABC was the chief beneficiary of Dumont's withdrawal.

A number of occasional and regional television network arrangements exist. Among them are specialized hookups such as the Hughes TV Network (a subsidiary of Paramount Pictures specializing in live sports and occasional special entertainment events), the Spanish International Network, and two religious chains, the Christian Broadcasting Network and the PTL Network. The latter three use satellite interconnection.

Also somewhat threatening to the full-service networks are several noninterconnected programming projects that developed in the 1970s, supplying prime-time programs to network affiliates as well as to independents. Although referred to as "fourth network" projects, they are actually special cases of *syndication* (§8.7).

---

*Of course a noncommercial fourth national television network does exist today, the Public Broadcasting Service, which is discussed in Chapter 10.

8.6 Changeover from Live to Recorded Entertainment

The "Live Decade": 1948–1957   If we look back with nostalgia to radio's "golden era" of the 1930s and 1940s, we may justifiably feel the same way about television's first decade. The networks put first priority on stimulating people to buy sets. Only attractive programs could provide the necessary stimulus:

It was the only time in the history of the medium that program priorities superseded all others. If there was an abundance of original and quality drama at the time . . . it was in large part because those shows tended to appeal to a wealthier and better-educated part of the public, the part best able to afford a television set in those years when the price of receivers was high. (Brown, 1971: 154)

Most programming, local and network, was necessarily live — a throwback to the earliest days of radio. Videotape recording had not yet been invented. Kinescopes, the filmed versions of television programs photographed off the picture tube (§4.3), were hopelessly deficient in quality. The motion picture industry, scared to death of television, kept all but its oldest and sleaziest feature films locked away in the vaults. Original television plays constituted the most memorable artistic achievements of television's live decade. "Talent seemed to gush right out of the cement," wrote the pioneer *New York Times* critic, Jack Gould (1973: 6). Robert Alan Aurthur, a young playwright at the time, recalls the challenge of producing 52 live, original plays a year — no network reruns in those days. Aurthur wrote the script for the last of the *Philco Playhouse* (1948–1955) series, "A Man Is Ten Feet Tall," for Sidney Poitier. It came at a low point in Poitier's career, when the distinguished black actor was running a barbecued rib joint in Harlem between acting jobs. The casting was tricky. Wrote the playwright:

Today it's no big thing for a black to play a leading part on television, but 1955 was something else. Two Southern newspapers printed editorials calling me a Communist, and several others condemned the network for airing the show. Six Philco distributors threatened to cancel franchises, and we received a rolled-up petition from Jackson, Miss., with more than 6,000 signatures of people who swore they'd never watch the Playhouse again. (Aurthur, 1973: 10)*

It is easy to become oversentimental about the live decade. A more realistic appraisal, perhaps, is that of Robert Saudek, producer of *Omnibus*, a prestigious series initiated in 1952 with Ford Foundation support as an experiment in high-quality television. Asking himself if the strain of live production was really worthwhile, Saudek concluded:

Any sane observer would have to say no, because it is both efficient and economical to put shows on film or tape. Not only does it provide profitable reruns, but also . . . the scheduling of crews, studios, lights, cameras, sound and all the other hardware can be computerized. In that way a whole season of shows can be frozen and stored away like TV dinners to be retrieved and served up on demand. (Saudek, 1973: 22)

In short, the economics of television drove it unrelentingly toward syndication and therefore toward recording. This was equally true at both the local and the network levels.

*There is a special irony in the source of this petition. The Jackson station, WLBT, was later denied license renewal for failing to meet the needs of the black segment of its audience (§18.3).

Coming of VTR   It was a foregone conclusion that the technique of magnetic recording, already well established in the audio field, would eventually be extended to video. All through the live decade RCA and other major manufacturers were experimenting with videotape recording (VTR) methods, but a small California firm, Ampex, was the first to reach a workable solution. Its *quadraplex* format achieved the necessary tape speed by combining transverse movement of recording heads mounted on a spinning disc with lateral movement of the tape (§4.3).

Ampex created a sensation at the first public demonstration of quadraplex VTR at the 1956 National Association of Broadcasters convention. In November, CBS put the new VTR to its first practical use in network operations by recording the nightly *Douglas Edwards with the News* program. The program originated in New York and was recorded off the network relay system in Los Angeles. In this way, CBS could delay the program for West Coast playback three hours later to coincide with the clock-time of the original East Coast release. Previously the news show, like most East Coast network programs, had to be produced live a second time for the later West Coast broadcast. "Ampex engineers literally slept in the VTR room to have access to the machines during the non-broadcast hours, between one and five a.m." (Roizen, 1976: 21).

RCA promptly gave up research on its own VTR system and accepted a license from Ampex, as did foreign manufacturers. This was one of the few times when competing manufacturers voluntarily put aside their rivalry at the introduction of a new technology, opting for compatibility from the outset.

Production Moves to Hollywood   Television programs could, of course, have been "recorded" from the very beginning by making them originally on motion picture film.

Economic, technical, and social barriers delayed adoption of this solution.

First, the slow and cumbersome single-camera production method traditional in Hollywood was far too expensive for television. Time was needed to adapt film technology to the physical limitations of television, with its lower resolution than film, its smaller projected picture area, and its much more restricted range of gray-scale values. Solutions to these problems, though not hard to achieve, were slow in coming because the motion picture industry regarded the upstart television medium with a mixture of overt contempt and secret fear. Moreover, many television specialists and critics wanted television to stay clear of the movies, counting on it to bring about a new breed of mass entertainment, independent of the familiar Hollywood fare.

The two points of view were as far apart as their two centers — television in New York and film in Los Angeles. But the economics of the two media drove them ever closer together. Inexorably, as the technical barriers to producing television programs on film were overcome, the production base for entertainment programming shifted to the West Coast.

A pioneer in this westward migration was the company formed in 1950 by Lucille Ball and Desi Arnaz, stars of *I Love Lucy* (1951–1961), one of the most successful television series of all time. The company they formed to produce the program on film in Hollywood, Desilu Productions, started as an interloper but eventually bought out the old-time RKO movie studios.

However, the leader in the move to the West Coast was, as we have seen (§8.5), the ABC network with its direct links to the movie industry. East Coast observers regarded ABC's defection as a betrayal. Wrote a *Fortune* commentator in 1958, ''The emergence of ABC as a fully competitive network brings into focus another of television's major influences for mediocrity: the film packagers. Without them as a source of supply, the network's evening schedule would be skimpy indeed'' (Smith, 1958: 168).

In the 1956–1957 season, 63 percent of all network programming was still being produced in New York, nearly all of it live, with most of the West Coast production on film. But in 1958 NBC moved *Studio One,* which for a decade had been the most prestigious of the New York live television drama series, to Hollywood. *Studio One* died within months, symbolizing the demise of the live decade.

Television's live production methods brought about changes in traditional film production techniques in Hollywood. Live television usually employs three or more cameras running at the same time, taking shots from different angles and at different focal lengths. The live action unfolds continuously, while the director edits simultaneously, selecting optional shots from the several cameras. Adaptations of this technique to film made possible much faster, more economical shooting than the traditional Hollywood method of staging and lighting each short scene separately for a single camera. After filming many ''takes'' of the same scene, the camera is moved to a new setup and the scene relighted before the next shot is taken.

Today, television series shot in Hollywood combine elements from both the film and live television traditions in varying ways. *All in the Family,* for example, used to employ a ''live on tape'' technique. Each episode was shot continuously by the live multicamera method in its entirety twice, with a studio audience reacting each time to the performances. Editors then selected the best shots from the two complete takes of the entire action to make up the on-air version. Inherent visual differences in the end products of tape and film products nevertheless remain, making one or the other preferable in specific situations in order to obtain given visual effects.

Film remains cheaper and easier to use for exterior, on-location shooting, but tape is nearly always used for interior shooting in conventional television situation comedy settings. When the choice between tape and film is not dictated by sheer economics it is influenced by custom and personal inclination.

Feature Films   In a replay of the newspapers' earlier fears about the inroads radio might make on the news business (§7.6), Hollywood withheld its better and more recent theatrical feature films from television for a dozen years. Only pre-1948 films were released to television, except for some foreign imports, and even these were released grudgingly by the film companies in fits and starts. The cutoff year was 1948 because after that year feature-film production contracts contained restrictive clauses taking into account the possibility of release to television. During the early 1950s, then, television stations had to content themselves with old ''B'' grade movies produced by minor companies. As for the networks, somewhat in the spirit of early radio, when networks disdained to use recorded sound, so in the 1950s television networks disdained to use feature films. For the time being movies served only as fillers in locally programmed hours. For example, the WCBS-TV (New York) movie series *The Late Show,* which started in 1951, is said to be the oldest feature-film series on television. Its producer recalled that the first break in the major studios' united front came in 1955, and by 1956 most of the big Hollywood studios had begun to offer him ''packages'' of old films culled from their vaults (Broder, 1976).

By 1960, however, Hollywood had concluded, as had the newspapers by 1940, that broadcasting could be a boon instead of a disaster to the older industry. As soon as better and more recent film features became available the networks began scheduling them. ABC led the way with *The Bridge on the River Kwai* in 1966. Feature films proved, in fact, to be the most popular fictional entertainment television could offer. By the 1970s the networks were paying astronomical prices for the right to show outstanding films on television. The movie classic *Gone With the Wind*, it is said, cost NBC $5 million for a single showing in 1976 — but it captured 65 percent of the audience for NBC. Such costly features cannot earn back their rental fees directly, but they are regarded as sound investments for the sake of their indirect rewards. It is especially rewarding to be able to clobber the opposition during a *sweep* week, a period when audience-measuring services are collecting viewing data (§14.2). An idea of the size of the backlog of feature films available to network and independent programmers is indicated by the fact that *TV Guide* keeps some 22,000 film titles and plot descriptions in its computer bank of program-listing materials.

Made-for-TV Features   The success of theatrical feature films and their high cost encouraged the networks to consider producing their own *made-for-television features,* or *tele-movies.* After all, the rental fee for a single showing of a major theatrical feature would more than pay for making a brand-new, low-budget feature just for television.

NBC led the way with a series called *World Premiere* in 1966, two-hour programs costing on the order of $800,000 each — small potatoes compared to the millions budgeted for even a run-of-the-mill theatrical feature film.

Though at first regarded as "a kind of grubby step-child of film" (Whitney, 1974: 21), during the 1970s made-for-television features became a staple part of the networks' programming. By the end of the decade, over a hundred were in production, some as ambitious in budget and scope as regular theatrical features.

8.7 Program Syndication

Definition   Development of television recording was essential to the economy of the medium because it made *syndication* easy. By its nature, television syndication is a global phenomenon: the parsimony principle (§7.4) ensures that wherever television exists the demand for programs exceeds the local supply. Only by means of networking and recording can programming rise above local limitations. This means that an important part of the market for U.S. syndicated programming is found overseas.

The FCC has defined a syndicated program as "any program sold, licensed, distributed, or offered to television station licensees in more than one market within the United States for noninterconnected (i.e., nonnetwork) television broadcast exhibition, but not including live presentations" (47 CFR 76.5p). As we pointed out in §7.5, networking and syndication are fundamentally simply alternative ways of dealing with the shortage of programs. An intimate economic link exists between network programs and syndicated programs. Most prime-time network entertainment programs cost more to produce than can be immediately defrayed by network advertising income (§12.5). Producers of such programs are willing, however, to suffer a loss in order to gain network exposure, counting on that exposure to enhance their future value in the syndication market.

How Syndication Works Distributors of television programs, the syndication companies, obtain programs from several sources and offer them, on tape or on film, to individual stations or to groups of commonly owned stations. The station or station-group buys the right to a stipulated number of "plays" over a fixed period of time, after which the rights to the programs revert to the syndicator. Such rights are awarded to the buyer exclusively within the buyer's own market.*

Syndicators obtain most of their new programs from networks (*off-network syndication*) and from independent and foreign producers (*first-run syndication*). Distributors showcase their new products at annual meetings of the National Association of Television Program Executives and other trade groups. The track records of syndicated programming already on the market are documented by the two major rating services, Arbitron and Nielsen, which issue special reports on the size and composition of the audiences attracted by existing syndicated series. The most popular series are sold in as many as 200 markets and so compete in physical coverage with network programs. The majority, however, reach less than a hundred markets in a given season.

The prices stations pay for syndicated programming vary widely according to market size, extent of competition among stations in

a market, age of the programs, and the bargaining skills of film buyers. A newly available, top-rated network series can bring $50,000 or more per episode, so that millions can be involved in a single buy (Bedell, 1979). At the other extreme, a much-played old-timer in a small market might go for $100 an episode. Some syndicated series have been running for over 20 years, replayed scores of times. *Little Rascals,* a series edited from *Our Gang* film comedies of the 1920s, started in 1955. *I Love Lucy* (1951–1956), the quintessential off-network syndicated series, dates back to the precolor television era. At times there have been as many as five Lucy episodes on the air the same day in a single market (Funt, 1974). *The Honeymooners,* another classic off-network comedy series, featuring Jackie Gleason and Art Carney, started as part of another series on the now-defunct Dumont Television Network in 1950, becoming a CBS staple in 1955–1956 (Jaffe, 1977).

Syndicated programs reach their purchasers by parcel delivery services. After airing a program, each station sends it on to the next customer. This "bicycling" keeps delivery costs of prints down and minimizes the number that have to be kept in circulation.

Off-Network Syndication After a prime-time network series has accumulated a sufficient backlog of episodes, it normally "goes into syndication" as an *off-network* series. Formerly the networks themselves syndicated their own programs through subsidiary companies, but effective in 1973 they were forced by the Federal Communications Commission to divest themselves of their domestic syndication operations. Contracts with producers for new programs usually give the network the right to only two "plays" of each episode — the initial presentation and one *rerun.* The right to rerun programs is essential because networks usually produce only 24 episodes of each prime-time series a year,

---

*Satellite distribution of television station programming to widely scattered cable systems tends to obliterate traditional market boundaries, throwing the exclusivity concept into confusion. In consequence regulation of exclusivity clauses in contracts has become a highly controversial subject (see §11.1).

filling out the remaining weeks of the 30-week season with repeats of episodes shown earlier in the season.

When weekly network series are released for syndication, however, stations usually *strip* them on a daily basis (the less usual alternate-day scheduling is known as *checkerboarding*). Buyers of off-network programs therefore need a large number of episodes, ideally at least 130, representing 26 weeks of stripped programming. At the production rate of only 24 episodes per season, it takes several years to accumulate sufficient programs to make an off-network series readily salable in the syndication market. This delay creates a shortage of off-network series, helping to stimulate the first-run syndication market.

Prime-Time Access Rule (PTAR) Programs not originally sold to networks but offered directly to the syndication market are known as *first-run syndication* programs. Before 1971 networks filled nearly all the best hours of their affiliates, leaving little opportunity for producers to sell programs aimed at the national market but not good enough (or not lucky enough) to be selected by the networks. The only times left open on affiliated stations for first-run syndicated material were the fringe hours. Prime time was available on independent stations, but these are generally the ones least able to pay high prices for programs. In part to broaden the market for first-run syndicated programming, the Federal Communications Commission adopted the prime time access rule (PTAR), effective in 1971. The PTAR confines network programming to a maximum of three of the four prime-time hours. *Prime time* is the segment of the television broadcast day when the maximum audience is available and hence the time when maximum program costs are justified. It is defined as the four evening hours between 7 and 11

P.M. (6 and 10 P.M. in the central and mountain time zones).*

Because affiliates generally used one half-hour of prime time for their own local news, the PTAR's effect was to open up one half-hour of prime time for nonnetwork programming each night of the week. The networks agreed to give up the 7:30–8 P.M. time slot; this period became known as *access time*. It may be filled with either locally produced or nationally syndicated nonnetwork programs. Most locally produced shows draw small audiences. Accordingly, stations usually consider access time too valuable to expend on such programs; therefore the great majority of access-time programming consists of syndicated material. Because of a variety of exemptions and exceptions to the rule, the networks usually still program Sunday access time (see Box). And on many stations Saturday access time is the period most often chosen for locally produced programs. Therefore, most syndicated access-time programming is stripped at 7:30 P.M., Monday through Friday.

One half-hour a day may not seem like much for the networks to surrender. However, when that half-hour of access time is multiplied by the 260 weekdays in the year and by the 150 network affiliates in the top 50 markets, PTAR yields an annual large-audience market for 39,000 half-hours of nonnetwork programming on major stations, times that were not before available to syndicators or local producers except at the price

---

*This is the FCC definition. Broadcasters sometimes define prime time differently. For example, the National Association of Broadcasters Television Code defines it in terms of *network* hours only: "a continuous period of not less than three consecutive hours per broadcast day designated by the station between the hours of 6:00 P.M. and midnight."

PTAR Fallacies, Exemptions, and Exceptions

The prime time access rule was not, as many people suppose, designed by the FCC to force stations into producing only *local* programs during access periods. This would be an economically unrealistic goal. The aim of PTAR, as the FCC put it, is "to make available for competition among existing and potential program producers, *both at the local and national levels,* an arena of more adequate competition for the custom and favor of broadcasters and advertisers" (25 FCC 2d 326, 1970, emphasis added). In practice, as was to be expected, the great majority of access time is filled with national-level syndicated programming.

Since PTAR aims at curbing the networks' control over prime-time *entertainment,* the rule also bars stations from scheduling off-network syndicated shows in access time. By the same token the FCC did not want to discourage the networks from scheduling *nonentertainment* programs. PTAR therefore exempts from the ban network programs for young children (age 2 through 12) as well as public affairs and documentary programs, except on Saturday nights. The FCC wanted to keep Saturday free of encumbrance by exemptions so as to encourage locally produced access programs at least once a week (Saturday being the traditionally favored timeslot for locally produced programs). Networks tend to schedule their major public affairs and documentary programs on Sundays; therefore the networks usually take advantage of the exemptions to use Sunday access time. For example, because of PTAR CBS moved *60 Minutes,* its prestigious news/documentary series, to the Sunday 7–8 P.M. time slot in 1975.

The rule also makes exceptions for news specials dealing with currently breaking events, on-the-spot news coverage, broadcasts by and for political candidates, regular network newscasts when preceded by a full hour of locally produced news or public affairs programming, runovers of live afternoon sports events, and special sports events such as the Olympic Games.

It must be borne in mind that the PTAR restrictions apply only to *affiliates* (including O&O stations) in the *top 50 markets.* This leaves independents in all markets and affiliates in the 150-odd smaller markets free to use off-network material during access time if they choose.

of canceling network shows. PTAR has therefore given a significant new incentive to producers of nonnetwork programming.

Programming produced for the access-time market is necessarily budgeted much lower than network prime-time programming. In the first place, early prime time is less valuable than the networks' time from 8:00 P.M. onward. Secondly, the many sellers of syndicated material must scramble to place their programs in access time, usually on relatively short lists of stations. Each network, on the other hand, is assured of placement on most of its 200-odd affiliates during the most valuable segments of prime time.

The best first-run syndicated programming is hardly distinguishable from network programming. For example, a 90-minute daily syndicated talk program such as *The*

Merv Griffin Show (1965–) has much in common with such network series as NBC's *Tonight Show*. Indeed, programs discarded by the networks often turn up in syndication. The best-known example is *The Lawrence Welk Show,* dropped after 16 years by ABC in 1971 because Welk's old-fashioned music-variety format appealed to an older audience segment than ABC wanted to reach (§8.5). Without missing a beat, Welk reappeared the following week on even more stations as a syndicated show than he had previously as a network offering (Whitney, 1976).

Sometimes a series planned for a network is turned down after production begins and goes into syndication instead. This happened in 1970 to *Mary Hartman, Mary Hartman,* a satire on soap operas originally designed by Norman Lear's T.A.T. Productions for CBS but turned down by all three networks because of its sexual candor.

Barter Syndication   In the 1970s a type of national-spot quasi-sponsorship called *barter syndication* began to get attention in the lively business of prime-time access syndicated programming. Also called *advertiser barter,* it involves the trade of station time for programs. Usually, national advertisers (or firms working on behalf of advertisers) obtain the rights to series of programs, either by purchase from a syndicator or by underwriting production.

Instead of buying national spot time outright, the barter syndicator trades (that is, *barters*) programs for station time, with the advertisers and the station splitting the spot availabilities within the programs. Thus stations gain programs of considerable popularity with no cash outlay, but can earn cash by selling spots in the programs. Advertisers gain station time with no cash outlay to stations and with assurance that their commercials will appear in a suitable program setting of their own choosing.

Perhaps the best-known example is again *The Lawrence Welk Show.* The barter syndicator, an advertiser specializing in products designed for the Geritol generation, reaches viewers who are passionately loyal to Welk's schmaltzy music. Other well-known barter series are *Hee Haw, Wild, Wild World of Animals,* and *Sha Na Na.*

There are several variations on the standard barter deal. *Time-bank syndication,* for example, refers to barter deals in which advertisers exchange programs for spots scheduled in other programs on the stations accepting the deal.

Prime-Time Syndication   A new type of prestigious syndicated programming evolved in the late 1970s, misleadingly referred to in the trade press as representing the beginning of a "fourth network." Among these ventures were Operation Prime Time, the Program Development Group, and the Mobil Showcase Network. Their distinctive feature was that they presented network-quality series especially produced for *prime-time* slots (rather than access-time slots) on major stations in major markets. In many instances network affiliates refused clearance to their regular network's offerings in order to make room for these syndicated specials. For example, in 1980 the Mobil Oil Corporation lined up some fifty major stations to carry a British-produced miniseries, *Edward and Mrs. Simpson,* which it sponsored.* The term "network" was associated with such productions because, though not interconnected, most participating stations scheduled them simultaneously, so that they had the appearance

*Mobile chose to sponsor a syndicated rather than a network series in this instance in order to use argumentative commercials of a type the networks would not accept. See the comments on *editorial advertising* in §18.6.

as well as the quality of prime-time network programming and could be nationally promoted in the network manner.

So far, however, network-like programming of the types just described is *not* typical of the great bulk of first-run syndicated material. It tends instead to concentrate on low-budget formats such as quizzes and game shows, semidocumentary wild-life programs, and voice-over travelogues. Nevertheless, the PTAR has created opportunities that did not exist before for producers not already in the elite group of companies that turn out the prime-time network series. For example, the networks all turned down *The Muppet Show* (1976–) as a regular series, but because of PTAR, Jim Henson, its creator, was able to get access to good time on 160 stations.

8.8 Ethical Crises

With unprecedented growth came unprecedented temptations for both television and radio. A series of ethical crises in broadcasting occurred in the 1950s — revelations about fraudulence in programming, tinkering with news, under-the-table payments to disc jockeys and others who control the selection of recordings for airplay, blacklisting of artists for political reasons, and even wrongdoing by members of the Federal Communications Commission.

Two of these scandals — the quiz-rigging episode and political blacklisting practices — deserve special mention here because of their historical significance and their long-term impact on television programming. They raised a fundamental question about the appropriate role of broadcasting in American society. Should broadcasting function merely as another vehicle for advertising and another form of show business? Or should it be regarded as also having a wider, more serious responsibility as a medium of information and a forum for the exchange of political opinion?

1950s Quiz Craze   In the mid-fifties high-stakes television quiz shows captured national attention. In fact they became almost a national obsession. The first big-time show of the type, *The $64,000 Question,* premiered on CBS in 1955. It is symptomatic that the program had begun its career as a radio show offering a maximum prize of only $64. Television magnified the prize a thousandfold. The show was the brainchild of Louis G. Cowan, inventor of the highly successful radio pioneer of the genre, *Quiz Kids.* In the midst of the quiz craze Cowan became president of CBS-TV. *The $64,000 Question* was followed by *Twenty-One* on NBC in 1956 and by dozens of others. At the height of the fad five new quiz shows were introduced in a single day.

Producers wrung the last possible drop of suspense out of the contests. They featured such colorful characters as a chorus girl who was an expert on astronomy, a clergyman expert on love stories, a shoemaker expert on opera, and a woman psychologist expert on boxing. (The last was Dr. Joyce Brothers, the one quiz show celebrity to survive unscathed and to build quiz success into a lasting career as a television performer.) Thousands of dollars hung in the balance as audiences awaited crucial answers from contestants enclosed in "isolation booths" to prevent prompting. Armed guards watched over steel safes containing the questions, which had been made up "under the supervision" of a professor of English. The caged contestants raised the suspense to almost unbearable heights with histrionic lip-biting and eye-rolling as they racked their brains for answers.

Most glamorous of all the contestants was Charles Van Doren, a handsome bachelor in his twenties, member of a famous literary family, and an English teacher at Columbia University (his father was Mark Van Doren, a Pulitzer prize-winning poet). He has been described by a historian of the scandal that ensued as "the quintessential contestant of the big-money quiz shows and one of the most meteoric folk heroes of the 1950s" (Anderson, 1978: 53). For fifteen breathless weeks Van Doren survived on *Twenty-One*, NBC's top-rated quiz show. At one point, he ran his earnings up to $143,000, and when finally defeated he walked away with $129,000. He became an instant media supercelebrity, with his face on the cover of *Time*, a five-year contract to appear on NBC's *Today*, and five hundred unsolicited offers of marriage. The worm in this paradise, the unbelievable reality, was that this gifted golden boy had been faking it all the time, conniving with the producers to rig the outcome.

The Scandal   By 1956 hints of "quiz fixing" had begun to surface. In 1957 a feature *Time* article mentioned that producers "may be taking great risks" to whip up flagging ratings. "The producers of many shows control the outcome as closely as they dare," wrote *Time* — carefully adding ". . . without collusion with contestants" (22 Apr. 1957).

Collusion was in fact the name of the game. In the midst of pious disclaimers from contestants, producers, and network officials, the New York district attorney started an investigation in the fall of 1958. Ultimately, ten persons pleaded guilty to having perjured themselves in denying complicity in quiz rigging. The official confirmation of fraud was not made until July 1959, but by then the first television quiz craze had already run its course — after earning millions

for drug and cosmetic sponsors (Weinberg, 1962: 46). Van Doren, along with the others who were indicted by the grand jury, received suspended sentences. He lost his appointment at Columbia University and NBC canceled his *Today* contract. Dave Garroway, anchorman of the *Today* show, was so overcome emotionally when he made the announcement on the air that he had to leave the set.

Jack Barry and Dan Enright, producers of *Twenty-One*, went into broadcasting exile. Louis Cowan, the CBS-TV president whose claim to fame was based on his success with quiz-type productions, lost his job. He had never been linked with the fraud, but the president of CBS itself, Frank Stanton, was particularly harsh in the measures he took to restore the reputation of the network. He not only canceled CBS's seven quiz shows; he went so far as to cancel Edward R. Murrow's highly successful interview program, *Person to Person*, on the far-fetched ground that it was presented as though occurring spontaneously but had actually been rehearsed. This abrupt decision embittered relations between Murrow and CBS, contributing eventually to the journalist's early retirement from the network in 1961 (Anderson, 1978: 161).

The ripples spread far and wide. The president of the United States requested a report from the attorney general, Congress held investigations, the FCC launched an inquiry. Ironically, the FCC had previously attempted to curb giveaway practices in broadcasting on grounds that they violate the law against lotteries, but the Supreme Court held that they were not lotteries in the legal sense (see §15.7). Congress considered a bill to license networks and to impose license suspensions and heavy fines for violation of regulations. By the time the bill reached the president for signature, however, its teeth had been blunted. All that remained was the addition of Section 509 to the Communications Act of

1934 threatening a $10,000 fine and/or a year in jail for complicity in rigging "contests of intellectual knowledge, intellectual skill or chance."

Return of the Quiz Big-money quiz shows were too lucrative to remain submerged forever. In 1970, his character having been cleared symbolically by the FCC when it granted him an FM station license, Jack Barry, co-producer of *Twenty-One,* returned from exile. "I condoned the coaching," he admitted in a later interview. "We lost sight of certain moral issues, which, in retrospect, I recognize as being wrong" (Russell, 1979: 21). Once more the giveaway/quiz format flourished on television. Viacom Enterprises, a syndicated program distributor and producer, even revived *The $64,000 Question* (perhaps not coincidentally, Viacom was once owned by CBS). The new version, introduced in 1976, made a concession to inflation — it had escalated into *The $128,000 Question.* A small tremor from the 1950s scandal could still be felt, however: three CBS-owned stations were reported to have canceled contracts for the show upon being reminded that CBS still had a policy, adopted in the wake of the scandal, not to air giveaway programs with prizes higher than $25,000.

In order not to violate Section 509 of the communications act, the revived quiz shows use carefully worded disclaimers and disclosures — with all the enthusiasm of cigarette companies imprinting their packets with the Surgeon General's warning. In the syndicated series *Celebrity Sweepstakes*, for example, a card momentarily flashed during the closing titles tells the viewer (in part) that "celebrities have been furnished with some joke answers as well as with some of the questions and answers." Mark Goodson, whose experience in producing quiz shows dates back to 1950, examined such disclaimers in an article for the *New York Times* headlined "TV Shows are Hoodwinking Viewers Again" (1976). Cryptic disclosures buried in the confusion of the final credits are meaningless to the ordinary viewer. At best they violate the spirit if not the letter of the law against deception.

Ambivalent Reactions Does anyone care? Would an event similar to the 1959 exposure of Van Doren cause a similar national outcry in the 1980s? Or has the sense of public morality become too jaded by the events of the 1960s and 1970s?

The quiz scandals dramatized divergent points of view as to what broadcasting is all about. This public ambivalence about the proper role of television in American society is at the root of much confusion about how the medium should be judged. To some, the quiz deceptions seemed like a massive betrayal of public trust, a symptom of widespread moral decay. To others, the quizzes seemed no more fraudulent than a stage pistol that fires blanks instead of lethal bullets. Opinion surveys taken just after the disclosure of the quiz rigging indicated that many people felt outraged at having been duped. Many others, however, still approved of the quizzes, and a quarter of the respondents saw nothing at all wrong with the deception (Kendrick, 1969: 130).

Ambivalence about the nature of responsibility of broadcasting goes back to the industry's very beginnings. David Sarnoff's original vision of network broadcasting in 1922 equated it with "a public institution of great value in the same sense that a public library, for example, is regarded today" (§6.5). The advertising agency people, on the other hand, saw broadcasting primarily as another vehicle for commercial copy. Many broadcasters themselves thought of it as show business pure and simple — a make-believe, escapist medium. Bill Stern, a nationally successful pioneer sportscaster, ingenuously volunteered a perfect illustration of the show-biz view of broadcasting. Attempting to justify the fact that in pursuit of ratings he had fabricated much of his "reporting" on the popular *Colgate Sports Newsreel*, he wrote:

I am certain that no harm was done to anyone through our recounting of these admittedly dramatized stories, which were aimed solely at entertaining those who listened to my show . . . I was living in the make-believe world of the theatre and the license I took was basically harmless. Diversion was my stock in trade and I thrived, rightly or not, on the same fanciful principles used by other communications media which lift audiences out of a humdrum, monotonous existence of mundane fact and insipid incident. (1959: 105)

Blacklisting The social role of broadcasting came into question from another perspective during the late 1940s and 1950s. This was the period of the Cold War, when some Americans feared imminent Russian takeover. One reaction in the United States was an intensive hunt for evidence of procommunist, subversive influences. People in the news and entertainment media became favorite targets of the hunters. Performers and writers suspected of leftist sympathies could find themselves on *blacklists* — privately (and sometimes publicly) circulated rosters, compiled by zealous investigators searching through newspaper files and other records for evidence of associations with causes and organizations suspected to have subversive intentions.

People whose names appeared on such lists suddenly lost their jobs and thereafter found themselves unemployable, usually with no explanation or opportunity for rebutting the evidence. Actors were especially

vulnerable because a few years before, during World War II, they had often been asked to appear at benefit performances and rallies in support of various aspects of the war effort. Because Russia was a wartime ally of the United States, often these conspicuous appearances could later be misinterpreted as evidence of communist leanings.

For example, actress Jean Muir, who had made such wartime appearances, was cast by NBC in 1950 as the mother in *The Aldrich Family*, a situation comedy about to be transferred from radio to television. Suddenly, for no apparent reason, NBC removed her from the show and offered her $10,000 to settle her contract. It was discovered that NBC, the sponsor (General Foods), and the sponsor's advertising agency had all received calls accusing Miss Muir of communist sympathies. As an actress reciting lines written by others she could have had no influence in turning the innocent *Aldrich Family* scripts into subversive propaganda, but the object of blacklisting seemed to be as much to punish those accused as to prevent the spread of propaganda.

After news of a few cases of such arbitrary dismissals became embarrassingly public, little more was heard about them. This meant not that the blacklisting had let up but that the networks and advertising agencies had "institutionalized" it in order to avoid unfavorable publicity. According to a study commissioned by the Fund for the Republic, they assigned top executives to comb through blacklists and to compile their own "black," "gray," and "white" lists as guides to safe casting and job-assignment decisions (Cogley, 1956). They found plenty of names in such publications as *Red Channels: The Report of Communist Infiltration in Radio and Television*, published by Counterattack in 1950. Scores of writers, performers, newspersons, and other broadcast employees found their careers abruptly halted. Many innocent people were permanently damaged, some even committed suicide.

Proving that listings were false (as many of the accused did), showing that circumstances were entirely innocent (as many did), or disclaiming any communist leanings (as many tried to do) did not suffice to "clear" names once clouded. Mere innocence was not enough. Private anticommunist "consultants" demanded that suspects purge themselves of "dangerous neutralism." AWARE, Inc., one of the self-appointed blacklist groups, published *The Road Back: Self Clearance*. It advised those who wanted to clear their names to actively "support anti-Communist persons, groups, and organizations" and "subscribe to anti-Communist magazines, read anti-Communist books, government reports and other literature." Religious conversion was suggested as a favorable sign of political redemption (quoted in Cogley, 1956: 136).

The broadcasting industry knuckled under with scarcely a murmur of public protest. However, when the Fund for the Republic polled broadcasting executives it found that only 11 percent considered the blacklisters as "sincere and patriotic." Other executives referred to them as "misguided," "crazy," "profiteers," and "pathological." Sixty-seven percent of the industry members interviewed believed the blacklisters were motivated by professional jealousy. But still no one wanted to be quoted by name (Cogley, 1956: 242).

Among the talent unions, only Actors' Equity took an antiblacklisting stand. The American Federation of Television and Radio Artists (AFTRA) was almost torn apart by controversy. Even though a problacklist group of officers was shown to represent only a minority of the members, AFTRA still failed to come to the aid of its accused members, who were facing the most serious crises in their careers.

The Faulk Case One AFTRA member who fought back was John Henry Faulk, a successful radio and television personality on CBS. Faulk sued the blacklisters and later wrote a book about his experiences (Faulk, 1964).

He had helped to organize an antiblacklist (but also anticommunist) ticket for the New York AFTRA chapter, winning election as second vice president. The problacklist faction included several officers of AWARE, Inc. Following the defeat of its slate in the AFTRA election, AWARE published a report accusing Faulk of seven instances of activities it considered politically suspect.

He brought suit against the blacklisters in June of 1956. Late in 1956 CBS abruptly discharged Faulk while he was out of the country on vacation. Upon his return he found his career suddenly at an end. Alleging a malicious conspiracy to defame him, Faulk proved in court that each of AWARE's seven charges against him were false. The viciousness of the libel so appalled the jury that it awarded even more damages than Faulk asked — a total of $3.5 million. "This unprecedented award," said the presiding judge, "was evidently intended to express the conscience of the community, represented by this jury . . . concerning a matter of fundamental rights" (quoted in Nizer, 1966: 459). On appeal, the defendants received another stinging rebuff when a five-judge New York appellate court unanimously upheld the guilty verdict, remarking that "the acts of the defendants were proved to be as malicious as they were vicious." The court did, however, reduce the damages to $550,000 (19 A.D. 2d 464, 1963), most of which Faulk was never able to collect. Louis Nizer, Faulk's lawyer, concluded his own story of the case by saying, "One lone man had challenged the monstrously powerful forces of vigilantism cloaked in super patriotism" (1966: 464).*

In point of fact the blacklisters only *seemed* "monstrously powerful." They gained their strength from the timidity of the broadcasters, advertisers, and agencies who surrendered meekly in order to avoid controversy. There were honorable exceptions to the rule that prove the point. Chet Huntley, for example, later a major network news personality, was then a local Los Angeles broadcaster, sponsored by a coffee company. When he was threatened with a boycott of his sponsor's product because he spoke favorably of UNESCO and unfavorably of Senator Joseph McCarthy of Wisconsin, the coffee company refused to drop its sponsorship of Huntley's program. Gypsy Rose Lee, the dancer, was attacked for alleged association with four subversive groups. She produced a list of some 300 benefits she had performed and asked how she could possibly have investigated the political complexion of every one; her network, ABC, refused to take action against her without more substantial evidence, and none was forthcoming (Cogley, 1956: 88, 24).

A Wider Responsibility   In the midst of all the publicity about the Jean Muir firing, General Foods commissioned a Gallup opinion survey. Less than 40 percent of the sample had even heard of the case. Of those who had heard of it, less than 3 percent could tie it in with the correct sponsor (Miller, 1952: 46).

---

*In 1975 Faulk's book was converted into a television special, "Fear on Trial," by CBS — an ironic vindication, considering that CBS had made the book possible by firing him 19 years before (Navasky, 1975). Later in 1975 he won a minor role for a short time on the comedy series *Hee Haw*.

In rebuttal, advertisers may well ask what rule of business requires them to take even so slight risk as this. The advertisers' position was expressed in The Fund for the Republic study by the president of the American Tobacco Company:

When a company such as ours uses its corporate funds to sponsor a program on television or radio, it does so with but one purpose — to reach the largest possible number of the public as its audience, and to present its products to that audience in the most favorable light . . . We would be wasting shareholders' funds were we to employ artists or other persons who, under company auspices, are likely to offend the public. (Cogley, 1956: 101)

This view would be completely reasonable if broadcasting were purely a business, responsible solely for returning a profit to shareholders. But broadcasting has a much wider social responsibility. That at least is the underlying assumption of American broadcasting policy as expressed in the Communications Act of 1934. Indeed, there is no country in the world, as we pointed out in Chapter 1, that does not view commercial broadcasting as bearing a social responsibility that extends well beyond the duty implied by the interest of shareholders in earning profits.

Acceptance of that wider responsibility was exemplified by another episode in the 1950s. The best-known exponent of the blacklisting approach to patriotism was Senator Joseph R. McCarthy. As chairman of a Senate subcommittee on investigations, McCarthy staged a series of flamboyant witch hunts. So notorious were his methods that the term "McCarthyism" has since entered the language as a synonym for public character assassination based on unfounded accusations.

One of those who took the risk of openly

opposing McCarthy was Edward R. Murrow, the CBS newsman whom we last met as he returned home in triumph after covering World War II in Europe (§7.6). Also at risk was the Aluminum Company of America, sponsor of *See It Now*, which stood firm despite threats of boycott. In television documentaries and radio commentaries Murrow had criticized specific instances of McCarthy's unfairness. Not until March 9, 1954, did he mount a direct attack on McCarthy's methods as a whole. That night, Murrow devoted his entire *See It Now* program to a devastating critique of McCarthyism.

Murrow and his producer, Fred Friendly, needed do little more than draw upon their film files. So outrageously inconsistent, illogical, opportunistic, and devious was McCarthy that they could assemble a program in which McCarthy condemned himself. As Murrow's biographer wrote, the senator acted "as his own executioner, in full view of tens of millions of Americans" (Kendrick, 1969: 35). "We will not be driven by fear into an age of unreason," said Murrow in his concluding remarks, "if we dig deep into our own history and our doctrine and remember that we are not descended from fearful men, not from men who feared to write, to speak, to associate, and to defend causes which were for the moment unpopular."

McCarthy accepted CBS's offer of rebuttal time, filming his reply on a Fox Movietone soundstage at a cost of $6,000, which CBS paid. With his usual wild rhetoric, McCarthy called Murrow "the leader and the cleverest of the jackal pack which is always found at the throat of anyone who dares to expose individual Communists and traitors" (quoted in Friendly, 1967: 55). Later in 1954 television dealt another blow to McCarthy by broadcasting in full the 36-day hearings of his Senate subcommittee during which he attacked the patriotism of the U.S. Army.* As in the *See It Now* broadcast, on camera McCarthy turned out to be his own worst enemy.

Murrow himself never claimed that the *See It Now* analysis played a decisive role in McCarthy's subsequent decline. Doubtless it helped the public to see McCarthyism for what it was. But press criticism was on the rise, and the mood of the country was changing. With the benefit of the *See It Now* analysis as background, more of the viewing public could recognize McCarthyism. In any event, within the year McCarthy's career was effectively brought to an end when the Senate passed a motion of censure against him.

In doing its part to expose McCarthy, broadcasting to some extent redeemed itself for having given in so tamely to the demands of the blacklisters. Nevertheless, as Murrow said, looking back in retrospect five years after the event, "the timidity of television in dealing with this man when he was spreading fear throughout the land is not something to which this art of communication can ever point with pride. Nor should it be alllowed to forget it" (quoted in Kendrick, 1969: 70).

Summary

Television broadcasting lagged two decades behind sound radio, delayed by the need to standardize high-resolution pictures, by World War II, and by the medium's high costs. Pre-electronic, low-definition systems were promoted in the 1920s and 1930s but gave way in the late 1930s to electronic sys-

*In those days the networks, especially the weaker ones, could find time for such extended coverage without undue sacrifice. Both the Dumont network and ABC carried the 187 hours of hearings in full, though ABC did not at that time have complete coast-to-coast coverage. NBC carried a few days of the hearings and CBS showed film clips in the evenings.

tems. In the United States, Farnsworth, Zworykin, and a team of engineers representing the major manufacturers were getting ready to introduce high-definition television when World War II interrupted developments. As a result, modern U.S. black-and-white television did not begin its growth as a mass medium until 1948. The original 12 VHF channels allocated in the U.S. proved unable to handle the demand for stations. After a 1948–1952 "freeze" on further station applications, the FCC added 70 more channels in the UHF band to the existing 12 VHF channels. Some channels in both bands were reserved for noncommercial use.

Intermixture of VHF and UHF channels in most markets put UHF stations at a disadvantage because of the inherently shorter propagation range of UHF waves. The FCC used a variety of strategies to equalize UHF/VHF coverage, but not until the 1970s did UHF commercial stations as a group begin to show a profit. After a battle between rival systems, the FCC adopted the RCA color system in 1953, but it took about two decades for color to come into general use.

In network programming, NBC's Weaver introduced important innovations in the early 1950s. However, CBS took the leadership in ratings in 1955 and was not displaced until ABC forged to the front in 1976. ABC's success after so many years of running a weak third among the networks is ascribed to its use of Hollywood-style entertainment and filmed rather than live series, its focus on audiences with the greatest buying power, and its emphasis on sports. A pro-posed merger of ABC with conglomerate ITT fell through in 1967, leaving ABC still far behind NBC and CBS in corporate size. NBC, as a subsidiary of RCA, has the most powerful corporate backing of the three.

Network television programming at first originated almost entirely from the East Coast and was produced live. In the late 1950s videotape recording and film displaced live entertainment, and the film industry, after an initial period of reluctance, became heavily involved in television. The center of entertainment production gravitated to Hollywood, though news and public affairs programming remained centered in New York, where the networks continued to maintain their headquarters.

The alternative to networks as a source of nationally distributed programming is syndication. Syndicated programs consist of off-network series, programs made especially for sale in the syndication market, feature films, and miscellaneous programming, including imports.

Television experienced several ethical crises during the 1950s. A scandal erupted when it was discovered that the outcomes of extremely popular network quiz shows were being rigged. Public reaction to the scandal suggests an ambivalent attitude about the role television should play, whether as simply a form of show business or as a responsible medium of information. Similar ambivalence was suggested by capitulation of networks, advertisers, and advertising agencies to blacklisting practices during the Cold War era.

CHAPTER 9

Commercial Television Programming

Having reviewed the development of the commercial television system, we turn now to the end result — the system's program output. Of the many program types, we have singled out five that for various reasons seem to have significance that merits giving them special attention: network entertainment, news and public affairs, sports, religion, and children's programs.

9.1 Scheduling Strategies

Most media reach consumers in individually packaged units — a film, a phonograph record, an edition of a newspaper or book, an issue of a magazine. Only broadcasting offers the consumer a *continuous* experience. Programming unfolds, minute by minute, as the day unfolds. It provides not merely a succession of information packages but also a coherent program *service*. For this reason, *scheduling* plays a major role in the strategies of effective broadcast programming.

In devising schedules, programmers take into account changing audience availability, occupations, needs, and interest as the cycles of days, weeks, and seasons progress. They also take into account competition from other stations, using scheduling changes as their primary competitive weapons.

Day Parts For scheduling purposes, programmers break air time down into *day parts*. Although definitions vary as to details, by general agreement television programmers divide the day into segments called prime time (including access time), fringe time, daytime, and "all other" time. Each day part has its characteristic audience potentialities. Exhibit 9.1.1 shows how one of the major research companies defines day parts.

Prime time affords access to the largest and most varied audiences and therefore justifies the most expensive programming with the broadest program appeals. By the same token, prime time also invites the keenest competition among television stations and networks. Because of the high cost of such programming and the need for flexibility in scheduling to outflank the competition, prime-time series are normally scheduled on a weekly basis, whereas in other day parts most programming is *stripped* — scheduled "across the board," Monday through Friday.

Audience Flow Programming strategies center on the goal of controlling *audience flow*. Occurring mostly at the junction points when one program ends and another begins, audience flow includes both *flowthrough* on the same station and *outflow* or *inflow* to or from competing stations. A. C. Nielsen, the ratings research company, made a special study of prime-time audience flow in 1977. It found that on the average 86 percent of a network's audience flowed through from one half-hour to the next when the same program contin-

Exhibit 9.1.1
TV station day parts

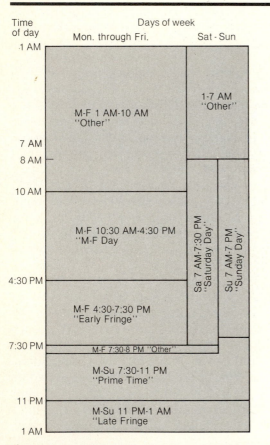

This division of the broadcast days of the week into prime, fringe, day, and "other" day parts is used by the A.C. Nielsen Company in reporting national audience data. It reflects the network outlook on day parts, with the prime-time access half-hour classified as "other". Note that the networks recapture the access half-hour on Sundays, as explained earlier in §8.7.

ued; flowthrough dropped to 68 percent when a new program of similar type followed in the next half-hour, and to 50 percent when a program of a different type started in the next half-hour (Nielsen, 1978: 56).

Some of the typical prime-time scheduling strategies that exploit audience flow include:

1. *Counterprogramming:* seeking to cause audience flow away from the competition and toward one's own station. Example: scheduling light entertainment against the opposition's news programs to attract segments of the audience not seriously interested in news.

2. *Block programming:* seeking to maintain audience flowthrough by scheduling programs with similar appeal next to each other. Example: an entire evening of comedy programs.

3. *Strong lead-in:* seeking to establish maximum initial audience size by starting the day part with a particularly strong program. Example: high-rated local news as lead-in to network news.

4. *Creating a hammock:* seeking to establish a new program, or to recover the audience for a program already slipping in popularity, by scheduling the program in question in a "hammock" between two strong programs. Flowthrough from the previous (lead-in) program may enhance the initial audience for the hammock program; later, flowthrough and premature inflow from other stations in anticipation of the strong following program may also help to bolster the audience for the hammocked program.

5. *Stunting:* seeking to keep the opposing networks off balance in the short term by such stratagems as making rapid schedule changes, opening a new series with an extra-long episode, and interrupting regular programming frequently with special programs.

Network Scheduling Each of the three national television networks offers its affiliates approximately a hundred hours of programs per week (Exhibit 9.1.2). Network programming fills about 70 percent of the air time of an affiliate that stays on the air 20 hours a day (say from 6 A.M. to 2 A.M.). The main arena of network rivalry is the 22 hours of prime time each network fills each week.* The profit margin for network daytime programming is greater than that for prime-time programming because of the extraordinarily high cost of the latter. Nevertheless, it is the network's performance in the prime-time arena that establishes its prestige and defines its leadership role.

The broadcast "season" has been growing progressively shorter. Originally 39 weeks (leaving 13 weeks for a summer hiatus), the television season has shrunk to 30 weeks, only 24 of which are filled with new episodes in prime-time series. The remaining weeks

*The 22 hours of network prime time represent the three hours from 8 P.M. to 11 P.M. nightly (21 hours) plus the 7 P.M.–8 P.M. Sunday hour, which the networks recapture under exceptions to the PTAR (§8.7).

are filled with *reruns* of episodes already shown earlier in the season.

At one time networks committed themselves for the entire season to the programs in their fall schedule when it was introduced in September soon after Labor Day. In recent years, however, competition has become so fierce networks cancel shows after only a few episodes if they fail to start earning good ratings from the outset. Critics complain that this practice kills off promising shows that need a longer run to establish a following. *All in the Family,* one of the most popular series of all time, came into its own only after 15 episodes had been aired. Had it been launched a few years later it might easily have been prematurely canceled after three or four episodes with unpromising ratings.

Selection of prime-time programs that form the basic framework for the fall season is preceded by a long gestation process. William Paley described the steps in his autobiography (1979: 261). In preparation for the 1978–1979 season, CBS bought over 200 scripts. Only 40 of these survived initial selection to be designated for pilot production. A *pilot* is the first, showcase episode of a

Exhibit 9.1.2
Amount of TV network programming by day part

	Daytime	Day parts Weekend daytime	Early news	Prime time	Late night	Weekly total
Hours per week	41	12.5	5.5	22	13	94
Percentage	44	13	6	23	14	100

Comment: The table averages the three national television networks. Weekly total for individual networks ranged from 86 hours (ABC) to 100 hours (NBC).

Source: FCC Network Inquiry Staff. *An Analysis of the Network-Affiliate Relationship in Television.* Preliminary Report. FCC, Washington, DC, October, 1979.

potential series. Usually longer and more lavishly produced than the rest of the episodes, a pilot gives researchers a chance to test audience reaction to the characters, the casting, and the basic story line. On the basis of research findings and executive hunches the final selection of shows for the fall season is made, usually in March, by a program committee.

Only 11 of the 40 series considered by CBS were actually scheduled to open in September — a survival rate from script to schedule of about 1 in 20. The remaining 29 pilots served for summer replacements and fill-ins. Sometimes pilots are produced in the form of made-for-television feature films (§8.6) so as to enhance their earning power even if they do not become the lead-off episodes in prime-time series.

Local Scheduling   Nonnetwork programs scheduled by individual stations may be divided into locally *selected* programs and locally *produced* programs. The former refers to the various types of syndicated material discussed in §8.7 — feature films, off-network series, and so on. For affiliated station programmers, local scheduling is largely a matter of filling in the blanks between network day parts with such material. The programmers' most important decision in this connection is deciding what to schedule in the prime-time access segment at their disposal.

Locally produced programs play a very small part, accounting on the average for little more than 9 percent of all television programming, and most of that consists of locally produced news. The evening news, by all odds the most important locally produced program, is the focus of local scheduling strategies for affiliated stations.

At the 14 percent of television stations that are not network-affiliated, programmers have many more scheduling options. Their chief scheduling stratagem, *counter programming*, takes advantage of the network affiliates' inflexibility. For example, their greater freedom of choice enables independents to schedule sports events that come at awkward times for affiliated stations. Networks can afford to devote prime time to only a few top-rated games that have great national interest; independents, however, can afford to schedule lesser sports events of high local interest, even though they may occur during prime time.

9.2 Prime-Time Network Entertainment

Dimensions of Prime Time   For the 22 hours of prime time each week the three national networks vie for audiences of awesome size, unprecedented in the history of communication. Collectively the networks capture about a 90 percent share of the households-using-television (HUT) during prime time.* This means that each network needs a share of 30 percent to stay even with the other two. Network prime-time programs that continue to fall below the 30-percent-share level are almost certainly headed for oblivion. The most popular programs attract nearly 50 percent of the prime-time audience, and major events carried by all three networks can reach as much as 90 percent of the entire adult U.S. population.

---

*See §14.3 for discussion of the HUT concept. Because of the factor of simultaneous viewing in multiset households, nonnetwork stations reach a somewhat higher percentage of the HUT than the 10 percent share that would be left if there were only one receiver in each home. During the 1980s cable television will probably cut back on the networks' accustomed 90 percent share.

Program Procurement About two dozen Hollywood companies create prime-time entertainment series. Some of these producers are associated with such traditional movie companies as Columbia and Warner Brothers. Less well known to the public are *independent* producers such as Spelling-Goldberg, Lorimar, and TAT/Tandem/PITS. These packagers specialize in prime-time series; other firms (and sometimes advertisers) are responsible for creating daytime series.

Generally networks go through four stages in arriving at a contract with a supplier:

1. The network program development department sifts through and evaluates hundreds of proposals a year that come from production companies, from the network itself, and from people outside the industry. Promising ideas are singled out for further exploration.
2. The network business affairs department negotiates a *development agreement* with a proposer, leading to the preparation of a script or a *treatment* (outline and description).
3. Top network officials evaluate scripts that result from development agreements and select a few for production as *pilots*.
4. The network program committee studies the success of pilots, both as on-the-air productions and as the subjects of special test screenings; the committee also considers how a new series would mix with the programs already penciled into the upcoming schedule and how it would affect audience flow. Finally, if the committee is satisfied, the producer gets the go-ahead, subject to negotiation of a mutually satisfactory contract.*

Program Diversity Critics often fault network television for lack of *program diversity*.

In fact they cite this limitation of network programming as one of the major reasons for urging development of cable television and other new delivery systems that promise to enlarge the viewer's choice.

As many as a third of the new prime-time series each season fail to return the next season. Despite such rapid turnover, prime-time entertainment program types remain remarkably similar from year to year. The popularity of particular subclasses (cowboy or police/detective plays, for example) runs through cycles, but beneath these superficial changes, programs tend to be confined to a few well-established formats, most of them variations of the dramatic format. A study of more than 2,000 prime-time programs broadcast by the networks between 1953 and 1974 revealed not only a narrow range of types, but a continuing decline in the number of types over the years (Exhibit 9.2).

Networks try to vary their offerings by frequent interruption of normal schedules with *specials*, which have been growing in frequency (upward of a hundred by each network each season by 1980), to the point at which they no longer seem particularly special. The fact is that lack of diversity arises from the networks' drive for rating supremacy. To compete they have to stick to the program types that have the broadest mass appeal. A study of the 1950–1975 period by A. C. Nielsen, the audience research company, analyzed the 15 all-time network favorites during that 25-year span. Among the top 15 only six program types were represented: situation comedies, westerns, talent shows, a police show, a comedy variety show, and a quiz show. No less than eight of the 15 favorites were situation comedies, led by *Lucy*, which ranked among the top 15 for 17 of the 22 seasons it was on the air as

*This description is based on an FCC Network Inquiry Staff Study (June, 1980).

a network prime-time offering (Nielsen, 1979: I-67).

Quest for Novelty Although prime-time network programming lacks diversity, network programmers nevertheless desperately seek *novelty*. The explanation of this seeming paradox is the fact that they want to be "different" without taking chances. So much is invested in prime time (in terms of network image-building as well as in terms of program costs) that program decisions have to be made at the highest corporate level.

William Paley, long after he had advanced from the position of CBS corporate president to that of chairman of the board, still participated actively on the network program committee that selected shows for the upcoming season. The committee included not only program and research executives, but also

Exhibit 9.2
Decline in diversity of prime-time network programming

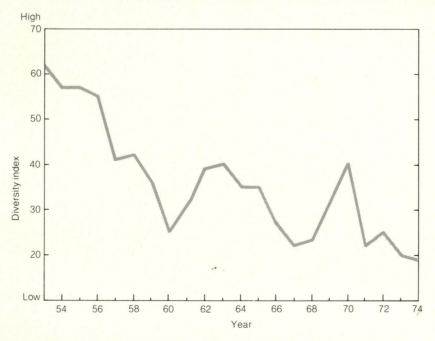

Prime-time network programming was categorized into 14 types including newscasts and documentaries as separate categories. The chart is based on a "diversity index," which ranges from zero to 79. A score of zero would mean that all of a season's programming consisted of no more than three categories; and a score of 79 would mean that programming that season was divided equally among all 14 program categories.

Source: Reprinted from "Trends in Network Programming" by Joseph R. Dominick and Millard C. Pearce in *The Journal of Communication* (26:1), Winter. Copyright 1976 Annenberg School of Communications.

both the network and the corporation presidents as well as the board chairman (Paley, 1979: 253). Program decision-making by corporate committees is not likely to favor daring experimentation. Instead new programs often tend to be *spin-offs** from already successful shows, if not outright imitations.

Relevance During the 1960s the quest for novelty encouraged the introduction, at least tentatively, of more realistic, contemporary material into prime-time entertainment. *The Smothers Brothers Comedy Hour* (1967–1969) and *Laugh-In* (1967–1973) dared to make satirical comments on previously sacrosanct topics of the day. CBS canceled the Smothers program in 1969 under controversial circumstances. "The *Comedy Hour* got too relevant," wrote Tommy Smothers. "We wanted to make it a platform for a dialogue between many people; the young, the old, the black, the white, even the dissident, because we felt that frustration finds a much healthier outlet in laughter. We are proud that our program touched on many relevant things, both humorously and seriously" (1969: 9). CBS ascribed the cancellation to the brothers' failure to submit a program tape in time for network preview, but it was also evident that CBS feared its affiliates might not be as ready for relevance in comedy programs as were the Smothers brothers.

By 1970, however, the social climate had changed enough to make a degree of relevance tolerable in prime-time entertainment. Norman Lear's situation comedy, *All in the Family* (1971–1979) has been credited with

playing a major role in breaking down the traditional barriers to realistic comedy. Lear earned widespread praise for this achievement. Les Brown of the *New York Times* called him "the most successful and most daringly innovative television producer in Hollywood" (9 Apr. 1978). *Time* remarked that "not since Disney has a single showman invaded the screen and the national imagination with such a collection of memorable characters" (5 Apr. 1976). Fred Silverman, the leading program executive of the 1970s, wrote:

All in the Family *marked the first time that television comedy tried to treat the world as it really is. It is a tribute to the brilliance of the cast and the scripting that subjects from bigotry to rape could be presented in a comedy context, without either trivializing the subject or overwhelming the comedy. . . . The unreality of happy people with happy problems was forever over. Writers and producers with something to say found they could say it in a comedy format. (Quoted in Adler, 1979: 261)*

The name of the leading character, Archie Bunker, entered the language as a synonym for the outspoken and unashamed bigotry of the traditional WASP blue-collar working man, with his predictable hangups about sex, women, homosexuals, ethnic minorities, intellectuals, and religion. The timidity with which prime-time television approached this thorny character is suggested by the fact that the first episode seen by the public was the third pilot production. ABC had paid for, and turned down, two previous versions in 1969. Moreover, CBS preceded the airing of its version with a carefully worded warning: "The program you are about to see . . . seeks to throw a humorous spotlight on our frailties, prejudices and concerns. By making them a

---

*Spin-offs are a parsimonious and relatively safe way of capitalizing on the favorable image of an already-successful series by starting a new series using a well-established character from an old series. *All in the Family*, for example, yielded *Maude* and *The Jeffersons*. Similar to spin-offs are sequels to successful ventures, such as *Roots: The Next Generations*.

source of laughter we hope to show — in a mature fashion — just how absurd they are."

All in the Family received mixed initial reviews, but as word-of-mouth publicity spread, it began to catch fire. "It became a historic breakthrough," wrote CBS's Paley, who is said to have been less than enthusiastic when he agreed to schedule the series. "The next season we became bold enough to schedule it for Saturday in the 8 p.m. slot, where it could make or break the evening for us. There, it became the number-one show on television" (1979: 267).

Docudramas and Miniseries

The relevancy fad of the 1970s led to the popularity of that controversial mixture of fact and fiction known as the *docudrama*, which blends real people and real events with fiction for the sake of dramatic effect. Even the Bible was "improved" in the docudrama *The Day Christ Died* (Murphy, 1980).

A 1978 study of the evolution of the docudrama found that, in one form or another, the format had been used since the beginning of television drama itself but became conspicuous only in the 1970s. The researchers ascribed the popularity of the form to the interest in history, recent and remote, stimulated by Watergate news coverage and the U.S. Bicentennial celebration of 1976, among other things (Hoffer and Nelson, 1978).

Also important, however, was the networks' obsession with relevancy, aided and abetted by growing social permissiveness that countenanced ruthless intrusion into private lives. This permissiveness encouraged the exploitation of the public's natural curiosity, perhaps even of its envy (Arlen, 1977: 124).

Growth of docudramas coincided with a fad for *miniseries* — dramas too short to figure as regular continuing series, but too long to

schedule in a single evening. Their use was encouraged by the success of the short-run series imported by public broadcasting under the general title *Masterpiece Theatre.** The first commercial experiment came in 1973, but the format caught on in 1976 when ABC's *Rich Man, Poor Man*, a 12-hour dramatization of an Irwin Shaw novel, proved highly successful. Miniseries disrupt regular schedules, but such disruption had already been found effective as a competitive tactic in the scheduling of specials (§8.5).

By the end of the 1970s network programmers were said to be considering hundreds of topics for docudrama miniseries. They ransacked history — primarily current or recent history — for likely topics. Among the subjects used in the late 1970s were the holocaust in Germany during World War II; the assassination of President John Kennedy; the kidnapping of Patty Hearst; the death from "friendly fire" of an American soldier in Vietnam; the life of Martin Luther King; several Watergate-related dramatizations; and a fictionalized story of a black family's survival, starting with the enslavement of a forebear in Gambia, West Africa.

Roots, the most phenomenally successful entertainment program in television history, ran for eight nights in a row in one- and two-hour episodes on ABC in 1977. The final episode achieved a rating of 51.1 and a 71 share — an all-time television record. Based on family recollections and 12 years of research by a black writer, Alex Haley, *Roots* had a spectacular impact. It was more than simply the all-time most popular television show; in

---

*One of the oft-noted differences between British and American television is the fact that British networks do not press writers to continue television drama series beyond their natural life-spans in order to fit the demands of prime-time scheduling patterns. British writers are free to terminate a project as soon as their inspiration or the subject begins to wear out.

the words of a *Time* critic, it galvanized the country:

Suddenly both the history of slavery and genealogy were national obsessions. Theaters and restaurants emptied out during the show; hundreds of colleges started Roots *courses; the National Archives in Washington found itself flooded by citizens' requests for information about their ancestors. Writer Alex Haley . . . became a folk hero. A TV smash hit became a cultural landmark. (Rich, 1979: 84)*

In 1979, a 14-hour, seven-part sequel, *Roots: The Next Generations*, scored almost as great a success as the original.

Critics have deplored the docudramas' tendency to mislead viewers. *Roots* was taxed, for example, for misleading by oversimplification — Haley himself called it "faction," a blending of fact and fiction. *King* (1978), a docudrama about the life of Dr. Martin Luther King, was faulted for mixing actual newsreel footage with staged footage. *The Trial of Lee Harvey Oswald* (1977) contained many assumptions, presented as undisputed facts, about the assassination of President John Kennedy.

Defenders of the form point out that history has always afforded a mine of ideas for fiction writers. But television is not perceived as exclusively a medium of fiction like the theater or the novel; it functions also as the most widely used source of real history in the form of news and news documentaries. Moreover, television is also an advertising medium, and that can lead to jarringly inappropriate pairings of history with salesmanship. *Holocaust* (1978), for instance, a docudrama about the fate of Jews in Nazi Germany, was guilty of sudden switches to grotesquely inappropriate commercials — from the death camp to panty hose, for example (Morrow, 1978: 53).

Bimodal Appeal   Both *Roots* and *All in the Family* illustrate another important fact about prime-time television entertainment: attracting and holding the attention of tens of millions of people night after night demands programs of extraordinarily broad appeal. The most successful programs attain this breadth by appealing on two or more different levels. Paul Klein, a specialist in audience demographics, called this quality *bimodality* (1971: 22). He cites the example of age bimodality. Some programs tend to attract both young and old viewers, but not the age group in between. A graph depicting audience age against program popularity would show a bimodal curve, with two distinct peaks at lower and higher age levels.

Multidimensional appeals cut across differences that otherwise set people poles apart. The ability of *All in the Family* to draw such large audiences year after year hinged on bimodal perceptions of Archie Bunker's prejudices. Large numbers of viewers agreed with Lear's overt antibigotry message; others, perceiving the opposite message, enthusiastically endorsed what they saw as Bunker's courage in "telling it like it is." Neither group by itself would have been large enough to account for *All in the Family*'s high ratings. Working together in unconscious and ironic harmony they made the series unbeatable. A similar bimodality can be discerned in *Roots*, which had irresistible attraction for both blacks and whites, but for entirely different reasons.

9.3 Non-Prime-Time Network Entertainment

Weekday daytime programs, unlike prime-time series, are nonseasonal. They are scheduled year-round and on a Monday-through-Friday basis. Instead of the 20-odd new episodes a year of a prime-time series, a daytime series needs 260 new episodes. This grueling production schedule requires the most parsimonious use of program resources (§7.4). Soap operas, for example, are rigidly limited as to the number of characters and the number of sets that can be afforded for each episode. They make exacting demands on actors and production crews, who must be capable of turning out a complete episode in a single day's shooting.

Game shows, even cheaper to produce, record as many as five episodes in a single day's concentrated work. Other weekday non-prime-time formats include early morning news magazines and late-night talk shows. And the networks wring additional income out of some of their most popular prime-time series by stripping them as daytime reruns on a daily rather than a weekly schedule. On weekends, daytime programming reverts to weekly scheduling, with emphasis on children's programs, news and public affairs features, and sports events.

TV Soap Operas One of the classic radio formats, the soap opera (§7.4), made the transition to television as early as 1947, though the big growth in numbers of "soaps" came in the early 1950s. NBC's *The Guiding Light* has had the longest combined radio-television run of all network programs, having started on radio in 1937, switching to television in 1952. It began on television with 15-minute episodes, but the trend has been to longer and longer episodes. *The Guiding Light* was the first soap to extend to a full hour. That came in 1975, and in 1978 it went to 90 minutes.

Other modern soap-opera trends include a tendency to speed up plot developments (contemporary viewers apparently have less patience than their parents had) and a willingness to deal with increasingly realistic themes — another evidence of the demand for relevancy which has affected prime-time

programming so markedly (§9.2). "The search for relevance has led daytime drama to deal with social issues like drugs, venereal disease and the Vietnam war, to take feminist positions on questions like abortion and women working, and to bring blacks and ethnics into the WASP population of Soapland" (Astrachan, 1975).

Increased tolerance for controversial topics in soap operas is also due to changes in audience composition. It is estimated that over ten percent of the contemporary soap opera audience consists of men. There has also been a growth of interest on the part of younger, college-age viewers. Still the core of the soap-opera audience remains the housewife — an ideal target for manufacturers of soap and other household products. Another plus from the advertisers' viewpoint is the extraordinary loyalty of dedicated soap-opera viewers, who support several fan magazines, attend conventions, and patronize newspapers that give daily summaries of soap-opera plots.

Game Shows Soap operas are distinctively a *network* genre, whereas the second largest category of network daytime programs, the *game shows*, lend themselves readily to syndication. They have not, like the soap opera, gone to longer formats but have stayed with the half-hour length, a format strongly favored by the syndication market, because it fits into the access slot (§8.7) and enables more flexible scheduling than longer shows. Emphasis on real knowledge and the use of extraordinarily well-informed participants went out with the quiz scandals of the 1950s (§8.8). Modern game shows tend to use frivolous questions, often with risqué overtones.

Game shows have been described as

"among the oldest and most primitive of television programming forms, a survivor of the archaic days of big-time radio." They are also, the same critic points out, "the biggest bargain on television" (Buckley, 1979). One of the most parsimonious of formats, the game show is cheap and easy to produce once a winning formula has been devised. A handful of specialists produce most of the successful game shows. Goodson-Todman Productions, for example, is said to gross about $50 million a year. Mark Goodson, the surviving member of the team, which was formed in 1946, has pointed out that "soap operas and game shows are the great indigenous television forms and they are alike in one important way. There are no endings. They go on and on and on" (quoted in Buckley, 1979).

Game shows are highly profitable, not only because they are cheap to produce but also because the giveaway format justifies expanding commercial content far beyond normal limits. Advertisers welcome the opportunity to donate their products and to pay a cash fee in addition for the sake of a seven-second glimpse of the product plus a 20-word plug. So active is the television giveaway business that several companies specialize as prize brokers (called in the trade "schlock-meisters") to handle the collecting, warehousing, and dispatching of game show prize merchandise. The brokers get 40 percent of the retail value of prizes.

Talk Shows The networks' early morning programs — *Today* (NBC), *Good Morning America* (ABC), and *Morning* (CBS) — serve a news function but also use interviews in the basic talk-show manner. The quintessential network talk show is NBC's *Tonight,* a post-prime-time offering called by Les Brown "the premier desk and sofa show" (1977: 437).

An invention of NBC's pioneer program-mer Sylvester Weaver (§8.5), *Tonight* started in 1954 as a showcase for the comic talents of Steve Allen. In 1957 Jack Paar succeeded Allen as the host, and he in turn was succeeded by Johnny Carson in 1962. After 17 years of monologues and interviews, Carson became restless and threatened to leave the show in 1979.

Incredible though it may seem, not only the NBC network but even its parent company, RCA, was shaken by the threatened loss of one performer whose talent is virtually undefinable and whose main previous broadcasting experience had been as MC of a quiz show. It was estimated that as much as 20 percent of NBC's income came from the 90-minute *Tonight* show. Advertisers paid $25,000 for a 30-second announcement to reach Carson's 15 million-plus viewers. At the time Carson was already the highest-paid performer in television, with a salary reported to be on the order of $3 million a year.

In 1980 Carson signed a new three-year contract, reportedly at $5 million a year. NBC agreed to cut the show back to 60 minutes, but Carson agreed to do four shows a week, one more than he had been doing under the old contract.

Although the soap opera is often cited as the unique broadcasting format, a better candidate might be Carson's type of talk show. The British critic and playwright Kenneth Tynan pointed out that despite his unique achievement in American television, Carson is nowhere near as well known in other countries as many lesser pop-culture personalities. "The job at which he excels," said Tynan, "is virtually unexportable . . . most of what happens on the show would be incomprehensible or irrelevant to foreign audiences, even if they were English-speaking" (1979: 114).

9.4 Television News

Importance of News News has been called "television's noblest service, the major source of its prestige" (Brown 1977: 303). According to a series of national surveys sponsored by the broadcasting industry, by 1961 the public began to think of television as the most trustworthy source of news. Two years later, 55 percent of the people surveyed said television was their *main* source of news. By 1980 this percentage had risen to 64 (Roper, 1981: 3, 4).

The Federal Communications Commission has always regarded news as having key importance as an ingredient in broadcast schedules. In fact the commission went so far as to cite the news function as the main justification for allocating spectrum space to broadcasting in the first place:

One of the most vital questions of mass communication in a democracy is the development of an informed public opinion through public dissemination of news and ideas concerning the vital public issues of the day. Basically, it is in recognition of the great contribution which radio can make in the advancement of this purpose that portions of the radio spectrum are allocated to . . . radiobroadcasting. (13 FCC 1249, 1949)

Access to News Like radio, television had to struggle to establish its legitimacy as a news medium. Even though radio had won full access to newswire services in 1940 (§7.6), in the early 1950s the print news media still tended to regard television as an interloper — a medium basically devoted to entertainment and therefore not to be taken seriously as a purveyor of news and public affairs information.

The single event that did the most to give television equal access to news was a showdown in 1952, remembered since as "The Battle of Abilene." Presidential candidate General Dwight D. Eisenhower attempted to bar television cameras from an important press conference he was to give in his Kansas hometown of Abilene. Edward R. Murrow's producer, defying the Eisenhower ban, forcibly led the television camera crews into the meeting. "The newspaper and wire services protested vehemently. They said that by filming their expert reporters asking questions, and getting the candidate's answers, television was misappropriating what did not belong to it" (Kendrick, 1969: 350). Eisenhower, accepting the advice of his press secretary, James Hagerty (who later became a top news official with ABC), dropped his opposition to television coverage. Moreover, the following January, one of Eisenhower's first acts as president was to give a press conference at which television news teams had full access and freedom to report the president verbatim (though at first only after White House clearance).

Although television's access to news rapidly improved, one major barrier lingered on. The American Bar Association's Canon 35, later redesignated Canon 3(A)(7), recommended that courts should prohibit on-the-spot broadcast coverage of trials (§17.2). At first the courts almost universally observed the ABA canon, but in recent years more and more state judicial systems have begun experiments allowing controlled coverage of court trials. By early 1980, 21 states had either removed the barrier or started to allow experimental television coverage (Kowet, 1980). Broadcast television crews are still banned from the federal courts, the proceedings of many government agencies, and the floor of the Senate (though the House now televises itself, making the coverage available to broadcasters).

Sources of News Physical access is important to television news teams because the networks and most stations depend primarily on their own camera crews for gathering most of their pictorial material. The established news agencies, AP and UPI, provide a written news agenda and still pictures (including color slides), but not motion pictures. The networks send their own camera teams to cover foreign news,* though they also buy occasional items from the European Broadcasting Union's Eurovision network and other foreign sources. They also sometimes acquire coverage of nationally significant stories from their own affiliates when such events occur in their vicinities.

In turn, affiliates can obtain what amounts to a syndicated television news service from their own networks. This network-syndicated service feeds the news over regular network relay facilities to affiliated stations during daytime hours when the facilities are not tied up with scheduled network programming. Affiliates can record these feeds, selecting items for later use and paying their networks a fee for the service. They can also obtain the right to record regular network news programs as sources of stories for later insertion in local programs (Graf, 1972). Still another nonlocal syndicated source of news material emerged in 1980 when the Cable Network News (CNN) service offered to exchange news stories with television stations (§11.4).

The CNN exchange offer is available to independent television stations, but the main syndicated source of nonlocal news stories for independents is UPITN, a combined operation of United Press International and Independent Television News, the British commercial television companies' commonly owned news service (§1.3). In 1980 a syndicated news-program service, Independent Network News, began relaying a daily half-hour packaged newscast via satellite to subscribing independents at 9:30 P.M.

Local News Despite the prestige value of news and current affairs programming, television stations at first tended to regard it more as a burdensome chore than as a glorious opportunity. Such programs cost a lot to produce but rarely won high ratings.

During the 1960s, however, as viewers became more and more dependent on television, a remarkable change began to occur. Stations discovered that their nightly local news programs could play a pivotal role in both audience building and image building and therefore also in moneymaking. As audiences for — and advertising revenue from — news programs grew, stations began investing heavily in their news operations. Local news department budgets in the millions of dollars became commonplace, enabling stations to purchcase or lease helicopters and other special facilities for newsgathering. Large stations developed their own local investigative reporting and documentary units. In 1980 they even began sending news teams to distant places to get local angles on national news events, sending stories back to their home bases via satellite. So important had local news become that, for network affiliates at least, being number-one in local news usually meant being the number-one station in the market.

The central role of news in local programming is indicated in Exhibit 9.4.1, which shows that television stations as a whole devote less than 10 percent of their schedules to locally produced programs, most of which

---

*Relatively few of the world's television systems can afford the luxury of covering foreign news with their own cameras. Most subscribe to Visnews, a television news service run by a consortium of British and Commonwealth interests, serving over 200 subscribers worldwide.

are news and public affairs. Locally produced *entertainment* programming amounts to less than one percent of the total.

Network News Although the networks gave up production of prime-time entertainment series to outside suppliers, they retained control of news and public affairs production. The policy of refusing to accept such programs from outsiders is maintained as a jealously guarded prerogative, despite criticism from independent producers and the occasional loss of a scoop.

For example, in 1977 all three networks turned down David Frost's offer of his independently produced series of 90-minute interviews with Richard Nixon, the first such public appearance since the ex-president's resignation. This refusal was costly to the networks, for 165 stations, most of them affiliates, preempted network programs to clear time for the Frost/Nixon series on a syndicated basis. It drew the largest audience ever attracted by a syndicated series (Barrett, 1978: 84).

The networks — especially CBS and NBC — argue that in order to function responsibly in the news and public affairs realm they must control the production process (Reel, 1979: 89). Each network operates its own news division, entirely separate from its entertainment divisions and headed by its own president. Each of these news operations employs on the order of a thousand persons.

Exhibit 9.4.1
Local and nonentertainment TV programming[a]

Percentage of all programming by category, 6 A.M. to midnight

Program source	News	Public affairs	Other non-entertain-ment	Total non-entertain-ment	Entertainment	Total
Locally produced	4.8	1.8	2.0	8.6	0.9	9.5
Nonlocal	4.6	2.7	10.0	17.3	73.2	90.5
Total	9.4	4.5	12.0	25.9	74.1	100.0

Comment: The FCC derives this information by tabulating a composite week of commercial station programming, reported by stations each year on FCC Form 303-A. Locally produced programming, less than 10 percent of the total, was mostly devoted to news and public affairs; less than 1 percent of programming was devoted to locally produced entertainment. The table shows averages for all stations, but examination of the station-by-station data in the full report generally reveals little variation from these averages.

[a]Average of 711 commercial stations reporting for 1978.

Source: Based on data in FCC, *Annual Programming Report for Commercial Television Stations: 1979*, FCC, Washington, DC, 15 Dec. 1980.

They maintain news bureaus in major U.S. and foreign cities. Each network is said to spend over $100 million annually on its news operation. The networks do not release financial details, but it is believed that not until 1979 did their news operations begin making a profit for all three networks (Pearce, 1980).

ABC News, historically the weakest of the three (§8.5), began to strengthen its position in the 1970s. One stratagem was to exploit the graphic resources of television in news programs more than had been customary. But ABC relied mainly on a maneuver learned from CBS (§7.5) — talent raids on the other networks (Gates, 1980). Harry Reasoner, long a CBS fixture, moved to ABC, becoming its chief anchor in 1970. In 1976, in its most talked-about move, ABC News lured Barbara Walters away from NBC, making her the first network anchorwoman as well as the highest-paid newscaster, at a million dollars a year. In other talent raids in 1978, William Small, long a distinguished CBS newsman, became president of NBC News. And Richard Salant, upon his retirement as CBS news chief at age 65, became vice chairman of the NBC board of directors.

The network anchorperson, as the up-front public representative of the entire network news operation, took on extraordinary significance. The "anchor" title seems to have been invented for Walter Cronkite, who became the chief news presenter for CBS news in 1962 (Exhibit 9.4.2). After a distinguished career as a wire-service correspondent and bureau chief during and after World War II, Cronkite joined CBS in 1950. He surged to the forefront at the 1952 Republican national political convention. Cronkite came to the convention

knowing that it was his big chance. He had come thoroughly prepared, he knew the weight of each delegation and he was able to bind the coverage together at all times. He was, in a field very short

on professionalism, incredibly professional, and in a job that required great durability, he was the ultimate durable man. By the end of the first day, in the early morning, the other people in the control booth just looked at each other; they knew they had a winner, and a new dimension of importance for television. (Halberstam, 1979: 243)

As a newspaperman in the old tradition, Cronkite fought against the show-business aspects of broadcast journalism. From the outset of his assignment as anchor for CBS nightly news he insisted on both the title and the active role of "managing editor." So influential did the job of anchorperson of the leading network nightly news become that, according to a national poll, the public came to esteem Cronkite as "the most trusted man in America" (Shaw, 1979: 38). The announcement that Dan Rather, after receiving bids from all three networks, had agreed to succeed Cronkite upon the latter's retirement in 1981 ranked as front page news. Within months of the changeover, ABC's evening news rating edged ahead to complete ABC's triumphant rise to network leadership.

Expansion of News CBS launched nightly television network news modestly in 1948 with *Douglas Edwards with the News* — essentially not much more than a 15-minute illustrated radio program. Edwards, unlike his successor at CBS, Walter Cronkite, came from a radio news background. In 1948 not many successful radio newspersons were willing to take the gamble on switching to the more demanding, little-understood medium of television.

Fifteen minutes remained the standard newscast length until 1963, when the networks expanded to a half-hour news format (actually only about 22 minutes, after time for commercials and opening and closing announcements is deducted). Despite the fact that the wordage of an entire half-hour newscast could fill less than a single page of a full-sized newspaper, the move to the half-hour format was a major factor in elevating network television to the status of the most widely accepted source of news in the country.

In 1976 Cronkite and others argued strenuously for expansion of network evening news to a full hour. All three networks explored the possibility. CBS went so far as to relay a sample one-hour newscast to its affil-

Exhibit 9.4.2
"The most trusted man in America"

Successor to the fabled Edward R. Murrow as the leading figure in broadcast news, Walter Cronkite's avuncular manner and great credibility earned him the title "the most trusted man in America." He started his career in print journalism, first as a part-time reporter while a student at the University of Texas, later as a wire service correspondent. He served as managing editor as well as anchorman for CBS Evening News from 1962 to 1981.

Source: Courtesy CBS Evening News.

iates in the hope of persuading them to accept the change. They nevertheless voted overwhelmingly against the expansion.

The failure to expand network news to an hour-long format was called "a major setback for the forces of responsible broadcasting" (Barrett, 1978: 8). But affiliates wanted to retain the prime-time lead-in slot for their own highly profitable newscasts. This meant that network news could expand only by encroaching into the primest of prime time, the 8:00–11:00 P.M. period. Nevertheless, it seems inevitable that, in one direction or the other, evening network newscasts will eventually be extended at least to 45, if not to 60, minutes.

Meanwhile, the networks increased their news schedules in other ways. CBS gradually expanded its morning news, first to a half-hour in 1963, then to a full hour in 1969. All three networks now schedule morning news or news-magazine programs as well as short news summaries throughout the day. In 1976 they began inserting one-minute news capsules in breaks between prime-time entertainment programs. These subminiature newscasts consist of 42 seconds of news, a 10-second commercial, and 8 seconds of announcements. Because of their adjacency to high-rated entertainment they draw the largest audiences that regularly scheduled newscasts have ever received.

Late in 1979 ABC found that sizable audiences gathered to watch its temporary 11:30 P.M. nightly news roundup on the crisis that arose from the Iranian seizure of American embassy personnel in Teheran as hostages. This experience led ABC to schedule a regular 20-minute late-night network news program, *Nightline*, each program concentrating on a single story.

At the station level, however, longer evening news formats flourished, extending in some cases to as long as two hours. A UHF station in Los Angeles went so far in 1973 as to attempt a daytime all-news format, but the venture lasted only a few months. More recently an Oklahoma City station revived the idea, planning all-news from noon to 5 P.M., followed by subscription television in the evening (*Broadcasting*, 3 Nov. 1980).

Electronic News Gathering One reason local news teams could generate enough material to fill longer news programs was the advent of *electronic news gathering* (ENG), sometimes also called *electronic journalism* (EJ). ENG was made possible by the development of the time-base corrector (§3.11) in 1973, which enabled mixing input from small video cameras and videotape recordings with program material from studio and network sources. Before ENG, stations depended primarily on 16-mm films for on-the-spot coverage of local news events. Film equipment is cheaper, but its operational costs are higher, it is slower because film takes time to develop, and it is less versatile than tape.

Mobile equipment had been a feature of television's production resources from the beginning, but at first it involved a large moving-van type of truck, loaded with heavy, bulky equipment. ENG equipment is not only mobile but also *portable* (Exhibit 9.4.3). It can be carried in an automobile, a small panel truck, or a helicopter, and it can be operated by a three-person crew. An ENG unit can travel quickly and economically to the scene of a news story. It can be rapidly deployed so as to start feeding an on-the-spot story back to the studio immediately by means of a microwave link. Alternatively, it can record material for later editing at the studio. ENG caught on rapidly. Only 3 percent of the commercial stations used it in 1973, but by 1979 86 percent were using it. By that time only 11 percent of the stations reported that they still relied on film alone (Stone, 1980).

Line-of-sight terrestrial relays are subject to many problems of signal blockage, reflections, and excessive distance. Eventually ENG equipment will probably beam signals up to satellites for relay back to the studio. Satellite relays will make it possible for ENG teams to deliver stories from virtually anywhere, at unlimited distances from their home studios.

Issues Broadcast news, Edward R. Murrow once told a meeting of broadcast news directors in 1958, is "an incompatible combination of show business, advertising, and news. Each of the three is a rather bizarre and demanding profession. And when you get all three under one roof, the dust never settles" (Murrow, 1958: 256). Three years later Murrow left commercial broadcasting, disillusioned because, as he saw it, show business and advertising had come to domi-

Exhibit 9.4.3
Electronic news gathering (ENG)

The unwieldy remote vehicle in the background contrasts with the compact, lightweight ENG van in the foreground. The machine-gun-like object on top of the van is an antenna for relaying pictures back to the studio.

Source: Photo courtesy of WTVJ (TV), Miami, FL.

nate broadcast news. His resignation was due not to any single slight but to an accumulation of setbacks:

Quite systematically, CBS moved to emasculate Ed Murrow. First to limit the number of "See It Now" shows. Then to control the hour they were shown. Then to change the name. Then to take the show away completely. Then to separate him from his producer, Fred Friendly. It was all done very deftly, and perhaps not even that consciously; corporations are often good at this, the increments of limitation were small, just enough to cut him steadily down but never really enough to drive him away in anger. (Halberstam, 1979: 147)*

Since Murrow's time, the rise to commercial success of news and news-related programming has assured it more respectful treatment from network and station managements. But the show-business influence to which Murrow referred has continued to be an issue. It surfaced, for example, in the controversy over "Happy Talk." The term refers to the jazzing-up of local news presentations with informal banter among members of on-air television news teams — usually an anchorperson, a sports reporter, a weather reporter, and varying numbers of other on-camera reporters. These calculated diversions create, as one critic put it, "an aura of exaggerated joviality and elbow-jabbing comradeship" (Powers, 1977: 35).

In part, at least, "Happy Talk" resulted from the advice of *news consultants*, a new breed of marketing specialists that rose to prominence in the 1970s. The best known are Frank M. Magid Associates, a marketing research firm that turned to news consultancy in 1970, and McHugh-Hoffman, Inc., which

turned from entertainment program consulting to news specialization in the late 1960s. The consultants' job is to jack up the ratings of news programs, a goal that took on vital importance when it was discovered that the ratings of a station's local evening news crucially affected not only its public image but also its competitive position in its market as well as its earning power.

News consultants move in with a battery of sophisticated psychological tests with which to analyze public perceptions of a station's news and news personnel and the organizational relationships within the station. Their advice can range widely, from wholesale firings of news personnel to the adoption of an on-the-air dress code. But the advice most resented by conscientious television journalists has to do with the news itself — though consultants vehemently deny that they interfere with professional journalistic judgments.

The 1975 DuPont-Columbia survey of broadcast journalism included a chapter entitled "The Trojan Horse" severely criticizing the news consultants. The title came from a report to the survey by Ralph Renick, one of the country's leading local news directors. Renick, vice president for news of WTVJ-(TV) in Miami, Florida, said the news consultants "are really a Trojan horse. They roll it in and suddenly the enemy troops are in your camp. Too often the service is put to political use to permit management to get control of the news when the news director is in conflict with management. What it really is, is franchised news — like McDonald's" (Barrett, 1975: 97). Ron Powers, in a book highly critical of the consultants, concluded:

When local stations create and choreograph entire programs along guidelines supplied by researchers — toward the end of gratifying the audiences'

---

*In his autobiography, CBS's William Paley said he was "extremely hurt" by Murrow's criticism of broadcasting in the 1958 speech quoted above. While admitting that he and Murrow had had their differences, Paley complained that they had been "distorted by careless writers" (1979: 297).

surface whims, not supplying its deeper informational needs — an insidious and corrosive hoax is being perpetrated on American viewers. . . . The hoax is made more insidious by the fact that very few TV newswatchers are aware of what information is left out *of a newscast in order to make room for the audience-building gimmicks and pleasant repartee. (Powers, 1977: 234)*

Another news director who reported to the DuPont-Columbia survey put the controversy in perspective by pointing out that, properly used, consultants could be useful. "The problem arises," he went on, "when the consultants try to run a newsroom and make editorial decisions. . . . In a good station that really cares about covering the news — as well as [about] the ratings — this is no problem" (Barrett, 1975: 98). In any event, as the decade wore on, reputable news consultants came to be widely accepted. A survey of the hundred top television markets in 1979 indicated that half of the stations had used consultants and seven out of ten news directors said they would not resent their advice (American University, 1979).

News consultants have been charged with aggravating two natural limitations of television journalism — its brevity and its dependence on pictures — by urging stations to concentrate on "action news" that lends itself to photography, such as fires and accidents, and to edit news stories to be as short and "punchy" as possible.

Although such deliberate distortions are to be deplored, it remains a fact that television is not well adapted to dealing at great length with hard news stories, nor can conventional photography add anything to stories that lack intrinsic visual content. More imagination might be used in exploiting television's graphic resources to clarify such stories, but the fact remains that television is not able to handle some types of news as well as newspapers. But brevity should not be despised. Viewers who want more depth can always turn to other media better adapted to their purpose.

9.5 Public Affairs Programming

Definition   News and public affairs are usually linked together by stations and networks, but the FCC in its license forms distinguishes "Public Affairs" as a separate class of programs, defined as follows: "local, state, regional, national or international issues or problems, including, but not limited to, talks, commentaries, discussions, speeches, editorials, political programs, documentaries, minidocumentaries, panels, roundtables and vignettes, and extended coverage (whether live or recorded) of public events or proceedings, such as local council meetings, congressional hearings and the like."

The television networks and most stations maintain at least one weekly public affairs discussion series and a news documentary series (the latter not always affordable by stations). Enthusiasm for documentaries waxes and wanes according to the degree of heat the networks feel from critics and the FCC. They are expensive to produce, cause a great deal of controversy, and rarely attract large audiences. For those very reasons as well as for their intrinsic informational value, broadcasters regard news documentaries as symbols of achievement, signs that when it wants to, television can be responsible and mature about serious matters.

The Murrow Tradition   With *See It Now* (1951–1958) Edward R. Murrow and his producer, Fred Friendly, bridged the radio and television documentary traditions. This news documentary series set many precedents, tackling the most controversial issues of the day. Among its "firsts" were pioneer television studies of segregation, apartheid, McCarthyism (§8.8), and the link between cigarette smoking and lung cancer (the last coming before the Surgeon General's report).

Murrow and Friendly experimented for two years with *See It Now* before hitting on a documentary style significantly different from the older tradition of film. Fred Freed, a Murrow colleague and himself a distinguished producer of television documentaries, recalled the innovative character of a 1953 *See It Now* program, "Christmas in Korea":

It tried to show what was behind the news, beneath the surface, what it was like to be out there in the line in Korea at Christmas time. It was a radio documentary with pictures, not a film. It was journalism, not art. That turned out to be crucial. It settled the way we would make news documentaries for television for the next twenty years. They would be in the hands of journalists. The important decisions would be journalistic. Ideas would come first. (1972: 56)

Influence of Technology

When screened today the early *See It Now* documentaries still project some of their original fervor, but their style seems stiff and formal. This old-fashioned look is due to changed approaches to documentary making, both as to substance and form. Murrow's biographer commented on the changed approach: "The sharp, shrewd editing of film that enabled a Murrow-Friendly program to make point after point was replaced by a kind of cinéma vérité that substituted impressions for points. The dissecting table became a psychoanalyst's couch. . . . The New Wave offers the viewer a sensory experience rather than balanced judgment" (Kendrick, 1969: 28).

Abetting the cinéma vérité approach, changes in the technology of picture making

have enabled a less obstrusive use of camera and microphone. The Murrow-Friendly team inherited the 35-mm theatrical newsreel tradition, which frowned on wobbly hand-held cameras, fuzzy focus, distorting angles, and poor lighting as evidences of amateurishness. Synchronous sound shooting used to require bulky equipment that limited the camera's mobility, making filming an obstrusive, disturbing element in the scene being filmed. The physical intrusion of equipment became far less disruptive with miniaturization and other technological advances. Production style changed when it became possible to use small, concealable microphones, lightweight hand-held cameras, and easily portable sound recorders with remote synchronization (eliminating the need for an umbilical cord between camera and recorder). Natural lighting could be used, dispensing with the glare of artificial lights and their tangle of cables. Results were not always perfect, but audiences had become tolerant of technically imperfect pictures and sound. In fact, slickly professional results came to be regarded with suspicion, as a superficial gloss possibly hiding lack of substantial content.

At its worst, this new style encouraged matching fuzzy thinking with fuzzy pictures. One critic called it "the kind of earnest incompetence that equates bad technical quality with honesty and considers passing up a [cinematic] cliché to be a creative act" (Stein, 1972: 200). At its best, however, naturalistic style produced memorable documentaries that let the camera do the talking. Examples are Frederick Wiseman's series of films on such institutions as hospitals, police departments, and juvenile courts. He developed, said one reviewer, "almost incredible ability not to provoke self-consciousness with his camera, a major problem in many cinéma vérité projects" (O'Connor, 1973). Another example was Helen Whitney's "Youth Terror: The View from Behind the Gun," a startling visual record of real-life teen-age criminality in the slums of New York and Newark, broadcast by ABC in 1978. The spontaneous sound track carried street language never before heard on television.

60 Minutes The most striking development in news-related programming was the rise of CBS's magazine-format documentary series, *60 Minutes*, to the very top of the prime-time ratings. In the 1979–1980 season it led all network programs in popularity, scoring an average rating of 28.2 against 26.3 for the leading entertainment series of the season.

This success violated all conventional wisdom about documentary programs, which had always been considered to have a built-in repellent that drove audiences away. One reason for their failure to get high ratings may have been that network programmers always tended to put documentaries in less favorable times and to deny them the luxury of stable scheduling. After years of wandering, *60 Minutes* finally achieved stability at a good hour because of the prime-time access rule, which opened up the 7:00–8:00 P.M. Sunday time slot.

Another reason for the *60 Minutes* success story is its stellar team of correspondents: Dan Rather, Harry Reasoner, Morley Safer, and Mike Wallace. As a *New York Times* commentator put it:

Their gray or graying hair, their pouched and care-worn countenances, the stigmata of countless jet flights, imminent deadlines and perhaps an occasional relaxing martini, provide a welcome contrast to the Ken and Barbie dolls of television news whose journalistic skills are apt to be exhausted after they have parroted a snippet of wire

service copy and asked someone whose home has just been wrecked by an earthquake, "How do you feel?" (Buckley, 1978)

These four, with the chief producer Don Hewitt and a staff of some 70 producers, editors, and reporters develop about 120 segments annually (Stein, 1979). The magazine format allows for scheduling a great variety of subject matters and for varying segment length, adding to the program's popular appeal. Also important is the "confrontation" formula, a Mike Wallace specialty. Confronting his victims on camera with damning evidence of wrongdoing, Wallace grills them unmercifully. Audiences, already in the know, are fascinated by the victims' evasions, lies, and brazen attempts to bluff their way out of their predicament.

Other Public Affairs Formats Each network also schedules an old-fashioned public affairs question-and-answer session with newsworthy figures, usually on Sundays in midday hours. Those are times of generally low ratings, when the small audiences of such public affairs programs (usually on the order of only 2 or 3 rating points) do the least damage to adjacent programs. NBC's *Meet the Press*, the oldest program of its type, dates back to 1947 — the longest-surviving program on network television. CBS launched its *Face the Nation* in 1954, ABC its *Issues and Answers* in 1960. Small audiences do not discourage interviewees, who count on reaching opinion makers through such programs. Every politician of any consequence has made appearances, many more than once. Senator Hubert Humphrey held the record for repeat performances, having appeared on *Meet the Press* 22 times (Levine, 1973).

The greatest achievements of broadcast news and public affairs programming, however, take place outside the contrived environment of the studio. The memorable high points of broadcasting have been the *actualities* it has covered in real time. Their qualities of immediacy and unpredictability lend a special fascination to actualities, whether the story is the Olympic games, congressional hearings, the first steps on the moon, or the pageantry of great events of state.

Among such achievements, television's coverage of the assassination of President John F. Kennedy and subsequent events in 1963 set an unforgettable example. Even television's severest critics had to admit that on that fateful occasion the medium lived up to its full potentialities with dignity and extraordinary skill. "During those four fantastic, shocking days," said *Newsweek,* "television was as integral a part of the nation's life as food or sleep. . . . The greatest escapist medium ever devised made escape impossible" (1963: 51).

9.6 Sports Programming

Role of Sports   Sports provide television with ideal subjects — real-life events that occur on predictable schedules but that nevertheless are full of dramatic suspense. Fictional drama has wider audience appeal, however, and only a few world play-off sporting events such as the Super Bowls and the World Series games rank among the most popular programs of all time. These events have elements of pageantry that appeal to a broader audience than the year-round sports fans. A survey sponsored by *TV Guide* indicated that 60 percent of the public watched professional football. Next in popularity was pro basketball, and after that the number of viewers fell off abruptly, with less than 10 percent having watched such sports as auto racing, soccer, or bowling (Kowet, 1978).

Nevertheless, sports reports have a place in every complete newscast, and the industry spends hundreds of millions of dollars annually on the rights to on-the-spot coverage of sports events. ABC pioneered the weekend *sports anthology* format with its *Wide World of Sports* (1961–). By combining highlights of several sports events into a single program, this format avoids boring audiences with overlong coverage of minor sports — thus even such sports as cliff diving or surfing can be covered. ABC also pioneered the scheduling of major live sports coverage in prime time when it started *Monday Night Football* in 1969 (§8.5).

Scheduling Problems   The seasonal nature of sports events and the limited amount of broadcaster control over them make for scheduling complications. Scheduling football in network prime time was a daring innovation because it meant risking a long stretch of extremely valuable time on a single program with selective audience appeal. Moreover it meant committing the time for only part of the television season. Once football was over, replacement programming had to be found. Nowadays abrupt midseason disruption of network scheduling is no longer considered unusual (§9.1), but it was regarded as a daring gamble when ABC made the move in 1969. Independent stations find it easier to handle live sports on a local and regional basis than do networks and network-affiliated stations. A number of ad hoc networks exist expressly for the purpose of carrying the games of particular colleges, professional teams, and conferences.

Issues   Stations and networks are at times tempted to overcome some of the unpredictability of sports events by staging them expressly for television coverage. This kind of manipulation, which involves mixing reality with show business, is particularly prone to abuse. In 1977 the House Subcommittee on Communications held hearings on such abuses, including the manner in which ABC selected fighters for its "U.S. Boxing Championships," and the supposedly deceptive use of the title "Winner Take All" in a tennis playoff sponsored by CBS (House CC, 1977).

Ethical questions also arise because many teams and sports associations insist on having control over the hiring of play-by-play and color announcers. This practice raises the issue of whether sports events should be regarded in the same light as news events, or as belonging in the same category as entertaining fiction. The director of a consumer-oriented organization of sports fans asserts that broadcasters tend to surrender control over their coverage of sports events because of the need to please the people who govern the sale of rights to cover such events (Gruenstein, 1978). The FCC conducted an inquiry into biased sports reporting, reminding broadcasters that they have "a responsibility to refrain from engaging in or permitting others to engage in substantial deception or suppression of facts" in covering sports (48 FCC 2d 237, 1974).

9.7 The Electronic Church

At one time it would have seemed a contradiction in terms to include a section on religious broadcasting in a discussion devoted to commercial television. But in recent years a highly commercialized approach to religious broadcasting has received much notoriety. The "electronic church" has become an active and controversial element in commercial programming.

Early Policies　As we have seen, preachers and religious organizations were among the first to recognize the potentials of radio broadcasting (§7.9). One of the early network television religious series, *Lamp unto My Feet* (1948–1979), was presented by CBS on behalf of the Protestant Radio Commission. It was not narrowly Protestant in outlook, however; rather it tried to show how the major religions of the world shared common ideals.

The first preacher to win a prime-time slot on national network television was a Catholic bishop, Fulton J. Sheen. Starting in 1952, his *Life Is Worth Living* program ran for six years as a prime-time network series and appeared at various times thereafter in syndication. Sheen relied entirely on the spoken word, unembellished with the show-business trappings featured by current religious superstars. Nevertheless, he outdrew the best that entertainment television of the 1950s had to offer.

The bishop's persuasive powers depended a good deal on deep-set, piercing blue eyes that seemed to transfix his viewers, and a burnished voice that would soar, pause theatrically or plunge to a hushed whisper. Wearing a cape and a large pectoral cross, and with a blackboard as his only prop, he performed flawlessly without a script or cue cards. (Time, 24 Dec. 1979)

Broadcasters welcomed Bishop Sheen's sermons not only because he drew large audiences but also because he stuck to religion. They had been sensitized to the dangers of getting embroiled in controversial issues not of their own choosing back in the early 1940s by the right-wing radio crusade of Father Coughlin (§7.1). As a result of that experience the more conservative stations and networks had adopted a general policy of refusing to sell time to the promoters of any and all ideological viewpoints (Brown, 1980).*

---

*As time went on this distinction between the sale of ideas and the sale of goods and services became more and more difficult to maintain. Nevertheless, the legal

In keeping with the NAB Television Code recommendation against accepting payment for religious program time, most networks and stations traditionally gave sustaining (free) time to religious groups, tending to confine such gifts of time to the large, mainstream Catholic, Jewish, and Protestant coalitions. By these means broadcasters avoided religious controversy while protecting themselves from the demands of innumerable smaller sects.

An alternative solution, later adopted more and more widely, was to refuse to *give* time to any religious group. Typical was the reaction of the general manager of a small CBS affiliate in the Southwest, who told a reporter early in the 1970s, "We only *sell* time for religion. If you *give* time to the Baptists, then you have to give time to the Christian Scientists and the Presbyterians and the Catholics and the Methodists and you've got an impossible situation." Since none of these mainstream religious groups would buy time, the station solved the problem by selling six half-hours to evangelists every Sunday, each of whom paid $8,320 a year for the time (Bagdikian, 1973).

Origins of TV Evangelism   Televised religion arose as a natural outgrowth of the tent shows and mass rallies of fundamentalist revivalism, a long-standing American tradition. For example, Oral Roberts, famous as an itinerant faith healer since the early 1950s, carried on his revival meetings in what he called his "Canvas Cathedral." As television grew, he found it harder and harder to fill his tent (said to have been the world's largest). "'People were no longer attracted by its

novelty,' he said. Television cut into the entertainment value of an evening of singing and preaching. Moreover, his own constituency was becoming better educated and more sophisticated in its taste" (Fiske, 1973: 17).

Roberts realized that through television he could transform the whole country into a vast electronic tent. He finally folded away his great canvas cathedral for good in 1967. He is credited with having been the first of the major evangelists to exploit the full resources of television. His idol, Billy Graham, used television too, but originally more as a news medium, a way of reporting on "crusades" staged for audiences in auditoriums and stadiums. Roberts capitalized more fully on the medium's show-business techniques, using lights, costumes, music, cameras, scenery, and video effects to create programs expressly designed to capture the attention of home viewers.

If Oral Roberts represents the metamorphosis from tent to tube, M. G. "Pat" Robertson may be singled out to represent the new, television-bred generation of evangelists. The contrast between the two is vivid. Robertson is the son of a U.S. senator and a graduate of the Yale Law School. Now president of the Christian Broadcasting Network (CBN) and star of its principal syndicated series, *The 700 Club*, his skillful, low-key interviews with celebrated born-again Christians on a daily 90-minute talk/variety program inevitably remind his critics of the *Tonight Show*. In fact, Robertson is frequently referred to as the Johnny Carson of the electronic church.

Syndicated to many television stations (on time paid for by CBN) and fed to over 3,500 cable television systems, *The 700 Club* is only the most widely visible part of the Robertson communications empire, which includes at

right of broadcasters to refuse the sale of time for what came to be called "editorial advertising" was affirmed by the Supreme Court. The controversy over editorial advertising is discussed in §17.6.

its Virginia Beach headquarters the CBN University, elaborate program-production facilities, and two satellite ground stations for feeding affiliates and cable systems 24 hours a day. CBN owns WYAH-TV (a UHF station) in nearby Portsmouth, three other television outlets, and six FM stations.

Dimensions of Religious Broadcasting

During the 1970s commercialized religious broadcasting became one of the most rapidly expanding sources of industry income. Although the networks and the NAB Code retain their policy against selling time to religious broadcasters, 80 percent or more of the television stations have no such scruples. Nonpaid religious time almost disappeared from television schedules. In 1981 the number of stations classified as religious included 18 television outlets (all UHF) and 531 radio outlets (80 of them noncommercial). However, the larger impact of religious broadcasting came from the purchase of time from hundreds of other stations not predominantly religious in format. Millions of dollars are spent annually for time in which to schedule sponsored religious program series. These are referred to as syndicated programs, though they reverse the usual syndication transaction in which the stations pay the syndicators for the use of programs. In the case of sponsored religious shows, the syndicators pay the stations commercial rates for the use of time. So universal is this practice that the Standard Rate and Data Service, the publisher of station rate card listings, routinely reports for each station whether paid religious programming is accepted.

This active commercial market depends primarily on small voluntary donations from viewers, though religious broadcasters also realize income from the sale of publications and merchandise and from commercial operation of some of their broadcasting stations.

Some evangelists spend much of their air time imploring viewers to send in "love offerings" to assist in expanding their "television ministry." The FCC rule against program-length commercials does not apply to such appeals, though it does apply to sales pitches for specific objects, religious or otherwise. A Catholic critic pointed out that only two kinds of advertisers "have the option of producing 15- or 30- or 60-minute commercials" — politicians and preachers (Clancy, 1979: 272).

Issues The startling growth of commercialized religious broadcasting in the 1970s stimulated increasing criticism as the decade wore on. The established churches, seeing their congregations and the contents of their collection plates dwindle, blamed television for luring away both communicants and cash. Television evangelists reply that on the contrary they use their power to urge viewers to return to their local churches, along with their contributions. Statistics on the permanency of television conversions and the extent to which communicants return to their neighborhood churches are inconclusive.

With so many millions of dollars passing through the mails, questions about fiscal responsibility inevitably arose, especially because of the fact that churches are tax-exempt. But many religious organizations resent inquiries into their financial operations, seeing such questioning as an invasion of constitutionally guaranteed freedom of religion. Jim Bakker, star of the *PTL Club*, a syndicated religious talk/variety spin-off from *The 700 Club*, flatly refused to give the Federal Communications Commission information about the disposition of funds solicited on the program (71 FCC 2d 324, 1979). Bakker claimed, among other things, that the inquiry violated "First Amendment guaran-

Inside the Electronic Church

Their voices and images magnified by television, the fundamentalist stars of the electronic church have created the impression of having more widespread influence and support than they actually have.

A high proportion of the stations that sell time to religious syndicators are the smaller television outlets. Often the programs appear in day parts with the lowest audience potential. Audiences for *The Old-Time Gospel Hour* and other top-ranked syndicated religious shows are extremely small by ordinary television standards. Even the most popular of such programs earn ratings lower than routine kid series such as *Hopalong Cassidy*. Cable adds to their coverage, but they still reach a small minority of the television audience.

Nevertheless, the earning power of the syndicated religious shows is impressive. They achieve to an unusual degree the goal of every commercial broadcaster — ideal audience demographics. Audiences may be small, but they are loyal and include an extraordinarily high proportion of paying customers. Donors can be described as customers because the big religious shows function essentially as direct-mail businesses, spending even more for sophisticated mailing campaigns than for television time.

Though extremely efficient generators of donations (averaging $14 a correspondent), such campaigns are also extremely expensive to run. In the years 1977–1980, *The Old-Time Gospel Hour* brought in $115 million, but most of the money was reinvested in the collecting process itself, paying for "gifts," television time, production costs, mailing, and the hundreds of employees needed to keep the show on the road (Fitzgerald, 1981: 89, 92).

tees of the free exercise of religion and freedom of speech" (p. 328). He used the *PTL Club* program freely as a forum for attacking the FCC and urging viewers to protest its interference with the group's activities.

Radio had long been a favorite vehicle for extreme right-wing fundamentalists, but a similar blend of preaching and politics in television did not emerge as a noticeable trend until the 1970s. Typical of the issues on which syndicated television preachers advocated extreme conservative views were abortion, homosexual rights, the women's equal rights constitutional amendment proposal, the Supreme Court ruling against prayers in public schools, children's sex education, and the Panama Canal "giveaway." Television evangelists and their followers exploited such issues during the 1980 national elections to bring down several liberal candidates they had targeted for defeat.

Encouraged by this success, fundamentalist preachers stepped up their boycott campaigns against television programs that they regard as morally objectionable. Among the vocal opponents of these boycotts is Norman Lear, famed for such network series as *All in the Family*, but more recently producing only for cable and subscription television. Lear headed People for the American Way, one of several organizations opposing the tactics of the television preachers. It was an ironic confrontation, pitting religious and secular television stars against each other in a struggle to influence the future conduct of the medium that made them.

It would be easy to overstate the significance of the electronic church. It has been widely publicized because of its colorful and controversial aspects, but its actual audience is small (see Box). Not a united movement, it encounters opposition from within the evangelical camp as well as from the mainstream churches. Its apparent political success reflects the influence of a broad social trend, not the narrow sectarianism of individual television preachers. They neither created nor control the ground swell of conservatism of the 1980s, which was generated more by economic than by theological forces.

9.8 Children's Programming

Controversial programming of a different sort involves the question of regulating commercial programs aimed at children. Children have such easy access to television, and it exerts such a powerful hold on their attention, that programs designed to exploit children commercially raise special problems. Most broadcasting systems regulate children's programs in considerable detail; in some countries advertising to children is not permitted. The Federal Communications Commission first singled out children's programming for notice in 1960 when it listed certain program types as having special public interest significance. In its programming policy statement of that year, the commission listed children's programs as one of the types that should be given particular attention by broadcast licensees, but it issued no specific

rules. The Television Code of the National Association of Broadcasters also says that "broadcasters have a special responsibility to children," but, like the 1960 FCC statement, gives no guidelines, except to place certain limitations on advertising in children's programs (§13.4). These came as a result of consumer pressures on the FCC described later in this section.

Dimensions of Children's TV   In the late 1970s the average commercial station programmed about eleven hours of children's television a week.* Independent stations scheduled many more of these programs than network affiliates. The latter concentrated most of their children's programming on the weekend (half in the Saturday morning animated cartoon block alone), whereas the independents tended to spread them throughout the week.

Manufacturers of toys, cereals, and candies are the main supporters of commercial children's programs. They spend on the order of $600 million a year on television (*Broadcasting* 29 Oct. 1979). Although that represents only about 6 percent of television's commercial revenue, the economic importance of children's programming is enhanced by the fact that it can be scheduled at times (notably Saturday mornings) that have minimal value for reaching other types of viewers. Also as a scheduling stratagem, programmers often place a series of interest to children late in the afternoon on weekdays (fringe time), expecting that a high proportion of sets will stay on, flowing through to the local news that often follows.

About half the children's programs on the

---

*Unless otherwise credited, statistics on programs in this section refer to the 1977–1978 findings of the FCC's Task Force on Children's Television (FCC, 1979).

air come from syndicated sources. Among the most popular syndicated series are *Batman, The Flintstones, Gilligan's Island, New Zoo Review,* and *Popeye.* Networks accounted for about 45 percent of the programs. Each network has a vice president in charge of children's programs, who oversees such series as *Captain Kangaroo* (the longest-running network children's show, on CBS daily since 1955), *The New Fat Albert Show,* and *Space Academy.* Among network weekend innovations praised by experts on children's shows are *30 Minutes* (a teen-agers' version of CBS's *60 Minutes*), ABC's 30-second spots promoting safety, consumerism, and other prosocial messages, and *ABC Weekend Specials.* However, the Public Broadcasting Service produced six of the weekend series rated best by the experts (Safran, 1980).

Only about 6 percent of the children's programs on the air are locally produced. One of the oldest, *Romper Room* (1952–), is sold both as a syndicated program and as a syndicated format; in the latter case the station produces the series locally using a syndicated script. The oldest local children's program on the air is believed to be WOI-TV's *The House with the Magic Window* (1950–), a weekday half-hour program for preschoolers produced by the commercial station owned by Iowa State University.

ACT's Petition Consumer groups have long complained about what they considered to be the generally low quality of children's programming and the exploitative commercials it contained. Traditionally this type of programming has been full of sexist and racist stereotypes, laced with violence, and loaded with commercials designed to take every advantage of childish inexperience. Complaints were largely ineffectual until the formation in 1968 of a new and sophisticated

consumer group, Action for Children's Television (ACT).

In 1971 ACT persuaded the FCC to hold hearings on a petition asking the commission to make definite rules to govern certain aspects of children's programming. It asked the FCC to adopt rules requiring each commercial station to broadcast at least 14 hours of children's programming a week, scheduling them throughout the week. Moreover, such programs, ACT said, should be "age-specific," rather than being aimed shotgun-fashion at children of all ages simultaneously (the usual commercial practice). ACT suggested that programs should be tailored to meet the differing needs of three separate age groups — preschool (ages 2 to 5), primary (6 to 9, and elementary (10 to 12). Another aspect of ACT's petition dealt with advertising reforms, which are discussed in §13.4.

After holding extensive hearings, the commission rejected ACT's rule-making request. Instead it issued a policy statement in 1974 urging broadcasters to voluntarily improve children's programming along the lines of the ACT proposals (50 FCC 2d 1, 1974).* One immediate result was the NAB Television Code Board's adoption of special advertising rules for children's programs (§13.4).

A few years later the FCC, still under pressure from ACT and other consumer groups, appointed a Children's Television Task Force to check on the extent to which broadcasters had complied with the 1974 policy statement. The task force studies found some improvement in advertising practices but little in the programming area. The average amount of children's programming per station had grown from 10.5 to 11.3 hours a week, mostly because of individual station rather than network increases. Nearly half the programming

---

*ACT appealed the decision, but the court upheld the commission's right to issue a policy statement instead of adopting specific rules (564 F 2d 458, 1977).

was still concentrated in the weekends and few attempts had been made to create age-specific programming.

In view of the limited effectiveness of its 1974 policy statement, the FCC reopened the rule-making question in 1979, inviting comments on a number of possible steps that might be taken. Among the options suggested by the FCC's own staff was a proposal to require each commercial station to schedule at least 7 to 12 hours of age-specific children's programs a week, Monday through Friday. However, the trend toward deregulation, along with changes in FCC outlook as the new Republican administration began making appointments in 1981, meant that the long-fought attempt to regulate children's programming was lost, at least for the time being.

9.9 Appraising the TV Program Service

So far in this chapter we have touched upon specific issues that arise in appraising particular program types. What about the programming as a whole? What sorts of generalized issues arise concerning television as a program service?

A "Vast Wasteland"? The best-known generalization about television programming was made by Newton Minow, a former chairman of the Federal Communications Commission. In his first address to the National Association of Broadcasters back in 1961, Minow challenged the station owners and managers to sit down and watch their own programming for a full broadcast day. They would, he assured them, find a "vast wasteland" of violence, repetitive formulas, irritat-ing commercials, and sheer boredom (1964: 52). The phrase caught on and became a part of the language of broadcasting.

Fifteen years later Minow (by then a lawyer in private practice and an executive of the Public Broadcasting Service) spoke on a panel at another NAB convention. Asked to comment on his famous "wasteland" phrase, he admitted that advisers had warned him against using it. Nevertheless, he said, he had no regrets: the criticism had jolted broadcasters out of their complacency, at least momentarily. In the intervening years said Minow, "there has been enormous improvement, particularly in the area of news and information" (Terry, 1976: 5).

Normally neither Minow nor other discriminating viewers watch *everything* on television. Nevertheless, commentators make sweeping judgments about television as a whole. They refuse to concede that television sometimes rises to peaks of excellence, even though — given the nature of things — between the peaks must lie broad valleys (or vast wastelands) of routine programming. How green the valleys depends on the viewer's own tastes and standards.

Television aims to please not just FCC commissioners but all sorts of people at all sorts of times of the day and night. No previous medium has faced such a demanding task. In attempting it, television makes apparent something that was never before exposed so blatantly — the common denominator of popular taste. As Daniel Boorstin, an authority on American cultural history, explains it:

Much of what we hear complained of as the "vulgarity," the emptiness, the sensationalism, the soap-serialism, of television is not a peculiar product of television at all. It is simply the translation of the subliterature onto the television screen. . . . Never before were the vulgar tastes so conspicuous and so accessible to the prophets of our high culture. Subculture — which is of course the dominant culture of a democratic society — is now probably no worse, and certainly no better, than it has ever been. But it is emphatically more visible. (Boorstin, 1978: 19)

It makes no sense to measure television with traditional yardsticks, as though broadcasting were not much different from the library, the theater, or the art gallery. Book reviewers do not make such all-inclusive judgments about "print" or art critics about "paint" as they do about "television." One cannot reasonably expect to be able to turn on the radio or television set at any time, day or night, to immediately find a program suited to one's particular tastes and needs of the moment. No more would one expect to be satisfied with the first book that came to hand on the shelf of a library.

Limits on Choices   On the other hand, in the library we can put the first book back on the shelf and keep on browsing until we find just the book to suit our needs of the moment. For a number of reasons, traditional television offers no such range of immediate choices: (1) most viewers can tune in only a few over-the-air stations; (2) at any given moment several of the available stations are likely to be airing the same sort of program; and (3) television is a *prisoner of time* — viewers cannot browse through shelves of past programs to select the one that best serves the needs of the moment. Discriminating viewers must have the patience and foresight to plan ahead to gain access to just those programs that suit their tastes and interests. Cable television and home video recording overcome these limitations to some extent by offering a wider range of immediate choices and the possibility of putting programs on the shelf for later use, but only at additional cost.

Viewer Expectations   This is not to suggest that broadcasting should be exempt from criticism, only that criticism should take into consideration the nature of the medium. Each medium has its characteristic limitations and potentialities.

Nevertheless, we have a tendency to expect broadcasting to serve all needs and all moods, at all times. These unreasonable demands arise, perhaps, because of the medium's unique qualities. Broadcasting comes directly into the home as an ever-present, ever-ready source of potential pleasure and information. As a federally licensed medium, it comes with a kind of implied government approval. Moreover, it enters the home only because audience members have themselves invested in the medium. No one has to buy part of a printing press to enjoy a newspaper or a seat in a movie theater to enjoy a film. In order to enjoy broadcasting, however, audience members invest in the technology of the medium by purchasing, maintaining, and operating receivers. This public investment exceeds by far the entire investment of the industry in the means of production and transmission.

The unique nature of broadcasting thus tends to give audience members a special proprietary feeling about it. Consciously or not, they feel that broadcasting has a positive obligation to serve their personal needs — not just occasionally with individual programs, but continuously with an ever-present service.

Summary

Strategies of program scheduling take into consideration the characteristics of audiences for different day parts, and the effects of audience flow. Networks typically fill about 70 percent of the time of their affiliates. The rest of programming comes mainly from syndication and local production. For economic reasons the latter is confined mostly to local news programs.

The main arena of network competition is the prime-time period. The number of new episodes in prime-time series each season has been shrinking, as has the variety of program types chosen by the networks.

Internetwork competition demands novelty without radical change. Recent prime-time programming tends toward relevancy in subject matter and the miniseries in format. Bimodal appeals help give prime-time programs the ability to draw audiences of the great size needed for successful network competition.

Nonprime-time network entertainment, consisting mostly of soap operas and game shows, is profitable because it is economical to produce. Its program series are scheduled on a year-round rather than seasonal basis and on a Monday-Friday rather than a weekly cycle.

Although occupying only a small percentage of television program time, news-related programming assumes great importance, both because it is regarded as socially desirable and because it has become a major source of prestige and income. The trend is toward longer news programs and more on-the-spot coverage by means of ENG. Brevity and concentration on pictorially interesting news have been emphasized by news consultants. Their advice has been controversial because it stresses show-business aspects of news presentation in pursuit of high audience ratings.

Public affairs programming has been encouraged in recent years by the success of the news-documentary magazine, *60 Minutes*, the first such program to achieve top prime-time network audience ratings. Single-topic news documentaries are regarded as an important television contribution to public understanding, but often create controversy.

Sports programming has a natural affinity for television because of the public's interest in live actualities. Sports schedules, however, are not always compatible with the needs of broadcast schedules. For this reason sports is a major program resource of independent (nonaffiliated) stations. Most network sports is scheduled on weekends with the notable exception of *Monday Night Football*, an ABC innovation.

Commercialized religious programming has assumed an economic role in contemporary television. Traditionally most broadcasters opposed the sale of time for religion, and the networks still follow the policy of giving sustaining time to representatives of the larger, established church organizations. Most stations, however, now are willing to sell time for televised religion. The stars of such programs attract small but loyal audiences from which they collect millions of dollars in donations. Much of the money goes toward buying still more broadcast time. Critics question the economics of televised religion as well as the political activities of some television evangelists and their economic boycott campaigns against television programs of which they disapprove.

Consumers petitioned the FCC to adopt special rules governing children's programs, but the FCC issued only a policy statement. Broadcasters modified their commercial practices and introduced a few program improvements. Consumers were not satisfied with the voluntary changes, but the FCC declined to go further.

In appraising television, critics sometimes

tend to condemn it as a whole, without taking into consideration the limitations imposed by its unique characteristics. The
choices television offers at any one moment
are limited, but over time the choice is wide
for the viewer who plans ahead. Nevertheless, because of television's presence in the
home, its cost to the viewer, and its status as
a government-licensed medium, viewers
tend to feel justified in expecting instant gratification.

PART IIII

Noncommercial and Nonbroadcast Systems

We pause now to trace the evolution of alternative systems that have emerged to challenge the dominance of the commercial broadcasting system described in the previous chapters. Side by side with commercial broadcasting a noncommercial alternative evolved, though at a slower and somewhat uncertain pace. At the same time, new applications of communication technology were being developed, offering a variety of optional methods for relaying, storing, and delivering programs on a nonbroadcast or quasi-broadcast basis.

These alternative systems form the subject matter of Part 3. Challenging the hitherto secure position of the traditional commercial system, they are exerting influences that may significantly change the future of broadcasting in America.

CHAPTER 10

The Noncommercial Alternative

The majority of this book deals with commercial radio and television because they were and remain the primary bases of broadcasting in this country. But commercial broadcasting has met with considerable criticism over the years. One of the key concerns voiced by critics is the need for services other than entertainment, which takes up the majority of commercial air time. The recognition that such service is unlikely to come from commercially oriented stations has been one impetus leading to a parallel public broadcasting system.

10.1 Why "Public" Broadcasting?

Before exploring the development and present-day operation of public broadcasting we need to understand a basic problem surrounding it — the lack of agreement on just what it is or what it is supposed to do. The confusion is even evident in terminology. Until 1967 such public-service operations were called "noncommercial" or "educational" stations, terms which only partially described their content and most assuredly

helped to drive away potential audience.* Since 1967 the term "public" has been used to denote both the noncommercial (and increasingly tax-supported) nature and the broader audience aim of such stations. The continuing intermixture of terms and confusion over what they mean is only a demonstration of what anyone dealing with the system must face — disagreement on the definition, the role, and the impact of public stations in a commercially dominated system.

The Defenders Those long active in or newly won over to public broadcasting point out its many better qualities. Foremost among them is the provision of types of programming usually not available on commercial stations: fine arts, music, dance, important foreign language films, superior dramatic programs, public affairs discussions, and the like. Further, there is a widespread feeling that public stations can better meet the needs of specific subgroups in society, whether ethnic minorities or children or other special interest groups. In addition, public stations are seen by many as the last true demonstrations of "localism," in which a station reflects and projects its local com-

---

*Officially, public broadcasting remains "noncommercial educational broadcasting" in the Communications Act and FCC Rules and Regulations.

munity rather than merely relying on .network or syndicated material. Those active in public broadcasting claim that actual public participation in station and system policy helps to define the difference between public and commercially dictated programming service. The very existence of a thriving debate on the role of public broadcasting, says the defender, is an indication of the widespread input into system operations. The only real problem is a lack of sufficient funding with which to do the job. Give us a decent level of system income over a reasonable period of time to allow planning, say public broadcasting defenders, and we can quickly become a full-fledged competitive alternative to commercial stations.

The Critics Those critical of public broadcasting contend that its special programming is really a service by elite groups for fellow elites. The critic notes the minuscule size of the public broadcaster's audience, as well as its makeup, and suggests that fine arts and high culture are merely more narrow-interest content provided for those easily able to get such material from sources other than publicly supported broadcast channels. Critics liken tax support of public broadcasting to government subsidies for passenger ships on which only the wealthy can ride. Further, the critics point out that public broadcasting is as network-oriented as commercial stations — and that public participation in most public stations is a sham at best, the decisions being made by professionals, as in commercial broadcasting. The critics sum up their argument by suggesting that the funding problem always complained about by the defenders of public broadcasting is really an indication of the limited scope and value of the system. In this country, money flows to the provider of a recognized public service. Funding for public broadcasting is low because its audience aim and appeal is too narrow. Yet to widen

that appeal merely calls into question whether there would then be much difference between public and commercial stations other than how they are funded.

The key question that has emerged over the years is this: if public broadcasting can't attract a broader audience, do we really need public funding for an increasingly expensive alternate to commercial broadcasting? As we will see, many of the issues are not new. Commercial broadcasters still want many of the channels held by or reserved for noncommercial users, and they are increasingly resentful over the use of corporate funds to support public television rather than advertising on commercial television. Government agencies that have been a source of funds are under increasing budget pressure; the largesse of the 1960s is at an end.

10.2 Rise of Educational Broadcasting

The history of noncommercial radio and television, especially the latter, clearly divides at the year 1967. But some of the patterns and many of the problems already noted became evident in the early years.

Early Educational Radio Several colleges experimented with wireless telegraphy in the years before World War I. Members of the University of Wisconsin's physics department, for example, began tinkering in 1902, had an operating experimental transmitter by 1909, and progressed to a licensed wireless telegraphy station, 9XM, by 1915. During World War I, 9XM remained on the air to assist training of navy radio personnel, while most other amateur and broadcast operations went off the air for "the duration."

With the boom in license applications in the 1920s, various educational institutions joined in the rush. Right from the beginning, however, their purposes and hopes varied: extension education, school or church promotion, use of radio as a fund-raiser for other activities, provision of education and culture, and so on. Most stations operated on a financial shoestring for but a few hours per week.

But the increasing success of commercial radio after 1927 created a demand for channels occupied by these educational organizations. Although a few of the latter capitalized on the situation and began to charge for air time to support their programming, most did not. Questions about the long-range purpose and funding of educational radio combined with the pressure from the commercial sector to turn the tide against noncommercial stations. Some turned in their licenses in return for promises of air time for educational programs on commercial stations — promises that dwindled with the rising value of air time for advertiser-supported entertainment. Those educational stations that tried to maintain service found themselves confined to low power, inconvenient hours (often daytime only, useless for adult education efforts), and constantly changing frequency assignments as the Federal Radio Commission made an attempt to bring initial order to channel allotments. A majority simply gave up the struggle and left the air. After 1929 the Depression hastened a trend already begun. In 1927 there were 98 noncommercial stations on the air (13 percent of all licenses), but by 1933 only 43 (7 percent) were left. "Commercial stations made money, convertible into political power; educational stations cost money. If their programming was not popular enough to attract sizable audiences,

they were hard to justify politically" (Blakely, 1979: 55).

As the number of noncommercial radio stations declined, however, concern over their fate increased. Pressured to do something to save educational programming (if not stations), the FRC and later the FCC responded with general statements calling for more such material from commercial licensees, but at the same time the regulators resisted reserving channels for noncommercial stations. This pattern persisted for more than 12 years.

The failure of most educational institutions to defend their original AM allotments against the raids of commercial interests confirmed what some had said from the first: at the very outset a share of the AM frequencies should have been set aside exclusively for educational use; educational interests could not reasonably be expected to compete with commercial interests in the open market for the use of radio channels.

FM Channel Reservations   In January 1935 the Federal Communications Commission reported to Congress that in its opinion existing commercial stations gave ample opportunity for educational programming, so no special reservation of frequencies for this purpose was needed. Faced with mounting evidence that education time on commercial stations was far too little to meet in-school needs, the FCC in 1938 reserved high-frequency space for 25 channels of special in-school AM broadcasting. In 1940, when the first FM allocation was made, the educational reservation was switched to the FM service. Thus five of the 40 FM channels were to be *reserved* for noncommercial users. A crucial precedent had been set. When the FM band was reallocated to 88–108 MHz in 1945, the commission set aside 20 of the 100 channels (88–92 MHz) for education. Slowly the years of talking about the potential of educational radio began to have a practical effect. Plans were announced in many states for statewide networks of FM stations. Schools that had not operated a radio station for 20 years, or had never had one, made plans to apply for a license on the new reserved band. To stimulate use of the reserved FM frequencies, the FCC in 1948 liberalized its rules to allow informal operation of noncommercial stations with as little as a mere 10 watts, thus allowing broadcasting at a fraction of the usual cost — but at the price of reaching only a fraction of the potential audience, because such low-power operations often reach out but two or three miles from the transmitter. Thus, noncommercial radio found itself even more seriously undermined by television than by commercial radio. Although the number of stations on the air continued to increase (Exhibit 10.2), most operated on low power and often for very short broadcast days. The Federal educational television facilities act of 1962 (§10.5) ignored radio's needs. With only a limited amount of program exchange and no network operation, educational FM stations (and the 25 or so AM educational survivors from the 1930s) operated almost totally on their own resources. Only Wisconsin succeeded in developing a statewide network of FM stations. The first comprehensive survey of modern educational radio was published in 1968 under the fitting title *The Hidden Medium* (Land, 1968). After a 15-month tour and study of educational radio stations in 1971–1972, another research team admitted being "confused, for no two stations are alike, and there are almost no models to which to point" (Robertson and Yokom, 1973: 115).

Early ETV In the initial 1941 allocation for television, the FCC made no reservation for noncommercial services. After the war, with the FM precedent in mind, there was some interest on the part of a few educators for television reservations. But not all agreed;

many noncommercial broadcasters wanted to get settled in the FM band first before facing the far greater expense of television — and the kind of pressures from commercial operators that had almost killed educational radio in the 1920s. The beginning of the freeze in 1948 (§8.3), however, turned that relative complacency into a concerted effort as commercial broadcasters lobbied increasingly against educational reservation.

Several factors were joined in the effort: a cadre of successful educational broadcasters convinced that a push for TV channel reservations should be made; an FCC commissioner sympathetic to the educators' interests; and the increasing effectiveness of the National Association of Educational Broadcasters as an organization in getting educators interested in and concerned about the possibilities of noncommercial television (Blakely, 1979: 3). These came together to create the Joint Committee on Educational Television (JCET) as the spearhead of a lobbying effort asking the FCC not to end the freeze before including some kind of channel reservation scheme. After extensive hearings in 1950, the FCC proposed a temporary channel reservation of 209 allotments for educational stations. Commercial interests leveled intense pressure against channel reservation. Their arguments stressed that channels would be unused while educators tried to get together funds to put stations on the air, although commercial firms stood ready to build stations as soon as the freeze ended. Further, commercial licensees and potential licensees promised time on the air for educational programs — just as they had with radio in the 1930s.

Finally, in April of 1952 with its *Sixth Report and Order* (§8.3), the FCC, among other things, reserved 242 channel allotments, 80 VHF and 162 UHF — but only for

Exhibit 10.2
Growth of educational stations: 1925–1980

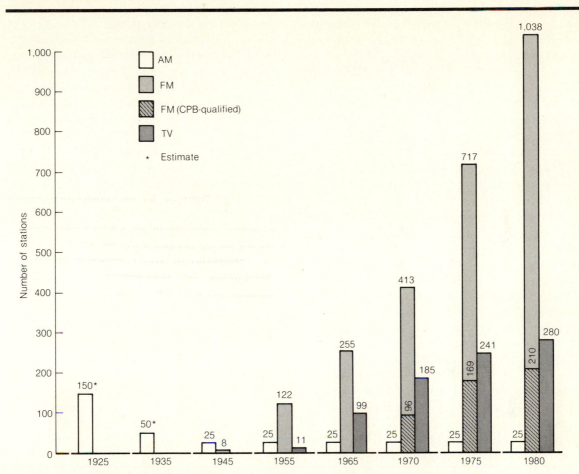

This chart shows the rapid and relatively recent expansion of public radio and television stations in the U.S. All data are as of January 1 of each year. The figures for AM educational or public stations are all estimates; there is no official, let alone accurate, count of such operations, which do not operate on reserved frequencies as do FM and television public facilities. Note that only a small proportion of the FM stations are CPB-qualified. The number of *new* public broadcasting stations is likely to drop off in the 1980s as available frequencies are taken up and as funding goes into other technologies.

Source: Data published with permission from the Corporation for Public Broadcasting.

a limited time of a year or so — "long enough to give . . . reasonable opportunity . . . [but] not so long that the frequencies remain unused for excessively long periods of time" (Blakely, 1979: 89). Unfortunately, because existing VHF allotments were already occupied by commercial stations, no VHF educational channel was possible in many major cities, including New York, Los Angeles, Philadelphia, Washington, and Detroit. A year later the FCC made the reservations permanent, subject only to petitions concerning individual channels. Over the years, the number of reserved allotments increased to about 600.

The decade from the end of the freeze to the passage of the first federal funding legislation in 1962 marked the initial slow expansion of educational television stations with local and foundation funding (§10.5). As shown in Exhibit 10.2, noncommercial television grew very slowly despite initial concern over loss of the reserved frequencies. Only one station got on the air the first year — KUHT at the University of Houston in May 1953 on VHF Channel 8. The second station was under the aegis of the University of Southern California and a local Los Angeles foundation, but it had to operate on UHF Channel 28. The lack of UHF receivers, along with funding problems, forced the station off the air in September 1954 after less than a year's operation — the only educational television station to go off the air in the early years of the medium. Channel 28 returned to educational television operation in 1964 under the control of a community group. By 1955, 11 educational television stations were on the air, and by 1960 44 (34 on VHF channels) were in operation, but there was still no educational television service in half the states.

A host of problems faced the stations going on the air, chief among them being that of putting together sufficient program material to fill even a limited schedule. Lacking a network program source, stations relied on their own resources, including local production of instructional and children's programs, purchase of educational films, and a limited exchange with the few other stations on the air (thus spreading production dollars as far as possible). The very emphasis on local and live material helped to make educational television stations an alternative to commercial stations right from the start, although the educational television station typically programmed only half as long as the commercial channels.

A small change in the purely local nature of educational television stations came in 1952 with the establishment in Ann Arbor, Michigan, of what became National Educational Television (NET). This program production and distribution center supplied up to five hours of programming per week, sent by mail to the few stations on the air. With financial support from the Ford Foundation (§10.5), NET slowly increased both the amount and quality of its material, and in 1959 moved to New York to gain easier access to highly skilled personnel. The Washington-based lobby for educational broadcasting was the NAEB, which had been active in radio since the 1920s and had moved to the national capital from the University of Illinois campus to gain increased visibility with policy makers. These relocations of the key national educational broadcasting organizations signified their growing awareness of the need to reach national power centers and produced a new awareness of their potential by those in government and national commercial broadcasting.

Carnegie Concept and CPB   1967 was a watershed in the development of noncommercial broadcasting. Substantial changes were made in the way educational television was organized, funded, and perceived. The needed thrust to raise the noncommercial service to a higher level of policy and audience impact came with the report of the Carnegie Commission on Educational Television (CCET). Made up of top-level representatives from higher education, media, business, politics, and the arts, the commission proposed that Congress establish a corporation for public television. The commission used the word *public* rather than educational to disassociate itself from what many regarded as the "somber and static image" projected by the existing educational television services. It also sought a term that would differentiate instructional or classroom television from a broader service intended for the general public. President Johnson supported the legislative proposals, and with few changes they were considered and passed by Congress as the Public Broadcasting Act of 1967 (47 USC 396–398) amending the Communications Act of 1934. The act created the Corporation for Public Broadcasting (radio was added at the last minute) as a nongovernmental entity. The major change from the Carnegie recommendations was omission of any system of long-range financial support (§10.5). The commission had recommended that the president appoint half the members of the CPB board and the board itself appoint the other half, but Congress gave all appointive power to the president. These two provisions left CPB at the mercy of any president who chose to interfere with its autonomy — an eventuality that soon developed (see Box, page 275).

Among the purposes and activities of the corporation, Section 396(g) of the act lists the following:

■ Facilitating "full development of educational broadcasting in which programs of high quality, obtained from diverse sources, will be made available to noncommercial educational television or radio broadcast stations, with strict adherence to objectivity and balance in all programs or series of programs of a controversial nature."

■ Assisting in setting up network interconnection so that all stations "that wish to may broadcast the programs at times chosen by the stations"; common carriers are authorized to give free service or reduced rates to such networks, subject to FCC approval.

■ Carrying out its work "in ways that will most effectively assure the maximum freedom . . . from interference with or control of program content or other activities."

■ Making contracts and grants for production of programs.

■ Establishing and maintaining a library and archives.

■ Encouraging development of new stations.

■ Conducting research and training.

In carrying out these functions, the corporation may not own any broadcast facilities itself.

10.3 National Organization

The basic structure that developed in 1967–1969 from the Carnegie Commission report and subsequent legislation has survived for better than a decade, though with some important changes in detail. We deal first with the national organizations because of their primary importance in the emergence of public television, then turn to the local stations.

The CPB-PBS Struggle With one important exception, public television in 1967–1969 consisted of local production and the continued operation of the NET "bicycle network" of program exchange. The exception, funded by the Ford Foundation (§10.5), was the *Public Broadcasting Laboratory,* hosted on Sunday evenings by Edward P. Morgan, a demonstration showcase of what could be done in public affairs and the arts with simultaneous scheduling and a higher national recognition factor. It provided a live interconnection for the first time, allowing some 50 educational facilities to become a part of a network system. It seemed logical to many within public television that the corporation would continue NET's networking role, but two things stood in the way. The stations had long disliked the centralized and sometimes arrogant approach of NET and pressured for a different approach. The corporation, new and politically vulnerable, didn't want to face a long-established organization in a contest for system supremacy. After a good deal of political wrangling behind the scenes, the corporation formed in 1969–1970 the Public Broadcasting Service (PBS), which despite its name would exist to operate only the interconnection facilities. Shortly thereafter, NET merged with New York's Channel 13 (a one-time commercial station which was sold to an educational group) to become a station operator and major program production facility.

The first five or six years of the PBS-corporation relationship (to 1974) were fraught with organizational infighting. PBS combined some of the functions of networking with station representation. Relationships between PBS and the other main elements of the system — the stations as program users or, in some cases, as major program producers; the NAEB as a representative of traditional noncommercial interests; and CPB itself as the umbrella organization and source of federal funds — underwent constant change as the new system struggled to establish its identity and to develop a working style.

In the fight to achieve the first noncommercial channel reservations and then for-

malized federal support, the constituency of noncommercial television had been much enlarged and diversified. Traditional educational radio leaders, who had kept the faith over the many lean years, found themselves jostled aside by the newly saved — the national educational establishment, politicians, the Washington bureaucracy, and activist citizen groups.

Out of this new matrix of forces emerged conflicting views of the nature of the noncommercial service. One group took "educational television " to imply a broadly inclusive cultural and information service; another construed it more narrowly as a new and improved audiovisual device whose primary importance would be to schools. Some favored a strong national network and a concern for audience building; others stressed localism and settled for limited audiences. Some wanted to stress high culture and intellectually stimulating programs; others wanted to emphasize programs of interest and value to ethnic minorities and the poor. As the man who drafted the Carnegie Commission report put it five years later, "It was hardly a system we were seeking to nurture at all, but rather a variety of broadcasting arrangements bearing a common name and yet widely differing in structure, financing, concept of role and degree of independence" (Cater, 1972: 10).

The role of the public broadcasting network organization provided a central source of disagreement. The Carnegie Commission had stressed the vital importance of having interconnection but at the same time had emphasized that it should not lead to a centralization of programming on the commercial network model. Public broadcasting was to differ from commercial broadcasting in having "a strong component of local and regional programming." It would "provide the opportunity and the means for local choice to be exercised upon the programs made available from central programming sources" (CCET, 1967: 33). The commission pictured the stations as picking and choosing among the offerings coming down the network line, recording them, and then making up their own uniquely localized broadcast schedules out of this and other material.

In its anxiety to keep public television from modeling itself on the centralized mass entertainment industry of commercial networks, the Carnegie Commission seems to have underestimated the positive role that a strong national network organization could play in shaping an effective program service that combines both local and national elements. The commission failed to appreciate the practical problems of asking the national network to provide a smorgasbord of programming from which affiliates would pick and choose at will.

In any event, opponents of a strong PBS seized upon the Carnegie Commission's localism doctrine as justification for dividing public television into opposing groups. They ignored the fact that the commission had also made the point that "there must be a system-wide process of exerting upward pressure on standards of taste and performance" (CCET, 1967: 36).

The Struggle Peaks The initial period of disagreement came to a head in mid-1973. Under pressure from all sides, especially from members of Congress who stated flatly that no new funding would be forthcoming until the CPB-PBS fight was ended, leaders of both organizations finally hammered out a "partnership agreement" intended to define clearly which group did what.

What emerged was a totally different PBS. It now represented and was controlled by station interests, rather than being an arm of CPB.

The partnership agreement established the legitimacy of PBS as the voice of the system in interconnection management and the editorial judgements which accompany that management. It established the legitimacy of CPB as a major program funder, while at the same time granting economic power to the stations giving them ultimate control of half the federal funds in the system. (Dort, 1980: 62)

But the underlying conflicting principles that had led to the battles remained. On the one hand, CPB was to protect the programmers from political pressure — which it had manifestly proved unable to do in 1971–1973. On the other, "a system which depends upon public money for its support needs disinterested leadership with a broad vision of system responsibilities in order to insure that the public is being served" (Dort, 1980: 62-3). By statute, CPB was accountable. But PBS was now supported by station dues rather than CPB funds (except for the interconnection itself) and thus began to assume a more co-equal position with the corporation. Naturally, the arguments both before and after the agreement of 1973 centered on funding levels (§10.5), but they led as well to some fundamental changes in the ways programming was chosen for the system (§10.6).

The very abbreviated version of the organizational disagreements between CPB and PBS given above provides only a hint of the repetitive and stubborn nature of the continued arguments centered on programming and funding decisions. A variety of problems became clear in the 1970s, all of them working to limit the role public broadcasting might play:

■ "Turf battles" arose as people tried to protect the personal role they had in their own organization. A good deal of functional overlap between CPB and PBS lasted for years mainly because neither organization appeared ready to give way to the other. So both spent time and funds on program development, research offices, some degree of system promotion, and constant meetings of one group or another.

■ National vs. local decision making underlay much of the confusion. Individual licensees operating under varied ownership and funding restrictions were more concerned about their survival than about which national group programmed what. Most stations sided with "their" organization, PBS, against CPB, which was seen as a creature of Washington politics.

■ Program disagreements were a continuing and real problem — determining the kinds of programs that would best serve the system. At the heart of this issue, of course, were questions as to the proper role of public television.

■ Finally, at the heart of the arguments was always the issue of funding. Who was to get how much money and for what purpose and with what kind of accountability always seemed to be the specific cutting edge of most institutional disagreements in the 1970s. The only agreement was that public broadcasting needed *more* money, though there was little common agreement on application of what money existed.

Carnegie II By the time the country was entering the 1976 election year, concern over what to do about this continuing soap opera was evident outside the public broadcasting "family." Efforts to rewrite the basic broadcasting statute, the 1934 act, were coming into focus in the House Communications subcommittee (§15.6). Such action would clearly affect the structure of public broadcasting. In the summer of 1976 the boards of the corporation and National Public Radio

along with others requested the Carnegie people to consider establishing another commission to reanalyze the structure and operations of public broadcasting. After a year's internal task force research, the corporation agreed to undertake the new study, with a special focus on the impact that changing technologies might have on public broadcasting. Columbia University president William McGill was named to chair the panel of 20 members, which was supported by a New York-based staff. The commission was given 18 months to prepare its report, which appeared in January 1979.

Entitled *A Public Trust,* but often referred to simply as "Carnegie II," the report called for the following measures:

■ A threefold increase in federal funding for public broadcasting (comparing 1978 and 1985), with a sharp increase in funding from other sources as well, to a total outlay of about $1.2 billion by 1985. Some of the federal funding would come from a fee assessed on commercial broadcasters.

■ Abolition of CPB and its replacement with a Public Telecommunications Trust to guide and maintain the overall system, with an independent subsidiary, the Program Services Endowment, to concentrate on program development. The trust would insulate the system from political pressures.

■ Public radio concentration on activating an additional 250–300 "qualified" stations (§10.4) to improve the national coverage of the aural service.

■ Greater interest in, funding, and adoption of new technologies to supplement (and eventually possibly supplant) broadcasting.

But Congress was not in the mood for a vast increase in public expenditures — especially while congressional committees were in the throes of work on rewrites of the 1934 act. While many of the Carnegie II proposals found their way into those rewrites, their failure to be passed in 1979 deleted the immediate pressure for structural change from the public television organizations.

Still, there was change. Sparked mainly by the wider opportunities brought about by use of satellite distribution after 1978, PBS reorganized along program service lines. It spun off its previous activities of station representation (lobbying, research, and similar functions) to a new Association for Public Broadcasting (shortly thereafter renamed Association for Public Television). CPB, which had been marked for extinction by both Carnegie II and the rewrites, underwent a split into two largely independent halves — one dealing with program matters, and the other covering all other CPB concerns. As mandated under its new president, Robben Fleming, CPB's split was an attempt to enact internally some of the suggested changes in order to allow more insulation between funding and program decisions. But long-time observers of both organizations felt that the split was merely the latest in a string of reorganizations and that it signified too much time and effort spent on internal delineation of structure rather than on facing and dealing with the system's serious shortcomings.

Much of the change in PBS came about through its new president, Lawrence Grossman, appointed in 1976. Grossman's background was in commercial broadcasting. Previous PBS heads such as Hartford Gunn, who had helped to shape the system through its survival of the Nixon years, came from public service and public broadcasting backgrounds. From the start, Grossman's primary concern for PBS was, as he put it, "programming, programming, and programming." PBS offices soon blossomed with scheduling boards showing PBS programs against the commercial network offerings — suggesting that the public system, on the national level

at least, was thinking competitively. Grossman accelerated the shift to satellite interconnection of stations. He also stressed American productions instead of relying heavily on British material (§10.6).

To summarize, changes in CPB and PBS, though motivated in part by survival instincts, came about primarily because of pressure from local stations, concerned that insufficient funding was devoted to (1) their individual facility and operational needs, and (2) national and local programming. In part, the long-time stresses throughout the 1970s reflected the local vs. national conflict that has always been more evident in public than commercial broadcasting. The trends and changes suggest that local stations are supreme in public broadcasting in almost the same measure that they are subdued to national programming sources in commercial television.

NPR The trends and approaches to public radio provide an interesting contrast to those in public television. Radio acquired a name change from the first Carnegie report in 1967, but little else. In 1970 CPB set up National Public Radio (NPR) both to interconnect stations (like PBS) and to produce programs (unlike PBS). With its low profile and budget, public radio managed to stay out of the political infighting during the Nixon years. As Carnegie II noted:

NPR, therefore, now combines national production and distribution capability with political representation, in a way which many feel is unthinkable for television. In addition, the production activities of NPR are funded directly by CPB and are not, therefore, entirely controlled by the licensees. Unlike the situation in public television, the public radio stations have been quite willing to have national program production and distribution centralized and under the financial oversight of CPB. Public radio stations supported the creation of NPR from the beginning, and they retain control over it through its board. Sorely underfinanced, the stations have recognized the benefits of centralizing program functions. (CCFPB, 1979: 61)

The same report concluded "The major reason we have not witnessed the strain within public radio that has characterized public television over the last few years is the underdeveloped nature of the [radio] system." NPR provides only about 20 percent of daily programming for its member stations, which, in turn, are but a minority of all noncommercial stations on the air (§10.4).

With the newly constituted NPR came a new president — Frank Mankiewicz, a former broadcaster and filmmaker and political aide to Senators George McGovern and Robert Kennedy. He thus combined three essential qualities: background in the business of broadcasting, political connections in Washington, and a new face not connected with the old NPR. Under his feisty leadership, NPR struck out to increase its public visibility (when first approached about the job, Mankiewicz had to ask what NPR was) and thus its clout and funding. NPR became increasingly a competitor of PBS for a fair share of public broadcasting money and often argued its case directly to Congress.

Satellite Interconnection   Even before Carnegie I, the Ford Foundation suggested (in 1966) that public television programs be nationally distributed by means of communications satellite rather than by land lines and microwave (§11.4). The foundation pointed out that a satellite system could offer several channels of material at once and would likely save substantial delivery costs over time.

A decade later PBS announced a plan to interconnect public television stations by using three transponders on the Westar I domestic communications satellite. Benefits claimed for the system included better quality reception, ability to send signals east or west or within given regions, transmission of several signals at a time, allowing stations to pick and choose what is best for them, and cost saving. Stations would have to contribute about $25,000 each (a hefty sum for most) but in ten years would have full ownership of their receive-only earth station.

Aside from cost, a major factor in the debate over initating a satellite distribution system was increasing station concern over the centralized near-network role being performed by PBS under Lawrence Grossman. After considerable debate over control of the satellite scheduling process, a Transponder Allocation Committee (TAC) was set up as a part of PBS, though in reality it was controlled by the licensees. In the course of 1978, public television stations sequentially disconnected themselves from the terrestrial network and began use of the satellite interconnection.

PBS's system is built around 150 receive-only ground stations located around the country near public TV stations. The ground stations are licensed to the local outlets. Six ground stations can send programming to the satellite as well as receive it. One of these, located outside Washington, D.C., provides the main PBS feed while the other five serve regional networks from centers in Colorado, Nebraska, Florida, South Carolina, and Connecticut. These regional satellite uplinks can be used for regional feeds through one of the satellite transponders (Exhibit 10.3). By the early 1980s PBS and the stations working through TAC had evolved a simultaneous three-tier system:

■ PTV I is the main PBS network providing service similar to the old land line system. It allows for coordinated national publicity, especially in prime time when most stations carry the same program simultaneously.

■ PTV II is a distribution service that is not designed for direct broadcast but rather sends material of all kinds to stations for their later use. Programming serves the needs of specialty audiences, regional networks, and experimentation.

■ PTV III is a general education programming channel with material for children, plus instructional programs aimed at all age groups.

Exhibit 10.3
The PBS satellite distribution system

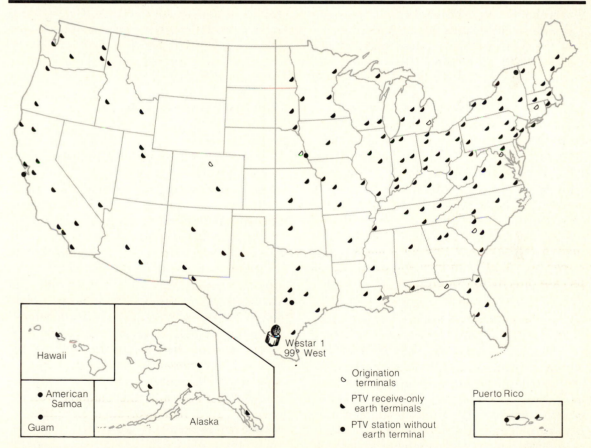

Westar 1
99° West

◦ Origination
  terminals

● PTV receive-only
  earth terminals

● PTV station without
  earth terminal

Hawaii

American
Samoa

Guam

Alaska

Puerto Rico

The map provides a simplified diagram of the earth station locations by which public television stations receive signals from the Westar I satellite. Six uplinks to the satellite allow programs to be originated at six different locations for regional or national feeds.

Source: Public Broadcasting Service.

Each of these services makes use of a separate transponder; the system can eventually expand to a fourth if needed. PTV I is under PBS operational control; PTV II is more a passive pipeline run by, but not controlled by, PBS; and PTV III is controlled mainly by advisory councils for each of its three main elements: children's programs, elementary and secondary instructional, and adult programming. Given that PTV II and PTV III act as "pressure valves" for specialized and overflow programming, some observers have predicted that in time PTV I will become a more centralized network operation essentially shaped by PBS rather than by the stations (Dort, 1980: 122–130).

Inception of the satellite system placed PBS at the forefront of network technology — but only for a year. National Public Radio followed suit with a Westar I-based satellite delivery system in mid-1980, becoming the first radio network to drop land line interconnection. With 17 uplinks around the country in addition to the receive-only earth stations (some shared with local public television stations), NPR began to program four audio channels while establishing plans to expand to as many as 12. Audio quality was vastly improved, with capability of networking stereo and even quadraphonic music programs. And, as with the television system, NPR could now send out a variety of programs simultaneously, feeding more material to member stations for them to pick and choose from as needed — at a substantial cost saving over the land line system used since 1971.

The satellite systems have an important impact aside from those mentioned — that of increasing the program input to and therefore the programming decisions of the local public outlet. Member stations now have greater control over what they receive and use — they have been largely freed from the time and schedule constraints still in force with single-feed commercial networks. This system can be more quickly and inexpensively expanded to remote areas than can land line-based networks. Technical quality of both picture and sound is vastly improved with satellite distribution and provides sufficient capacity for further experimentation with both signals. The three satellite channels can be used to expand the variety of material provided in order that public radio and television stations can appeal to a wider audience. Of increasing importance, the satellite facility system opens the way to new fund-raising possibilities through sale of unneeded satellite capacity to other users.

10.4 Types of Public Stations

To understand the confusion over the role of public broadcasting, one must understand the wide variety of types of local public radio and television stations. Although much of the controversy has swirled around the national organizations, local stations daily face quite different problems of political survival. There are four distinct types of television station ownership, and two very different classes of public radio stations. Their priorities differ and often conflict. The four broad categories of public television stations are: (1) state- or municipal-controlled stations, (2) college and university stations, (3) public school system stations, and (4) community stations.

State or Municipal Control There are more than 100 of these stations (about 35 percent of the total), and many are organized into state-operated networks. One city (New

York) owns and operates a station (WNYC-TV) as a municipal service. Of the statewide networks, typically only one station, usually in the state capital, does most of the programming; the other stations are, in effect, auxiliary transmitters of that signal. Alabama began what became a network of nine stations in 1955, and soon similar state authorities in Georgia, Kentucky, Mississippi, Nebraska, South Carolina, and others followed. In some states such as Pennsylvania an informal state network exists, though the stations are actually licensed to different (usually local) groups. But even states as licensees can get into trouble with the FCC. When the Alabama Educational Television Commission (AETC) applied for routine renewals of its eight stations in 1970, the FCC considered a complaint from 60 petitioners at the University of Alabama who claimed that the state system had steadily deleted PBS network programs dealing with blacks and the Vietnam controversy. The AETC replied that it gave priority to local programming and that, in any event, the omitted network programs contained "lewd, vulgar, obscene, profane or repulsive material" that the licensee was justified in deleting (25 FCC 2d 343, 1970). After first dismissing the complaint the FCC eventually refused renewal by a 4-2 decision — the first instance of such harsh action against a noncommercial licensee. However, the FCC allowed the Alabama network to continue operating the stations, pending a decision on who would become the licensee or licensees (by that time the state network involved nine stations). The FCC also waived its rules permitting AETC to reapply. In the long run, and at considerable expense for lawyers and filings, the AETC got all its licenses back.

College and University Stations The second largest group of facilities (about 30 percent) are licensed to institutions of higher learning, nearly all of which are publicly sup-

ported. Such stations were among the earliest public television stations on the air (§10.1). They are usually closely related to college curricula and often to previously established university educational radio stations (the University of Wisconsin's WHA-TV on Channel 21 in Madison built on four decades of radio experience). Station staffs are often heavily made up of university students or others on internships so that the station becomes a training ground as well as a program service. College stations, although usually state tax-supported, have the intervening layer of university administration between station decisions and the funding process. Most universities respect academic freedom and do not directly meddle in station affairs. Controls do exist, however, given the fact that station management must still seek funds from a single administrative source that may fear adverse reactions from *its* funders if the station becomes too outspoken.

An example of what *can* happen took place at pioneer public station KUHT, licensed to the state-supported University of Houston. The station had been scheduled to air the controversial docudrama *Death of a Princess* in 1980 when PBS put the program on the network feed. Based on a 1977 incident in which a Saudi Arabian princess and her illicit lover were publicly executed, the BBC telecast brought howls of protest from the Saudis (and temporary departure of the Saudi ambassador), who complained that the program was a totally unfair portrayal of real conditions in the country. Oil interests and others placed pressure on the Department of State, which in turn asked that PBS consider carefully whether to air the program in view of the potential damage it could bring to an American ally and chief source of oil imports.

Reports in the press quickly fanned this to a government-control-over-public-television issue. The university president overruled KUHT management and demanded that the station not air the program — allegedly because the university maintained oil interests and an educational arrangement with the Saudi Arabian royal family. Angry viewers took the case to court, and late in 1980 a district court judge ruled that because the station is licensed to an element of the state government it is a *public forum* like a street or park, where the First Amendment protects freedom of expression from arbitrary government suppression. The judge ordered the program aired. With the support of national public broadcasting organizations the university appealed that decision, which if upheld could have far-reaching consequences for state-owned stations.

Several years earlier, another university administration took the opposite role — essentially ignoring what its station was doing — and nearly lost its license. The University of Pennsylvania's WXPN (FM) in Philadelphia was operated mainly by and for students with little supervision for years. When the FCC investigated complaints and discovered lewd and explicit call-in talk shows and lack of licensee control, WXPN was ordered off the air. Only on appeal did the university manage to retain the license, promising far stricter control of programming.

Public School Systems By far the smallest category of stations (about 7 percent in recent years) are those operated by or as auxiliaries of local school systems or school boards. The prime role of such operations is naturally in-school instructional programs, many of them produced by and for the school system. In recent years several such stations have left the air (or been transferred to other licensees) as school board budgets have gotten tighter.

Community Stations The most interesting ownership category of public television stations is also the most important for the system as a whole. These stations, accounting for about 27 percent of public television operations, are controlled by organizations made up of representatives from various community groups including service groups, schools, colleges, art and cultural organizations, and the like. Their operating authority is nonprofit and does not usually receive direct tax support — rather it operates on foundation, business, and listener funding.

The drawback, obviously, is financial insecurity: there is no easy and reliable guarantee of where next year's budget is coming from. The advantage, on the other hand, is much greater flexibility and freedom in programming; no single financial kingpin can tell the community station how or what to program. Diversity of funding resources results in freedom of programming policies. (Wood and Wylie, 1977: 77)

This very freedom accounts for the importance of these stations, for every one of the major program-producing stations is operated by a community group. Such operations as WGBH in Boston, WQED in Pittsburgh, and KQED in San Francisco were on the air by the mid-1950s on VHF channels. They were joined later by WNET in New York, plus UHF stations WETA in Washington and KCET in Los Angeles. These are among the wealthiest of all public stations, though they too lack sufficient funds for ideal levels of operation.

These four differing ownership structures strongly influence the funding and programming of public television. They clearly also affect the stations' basic philosophical view of the role the public system should play. The school- and university-run stations have the strongest educational/instructional approach, as one might expect, whereas the community stations are most dedicated to the broad cultural-arts-entertainment-educational program mix aimed at a generalized audience.

Two Classes of Radio Technically, public radio licensees fall into the same categories as television stations, with universities holding nearly two-thirds of all "CPB-qualified" licensees. But that "qualified" phrase is the most important classification factor in radio, breaking the better than 1,000 noncommercial radio stations into a fairly small "have" class and a much larger "have not" group.

The expansion of television after the channel reservation fight, as well as the post-1967 concentration on development of a television system, led over the years to disarray and confusion among radio's long-time leaders. CPB realized that the only way out of the existing confusion was to select a cadre of professionally run full-service stations on which to build a more centralized system, using NPR as a core service. Thus arose a means of dividing potentially stronger stations (relatively speaking) from hundreds of small operations. To be "CPB qualified," radio stations must meet minimal standards: FM power of at least 3,000 watts; at least one production studio and a separate control room; at least five full-time employees; an operational schedule of 18 hours per day; a total operating budget of at least $80,000 a year; and some general strictures concerning local and generalized public service programming. By 1980 about 220 stations met or exceeded those standards and thus became eligible for grants from CPB and affiliation with NPR. The other 800 or so stations are generally outside the CPB-NPR axis and provide a strictly local and often very limited service. A major intention of NPR planners in the

1980s is to expand the number of CPB-qualified stations so that NPR programming can reach a larger number of people.

A key stumbling block is the result of the earlier FCC decision to license 10-watt noncommercial FM stations (§10.1). Several hundred of these stations were on the air by the 1970s, taking up frequency space and providing "electronic sandboxes" rather than serious broadcast training or service. With the expansion of demand for public radio service, the FCC in 1978 began to reverse course, ordering all 10-watt stations either to raise their power to a minimum of 100 watts or to assume a secondary status on a commercial frequency, with the possibility of having to give way to an applicant for full-power service.

But the "two-class" system of public radio stations persists. Funding grants go to the core qualified stations while the remaining stations operate in a kind of never-never land, not quite "public" but certainly not commercial. Whereas virtually all public television licensees have a part and often a voice in PBS decisions, the majority of public radio stations are not even part of the system, let alone having a say in its development. The exclusive club atmosphere naturally helps to assure NPR's dominance over affiliates with a minimum of the frictions that have afflicted television.

10.5 The Search for Funding

Ask virtually anyone in public broadcasting what the most serious problem is, and the answer invariably is insufficient funding to allow a quality job of broadcasting. As far back as the 1930s, some advocates proposed nonprofit rather than noncommercial operation, allowing sale of time sufficient to defray operating costs. The nonprofit notion came up again in the 1951 FCC hearings that eventually led to the reservation of noncommercial television channels, but educational interests realized that their only hope for winning approval of reserved channels lay in complete disassociation from commercialism. Volunteer sources of funds helped get educational television started but proved inadequate either to meet all current costs or to offer long-term fiscal security. These sources included foundation grants (the major component of income), gifts from business firms (both cash and equipment), viewer subscriptions, annual public fund drives, business underwriting of programs, production contracts, and rental of facilities.

The noncommercial character of public television stations does not preclude selling goods by auction and crediting donors (usually businesses), contracting with school systems to receive payment for telecasting over-the-air classroom instruction, commercial sale of production services, or even sale of advertising in printed program guides.

Funding Sources The result of many conflicting pressures is a public system funded both differently and at much lower financial levels than commercial television. Exhibit 10.5.1 diagrams funding for public television, showing the diversity of sources. As suggested above, each of these sources brings different obligations with its funding, has different system costs and resultant benefits, and has its own biases of just what it wants to fund and what it hopes to see result from its support. These often-conflicting goals of funders are one reason public television is so often accused of being bland and conservative in its programming — it has so many masters to please. Although no one in public broadcasting would want to be beholden to one source of income (whether government or nongovernment), considering the

potential for system abuse such support could bring, the existing diversity of sources leads to problems nearly as serious: inordinate amounts of system executives' time spent on fund-raising; inability to depend on a funding source over time (except for long-range congressional funding); conflicting obligations to different funding sources; and so on. Some of the funding is "designated," or limited as to use — the equipment grants from the Department of Education, for example, may not be used for operational costs. But station pressure on Congress has assured that Community Service Grants to stations (half of CPB's federal grant each year) may be used for whatever need the station selects. In the end, however, a substantial chunk of system funding goes to the production of programs, whether by other stations, outside producers, or independents.

The poverty that public television officials constantly plead is convincingly demonstrated in Exhibit 10.5.2, which provides a financial comparison of commercial and public television. Public television is trying to provide an alternative program service with but a fraction of commercial television's income — even though such things as prime-time network program costs are nearly as great. Perhaps the second row says it best: revenue to public television on all levels amounted to $2.15 for every man, woman, and child in America, while in the same year commercial television received better than $31 per person. The difference in funding shows in the technical proficiency and gloss of commercial programming, if not its intellectual depth.

Ford Foundation Years Next to tax sources, foundations have provided the largest share of public broadcasting support — and in the years prior to 1962 this was especially true. During the formative years of educational television, its chief foundation support came from the Fund for Adult Education, an agency of the Ford Foundation. The Fund's areas of concern — the American heritage, social anthropology, international understanding, and community self-development — automatically became educational television's areas of concern as well. As a

Fund-sponsored survey of this period declared:

Out of the Fund's own philosophy of adult education arose a requirement that a reasonable proportion of the programming should be in the area of adult education in the liberal arts and sciences. The [Educational Radio and Television] Center

Exhibit 10.5.1
Public TV funding flow

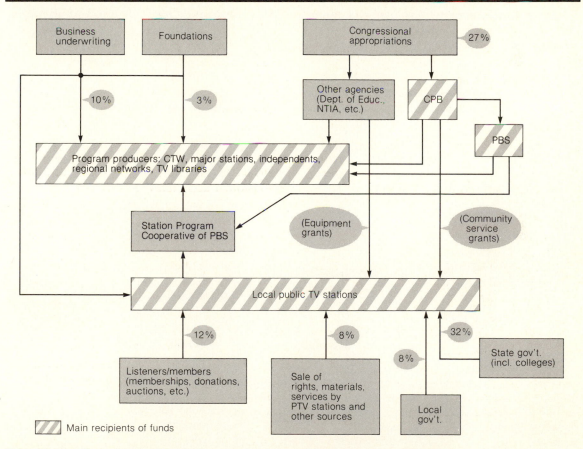

This diagram illustrates the "flow" of money between institutions in the system (see also Exhibit 10.5.3). A chart illustrating funding for public radio would be similar but would show a larger federal share.

Source: Data published with permission from the Corporation for Public Broadcasting.

was given the corresponding mandate, that this should be the area of its program production for the stations; and in a high proportion of cases the only "liberal education" that the stations offered in their early years was that furnished by the Center. (Powell, 1962: 70)

In short, the economic power of the Fund was a key to determining the very nature of educational television, let alone its emerging national structure. The Fund played a crucial role in securing the reserved channels (by funding of the various groups pressuring for the reservation); in activating many of them

(with substantial seed money grants for equipment); and in providing a small core of programming for the initial operations (by helping set up the predecessor to National Educational Television).

Without the backing of the Ford Foundation money, educational television would probably not have survived its first decade. In the years 1951 through 1962, the foundation provided some $82 million for the system. Some of this was directed at uses of television in instruction, including in-school experiments in several communities. After 1963, Ford funds were devoted to strength-

Exhibit 10.5.2
Comparison of public and commercial TV economics

Basis of comparison	Public TV	Commercial TV	Public as percentage of commercial
Revenues (1978)			
Total for system	$469,800,000	$6,913,000,000	7
Total per person	$2.15	$31.64	
Expenditures (1977)			
National network program expenditure per network	$ 67,500,000	$ 506,000,000	12
Average per-hour prime-time program cost	$200,000	$460,000	43

Comment: The huge difference in funding levels between public and commercial television is evident in these figures. While the dollar data change each year, the percentages change far more slowly. Radio is not compared here, for the only good statistical information on public radio refers to the "CPB-qualified" minority of stations — about 200 of 1,000 — and thus any comparison with commercial radio would be misleading.

Sources: Revenue data from S. Lee, *Status Report of Public Broadcasting 1980* (Washington: CPB, 1981), Table 9, p. 23. Expenditure information from Carnegie Commission on the Future of Public Broadcasting, *A Public Trust* (New York: Bantam, 1979), pp. 346 and 348.

ening the national program distribution process through NET and to supporting stations with direct grants.

Ford money was planned from the start as a seeding process — initial money to get a station or support service going and running for a few years in the hope that other means of funding would be found eventually. Other foundation money, especially from local groups in support of local stations, contributed a good deal in the 1950s, but the Ford Foundation support was crucial.

Increasing Government Role From the beginning of public radio, state and local governments were important supporters of the system, through their initiation and support of both stations and state networks. This support expanded with the higher costs of public television stations such that, by the mid-1960s, local and state tax funds provided about half of all system income. Into the 1970s, while the state proportion of support held steady at about 25 percent of total system income, local government (predominantly school board) support declined to well under 10 percent by mid-decade, in line with the diminishing proportion of school-run stations as budgets tightened (Exhibit 10.5.3). Until 1962, there was no federal financial input into the system.

Although the FCC had previously set up the noncommercial FM and TV educational class of licenses, public broadcasting did not receive legislative recognition in the Communications Act until the latter was amended by the Educational Television Facilities Act of 1962. This was the first explicit expression of federal responsibility for noncommercial broadcasting. It authorized $32 million to be awarded over a five-year period by the Department of Health, Education and Welfare for the construction and equipping (but not operation) of educational television stations. A driving force behind this law (which had

been in the works for six years) was the need to get more educational stations on the air to "hold" the reserved channels from commercial pressures. Funds were limited to a maximum $1 million for any one state and, further, were to be awarded only on a matching basis — one federal dollar for each dollar raised locally. This act, extended and revised, still provided equipment and facility funding annually in the early 1980s.

A major force leading to the first Carnegie Commission in 1967 (§10.2) was concern over needs not covered by the federal grants — funding for operations, including programming. Thus a key recommendation of the Carnegie report dealt with funding. It proposed an excise tax on new television sets, the funds from the tax to go to a trust fund designated solely for support of the Corporation for Public Broadcasting. The commission thus attempted "to establish an institution of information and ideas for which there was no American precedent — an institution which could be financed by government and responsible to the public but at the same time free from political interference" (McKay, 1976: 147).

Congress did not accept this crucial part of the Carnegie plan, in part because of traditional concerns about congressional control over federal appropriations, concerns over funding of the Vietnam War (then at its peak), and political disagreements. The result, of course, was an annual trek by officials of CPB to Congress for appropriations, opening the system to the kind of political pressures many had feared and which the Nixon administration provided.

Long-Range Funding During this period (1967–1975) a large number of funding alternatives were considered by Congress, special citizen groups, and think tanks. Among the proposals were: license fees on ownership of television receivers, acceptance of limited advertising on public stations, conversion of public television to pay-TV operation, some kind of tax on commercial broadcasting or earmarking of regular income taxes for public television, leasing access to spectrum space (some kind of annual fee on broadcast and other use of spectrum), the Carnegie-proposed tax on new sets, ownership and leasing of a satellite, etc. Although there was little agreement on any one of these proposals, there was agreement on the goals: (1)

insulation of funding from political pressures of annual funding; (2) an *adequate level* of funding to allow system growth; (3) year-to-year *stability of income*; and (4) funding over the *long-range* (generally defined as five or more years) to allow for more orderly planning, especially of program and technical development.

Several attempts at a congressional bill for even two-year funding had achieved no success — and in one case a Nixon veto (see Box). Added pressure came when the Ford Foundation, having spent nearly $300 million

Exhibit 10.5.3
Public broadcasting revenue by source: 1979

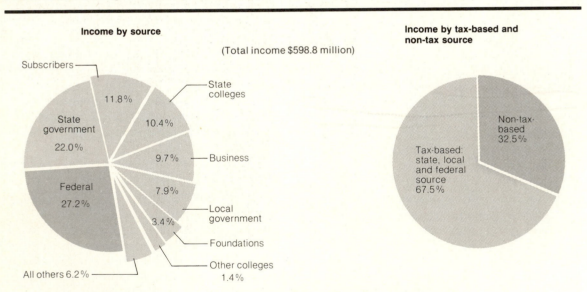

Income by source

(Total income $598.8 million)

Subscribers 11.8%
State colleges 10.4%
State government 22.0%
Business 9.7%
Federal 27.2%
7.9%
Local government 3.4%
Foundations
Other colleges 1.4%
All others 6.2%

Income by tax-based and non-tax source

Non-tax-based 32.5%
Tax-based: state, local and federal source 67.5%

Although the specific figures change from year to year up to the early 1980s, the overall percentages have changed little. Public broadcasting depends on tax sources for two-thirds of its income, with about 40 percent from state and local governments and under 30 percent from federal sources. With decline in Ford Foundation activity in this area, foundation contributions have dropped sharply over the past decade. Of the total income for the year, 84 percent went to public television stations. The federal portion of tax support is likely to decline sharply in the 1980s, leading to wider diversity of income sources (pay television for one), and less tax reliance generally.

Source: Data published with permission from the Corporation for Public Broadcasting.

How the Piper Called the Tune

Incidents during the presidency of Richard Nixon provide a textbook illustration of the difficulty of insulating a broadcasting system from politics when it depends on government for substantial economic support. Section 398 of the communications act tries to prevent political influence by expressly forbidding any "direction, supervision, or control" over noncommercial broadcasting by officials of the U.S. government. This legal detail did not stop the Nixon administration from manipulating public television for its own ends.

Around 1970 PBS started beefing up the noncommercial network's news and public affairs programming. For example, it hired a well-known NBC news reporter, Sander Vanocur, paying him a very high salary by noncommercial standards — a sore point with some affiliated stations and the Nixon administration.

The White House, regarding the PBS network as far too liberal, strongly objected to its intrusion into political commentary at the national level. The administration's attack began with a speech by Clay Whitehead, the president's chief telecommunications advisor, in 1971. He scolded the noncommercial broadcasters for neglecting their local responsibilities, charging them with having wrong-headed ambitions to create a "fourth network" to compete with commercial broadcasting. The administration used this same tactic of driving a wedge between affiliates and their networks against commercial broadcasting. The maneuver had relatively little success with commercial broadcasters, but it was effective against public broadcasters. They had only one network, heavily dependent on government funding. Moreover, some of the noncommercial station managers already felt resentful of the increased centralization of program decision-making at the level of PBS and the Corporation for Public Broadcasting.

In 1973 the administration sent a more explicit message: President Nixon abruptly vetoed the public broadcasting two-year funding bill that had been patiently nursed through Congress. Several board members of PBS and CPB — all presidential appointees — resigned in protest at the administration's interference in public broadcasting matters in defiance of the communications act. Nevertheless, the White House attack achieved its goal of weakening the national impact of public broadcasting, worsening existing divisions between CPB and PBS and between station managers with conflicting philosophies about the role of their medium.

on public broadcasting since 1951, announced a series of final terminal grants as it phased out its support. Ford officials felt that, with the system in place and the worst of the political in-fighting over, public broadcasting should be able to survive on its own. Finally, a funding bill was agreed to in Congress. The Public Broadcasting Financing Act of 1975 authorized funds for five years though it actually appropriated funds for only three.

The new act was based on a matching principal — congressional money would be released at the ratio of $1.00 for each $2.50 raised by the public broadcasting system from other than federal sources. The legislation also called for half the federal money accruing to CPB to pass through that organization directly to the stations in the form of unrestricted grants for the stations to use as they saw fit.

The 1975 act created a climate in which all the money CPB had to spend came to be viewed by the stations as "their money," since the level of federal funds was determined as a match of the stations' locally raised funds. This situation led the television stations and PBS to oppose a CPB plan for strengthening public radio, since television licensees, that raised most of the nonfederal funds, saw radio expenditures as a diversion of their own hard-earned funds. It also led PBS and the television stations to question many CPB program-funding decisions, as well as the Corporation's allocation of funds for nonprogramming activities. (CCFPB, 1979: 52)

Even so, the new bill provided sufficient time for PBS to initiate serious planning for its satellite interconnection. Three years later Congress approved a follow-on bill, the Public Telecommunications Financing Act of 1978, which carried funding authorizations through 1983 — but again with strings attached. This time the bill called for greater public participation in local station operations (by requiring that board meetings be held in public and by calling for public advisory committees for all public stations receiving funds from the bill's provisions). A ceiling was imposed on salaries of CPB, PBS, and NPR officers (essentially the level at which congressmen were paid). The "match" provision was revised to $1.00 of federal funds for every $2.00 of nonfederal system income. Certain specific equal employment opportunity provisions were required. Again, the bill called for specified levels of authorized federal

spending, but in practice the appropriations (when Congress actually *spends* the money) were for only three years at a time and almost always for less than the authorized levels.

Therefore public broadcasters have had to continue actively seeking financial input from all possible sources — both to earn the federal funding "match" and to expand system income to allow new program and technological initiatives. Public broadcasters continue to devote a disproportionate amount of energy to their money-seeking activities.

Program Underwriting The most controversial aspect of public broadcasting money-raising is the underwriting of television programming by business concerns. A program's producer, in assembling financial backing for a projected or continuing series, approaches some of the country's large business corporations and requests a grant. All that FCC regulations allow the company in return for this grant is brief credit in the form of short announcements at the beginning and end of a program to the effect that "This program is made possible by a grant from [corporation name]." Until 1981, FCC rules even prohibited use of corporate "logos" or trademarks. The search for funds led to multiple underwriting. Stations often also add local underwriting to cover costs of acquisition and distribution. The result in the 1980s is often a long credit "crawl" before and after programs. Mobil Corporation began underwriting public television programs in 1971 and has spent millions, including its underwriting of the popular Sunday evening *Masterpiece Theater* anthology series of British television dramas. From the company point of view, such underwriting is a form of high-level institutional advertising, especially because public television's audiences include a high proportion of influential and decision-making government and business leaders.

But during the 1970s underwriting became

an increasingly controversial issue. For one thing, underwriters generally are most interested in programs that will attract sizable (for public television) audiences; thus some of the very programming that an alternative service must provide does not stand to gain corporate funds. For another, there is concern about possible conflicts of interest between underwriters and the content of some programs that deal in issues of interest to underwriters. In 1980, for example, facing a large budget gap in a projected ten-part series on the history of the American labor movement, PBS waived some of its normal conflict of interest restraints on allowing underwriting of topics when it agreed to accept a large grant from several unions, so long as there were no strings attached and so long as the unions' support did not become the major financial underpinning of the series. Yet in most cases underwriters will not associate themselves with programs containing highly controversial subject matter, thus making many public affairs programs difficult to fund. In addition, commercial broadcast interests, spearheaded by the trade weekly *Broadcasting*, speak out strongly on the unfairness of allowing a government-supported, tax-exempt medium to compete with advertising-supported business for advertising dollars.

Other Approaches   Another example of competition with commercial interests arose in 1980 when four community public television stations combined forces and issued a new program guide magazine called *The Dial*. It is not unusual for noncommercial stations to earn income by selling program guides. *The Dial* project enraged commercial media because the noncommercial stations not only sold advertising in the magazine, they also used air time to promote sale of subscrip-

tions. Regional and city magazines affected by this competition complained to the FCC and the courts. *The Dial* won tax-exempt status and the FCC allowed the stations to continue over-the-air plugs, but opponents appealed those decisions. Beginning with four public television stations, *The Dial* soon attracted other participating stations, and, although reported to be losing money in 1981, appeared to be taking hold as a unique national magazine with local station program inserts.

Facing the inflationary pressure of the 1980s, even the largest and best-funded public television stations were forced to take drastic measures. KQED in San Francisco, for example, severely cut its local production of programs and laid off many staff members. The action ironically brought about competing applications when the station's license renewal came up — filed on the grounds that the station was no longer serving the public interest. New York's WNET divided into income-generating and not-for-profit sections and began vigorously to seek ways of raising funds. Some of the approaches considered or used by WNET and other stations included:

- Sale of commercial rights to materials from public television programs (the Children's Television Workshop provided a good deal of *Sesame Street*'s production funding from such sales).
- Production of limited-audience specialty-interest programming for distribution and sale by means of satellite or cable delivery (§10.3).
- Sale of programming to pay television for initial showing before release to public television (the PBS Cable proposal, §10.9).
- Rental of station facilities to commercial producers.
- Sale of videotapes to viewers.
- More intensive seeking of sales of productions overseas.

The constant search for funds to meet the federal "match" has caused many public television stations to push membership drives to the saturation point. Several times a year, often running for a week to 10 days at a time, station staff members and an army of volunteers operate telephone banks while on-air personalities sell membership at least as hard as commercials are sold on advertiser-supported television. Public television polls indicate viewer resistance to this means of fund-raising, which delays programs (and even interrupts some, again copying from commercial television) and strikes many within public broadcasting as demeaning. Even more objectionable from this point of view are over-the-air auction sales. Donated articles and services are promoted on the air at such length that the actions amount to program-length commercials, illegal in commercial broadcasting (§13.4).

10.6 Programming

Nowhere else does the confusion over public broadcasting's role show up more clearly than in what the networks and stations program. Because public radio and television operate quite differently, we consider television first, exploring both the local station and national service, and then turn to public radio. Just exactly what public radio and television are supposed to *do* within a basically commercial system is a matter of endless debate reflected in the varied trends in programs aired nationally and locally.

Where It Comes From As with commercial television, public television programming comes from a variety of sources (including commercial television). The national public television "network" (many in the organization dislike use of that term), the Public

Broadcasting Service, obtains the programs it feeds to member stations from three main sources:

(1) major production-oriented stations within its own membership; (2) specially focused supplier organizations like the Children's Television Workshop (§10.7); or (3) outside suppliers ranging from several large educational program "libraries" (§10.7) to government agencies.

Among the contributing producer-stations, WGBH-Boston, WNET-New York, and KQED-San Francisco stand out. Each has a long history of creative innovation in the public broadcasting field. WGBH introduced Julia Child's *The French Chef,* the first nationally recognized educational television series. WNET represents a fusion of the original educational network organizations, NET, with New York's public television station. Similarly, the corporation that operates the District of Columbia public television station, WETA, acts for the network in supplying PBS with timely news and public affairs programming, with direct financial support from CPB and the Ford Foundation.

The most important overseas source of programming has been British television, both the BBC and some of the independent (commercial) program companies. The popular Sunday evening PBS dramatic feature of the 1970s, *Masterpiece Theatre,* produced for the system by Boston's WGBH with underwriting from the Mobil Corporation, made use exclusively of British material — until 1981, when the BBC signed a contract limiting initial use of its programs to American pay television distribution. A number of popular documentary series have been co-produced in Britain — meaning that some of the personnel and funding is American, while much of what is actually seen and heard has a decidedly British tone. *Civilisation* is one example and *Connections* is another (both are discussed in more detail below). A small amount of Canadian and Australian content is also used, and some foreign language material finds its way into public TV schedules.

Independent producers have long complained they do not have sufficient access to public television stations, let alone PBS distribution. By independents, we mean individuals and institutions not affiliated with a public television station or organization. The independents, who are also substantially shut out of commercial television distribution, have argued that a public system should have diversified program input. Meetings have been held and guides published in an attempt to ease the path of independents — and their proportion of public television programs (mostly documentaries) has slowly increased in recent years.

The typical public television station produces and uses more material of its own than is the case with commercial television. Much of the local production is of two types — local news and public affairs programs and locally generated educational/instructional material telecast in daytime hours.

All this content reaches the local station by one of four distribution channels — the PBS satellite feeds, regional networks, "libraries," or the local station itself. Of these, by far the most important in terms of hours per day is the PBS satellite system.

In its operational structure PBS differs sharply from commercial network television. Affiliates sign contracts with PBS agreeing to pay varying amounts of dues according to each affiliate's overall budget and market size. But rather than being paid by the network for their time as is the case in the commercial system, public television stations pay the network for the programs. Unlike the commercial networks, PBS does no program production of its own — it provides a delivery service for programming produced by others and largely selected by the affiliate stations. This occurs through a funding mechanism termed the Station Program Cooperative (SPC), introduced in 1974. PBS offers affiliates a proposed list of programs for the coming season. Some are fully paid for by national underwriters, some are only partially funded, and some lack funding of any kind. The partially funded and unfunded programs will be carried by PBS only if sufficient stations "vote" for those programs in a series of rounds in which stations commit their programming dollars. These station commitments are based on such factors as which programs will appeal to local viewers, potential programs for which local underwriting may be available, and, perhaps most important, what any program will cost to carry (each station's share is prorated on a basis of station size and the number of stations voting to help fund the program). PBS acts as a clearing-house, providing a core schedule of prime-time programs, some of which are paid for, and "nominating" underfunded programs for stations to "elect." Such a system has been both praised for increasing democracy within the process and criticized for its emphasis on lowering financial risk, leading to little program innovation but rather a continuation of long-established series and a stress on what some critics have referred to as a program schedule made up of "the safe, the cheap, and the known" (Reeves and Hoffer, 1976).

The regional and state networks vary as to importance depending on location. Two regional networks are especially important: the Eastern Educational Network (EEN), serving stations on the East Coast down to Virginia; and the Southern Educational Communications Association (SECA), which covers the southern states from Maryland down

Exhibit 10.6.1
Public TV program production and distribution flow

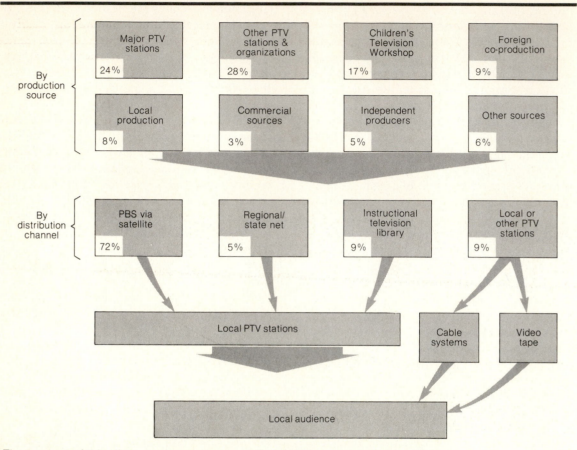

The top part of this diagram shows where public television programs come from; the middle portion shows how they are distributed to local stations. Note that the percentages (which vary only marginally from year to year) add to 100 for production source, and also to 100 for distribution channel. Cable systems and home video were of little importance in the 1970s but show great promise for taking on more of the distribution load in the 1980s.

Source: Data published with permission from the Corporation for Public Broadcasting.

through Texas. These stations exchange material of more regional interest among themselves and now make use of one of the PBS satellite channels for distribution.

The pages that follow focus on some of the more important types and examples of public television programming. Exhibit 10.6.2 shows the breakdown by hours first for all public television time, and then for prime time only (most of the latter from PBS and broadcast simultaneously by most stations). In the general schedule a considerable portion of time is given over to educational material, most of it aimed at children and much telecast during school hours. The program categories most often discussed by the critics and general public show up in the prime-time schedules: drama taking up nearly a quarter of the schedule, music and dance providing a fifth, and news-public affairs-general information taking up approximately a third.

Entertainment and Culture The best long-running showcase of public television is probably the popular *Masterpiece Theatre* telecast on Sunday evening. Foreshadowed by the NET telecasting in 1969–1970 of the

Exhibit 10.6.2
Public TV program types: 1978

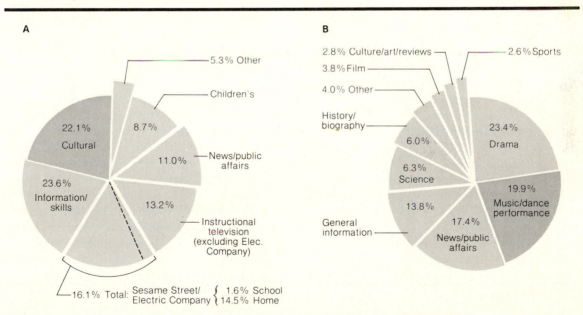

These two pie charts show different aspects of the average program week for public television stations. The left-hand diagram shows the percentage of total broadcast hours by program type; the second chart shows the percentage of *prime-time* hours by type. Notice the heavy proportion of drama and music/culture material in the evening hours as opposed to the heavier amounts of children's and educational programming overall, most of which runs in weekday daytime hours.

Source: Data published with permission from the Corporation for Public Broadcasting.

26-part BBC production of Galsworthy's *The Forsyte Saga* detailing a half-century in the lives of an upper-class English family, *Masterpiece Theatre* provides a glimpse for Americans of the best of British video drama. *Theatre* began in 1970 with 12 historical dramas relating the story of *The First Churchills*, combining superb acting, lavish costumes, and a smattering of real English history to educate viewers along the way.

Later series depicted the lives of the six wives of Henry VIII and the later years of Queen Elizabeth I. But the historical fiction programs were even more popular. Taking American viewers by storm, four seasons of the charming *Upstairs, Downstairs* detailed two decades of an Edwardian family, following in loving, gossipy detail the doings of the family (upstairs) and its servants (downstairs). Some critics suggested that this was merely high-class serial drama (high-class because of the quality of the scripts and acting — and because it was on public television) but still basically soap opera. From 1974 to 1977, running about 14 episodes a year, *Upstairs, Downstairs* was probably the most popular program on public television, with the possible exception of *Sesame Street.* On the lighter side, although also well-produced and acted, were dramatizations of Dorothy Sayers's Peter Wimsey mysteries, as well as the swashbuckling adventure series *Poldark,* which took place in eighteenth-century Cornwall with a full complement of villains and heroines. Each episode in the various *Masterpiece Theatre* productions was introduced by journalist and critic Alistair Cooke, born an Englishman, now an American citizen. These introductions — delivered casually and with great charm by Cooke — can be considered social essays in their own right; they establish a continuity in one of the most

outstanding examples of entertainment programming ever to appear on television.

Some British productions aired on PBS were critically acclaimed for content but criticized for having originated in Britain, thus ostensibly suggesting that the public system was both elitist and uninterested in American production. One case, a cycle of all the Shakespeare plays, began airing in 1979, two-thirds funded by the BBC and one-third by three American corporations underwriting the PBS portion of the co-production. It seemed fitting for the British to do Shakespeare, so complaints were muted.

In response to the criticism that *Masterpiece Theatre,* its most popular adult program, was British in origin and content, public television planners developed some popular though expensive domestic program options. *Great Performances* helped to showcase American plays and musical performances, often taped in actual presentation before theater audiences. Its irregular scheduling did not help to build television viewing. But these performances helped very much to build American audiences for opera and ballet: Sills, Pavarotti, Sutherland, Horne, Baryshnikov, Nureyev, Makarova, and Kirkland — these are only a few of the now genuinely familiar faces. On the other hand, the 13-part *Adams Chronicles* of 1976 demonstrated the system could produce excellent historical drama based on American themes, every bit as lavish and cultural as the British imports — but in this case at least at a very steep cost. The *Chronicles* detailed the lives of one of this country's most politically important families from 1750 to about 1900. Produced by WNET, the series ran up so extraordinary a cost ($7 million) that the station was accused by some of its own staff of cutting local public affairs material to meet the *Chronicles'* budget. Well received by critics and achieving good audience response, the series showed that if the expenses could be borne, American producers for public television could provide a high level of dramatic entertainment. But given budget limitations, imports of British materials provided equal or better quality at a fraction of the cost.

As well as supplying a considerable number of public television's dramatic and cultural offerings (numerous musical and dance performances are shown, many of them American in origin), the British provide many documentaries as well. Pioneered by Sir Kenneth Clark's *Civilisation*, which reviewed the development of the arts in Western Europe, documentaries in five to fifteen parts have run in prime time to considerable (for public television) promotional bally-hoo in the print and broadcast media. Most have been heavily underwritten by corporations. Among the most acclaimed were *The Ascent of Man* (a 1975 series reviewing anthropological knowledge and recent findings); *Connections* (a 10-part review of the development of selected inventions); *The Age of Uncertainty* (John Kenneth Galbraith's view of the development of economic issues and thought); *The Body in Question* (13 hour-long segments on new findings in human medicine); and *Cosmos* (the lavishly produced review of science and the universe featuring the ideas and narration of Carl Sagan).

Only two American-produced series demonstrated the same kind of audience impact: the weekly science series *Nova*, produced by Boston's WGBH, and the irregularly scheduled specials produced by the *National Geographic* magazine, programs once seen on commercial television but transferred to PBS when commercial network concern about their small audiences (by commercial standards) led to cancellation. Well produced and advertised by the magazine, the series scored an impressive audience feat when WNET's airing of an episode on the human body out-rated several New York commercial stations' fare.

News and Public Affairs There is a feeling among many in public broadcasting that public affairs programming is the key part of any alternative role in an essentially commercial system. For one thing, public television provides a different source of news and public affairs programs from the commercial networks that dominate audience attention. Many critics have accused the networks of devoting too little time to news and documentaries with too much entertainment content and too little real controversy. Public and commercial broadcasters share one problem, however — getting support for such programming. Just as commercial sponsors do not want to be associated with controversy on the networks, neither do underwriters wish to get too close to controversy on PBS.

Certainly the most crisis-ridden period of public affairs on public television was 1970–1974, the peak years of the Nixon Administration's assault on the media. For some time public television was a specific target of that assault with resultant administration pressure to limit funding legislation. That political tempest had a number of origins. The chief programming origin was the alleged liberal bias of PBS news and public affairs presentations. A related issue was PBS's employment of ex-network news reporters as correspondents whose apparent liberal outlook had been purchased with what were for public television high salaries. And specific documentaries and/or commentary — especially concerning the 1972 election — occasioned still more anger on the part of the administration. Surveys of public television station managers at the time showed that the political pressure was having an effect — nearly half registered their belief that the system should focus on culture and education, leaving out controversial public affairs programs entirely. The end of Nixon regime pressures, however, helped to bring about a revival of public affairs concerns in public television. Live coverage of the Senate Watergate hearings in 1973 showed what impact such coverage could have, and the potential to public television for showing more of the same.

One result of the Senate coverage was inception of the *MacNeil/Lehrer Report* in 1975, using as anchors two of the reporters who had covered the Watergate hearings. Unlike commercial network newscasts, this half-hour program is essentially an interview show, devoting each issue to a single topic: "a leisurely thirty minutes of agreeable conversation among several reasonably articulate people" (Kopkind, 1979: 31). Robert MacNeil operates from New York and Jim Lehrer hosts from Washington, thus giving the program a base in two important news centers and easy access to both business and governmental figures. The program aims at a more limited audience — those actually involved with decision making or vitally concerned with it. PBS President Lawrence Grossman encouraged the news role of PBS with his support of often controversial documentaries distributed by PBS though usually produced by local stations or independents. Late in 1977, for example, the Philadelphia public station, WHYY, produced an hour-long version of its weekly *Black Perspective on the News* featuring a panel of blacks quizzing a member of the Ku Klux Klan and one of the American Nazi Party as to their racial views (§17.1). There were widespread verbal protests, and some attempted court action, to keep such views off the air. None succeeded, and the program aired — with a larger audience, thanks to the controversy.

In 1978 Grossman brought in Richard Wald, a former president of NBC news, to analyze the role and performance of public

television in television news. Wald's report called for several weekly series of public affairs programming, including live coverage of important events, and expansion of existing programs. He placed stress on the live-coverage question, noting commercial networks were doing less and less of it, thus opening up an alternative role that public television should take on. Bill Moyers, a journalist well respected for his five-year series, *Bill Moyers' Journal*, for WNET, explained the contrasting problems of public affairs coverage on commercial vs. public television in 1978, when he had just returned to public television after a two-year sojourn with CBS:

The commitment to quality is high in both places. On CBS there are first class journalists, but they don't get the time on the air. On public broadcasting, they have the time on the air, but they don't have the resources. The one has the money but not the time, the other has the time but not the money. (NYT 11 Apr. 1978)

Public Radio Services   A discussion of programming on public radio is necessarily incomplete because of two factors: (1) consistent statistical information is available only for CPB-qualified stations, or about 200 of more than 1,000 licensees (§10.4), and (2) a considerable variety of formats and specializations exist among stations. Many of the non-qualified stations are inconsequential. Data on the qualified or larger stations is fairly easy to summarize (Exhibit 10.6.3). About three-fifths of their total hours on the air are taken up with some kind of music, usually classical, sometimes popular; about a fifth is comprised of news and public affairs, and another fifth consists of "culture." Fully 60 percent of station programming originates locally; about 20 percent comes from NPR. Nearly two-thirds of the typical daily schedule is in stereo, another indication of the importance of music on these stations. These CPB-qualified outlets are on the air over 18 hours a day, comparable to commercial radio (Katzman and Katzman, 1980).

But hidden within such summary statistics are some interesting trends. For one thing, public radio is the focal point of network experimentation to a far greater extent than either commercial radio networks or even PBS. Given its structural difference from PBS (§10.3), NPR has been able to develop a distinctive image. The program with which NPR began to develop an identity was a late afternoon news and public affairs show, *All Things Considered*, which has been showered with awards since its beginning in 1971. The program consists of a daily 90 minutes of news reports, interviews, dramatized comment on news events, and other features, about a third of which come from member stations. The result is a program that approaches cult status among its listeners, partially because it is so clearly different from the commercial station headline news service. *All Things Considered* in 1980 spun off *Morning Edition*, which provided an early morning version with a similar approach. As well as offering these regular programs, NPR distributes classical music concerts and provides other coverage of public and cultural events. Local stations often record these and broadcast them at hours of their own choosing. NPR also presents live if not lively coverage of governmental affairs (among high points: the first live coverage of a Senate debate, when that body considered the Panama Canal treaties in 1978, and a complete verbatim reading of the Nixon tapes during the Watergate crisis in 1973–1974).

Dramatic programming, though heard to a limited degree on commercial radio, is actively developed on public radio, spearheaded by the *Earplay* production unit at the

University of Wisconsin, which for nearly 15 years has experimented with the application of stereo techniques to dramatic formats (for example, characters in conversation are heard on different stereo channels).

But the most important role of public radio is as a bastion of classical music and fine arts programming — often the only such service in a given market. Exhibit 10.6.3 shows that nearly two-thirds of average station program hours (on the large, CPB-qualified licenses, at any rate) is devoted to music. And of musical programming, nearly two-thirds is classical (including opera), and another fifth is jazz (Katzman & Katzman, 1978: 33). Paralleling commercial radio, most public radio

Exhibit 10.6.3
Public radio program types: 1978

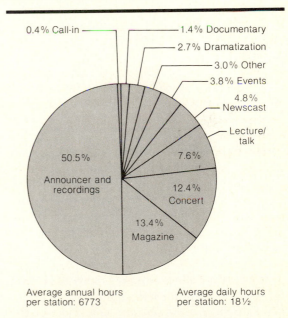

0.4% Call-in
1.4% Documentary
2.7% Dramatization
3.0% Other
3.8% Events
4.8% Newscast
Lecture/talk
50.5% Announcer and recordings
7.6%
12.4% Concert
13.4% Magazine

Average annual hours per station: 6773

Average daily hours per station: 18½

Note that nearly two-thirds of public radio programming is devoted to music, most of it classical in nature.

Source: Data published with permission from the Corporation for Public Broadcasting.

music is in stereo (about 64 percent), and most of it derives from the local station's record library or from live origination, though NPR offers a few musical series. The fine arts programming often includes cultural interviews and features on dance, art, and local cultural events in a community.

In the late 1970s a subclass of public radio began to provide cohesion among the smaller affiliates of NPR. These "community" stations, funded by listener donations, provide more drastically alternative programming, often appealing to college-age listeners rather than an older cultured elite. Small in number (about 50) and more underfunded than other noncommercial radio stations, they provide a good deal of local program material, often from groups with widely varied views on politics and cultural matters (§7.9).

10.7 Children and Classrooms

There is little disagreement in or out of public broadcasting that one of its major functions is to provide educational material — ranging from in-school or instructional programming to more generalized at-home educational material — to adults and children. A large proportion of television daytime hours on public stations is taken up by school programming, with additional special programs for children early in the morning and again in the late afternoon hours.

Children's Television Workshop (CTW)
Public television's most celebrated program series, *Sesame Street*, began as a reject of the commercial networks, which had first crack at this unique approach to television for three-to-five-year-olds. The three networks turned down the show because they felt that commercial sponsors would have little or no interest in a program narrowly focused on such a small specific age group. Launched on public television in 1969, it was developed and produced through an independent non-profit corporation, Children's Television Workshop (CTW). Funded initially by foundation and government grants, CTW now earns about half its income from sale of articles franchised to use the program's name and characters.

It is difficult to overstate the impact of *Sesame Street*. The program appeared just as the transition from educational to public television was taking hold — and it brought the first large audiences to the system, often disadvantaged households (to which the programs were specifically aimed), which had previously ignored public television. The series changed relationships among home, school, and television and also within the system. Independently funded and directed, CTW could rise above station and even PBS quarrels to stick to its own research-backed course. For the first time the entire technical resources of the medium were brought to bear on a series directed to children. A wonderfully original series of large-scale puppets called Muppets became a hallmark of the program, providing both entertainment and education in their short bits.

No series on either commercial or public television has been given the amount of scheduled air time as has Sesame Street. *Throughout the 1970s, local stations have consistently devoted 29 percent of their weekday school-hour schedule, 14 percent of the weekend daytime schedule, and about 47 percent of their weekday after-school broadcast hours to* Sesame Street. *As the decade came to a close, an average 11.4 percent of the total broadcast hours of each public television station featured* Sesame Street, *with each program aired four times during the year. (Sikes, 1980: 9)*

Some segments were taken out of certain programs and used in others, a kind of interchangeable parts approach to programming that stretched the series into its second decade and easily its third or fourth audience "generation." Yet the basic aim of the series has remained the same: to lessen the gap between inner-city disadvantaged children and their suburban counterparts in basic reading (letters and numbers) and social skills. Programs are divided into short segments to maintain attention, with a variety of formats and even "advertisements" ("This segment of *Sesame Street* has been brought to you by the letters A and L and the numbers 3 and 7 . . ."). Even the entertainment segments with the Muppets or animated material serve some educational goal.

Building on its initial success, CTW branched out with *The Electric Company* for older children, drawing on the methods and research of *Sesame Street*, though with more advanced reading concepts built in. In 1980 CTW began providing a daily science program, *3-2-1 Contact*, in a half-hour format, aimed especially at those not previously thought to be interested in science, particularly girls and minorities. As in *Sesame Street*, segments of these series can be pulled apart and reassembled for updated use again, stretching the production dollar.

By the very attention they have received — and the high quality of their programming — the CTW productions create an ironic dilemma for public broadcasters. The cultural spread of CTW's audiences does not extend to adult programming; the lower socioeconomic groups drop away as they outgrow children's programs. The very quality of CTW's production makes any other programs seem pale by comparison, and few others have anywhere near the budget of CTW with which to work. Producers of adult programming look wistfully at the continuing success of *Sesame Street* and its spin-offs and ask why public television can't have an adult program as popular.* The very success of CTW made it extremely difficult to get funding for other children's programming from funders who felt little need for still more "kidvid," as children's television (kid video) is known in the business.

When *Sesame Street* began to expand to overseas distribution, the American product did not always hold up under scrutiny of different cultural needs. The BBC, for example, turned the series down cold, complaining that its similarity to American commercial television in format (short commercial-like segments) simply reinforced the short attention span of children rather than furthering education. But many other countries found the program idea and some of its characters highly useful. *Sesame Street* now airs in many foreign countries, in all cases in the local language, and in many instances with locally produced inserts more closely reflecting local cultural interests or priorities.

Other children's programming has also won both audiences and awards. *Villa Alegre* and *Carrascolendas* are young children's programs aimed at Hispanics. For more than 25 years, versions of *Mr. Rogers' Neighborhood* have taught social niceties to preschoolers, making that program second in viewing popularity only to *Sesame Street*. Beginning in 1972, but fading by decade's end for lack of funding, was *Zoom!*, which was produced for and by children, based mainly on thousands of letters from child viewers.

*CTW discovered itself to be not wholly infallible when it tried to produce its first adult program, *Feeling Good*, which was built around medical knowledge and advice. The program was withdrawn after a single season, despite considerable midyear reworking. Researchers found the show tried to cover too much with widely varied formats, making it hard to build a consistent audience.

Broadcasts to Classrooms   One of the important factors behind early interest in educational radio, and later television, was the feeling that the broadcast media could be masterful educators in and out of classrooms. Serious experiments and research on instructional, or in-school, radio began in the late 1930s and carried over to television early in the 1950s.

One fundamental characteristic distinguishes instructional television programming from general television programming for children. Instructional television . . . is expected to help students achieve identified, specific learning goals under the administration and supervision of professional educators in a formally structured learning environment. ITV requires active, intellectual participation of its viewers. The "success" of a program does not depend on the size of the audience. Rather, the skill of the classroom instructor and the receptivity of students combine to use television for learning. (Sikes, 1980: 19)

Inherent in this description/definition is the idea that television (or instructional radio for that matter) is *supplemental* to regular classroom instruction — a matter of enrichment in an educational program rather than solo media performance. It took years of often repetitive experimentation in both radio and television to prove that broadcasting was not a "hypodermic" educator that could replace teachers and classrooms. Time and again the use of radio or instructional television has been found no better or worse than use of a live teacher — but television along *with* that teacher can be especially effective.

Indeed, the raw statistics are impressive. A 1976–1977 CPB survey of users reported that 72 percent of all primary and secondary teachers had instructional television facilities available for use in their classes, though only 60 percent actually used them, with 46 percent using one or more series of programs regularly. CPB estimated that 15 million stu-

dents got a portion of their regular education from instructional television, virtually all of it integrated with other classroom activities. Usage was concentrated in the primary grades. The survey noted increasing classroom use of videotape, which is more flexible than broadcast programs.

Much of that taped material (some of which is also broadcast) comes from one of several large libraries of instructional material that act as centers of syndication. The two largest and best known are the Agency for Instructional Television, based in Bloomington, Indiana, and the Great Plains National Instructional Television Library in Lincoln, Nebraska. Both produce, store, and distribute series of instructional programs for all levels of education.

Following the example of the British Open University, several American "distant-learning" projects now concentrate on use of television for adult education. The University of Mid-America (UMA), headquartered in Lincoln, Nebraska, has no campus but rather exists as a consortium of 11 midwestern universities, providing over-the-air and for-credit college courses. Students watch the material on a local public TV station, pay a registration fee to a local administering college, and thus can learn at home. UMA gets its income from the stations showing the program and from the administering colleges, which are charged a per-student fee. A newer project, headquartered at the University of Maryland, is known as the National University Consortium. The Corporation for Public Broadcasting entered this activity with the aid of a $150 million grant in 1981 from Walter Annenberg (publisher of *TV Guide*), to be paid out at the rate of $10 million in each of 15 years. The shared hope of all these projects is to reach nontraditional (older adult) students as well as those not interested in credit.

Despite these approaches, it has become increasingly obvious that broadcast channels do not constitute an efficient means of distributing in-school instruction. For most such applications, broadcast television offers too little time or subject flexibility while at the same time filling valuable spectrum space. Educational situations call for more individualized instruction than open-circuit television can furnish. Thus the use of various closed-circuit systems such as Instructional Television Fixed Services (ITFS, §4.7), relay networks, home video systems, and cable television channels increasingly make more sense both educationally and economically. Several of the new open university projects and long-range funding bills have encouraged use of other means of delivery in addition to public television. Such thinking is prompted by the increasing budget pinch of schools and universities seeking new ways to disseminate education while cutting costs.

10.8 Impact of Public Broadcasting

Arguments about the role of public broadcasting in a pluralistic system are increasingly focused on the size and character of the public radio and television audience. For years accused of catering to a small elitist audience, public broadcasting has made a strong attempt in recent years to reach more people by broadening its appeal and widening its constituency. Considerable pressure to that end has come from Congress as the source of federal funds and from foundations and corporate underwriters concerned about the impact of their dollars. Under this pressure,

public broadcasting has finally begun to develop the "numbers" research long common in commercial operations.

Who Tunes In   For many years the audience for public radio and television was small, no matter how one defined that word. And many in public broadcasting seemed to revel in that very limited size, speaking of their elite and upscale audience, which supported public broadcasting as a kind of cultural oasis in the midst of the commercial wasteland. To some degree, this already-educated audience led programmers to assume a certain background on the part of listeners: programming was not designed to appeal to those of lesser educational attainment. The first important audience study of noncommercial television concluded that educational stations might well be "condemned forever to program ratings of 1, to minority audiences heavily skewed toward high education and his social status, and to viewers who come purposefully to ETV for one program and then turn off the set" (Schramm, Lyle, Pool, 1963: 171).

Until the 1970s there were few figures on the audience of public television simply because there was little demand for such data. With rising federal funding and more corporate underwriting, however, public broadcasting had to prove its "success" in terms of hard audience numbers. A concern with audience *size* became increasingly important.

A summary of early studies that appeared in 1974 concluded that about a third of all television households tuned to at least one public television program in a given week, while nearly half did in a month. In markets with a VHF public television outlet, the weekly audience might approach half the television homes (Lyle, 1974). These figures on public television's reach were minuscule when compared to those for commercial fare. Measuring audience over a week or month instead of per day or day part as in commercial television was necessary: the audience for most individual public TV programs was simply too small to measure except cumulatively. Further, there was a philosophy evident in public television circles that the role of the system was to reach large audiences cumulatively through many specialized interest programs for small audiences.

By 1977 CPB reported 60 percent of the country's households tuned to a public TV program at least once in a given month; by 1980 research showed better than half the homes now tuned to public TV in the course of a *week*, some 41 million households watching an average of three and a half hours' worth. Of households with children, no less than three-quarters tuned to public television — an indicator of the drawing power of *Sesame Street* and other children's programs. As for prime-time viewing only, the late 1980 data showed that nearly 30 percent of the country's homes tuned in for an average of just under two hours per week — a 30 percent improvement over the year before (*TV/Radio Age*, 26 Jan. 1981).

Part of the limited impact of public television in the 1960s and 1970s was limited system penetration. Only some areas of the country could even receive a public television signal. By 1977, however, CPB reported that nearly 90 percent of the country could receive public television programming, some of that delivered by cable rather than over the air.

With the important exception of the audience for children's programs, the audiences for commercial and public television differ from one another. Compared to commercial television's average viewer, the public television/radio listener has higher education, higher income, and higher social status. Indeed, this basic profile of the public television viewer has changed little in 20 years of research. Most research reports of recent vintage merely reiterate what is already known.

Those involved in audience research for CPB or PBS have therefore been caught in the middle of a policy controversy — whether to serve the system's "upscale" listeners (who would most appeal to potential corporate underwriters) or the larger and demographically broader audiences slowly being developed (who would be of interest to government and some foundation funders).

Research   Beginning in 1970 PBS began to purchase special audience research from commercial firms, especially A. C. Nielsen. The research was "special" partially because the very low ratings of public TV programs (by the end of the 1970s, the average prime-time program earned only a 2 rating while commercial programs averaged eight times that) made it hard to judge accurately the overall size of public television audiences. The special studies sought to measure the changing and somewhat wider demographic pull of public programming. In this goal they were only marginally successful, prompting CPB researchers to try a different research approach.

Commercial ratings are quantitative; they measure the size and to some degree the characteristics of the audience (§14.7). For several years, CPB has underwritten research studies and conferences exploring possible systems of "qualitative" ratings that would seek more information about why viewers select and stay with certain programs. This research has the dual intent of improving programs on the basis of more specific audience research and providing another means of demonstrating public broadcasting's impact other than that of size alone.

The model of what can be done is CTW's *Sesame Street*. With federal and foundation funding, research began two years before the series first aired in 1969. Extensive research was built into planning the program, with several years of detailed "before and after" comparisons of what children had learned, which segments were most effective, how children's demographic backgrounds affected their learning, and so on. The results of the research were fed back into the program production process; segments that were not effective were altered and new ones were designed — a kind of feedback between audience and program content not typical in either public or commercial television. Few programs or organizations, however, can afford this kind of intensive ongoing research program.

National Public Radio developed a small informal audience research capability in the late 1970s. Findings paralleled those of television — the audience was very small and not even especially loyal to public stations, as had been previously supposed. Listening to public radio, like viewing public television, was generally listening in *addition* to (rather than *instead* of) commercial programming.

Few local noncommercial stations can even afford regular Nielsen market ratings (and half of the stations have audiences so small they are not readily measured). Differences in the aims of individual programs, to say nothing of the ongoing disagreements about the public system's mission, have impeded consistent research on both national and local levels. After two decades the question remains: do policy makers, and the researchers who support them, want to stress greater impact among a small number of viewers (the elitist programming approach) or a lesser impact spread over a vastly larger audience (the alternative but more popular programming approach)? At the moment, research suggests that public television and radio have considerable impact on their small but often influential audiences. But whether

that fact is sufficient to justify funding the public system in the face of coming competitive technological options is an open question.

10.9 The Outlook

In the 1980s the whole role and structure of public broadcasting face a combination of new threats more potent than those of the past. The prime concern is still financial, but technology raises both options and pressures for change at the same time — and the combined effects of funding and delivery system changes promise to transform public broadcasting.

The Money Crisis The worsened economic conditions of the early 1980s spell serious trouble for the financing of public broadcasting. The Corporation for Public Broadcasting, which was under considerable pressure from the Carter administration, was earmarked by the Reagan administration for a substantial funding cut (on the order of 25 percent, not counting inflation) and perhaps even for abolition. There is general agreement in and out of government that increased federal funding is unlikely. Thus the system is forced to consider other means of financial survival. Federal funding in the mid-1980s is projected at static or falling levels, not even taking inflation into consideration.

Seeing some of this coming, the Carnegie II task force spun off a more specialized report in 1980 suggesting that public television consider a pay television scheme as a way of developing increasingly expensive programming. The plan capitalized on the elite appeal of much public television fare.

Programming would be developed initially for this premium pay cable service; only later would it be provided to public television stations at no extra cost to those viewers. The income from the pay cable showings would help to fund the program productions. Though sharply attacked at first as being the antithesis of what public television had long been trying to do, the idea was soon embraced by PBS under funding crisis conditions. Early in 1981 PBS announced plans for the 1983 inception of PBS Cable, a pay service which would provide from 90 minutes to three hours per evening of cultural, documentary, and other programming, as well as daytime professional and instructional courses, for $10 to $13 in monthly subscriber fees. Unfortunately for PBS, it was not alone in announcing a new cultural specialty program service for cable; accordingly, the success of the PBS plan was by no means assured, given likely limited audience demand for "pay culture" programs. PBS planned to offer such fund-raising options as the sale of recordings of programs, program guides, and cultural event tickets at a discount. Distribution would use PBS's satellite transponders to feed cable and other pay television sources. PBS stations would pay $20,000 per year to be part of the "consortium," and cultural institutions around the country would also pay small fees and provide material. The stations and institutions would therefore be able to use programming that had been developed while sharing the revenues that had been raised.

Early in 1980 the FCC approved PBS's plan to lease access to the 12-channel reception capacity of its 150 receiving ground stations around the country to commercial television program distributors, thus opening up another avenue for syndicated program access to commercial stations while helping public stations meet costs of the satellite interconnect. In a related move, Western Union was

given access to the PBS ground stations, providing further rental income to the PBS operation.

Despite these initiatives, it appears that public broadcasting will have to rely heavily on already-existing and new private financial sources — listeners and underwriters — and less on local and federal tax funds. This inflationary budget pressure, along with increased competition and a political mood calling for less government role in the economy, forces the system to focus on the basic question of its role in a time of lowered public support for noncommercial social programs. Public broadcasting, with a confused image of its own role, is caught between conflicts in budget and technology.

Increasing Competition   Development of the new technologies discussed in Chapters 4 and 11 are looked upon with some concern by those in public broadcasting.

While the new television services are expected to decrease audience share for all types of broadcasting, the decrease is expected to be felt by public TV earliest and most severely for two reasons. First, the specialty productions and targeting of small audiences characteristic of the new media invade what had been the exclusive province of public TV. By the late eighties public TV may be one of a dozen sources of specialty programming. Programs are needed to fill the schedules of the new media, and so producers of specialty material such as live music, nature, science, and documentary programs, accustomed to the lean public TV market, will be invited to the feast of the new distribution systems. This will result in rising costs for programs of this type, forcing public TV to offer fewer of its traditional kinds of programs. Second, the public TV audience for these programs will be siphoned away to the other media. This shift will challenge the status and rationale of public TV as the principal "alternative" to real-time commercial broadcast programming. (Agostino, 1980: 200)

An example of this process was the purchase in 1980 of first-run rights to all BBC television productions shown in the United States by a Rockefeller Center-based pay cable service termed *Bluebird*. After January 1982, the only British first-run material still available for purchase by public television is that of the independent firms. Given that BBC drama and documentaries had become a staple of PBS prime time in the 1970s, observers feared for the noncommercial service's future if such siphoning were to become widespread.

The sale of BBC rights helped to focus the arguments over the impact of technology. Some observers see the sale as a good omen, forcing PBS to turn to more American and independent production sources. They argue that if public broadcasters retain flexibility, the system can change with the times and remain viable. Others, noting the conservative nature of local stations, are less optimistic and fear being priced out of operation in a short time.

Partly to stem a rash of negative press reports and the rising concern within the public television system itself, the National Association of Public Television Stations (the lobbying groups that split off from PBS in 1980) began a counterattack. The NAPTS noted the areas of public television's strength:

■ The presently operating television stations could reach in 1980 a larger proportion of the population than any cable-delivered program service would reach even a decade later.
■ Such services as multipoint distribution systems (MDS) or tape or disc home video options are even more limited in their audience projections for the late 1980s.
■ Public television certainly costs less than the various pay-TV options.
■ Many public television stations are actively becoming a part of cable and other media options in their local markets, hoping to en-

sure their continued viability as program suppliers whatever delivery system is used.

Summary

Public broadcasting is as old as commercial radio and television but has developed in its modern organization only since the 1967 Carnegie I report and resultant legislation.

Throughout its development, there has been debate within and outside the system over (a) just what service the public broadcaster is to provide, (b) the comparative roles of the stations versus the central national organizations, (c) how to fund the system adequately, and (d) how to insulate public broadcasting from political and other outside pressures.

The question of role has been basic and most difficult to answer. Some feel public broadcasting should be an alternative to commercial stations, focusing on cultural and educational material for an elite audience. Others see the need for a broader public acceptance of and support for public broadcasting; they encourage children's and specialty programming mixed with more popular fare. And still others feel there is no need at all for a separate, partially tax-supported system merely duplicating what commercial stations can or do provide already.

Public radio and television stations operate on reserved frequencies (except for the few AM educational stations), assuring that the more slowly funded educational institutions, which are usually licensees, would have time to establish stations to supplement the commercial service. The reservations also seek to provide at least one public radio and television signal in most of the country.

The Corporation for Public Broadcasting (CPB), set up in 1967, acts as the funding agency for public broadcasting. It receives funds from annual congressional appropriations and directs those funds to the Public Broadcasting Service (the television interconnection), National Public Radio (the radio network), and directly to individual stations.

In 1979–1980 public television and radio stations went to a satellite rather than land line interconnection. This allowed for greater program diversity in that stations could pick from three signals at a time, thus allowing more specific picking and choosing of what to air. As well as providing considerable cost saving, use of the satellite allowed expansion of public broadcasting to more remote areas.

The largest category of television station ownership is that operated by colleges and universities, the smallest that operated by school boards. In the middle numerically, but highly important for the program production and system operation roles they perform, are the stations operated by state and municipal governments (including the several state-owned public television networks), and the community organizations that exist solely to operate public radio and television stations.

Public radio stations are similarly owned but break into two categories: about 225 that are CPB-qualified and actively participate in national funding and NPR, and another 800 that are much smaller and subsist on local community support.

About 30 percent of funding for public broadcasting has come from the national government, nearly 40 percent from state and local tax funds, 10 percent from listeners who "subscribe" to local stations, about 10 percent from businesses that underwrite some programming, and the rest from other sources. In the 1980s the federal portion of the funding pie began to shrink markedly.

Key issues in funding include: the total amount of money available (never enough); its source (tax money is becoming less important, forcing greater reliance on station listeners and corporate underwriters); and the degree to which funders have a say in system operation, especially programming.

A great deal of public radio and television program time is devoted to daytime instructional programs for use in school. In addition, public television allots a substantial portion of its typical broadcast day to programs for children. PBS evening programs lean heavily to dramatic entertainment, cultural presentations, and documentaries.

Public radio programming is mainly devoted to music (60 percent of the typical station schedule); NPR provides a number of news and discussion programs.

The audience for public broadcasting is minuscule when compared to that for commercial stations. It is an "upscale" audience with higher levels of education, income, and social status than the commercial broadcasting audience. Only with its children's programs does public television reach the homes of a wider general audience.

Expanding technological delivery options and a murky financial outlook appear to be major threats to public broadcasting in the 1980s.

CHAPTER 11

Cable and Newer Technologies

Broadcasting will undergo more change in the coming decade or so than in its entire history thus far. The main cause of that change is the development of a number of alternative delivery technologies, which in the 1970s began to develop into viable commercial competitors to traditional broadcast stations. This chapter, which should be read in conjunction with the more technical background material of Chapter 4, provides an overview, from the stance of the early 1980s, of the operation of cable television and newer delivery systems. Given its size and the fact that it developed first, we devote most space to cable television, but all the new technologies share a common need — access to the home television set.

Such alternative services can be regarded as "parasitic" in that they take advantage of a situation created by commercial television without contributing to the profitability of station owners (though an argument can be made that program production has been substantially expanded by these services). Broadcast television, whatever its failings, created the almost universal demand for receivers — and thus the market potential for those sets now being exploited by the services discussed in this chapter.

11.1 Evolution of Cable

Origins Community antenna television was inconspicuously introduced soon after television itself began as a mass medium. One of the first, if not the first, systems began operation in 1950 at Lansford, Pennsylvania. It picked up three stations not otherwise receivable in the hilly community and delivered the signals to subscribers via coaxial cables, using amplifiers between the headend and the drop-off points. It thus met the basic criteria that distinguish cable from other systems that use a common antenna, such as apartment house master antenna systems: it used intermediate amplifiers, fed more than one signal simultaneously, and was sold on a subscription basis.

During its first decade cable remained primarily a local concern. At first the only regulation was by municipal governments, which had to be consulted in order to get permission to run cables over public property. With time, a three-tier system of control developed — municipal, state, and federal. Municipalities generally issue franchises to cable companies, giving them exclusive rights for a limited period of time to install and operate cable systems. Larger communities franchise several companies by dividing their areas into zones. New York, for example, divided Manhattan Island at about

80th Street, awarding different franchises to the northern and southern halves of the borough. The municipalities receive a fee from each franchisee, usually no more than 5 percent of the franchise's gross income.

Cable Augmentation   After their initial success at answering the existing demand for access to television broadcast programming, cable operators began to cast about for ways to augment this service in order to make subscriptions more salable. After all, once the franchised system makes the capital expenditures for installing the cable, new services can be added at relatively little cost.

Augmentation takes several forms. One form simply broadens the range of broadcast services on the cable by importing signals via microwave relays from stations more distant than the ones in the immediate vicinity. Another form, called local *origination* supplies closed-circuit nonbroadcast materials at no extra cost (§11.2). A third form is that of extra-cost "box office" types of syndicated programs, usually feature films and major sports events (§11.5).

The proven workability of all these forms of augmentation, at least on a preliminary basis, stimulated still more entrepreneurial interest. The initial success of cable had oc-

Exhibit 11.1
Indicators of cable TV growth: 1955–1981

							System size	
Year	Number of systems	Number of subscribers (add 000)	Average number of subscribers per system	Percentage of TV homes with cable	Percentage above 5,000 subscribers	Percentage below 2,000 subscribers	Percentage having 12 or fewer channels	Percentage having 13 or more channels
1955	400	150	375	.5	na	na	na	na
1960	640	650	1016	1.4	na	na	na	na
1965	1325	1275	962	2.4	na	na	na	na
1970	2490	4500	1807	7.6	8	65	90	3
1975	3506	9800	2795	14.3	16	61	78	22
1981	4637	19800	4270	27.0	21	70*	62	38

Comment: The major trend in cable TV has been increasing size of individual systems, followed by increase in channel capacity. Substantial growth of cable audience penetration did not come until the late 1970s and early 1980s, stimulated by pay cable service availability.

Source: Christopher H. Sterling and Timothy R. Haight, *The Mass Media: Aspen Institute Guide to Communication Industry Trends* (New York: Praeger, 1978), pp. 56, 58, and 322 for data through 1975.; and *TV Digest* for 1981 information. All data as of January 1, except 1981, which is June 1. *1981 data refers to systems with under 3500 subscribers.

curred mostly in small communities that supported only small systems. When entrepreneurs began to look for ways of using the underlying cable concept on a massive scale, the obvious next step was to invade the large cities, where very large concentrations of potential subscribers could be found. Big-city television viewers often experience direct-reception difficulties because of electrical interference and the tendency of large buildings to screen out television signals or to cause "ghosts." In the main, though, city dwellers already receive a full complement of broadcast services. The primary motivation for subscribing, lack of access to stations, no longer works for them. To recruit city subscribers cable operators must use especially attractive augmentation.

One of the major problems urban cable operators encounter, however, is that initial enthusiasm quickly wears off, causing far greater turnover in subscribers than efficient business operations normally tolerate. Moves to augment the original cable function combined with moves to invade big urban markets brought forth complex new legal, economic, and social problems.

As long as cable acted as a neutral redelivery system in small towns, filling in shadow areas, beefing up fringes, and overcoming local interference, television stations welcomed cable. Some stations found themselves being relayed by 30 or 40 different cable systems and reaching substantially larger audiences than before. By 1967, however, broadcasters had begun to wonder if their initial welcome to cable had not opened the door to a dangerous predator rather than merely a benign parasite.

The growing practice of importing signals from distant stations tended to obliterate the fixed market boundaries previously imposed by the inherent limits of over-the-air signals. For example, if for some reason a cable system failed to carry the programs of a local

television network affiliate and instead imported those same programs from an affiliate in a distant market (a process called *leapfrogging*), the local station's audience would decline. Even without such duplication, importing distant signals divides the available audience into smaller fractions for each local station.

Protectionist Regulation Threatened regulatory attention from the Federal Communications Commission was directed toward cable several times in the 1950s, but in each case the FCC eventually backed off, finding that cable was not legally defined as broadcasting and was therefore not subject to existing broadcast regulation. Specifically, cable was seen simply as an extension of the local home viewer's antenna, which certainly did not call for regulation; furthermore, it was not generally deemed an important economic threat to then rapidly expanding television.

Eventually, cable began to have so much impact on broadcasting that the FCC was obliged to intervene. For years it had been nurturing UHF television, only now to see its shaky foundation undermined by cable, which tends to hurt the weakest stations first. Educational stations, too, felt themselves vulnerable to cable audience splitting. Denver public television interests, for example, opposed importation of educational signals from California.

The FCC based its first claim of jurisdiction over cable on the fact that many systems were beginning to import distant signals by using microwave relays (which required FCC licenses). Such imported programs, the FCC concluded, threatened economic hardship to broadcast stations, whose audiences would be reduced by competition from stations not normally part of their markets. Accordingly, in 1962 the commission began to impose

case-by-case restrictions on cable systems using microwave relays.

In 1966 the FCC asserted general jurisdiction over cable systems, including those not using microwave relays. The rules adopted that year included requirements that a cable system must carry local television stations and must not duplicate local programs with imported programs on a same-day basis. The 1966 rules also prohibited importation of any signals at all into the top 100 markets without prior hearings as to the probable effect of such importations on existing broadcast stations. The Supreme Court affirmed the FCC's jurisdiction over cable in 1968 in the *Southwestern Cable* case (392 *US* 157).

A period of intense effort to create a comprehensive system of regulation followed. The debate centered on the issue of cable development in the largest urban centers. At one extreme cable proponents argued for unrestrained growth, contending that broadcasting represented an outmoded technology, artificially propped up by FCC protectionist policies. At the other extreme broadcasting interests argued that if the FCC allowed unrestrained cable development, the public would eventually find itself paying for the entertainment programs that it had previously received "free" from over-the-air broadcasting and would be denied public service programs of a type only national networks can produce.

The result, in 1972, was the issuance by the FCC of so-called definitive cable regulations dealing with most of the problem areas. The 1972 cable order (36 FCC 2d 143) incorporated a compromise of the many conflicting views. The commission severely restricted cable television program carriage and expansion with the following requirements:

■ Signals from local television stations (local market to be defined by the FCC) were to be carried.

■ Distant signal importation was to be limited essentially to three network signals (imported only if not locally available), plus one or two independent television stations, and an unlimited number of educational/public stations. In other words, importation of distant signals was limited in number to prevent excessive dividing up of the available audience. Further, there were very specific rules protecting syndicated broadcast programming from being freely imported on cable.

■ Cable systems had to provide a minimum of three local channels — one for local government use, one for educational application, and a third for general public access. If any of the three "filled up," an additional channel was to be provided. The commission required that the channels be made available in an almost common carrier fashion, in which the system operator merely provides facilities but has nothing to say over use of the channels. The requirement emerged from the FCC's feeling that cable offered an opportunity for expanded local expression.

In summing up the federal regulatory status of cable in mid-decade, one observer noted:

No broadcast signals could be added by cable systems without obtaining prior approval from the FCC; there were severe restrictions on the programming cable systems could offer for an extra per channel or per program charge (pay programming); all new local franchises and most franchise amendments had to be submitted to the FCC for review and certification as consistent with federal franchise standards accepted by the FCC; and cable system compliance with elaborate channel capacity and access requirements was reviewed whenever the FCC approved the addition of new broadcast signals or passed on the validity of new franchises or amendments. (Shapiro, 1980: 20)

The rules were detailed, varied by the market size served, and generally treated cable television as distinctly secondary to local broadcast television. Cable was seen as a distinct economic threat to local television broadcasters, the dominant piece in the FCC's local service puzzle. As long as cable served primarily to expand coverage of broadcast stations, or provided new services (such as access) to viewers, it would be allowed (if not encouraged) to expand.

No sooner were the so-called final rules in place than various pressures and institutions began to chip away at the edifice the FCC had built to contain cable. Two important events external to the commission pushed this change: (1) the passage of new copyright legislation by Congress in 1976 and (2) the *Home Box Office vs. FCC* decision. The copyright question is treated in more detail below, but essentially the new law changed the relationship between cable and broadcasting by calling for a copyright fee from cable operators in return for a mandatory right to carry broadcast signals.

FCC Deregulation The *Home Box Office* decision (567 F 2d 9, 1977), although it dealt specifically with pay cable (§11.5), strongly chastised FCC regulation of cable. The court held that the commission "has in no way justified its position that cable television must be a supplement to, rather than an equal of, broadcast television." This decision led the FCC to reconsider totally its approach to cable by initiating a massive investigation of the economic relationship between cable and broadcasting. The inquiry yielded considerable statistical research, allowing the commission to conclude that cable penetration had and would for some years continue to have little impact on audiences or revenues of broadcast stations. In response to those findings, the FCC in 1980 lifted two of its long-standing rules that had previously

banned most importation of distant signals and had mandated protection of some types of syndicated programming from free cable competition. Clearly, then, the commission had moved 180 degrees from its position of a decade earlier; it now sought not to protect broadcasting from cable but to encourage competition between the two.

Under other court orders, and to some degree on its own initiative, the commission removed itself step by step from other aspects of cable television regulation. By the end of the 1970s, for example, the FCC had eliminated its oversight of local franchise requirements. No longer did cable systems have to meet set federal standards of construction or channel capacity (how many channels must be provided). The requirement that large cable systems (those with more than 3,500 subscribers) originate programming to supplement carriage of broadcast signals was abandoned.

Substantial controversy surrounded this trend. Broadcasters feared that cable systems, with their increased carrying capacity would draw ever larger chunks of the viewing audience away from over-the-air stations, leading to drastic change in the broadcast business. They complained to the FCC and Congress that cable was being freed of most federal regulation while they still operated under it.

The decreased federal intervention in cable was, of course, part of a general trend to deregulation in communications, and government generally (§21.5). But cable regulations disappeared in large part because of changes in the cable business itself. The advent of satellite-distributed services (§11.4) allowed local cable systems to become outlets for an increasingly wider choice of programs in addition to those broadcast over the air. Cable systems were seen by the courts and the FCC to be more like newspapers in their editorial role — and in their relative lack of need for any federal regulation. In addition, both broadcasting and cable find themselves under increasing competitive pressures from still newer means of content delivery (§11.7 and 11.8), a situation that causes those who advocate marketplace rather than government regulation to espouse a lower federal regulatory profile in favor of competitive balance.

Local Franchise Regulation　The decline in federal regulation of cable left more scope for state and municipal authorities. The most important local regulation of cable is the *franchise* process, in which a cable system is given its initial legal authority to build in a given political jurisdiction — a city or town, or part of a metropolitan area. Such a franchise is necessary because cable lines may have to cross or be built under such public facilities as streets and parks. In addition, cable systems are generally monopolies in their service areas, and as such they generally fall under utility regulatory policies in most communities.

The franchise process begins when the mayor or city council or other local governing body decides cable service should be provided locally. As a rule, this governing group first develops an *ordinance* or formal legal document describing the conditions under which a cable system will be allowed to operate. Designed in many cases by consultants or nonprofit advisers, the ordinance provides for (1) a term of the franchise (usually 10 to 15 years); (2) specific quality of service to be provided; (3) technical standards (minimal number of channels, interconnection with other systems); (4) minimal signals to be carried; (5) level of return from the system to the governing body (usually 3 to 5 percent of

gross revenues) as a franchise fee. Equipped with the ordinance, the community then seeks bids from cable system operators for the new franchise.

The bidding process that then takes place has become a highly controversial aspect of cable television. In a number of areas it became common practice for the competing applicants for a lucrative franchise to "rent a citizen" by providing key politicians and others with stock in the firm, which would become very valuable if that company won the franchise. Sometimes the citizen paid a nominal amount for the stock, sometimes it was an outright gift. The citizen, in turn, was expected to speak favorably of the merits of that firm in the competition. Sometimes, however, the process involved even closer "cooperation" between politicians and applicants. In Houston, for example, a court found in 1981 that public officials had secretly cooperated with one or more applicants to close out other applicants in return for favors.

After comparing the promises (and possibly the performance in other markets) of the competing applicants, a franchise is awarded, and construction of the system can begin. Most franchises include regulations requiring steady and fairly rapid construction in the franchise area. In addition, citizen complaints about technical or program service are dealt with under franchise rules, which often go so far as to enumerate conditions under which the community may buy out the franchise and award it to somebody else. Seeking to avoid the commercial franchise hassles, a few communities have operated cable television systems as municipal services run like other local utilities (§11.2).

State Regulation　A few states have also asserted authority over cable television. State interest dates to the 1963 Connecticut statute granting jurisdiction over cable to the state public utilities commission. Up to 1981, however, only 11 states had adopted a comprehensive regulatory policy toward cable, the last being Delaware in 1974. About half the states delegate regulation of all aspects of cable to local authorities, sometimes suggesting or mandating minimal standards that must be observed. A number of states have imposed taxes on cable, which is variously perceived as a public utility, a kind of broadcast service, or even a luxury.

In only two areas have state and local authorities been banned from a regulatory policy role — pay cable and copyright. When, in the late 1960s, the FCC asserted control over pay cable, it automatically excluded any state regulation of programming carried or fees charged for such a service. On appeal, this assertion of authority was upheld — at almost the same time that FCC regulation of pay cable was virtually eliminated. Thus pay cable expanded in the 1980s, protected from local or state controls by a federal agency which itself could no longer regulate! This "Catch-22" situation was seen by many as a chief cause of the growth of pay cable (§11.5).

Copyright Fee Payment Until 1978, cable television systems were in an odd position as regards copyright. Broadcasters pay for use of copyrighted materials in the form of music-licensing fees (§15.7), scriptwriter fees, and so on. In 1968 the Supreme Court, basing its decision on the 1909 copyright law then in force, found that cable systems, as an extension of the home antenna, were not liable for payment of copyright fees to broadcasters or anyone else. Revision of the copyright law in 1976, effective at the beginning of 1978, changed the picture.

Section 111 of the revised copyright act, which deals with cable television as one of several "secondary transmissions," calls for a compulsory license for cable systems.

Rather than having each cable system individually contract with each copyright holder and each station for "retransmission consent," Congress instead provided for a blanket permission in the form of a license subject only to payment of a blanket fee administered by the Copyright Royalty Tribunal (CRT), a government agency set up by the act. More specifically, Congress felt such payment was due only for importation of distant nonnetwork signals. The CRT administers collection and subsequent division and payout of cable license fees to copyright holders, chiefly program producers and holders of rights (such as sports teams).

When the CRT began to set rates and determine which group would receive what proportion of the cable license "pot," controversy arose among those slated to collect some portion of the money. Barely meeting the deadline set by Congress for a decision, the CRT finally decided who would get what — and nearly everyone was unhappy. Broadcasters would get just over 3 percent of the total, program syndicators would get the lion's share of 75 percent, sports interests would get 12 percent, the Public Broadcasting Service would get just over 5 percent, and music-licensing societies would get nearly 5 percent. Appeals filed by several of these groups delayed the process. Complaints were also heard about the extremely low levels paid by cable systems — some as low as .7 percent of revenues, or a few hundred dollars per year. In 1981 the CRT raised the rates paid by 20 percent to meet complaints and inflation, though at the same time its administrator told Congress he felt the whole process was unworkable and unfair and that Congress should reconsider the whole treatment of cable in the act.

Violation of copyright in cable communication includes several kinds of piracy. Oldest and probably most common is tapping into the cable system's local feeder cable

(§4.8) to receive its channels without paying the usual monthly fee. The piracy problem became more complicated with the sale of decoding "black boxes," which allowed the user to receive scrambled pay television signals (either on the cable or over the air; §11.5 and 11.6). The most technically sophisticated piracy (although limited, in view of the costs involved) was practiced in the early 1980s by those who set up their own earth stations (§11.4) to pluck pay television signals from satellites — without, of course, paying the normal monthly subscriber license fee. Violators were often hard to find. Pressure mounted for Congress to modify the copyright or communication acts to make clear its intent on such unlicensed reception of premium (for pay) signals (§15.3).

11.2 Cable Economics

For a brief period in the late 1960s cable was a growth industry, but imposition of federal and state regulation, along with economic uncertainty, slowed the growth trend. However, the decline in regulation, the growing financial prospects of pay cable services, and the infusion of needed construction capital by conglomerate owners all converged in the 1980s to make the cable business organizationally and financially secure. It also became increasingly independent of its former reliance on broadcast signals.

Ownership For many years cable was typified by small systems — often only a few hundred subscribers in a small town, serviced by a company that was often more of a public service than a profit-making institution. But these "Mom and Pop" outfits (often run as sidelines to other businesses, recalling the early days of radio) gave way in the 1960s as cable penetrated larger markets. The trend

to ownership of more than one system by Multiple System Operators (MSOs) was caused partially by the franchising of companies to serve large urban areas, with their resultant need for very large amounts of construction capital. Small operators sold out to the MSOs, repeating the pattern seen earlier in other media. Yet even in 1980 the largest cable MSO, Teleprompter, served less than 10 percent of all cable homes, whereas the largest television multiple station owners could reach more than 20 percent of all television homes.

Exhibit 11.2 shows the extent to which other media businesses controlled cable systems in the 1970s. Broadcasters have long been the biggest single group of owners in cable, although publishers and television program industry companies have increased their ownership proportion of the cable business during the decade. This pattern likewise recalls earlier broadcasting history: older media building or buying into a newer service, both in order to protect their existing investment and to get in on an expanding new technology.

Mergers among MSOs were common in the early 1980s as the costs of wiring larger cities — and competing for their franchises — rose sharply with inflation. The competition for the Dallas franchise, for example, cost the competitors some $500,000 each before any award was given, and the Cincinnati contest cost about half as much. Of course, companies that lost the franchise lost that initial expenditure. Faced with such costs, companies sought well-heeled merger partners — American Express merged with Warner Cable, and Westinghouse took over number-one MSO Teleprompter. Investors generally welcomed such mergers because they promised greater managerial and financial stability. On the other hand, the FCC and the Department of Justice watched warily, concerned about potential monopolistic control.

Regulatory limitations on cable system ownership are few. FCC rules set in 1970 disallow ownership of cable systems by the broadcast networks, although in the early 1980s pressures were building to allow the competitively pressed networks entry into cable system ownership once again. Television stations and telephone companies may not own cable systems in their areas of prime coverage or service, but they may own systems elsewhere. In recent years the FCC has followed a liberal policy of waivers on the cable-telephone company rule, allowing

firms in rural areas (usually defined as having less than 30 homes per route mile) to build systems where independent (non-telephone-company-owned) firms would be unlikely to survive economically. There are no limits on newspaper-cable cross-ownership (as there are in broadcasting), nor is there any limit on the number of cable systems or subscribers that can be served by a single MSO.

One policy option that has long been considered is the separation of ownership of cable facilities from the programming function. The goal of such a separation is to diversify the ownership of cable by having a different "voice" for each cable channel. This policy would apply to those channels providing

Exhibit 11.2
Types of cable TV system owners: 1972 and 1979

Owner category	1972, in percent (N = 2,839)	1979, in percent (N = 4,180)
Broadcast stations	38	33
Newspapers	6	13
Other publishers	3	11
TV program producers and distributors	8	18
Movie theaters	3	4
Community or subscriber-owned	3	2
Telephone companies	2	3
Equipment manufacturers	11 (1973)	7
Other	26	9

Comment: To a significant extent, cable systems in the U.S. are owned by owners of other — especially broadcast-connected — media. Although networks are banned from owning cable systems, broadcast stations and programmers own the largest share of cable systems. A major trend in the 1970s was the increase in ownership of cable by publishers of all kinds.

Source: *TV Factbook* (Washington: TV Digest, 1973 and 1980).

original or pay programming as opposed to off-air broadcast signals, which might remain under control of the facilities' owner. Policy-makers have expressed concern about a single owner controlling all channels in a multiple-channel delivery system (the FCC usually allows broadcasters to own only a single channel in each broadcast service). On the other hand, some researchers suggest that the multitude of competing delivery systems for video programming (broadcast stations, cable, Multipoint Distribution Systems, subscription television stations, and even home video options) makes any kind of ownership limitation unnecessary because the marketplace will provide regulation through competition.

Programming Cable began as a simple extension of listeners' antennas to bring distant television broadcast signals to their home. For the first 15 years or so of cable system operation, there was little offered other than local and distant broadcast signals. Beginning in the late 1960s, however cable operators began to seek and offer new services, partly in compliance with FCC restrictions on the number of broadcast signals that could be carried, and partly to build subscriber interest. Typically providing news, weather, stock information, and sports scores, some systems included crude advertising and most provided a musical soundtrack. As new program options became available, especially those distributed by satellite (§11.4), cable operators began to plan and build systems with more than the standard 12-channel capacity. Franchise authorities, hearing of systems with 30 and even 80 or more channels, required higher channel capacities — and this helped intensify the cable search for more program options.

In the 1970s "true origination" developed.

Larger systems began providing material on one or more channels, in a manner somewhat akin to local broadcasting. These "nonautomatic" programs included live or taped local studio and remote material, syndicated films and tapes, and the like. Content consisted of community news, bingo games, local high school or college sports, amateur hours, local cultural events, and political speeches.

By 1980 syndication of original program material for use by cable systems was becoming an important business. Although there was often not much difference in the content of cable and broadcast material, many programs or series were made especially for cable system use. Cable system audiences add up to a salable commodity for the system owner. Owners are therefore willing to provide quite specialized programming for minority and special-interest groups, sometimes supported by advertising, sometimes provided as a service. Some minority programming was even provided by satellite for cable system use all over the country.

Cable Access An interesting, though short-lived, experiment on many cable systems was the *access* channel. Made available on a first-come, first-served basis to the local community as a kind of electronic soapbox, access channels allowed expression of many points of view and provided an outlet for local culture and entertainment. Typically a cable system provided a very rudimentary studio setup, often a cinderblock room with lights and a camera. This could be used (sometimes free and sometimes at cost, it varied with the system) for self-expression of any kind, subject only to rules of libel and obscenity. In many communities it became a kind of electronic letters-to-the-editor outlet allowing the town to talk back to itself rather than simply receiving media messages.

In principle, access is an important potential of cable because it capitalizes on the sys-

lower cost and eased regulation prompted rapid expansion of earth station use by cable systems and broadcast stations as well as other users of domsat signals. The satellites and the growing availability of ground stations made possible whole new patterns of program distribution (Exhibit 11.4.1).

Cable Networks With the pioneering of Atlanta's Ted Turner and his independent "superstation" WTBS (§12.1), along with pay

Exhibit 11.4.1
TVRO Earth Station

The most important technical development in the use of satellite distribution of video signals was the relatively small and inexpensive receive-only earth station, or TVRO. The dish collects and focuses the weak satellite signal for processing and boosting at the TV station, cable system, motel, or residence. Such dishes, thousands of which were in use in the early 1980s, are usually aimed at a single satellite (to cover two or more would add greatly to ground station costs).

Source: Eric A. Roth.

television distributor HBO (§11.5) the term "network" took on new meaning. No longer was it necessary to rely on landline or microwave interconnection. A satellite uplink ground station could get any signal to a satellite transponder and it could then be received anywhere in the country by anyone with a receive-only station.

Virtually all the programmers using satellite operate like Turner's WTBS, as shown in Exhibit 11.4.2. The distribution of receive-only earth stations is the key to the size of a programmer's potential audience. But the satellite is also important. Into the early 1980s the RCA domsat Satcom I was the primary satellite for cable use, to the extent that it was often called "Cable I" in the business. As earth stations can generally only "see" one satellite at a time, because satellites have slightly different orbital positions, demand from cable programmers for access to the "prime" cable satellite is heavy. Several battles were fought before the FCC and in the courts over just who had contractual rights to use the 24 transponders on Satcom I.

As more programmers seek access to satellites, the demand will force use of one or more additional satellites. In turn, that will force cable systems to purchase additional receive-only ground stations aimed at the new satellites, or to buy movable dishes that can aim at different satellites (one at a time). A more basic bottleneck to this flood of new cable programming is the channel capacity of the cable system. Most systems operating in the early 1980s could carry only 12 channels. Given the off-air signals they must carry (local television stations) plus some imported station signals, many cable systems simply lack the channel capacity to carry any of the new services. They usually offer a pay service if possible, because it is a source of additional revenue. Only by costly reconstruction can

Exhibit 11.4.2
Satellite distribution of superstation programming to cable TV systems

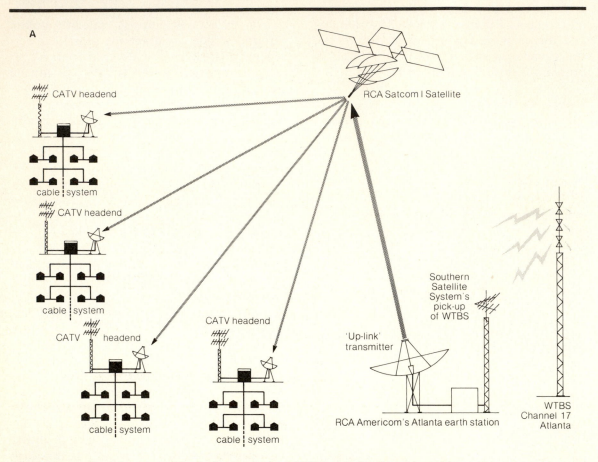

This diagram illustrates how Atlanta "superstation" WTBS gets its signal to cable systems all over the United States. The programming is picked off air by the satellite carrier, in this case Southern Satellite System, and is sent to the Satcom I satellite transponder by means of a large uplink earth station about nine miles from the television station. The signal is then beamed down by the transponder for pick-up at receive-only earth stations located near the headend of cable systems across the country (see map).

Source: Turner Broadcasting System.

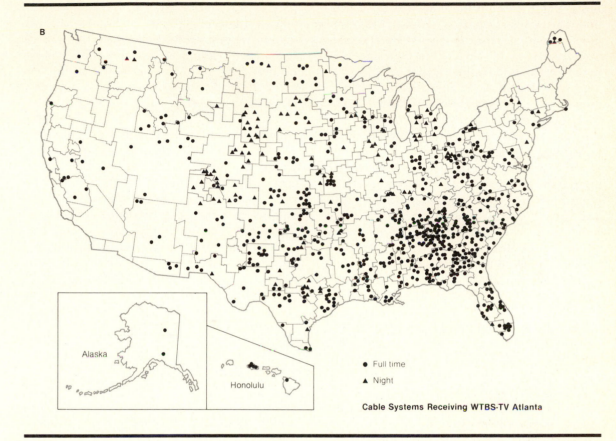

Cable Systems Receiving WTBS-TV Atlanta

• Full time
▲ Night

their capacity be increased to carry more of the program services already available, let alone those coming on line in the 1980s.

Building on his success with WTBS, Ted Turner began in mid-1980 to provide another service for cable systems — a 24-hour news feed, the Cable News Network (CNN). Based at WTBS studios in Atlanta, with stringers and studios elsewhere, CNN's staff of 400 provides a mixture of hard news and feature material. It offers a two-hour newscast in prime time each evening, plus news updates

hourly. A variety of feature and interview programs fill in the rest of the time. CNN is so expensive that Turner charges cable systems 15 cents per subscriber to carry it, a very high rate for a supposedly basic service for which system owners make no extra charge to their subscribers. Reports suggested that Turner was sinking some $25 million into the venture. Although it lost heavily in 1980–1981, by the end of that period it was reaching better than 5 million cable subscribers, and one major television advertiser, General Foods, had decided to invest some $40 million in a multiyear CNN advertising contract.

Spanish International Network (SIN) and

Black Entertainment Network (BET) distribute advertiser-supported ethnic programming, some of which is carried by specialty broadcast stations as well as by cable systems. The Cable Satellite Public Affairs Network (C-SPAN) feeds full coverage of the House of Representatives, National Press Club speakers, educational programs, and the like on an underwritten basis (neither advertising nor subscriber fees). Several conservative religious organizations lease transponders to provide feeds of variety and entertainment/inspirational material to stations and cable systems, paid for by listener donations and some advertising. Two services provide programming exclusively for children. *Nickelodeon* and *Calliope* program children's films, dramatic programs, documentaries, and the like (Exhibit 11.4.3).

DBS   The most significant next phase in the exploitation of space relays promises to be satellites capable of being received directly by people in their homes. These *direct broadcast satellites* (DBS) will combine the relay and delivery functions, bypassing the entire present distribution/delivery system.

In principle, any home could have its own ground station at the present time. As a practical matter, costs are still too high to compete with existing broadcast and cable delivery systems. But this is only because present satellite designs make a deliberate trade-off, sacrificing signal strength in the satellite for the sake of light weight (§4.6). The NASA space shuttle promises to make possible orbiting larger, heavier, more powerful satellites than any sent up by rocket-launchers. The need for larger-scale, extremely sensitive receiving facilities on earth will then be eliminated.

Then, in 1979, a subsidiary of Comsat, Satellite Television Corporation, announced plans to launch a DBS to provide three channels of pay-television content to the eastern part of the United States. The experiment was to span the eighties, leading to national service from several satellites by the end of the decade (Exhibit 11.4.4). The DBS system proposed was for an audience-supported service (about $20 per month plus purchase of rooftop antenna and down-converter equipment) aimed chiefly at rural areas and communities with less than three network services from other sources. One channel would feature typical pay-television films and other entertainment (without advertising), a second would offer educational and cultural material, and the third would provide sports, adult education and lectures, and experimental theater. Construction and launch costs of the system were forecast at $250 million, with about $180 million more in the first year for equipment and program costs. And all of this would appear in the mid-1980s if approved by the FCC. Skeptics and critics of the DBS plan were numerous.

They came in two general groups. A number of economists claimed the DBS system as proposed could not survive on basically rural audiences alone — and that, as cable penetration increased, the viability of DBS pay television would proportionately decrease. Other critics, mainly those worried about new competition, wondered what the Comsat plan offered that was not already being provided on STV (§11.6) pay cable systems or conventional broadcasting. Using every procedure possible, they tried to short-circuit the DBS proposal at every decision point at the FCC and in Congress. Both groups suspected that the DBS idea, exotic though it seemed when first offered, might already be outmoded in a nation rapidly developing so many alternative systems of television content delivery. Despite its capital cost, it might not provide anything new to its intended audience, let alone financial return to its back-

Exhibit 11.4.3
Examples of satellite-distributed video program services

Name	Content	Satellite operation began	Systems	Households (millions)	Hours per day
Basic Services					
Black Entertainment Network (BET)	entertainment and sports of interest to black audience	Jan 80	685	7.2	15 (Fridays only)
Cable News Network (CNN)	news and talk/feature service	Jun 80	1,270	7.0	24
Cable Satellite Public Affairs Network (C-SPAN)	House of Representatives proceedings and Press Club speakers	Mar 79	1,150	8.1	8 (weekdays only)
Christian Broadcasting Network (CBN)	*700 Club* and other Christian/family programming	Apr 77	2,800	11.8	24
Spanish International Network (SIN)	Spanish language films, sports, drama, news	Sep 79	106	2.7	24
Nickelodeon	children's shows (thru teen years)	Apr 79	1,200	4.8	13
WTBS (superstation)	movies, sports and general programming	Dec 76	3,170	12.5	24
USA Network	75% sports plus *Calliope* children's program, etc.	Sep 77	1,425	8.0	10
Pay Cable Services					
Home Box Office	first-run films, specials, sports	Sep 75	2,500	6.0	24
Showtime	first-run films, specials, sports	Mar 78	1,100	2.0	24
The Movie Channel	films	Jan 80	1,175	1.1	24

Comment: This table provides but a selection of the more than 30 satellite-delivered video services available by mid-1981. "Basic" services are usually advertiser supported and do not directly charge viewers; pay services have monthly surcharges. Not shown here are a number of announced or just-begun cultural programming pay services.

Sources: data on program content hours on air and inception date from "They're Free and Clear," *Panorama* (April 1981), 54–55, 68–69; and "Pay Cable: What You Get for Your Money," *Panorama* (June 1981), 42–43. Subscriber count from *Cablevision* (20 July 1981), p. 24.

ers. Sentiment in Washington was divided as to whether such a system needed much official regulation, or whether the marketplace should be allowed to function with competitive forces.

In 1981 the FCC undertook a preliminary assessment of how DBS might fit into tele-

vision delivery in the mid-1980s. At the same time, other companies came forward with DBS proposals significantly different from Comsat's, including one proposing to carry advertiser-supported programming at no charge to viewers, and another planning to operate as a common carrier providing a large

Exhibit 11.4.4
A direct broadcast satellite system

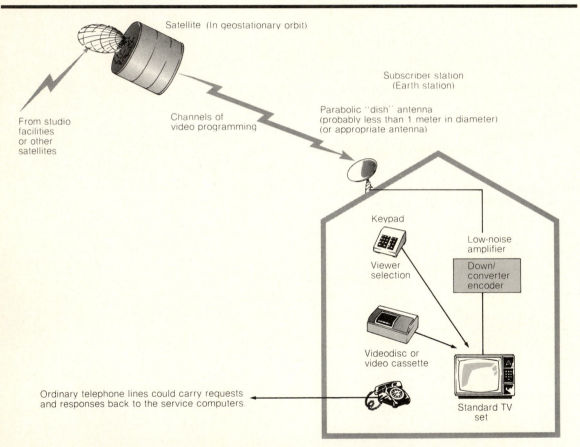

Unlike the present-day use of satellites to transmit programs to cable systems or even local TV stations, a DBS system sends signals directly to viewer homes, each of which is equipped with a small receive-only antenna. Such services are likely to be offered on a pay basis, with subscribers buying the equipment and paying a monthly reception fee for the right to decode scrambled signals (see Exhibit 4.6.2).

Source: Federal Communications Commission.

number of channels to programmers who would lease access. Faced with such variety, the commission decided to allow DBS to begin operation with minimal regulation, letting marketplace forces dictate its role and degree of success.

11.5 Pay Cable

The most popular form of cable augmentation (§11.1) is the growing number of satellite-carried syndicated program services. Cable systems welcomed them because they both attract new subscribers and bring in additional system income in the form of pay cable.

How It Works   All cable subscribers pay an initial installation charge and then a monthly fee — by the early 1980s these averaged about $25 and $8, respectively. So in a way all is "pay cable." But there is an additional level of payment over and above the basic charge to receive specific programs or channels. Such added-charge services are referred to as *pay cable*.

Once a home subscribes to basic cable service (the off-air signals plus some additional services supplied at no additional charge), the subscriber is usually offered a chance to pay a further monthly fee for the right to view one or more *premium channels*. These channels offer programming (mainly movies and sports events with no advertising) at a set fee per month — usually about $10, no matter how much is viewed. This simplifies bookkeeping for the pay program distributor (who gets part of the proceeds) and the cable operator (who gets the rest).

Although initially only one pay channel was offered, cable systems soon began to offer several tiers of service, much like Warner-Amex's Qube system (§11.3). The first tier was the basic service. The second and subsequent tiers were premium services charged for on a per channel monthly rate. Sometimes the subsequent tiers are regional services. In Philadelphia, for example, cable subscribers often take one of the national pay services and can also sign up for PRISM, a regional service in the Delaware Valley, which offers more advertising-free movies and provides a full schedule of local professional sports events as well. None of the premium programs can be received until the cable operator provides the technical means (coded number, key card, etc.) for the home receiver decoder to unscramble the pay signal (in other words, the premium channels are "locked out" of homes not paying for them — or seriously behind in monthly payments).

HBO   The pioneer pay cable program supplier, Home Box Office (HBO), a subsidiary of Time, Inc., began in 1972. It served a number of interconnected cable systems in the Northeast, linked by microwave. While several other suppliers of pay material for cable systems existed, most had but a few thousand subscribers because of the difficulties of scheduling programming on noninterconnected affiliate systems. HBO succeeded because it solved the distribution problem. Gerald Levin, then head of HBO, announced early in 1975 that HBO had leased a satellite transponder. In this way, pay cable programming was offered on a simultaneous basis to systems across the country. Satellite delivery sharply reduced distribution costs, while allowing for national promotion. "Rarely does a simple business decision by one company affect so many. . . . In deciding to gamble on the leasing of satellite TV channels, Time, Inc. took the one catalytic step needed for the creation of a new national television network designed to provide pay TV programs'' (Taylor, 1980: 142).

For the next four years HBO dominated the industry, growing into the major force in pay cable (Exhibit 11.6.1). First to use satellite interconnection, HBO had no serious competition until the 1978 debut of rival Showtime. HBO concentrated its programming on films and sporting events, repeating each film throughout the month at different times of the day. In mid-decade subscribers often complained about the quality of the films. Subscriber turnover was said to be high. But after 1978, when HBO finally began to make a profit, the films improved greatly.

HBO went into the movie-rights purchase business in a big way, buying the rights to hundreds of old and new Hollywood feature films, as well as hundreds of short films. With its dominance of cable and its national circulation, HBO was able to all but dictate film prices to the Hollywood producers. Prices were calculated on a certain amount of money per subscriber (usually about 20 cents), combined with a set flat rate determined by the value of the specific film to HBO. Hollywood producers felt HBO paid too little for film rights, but there was little they could do (aside from withholding films from sale) — HBO was the only cable customer big enough to make such purchases.

HBO's bargaining position was weakened a bit in 1978 with the formation of Showtime, which also uses satellite transponders to distribute its films and other special events, both sports and cultural. Viacom, the operator of Showtime, sold a half interest in the distributor in 1979 to then number-one MSO Teleprompter, providing more cable systems for the new service (and as 25 Teleprompter systems had been contracted to carry HBO, the loss was direct) and more financial clout.

But despite aggressive marketing, Showtime remained second to HBO in the competitive race.

Programming   HBO, Showtime, and the smaller competitors all utilize a basically similar mass appeal format built around current Hollywood feature films, shown uncut and with no commercials. A typical evening's fare includes two or three films, separated by short filler films. A dearth of sufficient films, plus competition from over-the-air subscription television (§11.6), prompted a broadening of program offerings on pay cable to supplement the film emphasis. The new forms included Las Vegas-type stage reviews, special cultural or theatrical presentations, and sporting events not shown on commercial television. In the 1980s pay cable distributors provided original made-for-cable shows to increase audience appeal.

In 1980 four major film-producing companies decided to try to enter the pay cable market. With funds from the Getty Oil Company they formed a venture called Premiere. The four companies (Paramount, MCA, Columbia Pictures, and Twentieth Century Fox) gave Premiere first-call on their productions; the films would be withheld from sale to HBO or Showtime for nine months. Ironically, considering its own dominant market position, HBO cried foul, and the Justice Department, after conducting its own investigation, filed an antitrust suit. On the last day of 1980 a judge ruled against the Premiere firm, and the film companies' attempt to challenge HBO dominance collapsed. The film companies resumed selling pay cable rights to their products.

Early in the 1980s several companies announced plans to offer cultural and arts programming for cable systems. The aim of these services was to present (usually on a pay cable basis) symphony concerts, operas, theater, dance, and other material generally unavailable on cable and only occasionally on broadcast services. All three of the commercial television networks announced plans to produce material for cable, although they no longer provided much cultural material for broadcast. Indeed, the "counter-programming" potential of cable, with its ability to target audiences more narrowly than broadcasting, is a key reason for the emergence of cultural services. ABC, in conjunction with Warner-Amex, premiered its cultural material early in 1981, directed to that portion of the television audience (roughly 16 to 20 percent) they found expressing an interest in such programming. CBS had announced even earlier its entry into the same field, and both networks expected to put tens of millions of dollars into development of original theatrical and musical material, hoping to recoup some of the costs, primarily from advertising but also to some extent from subscriber fees.

Rockefeller Center announced in 1980 that it had purchased first U.S. rights to BBC television productions for a decade-long period as part of a new program service called *Bluebird*, which, on a pay basis to both cable and STV subscribers, would provide U.S. drama, children's programming, and other cultural programming for about 48 hours per week. *Bluebird* includes some advertising between offerings. RCA (owner of NBC) entered into a partnership with Rockefeller in 1981, the last of the conventional networks to enter the "culture" market. *Bravo*, a program service developed by a consortium of cable MSOs, began in late 1980 to provide an odd mixture: an arts magazine with music and dance for 12 hours per week, tied to "adult" entertainment (called *Escapade*) five nights a week. The service planned to operate totally on a pay-cable basis without advertising.

Such specialized services aimed at such limited audiences were designed to test a basic assumption of pay cable: that uneconomically small *local* audiences could be built into an economically significant *national* audience when aggregated by means of satellite-connected cable systems.

11.6 Subscription Television (STV)

Subscription, or over-the-air (broadcast) pay television, though developed earlier than pay cable, emerged as a commercially viable option much later than pay cable. Because it is broadcast, it is regulated differently from cable — a fact that accounts in some measure for its slower growth.

How It Works   For much of its broadcast day, an STV station operates like any ordinary independent television station. To meet both FCC requirements and the need for advertising revenues, most daytime and some evening hours are filled with the usual off-network shows, feature films, game shows and the like, all advertiser-supported. But in the prime-time evening hours and often through the entire weekend, STV stations switch to the subscription mode.

In this mode the station transmits its audio and video signals in a scrambled form so that nonpaying viewers receive unintelligible sounds and images. Subscribers pay a set monthly fee to rent a *decoder* on their home receiver that picks up unscrambled signals. While some STV stations charge on a per-program basis much like the Qube cable system (§11.3), most charge a flat monthly fee regardless of how much is viewed.

STV stations can, of course, transmit only a single "channel" of program service. Once in subscription mode, the station offers programming similar to that offered on pay cable. Indeed, HBO and other program distributors supply STV stations as well as cable systems.

A number of over-the-air pay television experiments took place in the late 1940s and 1950s; all received a great deal of press attention and caused major debate in and about the television business. Most of these experiments failed to achieve convincing results because their scope was too limited — they provided service only to a local audience, rather than the regional or even national audiences required to make pay television economically viable. Though STV backers spoke of providing minority-interest programming, it quickly became clear that to keep subscription prices low, pay television needed a large mass-appeal audience. None of the experiments was on a large enough scale to make money.

Only in 1968, after years of controversy, did the FCC adopt its first rules allowing regular, nonexperimental STV to begin, but a stringent set of regulations resulted. Partially because of the fear that pay television could *siphon*, or take away, programming from advertiser-supported television, and partially because of pressure from Congress, the FCC's rules were strict in controlling the kinds and amounts of material that STV could program. Initially, STV could operate on only one station per market, and then only if there were at least four other commercial stations already on the air. Given the FCC and court deregulation of cable and pay cable, both competitors of STV, such harsh rules helped hold back commercial inception of over-the-air pay television. Only in 1977–1978, as a part of its general deregulatory thrust (§16.10), did the FCC eliminate many of the restrictions on STV programming. In

1979 the one-STV-station-per-market rule was dropped, and other restrictions were lifted in the 1980s.

STV Economics The eased regulatory situation, plus the lower cost of providing premium programming to cities by STV rather than cable, helped bring about the inception of regular STV in 1977, when the first two stations went on the air in Los Angeles and New York. By 1981 sixteen were already operating with about 30 or so in various stages of planning and construction (Exhibit 11.6.1).

STV stations typically charge their subscribers an initial fee of $25 to $50 and then a flat monthly charge of $15 to $20. This is essentially a rental fee for use of a decoder. STV has survived only in large urban markets where the small proportion of viewers agreeing to pay those rates is large enough to warrant operation.

A possible change in that situation may develop with the introduction of low-power television (LPTV). With its limited facilities and power, the LPTV covers 12 to 15 miles (§8.4). Many applicants for LPTV facilities consider subscription operation the only economical way to provide specialized programming for audiences that are too small to interest advertisers. LPTV subscription networks utilizing satellite transponders are planned; they would allow specialized programming to reach groups of people with special needs all over the country. Specialty advertisers may be sufficiently attracted to support a hybrid operation of LPTV, with both advertising and subscription income, as on full-size STV stations.

Virtually all existing STV stations provide more than the FCC-mandated 28 hours per week of nonsubscription programming simply because they realize more income that way. STV has not proved successful thus far in daytime hours (even pay cable operates mainly in evening hours). One way such

Exhibit 11.6.1
Growth of pay TV subscribers: 1977 and 1981

	1977	1981
Pay Cable		
Subscribers	1,174,000	11,320,000
As percentage of homes passed	12	52
Number of systems	459	na
Average rate charged	$7.81	$8.80
MDS		
Subscribers	65,000	500,000
As percentage of homes passed	21	3
Number of systems	18	54
Average rate charged	$10.69	$15.08
STV		
Subscribers	5,000	972,000
As percentage of homes passed	4	4
Number of stations	2	24
Average rate charged	$14.98	$19.38

Comment: Among the pay television services available, pay cable, thanks to its satellite distribution, is larger by far than Multipoint Distribution Systems and Subscription (over the air) television. All three, however, have grown up at the same time — since about 1975. In the table, "percentage of homes passed" means homes either passed by a cable system, or within the coverage area of MDS or STV signals — i.e., potential subscribers.

Source: *The Pay TV Newsletter* (Carmel, Ca.: Paul Kagan Associates), Census issue of July 15, 1981, p. 1. Data are for June 1977 and June 1981.

non-STV time has been made to pay off is *narrowcasting*. This refers to programming to appeal to a narrower or more defined group than television stations usually serve. Rather than aiming at the broad general audience, the narrowcasting STV station aims at the needs of specific cultural or ethnic groups, such as blacks or Spanish-surnamed Americans. Indeed, some station owners *broker*, or lease, large chunks of their daytime hours to programmers who want to reach these audiences. In brokered programming, the supplier provides the programming and sells the advertising time, using the proceeds to pay the STV station owner and gain a margin of profit. In fact, some STV stations operate almost as common carriers, providing facilities that are programmed by others.

STV vs. Pay Cable Because STV stations and pay cable provide similar pay-television programming in evening and weekend hours, the outcome of competition between them is difficult to predict. STV has lower transmission costs, but it can provide only one channel. Cable systems have higher construction costs, but once in place they provide not only a basic cable service but often several tiers of pay cable in addition. Viewers pay $15 to $20 for one channel of STV and about the same for both basic cable and an additional tier of pay programming. For the viewer, the cable option seems the better buy.

Some industry observers feel, therefore, that STV will thrive mainly (or perhaps only) in areas not wired for cable reception. As cable expands, STV may be limited in growth potential. Satellite-distributed pay programming is provided to both cable and STV by national distributors. Although tremendous investment is poured into both means of distribution, many observers feel that STV will eventually lose out, partly because its capacity is limited and partly because it is subject to broadcast regulation (which prevents carrying the sexually oriented programming that is very popular on some pay cable channels).

MDS Multipoint Distribution Systems (MDS) are a special kind of STV operation. Operating high in the frequency spectrum (§4.7), MDS systems require a converter to allow reception on normal television receivers. They are programmed by the same sources that supply content for pay cable and STV; like STV stations they charge a monthly fee for use of the decoding devices that enable viewing.

The principal advantages of multipoint distribution over broadcast STV include simpler regulation (common carrier vs. broadcasting), faster entry of new services [meaning FCC procedures are less cumbersome and faster for this common carrier service], lower construction cost, and lower breakeven expense. On the other hand, MDS transmissions have very limited reception range [up to 15 miles in most cases — much like LPTV stations] and are extremely vulnerable to obstructional interference. Even trees in the line-of-sight may prevent reception. (Howard & Carroll, 1980: 40)

MDS systems thrive in some major markets; in Phoenix, for example, they compete successfully with STV stations. Supporters of the MDS option have put pressure on the FCC to allocate more frequencies to MDS use. Other spectrum users argue that America has no need for so many different means of delivering the same kind of programming.

Teletext and Videotex Broadcast teletext and wire-delivered videotex systems provide a means of presenting printed text and graphic material on the television screen (§3.11). Developed in Britain, France, and Canada in the late 1970s, teletext and videotex systems became important in the United States in the early 1980s, as American firms began to line up behind one or another of the foreign systems to develop the American market. There was some confusion over whether these systems of text delivery were more suited for school and office application or home use. One evidence of that confusion is the disagreement over the proper technical system or standard to approve as "the" American system.

On the other hand, the potential of both systems is important to the notion of a home information utility built around the television screen (Exhibit 11.6.2). Whether delivered by broadcast or wire, these video print systems are a type of pay television in that the subscriber pays a set interconnect fee on a monthly basis and then is billed further depending on how many pages are "screened," or viewed. Thus the billing for teletext/videotex is very much like the monthly charges for a telephone.

In these systems the firm that controls the hardware and the actual delivery process acts as a common carrier, selling access to software (content) providers who fill the system with whatever kinds of information they choose, such as weather, news, sports, catalogue-ordering information for stores and services, consumer advice, video games, material on government and education, cultural and theater guides, lists of restaurants, travel services, and the like. Much of this information is already made available to business or consumers by other means (such as stock market data in newspaper financial pages or various kinds of business and service advertising in press and broadcasting), but teletext or videotex offers in-the-home instant retrieval convenience combined with constant updating of information provided.

Exhibit 11.6.2
Teletext and closed captions

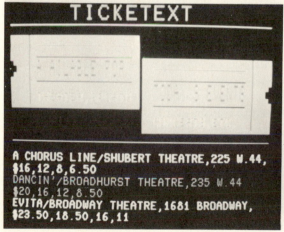

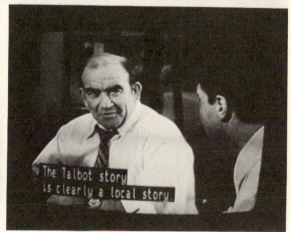

Broadcast transmission of text and graphics to the home or office TV receiver makes use of the vertical blanking interval (VBI) lines between TV pictures. The various systems can produce a variety of effects in multiple colors. Simple lists or computer graphics are the least expensive approach. The transmission of closed captions for the deaf (shown in lower right-hand screen) uses the same basic technology and VBI lines (see §3.11).

Source: CBS Television Network.

11.7 Home Video Center

Home video systems of all kinds differ from what we have discussed thus far in that, like musical recordings, they are individually purchased and used. They do not provide simultaneous delivery of a common signal to a large, widely separated audience. Briefly defined, home video systems include a player machine and the videocassettes or discs used by that machine. The home video market is based heavily on the appeal of broadcast programming, allowing consumers to record and play back material at will (videocassettes) or to buy prerecorded material for lesser cost, much of it former broadcast programming (video discs). Home video systems require a substantial financial outlay by the consumer — often two or more times the cost of a color set.

Videocassette Recording (VCR) The idea of home video recording dates back at least to the 1960s, when CBS tried to market its Electronic Video Recording (EVR) system, at a loss of perhaps $30 million. In 1972 Sony introduced the first videocassette (VCR) machine, its U-Matic, for the educational and business market. Three years later, the same firm introduced its Betamax home videocassette machine at an initial price of $1,300. It was ballyhooed as a "time shift" machine because it enabled users to look at television programming whenever they liked (Agostino, et al., 1979: 11). Pundits predicted a new video revolution was coming now that consumers could not only pick *when* they would view something, but could even pick and choose *what* they would view from broadcast, prerecorded, or their own home sources. For two years, Sony had the market to itself; it sold some 50,000 units.

This monopoly ended in 1977 with the introduction of a different and technically incompatible cassette format, the *VHS* system,

also developed in Japan. The newer system, which provided longer recording time, gradually acquired about 60 percent of the videocassette market. Beta machines, which also developed longer recording time for its cassettes, took the remainder. Several firms, both foreign and domestic, marketed each type, adding special features as inducements to buy. In 1981, a third format, incompatible with the first two, was announced by Philips, a Dutch firm. By 1981 about 2 percent of the nation's homes had one of these machines, and annual sales were expected to break a million units for the first time. Sale of blank tapes ran ahead of prerecorded material by six to one (*Television/Radio Age,* 12 Jan. 1981).

Video Discs A technically limited but less expensive alternative to the videocassette appeared in the 1970s in the form of the video disc. Limited to playback-only (consumer recording was not possible on the initial video disc systems), video disc dated in theory back to the 1920s, though the first modern system was only introduced in the 1970s. Marketed in Atlanta on a test basis by Magnavox beginning in 1978, the initial video disc used a sophisticated laser system (§4.3). The market competition heated up with introduction of a noncompatible laser system from Pioneer and a capacitance (or non-laser electronic) system introduced with huge fanfare by RCA in 1981. Each of the competitors could only play recordings designed for that system. Both the player machine and the discs were cheaper per unit than their VCR counterparts.

The Home Video Center Some manufacturers and social planners are touting a whole complex, probably occupying its own room, built around the home television receiver. Making use of a substantially larger, even wall size, screen, home designers and electronics manufacturers concentrated on planning "video environments" with many inputs, all keyed to the screen in a room with little else other than seats or cushions to sit on. Conceived of primarily as a place of entertainment, the facility naturally could replace the home library as well with cassettes or discs of informational material, teletext or videotex capability, and the like (Exhibit 11.7).

Summary

Until about 1970 cable television was essentially an extension of over-the-air television, providing reception in communities that could not otherwise get good television service. The FCC asserted regulation over cable in 1966 and set up so-called definitive regulations in 1972.

Since 1972 regulation of both cable and pay cable has been substantially undone. Court decisions and FCC actions have removed the requirement for access channels (though many local franchises still require them), eliminated restrictions on distant signal importation, removed the FCC's supervisory role over local franchises, and lifted any controls on pay cable content or rates.

A few states regulate cable; the all-important franchise process is controlled by local communities, which determine how long a cable system will serve, what area it will cover, and what minimal services it must provide.

Under the copyright act of 1976, cable systems may carry television signals without seeking prior consent of broadcasters. In return, however, they must pay a set small proportion of their revenues to the Copyright Royalty Tribunal for distribution to copyright owners.

Exhibit 11.7
Costs of home video center inputs

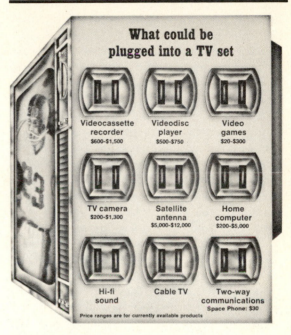

The diagram illustrates the growing number of input options that display through a television receiver. The costs are as of 1981, and in many cases will drop substantially as mass production grows. For example, satellite antennas are already available for considerably under $5,000 (for relatively simple TVROs). The cost of hi-fi sound varies from $200 up to thousands of dollars, depending on what is included. The monthly cost for cable TV usually includes both a base rate and one or more monthly premium channel rates — ranging in total from $8 up to $30 and more.

Because of the costliness of seeking franchises and building cable systems with higher channel capacity, cable ownership is becoming more concentrated in the hands of multiple system operators (MSOs). A substantial number of cable systems are owned by broadcasters and firms with other media interests. There are few restrictions on cable system ownership.

Although once thought of as an ideal medium for enabling the general public to express its views, cable systems, no longer required to provide access channels, now often make available channels on a leased access (rental) basis for high-volume users. Advertising on cable is thus far a very small business compared to broadcasting advertising.

Interactive, or two-way, cable is offered commercially on several Qube (Warner-Amex) cable systems and is experimented with elsewhere, but thus far shows more promise than economically viable performance.

Development of domestic satellite distribution of broadcast and cable signals is dramatically expanding the program options for both services. An increasing number of new basic (free to subscribers) and premium (subscriber pays) services are offered on a continuing network basis.

Direct Broadcasting Satellites, under development in the early 1980s, would provide programming directly to homes, by-passing cable and/or broadcast stations.

Pay cable services (of which HBO is the largest) provide movies and other entertainment without advertising, for a monthly viewer charge. Faced with a limited output of Hollywood films, pay cable distributors in the 1980s are increasingly turning to original programming of their own, including several services providing cultural and educational material.

Subscription, or over-the-air, television (STV) stations operate as advertiser-supported independent stations in daytime hours. STV programming is very much like pay cable programming, although because it is a broadcast service, STV is somewhat more closely regulated.

Special kinds of STV service include MDS systems, which use high frequencies to send their microwave pay television signals to subscribing homes, and teletext/videotex, two technical means of delivering alphanumeric information to homes and businesses.

The home video market, which began with video games, has more recently expanded to videotape and video disc equipment and programming.

The home television receiver, now the focal point for a vastly increased number of inputs over the past decade, is becoming a home video center with broadcasting being merely one source of content.

PART IV

The Business of Broadcasting

In Parts 2 and 3, we traced the evolution of commercial and non-commercial broadcasting and the coming of cable television and other alternative sources of programs and services. Now in Part 4 we focus on the economy of commercial broadcasting — its financial organization and its reliance on advertising.

Though commercial broadcasting shares most of the traits of other business enterprises, it has some unique features that set it apart. Its economic units are relatively small when compared to the largest corporations because public policy limits the number of stations that any one company may own. Stations are bound together into larger units by means of networks, but the ties that bind are again subject to public policy rules that prevent undue centralization of controls.

The manufacturing of programming is often compared disparagingly to the assembly line manufacturing of machine-made products. But program making involves risks, uncertainties, and problems of supply that are not shared by makers of toasters or Post Toasties. It is also said that programs are only a means to an end, the real business of commercial broadcasting being the manufacture of audiences for the benefit of advertisers. Certainly the broadcasting industry spends a great deal of time and money on measuring and analyzing its audiences to prove the value of broadcast advertising. The final chapter in this part deals with the ways of collecting this information and putting it to use.

CHAPTER 12

Administrative and Financial Organization

it's now 36 {12 AM, 12 FM, 12 TV

12.1 The Station

Definition Although individual owners may legally control as many as 21 broadcasting stations, every station is licensed as a separate, unique entity designed to serve a specific community.* Moreover, each license encompasses the transmission as well as the programming functions.

A station therefore normally combines four facilities: business offices, studios, transmitter, and transmitting antenna. Often the offices/studios are located separately from the transmitter/antenna because each works best in a different environment, but all come under common ownership (although in a few cases transmission facilities are leased). This point is made because in many countries one authority operates the transmitting facilities while entirely different authorities operate the programming and production facilities. In some countries yet another authority has charge of selling advertising.

*The limitation to 21 refers to full-scale commercial stations. One licensee may control larger numbers if a new class of low-power television stations is included. Initially the FCC set an ownership limit of 15 on these stations (§17.7).

In the United States, a broadcast station might be formally defined as an entity (individual, partnership, corporation, or nonfederal governmental authority) that is licensed by the federal government to organize and schedule programs for a specific community in accordance with an approved plan and to transmit them over designated radio facilities in accordance with specified standards.

Station Organization Broadcasting stations vary enormously, conforming to no standardized table of organization. Nevertheless, all stations need to perform the four basic functions that are reflected in the expense categories the Federal Communications Commission uses in its annual financial report forms: (1) General/Administrative, (2) Technical, (3) Programming, and (4) Sales. These functions are so basic that they have to be performed at noncommercial as well as commercial stations, though in the former the money-gathering function is called "development" instead of "sales."

The chart in Exhibit 12.1 shows some of the subordinate functions that fall under the

NAB   *Radio Adv. Bureau*

four main headings. References to contractual services in the chart are reminders of the extent to which stations depend upon syndication in its various forms. Not only are program materials obtainable from external sources — so too is the expertise of consultants on problems of finance, management, programming, promotion, sales, and technical operations. Over a thousand firms offer such program and consulting services.

1. *General/Administrative* functions include the services that any business needs to provide in creating an appropriate working environment. Services of a specialized nature peculiar to broadcasting are most likely to be obtained by contract with external organizations. For a network affiliate, the main such external contract is the one with its network.

Broadcasters are untiring joiners. The timely nature of their work requires keeping

Exhibit 12.1
Station functional organization

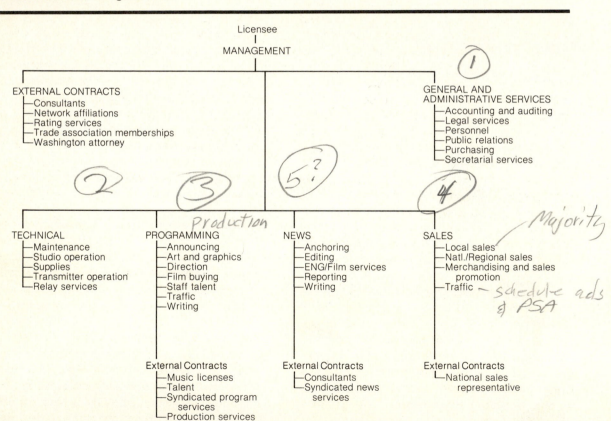

The chart does not represent any particular station but rather depicts major functions usually performed by all stations. In smaller operations, several functions are often carried out by a single employee. Stations also vary widely as to the types and the extent of the services they obtain under contract from outside sources.

up to date with constant new developments. Management is likely to join trade associations such as the National Association of Broadcasters, the Television Bureau of Advertising, and the Radio Advertising Bureau. There are specialized station associations for independent television, daytime radio, UHF state networks, and for farm, religious, and Spanish-language broadcasters. Individuals can join associations of blacks, engineers, financial managers, news directors, program executives, promotion specialists, pioneer broadcasters, and women broadcasters.

2. *Technical* functions center on transmitter operation, which is subject to strict Federal Communications Commission rules. Technical operations at a station are headed by a chief engineer. In the smallest stations the chief may be the only technically qualified staff member, but in most cases the chief supervises a staff of operational and maintenance personnel. Chiefs at large television stations spend most of their time on administration and on keeping up with the rapidly developing technology of broadcasting.

3. *Program* functions fall into planning and implementation phases. Major program planning decisions usually emerge from interplay among the heads of programming, sales, and management. Because in most cases relatively little locally produced programming originates at the station, a major role of the program department becomes the selection and scheduling of prerecorded material — music in the case of radio stations, syndicated series on film or tape in the case of television. Implementation of program decisions is the role of *production*, which has the day-to-day task of putting the program schedule on the air.

News, although a form of programming, is usually treated as a separate department with its own head reporting directly to top management. This separation from entertainment programming arises because of the timely nature of news and the special responsibilities it imposes on management. The news department usually also has charge of station editorials and of public affairs programming generally.

4. *Sales* departments have their own staff members for selling time to local advertisers, but to reach regional and national advertisers most stations contract with a national sales representative firm to speak for them in the out-of-town centers of business. Network affiliates benefit from a third sales force, that of their network organization.

The sales function and its coordination with programming involve processing a vast quantity of detail, which is handled by a special unit, the *traffic* department. Traffic necessitates the daily scheduling of facilities, personnel, program items, and announcements. These assignments appear in the daily *program log*, which is prepared by the traffic department.

Traffic personnel monitor fulfillment of commercial contracts, stopping and starting schedules on time, and arranging for "makegoods" of spots that are missed or technically inadequate. Traffic also maintains a list of "availabilities." This list informs sales personnel of commercial openings in the schedule as they become available for advertisers. Until these openings are sold, traffic usually fills them with public service announcements.

Group Ownership   As do other enterprises, broadcasting businesses benefit from "economies of scale." Ownership of several stations enables bulk purchasing of supplies and equipment; retaining specialized experts in management, programming, engineering, and other fields; and sharing of experiences and new ideas.

If it were not for legal constraints, doubtless great chains of commonly owned stations would have evolved, just as in the newspaper business. For reasons of public policy (§17.7), however, broadcast ownership is limited by regulation. The overall ceiling, imposed by the "Rule of Seven," limits owners to a maximum of seven AM, seven FM, and seven television outlets, or a total of 21 stations. Of the allowable seven television stations, only five may be VHF. Other rules impose still further restrictions to prevent regional and single-market concentrations and to limit newspaper-broadcasting combinations.

There are over 450 commonly owned station groups, each consisting of three or more radio stations and/or two or more television stations (licensees of single AM/FM or AM/FM/TV combinations are not considered group owners). Most of the groups consist of three to five small stations, but a few, such as the network-owned-and-operated (O&O) groups are very powerful combinations. However, excluding the O&O groups, common ownership does not necessarily mean that all members of a group are affiliated with the same network.

Television network O&O groups serve the networks in several ways: (1) O&Os are extremely profitable, each group reaching more than 20 percent of the nation's television households and representing over a third of total network revenue; (2) they give the networks their own prestigious voices in the major markets; and (3) like other powerful groups, the O&O stations benefit from economies of scale in dealing with suppliers.

Networks administer their O&O groups separately from their network operations. Each O&O station is headed by a vice president who, as general manager, has a good deal of autonomy in operating the station.

This ensures compliance with the FCC requirement that each station must serve its own community of license. Independence is sufficiently real to enable O&O station general managers to reject occasional network programs that they judge would be contrary to the interests of their local communities.

Among the best known of the large non-network group owners are the following:

Capital Cities Communications, Inc. (7 AM, 6 FM, 6 TV)

Cox Broadcasting Corp. (5 AM, 7 FM, 5 TV)

Metromedia, Inc. (6 AM, 7 FM, 7 TV)

Taft Broadcasting Co. (6 AM, 6 FM, 7 TV)

Westinghouse Broadcasting Co. ("Group W," 7 AM, 2 FM, 5 TV)

Westinghouse, noteworthy for leading persistent attacks on what it regards as network encroachments on affiliates, was responsible for proposing the prime-time access rule (§8.7).

Group W also led in efforts to use the leverage of group ownership to produce local programs. In 1976 one member of the group, KPIX in San Francisco, started a locally produced magazine program called *Evening*, designed especially for access-time scheduling (§8.7). Group W stations in four other major cities adopted the format, each city contributing local segments of its own to make up a composite magazine, hosted in each city by two local interviewer-guides. *Evening* was so successful that in 1978 Group W began syndicating the series to stations outside its own group, but on a *cooperative* rather than one-way basis. Each purchaser agreed to contribute its own locally produced segments to the show, rechristened *PM Magazine*, as well as to use segments from other cooperating stations. Group W expected eventually to syndicate it to as many as a hundred stations (Droesch, 1980). This hybrid of local and syndicated production has been widely imitated.

Affiliation vs. Independence About 85 percent of all commercial television stations are affiliates of the major networks. Most are *primary affiliates,* serving as the sole, or main, affiliate of ABC, CBS, or NBC in their markets. *Secondary affiliates* share affiliation with more than one network. For example, Topeka, Kansas, has only three stations, one a primary affiliate of CBS and a secondary affiliate of ABC; the second station is a primary affiliate of NBC, and the third is noncommercial. A few small markets have only a single station. Affiliates in Twin Falls, Idaho, and Presque Isle, Maine, for example, have the unusual privilege of picking and choosing programs from all three networks (Nadel, 1977).

Approximately a hundred stations, most of them UHF, are *independents,* meaning they have affiliation with none of the three major networks, though they may affiliate with smaller networks. About a dozen of the VHF independents located in the top markets are very profitable. Examples of these prominent independents are WOR in New York, WGN in Chicago, and KTLA in Los Angeles. On the whole, however, independent stations have had a difficult economic struggle. As a group they lost money until 1975, when they first reported a small profit.

Independents benefited from the introduction of the prime-time access rule in 1971 (§8.7), which weakened network affiliates' early ("fringe") prime-time programming, giving the independents a chance to counterprogram effectively with the off-net syndicated programs denied by PTAR to the affiliates. Also helpful was the establishment of the Association of Independent Television Stations (INTV), founded in 1972. INTV sponsored an Arbitron study of the independent stations' audience in 1977, giving them much-needed favorable evidence about their viewers with which to overcome the negative image of independents in the minds of advertising agency time buyers. Some of the independents have enhanced their viability by specializing in Spanish and religious programming. But affiliation with one of the three major networks remains the most valuable asset a television station can have.

Superstations The most notable recent development among independents, however, has been the emergence of a tie-in between broadcast stations and extensive networks of cable systems. An independent that offers an especially attractive program service not otherwise available from broadcast stations is valuable to cable operators as an enhancement of their services. Stations that attract an extraordinarily large number of widely scattered cable systems in this way have come to be called *superstations.* There was nothing new in a station being picked up by a number of cable systems, but at some undefined point, being picked up by a large enough number of cable systems with wide enough dispersal justifies the label "superstation."

The big-city VHF independents previously mentioned were obvious candidates for such status — not because they consciously programmed for distant cable viewers, but simply because the size of their home markets made it economically possible for them to afford unusually attractive nonnetwork programming. Some of these VHFs, such as WGN in Chicago, found themselves becoming *unintentional* superstations, simply because so many distant cable systems chose to pick up and redistribute their signals.

But the first outlet to intentionally cultivate superstation status was not a VHF in a large market at all. Instead it was a small outlet in a medium-size market that took the innovative step of deliberately shaping its program schedule to attract distant cable viewers' interest. WTBS (formerly WCTG), a UHF station in Atlanta, the nation's sixteenth market in size, is owned by a swashbuckling entrepreneur, Ted Turner. He also owns the Atlanta Braves baseball team, part of a professional basketball team, the yacht *Courageous* (with which he won the America's Cup race in 1977), and Cable News Network, a 24-hour news service started in 1980 exclusively to serve cable systems. By his own description a "multifaceted person," Turner had the bravado to envision his insignificant Atlanta UHF station becoming the heart of what he called the "fourth national network" — a network of cable systems.

Turner not only capitalized on the hunger of cable systems for an additional program source, he also made the WTBS service cheaply and easily available. Counting on the cable systems to install their own satellite terminals, he contracted to relay WTBS programming by satellite, starting in 1976. Cable systems that buy the WTBS satellite feed pay only a few cents per subscriber per month for the services, making no extra charge to their subscribers (§11.4). The money goes to pay for the satellite uplink in Atlanta and the use of a transponder, not to support WTBS. Turner counts on getting his share of the pie in terms of higher advertising rates on WTBS, justified by the increase in its audience represented by the cable subscribers.

What is the secret of Turner's programming strategy? Simply sports and movies, 24 hours a day. Of course WTBS also schedules other entertainment as well as public service programs, such as local news, to serve its own community. But it carries far more sports and feature films than any UHF station in a market the size of Atlanta would normally schedule.

Superstation Issues Superstations raised issues profoundly disturbing to con-

ventional broadcasting. They struck at fundamental assumptions that had previously ruled the industry. The natural physical limits of broadcast signal coverage normally impose well-defined geographical boundaries on a station's service area. Using this fact, audience research firms have divided the entire country into 200-plus distinct television markets.

Traditionally, when the controllers of program rights — primarily syndicators, but also the owners of the rights to such resources as college sports events, for example — sold such rights to a station, both buyer and seller took it for granted that the station was paying for the right to deliver the programs to its own market *exclusively*. Exclusivity worked both ways: it prevented the controller of rights from selling the programs to competing stations in the same market and the buyer of rights from releasing the programs to markets other than its own.

A program owner or syndicator who leased program rights to a superstation, however, found that, although the superstation paid for only its own market, the program actually reached scores of distant markets via relays to cable systems. Moreover, the syndicator may well have sold the same program in some of those distant markets to other stations — stations that thought they were buying exclusive rights to the program in their own markets, only to find themselves in competition with a cable system carrying the same program.

How is it that cable system operators may legally pick up and use television signals without getting permission from the originating stations? This privilege came into being when Congress passed the new copyright law of 1976. The act included a provision *requiring* copyright owners to grant *retransmission rights* to cable operators at a very low fee, fixed by the federal Copyright Tribunal (§11.1). Most owners of copyright material and broadcasters advocate changing this law so as to require cable system operators to bargain with copyright owners and stations for *retransmission consent*. This, as the president of a broadcast station group put it, "would have the merit of putting distant stations and cable into a true marketplace, rather than the fictional marketplace in which they now pretend to operate" (Chaseman, 1979).

Superstations worry networks, too, which see them as a potential threat to their position of dominance. ABC's board chairman described the superstation as "an entrepreneurial effort to have the best of both worlds — the requirements and program costs of only a single station [and] the profit opportunity of a full network" (Goldenson, 1978). His words allude to another of the paradoxes posed by superstations' blending of broadcasting with cable — the fact that each broadcasting station is licensed to serve a specific community, yet the superstation uses that license to turn itself into a kind of network, reaching scores of other communities as well.

12.2 Networks and Affiliates

Definition of Network Two or more stations interconnected by some means of relay (wire, cable, terrestrial microwaves, satellite) so as to enable simultaneous broadcasting of the same program constitute a minimal network in the legal sense. In addition to the major national networks there are over a hundred smaller networks. These are mostly part-time or occasional hook-ups, usually designed to share programs within a region or single state. Some have a common program orientation, such as religion (the Christian Broadcasting Network), language (the Spanish International Network), and sports (Hughes). In the case of the Spanish-language network, most of its 50-plus affiliates are translators (§4.7) rather than full-scale stations.

Our concern here, however, is with the national *full-service networks*, whose emergence has already been discussed (radio in §7.5, television in §8.5).* Because networks contribute only about one percent of radio's total revenue, our interest in this chapter lies with the three major commercial television networks, which generate over 40 percent of commercial television's total revenue.

Network Organization Like the stations, networks vary in their organizational structure, yet each must fulfill the same four basic functions as stations — administration, programming, engineering, and sales. Networks enjoy the luxury of a much higher degree of specialization than do stations. NBC, for example, has separate units, each with its own president, for entertainment, news, O&O stations, sports, and the television network (NBC's radio network makes do with an executive vice president).

The networks are notorious for appointing droves of vice presidents. NBC has well over a hundred. In NBC sales there are vice presidents for the central, eastern, and western regions, and even one just for Detroit; other vice presidents for sales concentrate on sports, daytime, and special programs. In

---

*The FCC uses varying definitions of "network" depending on the context. What we are calling a "full-service" network is referred to by the FCC in its rules dealing with television affiliation agreements as "a national organization distributing programs for a substantial part of each broadcast day to television stations in all parts of the United States, generally via interconnection facilities" (47 CFR 73.658).

NBC Television's Entertainment Division vice presidents supervise units specializing in children's programs, daytime serials, daytime programs, prime-time series, and variety programs; others head the story, drama, and comedy development units.

Distinctive network responsibilities deal with arranging the relay facilities that deliver programs to stations and with maintaining good relations with the affiliates. NBC's Affiliate Relations Department keeps five vice presidents busy. In addition, separate advisory boards representing NBC's radio and television affiliates help maintain the working relationship. In the spring of the year each television network organizes a plush convention for its affiliated stations at which it shows pilots of new shows and unveils program plans for the coming season. These efforts at building affiliate morale and creating an atmosphere of loyalty are vital to the networks' long-term success.

Network-Affiliate Contract   The economic link between a network and an affiliate is formalized in an *affiliation contract*, by law renewable every two years. At the heart of the contract is the clause that defines the terms on which the network will pay the station in return for the right to use the station's time. Called *network compensation*, this payment represents in effect a discount price conceded by the affiliate in consideration of the network's services in obtaining or creating programs, promoting programs, selling advertising, and relaying the programs to the station.

Each television network uses a slightly different formula for calculating compensation, but all arrive at about the same rate of payment. The contract assigns a hypothetical base value to an hour of each affiliate's time. This rate varies from station to station, reflecting differences in market size, station popularity, and other factors that affect the value of the affiliation to the network. The New York flagship stations of the three networks are valued at about the same rate — $9,300 per hour for ABC, $9,500 for CBS, and $10,000 for NBC. Rates go down to as low as $50 for the smallest markets. ABC also lists *bonus* stations that get no compensation at all.

The first step in calculating a station's monthly compensation deducts an amount for network operating expenses. CBS, for example, deducts the equivalent of between eight and nine hours of time at the full network station rate for each monthly payment. After this "up front" deduction, compensation for each segment of network programming that an affiliate carries is calculated as a percentage of the network hourly station rate. The formula takes into account (1) the number of hours in the segment, (2) the number of spots sold in the segment (compared to the number available), and (3) the day part. The last factor reflects the fact that audience potential varies drastically from one day part to another (§9.1). CBS, for example, pays only 5 percent of the network hourly rate for the 8 A.M. to 9 A.M. hours, but 32 percent of the rate for the hours in the 6 P.M. to 11 P.M. day part. On the average, network compensation to affiliates amounts to about 15 percent of their theoretical network hourly rates.

In some instances special circumstances arise requiring adjustments in compensation. For example, NBC pays no direct compensation for the two-hour early-morning *Today* program; instead affiliates get their compensation by selling advertising in the first and third half-hours, retaining all the income; the network in turn keeps all the income from sales that it makes in the second and fourth half-hours.

The financial significance of network compensation to affiliates can be viewed either from the point of view of the networks (what proportion of their revenue do they turn over to affiliates?) or from the point of view of stations (what proportion of station revenue comes from network compensation?). Measured from either viewpoint, television network compensation to affiliates amounts to only about 8 percent of gross revenues (including network payments to their own O&O stations).

This division of the spoils — 92 percent to the networks and only 8 percent to their affiliates — would seem remarkably one-sided if one did not take into account the fact that the network bears all the expenses of program procurement and distribution and of selling affiliates' time. Moreover, stations measure the value of affiliation not in terms of compensation alone, but also in terms of the audiences that network programs attract. Affiliates profit spectacularly from the sale of spots in the 90 seconds or so the network leaves open for affiliate station breaks in each prime-time hour of network programming (increased to seven or eight minutes at other times). And of course audiences for the stations' own programming (locally produced or syndicated) are much enhanced by the flow of audiences to and from network programs.

12.3 Network-Affiliate Relations

Power Balance This does not mean that the relations between networks and their affiliates are without controversy. Theirs is a somewhat uneasy, paradoxical sharing of power, complicated by political and eco-nomic factors too subtle for contracts to define.

In one sense the networks have the upper hand. Affiliation is vitally important to the economic success of television stations. Although the law says networks may not coerce stations into accepting programs and running them as scheduled, the threat of nonrenewal of network contracts is an ever-present reality. The threat rarely needs to be carried out. When CBS ended its 23-year relationship with KXLY-TV in Spokane in 1976 because of repeated rejection of programs and frequent delayed broadcast of those that were accepted, the decision was regarded as newsworthy.

On the other hand, without the voluntary compliance of affiliates, a television network amounts to nothing but a group-owner of five stations instead of being the main source of programming for 200 stations. In that sense affiliates have the upper hand, and woe to the network that fails to please them. The defections of CBS and NBC affiliates to ABC that occurred when ABC forged into the ratings lead (§8.5) is a convincing example of what can happen. Nevertheless, such rare upheavals aside, network-affiliate bonds have been remarkably stable. In the decade 1968–1977 only 46 television affiliates changed networks, and 15 of those changes occurred in 1977.

Clearance The fulcrum at the balance of the complex relationships between networks and their affiliates is the act of *clearance*. This is the voluntary agreement by an affiliate to keep clear in its program schedule the time needed to run network programs. Even after an affiliate has cleared time for a network series, it still has the right to *preempt* the time of scheduled episodes and to substitute programs from other sources.

Networks rely on affiliates not only to carry their programs, but to carry them *as*

scheduled. Delayed broadcasts by affiliates reduce a network's immediate audience for the delayed programs, in consequence reducing their national ratings. Moreover, networks need simultaneous coverage throughout the country in order to get the maximum benefit from their efforts at promoting and advertising their program offerings. These efforts are vitally important to network success.

In practice, affiliates accept about 90 percent of all programs offered by their networks, most of them on faith. Stations feel no need to preview all network offerings, despite the fact that as licensees, they, not the networks, have the ultimate legal responsibility for programs. Because most television programs come in series, however, their general tone is already well known, so that the acceptability of future episodes can usually be taken for granted. Questionable or controversial programs can be screened in advance for affiliates, but previewing is not a universal practice.

Thus affiliates have little or no influence over the *day-to-day* programming decisions of their networks. In the long run, however, they do exert a powerful influence. Network programming strategists take very seriously the feedback that comes from their affiliates. It comes to them from the affiliate-relations departments, station advisory boards, annual affiliate conventions, and individual contacts with managers and owners, reinforced by the statistics of affiliate refusals.

Nonclearance Failure to clear and preemption of already cleared time can occur for several reasons. Sometimes stations opt to skip low-rated network programs in favor of syndicated materials that keep audiences from flowing to competing stations and earn added revenue from the sale of spots (station revenue from network programs is based on the network service as a whole, not on individual programs, as explained in §12.2).

At other times affiliates want to protect their local audiences from what they regard as morally or politically offensive network offerings. Less frequently, affiliates take the risk of offending their networks and losing audience members for the sake of being able to schedule local programs in desirable time normally cleared for their network.

An inkling as to which motive dominates was offered by a detailed study of preemptions: more than half the replacement programs in a sample month of preemptions were either syndicated shows (35 percent) or movies (21 percent). Sports replacements ranked third (16 percent). Local programs were at the bottom of the list, representing only 9 percent of the replacements for preempted network programs (Osborn et al., 1979).

Low-rated network programs traditionally consist, almost by definition, of public affairs and other nonentertainment offerings, which therefore are the ones most often denied clearance. *Camera Three*, a prestigious sustaining series on the arts, which began as a network series in 1956, was being carried by only 40 stations, about 20 percent of the network, when CBS finally gave it up in 1980. Fortunately for its small but devoted following, *Camera Three* stayed on the air as a public broadcasting offering.

One of the reasons ABC's evening news used to run such a poor third to CBS and NBC (§9.4) was that over a score of ABC's major affiliates failed to clear time for it, guaranteeing continued low ratings by denying ABC's news access to some 14 percent of the network's potential audience. CBS could persuade less than half its affiliates to clear time even for the highly respected, though often controversial, news documentaries of Edward R. Murrow (§9.5).

A new temptation to preempt network time emerged in the 1970s with the development of first-run syndication series designed to compete with networks for prime time (§8.7). The 25 major affiliates that preempted network time to run the presponsored miniseries, *Edward the King*, received about 25 percent higher payment for the time than they would have from their networks. CBS lost time worth $5 million or more because of defections by 19 affiliates to carry this series (Bergreen, 1979).

Innumerable pressure groups seek to influence programming, primarily in the negative sense of trying to keep programs they regard as objectionable off the air. These groups object to material they allege to be immoral, unpatriotic, politically one-sided, insulting to ethnic or occupational groups, violent, harmful to children, and so on. They sometimes attempt to *boycott* offending stations, networks, and advertisers (§18.2 evaluates this tactic). Generally speaking, stations and advertisers give in to such pressures more readily than networks.

An extreme example of nonclearance owing to politically objectionable material in entertainment programs occurred in 1973, when CBS canceled a scheduled telecast of a play called *Sticks and Bones*, one of a series of prestigious productions by Joseph Papp, an outstanding theatrical producer.

The play depicted, in harrowing and violent terms, the poisoned relations between a blinded Vietnam veteran and his uncomprehending family. By chance, its playdate fell at the very moment that Vietnam prisoners of war were arriving home to star in a real-life drama staged by the government. The Nixon administration maximized the political benefits it hoped to gain from the POW release by arranging for the televising of the POWs' arrival and their joyful reunions with their families in an atmosphere of triumph and patriotic enthusiasm.

The contrast between these happy televised scenes and the bitter disillusionment in *Sticks and Bones* was too strong for many affiliates. "Offensive to local audiences" was the reason most frequently cited for noncarriage (Pekurney & Bart, 1975). In the face of an unprecedented level of affiliate defections, William Paley, chairman of CBS, himself postponed the performance.

Four months previously an administration spokesman had publicly warned licensees to be more critical of network offerings. He told stations they could "no longer accept network standards of taste, violence, and decency in programming," urging them to "jump on the networks" (Barrett, 1973: 232). Doubtless these signals from the White House prompted, or at least reinforced, adverse reactions to *Sticks and Bones*.

About six months later, after the euphoria of the POW returns had subsided, CBS rescheduled the play. Half its affiliates still refused to clear for it, and nearly a quarter of them carried it only on a delayed basis. Not one advertiser could be found to buy the participating spots. The play went off without incident. By then it seemed relatively tame. Most critics agreed it was not a particularly good play, but practically everybody granted that it was "abrasive."

An example of conspicuous failure to obtain clearance on moral grounds for an entertainment program also involved CBS. Two episodes in the comedy series *Maude* dealt with a decision of the title character to have an abortion. The abortion episodes, originally telecast late in 1972, came up for rerun in August 1973. Catholic Church organizations led a campaign to persuade CBS to cancel, or affiliates to refuse clearance for, the reruns of the two episodes. CBS would not back down, but about 20 percent of the affiliates complied by refusing clearance.

Issues   The foregoing description of the network-affiliate relationship suggests that the image of the network programmers as all-powerful dictators, imposing their will on helpless affiliates, is a myth. Far from being helpless, affiliates in the final analysis have the upper hand when they mobilize their collective strength. It might be argued that in refusing to carry certain network programs, station licensees are doing no more than their undoubted duty to be responsible to their own local audiences. However, this argument carries little conviction when the pattern of nonclearance indicates that the real motive is money. As an FCC member once complained, some affiliates "refuse to carry network news and public affairs in the name of 'local autonomy' and then refuse to provide this programming from any source whatever" (14 FCC 2d 18, 1968).

Responding to the claim that networks shift the blame for the cancellation of high-quality programs to the audience, Les Brown suggested that the real culprit is "the unwillingness of affiliates to clear for them; it was not that the shows were rejected by *people* but that they were *prerejected* by stations" (1971: 359, emphasis added). More recently another critic, in listing the influences other than networks and program producers that affect the quality of television programming, put affiliates at the top of the list, pressure groups near the bottom (Reeves, 1979).

As a matter of fact, despite their surrender to blacklisters in the 1950s (§8.8), the networks deserve some credit for at times standing firm against pressure-group tactics, often setting an example for their affiliates, as in the cases of *Sticks and Bones* and *Maude* previously described.

12.4 Regulation of Network-Affiliate Contracts

The degree of independence and clout enjoyed by affiliates did not come as a gift from the networks. Ever since the late 1930s, government agencies have been busy trying to counteract the inevitable tendency, first of radio then of television networks, to exert what the government perceived as undue control over affiliates, programming, and other aspects of the industry.

Chain Broadcasting Regulations   Regulation of business relationships between networks and their affiliates began in the radio era when the Supreme Court upheld the FCC's chain (i.e., network) broadcasting regulations in 1943 (§7.5). Later the rules were extended to the television networks.

The rules forbid stations from entering into contracts with networks that would restrict affiliates' freedom of action in several areas, the most critical of which are:

1. *Exclusivity*. A network contract may not include *exclusivity rules* aimed at preventing an affiliate from accepting programs from other networks; nor may an affiliate prevent its network from offering rejected programs to other stations in its market. In practice, independent stations often enter into agreements with networks to have first call on programs that affiliates in their markets reject.

2. *Length of Affiliation Contract*. Affiliation agreements must be renewed every two years, and must bind the two parties equally (previously the radio networks had tied up affiliates for five years but themselves for only one).

3. *Network Ownership*. A network may not own two or more networks covering the same territory (aimed at the NBC Red-Blue network combination).

4. *Program Rejection.* A network may not coerce an affiliate in any way to ensure clearance of time for its programs. The allowable reasons for rejection are broad: "unsatisfactory or unsuitable"; "contrary to the public interest"; time needed for another program "of outstanding local or national importance." In effect, the affiliate has complete freedom of choice.

5. *Rate Control.* A network may not influence an affiliate's nonnetwork advertising rates (at one time the radio networks tried to ensure that network advertising would be more attractive to national advertisers than spot advertising arranged by direct contracts with stations).

In 1977, recognizing that the original chain broadcasting rules no longer had much relevance to modern radio networks, the FCC freed them of most of the old rules, the main exception being the nonexclusivity rule. At the same time the commission broadened the definition of radio network to include the audio news services offered on an interconnected basis by news agencies (63 FCC 2d 674, 1977).

TV Prime-Time Access Rule (PTAR)

While giving the radio networks more freedom, the FCC imposed still more restrictions on the television networks. In 1971 it adopted rules to lessen the networks' hold over prime-time entertainment programming. The *prime-time access rule* (PTAR) imposed a limit of 2½ hours that affiliates in the top fifty markets would be allowed to clear for network entertainment (details of how PTAR works are discussed in §8.7). Along with the access limitation came a rule forbidding the networks to engage in domestic syndication of their own programs; even their overseas syndication activity is limited to nonenter-

tainment programming (for which there is little foreign market compared to the overseas appetite for U.S. entertainment programs). Networks are also forbidden to function as national spot (nonnetwork) sales representatives for stations other than their O&O stations.

12.5 Program Economics

All broadcast program production activities face an ever-present and ever-increasing problem of costs. This problem, as we have pointed out, is manageable only by applications of the parsimony principle (§7.4), the rule that program materials must be conserved by shared and repeated use. In practice this means syndication in its many different forms.

Station Program Departments In radio the average program department expenses amount to 28 percent of the total station expenses, but in television program department costs rise to 43 percent of the total. Television program departments also cost more to run in dollar terms — a yearly average of over $1.5 million per station compared to a little over $100,000 for radio. Putting it another way, television stations spend 15 times as much on their program departments as do radio stations.* Television stations spend a much higher proportion of their program budgets on syndicated materials and services than do radio stations; on

*Financial data in this chapter, unless otherwise attributed, are based upon information given in the FCC's 1978 annual financial reports (FCC, 10 Dec. 1979 and 17 July 1980). The FCC compiles these summaries from official annual financial statements that all stations must submit. The National Association of Broadcasters compiles more current annual estimates based upon voluntary reports from a sample of stations.

the other hand, radio depends more heavily on live performers in the form of DJs and talk hosts. These contrasts are brought out in the following analysis of total program department expenses as reported to the FCC:

Salaries and talent fees: radio 63%, TV 40%
Syndicated services and materials: radio 23%, TV 42%
Other program expenses: radio 14%, TV 18%

We have categorized as "syndication" expenses in the above analysis payments for music licenses, news services, audio recordings, taped and filmed programs, and miscellaneous performance and program rights.

Local TV Production We have already pointed out (§9.4) that local television production is in most cases confined almost exclusively to news programs. As a station official put it, "after budgets are set for the news effort, little is left for other local programs. Besides, news shows are usually profitable, while other local programs rarely are. . . . the best the average broadcaster can hope for is the occasional special" (Schofield, 1979: 42).

Stations in the larger markets with better-than-average resources do somewhat more. Some, for example, produce a weekly access-time local series. Saturday evening is a favorite time for such locally produced programs, a fact acknowledged by the FCC in setting up the prime-time access rule (§8.7). Few, however, accomplish as much as WCVB, Boston's Channel 5, which in 1981 produced 47 percent of its programming locally, compared to a national average of about 10 percent. Its innovative programs even included an informal post-midnight local television talk show (Schwartz, 1981).

Ironically, so powerful is the parsimony principle, locally originated entertainment programs that prove to have broad audience appeal soon move into syndication, losing their status as local programs. This happened to the nationally syndicated Mike Douglas and Phil Donahue shows, for example, both of which started as local productions, Douglas at a station in Cleveland, Donahue in Dayton. *PM Magazine* developed from a local daily show into a widely syndicated show with continuing local input (§12.1).

Network Program Procurement Television networks, like stations, obtain most of their programming from outside their own organizations. Only 17 percent of network program budgets goes toward their self-produced news and public affairs programs. By far the biggest item of program expense, 63 percent of the total, goes to pay for entertainment programs created by outside production companies. The networks spend well over a billion dollars a year to purchase not programs but *licenses* — merely the right to use programs for a limited number of plays (§8.7).

Large as this amount may seem, it barely covers the cost of production. Producers are willing (grudgingly, to be sure) to sell the use of prime-time entertainment series — the only ones with high residual value for syndication — to the networks at cost or even less, counting on subsequent syndication fees to bring in the profits. This maneuver, known as *deficit financing*, capitalizes on the peculiar dynamics of the syndication market. Initial showing on a network, instead of lowering the future value of a series, actually enhances it because network exposure gives the series prestige and a proven track record when it is offered for syndication in the foreign and domestic markets.

Production Budgets The main variables affecting prime-time program costs are the production method (taping performances before a studio audience is cheapest, single-camera film most expensive) and cast salaries. Production expenses are divided for budgeting purposes into two categories — above-the-line and below-the-line expenses. The "line" represents the division between the creative aspects of production and the craft aspects. Typical above-the-line items are salaries for writers, performers, and directors. Typical below-the-line items are payments for scenery, costumes, props, lights, camera operators, editing, film and/or tape stock, film processing, and facilities rental or overhead.

12.6 Financial Framework of Broadcasting

A Money Machine? Broadcasting is so profitable that it is often likened to a "license to print money," or a "license to steal." This is only a half-truth as far as stations are concerned, although it is true that the dominant forces in the industry, the television networks, have been both highly profitable and relatively immune from the financial ups and downs that affect most businesses.

A high proportion of stations actually report losses rather than profits. In 1978 a third of the AM and AM/FM radio stations claimed to lose money, as did 43 percent of the independent FM stations. In 1978, 8 percent of the VHF and 27 percent of the UHF television stations reported losses. Such high numbers of unprofitable operations may be explained in two ways: (1) Many reported losses are only on paper because the FCC allows stations to count depreciation and payments to owners as "losses"; moreover, many stations are owned by conglomerate firms that may use them as tax write-offs. (2) Even genuinely

unprofitable stations tend to hang on because of their owners' or prospective owners' optimism about an eventual payoff.

The current overall profitability of FM radio and UHF television after years of losing money shows that in broadcasting it often pays to keep trying against formidable odds. Failing broadcast properties attract investors not only because the owners have confidence that losers can be converted into money machines if only the right formula can be found, but also because station ownership confers a certain aura of glamor and community prestige that satisfies the ego.

Role of Market Size Profitability is closely associated with market size, which tends to affect all aspects of the broadcasting enterprise. Generally speaking, the larger the market the larger the station staff, the higher the salaries, the longer the program day, the more network programs are carried, and the more local production occurs — and of course the higher the profits. Exhibit 12.6.1 compares markets of widely differing size, showing, for example, that the average television station in the 4th market earns *fifty* times as much as the average station in the 147th market.

Television stations, because of their irreducibly high cost of operations, can survive commercially only in relatively large communities. The majority of radio stations, however, are located outside metropolitan areas; in fact more than 2,000 radio stations operate in communities where they are the only outlet and average only about $8,000 income a year.

This is not to say that the correspondence between market size and profitability is absolute. Economic conditions vary among markets of identical size (in terms of numbers of households, the measurement used in broadcasting), and of course broadcast managements vary in their efficiency. Cleveland, for example, a somewhat depressed industrial city, ranks 9th among U.S. markets in size, but only 11th in broadcast revenues. Phoenix, on the other hand, a flourishing Sunbelt city, ranks 33d in size but 26th in revenues (Blair, 1979).

Capital Investment   The broadcasting industry's investment in tangible property is small relative to its revenue and income. As a whole, the industry earned 73 percent of its original capital investment in just the one year of 1978, according to the FCC's annual report. As Exhibit 12.6.2 shows, the total investment of television is less than twice that of radio, despite the fact that the average cost of individual television stations is about 13 times the cost of individual radio stations. The aggregate investment in radio mounts up, however, because of the far greater number of stations in the total.

Exhibit 12.6.2 fails to disclose an important aspect of the industry's economic base — the capital investment of the general public in broadcasting. Unlike most other media, broadcasting counts on the consumer to supply the largest part of its basic capital equipment — the broadcast receivers. The public's capital investment in broadcasting amounts to many times the total investment of the industry itself. Some estimates place the public's investment at more than 90 percent of the total. Involvement of the consumer in the essential capital investment of an industry to this extent has obvious implications regarding the broadcasting industry's unique obligation to its audiences.

Income   If any broadcasting organizations are in fact "money machines" it is the television networks that most nearly qualify. In 1978 the three networks collected nearly $3

Exhibit 12.6.1
Broadcast income and market size

| Market | Market rank | Radio stations[a] | | TV stations | |
		Number	Average income	Number	Average income
Philadelphia	4	39	$148,480	7	$6,002,614
Toledo	56	17	93,083	3	1,905,267
Amarillo	107	11	26,803	3	319,328
Bangor	147	5	14,373	3	272,659

Comment: As market rank (in terms of number of households in the market) goes down, so does average income for both radio and television stations.

[a]Includes only stations licensed to that market specifically and reporting income. Stations from other markets can normally also be heard.

Sources: Based on FCC, *AM and FM Broadcast Financial Data, 1978* (Washington, D.C., 10 Dec. 1979), Table 15; and FCC, *Revised TV Broadcast Financial Data, 1978* (Washington, D.C., 17 July 1980), Table 19.

billion. After deduction of expenses, they were left with pretax income of $373 million. When pretax earnings of the network O&O stations are included, the networks garnered 34 percent of the industry's entire income. As Exhibit 12.6.3 shows, this contrasts sharply with radio, in which the networks, together with their 36 O&O stations, earned only 14 percent of the total radio income.

12.7 Employment in Broadcasting

Size of Work Force Networks and stations employ a relatively small number of people. The entire commercial broadcasting industry has fewer than 150,000 full-time employees. Once more we see the pervasive effects of syndication: a large part of broadcasting-related work is done by highly specialized outside firms that produce basic program materials ranging from station identification jingles to prime-time entertainment series.

Most of the opportunities for creative work in the performing arts, writing, directing, designing, and so on are found with firms that supply the broadcasting industry. Many other types of work related to broadcasting take place in advertising agencies, station representative firms, program-syndicating organizations, and the like.

Aside from the television networks, most broadcasting organizations have small staffs. Exhibit 12.7 shows that radio full-time station staffs average 12 persons, television 72. According to the National Association of Broadcasters' annual financial reports for 1979 typical radio full-time station staff sizes varied from 52 for the largest markets down to five for the smallest. Typical television station staff sizes range from 273 to 20 persons.

Radio staffs of only one person are not unknown. An FCC official commended the "selfless dedication" of the owner of a Massachusetts one-man classical music FM station where the owner worked 85 hours a week, earning only $5,000 a year (*Broadcasting*, 3 July 1978). KYUS, an exceptional television station in Miles City, Montana, serving an area of about 20,000 households, is run almost entirely by a husband and wife team

Exhibit 12.6.2
Tangible investment of broadcasting industry (original cost, in millions)

	Average investment			
	Networks	O&O stations	All other stations	Industry total
Radio	$ 1.5	$1.2	$0.26	$1,510.3
Television	$147.5	$9.1	$3.1	$2,691.4

Sources: Based on data in FCC, *AM and FM Broadcast Financial Data, 1978* (Washington, D.C., 10 Dec. 1979), Table 13; and FCC, *Revised TV Broadcast Financial Data, 1978* (Washington, D.C., 17 July 1980), Table 12.

with the help of three young technicians — a true "Mom-and-Pop" operation. In 1980, the station was producing as many as five local shows a day and three hours of local remotes a week.*

Salary Scales The huge salaries reported in gossip columns are reserved for top creative persons and executives, most of them at network headquarters and the production centers of New York and Hollywood. Average salaries for most jobs at most stations are moderate at best. News jobs are the top-paying nonsupervisory positions in television and sales jobs the top-paying supervisory positions below the general manager level.

*Said the owner to a consulting engineer brought in for a technical emergency: "This must be the slaphappiest operation in the world." "On the contrary," replied the engineer, "this is without a doubt the most efficiently operated television station in existence." (Personal letter from David G. Rivenes, 29 July 1980.)

Employment Opportunities Surveys of students enrolled in college broadcasting curricula indicate that most would-be broadcasters initially think in terms either of on-camera and on-mike positions or of creative behind-the-camera positions. These are the jobs *least* accessible to beginners because of the oversupply of candidates. The aforementioned delegation of creative work to specialized production firms means that such creative work is concentrated in a few centers where competition is fierce and where unions control entry.

An exception to this rule is the news field, the one field in which *local* production still flourishes (§9.4). All networks and nearly all stations employ news specialists. Surveys by the Radio and Television News Directors Association indicate that three-quarters of the radio stations employ at least one full-time newsperson, while the median television station news staff size is 11 persons. Moreover, a substantial number of news personnel are

Exhibit 12.6.3
Broadcast pre-tax income (in millions of dollars)

	Radio		Television	
	Amount	Percentage	Amount	Percentage
Networks	$ 15	5	$ 374	23
O&O stations	29	9	186	11
Other stations	267	86	1,093	66
Total	$311	100	$1,653	100

Comment: This table brings out the marked difference between the role of networks in radio (about 5 percent of the income) and their role in television (about 23 percent). Also notable is the great profitability of the network O&O stations.

Sources: Based on data in FCC, *AM and FM Broadcast Financial Data, 1978* (Washington, D.C., 10 Dec. 1979), Table 6; and FCC, *Revised TV Broadcast Financial Data, 1978* (Washington, D.C., 17 July 1980), Table 3.

hired directly out of college (Stone, 1978). A group of broadcasting executives predicted that news would be one of the fields of employment most likely to expand in the 1980s (see Box).

The same executives placed *sales* at the top of their list of expanding employment opportunities. Every commercial network and station necessarily employs people in the sales areas; moreover, the highest managerial positions in both networks and stations are usually filled from the ranks of sales personnel. Nevertheless, one of the most frequent complaints of station personnel directors about college-trained job applicants is that they fail to comprehend the financial basis of commercial stations' existence and its profound influence on every aspect of operations.

If would-be broadcasters looked only to networks and stations and their suppliers for jobs, however, they would seriously underestimate the actual employment opportunities. Radio and television have become so pervasive that virtually every large organization that has any contact with the public uses these media in one form or another. Broadcasting specialists find employment with cable companies, retail firms, religious institutions, educational and health organizations, foundations, government agencies, and the armed services. Many such organizations make extensive in-house use of closed-circuit television and produce videocassette programs. They apply broadcast techniques to job and skills training, management development, sales presentations, and public relations. Such nonbroadcast uses of television require trained personnel for producing, directing, writing, studio operations, program planning, and other tasks that originated as broadcasting occupational specialties.

Women in Broadcasting The Federal Communications Commission enforces Equal Employment Opportunities Act standards for stations with five or more employees. These

Exhibit 12.7
Employment in commercial broadcasting

Broadcasting service (units)	Full-time[a] employees	Average per network or station
Radio networks (8)	876	109
Television networks (3)	12,983	4,327
Radio stations (5,478)	67,862	12
Television stations (714)	51,153	72
Industry total	132,874	

[a]In addition TV had 5,110 part-time employees, radio 22,942.

Sources: Based on data in FCC, *AM and FM Broadcast Financial Data, 1978* (Washington, D.C., 10 Dec. 1979), Table 13; and FCC, *Revised TV Broadcast Financial Data, 1978* (Washington, D.C., 17 July 1980), Table 13.

Advice for Job Seekers

A 1979 survey of broadcasting employment in the state of Virginia was unusual for achieving responses from every one of the 222 radio and television stations in the state. Virginia's 2,593 broadcasting jobs broke down as follows:

Primary job (percentage of total)	Total positions	Proportion held by women
Announcing (21)	545	6%
Sales (19)	485	18%
Traffic-Clerical (18)	419	46%
News (13)	340	12%
Management/ Administration (10)	270	5%
Engineer (10)	253	1%
Other (11)	281	12%

Asked to predict personnel needs ten years in the future, Virginia broadcasting executives gave top priority to *news* (59 percent expected increase), second priority to sales (53 percent increase). As to education, 40 percent of the chief executives and 24 percent of the staff had college degrees. The staff category with the highest percentage of college graduates was news (61 percent).

As always in such surveys, the broadcasters differed in their assessments of the value of college training for their field, but they did agree on the importance of getting *practical experience*. Executives who favored college training gave such advice as:

■ "Study the 'people' subjects carefully. Psychology, sociology are good, and English composition is a must."
■ "Get plenty of education — it's a highly competitive field. And above all, *learn the English language.*"
■ "Get as broad an education as you can. You've got to have at least a surface knowledge of many things to be a successful communicator. You can *never* know enough."

From the anti-college executives came such blunt advice as:

■ "Get out of broadcasting courses. Every one I've seen, the student leaves with unrealistic attitudes, with rose-colored glasses."
■ "Forget the college stuff. I'll hire one year of experience before a doctor's degree."

Source: Gordon A. Sabine, "Broadcasting in Virginia: Benchmark '79," Blacksburg, Va.: Department of Communications, Virginia Polytechnic Institute and State University, 1980. Used with permission.

standards require licensees to submit an annual report (FCC Form 395) classifying their employees according to nine major job categories and according to sex and minority status. The U.S. Commission on Civil Rights made a detailed study of the 1975 reports coming from a sample of large stations, both commercial and noncommercial. At that time women predominated in the office and clerical job category, but held progressively lower proportions of the professional, managerial, and technical jobs.

In its 1979 annual employment study of stations with five or more employees, the FCC reported that women occupied 32 percent of the broadcasting jobs. The proportion of women was slightly higher in noncommercial stations and the networks than in commercial stations. Radio and Television News Directors Association Studies, based on sample surveys of stations, indicated steady growth in employment of newswomen. Its 1979 study indicated the following percentages (Stone, 1980):

Stations with newswomen on staff: Radio 50%, TV 94%
Women as percentage of news staff: Radio 26%, TV 26%

Minorities EEO rules also require stations to report on their efforts to upgrade the employment opportunities of minority group members. In the sample of stations studied by the U.S. Civil Rights Commission in 1975, one out of every five employees was a member of a minority group. However, only 11 percent of the jobs in the upper four categories were held by members of minority groups. The FCC's 1979 report on the industry as a whole indicated that minority group members constituted 15 percent of the broadcast work force at stations employing five or more persons.

Unions Unionization in broadcasting is complete at the level of the networks and the national production centers, less so at the individual station level. The industry is fragmented into so many units — mostly, as we have seen, with relatively small staffs, involving personnel performing more than one type of job — that unionization at the small-station level is not usually practicable. For example, a small radio station cannot afford to assign two employees to record interviews, one a technician to operate the equipment, the other a performer to do the talking,

when the job could just as easily be done by one employee.

Unionization of the broadcasting industry is also affected by the fact that the medium draws upon personnel from older established electrical, musical, motion picture, stage, and newspaper industries that already had their own unions. Most of the 40-odd unions that affect broadcasting therefore cover workers in other media as well. Thus the American Federation of Musicians, whose marathon battle to control the use of recorded music was described in §7.7, covers every kind of professional musician, from players in symphony orchestras to pianists in bars.

People who work in broadcasting can be classified in broad categories — the creative/performing group and the crafts/technical group. Unions divide along similar lines, the former usually avoiding the word "union," calling themselves "guilds," "associations," or "federations."

The first purely broadcasting union to arise was the American Federation of Television and Radio Artists (AFTRA), which was formed originally (as AFRA) in 1937 to represent that universal radio performer, the announcer. Most of the creative/performing unions, however, came from the stage and motion pictures. Examples are the Writers Guild of America, the American Guild of Variety Artists, and the Screen Actors Guild. When videotape came to rival film as a medium of production, SAG and AFTRA both claimed jurisdiction over the new medium. The dispute was finally settled in favor of AFTRA. Many actors now belong to both unions, each of which has about 45,000 members.

The creative unions have played a significant role in forcing adaptation of contract terms to take belated account of developments in technology. It will be recalled that feature films were kept off television at first because film-making contracts had no provisions covering performance in the new medium (§8.6).

SAG went on strike in 1960 (when Ronald Reagan was president of the union rather than president of the United States) to force higher scales for *residuals* — the payments made to performers and others for repeat performances of recorded programs on television. SAG has collected residuals on behalf of its members since 1954, much as ASCAP and BMI collect copyright payments on behalf of composers (§7.7). In 1979 SAG handled residual payments of nearly $38 million. In fact some performers lucky enough to be in particularly popular syndicated series became known as "residuals millionaires" (Henderson, 1979). New technology triggered strikes in 1980–1981 involving several unions. This time the issue was the sharing of the income realized from the sale of recorded programs to the pay-television, videocassette, and videodisc markets.

Technical unions became active in broadcasting early in its history. The first successful strike against a broadcasting station may have been the one organized in 1926 against a CBS owned-and-operated radio station in St. Louis by the International Brotherhood of Electrical Workers (IBEW), a technicians' union founded in the late nineteenth century by telephone linemen (Koenig, 1970: 22). The IBEW later obtained a network contract with CBS.

In 1953 NBC technicians formed a separate association of their own that ultimately became the National Association of Broadcast Engineers and Technicians (NABET), the first purely broadcasting technicians' union. Later the word "Engineers" was changed to "Employees" to broaden the union's scope. Competition between NABET and IBEW caused many jurisdictional disputes. A third technical union, an old rival of IBEW, entered the

television scene from the motion picture industry, the International Alliance of Theatrical Stage Employees and Moving Picture Machine Operators of the United States and Canada (IATSE).

Summary

Broadcast station expenses are divided along functional lines into general/administrative, technical, program, and sales. Station organization follows the same pattern, with subheadings for news, production, traffic, administrative services, and other specialized functions. Much of the work is done under contract by external specialists. Stations differ in terms of affiliates vs. independents and single-ownership vs. group-ownership. Some independent stations that serve many cable systems have become identified as "superstations."

Networks are organized along the same lines as stations, with added responsibilities for program distribution and station relations. Network station ownership is limited, so that most affiliates have only a contractual relationship with their networks. The most important provision of affiliate contracts concerns station compensation for time used by networks. Such compensation amounts to only a small percentage of affiliates' revenues.

Affiliates have the legal right to refuse to clear time for network programs and to change networks at the expiration of contracts, which are limited to two years' duration. The relationship is therefore one of mutual trust, with networks and affiliates sharing power. This sharing comes about because of legal constraints that prevent networks from unduly dominating affiliates and that limit the amount of prime time that stations may clear for network programs.

Despite the fact that stations *produce* few local programs, programming nevertheless represents their main expense. News and public affairs programs are the principal types of self-produced programs of both networks and stations. Most other programming comes from external sources, either from network suppliers that specialize in various types of production, or from syndicators that distribute programs already recorded on discs, tapes, and films.

Although commercial broadcasting as a whole is very profitable, many stations report losses rather than profits. Profitability is closely related to market size, especially for television. Profitable operations receive high returns on capital investment in equipment and facilities; moreover the general public invests heavily in the physical system in terms of broadcast receiver purchases.

Broadcasting has a small work force relative to its social impact. The best employment opportunities for newcomers to the industry are in sales and news; there are also many opportunities for production work in the widespread nonbroadcast use of radio and television. Broadcast employees are unionized at the network level and in the major production centers, but most stations are not targets for unionization because their employees are few in number and often do several jobs that if unionized would come under several different jurisdictions.

CHAPTER 13

Broadcast Advertising

Although they were the youngest of the major advertising media, first radio and then television quickly earned places among the top five. Today only newspapers surpass television in total advertising dollar volume, and television is tops in national advertising. Radio comes fourth, after direct mail advertising but ahead of magazines (Exhibit 13.1).

Rapid commercial success of both radio and television in the face of entrenched competition is explained by their flexibility and persuasiveness. Broadcasting's extraordinary flexibility enables the same stations to serve the needs of both local and national advertisers almost equally well. And television is so persuasive that, as one commentator observed, when it advertises dog food it makes you wish you were a dog.

13.1 Psychological Advantages

Access to Consumers Because radio and television receivers are found in virtually all homes, broadcasting has unrivaled access to all members of the family under all the changing circumstances of daily living. At the same time, car radios and portables enable broadcasting to compete with magazines and newspapers as a medium that can travel with the consumer outside the home. Above all, however, the constant availability of broadcasting as a companion and provider of entertainment and information gives it a great psychological advantage.

Timeliness Then too, programming *unfolds* continuously, as we pointed out in speaking of the importance of program scheduling (§9.1). For advertisers this attribute offers a unique advantage because it lets them time their messages to coincide precisely with activities relevant to their products. Commercials for household products can be scheduled just when the homemaker is actually using such products, food commercials just when people are preparing or consuming food, sportswear commercials at the very moment sports fans are engrossed in watching their favorite sports.

Ability to Demonstrate Advertisers find television's ability to show how products work and how they affect consumers a unique asset. For example, they can "prove" claims made for their products by means of vivid demonstrations. Color adds to the effectiveness of demonstrations, as does participation by celebrity endorsers.

Entertainment Value Commercials often take the form of tiny plays that exploit all the entertainment values of the theater — character, conflict, suspense, and resolution. There is some truth in the wry comment that commercials are often more entertaining than programs. If the skill, craftsmanship, attention to minute detail, and lavish expenditure of money that go into creating the best com-

mercials went into the production of programs, the "vast wasteland" might be made to bloom. Unfortunately, multiplying the cost of making a top-quality 60-second commercial (up to half a million dollars) by the number of minutes in programs would make an ordinary situation comedy as costly to produce as *Star Wars*.

Attention-holding Value A great deal of research and planning goes into planting commercial messages at just the right moments to maximize their chances of being seen or heard. The newspaper reader can skip over advertisements, the commuter can ignore billboards; mail addressed to "occupant" can be dropped unopened into the wastebasket. But once their attention has been engaged, listeners or viewers find skillfully placed broadcast commercials hard to evade.

Status Value The very fact that a product is advertised in a major medium confers a certain status. Some of the feeling of confidence that people have in a medium may be unconsciously transferred to the products it advertises. Taking advantage of this transfer, advertisers sometimes use the phrase "As seen on television" in supermarket point-of-sale displays and newspaper ads.

13.2 Flexibility of Coverage

In addition to its psychological advantages as an advertising medium, broadcasting has the physical advantage of functioning almost equally well as either a local or a national/regional advertising medium. The same stations that at one moment serve as

Exhibit 13.1
Advertising volume of major media, local vs. national

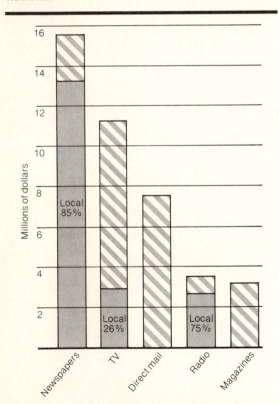

Newspapers retain the lead as the principal medium for local advertising, but television leads all other media in nonlocal advertising.

Source: Reprinted with permission from the January 5, 1981 issue of *Advertising Age.* Copyright 1981 by Crain Communications, Inc.

local outlets at another moment may serve as outlets for national or regional networks.

Local Advertising   All stations are by their nature essentially *local* media, though their individual coverage areas vary a great deal (§3.10). Even network stations are necessarily local because each covers only one market and must by law devote some of its programming to its own community.

As Exhibit 13.2 shows, radio depends for three-quarters of its revenue on local advertisers, whereas television derives 44 percent of its revenue from local billings. This difference reflects the historical fact that television captured most of the national advertisers, driving radio to cultivate local sources of revenue. Moreover, since radio is a much less expensive medium, it is more affordable than television for small local businesses.

Daily newspapers, broadcasting's chief rival for local advertising dollars, have far less flexibility of coverage. Of the 1,500 communities with daily papers, over 97 percent are one-paper towns. Daily newspapers attempt to adapt their coverage to advertisers' needs by using add-on suburban supplements; but in many a one-newspaper town, local advertisers may choose among two dozen or more radio and television stations with varying coverage areas.

Nevertheless, despite broadcasting's advantages, newspapers in fact remain the leading medium for local advertising in the country as a whole, as shown in Exhibit 13.1. Newspapers have three major advantages: (1) Broadcasting can offer no effective substitute for the large display ads of department stores and supermarkets (with their clip-out coupons). (2) Broadcasting cannot compete effectively with newspapers' classified "want ad" sections (though some radio stations do offer want-ad segments in their programming as a public service).* (3) A broadcasting station has only 24 hours of "space" each

---

*An attempt in 1966 to convert a Los Angeles FM station to a want-ad format, under special FCC authorization, failed after a year of experimentation and the loss of several million dollars (Kushner, 1972).

Exhibit 13.2
Network, spot, and local station revenues

	Percentage of revenue obtained from		
Type of station	Network compensation	National spot sales	Local sales
Radio	1	21	78
Television	7	49	44

Comment: Note that these percentages reflect what stations receive rather than what advertisers pay. The amounts retained by the networks for their own expenses and profits make up the difference.

Sources: Based on 1978 data in FCC, *AM and FM Broadcast Financial Data, 1978*, Washington, D.C., 10 Dec. 1979; and FCC, *Revised TV Broadcast Financial Data, 1978*, Washington, D.C., 17 July 1980.

day, whereas print media can expand their space indefinitely. Broadcasting has nothing comparable to the multipage inserts that advertisers can buy in newspapers.

The chief local clients for broadcast advertising are food stores, auto dealers, department and furniture stores, banks, restaurants, and movie houses. Many local firms act as retail outlets for nationally distributed products. In such cases the cost of local advertising may be shared between the local dealer and the national manufacturer. This is often the case with local automobile dealers, who may share the cost of advertising with the Detroit companies that build the cars they sell. This type of cost sharing, known as local *cooperative advertising*, or just "local coop," is a major source of radio revenue, so much so that some stations appoint a special staff member to coordinate cooperative advertising.

Network Advertising   When a station throws the switch that connects it to a network, the station instantaneously converts itself from a local into a national advertising medium. For advertisers of nationally distributed products, network advertising has four significant advantages.

(1) In a single transaction, the network advertiser can place messages on several hundred stations of known qualities, located strategically to cover the entire country. (2) Network advertisers can have centralized control over their advertising messages and assurance that they will be delivered at the times and in the program environments of their choice (barring, of course, "circumstances beyond our control"). (3) Network advertisers also benefit from sophisticated audience research by their networks. And (4) they benefit from the prestige that attaches to the very fact of being network advertisers.

Traditionally, two basic ways of presenting network messages were available to ad-

vertisers. They could either *sponsor* entire programs, inserting their messages where and how they chose, or they could buy *participations* in network programs over which they had no control. In a slight variant on the latter, *network cooperative* advertising permits affiliates to sell spots in certain network programs. NBC's *Today* is a case in point (§12.2). Affiliates pay a fee to their networks for the cooperative spots they sell; any left unsold are filled with public service (free) announcements.*

Sponsorship, once the principal type of network advertising, had the advantage for advertisers of identifying them closely with sponsored programs and their stars as well as giving advertisers a great deal of control over programs. But sponsorship disappeared from network radio after television drained away national advertising, and from television during the 1960s, when rising program costs made it too expensive for most advertisers. The term "sponsor" now usually means *any* advertiser, though historically it meant only those who assumed responsibility for entire programs. Today sponsorship in the original sense survives only for occasional specials, underwritten by large corporations desiring a particularly prestigious type of image-building exposure.

Participating advertising is sold as announcements ("participations") scheduled in slots made available by the network within its programs. Most advertisers use *scatter buying* strategies, distributing their ads over a number of different programs. In this way, they avoid risking too much on any one pro-

---

Network cooperative advertising should not be confused with *local* cooperative advertising, the sharing of local advertising costs between dealers and manufacturers mentioned earlier in this section.

gram and also gain the advantage of exposure to varied audiences.

Network advertising also has its drawbacks. (1) The high demand and the high price for network advertising puts it beyond the reach of many firms. (2) Network affiliates may not be the stations best able to tap the particular audience an advertiser wants to reach. (3) Networks cover virtually the entire country through a fixed number of affiliates, but some advertisers would rather concentrate their messages in certain regions and use fewer stations. (4) Networks have relatively high standards that forbid acceptance of some products and of some commercials which individual stations may nevertheless be willing to accept. For these and other reasons, an alternative *nonnetwork* method of serving national advertisers emerged.

National Spot Advertising   The alternative to network advertising for clients who need to reach national audiences is known as *national spot*, or simply as *nonnetwork national* advertising. The major difference lies in the fact that in national spot advertising the stations that participate do not constitute a true network, a group of *interconnected* stations. National spot advertisers use ad hoc collections of nonconnected stations chosen to suit their particular needs. Advertisers may choose network affiliates as well as independents to participate in national spot campaigns. The commercial announcements are sent out to the chosen stations by mail or similar delivery methods. This means, of course, that spot advertisers lack the centralized control of message, timing, and program environment that station interconnection makes possible for network advertisers.*

*One of the attractions of barter syndication (§8.7) as a form of national spot advertising is that it gives bartering advertisers control over the environment in which their commercials appear.

The national spot advertiser puts together the combination of stations that best fits the needs of the advertised product or service. If, for example, the product is of interest only to farmers, the spot advertiser can select only stations located in farm areas. Moreover, spot advertisers are free to select any kind of advertising vehicles (other than most network programs) that suit their needs. This could mean station-break spots between network programs, sponsorship of either local or syndicated programs, or participating spots in such programs.

In the example of a farm-related product, a spot advertiser might choose to sponsor a respected local weathercaster or to buy participations in a popular local farm-and-home hour. In this way national spot advertising can capitalize on *local* program interests, something the network advertiser cannot possibly do.

Although many companies use spot advertising because they cannot afford network prices, the biggest spot advertisers are all familiar names on network advertising as well — such companies as Procter and Gamble (by far the biggest spot advertiser), General Foods, Coca-Cola, General Mills, and Lever Brothers. Such firms use spot and network advertising in combination, as shown in Exhibit 13.7.1, to achieve better coverage than either could yield on its own.

National Representative Firms   Loss of the network's unique ability to offer the convenience of a single transaction could be a problem for the national spot advertiser. A manufacturer located in Dayton is in no position to evaluate the thousands of stations scattered across the country and to negotiate separate contracts with each of several dozen selected for a spot campaign.

This gap is bridged by specialized intermediaries — *national sales representative* firms ("reps" for short). A rep contracts with a string of stations (the top firms have about a hundred stations on their lists), selling their time in the national market, functioning as an extension of their client-stations' own sales staffs. Some radio reps sell their client-stations to national spot advertisers as groups, referring to them as "non-wired networks."

Reps perform many other services in the course of carrying out their primary mission of sales representation. Their national perspective provides clients with a broader view than stations get from the perspective of their local markets. Reps often advise clients on programming, conduct research, and act generally as all-around consultants. In return for their services, rep companies collect a commission of from 10 to 15 percent on the national spot sales of their client-stations.

Network sales staffs and national reps are natural rivals. Each group aims at the same target — advertisers with a need for reaching national audiences. The major nonbroadcast medium competing for these advertisers is national magazines. They too try to satisfy advertisers who do not want to buy the entire "network" of a magazine's national distribution list. Their version of spot advertising is regionalized editions. Editorial and most of the advertising content remains the same, but room is left for inserting advertising of regional interest. *Time* has carried this process to the extreme of offering 228 editions with specialized circulation, either as to regions or as to types of readers.

13.3 Integration of Commercials in Programming

Sponsor Identification   Section 317 of the Communications Act of 1934 requires that commercials be recognizably distinct from programs. Disclosure must be made as to the source of anything a station puts on the air for which it receives payment, either in money or some other "valuable consideration." Known as *sponsor identification*, this disclosure is intended to prevent deception of the public, which might otherwise be subjected to propaganda or "disinformation" from unknown sources.

The sources of ordinary commercials are, of course, self-evident. Anonymity is the last thing commercial advertisers desire. But propagandists who use what is called *editorial advertising* may not always be so anxious to reveal their true identity. And of course the sources of any under-the-table payments to disc jockeys or others for on-the-air favors certainly have no wish to be identified.

Thus the integration of commercial matter into the programming must be handled in systematic ways to ensure its proper identification and to prevent violation of the communications act as well as for the convenience of sales departments.

Trafficking of Commercials   After sales have been made to advertisers, the *traffic department* has the responsibility of scheduling commercials in accordance with contracts. For this reason the system of scattering commercials throughout the broadcast day is referred to as *trafficking* commercials. The alternative system, used in many other countries, clusters all advertising in designated time-periods, leaving programs free of commercial interruption.

Because the placement of commercials with regard to programs, other commercials, and other types of announcements is of the greatest interest both to advertisers and programmers, the trafficking of commercials takes on considerable importance. It requires specific, predictable points when commercials can be logically inserted in the flow of programming.

Sponsored Programs   An advantage of sponsored programs was that advertisers could control when and how commercials were to be inserted and could shape programs so as to integrate commercials smoothly and logically. In the few instances of fully sponsored programs that now occur, the sponsor often clusters commercials at the beginning and end so as not to interrupt program flow.

Participation Programs   When stations took over the responsibility for programs from advertisers, they at first maintained the fiction of sponsorship by referring to advertisers whose commercials occurred during breaks within programs as "participating sponsors." For this reason the term *participations* (or *participating spots*) was adopted.

Vestiges of this concept survive in the *billboards* seen at the open and close of some television programs — lists of "participating" advertisers thrown in at no added cost as an incentive to buyers of spots. Billboards are often used to introduce major sports events for which buyers pay premium prices; the higher prices entitle them to special treatment, such as the extra exposure they get from billboard listings.

Today most broadcast advertising is sold simply as *spot announcements* (more briefly, just *spots*). In its published directories of media rates, Standard Rate and Data Service (§13.6) offers stations four different ways of stating their rates: in terms of spots, participating announcements, packages (spots sold in groups), and programs (sponsored adver-

tising). Most stations devote most of their space to listing their rates for spots, paying little attention to the other three classifications.

Some types of programs have natural breaks, allowing for insertion of spots without interrupting the flow. The breaks between rounds of a boxing match or between record cuts on a DJ show are examples. In other cases the break must be artificially contrived. Part of the art of writing half-hour situation comedies lies in building the plot to a suspenseful but nevertheless logical break-off point halfway through for inserting the middle commercial.

Opinions on what qualifies as a "natural" break can differ. The industry now regards breaks between stories in news programs as natural, but originally the interruption of news with commercials was regarded as highly unprofessional and not at all "natural." Certainly viewers often complain about the arbitrary breaks made in theatrical feature films, which were not, of course, written like television shows with seemingly natural climaxes in the action every ten minutes where breaks would be appropriate.

Sustaining Programs   Some programs are neither sponsored nor subject to participating spot advertising. These are *sustaining* programs, now limited almost exclusively to public affairs programs of a type that could not, without a serious breach of taste, be subjected to commercialization. Presidential addresses and state funerals are examples.

At one time the FCC urged stations to devote 20 percent of their time to sustaining programs, looking upon them as having a "balance wheel" function. The range of program types would be wider, the FCC reasoned, if not all of them had to meet the test of being suitable for sponsorship. Later, the commission decided that commercial motives, in the absence of widespread sponsorship of programs, were no longer as restrictive as they had been originally. "Sponsorship fosters rather than diminishes the availability of important public affairs and 'cultural' programs," wrote the FCC in lifting its previous emphasis on sustaining programs (44 FCC 2315, 1960).

Station Breaks   Partly as a matter of law and partly as a matter of custom, stations insert *identification announcements* (IDs) between programs and between the major segments of very long programs.* Because ID announcements represented breaks in the program sequence they were called "station break announcements." They opened up convenient slots into which to insert commercials for advertisers other than sponsors.

Networks had to observe the legal ID requirement by interrupting their program feeds periodically to allow affiliates to make station break announcements. Thus grew up the practice of cutting network programs a bit short to allow affiliates time not only for ID announcements but also for one or more commercial announcements. When station break commercials come between high-rated network programs they are, of course, extremely profitable to affiliates.

Promos and PSAs   Also figuring in programming at the junctures where commercials normally appear are two types of announcements that are quasi-commercial in nature, promos and PSAs.

Promos (for "promotional announcements") call attention to future programs of networks and stations. Although the FCC does not require them to be logged as commercials, they are in effect self-advertisements for stations and networks, and are considered to be crucially important elements in the strategies of competition (Lipton, 1978).

PSAs ("public service announcements") resemble commercials but are devoted to noncommercial ends and are therefore broadcast without charge by stations and networks. They give broadcasters a convenient way of fulfilling some of their public service obligations and are useful as temporary fillers for unsold commercial openings.

13.4 Time and Taste Standards

Evolution of Standards   In addition to agreed-upon ways of integrating commercial matter in the flow of programming, general consensus is also needed on the amount of time commercials may be allowed to occupy and the standards of taste they should be expected to meet.

Far from being permanently fixed, such standards constantly evolve, reflecting changing conditions in society generally as well as within the broadcasting industry. Society grows more permissive, the industry more competitive. Products that only a few years previously could not possibly have been advertised on television ("feminine hygiene" aids, for example) became routine in the 1970s. Increased competition, not only from new broadcast stations but also from other sources such as cable television, de-

*The rule requires IDs, consisting of station call letters and community of license, at hourly intervals, or at a "natural break" if a program runs longer (47 CFR 73. 1201). When regulation first began, ID requirements were more stringent, making it easier to track down improperly operated and unauthorized stations.

mands increasingly flexible time and taste standards.

A constant tension exists between the urge to cram ever more commercial material into the schedule and the need to avoid alienating audiences by intolerable levels of interruption. At the same time, the desire to exploit every tactic of persuasion and to capitalize on every available source of advertising income collides with the need to stay reasonably close to the socially acceptable.

These are not struggles between crass commercialism and pure idealism. They are pragmatic encounters between the points of view of sales directors and program directors, striving to reach an accommodation that will maximize present income without endangering future income by driving away the audience.

Mandatory Time Standards Contrary to what many people think, the Federal Communications Commission does not explicitly set a maximum number of commercial minutes per hour of programming. True, the commission once proposed to start regulating commercials, but quickly dropped the idea when a bill to forbid such regulation was introduced into Congress (House CIFC, 1963).

Nevertheless, from its earliest days the commission regarded the relative prominence of commercials as having a significant bearing on operation in the public interest. Television license applications and renewal forms require applicants to state the number of commercial minutes per hour they plan to allow, or have allowed in the past (similar radio requirements were dropped in 1981). Applicants who exceed the industry's own time-standards code may be asked to justify the excess. Thus the FCC tacitly endorsed the

industry code governing amount of commercial time without officially adopting it, leaving open the possibility of case-by-case variations.

The FCC forbids what it calls "program-length commercials." The term refers to productions in which "the non-commercial segment of the program is so closely interwoven with the sponsor's commercial messages that it is apparent that the program as a whole promotes the sponsor's products or services" (39 FR 4043, 1974). Radio programs that originate from shopping centers or sponsors' premises are typically prone to this abuse.

Voluntary Time Standards The industry standards tacitly accepted by the FCC are those of the National Association of Broadcasters (NAB), the largest trade association of the industry. It has set up voluntary standards for both advertising and programs for the industry as a whole. The NAB Code Authority, a relatively independent unit of the association, administers the two codes, one for radio and one for television.

Stations and networks may subscribe to the codes even if they choose not to be members of the NAB itself. Subscriptions are voluntary and the Code Authority has no enforcement powers. A higher percentage of television than of radio stations belong to the NAB, but of those that do belong, a higher proportion of radio stations than television outlets subscribe to the code (Exhibit 13.4).

The NAB codes cover two aspects of broadcast operations — programs (discussed later, in §18.6) and commercials. Setting time standards for commercials is complicated by the fact that seven types of material not technically classified as commercials may interrupt the flow of television programs, contributing to the impression of "commercial clutter." These include:

1. *Billboards*: brief listing of participating advertisers at the open and close of a program.

2. *Bumpers*: transitional material used to separate program matter from commercials (for example, "Don't go away! We'll be right back after these announcements.").

3. *Credits*: names of cast members and other program participants, most of which are required by union rules.

4. *Plugs*: short identifications of prize donors in game shows.

5. *Promos*: information about upcoming programs (§13.3).

6. *Public service announcements*: sustaining equivalents of commercial announcements (§13.3).

7. *Station IDs*: station identifications, some required by law (§13.3).

The NAB Television Code deals with the problem of definition by lumping several of these types of announcements with commercials and calling them collectively "nonprogram material" (the radio code speaks simply of "advertising"). There are many exceptions and qualifications, but in brief the nominal code limits on nonprogram material per hour are as follows:

- Radio: 18 mins.
- TV affiliates: prime time, 9½ mins.; other time, 16 mins.
- TV independents: prime time 14 mins.; other time, 16 mins.*

Lack of uniform time limits reflects the fact that radio and independent television stations have smaller audiences than network affiliates and try to compensate by selling more advertising (at lower rates of course). The same reasoning applies to the fact that more time for advertising is allowed in non-prime-time television than in prime time. This distinction may also reflect the industry's awareness that business executives and political leaders (the opinion makers who might influence legislation to impose limits on commercials) usually watch television only after business hours.

*References to the codes in this chapter are based on the 22d edition of the radio code (1980) and the 21st edition of the television code (1980). Single copies of the codes can be obtained free from the NAB, 1771 N Street, N.W., Washington, D.C. 20036.

Exhibit 13.4
NAB membership and code subscribership

	Radio	Television
Commercial stations on the air	7,757	737
Percentage NAB members	60	89
Percentage code subscribers	50	69

Comment: Among the vast number of commercial radio stations on the air many are too marginal economically to be able to afford either NAB membership or code membership. Some, of course, decline to join or subscribe for other reasons as well.

Sources: NAB/Code data, as of June 1, 1980, courtesy NAB Code Authority.

Decoding the Code

It would seem to be a fairly simple task to set up quantitative rules to limit television commercials. Of course, the code makers had to make allowances for differences between prime time and nonprime time and between affiliates and nonaffiliates; and decide which of the seven types of noncommercial or quasi-commercial announcements should be counted in the allotted commercial time; and calculate how many interruptions per hour should be allowed (the code says four); and decide how many consecutive announcements should be allowed per hour (the code says five). Even after all that, the code makers had to satisfy a variety of claims for exceptions and special rules for special cases. Some examples:

■ *Not counted* as "nonprogram time" are public service announcements, program credits (unless especially long), and certain voice-over announcements and other special material.

■ *Exceptions to length limits* include those short announcements (often numerous) about donors of prizes in game shows.

■ *Exceptions to commercial interruption limits* include news, weather, and sports programs.

■ *Exceptions to consecutive announcement limits* include sponsored programs in which sponsors have reduced the allowable number of interruptions.

■ *Waivers* of time standards may be granted on a case-by-case basis for programs that "provide a special service to the public in which certain material normally classified as nonprogram is an informative and necessary part of the program content."

There are other special exceptions, too involved to explain in a brief space. Decoding the code is far from easy for the ordinary viewer. After monitoring an hour's programming on a code-subscriber station, such a viewer would almost certainly find the station seeming to violate the code — not because the station actually flouted the rules, but because the code is so loaded with exceptions and qualifications that only an expert can interpret it.

The time limits referred to above are only nominal because of the many exceptions the codes allow. Radio's 18-minutes-per-hour limit was compromised by a 1977 amendment saying that "for good cause and when in the public interest broadcasters may depart from this standard in order to fulfill their responsibilities to the communities they service" (not, it should noted, merely in order to make money!). The television code's more complex time limits are qualified by exceptions too extensive to enumerate (see Box).

Individual Announcement Length Implicit in the very word *announcement* is the idea of brevity. Commercials that occupy all or most of a program's time violate FCC rules against program-length commercials. The most common announcement length is 30 seconds, the preferred standard adopted by the networks in 1972 when they abandoned the previous 60-second length in order to schedule more announcements without increasing the minutes-per-hour maximum. Announcements varying from about 10 seconds to about three minutes are also used. Extremely short announcements that might take advantage of *subliminal perception* (an alleged tendency of listeners and viewers to absorb messages unconsciously) are ruled out by the FCC.

Announcements as short as seven seconds are used in game shows to repay advertisers who donate merchandise and services for the sake of brief mentions and pictorial displays. The FCC does not consider these mentions, called *plugs*, as commercial matter as long as the donors do not pay any fee and the identification of the donors is "reasonably related" to the use made of the gifts in programs (47 CFR 73.1212). By this ruse, game shows can greatly exceed the nominal NAB code limits, both as to total commercial time and as to number of consecutive announcements.

Excessively long commercials are regarded as *pitch advertising*, a term derived from "pitchmen," slick-talking street or carnival vendors of sleazy merchandise. A common type of broadcast pitch describes or demonstrates a product at great length, usually making exaggerated claims and promises. The NAB Television Code states that pitch advertising is "inconsistent with good broadcast practice and generally damages the reputation of the industry and the advertising profession."

Loudness　Commercial salience is affected by style as well as by length. Harsh voices, rapid delivery, excessive repetition, and loudness are examples of stylistic aspects of commercials often deliberately used to make them more obtrusive.*

One of the most persistent subjects of complaints to the FCC is the loudness of commercials. After a study, the commission

issued a policy statement in 1973, declining to set up hard-and-fast rules because of the difficulty of measuring loudness objectively. The commission made a new study in 1978 and reopened the subject the following year (Hassinger, 1978). In issuing the notice of inquiry, the commission noted that "loudness is a very complex phenomenon. It has both sensory and psychological aspects and is perceived differently by men and women, and by young and old. Even within individuals it is affected by interest, time of day, tolerance, semantic content and health" (72 FCC 2d 679, 1979).

Standards of Taste　Many products and services not usually advertised on broadcasting stations are nevertheless perfectly legal and are advertised without hindrance in the print media. This double standard of taste is one more evidence of the special obligations that society lays on broadcasting because of its unique nature as a home medium accessible to all.

Few legally advertisable products and services are designated as flatly "not acceptable" by the NAB codes. The most conspicuous example of self-imposed advertising abstinence is hard liquor. Beer and wine are acceptable, but "only when presented in the best of good taste and discretion." This means, for example, that performers in beer commercials may not quaff their brew on camera. Not only is the gusto that drinkers of soft drinks portray forbidden — even sober sipping is considered indiscreet.

A second major area of concern for the codes in the advertising arena is what they call "personal products," a term covering such touchy subjects as deodorants, feminine hygiene, toilet tissue, and contraceptives. To keep abreast of changing social mores, the

---

*Simulating a news flash to capture attention as an attention-getting device was ruled out in 1938, when a drama about an "invasion" from Mars presented in a news-program format caused a dangerous panic (§20.2).

Code Authority issues frequent interpretations and minor changes in its rules governing such advertising. So far, contraceptives have not been cleared, although some maverick stations experimented with condom advertising as early as the mid 1970s (*Broadcasting*, 14 Aug. 1975). In 1980 the code board was conducting surveys to test public acceptance, and it seemed likely that contraceptives would soon be discreetly advertised on television.

Additional areas that the codes single out for cautionary comment are fortunetelling (not acceptable), medical products (and the use of simulated doctors, nurses, and laboratories in advertising such products), contests, testimonials, and children's advertising.

Children's Advertising Standards

Consumer groups such as Action for Children's Television (§9.8) contend that because young children have not yet learned to understand the difference between advertising and entertainment, they need special protection from commercial exploitation. After conducting hearings on this and related questions, the FCC issued a statement of policy in 1974. The statement recommended that broadcasters voluntarily adopt special standards for children's advertising in four areas: amount of advertising per hour, separation of commercials from program content, use of program hosts as salespersons, and tie-ins between products and programs. A follow-up study in 1979 by the FCC Children's Task Force appraised the results of the 1974 statement:

1. *Time Standards.* The FCC recommended that stations follow standards added to the NAB Television Code shortly before the policy statement was issued. The NAB reduced allowable nonprogram material in children's nonprime-time programs from 12 to 9½ minutes per hour on weekends, from 16 to 12 minutes on weekdays. The task force reported that compliance with these standards had not been complete but was generally satisfactory.

2. *Separation.* The most frequently used bumper — simply a fade to black between program material and commercials — was not considered adequate separation by consumer advocates. ABC, however, received praise for developing 5- to 10-second bumpers consisting of animated spot announcements that conveyed useful messages to children.

3. *Host Selling.* The FCC agreed in 1974 with consumer complaints that it was unfair to children for the hosts of their programs to deliver sales pitches in the same programs. The task force reported that this practice had been discontinued.

4. *Product Tie-ins.* In its 1974 statement the FCC noted with disapproval the sneaky exploitation of children by slipping mentions of advertised products into the body of programs. For example, the hostess of a children's show ended a prayer by saying to children in the studio, "Now you can have your [Brand Name] or any juice from the XYZ Dairy." The task force reported that this type of exploitation had been eliminated.

Commercial Clutter Advertisers became concerned about the marked increase in television *clutter* that started in the late 1960s. Clutter refers to the feeling of disorder and confusion that arises from long strings of commercial, quasi-commercial, and noncommercial announcements. Clutter increased because of several developments, including the decline of sponsorship, the change from 60 to 30 seconds as the standard length for network commercials, and an escalation in the intensity of program promotion as a result of ABC's challenge to the older networks (§8.5).

In any event, historically the codes have steadily increased permissible commercial length. Between the first television code in 1953 and the nineteenth in 1976, the allowable time for nonprogram material rose by 35 percent in prime time and 68 percent in other periods (Ray & Webb, 1978). The only instance of *reduction* in commercial time allowances by the code board occurred when, in response to pressures from consumers and the implied threat of FCC action, it cut back on children's television advertising, as noted in the previous subsection.

During the 1970s complaints about clutter by advertising agencies, station representatives, and advertisers steadily mounted. It was possible to count 37 interruptions in only seven minutes of programming (Meyer, 1970) and 30 commercials in a typical daytime television hour-long news program (Doan, 1973). Advertisers object because clutter undermines the effectiveness of commercials. A 1978 study, for example, confirmed that the longer the string of nonprogram items, the less people can remember about commercials in the middle of the string (Ray & Webb, 1978). It should be noted, however, that such research focused on clutter's adverse effects on *commercial* messages, not its adverse effects on the enjoyment of *programs* by the long-suffering public.

Responding to pressure from the advertising community, the NAB revised its television commercial standards in 1978 by slightly broadening its definition of nonprogram materials.

13.5 Deceptive Advertising

Federal Trade Commission Prosecution for outright deception in advertising falls under the jurisdiction of the Federal Trade Commission (FTC) rather than that of the FCC. Use of fraudulent advertising by a broadcaster can be cited by the FCC as showing lack of the necessary character qualifications to be a licensee, but the FCC cannot prosecute licensees for violating the fair trade laws.

The FTC's responsibilities extend to all media, not just broadcasting, and to all types of unfair trade practices, not just deceptive advertising. Its duties are too multiple and too varied to leave time for a thorough screening of the tens of thousands of commercials that reach the air each year. Indeed, it was not until 1958, after television advertising became a major force, that the FTC took much notice of broadcast commercials. At about that time, blatant misuse of demonstrations in television advertising finally compelled FTC attention.

Demonstrations The FTC won its first deceptive demonstration case after a four-year battle against Colgate-Palmolive for deceptively "proving" the superiority of a brand of shaving cream. The demonstration claimed the product was so effective that it could be used to "shave" sandpaper. But the demonstration shown as proving this claim used a Plexiglas mockup, not actual sandpaper. It took 80 minutes for the cream to soften real sandpaper. An appeals court twice reversed the FTC's finding that such a demonstration was unlawful. Finally the Supreme Court vindicated the FTC's claim. By that time it had been conceded on all sides that the original sandpaper claim could not be proved. The Supreme Court focused on a more fundamental question: is it unlawful to use substitute "props" for real items in staging television commercial demonstrations? The Court said it was (380 US 374, 1965).

Corrective Advertising The FTC settles most cases of alleged advertising deception *by stipulation*, an informal (and hence time-saving) way of getting advertisers to drop objectionable practices voluntarily. If a formal complaint becomes necessary the FTC can seek a *consent order*, another nonpunitive measure under which the advertiser agrees to stop the offending practice without admitting guilt.

Actual guilt has to be proved before the FTC can obtain a *cease and desist order* forcing compliance with the law. These orders can be appealed to the courts, which usually means considerable delay in bringing the objectionable advertising to a halt.

In the early 1970s the FTC introduced a new penalty, designed to go beyond merely forcing false advertisers to "cease and desist." Called *corrective advertising*, it required offending advertisers (if they wished to continue advertising the products in question) to devote some of their future advertising budgets to setting the record straight.

The first such corrective campaign occurred in 1971, when ITT Continental Baking Co. agreed to begin a 12-month series of corrective commercials for Profile Bread. The company agreed to devote a quarter of the year's advertising budget for Profile to announcements that read in part as follows:

Does Profile have fewer calories than other breads? No, Profile has about the same per ounce as other breads. To be exact, Profile has seven fewer calories per slice. That's because it's sliced thinner. But eating Profile will not cause you to lose weight.

A reduction of seven calories is insignificant. It's total calories and balanced nutrition that counts.

Not until 1978 was the legal right of the FTC to require such corrective advertising confirmed by the Supreme Court, which refused to review a lower court's decision in favor of the FTC (562 F 2d 749, 1977). The case involved Listerine, a mouthwash sold by Warner-Lambert Co. For nearly a hundred years Listerine had been on the market as a preventative for colds and sore throats. In 1972 the FTC concluded that the claim was false because Listerine affects only bacteria, not the viruses that cause colds.

The appeals court approved the FTC's requirement that Warner-Lambert either cease advertising Listerine or include a corrective statement in ten million dollars worth of future advertising (the amount was based on the company's average annual expenditure for Listerine advertising during the decade previous to the FTC suit). However, the court softened the impact of the corrective statement by deleting the phrase "Contrary to prior advertising," which the FTC wanted included with the disclaimer that "Listerine will not help prevent colds or sore throats or lessen their severity."

As the court's tenderness for the feelings of the offending advertiser suggests, corrective advertising has hardly amounted to sackcloth and ashes for those found guilty of deception. The FTC has imposed the corrective penalty in only about a dozen cases since the first one in 1971. And the rectifying messages have been so skillfully worded that probably few consumers recognized corrective advertisements as admissions of prior misrepresentations. Nevertheless, corrective advertising represented a positive move in the direction of consumer welfare by an agency that had previously been regarded as ineffectual in this area of its responsibility.

Self-Regulation   The NAB Television Code advertising standards include warnings against misleading demonstrations. At the Code Authority's request, advertisers must turn over to it "documentation adequate to support the validity and truthfulness of claims, demonstrations and testimonials contained in their commercial messages." The Code Authority reviews thousands of commercials a year, using a panel of medical and scientific experts to analyze the often highly technical research reports upon which advertisers base their claims.

The major networks subscribe to the NAB codes, giving the codes far more clout than station subscription alone would confer. The networks also have their own standards departments to screen both commercial and program materials to ensure conformity with their corporate policies. The former head of the NBC broadcast standards department said that advertiser claims offered the most difficult problems to screeners of the 45,000 commercials that were submitted for clearance annually. Only about a third of these finally went on the air, though most were withdrawn for reasons other than unresolvable conflicts with NBC standards (Traviesas, 1980).

Advertising self-regulation comes also from the National Advertising Review Board (NARB), which evaluates complaints about advertising in any of the media that are forwarded to it by the National Advertising Division of the Council of Better Business Bureaus. The NARB was formed in 1971 in response to growing public cynicism about the truthfulness of advertising claims. It does not review advertising in advance as do the NAB and the broadcasting networks. Instead it deals with charges brought against advertisements after they are broadcast or printed.

Concealment of Sponsorship   A little-noticed but potentially dangerous type of de-

ception in broadcast advertising is failure to observe *sponsor identification* rules (§13.3). The mention of a trade name or a place of business provides automatic sponsor identification, but the purchasers of advertising time are not always advertisers in the business sense. Examples are government agencies, religious organizations, and political candidates. In 1977 the FCC found it necessary to issue a public notice, commenting on "widespread licensee failure" to observe the sponsor identification rules. It noted as an example an evangelical religious organization that financed a campaign of paid announcements featuring the phrase, "I have found it," without disclosing either that the announcements were paid for or that the source of the payments was a religious sect (66 FCC 2d 302).

13.6 Advertising Rates

Problem of Pricing   Putting a price tag on advertising time is complicated by the fact that time has value to advertisers only in terms of the audiences it represents. Because audiences constantly change, so does the value of time to the advertiser.

The most stable factors that affect prices of broadcast time are *market size* (§12.6), *station facilities* (frequency, power, antenna location, and other physical factors that influence coverage), and *network affiliation*. Within a given market and within limits imposed by a station's facilities, the major variable is audience availability. Audiences change with time of day, day of week, and season of the year. Station managers have no day-to-day control over these relatively stable factors.

The major dynamic factors — the ones that make one station successful and another similar station less successful — are the variables of *programming, promotion,* and *sales.* Good management can lure audiences away from competitors with attractive program schedules supported by effective promotion, while an efficient sales department can lure advertisers away from competitors with persuasive arguments and solicitous attention to advertisers' needs.

No standard way of factoring all these variables into a formula for setting appropriate broadcast rates has been devised (Besen, 1973). However, market forces eventually tend to bring prices to an economically rational level. The main test of reasonableness is the *cost per thousand* (CPM) standard — the cost of reaching a thousand people or households. It is calculated by dividing the number (in thousands) of people or households reached by a commercial message into the charges for disseminating the message. For example, if a spot costing $90 reached an estimated 30,000 viewers, the CPM of the spot is 90 divided by 30, or $3. CPM is useful for comparing one medium with another (newspaper vs. television, radio vs. television, etc.), or for comparing one station with another in any given market.

CPM measurements have their limitations: they can be no better than the research on which they are based, and in any event are based on past, not future, performance. Nevertheless, in the long run if a station's CPM is seriously out of line with the CPM of competing stations and media, it will be passed over by advertisers and advertising agencies.

Radio Station Rates Broadcast advertising depends for its effectiveness on its cumulative effect. Spots are therefore bought not singly but in groups (a *spot schedule* or a specially priced spot *package*). Thus the *Broadcasting/Cable Yearbook* in listing sample rates of radio stations in its directory gives the rates for one-minute spots scheduled 12 times a week in four different day parts. For example, a small, rural station in Georgia picked at random from the 1981 yearbook charged $4 per spot in each day part; a large, metropolitan station in Ohio, also chosen at random, varied its charges from a high of $94 per spot in the 6 A.M.–10 A.M. day part to a low of $40 in the 7 P.M.–midnight day part.

The small station in the example does not bother to price day parts differently because it would hardly pay to keep track of different rates when the basic charge is so low. The larger the station and market, the more expensive the time and the more refined rate differences become, reflecting even hour-to-hour changes in audience size and composition.

For detailed radio rate information, buyers consult either individual station rate cards or *Spot Radio Rates and Data,* a monthly publication of Standard Rate and Data Service (SRDS). This publication, especially valuable to national spot time-buyers, gathers rate-card information from stations all over the country, presenting it in a standardized format. A typical SRDS radio entry is shown in Exhibit 13.6.1. In addition to information on rates, rate cards contain such information as the following:

■ *Time Classes.* Typically radio stations divide their time into four day parts, with different prices for each. The station in Exhibit 13.6.1 also uses three subclasses within each time class.
■ *Spot Position.* Subclasses within time classes are usually based on the way spots are scheduled. *Fixed-position* spots have an assured place in the schedule and are sold at a premium rate. *Run-of-schedule* spots (ROS) may be scheduled anywhere within the time period designated in the sales contract. Some stations *rotate* spots to give each advertiser

Exhibit 13.6.1
Sample SRDS radio station rate listing

K A B L
1925
OAKLAND

K A B L - F M
1965
SAN FRANCISCO

Christal

NAB **RAB** NRBA

Subscriber to the NAB Radio Code
Media Code 4 205 7350 3.00
KABL-Shamrock Broadcasting Co., Inc., 632 Commercial St., San Francisco, Calif. 94111. Phone
415-788-5225. TWX 910-372-7489.

1. PERSONNEL
Pres. & Gen'l Mgr.—Bill Clark.
National Sales Manager—Tom Anderson.
Local Sales Manager—Mike Grinsell.
2. REPRESENTATIVES
The Christal Company, Inc.
3. FACILITIES
5,000 w.; 960 kc. Directional.
Operating schedule: 24 hours daily. PST.
FM-ERP 100,000. 98.1 mc. Stereo.
Operating schedule: Same as AM.
Simulcast Mon thru Sat 4-10 am.
4. AGENCY COMMISSION
15% net time if paid by 20th of following month.
5. GENERAL ADVERTISING See coded regulations
General: 1b, 2a, 2b, 3a, 3b, 3c, 3d, 4a, 5, 6a, 8
Rate Protection: 10e, 11e, 12e, 14e, 15a, 15b, 15e
Basic Rates: 20b, 21a, 21b, 21d, 24b, 24c, 25a, 28b,
29a, 33b.
Contracts: 40a, 41, 44a, 45, 46, 47a, 51c.
Comb.; Cont. Discounts: 60e, 60i, 60j, 61a, 62b,
62d, 62c.
Cancellation: 70a, 70c, 71a, 72, 73a, 73b
Prod. Services: 80, 81
Affiliated with Christal Radio Networks.
TIME RATES
No. 23 Eff 9/1/79—Rec'd 9/10/79.
Drivetime—Mon thru Sun 5:30-10 am & 3-8 pm.
Daytime—Mon thru Sun 10 am-3 pm.
Evening—Mon thru Sun 8 pm-midnight.

6. SPOT ANNOUNCEMENTS

GRID—DAYTIME—1 MINUTE

	6 ti	12 ti	18 ti	20 ti	30 ti
PER WK:					
PER YR:	52x	156x	312x	520x	750x
I	140	135	130	125	120
II	130	125	120	115	110
III	115	110	105	100	95

DRIVETIME

I	135	130	125	120	115
II	125	120	115	110	105
III	110	105	110	95	90

EVENING

I	80	75	70	65	60
II	75	70	65	60	55
III	70	65	60	55	50

30 sec: 80% of 1-min.

7. PACKAGE PLANS
TAP—MON THRU SUN—1/3DT, 1/3DR, 1/3EVE

	12 ti	18 ti	24 ti
PER WK, EA:			
PER YR, EA:	156x	312x	500x
I	112	107	102
II	102	97	92
III	92	87	82

IMPACT PLAN—MON THRU SUN 5:30 AM-8 PM

	12 ti	18 ti	24 ti
PER WK, EA:			
PER YR, EA:	156x	312x	500x
I	125	120	115
II	115	110	105
III	100	95	90

30 sec: 80% of 1-min.

SUPER EFFICIENCY PLAN

1 MIN/LESS, PER WK:	20 ti	40 ti
1/2 Mon thru Sat 8 pm-midnight; 1/2 Sat & Sun 6 am-8 pm, ea.	65	—
1/2 Mon thru Sat 8 pm-midnight; 1/2 Sat & Sun 6 am-8 pm, ea.		70

WEEKEND PLAN—SAT, SUN, MON 6 AM-8 PM
30 ti, 1 min/less...... 75   10 ti, 1 min/less...... 80
NIGHTTIME IMPACT—SUN THRU SAT 8 PM-
MIDNIGHT PREEMPTIBLE
20 ti, 1 min/less...... 50   10 ti, 1 min/less...... 55
AM non-simulcast only: Deduct 5.00.
FM only: 50% of above rates.
8. SPECIAL FEATURES
Newscasts—incl 10-sec open & close plus 1-min spot,
applicable 1-min plus 10.00.
Maximum discount: 12 ti per wk/312x per yr.

Stations pay SRDS to list their rates and other information of interest to advertisers and agencies in its national directory. In this example KABL (AM and FM) of Oakland–San Francisco starts by naming its national representative and noting that it is a member of the NAB, the Radio Advertising Bureau, and the National Radio Broadcaster's Association.

Listings must conform to a standard SRDS pattern, represented by the numbered sections. To save space, SRDS uses a number code for the various policies and contract terms listed in section 5. For example: the code number 4a in section 5 of KABL's listing means that it accepts beer and wine advertising; 6a means that it accepts sponsored religious programming; 8 means that it does not accept per inquiry advertising.

The actual rates, listed as dollar amounts without the dollar signs in section 6 and following, vary according to spot length, time of day, number bought, and other factors as shown.

Source: Reproduced with permission from Standard Rate and Data Service, *Spot Radio Rates and Data,* July 1980, p. 162.

the benefit of varying positions within a time segment.

■ *Preemptibility*. Another basis for varying the price of spots is the degree of *preemptibility* risk they face. In order to keep their inventories of spot availabilities as fully sold as possible, stations offer unsold openings at a cut rate. These are called *preemptible spots*, meaning that the station can cancel them when a full-rate customer is found. Spots that are sold as preemptible with no notice are offered at an even lower rate than spots preemptible after a stipulated period following preemption notice.

■ *Package Plans*. Stations offer a variety of cut-rate package plans that include several spots, scheduled at various times of the day. These can be helpful to time-salespersons, especially when they deal with small local merchants with little experience with broadcast advertising.

■ *Special Features*. Spots associated with particularly popular programs are often sold at a higher rate. Many stations list a number of such features, including both local programs and also *coop network* programs in which stations are entitled to sell cooperative spots (§13.2).

TV Station Rates   Brief information on television station rates can also be obtained from the *Broadcasting/Cable Yearbook*'s station directory, but many (including all the top-rank stations) prefer not to quote hard-and-fast rates for entire day parts, especially in a publication that comes out only once a year. In fact some television stations refrain from publishing rates in *any* form, relying instead on their sales personnel to negotiate rates with each client individually. Stations can get away with this somewhat high-handed treatment of potential customers because the demand for television time is high in major markets. An idea of the range of television rates can be gained from Exhibit 13.6.2, which compares prices for television spots in four markets of varying size.

Listings in the SRDS *Television Spot Rates and Data* books are similar to those for radio. The main difference is that television rates are far more variable. It is not uncommon for a station to list over a hundred different prices for spots, using a device known as a *rate grid*. For example, a station might list 20 different time periods or program titles down the left side of its grid. Across the top it might list six different rate levels, numbered I through VI. This arrangement would create 120 cells or boxes into which specific prices can be entered. Such a grid gives sales personnel great flexibility in negotiating deals without having to resort to under-the-table rate-cutting. The six rate levels can be defined quite arbitrarily, enabling the station to quote six different prices for essentially the same spot.

Network Rates   Extreme differentiation in rates is especially true of network television. Changes of rate occur even for the same spot position in the same program in the course of a single season if the audience for the program changes significantly. In the 1979–1980 season, 30-second network spots in regular prime-time programs averaged $67,000 each but the cost could rise to $150,000 for the most popular regular shows and as high as $200,000 for outstanding special programs (BBDO, 1979). It must be emphasized that these were *average* rates. Rates for specific spots in specific time-slots vary widely.

SRDS publishes a volume on network rates and data, covering both radio and television networks and including the nonwired radio networks operated by some of the large advertising agencies and national sales representatives. However, none of the major networks, radio or television, releases details on rates to SRDS, preferring to remain flexible, free to negotiate each sale individually.

Variant Rate Practices Three types of commercial practices fall outside the normal rate-card listings previously described: trade deals, time brokerage, and per inquiry.

(1) *Trade deals* (also called *tradeouts*), the exchange of time for goods and services, have always been a common practice in broadcasting. In the everyday type of trade deal, stations run commercials at no charge in exchange for office space, the use of a vehicle, office supplies, and so on.

A more specialized type of trade deal involves the exchange of prizes for mentions (*plugs*) from seven to ten seconds in length on game shows (§13.4). For costly prizes the advertiser receives one or more of the short plugs; for the less expensive prizes the advertiser pays a fee in addition to donating merchandise for a single plug. Advertisers can buy as many as 20 plugs for the price of a 30-second commercial on a network game show (Sanno, 1980).

In the 1970s another special type of television trade deal, *barter syndication*, began to become popular. It involves trading commercial time for programs, as described in §8.7. The annual FCC television financial report for 1979 indicated that only about 2 percent of industry revenue came from tradeouts and barter transactions. The actual amount may be larger because, it is said, stations tend to underreport these sources of revenue. Even so, such transactions represent only a small fraction of television sales; they receive disproportionate attention, however, because

Exhibit 13.6.2
Influence of market size on TV rates

		Price for 30-second spot in		
Market	Market rank	Prime time	Early fringe	Day time
Flagstaff, Ariz.	208	$ 70	$ 32	$ 17
Rockford, Ill.	105	200	180	45
New Orleans, La.	36	850	350	160
Sacramento, Cal.	22	1,800	700	300

Comment: Prices are quoted for a specific station in each market and refer to rates for national advertisers. The table shows the strong correlation between market size and rates. Because TV audiences vary more in size according to day part than radio audiences, TV rates vary more widely by day part than do radio rates. Unlike small-market radio stations, even very small-market TV stations vary rates according to day part.

Source: Based on data in station directory in *Broadcasting/Cable Yearbook, 1981*, Broadcasting Publications, Inc., Washington, D.C., 1981.

barter syndication looms large in the one field where station program directors have the most say-so, the field of prime-time access programming.

(2) *Time brokerage* refers to selling time in chunks to brokers who then resell it with whatever markup they can get. Foreign language programming is often brokered in this way. Time brokerage was once regarded as a somewhat questionable practice because it often meant surrender of licensee control over programming, in violation of one of the FCC's most emphatic rules (§16.5). However, in its 1981 report affirming radio deregulation, the FCC spoke approvingly of time brokerage as a means of giving groups access to air time. Those who cannot afford to operate a station might at least be able to afford a few hours of their own air time each week.

(3) *Per inquiry* (PI) deals, favored by mail-order firms in cut-rate, late-night time periods, commit the advertiser to pay not for station time but only for the number of inquiries or the number of items sold in direct response to PI commercials. Most broadcasters oppose PI advertising in principle because it underrates the value of broadcast advertising. Advertising's worth cannot be measured fairly by direct sales alone because it also produces such effects as creating a favorable image of the advertiser and product, imprinting trade names in the consciousness of audiences, and leading indirectly to sales at a later time, all in combination with other influences.

13.7 Selling Broadcast Advertising

Station Sales Departments The stars of commercial broadcasting may seem to be the performers the public sees and hears, but in the business of broadcasting the real stars are the salespeople who generate the revenue to pay the performers. They are rewarded accordingly.

Their major sales tool, aside from the personal qualities needed for success in any sales job, is audience research. Data from the standardized ratings "books" (as the periodic reports on each market from the national audience research companies are called) have to be reprocessed to serve the needs of each particular station. Armed with these data (often printed up in attractive brochures), with information on commercial availabilities supplied by the traffic department, with the local rate card, and with all information available on advertising needs and history of each prospect, the salesperson sallies forth to do battle. The fight is not only against the sales pitches of competing stations but also against those of competing media.

Among the selling aids available to the local sales department are the services of the Radio Advertising Bureau (RAB) and the Television Advertising Bureau (TvB). These New York-based organizations supply sales ammunition such as audience and product data and sales-promotion materials for their respective subscribers.

In a sense the broadcast salesperson's job really begins *after* a client signs the first contract. Thereafter *account servicing* by the salesperson nurses the client's interest in the medium, seeking to ensure renewal of the first contract and, better still, bigger contracts in the future.

National Sales Stations get access to national advertising business through sales representatives (§13.2) and, in the case of affiliates, also through network sales departments. As Exhibit 13.2 shows, national business accounts for only 22 percent of radio billings, but amounts to 56 percent of television billings.

Major national advertisers use many different media, so that the selling job of any one medium is to convince advertisers and their agencies to divert as much as possible of the firm's advertising budget in its direction. Exhibit 13.7.1 shows how firms that budgeted over a million dollars a year for advertising allotted funds to the major media. Allotments differed widely, but no advertiser put all its advertising money into a single medium. Deciding on the right *media mix* is the task of advertising agency media directors.

Advertising Agency Functions All regional and national advertisers, and most large local advertisers, deal with the media through *advertising agencies*. Some national firms have their own "in-house" agencies, but most rely on independent agencies staffed with highly trained specialists and able to handle a number of clients (Exhibit 13.7.2).

Advertising agencies employ a variety of specialists to advise clients on how to get the most out of their advertising budgets. They conduct research, design advertising campaigns, create commercials, buy time from stations and networks, supervise the implementation of campaigns, and pay the media on behalf of advertisers. Agencies become intimately familiar with each client's business problems, sometimes even assisting in the development of new products or the redesigning and repackaging of old ones.

Large advertisers rely almost entirely on advertising agencies for creating commercials. Indeed, designing and producing commercials are an agency's most crucial function. Anyone who doubts that making

Exhibit 13.7.1
How top advertisers spread their budgets

Rank	Advertiser	Budget (millions)	Net radio	Spot radio	Net TV	Spot TV	Other media
				Percentage of budget allocated to			
1	Procter & Gamble	$509	0	a	57	34	9
2	General Foods	355	2	2	57	26	13
3	General Motors	339	3	7	35	31	24
4	Ford Motor Co.	216	1	5	45	32	17
5	Philip Morris	212	0	2	41	8	49

Comment: Four out of these five premier advertisers chose network television for their major expenditures. Among the top one hundred advertisers, all but eight spent more on broadcast media than on all other media.

[a] Less than 1 percent.

Source: Based on 1979 data in Television Bureau of Advertising, "Top 100 National Advertisers," N.D.

commercials is a highly developed art need look no further than the homemade commercials of small radio and television stations for evidence. The most convincing proof can be found in commercials featuring local advertisers in person. Though the weird performances of used-car dealers and cut-rate store owners sometimes achieve a kind of bizarre local notoriety, they are living testimony that creating advertising needs a special kind of talent.

Financial Role of Agencies The traditional payment for agency services is a 15 percent commission on *billings* — the amount charged by the advertising *media*. An agency pays a station or network 85 percent of its time charges, billing the client the full amount and keeping the 15 percent difference as payment for its own services. Variations in payment method arise because a firm's own advertising department may do some of the work, or may retain specialist firms to do specific jobs such as research, time-buying, or production of commercials. Some agencies accept less than 15 percent commission or charge fees in addition to commission; some work on a straight fee basis; some on a cost-plus basis.

In any event, the fact that the media allow a discount on business brought to them by agencies creates an odd relationship: the

Exhibit 13.7.2
Top advertising agencies and broadcast billings

Rank	Agency	Annual broadcast billings as percentage of agency total
1	Young and Rubicam	60
2	J. Walter Thompson	76
3	Batten, Barton, Durstine & Osborn	60
4	Dancer Fitzgerald Sample	79
5	Leo Burnett	53
6	Ogilvy & Mather	57
7	Grey	57
8	McCann-Erickson	60
9	D'Arcy-MacManus & Masius	64
10	Foote, Cone & Belding	66

Comment: "Billings" refers to the amounts billed to clients by the agencies for their services. The top two agencies billed over a *billion* dollars in a single year.

Source: Based on 1980 data in *Broadcasting,* "Broadcasting's Top 50 Agencies and Their 1980 Radio-TV Billings," 26 Jan. 1981, p. 30.

agency is *working for* its client, the advertiser, but is being *paid by* the medium in the form of a discount on time charges. The fact that the agency actually makes the payments for time to the medium (as an agency service, but also in order to first deduct agency commission) can create problems if an agency falls on hard times. In the 1970s a large agency collected money owed to CBS from an advertiser, but before passing on the payment due to the network the agency went bankrupt, leaving CBS empty-handed. A court ruled that CBS could not collect from the advertiser and the network had to write off the debt. This incident reinforces the point, often misunderstood by the lay observer, that the agency works *for the advertiser*, not for the medium.

That being the case, it may seem strange that a medium would be willing to accept lower payment for its services when the business is brought to it by an agency. But there is good reason for this seeming generosity. Many of the services of the agency would otherwise have to be done by the media, which are not equipped with the specialists and facilities to do the agency's jobs. Even the indirect method of payment to the media through the agency is normally advantageous to the media because the agency assumes the burden of deciding on an advertiser's ability to pay. The intermediate role of the agency is shown graphically in Exhibit 13.7.3, which traces the routes taken by broadcast advertising in getting from advertiser to consumer.

Proof of Performance   Advertisers and their agencies need evidence to show that contracts have been carried out. The most universal documentation of broadcast performance is the daily program log. Formerly required of all stations by the FCC, it was deleted as an official requirement for radio in 1981. But all stations still need most of the previously mandated data for their own information and protection. Logging the time, length, and source of each commercial serves as documentary proof of contract fulfillment. Station sales departments rely on logs in preparing proof-of-performance warranties to accompany their billing statements.

Contracts provide for remedies when scheduled commercial announcements are missed or garbled because of technical failure, program overruns, or oversights. Compensation takes the form either of adjustment in billing or rescheduling of missed announcements as "makegoods."

Advertisers and agencies can get independent confirmation of contract fulfillment from Broadcast Advertising Reports (BAR), a firm that conducts systematic studies of radio and television commercial performance. BAR checks on commercials by recording the audio portion of television programs in 75 markets, sending the recordings to central offices for processing.

Along with other more specialized firms, BAR also uses *screeners* in New York and Los Angeles to check on the visual as well as the audio quality of television commercials. Screeners sit at home watching television to check and report on how clients' commercials are presented (Connor, 1973).

13.8 Unethical Business Practices

BAR exists more because of honest mistakes and technical failures than because of deliberate cheating by broadcasters. However, there are areas of commercial abuse in broadcasting that have been the subject of FCC and even of congressional action. Four types of unethical deals that have been particularly troublesome are plugola, payola, fraudulent billing, and clipping.

Plugola A conflict of interest situation comes about when a station or one of its employees uses or promotes on the air something in which the station or employee has an undisclosed financial interest. This practice, called *plugola*, usually results in an indirect payoff. For example, the FCC cited a station for plugging a live concert without revealing that the station itself sponsored the concert and stood to benefit from increased attendance. In an-

other case a station editorialized on subjects in which it had a financial stake.

Payola Direct payment in cash, goods, or services to the one responsible for inserting plugs is known as *payola*. It occurs most frequently in the form of under-the-table payoffs by recording company representatives to disc jockeys and others responsible for putting music on the air.

The legal basis for banning both plugola and payola is that they violate the *sponsor identification* law (§13.5). Plugola/payola can

Exhibit 13.7.3
Broadcast advertising sales flow

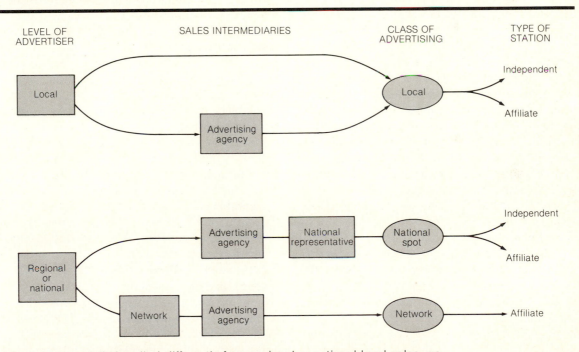

Local sales, usually handled differently from regional or national level sales, go either directly to stations or through advertising agencies. Regional and national sales usually involve not only advertising agencies but also either network sales departments or national sales representative firms. Network advertising is normally carried only by affiliates, but in specific instances when affiliates fail to clear time the networks may divert programs to independent stations.

also cause violation of commercial logging rules and excessive commercialization.

A 1959 congressional investigation uncovered a wide range of both plugola and payola practices. As a result of these disclosures, in 1960 Congress strengthened the sponsor identification law, adding Section 508 to the communications act, which prescribes a $10,000 fine or a year in jail (or both) for each payola violation. Despite these efforts, payola scandals continue to erupt every few years.

Double Billing Local cooperative advertising (§13.2) sometimes tempts stations into fraudulent *double-billing* practices. Manufacturers who cooperate in paying for local advertising by their dealers are easy targets for such deception. Being far away, they must rely on their local dealers to handle co-op advertising. Dealer and station may connive in sending the manufacturer a higher bill for advertising than the one actually paid. Station and dealer then split the excess payment. Double billing occurs often enough for the FCC to issue special notices warning licensees against the practice. Stations have lost their licenses for double-billing frauds compounded by misrepresentations to the FCC.

Clipping Network *clipping* occurs when affiliates cut away from the network programs prematurely usually in order to insert commercials of their own. Clipping not only defrauds the network, but also violates FCC sponsor identification and logging rules.

Summary

Broadcasting achieved relatively rapid success as an advertising medium because of unique psychological advantages, in combination with great flexibility in serving both local and regional advertisers. Current practice has shifted from sponsorship to insertion of commercial announcements in the schedule as spots, within and between programs over which advertisers have no direct control.

Standards governing the amount of time that may be sold for commercials are not rigidly controlled, but the industry set up voluntary codes of standards through the NAB. The standards also concern candor and taste in advertising. The impression of clutter created by the many announcements in addition to advertisements is worrisome to the advertising community because it decreases the effectiveness of commercials.

The rates for advertising reflect the fact that advertisers buy time only as a means of getting access to audiences. Because audiences change throughout the day, the tendency is to change prices for spots accordingly, especially at the larger stations where price variations can be wide. The sale of time is subject to a variety of contractual terms that reflect individual station and network policies, such as discounts for buying in quantity, protection of advertisers from sudden rate changes, proximity to commercials for competing products, and preemptibility.

Station sales departments are assisted in reaching national advertising clients by national representatives and (for stations that are affiliates) by network sales organizations. Most of the planning of advertising campaigns and the selection of media outlets is done by advertising agencies. Broadcasters provide proof of performance with their bills, but agencies also hire specialized firms that make a business of checking on fulfillment of advertising contracts on the air. The sale of advertising time is subject to several abuses such as double billing and plugola, offenses that can jeopardize station licenses if known to the FCC.

CHAPTER 14

Audience Measurement and Testing

In previous chapters we discussed such audience-centered topics as dayparting, audience flow, scheduling strategies, program ratings, station and network economics, and advertising rates, all of which presuppose knowledge about audience size and composition. How such knowledge is obtained forms the main subject of this chapter.

14.1 Feedback in Broadcasting

Definition As generally used, the term *feedback* means any kind of information coming from an audience. To researchers, however, the term has a deeper meaning: "the control of a system by reinserting into the system the result of its performance" (Wiener, 1950: 71). Thus feedback is both *circular* and more or less *continuous*.

In face-to-face conversation, as speakers pick up the numerous visual and auditory cues that tell them how their communications affect each other, they modify their conversation accordingly. Information comes back to the message originator about how the message receiver is reacting; in turn the message originator constantly modifies messages in response to that information. Feedback is taking place.

Broadcasting is often mistakenly called a *one-way* system of communication, as though no feedback occurred. Every time program executives discuss programs with taxi drivers, with their children, with clerks in shops, and with neighbors and friends, feedback is taking place. Every telephone call or card to a station about programs counts as feedback. Thus feedback in broadcasting inevitably occurs because program executives do not live in isolation chambers. It is delayed feedback, to be sure, and may be fragmentary, inadequate, and downright misleading. Nevertheless, it occurs.

Audience Mail Volunteer mail from listeners was the first source of audience information from beyond the immediate environment of station executives. When radio was still a novelty, listeners eagerly sent in reports on reception. After the novelty wore off, stations began offering gifts and prizes to motivate listeners to write in, thus stimulating the feedback process. Broadcasters still rely on audience mail to some extent, but it is now well recognized that because writers-in are not statistically representative of the *entire* audience, they can give very misleading impressions. Moreover, audience letters are not always genuinely spontaneous expressions of individual opinion; often they result from campaigns orchestrated by leaders with a specific cause to push (§16.6).

The biases of letter writers have been studied in detail. For example, research based on letters in the public files of stations (put there in compliance with FCC rules) found that letter writers differed significantly from the general population of the stations' market areas in terms of race, education, income, type of job, age, and marital status — all differences important to advertisers (McGuire & LeRoy, 1977).

Systematic Research   Broadcasters need feedback that is free of their own personal biases and those of their social surroundings. They need objectivity, consistency, and completeness, to the extent that these ideals can be obtained in an imperfect world.

For these reasons, most day-to-day audience research is conducted by independent commercial companies, using scientific methods for probing into human behavior and attitudes.* Over fifty such companies operate at the national level, many more at the local level. They use a variety of testing methods, first to assist in the preparation of programs and advertising messages, later to assess their outcome in terms of such effects as purchasing, brand recognition, and the "image" projected by performers, stations, networks, and programs. We hear more, however, about *ratings* — reports on the sheer numbers of people exposed to broadcasts.

We hear so much about ratings because of the inherent drama in reports from the battle front, telling which programs, stations, and networks claim to be ahead in their endless struggle for survival and supremacy. Because

they play such a decisive role in the selection of the programs we see and hear, ratings merit special study. For that reason most of this chapter is devoted to that one area of audience study — the theory and practice of ratings research.

In measuring this dynamic process there is no single method as simple as the print media's circulation counts. Networks offer different measurement problems from those of the stations of each separate market, radio different problems from television. Broadcast ratings are therefore generated by several different competing firms using several measurement techniques.

Ratings companies issue reports to subscribers at regular intervals in pamphlet form, called "books" in the trade. Frequency of issue varies in accordance with costs and the urgency of the "need to know." Ratings on a daily basis are available only for national network television programs, based on a small national sample. Daily reports can also be obtained in a few of the largest cities where ratings services have wired small samples of households to disclose instantaneous evidence of set use. Most stations rely on reports issued only two to four times a year.

14.2 The Ratings Business

Media Comparisons   We hear a great deal about broadcast ratings, but never about magazine story ratings, newspaper editorial ratings, or comic strip ratings. No national newspaper readership reports are issued. Magazine readership is reported once a year, but the service is not universally accepted. The Audit Bureau of Circulation checks on the paid circulation of newspapers and magazines. Few people are aware of it; yet prac-

---

*This is *applied* research. Theoretically oriented audience research is also conducted, mostly at universities and "think-tank" institutions (Chapter 20).

tically everyone has heard of Nielsen and knows that the networks are locked in a dramatic battle for ratings dominance. The rise or fall of each major prime-time network program becomes a news item in itself.

Again, we are reminded of the unique nature of broadcasting. Other media can measure their audiences inferentially by counting the number of newspapers or tickets of admission sold. But broadcasting has no readily countable physical output. Programs are "published" in a continuous process; audiences flow elusively from one program to another, coming and going at will.

Arbitron and Nielsen   Two ratings firms stand out because their reports are both local and national in scope and are the most universally accepted sources of measurements used by broadcasters and the advertising community.

According to a comparative study commissioned in 1978 by broadcasters and national sales representatives, subscriptions to services of these two leading ratings companies, Arbitron and Nielsen, cost $35 million a year.*

Revenue of the two services comes mainly from station subscriptions. About 90 percent of all television stations subscribe to at least one of the two services, and those in the top markets subscribe to both. Station subscription rates vary according to station revenue, ranging from a high of about $75,000 a year down to about $5,000. A major agency needs to subscribe to both network and local station ratings reports, thereby spending as much as $300,000 a year. Other purchasers of ratings

reports are networks, national sales representatives, program suppliers, and syndicators. Most advertisers rely on their advertising agencies' subscriptions.

The Arbitron Company is a subsidiary of a large conglomerate, Control Data Corporation. A. C. Nielsen, the biggest market research company in the world, has operations in a score of foreign countries as well as in the United States. Broadcast ratings are a comparatively small aspect of its market research activities, which are primarily concerned with food and drug marketing.

Local Ratings   Ratings data are gathered and published for each separate broadcast market. These local reports reflect the relative position of each station among its competitors. They estimate the sizes of local audiences for network programs as well as for nonnetwork programs in each market.

Data for local ratings are not collected continuously through the year. Instead, data are gathered in short spurts known as *rating periods.* The annual number of rating periods varies, with more frequent surveys made in large markets than small, and more for television than radio. The occasions when the ratings firms survey all (or nearly all) markets are the most vital because they enable making comparisons on a nationwide scale, an important factor in the sale of national spot (nonnetwork) advertising. These all-market surveys are called *sweeps,* of which there are two each year for radio and four for television. The larger individual markets are surveyed more frequently, the number varying according to market size and the demands of stations.

The local ratings reports generated by the sweeps are the primary tools used by stations in selling their time to advertisers and in evaluating both their own programs and those of

*Financial and usage data on the two services in this section are drawn from a 1978 study commissioned by the industry from the consulting firm, Booz, Allen and Hamilton, Inc. After surveying users of the ratings services, the consultants concluded that it was not economically realistic to encourage formation of a third national ratings service.

their competitors. Sweeps are also important to networks, however, because they give a more in-depth picture of network audiences than do the regular network ratings reports, which though issued more frequently are based on a relatively small *national* sample instead of individual market samples.

Five principal sources of local market ratings reports that have been approved by the Broadcast Rating Council (§14.7) are available:

- *Arbitron Radio Markets:* 253 local radio markets; all covered in the spring sweep, most in the fall. A few markets are also covered in summer and winter.
- *Arbitron Television Markets:* 216 local TV markets, covered 1 to 7 times a year, depending on demand and market size.
- *Nielsen Station Index:* 220 local TV markets, nearly all covered 4 times a year.
- *Arbitron Metered Markets:* 4 major cities (with more to be added), continuous measurement, daily "on line" reports and weekly printed reports.
- *Nielsen Metered Markets:* 6 major cities (with more to be added), continuous measurement, daily "on line" reports and weekly printed reports.

Network Ratings Network ratings present a much different problem for research firms than local ratings: (1) there is no need to survey every market in order to get a usable national picture of network audiences; and (2) there are far fewer competing network programs at any one time-period than there are competing stations. These simplifications are offset, however, by the fact that networks demand much more immediate and frequent reporting than do the stations.

Nielsen supplies the only continuous television network ratings, issuing them weekly

(Exhibit 14.2). Its customers can also get rough approximations of audience size from "overnights," daily ratings reports based upon data from a few key cities. Nielsen's regular network reports are based upon a *national* sample of metered homes (described in §14.4).

The only national radio network ratings service is RADAR (for Radio's All-Dimension Audience Research). It is financed by the networks themselves, which contract with an independent company, Statistical Research, Inc., to conduct the surveys and to prepare the reports, issued twice a year, in each case covering a week's listening.

Special Studies Both Arbitron and Nielsen publish a great many supplementary reports, based upon the data gathered in preparing their regular subscription reports. These include, for example, reports devoted exclusively to market-by-market analyses of syndicated programming (§8.7). In addition, clients can order special reports tailored to their particular needs.

14.3 Ratings Concepts

Market Delineation An essential prelude to any audience measurement project is to define geographically the local market covered by the radio and television stations belonging to that market. A national system of clearly defined markets is essential to the conduct of the broadcasting business. To be useful, the system must avoid overlaps so that markets can be grouped regionally or nationally for network and national spot sales planning without counting the same people more than once.

The most widely accepted system for defining television markets is Arbitron's *Areas of Dominant Influence* (ADIs), though Nielsen

Exhibit 14.2
Excerpts from Nielsen network ratings report

A-12

Nielsen NATIONAL TV AUDIENCE ESTIMATES — EVE.SAT. OCT.4, 1980

TIME	7:00	7:15	7:30	7:45	8:00	8:15	8:30	8:45	9:00	9:15	9:30	9:45	10:00	10:15	10:30	10:45

ABC TV

TOTAL AUDIENCE (Households (000) & %): 16,880 / 21.7 — 17,580 / 22.6 — 16,650 / 21.4

NAT'L LEAGUE CHAMP GM 4 PHILADELPHIA VS HOUSTON (4:23–8:27PM)(-OP) — LOVE BOAT SPECIAL (8:27–9:00PM)(R) — LOVE BOAT (R)(OP) — FANTASY ISLAND (R)

AVERAGE AUDIENCE (Households (000) & %): 13,850 / 17.8 — 13,930 / 17.9 — 12,760 / 16.4

SHARE OF AUDIENCE %: 24.6* / 47* — 26.1* / 48* — 33 — 17.4* / 32 — 18.4* / 33* — 16.4 / 32 — 16.4* / 31* — 16.4* / 33*

AVG. AUD. BY ¼ HR. %: 24.3 24.9 25.9 26.2 26.7 17.4 17.6 18.0 17.0 17.9 18.1 18.6 16.9 16.0 16.3 16.5

WEEK 2

CBS TV

TOTAL AUDIENCE (Households (000) & %): 12,600 / 16.2 — 20,070 / 25.8

TIM CONWAY SHOW (OP) — WIZ

AVERAGE AUDIENCE (Households (000) & %): 10,270 / 13.2 — 11,510 / 14.8

SHARE OF AUDIENCE %: 24 — 28 / 15.7* 29* — 15.1* / 27* — 14.5* / 26* — 14.9* / 28* — 14.0* / 28*

AVG. AUD. BY ¼ HR. %: 12.1 14.3 15.6 15.8 15.1 15.1 14.7 14.4 14.7 15.0 14.4 13.5

NBC TV

TOTAL AUDIENCE (Households (000) & %): 17,430 / 22.4

NBC SATURDAY NIGHT MOVIES CENTENNIAL, PART 7(R) (8:00–10:55PM)(S)(OP)

AVERAGE AUDIENCE (Households (000) & %): 8,640 / 11.1

SHARE OF AUDIENCE %: 20 — 8.3* / 15* — 10.1* / 19* — 11.0* / 20* — 11.9* / 22* — 13.0* / 24* — 12.7* / 25*

AVG. AUD. BY ¼ HR. %: 8.0 8.7 10.3 9.9 10.8 11.2 12.0 11.8 12.9 13.0 13.0 12.4

| TV HOUSEHOLDS USING TV (See Def. 1) | WK.1 | 47.8 | 49.7 | 50.6 | 51.9 | 51.6 | 52.5 | 53.7 | 54.0 | 54.3 | 54.8 | 54.6 | 54.3 | 52.6 | 52.1 | 51.3 | 48.6 |
| | WK.2 | 52.9 | 54.6 | 55.5 | 55.7 | 55.5 | 55.6 | 54.0 | 54.5 | 54.7 | 55.7 | 55.4 | 55.2 | 54.3 | 53.1 | 51.0 | 49.5 |

U.S. TV Households: 77,800,000 — For explanation of symbols, See page A.

A-13 — EVE.SAT. OCT.11, 1980

A-20

Nielsen NATIONAL TV AUDIENCE ESTIMATES — DAY MON.–FRI. SEPT.29–OCT.3, 1980

TIME	7:00	7:15	7:30	7:45	8:00	8:15	8:30	8:45	9:00	9:15	9:30	9:45	10:00	10:15	10:30	10:45

ABC TV

TOTAL AUDIENCE (Households (000) & %): 4,430 / 5.7 — 4,280 / 5.5

GOOD MORNING, AMERICA–730 (CO–OP) — GOOD MORNING, AMERICA–830 (PARTICIPATING) (S)(OP)

AVERAGE AUDIENCE (Households (000) & %): 3,500 / 4.5 — 3,660 / 4.7

SHARE OF AUDIENCE %: 26 — 27

AVG. AUD. BY ¼ HR. %: 4.3 4.7 — 4.7 4.7

WEEK 1

CBS TV

TOTAL AUDIENCE (Households (000) & %): 2,800 / 3.6 — 2,720 / 3.5 — 4,670 / 6.0 — 4,820 / 6.2

MORNING MON–FRI (CO–OP) (PARTICIPATING) — CAPTAIN KANGAROO — JEFFERSONS M–F (MTUWF)(S)(OP) — ALICE–M–F (MTUWF)(S)(OP)

AVERAGE AUDIENCE (Households (000) & %): 1,630 / 2.1 — 1,480 / 1.9 — 3,970 / 5.1 — 4,360 / 5.6

SHARE OF AUDIENCE %: 13 / 2.2* 13* — 11 / 1.8* 10* — 2.0* 12* — 28 — 31

AVG. AUD. BY ¼ HR. %: 2.0 2.2 2.2 1.6 1.9 1.8 2.1 4.8 5.3 5.5 5.6

NBC TV

TOTAL AUDIENCE (Households (000) & %): 4,750 / 6.1 — 5,060 / 6.5 — 1,790 / 2.3 — 1,710 / 2.2

TODAY SHOW–7.30AM (CO–OP) — TODAY SHOW–8.30AM (PARTICIPATING) — DAVID LETTERMAN–1 — DAVID LETTERMAN–2 (SUS–OP)

AVERAGE AUDIENCE (Households (000) & %): 3,580 / 4.6 — 4,120 / 5.3 — 1,400 / 1.8 — 1,480 / 1.9

SHARE OF AUDIENCE %: 27 — 31 — 10 — 11

AVG. AUD. BY ¼ HR. %: 4.4 4.9 5.6 5.1 2.0 1.7 1.7 2.0

Above, a Saturday prime-time report. ABC's schedule illustrates an exception to the prime-time access rule: a late afternoon live sports event spilled over into the 7–8 P.M. period that is normally barred to network programs. *Below,* an early-morning weekday report, showing how the three morning magazine shows compare.

(Abbreviations: OP = other short program items that occur in this time segment are rated elsewhere in the report; R = repeat; S = special program; *= ½ hr. rating for this and preceding ¼ hrs.). Week numbers refer to the fact that each report contains ratings for two consecutive weeks.

Source: A. C. Nielsen Co., *Nielsen National TV Ratings* September 29–October 12, 1980.
Used with permission.

has its own version, called *Designated Market Areas* (DMAs). An ADI is defined as the counties in which the *dominant share* of viewing goes to the stations belonging to that market ("home market stations" Arbitron calls them).

Arbitron assigns each and every one of the more than 3,000 counties in the United States to one, and only one, ADI. It updates the assignments each year, though conditions change but slightly from one year to the next. ADIs are ranked by size, from #1 (New York, with over six million television households) to #213 (Miles City/Glendive, Montana, with 28,500).

Units of Enumeration

Another preliminary step is to define what will be counted as "one" in enumerating an audience. In drawing a sample, researchers refer to this as the *elementary sampling unit.* In broadcasting it is usually defined in terms of either households or persons.

Households (defined as any housing units, such as houses, apartments, or single rooms) are the most convenient unit of enumeration to use. They are easier to count than persons because they stay in one place and are fewer in number (most households represent family groups of two or more persons). The fact that television viewing is largely a family activity makes the household a logical unit of enumeration. A diary kept by one household member can be used to record the viewing of all members. Ratings reports based on household counts therefore also report on the individual viewing activities of all persons in the households.

Enumeration by household has the disadvantage that it fails to account for viewing by persons in hotels, dormitories, barracks, and institutions. Enumeration by persons is preferred for radio audience measurement because radio listening is more of an individual activity and much of it takes place outside

the home. In the discussion that follows, however, we will assume that the household is used as the elementary sampling unit unless measurement by persons is expressly mentioned.

Derivation of Ratings

A rating is a *comparative estimate* of set tuning in any given market (or combination of markets as in the case of network ratings) at any given time.* The word *comparative* is used because a rating compares the *actual* estimated audience with *total possible* audience. A rating of 100 would mean that *all* (100 percent) of the households in the market were on and tuned to one particular program. But a rating of 100 could never occur in practice because not every set could possibly be in use at any one time. Not even the most irresistible program imaginable could recruit audience members who are too ill to use their receivers, away on vacation, unable to afford repair of a broken set, asleep, or otherwise unavailable. The most successful entertainment television program of all time, an episode of *Dallas* in 1980, had a Nielsen rating of 53.3. Prime-time television programs average a rating of about 17, daytime programs average about 6. Radio ratings are usually too low to be meaningful — often less than 1 and rarely more than 2 or 3. Radio therefore relies more on *cumulative* measurements, discussed later in this section under *cumes.*

A rating is an *estimate* because it is based on the sets used by only a sample of the audience, and samples can *never* yield absolute measurements, only approximations, for reasons explained in the next section.

The arithmetic of ratings is simplicity itself — a matter of dividing the number of house-

---

*Definitions used in this chapter conform to the NAB's *Standard Definition of Broadcast Research Terms* (1973).

holds tuned to a particular program by the total television households in the market. Thus if in a sample of 400 households 100 are tuned to a particular program, the rating of that program is found by dividing 100 by 400. The answer is .25, but the decimal point is dropped, resulting in a rating of 25. The concept is illustrated in Exhibit 14.3.

Ratings Projection A properly derived rating is *projectible*. Expressed as a percent-

age, it can be applied directly to the total population that the sample represented. In the example just used, let us assume the sample represents a total population of 100,000. We multiply this number by the rating with its decimal restored (.25), finding that the estimated total audience consists of 25,000 households.

HUTs and Shares A rating gives an estimate of the percentage of the *total possible*

Exhibit 14.3
Rating concepts

The pie shows television set-use information gathered from a sample of 400 households, representing a hypothetical market of 100,000 households.

Note that program ratings are percentages based on the entire sample (including the "no response" households). Thus Program A, with 100 households, represents a quarter (25 percent) of the total sample of 400. The rating is expressed as 25, without the percentage symbol. The formula is $100 \div 400 = .25$, the decimal being dropped when the number is expressed as a rating.

Projected to the entire population, this rating of 25 would mean an estimated audience of 25,000 households. The formula is .25 (the rating with the decimal restored) $\times$ 100,000 = 25,000.

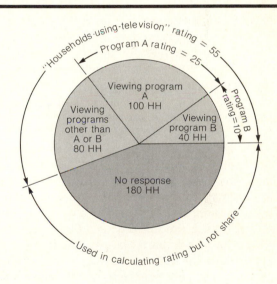

The smaller pie, 55 percent as large as the bigger pie, represents only the households using television, in this case 80 + 100 + 40 households, or a total of 220 (expressed as a households-using-television or HUT rating of 55 as shown in the larger pie). Shares are computed on the basis of treating the total number of households using television, in this case 220, as 100 percent. Thus program A's 100 households divided by 220 equals about .445, expressed in rounded figures as a share of 45.

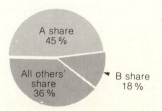

audience that is tuned to a program. A station's share of the audience is calculated on the basis of the percentage of *households using television* (HUT). A HUT of 55 means that an estimated 55 percent of all the television households are actually tuned in to *some* station receivable in that market at that time period. In other words, HUT measurements refer to the viewing in the market as a whole, not to any individual station or program receivable in that market. HUTs vary with day part, averaging nationally about 25 for daytime hours, about 60 for prime-time hours.

Shares are derived from HUT data by dividing each station's viewing audience by the market's HUT figure, as shown in Exhibit 14.3. A station's share percentage for a given time period is always larger than its rating. For example, while the top network programs during prime time usually earn ratings of about 30, their corresponding shares are about 45.

Share percentages are usually preferred to ratings as advertising sales tools. This is partly because share percentages are larger and therefore more impressive, but also because they give advertisers a more immediate estimate of their competitive position. The basic audience size is essentially predetermined by the time of day. Audience availability within day parts varies little from day to day unless extraordinary events cause people to change their normal habits. But changes in program appeal can cause audience flow (§14.6), thereby increasing or decreasing the audience share obtained by any particular program, even though the total audience in the time period remains about the same.

Cumes   In radio, because ratings are so small, the larger share percentage figures are usually preferred. Even more significant for radio are *cumulative audience* (cume) figures. Although a radio network or station reaches

a relatively small number of people in a given quarter-hour, over a period of many quarter-hours, or in the same quarter-hour over a number of weeks, radio reaches a surprisingly large number of *different* listeners when all are added together (cumulated). *Reach* is therefore another term for cume.

Demographics   Rating books report on audience composition in terms of sex and age. The *demographic breaks*, or simply *demographics*, as they are called, break down overall rating into subratings for men, women, teenagers (ages 12–17), and children. The men and women categories are further subdivided into age groups, typically 18–24, 25–34, 35–49, and 50–64.

In the stereotyped world of advertising, most products are seen as having primary appeal for specific groups (lipsticks for women, candy for children, beer for men, denture cream for the elderly, horror movies for teen-agers, and so on). For this reason advertising agencies "buy" demographics, not just audiences. Most advertisers would rather have moderate-sized audiences with exactly the right demographics for their product than much larger audiences with the wrong demographics.

14.4 Collecting Set-Use Data

The three main ways of collecting data on which to base ratings are diaries, meters, and telephone calls. Each has its own advantages and disadvantages, none is completely satisfactory.

Diaries   Researchers using the *diary* method for gathering data persuade listeners or viewers in sample homes to fill out printed forms, keeping a daily record of their set use. For radio ratings, Arbitron sends a separate diary to each *person* over 12 years of age in each sample household. The diary keepers are asked to write down their listening times and the stations heard, keeping track of out-of-home as well as in-home listening.

For television viewing measurements, Arbitron assigns a separate diary to each *receiving set* in each sample home. Diary keepers are asked to write down not only viewing information but also demographic information about all viewers, including visitors who may join them while a set is in operation.

Each radio or television diary covers an entire week's set use. Arbitron draws a different sample of homes for each week of surveying.

Meters A metering device attached to a receiver can record complete and precise information about set use. In eliminating the factor of human subjectivity, however, the meter also eliminates information on the composition of the audience. Nor does it give any assurance that anyone was actually present during the periods when the set was turned on.

The chief proponent of meters, the A. C. Nielsen Company, has evolved a sophisticated system of "instantaneous" meter reporting. For its National Television Index (network ratings reports), Nielsen connects all receivers in each sample household to a small computer located on the premises. This *Storage Instantaneous Audimeter*, as Nielsen calls it, stores data on the use of all sets in the household. It makes an exact record of tuning from station to station as well as on-off times. On cue from a Nielsen office in Dunedin, Fla., the home storage devices "dump" their stored data, sending the information by telephone line to Dunedin for processing.

To make up for the absence of audience composition information in measurements based on Audimeters, Nielsen supplements its metered homes with another, separate sample of homes using diaries. Devices the company calls *Recordimeters* are attached to sets in diary homes to give viewers audible and visual reminders to fill out their diaries every half hour while the set is turned on. The Recordimeters also keep a simple on-off record of set use. Recordimeter homes, entirely separate from the diary homes used by Nielsen for local market measurements, serve only to supplement and confirm the data derived from the national Audimeter sample of 1,200 metered homes used for network ratings. Nielsen activates about 700 of the diary home samples a week, reporting audience composition data only 34 times a year.

This elaborate method would be far too expensive to employ on a market-by-market basis throughout the country. Nielsen uses meters only for its NTI network ratings and for its instantaneous city ratings in a half dozen top markets. Arbitron has its own version of instantaneous meters for obtaining similar overnight local ratings in the largest cities. For its market-by-market ratings in the rest of the country, Nielsen depends entirely on diaries (without the aid of Recordimeters).

Telephone Coincidental Method If properly conducted, the *coincidental telephone* method is thought the most accurate source of audience-size data (ARMS, 1966). The method is called "coincidental" because the listening or watching *coincides* with the question about what is being heard or seen. Thus the factor of memory is entirely eliminated and the possibility of faking greatly reduced. The researcher simply asks whether *at this moment* a set is on in the vicinity of the respondent, if so what program or station the set is tuned to, adding a few questions to establish the number, sex, and age of people present in the room.

Because the coincidental method provides only *momentary* data ("What are you listening to or watching *now*?"), it requires a large number of calls, spaced out to cover each quarter-hour of the day, in order to build up a complete profile of listening or viewing. Another disadvantage is that it is not feasible to call people between about 10:30 at night and 8:00 in the morning, necessitating a switch to recall techniques for those hours.

Coincidental telephone surveys are widely used, but none of the major ratings companies employs the method at the present time for regular ratings reports. Nielsen offers a special, high-quality coincidental service for customers who require quick answers to specific questions.

Telephone Recall   Tricks of memory make the *telephone recall* method less reliable than the coincidental method. However, this problem has been minimized by modifications developed in a major comparative study of radio research methods (ARMS, 1966). This is the method adopted by RADAR, the source of radio network ratings. The main feature of the RADAR method is the use of *daily* telephone calls by prearrangement over a period of seven days, thus attaining a week's coverage while minimizing errors of memory. RADAR employs *random digit dialing* — a technique for generating telephone numbers at random by computer — to design a national sample of individuals (not households).

Personal Interview   The use of in-person, door-to-door surveys based on probability samples has faded in recent years because of the hazards of knocking on strange doors in strange streets. However, personal

interviews using nonprobability, *convenience* samples (also called *judgment* or *purposive* samples) are often used in studies other than ratings research. Typically, interviewers question people on busy streets, in shopping centers, or (for automobile listening information) at stoplights. Data gathered in such ways have limited significance, however, because the results are not projectible to the general population. If taken to be statistically representative, such data could be highly misleading.

14.5 Sampling

No matter which method is used, checking on the private listening and viewing behavior of millions of people tuning in thousands of stations in over 200 markets at all times of the day and night presents a formidable challenge. The task would be impossible without drastic simplification.

Ways of Simplifying   Rating research applies *sampling* to three aspects of the task to simplify it in terms of behavior, time, and people.

(1) *Behavioral Sampling.* Behavioral responses of audience members to programs can vary over an almost endless range of observable human reactions. What *minimum* and *universal* behavioral response is easiest to use in deciding whether to count a person as an audience member? Researchers decided that the behavior that best meets these requirements is the sequence of actions of turning a receiver on, selecting a station, and turning the receiver off. Each rating company has adopted an arbitrary span of time, rang-

ing from three to six minutes per quarter-hour, that the set must be kept turned on to count as being "in-use" by an audience member.

This simple *set-use test* leaves out of consideration much that we would like to know about audience members. It tells us nothing about whether listeners or viewers liked a program, whether they understood what they heard or saw, whether they chose the program after considering alternatives or merely passively accepted it because it was the one already tuned in, whether some family members imposed their choice on others, and so on. In fact, the set-use test does not even tell us for sure that anyone actually paid any attention to a program. Receivers can be left on, either deliberately or accidentally, after the user leaves the room. It is important to our understanding of what ratings mean to realize that they are based on the set-use test, not on any more revealing assessment of audience behavior.

(2) *Time Sampling.* The second simplification used in rating research relies on the fact that broadcast programs come in repetitive daily and weekly cycles. A sample taken from the continuous stream of programs every few weeks or months suffices for most purposes. As we have seen, only audiences for network programs and for stations in a few major cities are measured daily (§14.4).

(3) *People Sampling.* The third, and most controversial, simplification is the use of only a few hundred or a few thousand people to represent the program choices of hundreds of thousands and even millions. To the observer unfamiliar with the science of sampling, it seems a denial of plain common sense to claim, for example, that meters attached to sets and recording tuning in about a thousand households could be used to assess the tuning behavior of over 200 million people in 75 million families. Typical sample sizes for three of the major surveys are as follows:

■ *Arbitron radio market surveys* (diaries placed in each of 253 markets): from about 200 to 3,500 households per market, depending on market size.
■ *RADAR national radio network surveys* (telephone calls throughout the country): 6,000 persons.
■ *Nielsen national TV network surveys* (meters placed in households throughout the country): 1,200 metered households.

Role of Probability Theory Sampling works. We use it in a multitude of everyday practical situations. In many situations a complete census would be literally impossible. Broadcasting is one such case. Sampling works because when members of a population are *randomly* selected to serve as members of a sample, the laws of chance, or *probability,* ensure that a relatively small number will be *representative* of the entire population. The major characteristics of the population as a whole will appear in such a sample about the same way that they are distributed throughout the entire population.

Choosing at random is not as easy as it sounds. The "random" choice of passersby for street interviews by news teams is anything but random. Paradoxically, a high degree of systematic planning has to go into the making of random choices from human populations. This is because random selection means that ideally *every* member of the entire population being surveyed must have an *equal* chance to be selected. This condition can be met in drawing numbers for a lottery — a case of pure *probability sampling.* But sampling from general human populations always involves compromises on ideal randomness.

Sample Frames   For example, to draw a sample randomly from a large human population requires some way of identifying each member of the population by name, by number, by location, or by some other unique distinguishing label. In practice this usually means using either lists of people's names or maps of housing unit locations. Such listings are called *sample frames.* Ratings companies use either updated telephone directories or census tracts (maps showing the location of dwellings) as frames. But such frames never cover literally everybody; besides, they go out of date even before they can be printed.

Nielsen's national sample of television households (in which it places meters for deriving network television ratings) is drawn from U.S. census maps by a method known as *multistage area probability sampling.* This method ensures that the number of sample members chosen from each geographic area will be proportionate to the total population of that area. "Multistage" refers to the fact that, in the process of random selection, areas are successively narrowed down in several steps, starting with counties and ending with individual housing units. For its market-by-market ratings of stations, however, Nielsen uses special updated telephone directories, as do Arbitron and most other firms engaged in ratings research.

About 97 percent of the U.S. households have telephones, making telephone directories the most readily available sampling frames. Directories have drawbacks, however: many listed numbers represent business telephones rather than households and not every residential telephone is listed in a directory. The major research companies take steps to correct these deficiencies to the extent reasonably possible. Random digit dialing can solve the unlisted and newly installed telephone problem, which in a large city is

potentially serious, involving between a quarter and a third of all telephone-equipped households.

Sample Turnover   Ideally, each time a survey is made a brand-new sample is drawn so that imperfections in any one sample would not have a permanent effect. On the other hand, if the sampling and data-gathering methods are expensive it costs too much to discard each sample after only one use. Nielsen tries to retain each meter household in its national sample for five years. The company staggers its contracts with householders, replacing a fifth of the total each year. Thus the sample constitutes a relatively stable panel of viewers without becoming completely static.

Choice of Sample Size   Having obtained a frame from which to select sample members (elementary sample units), and having set up a method for making the selection randomly, the researcher's next task is to decide how large a sample to choose. In general, the larger the sample the higher its reliability. But reliability increases approximately in relation to the squaring of sample size (the sample size multiplied by itself: for example, to double reliability requires a fourfold increase in size). Thus a point of diminishing returns is soon reached after which increase in sample size yields such small gains in reliability it is not worth the added cost.

Researchers and their clients therefore have to balance the degree of certainty desired against the level of expense involved. At best sampling yields only estimates, never absolute certainty. The question becomes, how much uncertainty can be tolerated in a given sampling situation.

Sampling Error   The built-in uncertainty of all measurements based on samples arises from *sampling error.* This term refers not to mistakes made in gathering data, which are *non*sampling errors, but to the laws of probability. These laws say that any given sample-based measurement could be equally correct if increased or decreased by a certain known amount. Putting it another way, repeated sample-measurements would vary among themselves, but the chances are that *most,* but probably not all, of the measurements would be *near* the real amount. The *probable* amount of statistical uncertainty in ratings (that is, the amount of sampling error to be expected) can be calculated in advance ("probable" because there is uncertainty even about uncertainty!).

Nonsampling errors arise from a legion of mistakes, both intentional and inadvertent, that produce *bias* in the results. Bias can come from deliberate misrepresentation by respondents as well as from honest mistakes. Researchers may be consciously or unconsciously prejudiced. Both avoidable and unavoidable failures to fulfill sampling designs can occur. The wording of questionnaires can be misleading and mistakes occur in recording data and calculating results. Some degree of bias arising from nonsampling error is inevitable when sampling large human populations.

Response Rate   A sampling plan should contain precise instructions on how to choose or construct the sample frame and how to choose sample members from the frame. Responses from each and every sample member as specified in advance in the sampling plan should be included in the actual survey. In practice this 100 percent *response rate* is never achieved.

Ratings companies make special efforts to encourage participation of the preselected sample members and to ensure that those who agree to participate actually carry out their assigned tasks. Arbitron, for example, first writes a letter to prospective diary keepers, followed up with telephone calls before and during the sample week. Mailing in of completed diaries is motivated by a small cash payment.

Nielsen makes especially strenuous efforts to encourage the cooperation of its meter-equipped households because it costs so much to recruit households and to install and maintain the automatic meters. Nielsen field representatives visit prospective meter homes, giving a $25 gift to each householder who signs a contract to serve as a sample member. Nielsen encourages long-term cooperation of sample homes by paying half the costs of their normal receiver maintenance and giving a small cash award for each additional month of participation. Throughout the life of the five-year contract, "Nielsen families" receive frequent mailings and personal visits from field representatives.

Despite such efforts, no method of data collection succeeds in getting anywhere near a hundred percent cooperation from designated sample members. Diary and meter methods get a usable response rate of about 50 percent, the telephone method close to 75 percent. Some of the specific reasons for non-fulfillment of sample design that are typical of the chief methods of data collection are as follows:

Diaries: refusal to accept diaries, failure to complete accepted diaries, unreadable and self-contradictory diary entries, drop-off in entries as the week progresses ("diary fatigue"), failure to mail in completed diaries.

Meters: refusal to allow installation of meters; breakdowns of receivers, meters, and associated equipment; telephone line failures.

Telephone calls: busy signals, no answers, disconnected telephones, refusals to talk, inability to communicate with respondents who speak foreign languages.

Compensations for Sampling Deficiencies Ratings books contain supplements acknowledging the multiple problems involved in sampling. Arbitron, for example, lists a dozen "limitations," including those discussed in this chapter.

The fact is, no company attempts pure probability sampling. Instead, researchers take advantage of the fact that nonrandom sampling can be justified if the degrees and sources of nonrandomness can be identified and controlled. For example, *stratified sampling* ensures that sample members are drawn in such a way as to represent known characteristics of the populations in correct proportions. This procedure is possible because prior research, particularly the work of the U.S. Census Bureau, has caused a good deal to be known about populations. Nielsen's area probability sampling previously mentioned uses this device to match the size of subsamples to the known populations of areas being sampled.

A similar corrective is often applied to data after collection. Known biases can be minimized by *weighting* the data — giving extra numerical weight to the information received from certain sample members corresponding to their known weight in the total population. All ratings services use weighting in an effort to improve the representativeness of their data.

14.6 Broadcast Audiences

The cumulative result of years of intensive ratings research is a vast storehouse of knowledge about broadcast listening and viewing — surely the most analyzed mass activity in history.

Size Potential The most fundamental statistic about broadcast audiences is set *pene-* *tration* or *saturation*, expressed as the percentage of all homes that have broadcast receivers. This measurement defines the ultimate potentiality of broadcast audience size. In the United States penetration has long since peaked at between 98 and 99 percent for both radio and television. Indeed, most homes have more than one radio set and more than one television set. In short, for practical purposes it can be said that the audience *potential* is the entire U.S. population of over 70 million households.

Actual Size Of course, not every household has sets turned on at the same time. HUT measurements (§14.3) give an estimate of the percentage of television households in which sets are in actual use. Television viewing climbs throughout the day from a low in winter of about 12 percent of the households at 7 A.M. to a high of about 70 percent in the top prime-time hour of 9 to 10 P.M. Radio listening has a flatter profile, with the highest peak in the morning drive-time hours. Audience levels change predictably with the seasons: viewing is highest in January-February, lowest in April-June, reflecting the influence of weather on the choice of indoor vs. outdoor activities and hence on audience availability.

In the early years of television many observers predicted that as the medium matured and its novelty wore off the levels of set-use would decline. Instead, HUT levels continued to climb. The first hints that the growth curve might have flattened out, or even begun a downward trend, came in the late 1970s. In 1976 a drop in Nielsen network ratings caused a temporary panic, but the drop was not confirmed by other research and in the end was attributed to aberrations in data collection (Hickey, 1976). In 1978 another momentary drop in ratings shook the industry, but again it was explained as more apparent than real.

Nevertheless, the inroads of cable and home video *are* real. By 1981, 25 percent of all television homes were cable subscribers. No one seriously doubted that the audience for traditional over-the-air television will be increasingly affected by growing competition from cable, home video, and other technologies (§11.1).

Size Stability "The single most important thing to know about the American television audience," wrote Paul Klein, an expert on network programming, "is its amazingly constant size" (1971: 20). Long-term trends aside, in any particular season of the year people tend to turn on "the television" day by day in the same overall numbers, with no apparent regard to the particular programs that may be scheduled. Expressed in terms made famous by Marshall McLuhan, what matters is the medium, not the message.

Klein proposed a different terminology, the theory of the Least Objectionable Program (LOP). Half-jokingly, he theorized that people stay with the same station until driven away by an objectionable program. But even if they find *all* programs objectionable, according to the LOP theory they will still stay tuned in to the *least objectionable* one rather than turning off the set entirely.

This accounts, wrote Klein, for the steady 90 percent of the prime-time audience gathered in by the networks and the eternal struggle among the networks for a 30 percent share or better (§9.2). It also explains why seemingly excellent programs sometimes fail (because they are put up against even better programs) and seemingly mediocre programs sometimes succeed (because they oppose even more objectionable mediocrities).

Whatever the reasons, ratings data seem to confirm that audiences maintain an overall size stability, varying mostly because of changing day parts and seasons. This constancy of the audience pool forces each network to focus its programming efforts on prying audiences loose from the other two — on counter-programming strategies, in short. It is a rare program that forges ahead by virtue of enlarging the total sets-in-use figure; most succeed only by diverting existing audience members from rival programs.

Tuning Inertia A corollary of this phenomenon is *tuning inertia.* Whether because of its owner's loyalty to a station or network or because of sheer inertia, once a set is turned on, it tends to remain tuned to the same station. Usually the proportion of *flow-through* viewers (those staying tuned to the same station) is larger than the proportion that flows away to different stations (§9.1). Tuning inertia characterizes radio, too; in the large markets with as many as 40 stations to choose among, listeners confine their tuning on the average to only two or three favorite stations (*Broadcasting*, 9 Oct. 1978).

Time Spent Another measure of broadcasting's audience impact is the total amount of time people devote to listening and viewing. This is perhaps the statistic that arouses the most concern among critics of the media as social institutions. Any activity that takes up almost as much time as sleeping or working, they reason, surely has profound social implications.

Weekly average viewing per household was over 40 hours through the 1970s — on the order of six to seven hours a day. Of course this total represents the sum of viewing by all members of families. As a group, women are the heaviest viewers, followed by children aged 2 to 11. Teenagers are the lightest viewers. The fact is that on the average all age-groups view close to the same number of hours per week, the differences between groups depending more on the accessibility of receivers than on deliberate choice.

Demographic Influences Averages, however, conceal differences of detail. All audience set-use behavior is profoundly influenced by demographic characteristics. The following lists the demographic variables that hold the most interest for broadcasters, along with examples of the typical generalizations that audience research has made:

- *Age:* Among adults, viewing increases with age.
- *Education:* Viewing decreases with education.
- *Ethnic origin:* Blacks view more than whites.
- *Family size:* Large families view less than small.
- *Occupation:* Blue-collar workers view more than professionals.
- *Place of residence:* Urbanites view more than rural dwellers.
- *Sex:* Women view more than men.

Radio formats, for example, are highly selective in terms of age. Contemporary, rock, and Top-40 formats appeal most strongly to people in their late teens and twenties; classical, country, and MOR formats to people in their thirties and forties; and old-time music, news, and talk formats to people in their fifties and above. Interest in radio news and talk formats increases markedly with age.

Among television viewers, more women than men tune to the *Today* show, but more men than women watch the early fringe television news shows. Men outnumber women viewers for most sports, but nearly as many women as men watch horse racing and tennis. Teen-agers do not care much for sports, but the NCAA championship basketball games attract a much larger percentage of teen-agers than other sports events.

Demographic differences such as these could of course be predicted without benefit of research, but ratings data help by giving advertisers fairly precise measurements of their actual impact. Advertisers are willing to pay higher prices to reach specific audiences that are measurably more useful to them than undifferentiated audiences. The cost differentials are reflected in CPM data (cost per thousand, §13.6). Here are examples of CPM differences between undifferentiated households and specific target groups, based upon the cost of an average 30-second network spot (BBDO, 1978: 16):

- *Regular prime-time shows:* HH $3.61, Men $5.51, Teens $17.28.
- *Daytime shows:* HH $1.87, Men $7.43, Teens $14.16.
- *World Series Baseball:* HH $3.94, Men $4.70, Teens $32.79.

As these comparisons show, the more precisely the target audience demographics are defined, the higher the cost of reaching that audience.

14.7 Issues: Use and Abuse of Ratings

Ratings Investigation Complaints about the reliability of ratings mounted to such a pitch in the early 1960s that Congress launched an investigation. It confirmed charges of carelessness and ineptitude by some of the major ratings firms. The congressional hearings revealed cases of extensive doctoring, outright deception, and wildly contradictory ratings for identical programs. The subtitle of the committee's hearing report reflected its major concerns — *The Methodol-*

ogy, Accuracy, and Use of Ratings in Broadcasting (House CIFC, 1963–1965).

The committee commissioned a study of the statistical methods used in ratings research. The Madow Report, as the study came to be called, said that critics of ratings were putting too much emphasis on the issue of sample size; more emphasis, said the report, should be put on improving research methods and on investigating such unsolved questions as the significance of noncooperation among sample members. The report recommended complete and candid disclosure of the methods used in preparing each published ratings report, along with revealing the degree of sampling error associated with each rating.

While the congressional committee was conducting its hearings, the Federal Trade Commission made its own investigation. The FTC issued a cease-and-desist order in 1962, forbidding misrepresentation of the reliability of ratings. Specifically, the FTC ordered the companies to account for noncooperation in sampling, to cease making misleading claims about sampling, to cease mingling data from incompatible sources, and to cease using arbitrary "adjustments" on research findings.

Industry Self-Policing The industry responded promptly to the barrage of official criticism. The NAB, in cooperation with other industry elements, set up three study groups to make in-depth analyses of both radio and television ratings research, both national and local. These groups undertook a number of methodological studies that had considerable influence on subsequent research. For example, the NAB commissioned a study to find the most reliable method of gathering radio-listening data (ARMS, 1966); an industry committee studied ways of improving the coincidental telephone method (CONTAM,

1969); and another committee studied the feasibility of using random digit dialing to improve telephone sampling frames (Statistical Research, 1972).

Another industry response was to set up the Broadcast Rating Council (BRC), an independent auditing agency representing the users of ratings. The BRC accredits specific ratings services that meet its standards and submit to annual auditing. In addition to monitoring research methods, the BRC ensures full disclosure of those methods in the ratings report (Beville, 1981). Nowadays the ratings services withhold from public scrutiny only the details of the way they edit their raw data collected from diaries and meters. The Booz, Allen and Hamilton study of the ratings services (mentioned in §14.2) found that the companies "maintain a veil of secrecy around their editing procedure, and consistently declined to explain how the numbers are developed and edited."

Following the disclosures of the early 1960s, the industry eliminated the worst abuses — the gross discrepancies among ratings by different services, the shoddy procedures, the refusal to be candid about sampling and reliability standards. But this does not mean that criticism has fallen silent. Today's complaints focus on such problems as persistent failure to get ratings users to acknowledge the factor of sampling error, the tendency to underrepresent the segments of society most difficult to sample, and the practice of seeking to inflate ratings by scheduling especially attractive programs during weeks when ratings companies are gathering audience data.

Reliability of Ratings Perhaps the major cause of misunderstanding about ratings is the tendency to treat them as precise measurements, forgetting that they are merely *estimates*. Users of ratings in the industry tend to act as though differences of even fractions of a rating point have crucial significance, ignoring the fact that sampling error makes such precision utterly impossible.

It is true that the average of repeated measurements of programs in the same series has less sampling error variance than a single measurement. One commentator calculated that, with a given set of facts, a sampling error of plus or minus 2.6 rating points would be reduced to an error only plus or minus 1.8 points if ratings for the same series were averaged over a 13-week period. Even so, that small variability of only 1.8 rating points can make a shambles of program rankings. The program listed in the commentator's example as #19 (with a 20.4 rating) could with equal probability have ranked as high as #9 (with 22.2), or as low as #31 (with 18.7), or any rank in between (Chagall, 1978).

It is important to keep in mind that ratings by their very nature give us only limited information about the audiences they measure — and give it with only limited certainty. Hugh M. Beville, Jr., executive director of the Broadcast Rating Council and author of the best short introduction to the theory and practice of ratings, gives four warnings that every user of ratings should heed (1978: 4):

1. *Ratings are approximations.*
2. *All ratings are not equally dependable.*
3. *Ratings measure quantity, not quality.*
4. *Ratings measure [set-use], not opinion.*

Validity of Ratings   "Validity" in research refers to the degree of assurance that a measurement actually measures what it purports to measure. Ratings purport to measure *the* broadcast audience, but in practice they tend to measure only the broad middle range of the entire audience. People at the extremes, upper and lower, are less inclined to cooperate with ratings services than those in the middle. Thus ratings tend to underrepresent the very rich and the very poor and any other groups with unusual habits and life styles.

Black and Spanish-language-oriented station managers have long complained that the standard ratings reports grossly underestimate their audiences. Special studies and comparisons of census demographic data with survey sample demographics confirm this underrepresentation. Arbitron and Nielsen both acknowledge that measurement of minority audiences poses special problems, and both began in recent years to make extra efforts to give minority respondents designated in their sampling designs extra incentives to participate and to complete the reporting process.

The fact that, as a matter of both convenience and economy, television ratings research is based on households rather than individuals also affects validity. About a quarter of the households today are occupied by lone individuals who do not represent "households" in the traditional sense. Residents in group quarters such as college dormitories are omitted from household samples, much to the annoyance of stations located in college towns.

Tampering   The ratings system is vulnerable because, with such small samples, misrepresentation of listening or viewing by only a few sample members can have a marked effect. The ratings companies keep the identity of sample members a dark secret, taking every possible precaution to prevent tampering. There have nevertheless been cases of reported manipulation. For example, Arbitron threw out its radio report for an entire market when it discovered that two diaries had been filled out by an employee of a station in the market (*Broadcasting*, 7 Apr. 1980).

Hypoing   A far more widespread kind of tampering goes on quite openly. It is known as *hypoing*, the deliberate attempt by stations and networks to influence ratings by making extraordinary programming and promotional efforts during rating sweeps (§14.2). With advance knowledge of when the sweeps are scheduled, broadcasters choose these weeks to lay on their best programs, supported by heavy advertising and special promotions.

As a follow-up to its orders to the ratings firms in the early 1960s, the Federal Trade Commission also took notice of misleading use of ratings by stations. In 1965 the FTC issued a clarification of its views, pointing out that it was deceptive to knowingly use biased research findings or outdated ratings reports. Later the FTC lodged complaints against two stations for hypoing their ratings by means of special contests with unusually high prizes, saying "it is an unfair act or practice for a broadcaster to employ any short term and unusual promotional practice which has the tendency or capacity to temporarily destroy or inflate viewing levels in a broadcast market during a period when the market is being measured or surveyed" (quoted in Smith, 1970–1971: 109).

In 1975 the Federal Communications Commission proposed adopting anti-hypo rules, but withdrew the proposal, saying it would be too difficult to distinguish between hypoing and legitimate competitive strategies, leaving to the FTC the task of dealing with outright fraudulence.

Hypoing results in a roller-coaster programming profile, with attractive programs jammed into peak periods during the ratings sweeps. Because all stations and networks peak at the same time, hypoing creates a dilemma for viewers — at least for those without videocassette machines on which to preserve the good programs they would otherwise miss. In fact nobody likes the hypo roller-coaster, but competition keeps it going.

Stations have little to gain with everybody hypoing at the same time; yet any who refrained could find themselves unfairly penalized by below-normal ratings (and hence revenue) for the next few months because of the temporary loss of viewers drawn off by the competition during the last ratings sweep.

Qualitative Ratings Ever since ratings began to dominate programming strategies, critics have argued that the present ratings system encourages mediocrity by placing almost its entire emphasis on sheer size, to the exclusion of *qualitative* aspects of programs. Time and again a program seemingly of above average quality gets enthusiastic reviews and a substantial audience following but fails to meet the rigid minimum share requirements essential for commercial survival.

Critics question whether a program barely tolerated by a very large audience should automatically win out over a program with a somewhat smaller, but intensely interested, audience. Yet that is what quantitative ratings say must happen. They favor, as we have said, the "least objectionable" programs over the best possible programs.

The iron rule of set-tuning numbers need not be the sole test. In Britain and some other countries (§1.8), broadcasters are required by law to conduct research on qualitative as well as quantitative aspects of their programs and to take audience preferences into consideration. U.S. public broadcasters are in the forefront of a movement to establish a qualitative ratings system, as recounted in §10.8. Noncommercial broadcasting must, by virtue of its very nature as an alternative system, find evidence to support the need for a service that places audience satisfaction above audience size in its scale of values.

Commercial broadcasters have shown interest in only a very limited type of qualitative ratings research, aimed at measuring the likeability (as contrasted with the familiarity) of performers. Market Evaluations, Inc., regularly estimates ratings for the images projected by individual performers, based on national samples of 1,000 families. Respondents receive mail questionnaires asking all members of their families to answer questions about well-known television stars. From these data Marketing Evaluations constructs "familiarity" ratings and "likeability" ratings (it calls the latter "Performer Q"). These two ratings show the extent to which performers can be well known, as evidenced by familiarity scores, but not necessarily equally well liked ("Q" scores). Thus in early 1980, Robin Williams, Gary Coleman, and Jean Stapleton (stars in well-known prime-time situation comedy series) ranked high in both ratings. However, sportscaster Howard Cosell, for example, though extremely well known, ranked low in likeability (Stabiner, 1980).

Beyond such limited commercial uses of qualitative ratings research, however, there seems little prospect that the rule of numbers as determined by set-tuning will be replaced as the primary force controlling the choice of commercial broadcast programming. Generating continuous ratings is an extremely costly business, and the advertisers, agencies, networks, stations, sales representatives, and others that invest in the ratings system demand answers that are simple, clearcut, and as nearly irrefutable as possible.

14.8 Nonrating Research

Definition Nonrating research probes into the subjective reasons behind future as well as past audience behavior. It tries to find out what people like and dislike, what interests and what bores them, what they recognize and remember, what they overlook and forget.

For this subjective exploration, *attitudinal* research methods are usually employed. They reveal not so much people's actions (set-use) as their *reactions* — their *reasons* for action as revealed in their attitudes toward program material.

Commercial attitudinal research often makes no attempt to construct probability samples because it is usually not trying to make quantitative estimates of behavior projectible to entire populations. Instead, investigators choose respondents informally, assembling small panels called *focus groups* from which to gain insights about people's reactions and motivations.

Concept Research Program *concept* research, for example, tries out ideas for programs as described on paper. A small group's reactions to a two-paragraph written description can help in deciding whether to drop an idea, develop it further, or change some of its details.

Concepts for high-cost commercials are usually tested at intermediate stages of production, before final commitments to production costs are made. The AT&T "Reach Out" commercials, for example, were first shown to test audiences as *photomatics*. These are videotaped versions of still picture sequences based on the original story boards, enlivened with zooms and other camera effects as well as with sound. They look and sound something like full-scale commercials but cost far less to produce (Arlen, 1979).

Program Analysis To foresee the probable impact of new programs and to gather ideas about improvements in story, researchers show characterizations, casting, and so on in pilot versions to small groups. People watch, give their reactions, then discuss the reasons for their attitudes with a session director. Sometimes the discussions are videotaped so that writers and others concerned can study the reactions.

Minute-by-minute reactions to a program can be processed by the *program analyzer*, a device that enables members of a small test-group to express favorable, neutral, or unfavorable reactions by pushing buttons at regular intervals on cue. The machine automatically sums up reactions of the entire test-group, furnishing the discussion leader with a minute-by-minute profile. This reveals graphically the points of high and low interest throughout the program. In the group discussion that follows, the researcher probes for explanations as to why interest fell off or rose to new heights at specific moments in the script.

Theater Tests Less formalized previewing in theaters has long been practiced by the motion picture industry. Several firms specialize in staging previews of television programs and commercials in theater environments. Some viewing facilities are portable, capable of being set up in a shopping mall parking lot where shoppers can be easily recruited. Tests of commercials are usually disguised as tests of programs, the commercials seeming to be only incidental. Viewer reactions are usually explored by means of written questionnaires.

In-Home Testing All such staged preview sessions have the disadvantage of being conducted in an artificial environment, very different from the home environment in which people normally view television. Cable television introduced a new research tool, enabling researchers to conduct tests on viewers in their normal surroundings, using their own receivers.

One research company owns several small cable television systems which it uses for research on commercials. It splits cable subscribers into two groups, sending different test version materials to each. The company asks subscribers to keep diaries of their purchasing, thus giving concrete evidence of the influence commercials have on actual buying behavior. An even more realistic test situation is afforded by interactive cable systems such as Qube (§11.3). Audience members in their normal home environments can give immediate push-button responses to questions appearing on the screen. A computer at the cable headend analyzes their responses without delay, enabling researchers to alter their procedures as the test evolves. This kind of two-way facility opens up many new possibilities for designing realistic audience research procedures.

Physiological Testing Most methods so far described depend on self-analysis by panel members. In an attempt to eliminate this element of subjectivity and to monitor responses more subtly, researchers have measured a number of involuntary physical reactions as clues to audience response. Among the reactions that have been measured for this purpose are changes in brain waves, eye-movements, pupil dilation, breathing, voice quality, perspiration, and sitting position (the "squirm test").

For example, one researcher has capitalized on the well-known fact that the human brain is two-sided. Each side has its own specialized functions and emits different kinds of electrical impulses. Reasoning abilities seem to be centered in the brain's left side and emotions in its right side. It follows that commercials for products whose appeal is primarily emotional should, if correctly oriented, stimulate the right side of the brain more than those whose appeal is based more on logical considerations. Commercials shown to test subjects wired for brain-wave recording can be tested to find out if they elicit the desired brain-wave responses. Reviewing recent developments in such physiological testing for commercial effectiveness, a *TV Guide* writer concluded that it seems certain that eventually commercials "will be carefully designed to appeal more to our subconscious minds — once scientists figure out what it is that really turns us on" (Mariani, 1979).

Test Markets   Test markets perhaps are the most realistic device for appraising the effectiveness of advertising, but also one of the most complicated. Two or more markets, distant from each other but well-matched demographically, are selected. Each carries a different version of a proposed national advertising campaign. Researchers judge the effectiveness of each local version of the campaign by its influence on actual sales. Sales are measured by keeping track of the physical movement of goods in the market or (more easily) by using direct marketing, in which the advertised product is offered only through broadcast advertising and only in response to mail or telephone orders.

Research on Children   Several companies specialize in analyzing children's likes and dislikes and their influence on adult purchasing decisions. It is well known among marketers that children can have an impact on which brands and products adults buy for themselves as well as on the purchases made for children. One research firm gains insights into children's preferences and motivations by turning a group of kids loose in a miniature supermarket. As the children go on a shopping tour of the market, researchers secretly observe and record their behavior. This kind of research is little publicized, not only

to keep results confidential but also to avoid the possibility that the researchers will be criticized for taking unfair advantage of children (Chagall, 1977).

Summary

Applied audience research falls into two broad categories: studies designed to generate ratings and studies designed for pretesting and post-testing. Ratings research has the following salient characteristics:

1. It produces audience size measurements on both the local market level and the national level.
2. Ratings are percentages representing estimates of the proportion of the total possible audience tuned to a particular program. These data enable deriving households-using-television (or radio) and audience share statistics. When audiences are small, cumulative statistics can be used to show the aggregate reach of a program over a period of days or weeks.
3. In addition to audience size data, ratings also supply data on audience composition in terms of sex, age, and other demographic characteristics.
4. Data for ratings are usually gathered by means of diaries, meters attached to sets, or telephone calls. Each method has its own advantages and disadvantages.
5. Ratings depend on samples of behavior (usually the act of set-tuning is the behavior counted), time (most measurements are made only periodically), and people (all ratings are based on relatively small, representative cross-sections of the population).
6. Sampling requires the use of sample frames, systematic selection of sample members for representativeness, fulfillment of

sample design, and avoidance of bias in carrying out the entire project. Sampling procedures in the ratings business inevitably fall short of the ideal, increasing the probable range of error in the results.

7. Ratings research enables describing the broadcast audience in detail. Within given time frames, it is remarkably stable, with audience members tuning from station to station rather than turning sets off and on.

8. Ratings provide a reasonably accurate picture of broadcast audiences as long as the rather severe limitations on their accuracy and significance are kept in mind.

9. It would be desirable to have qualitative ratings that would measure the degree to which people liked programs as well as purely quantitative ratings, but there is little commercial demand for this alternative.

Nonrating research is widely used to test commercials, programs, and performers both before and after production. This research generally relies on small focus groups, probing them for personal motives and subjective effects such as recollection and attitude. One of the problems of this type of research is avoiding artificiality in the test situation; cable television provides researchers with an ideal natural setting in which to conduct certain kinds of audience effects research.

PART V

Social Control of Broadcasting

In Parts 1 through 4 we explored the physical, historic, and economic bases of broadcasting in America, noting their influences on the kinds and qualities of the programs the system produces. We turn now to a third set of influences, the constraints that society imposes on the system to ensure that it will reflect the nation's political ideology and its cultural identity. Most of Part 5 deals with formal legal and administrative controls and the constitutional issues that arise when such controls are put into effect. But social control is also exerted by political climate, public opinion, education, and organized pressure groups. Chapter 18 is devoted to these less explicit but more pervasive social influences.

CHAPTER 15

Law of Broadcasting

In the present chapter we explore the statutory basis for broadcasting regulation and the underlying organic law, analyzing its place in the constitutional scheme and its component parts.

15.1 National Communications Policy

Broadcasting as a federally regulated enterprise must be considered in the larger context of national communications policy. All users of electromagnetic energy share the same spectrum, and, as we have seen, there are many links between broadcasting and the other forms of electronic communication.

Spectrum Management The Communications Act of 1934 assigns responsibility for federal government users of the spectrum to the President of the United States. Under the act, the Federal Communications Commission regulates only civilian and state/local government users. Federal users are about equally divided between military and civil units. The latter include, for example, the Voice of America (under the International Communication Agency), the Coast Guard, and such cabinet departments as Agriculture. The entire list is shown in Exhibit 15.1.

The president delegates the coordination of federal spectrum users to the Department of Commerce. Within this department a specialized unit, the National Telecommunications and Information Administration (NTIA), was created in 1978 to bring together related functions that come under the president's executive responsibilities. The NTIA is the president's main telecommunications adviser. It helps to coordinate spectrum allocations and to further new technological developments. It also conducts research in the telecommunications sciences.

A special coordinating body, the *Interdepartmental Radio Advisory Committee* (IRAC), brings together representatives of all major interests concerned with gaining access to the spectrum — military, federal government, nonfederal government, private commercial, and private noncommercial. The FCC speaks for the last three and also represents the interests of Congress, in contrast with the NTIA, which speaks for the executive branch. The NTIA supplies the chairman and the executive secretary of the IRAC, although its role remains advisory (Exhibit 15.1).

Policy Trends During the 1970s national telecommunications policy stressed the benefits of competition. It encouraged the

Exhibit 15.1
Spectrum management

[handwritten: RADIO ACT of '27]

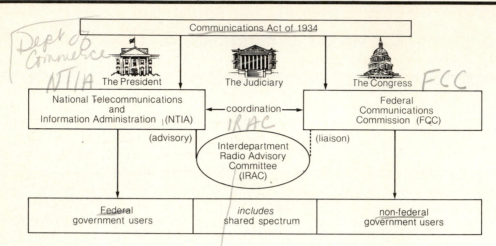

[handwritten annotations: "Dept of Commerce", "NTIA", "FCC", "IRAC"]

The Interdepartmental Radio Advisory Committee (IRAC) coordinates the demands of government users of the spectrum.

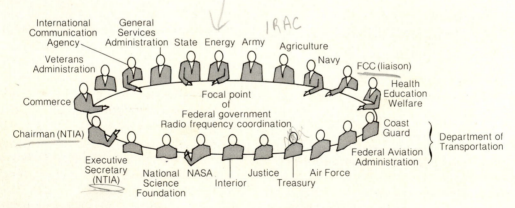

Membership of IRAC, shown around this symbolic table, includes representatives from over a score of government agencies. A representative of the FCC, as the government agency concerned with private users of the spectrum, sits on the committee for liaison purposes.

Source: International Telecommunication Union, *Telecommunication Journal*, June 1980.

emergence of new technologies to compete with the old, the breakup of old monopolies to give more competitors a chance in the marketplace, and the relaxation of government regulation.

We have already seen results of this policy as it affects broadcasting. Examples are the FCC's loosening of restrictions on cable television (originally imposed to protect broadcast television); rapid growth in the use of domestic satellites to relay programs, encouraged by the relaxation of FCC satellite regulations; plans for the addition of new channels in both radio and television broadcasting.

15.2 Constitutional Context

We left the history of broadcasting law at the point when the Radio Act of 1927 came into effect (§6.7). This first U.S. legislation to concern itself explicitly with broadcasting brought to an end a period of chaotic development that dramatized the need for federal regulation.

Scarcity Factor This intrusion by government upon the freedom of American citizens to communicate by whatever means they choose would ordinarily be forbidden by the Constitution, whose First Amendment explicitly prohibits Congress from making laws abridging freedom of speech. A major justification for this unusual abridgement was the *scarcity of channels*. Not everyone who wanted a station could be granted a channel without causing intolerable interference, as was proved by the experience before passage of the 1927 radio act. Scarcity meant that the government, as represented by the Federal Radio Commission (later the Federal Communications Commission), had to make

choices. When applications are "mutually exclusive," either because they make claims on the same channel or on adjacent channels whose activation would cause interference with existing stations, only one can be granted. The freedom of the rest must be abridged.

Today the scarcity factor as a justification for regulation is being challenged as never before. Opponents of traditional regulation point to the increase in the number of stations since the 1927 act was written — from about 600 to over 10,000. They argue that, even though there is still a demand for more channels in densely populated areas, cable television makes available unlimited numbers of supplementary channels, converting scarcity into abundance. We will analyze the validity of this argument against regulation based on scarcity in our final chapter. In the meantime, however, it needs to be understood that Congress and the courts relied on the scarcity factor as a major justification for government regulation throughout the evolution of broadcast law.

Broadcasting as Commerce Once it had been conceded that Congress has a right to regulate broadcasting, the next problem was to find a provision of the Constitution that could be interpreted as embracing the subject of this new medium. The specific constitutional justification for Congress to step in and take control of radio comes from Article I, Section 8(3), which gives Congress the power "to regulate commerce with foreign nations, and among the several States." This is the well-known *commerce clause*, which has played a vital role in U.S. economic development, preventing the individual states from undermining the unity of the nation by erecting internal trade barriers. Although not "commerce" in the original sense of the exchange of goods, the exchange of information by mail and wire had long been accepted as forms of commerce under the Constitution. Seen in this light, the statute governing radio could be regarded as one link in a chain of responsibility that extends down from the Constitution to the people and then back to the Constitution, as shown in Exhibit 15.2.

The commerce clause gives Congress ju-

risdiction over *interstate and foreign* commerce, but not over commerce within individual states. However, electromagnetic waves are regarded as *inherently interstate* in nature. Even when a radio service is designed to cover only a limited area within a state, as in the case of a radio taxi-dispatching service, for example, its radio signals cannot be cut off at the city limits. Zones of radio interference extend unpredictably far beyond

Exhibit 15.2
Chain of legal authority over broadcasting

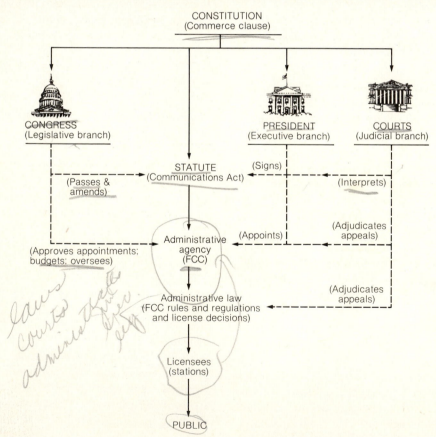

All three branches of the government play a role in controlling broadcasting under the general umbrella of the Constitution.

zones of service. Wire communication, on the other hand, can be cut off precisely at the city line or at any other geographic boundary.*

FCC's Relation to Congress

It would be impossible for Congress itself to attend to the endless details of regulation in the communications field. It therefore created the Federal Communications Commission to act on its behalf. Although the President appoints commissioners (with the advice and consent of the Senate) the FCC remains a "creature of Congress." Congress defined the FCC's role in the communications act and only Congress can change that role by amending the act. The FCC is constantly monitored by the House and Senate Subcommittees on Communications and must come back to Congress each year to justify its annual budgetary appropriation.

Licensees encounter the broadcasting law as it is expressed in the FCC rules and regulations. These carry the force of federal law, deriving their power from the Communications Act of 1934. Although the FCC has a good deal of freedom to use its own discretion, this freedom has its limits, spelled out in the act. Any FCC rule not fully justified by the act can be overthrown by appeal to the courts.

Constitutional Challenges

Congress in turn is ultimately ruled by the Constitution. The Radio Act of 1927 had scarcely been signed when the first challenges to its constitutionality began. Here are three examples of fundamental constitutional questions addressed to the courts in the first few years of the act's existence:

■ *Is broadcasting in fact interstate commerce?* In reply to this question, put by the American Bond and Mortgage Company in 1929 when its license was deleted because of interference, the appeals court said firmly:

It does not seem to be open to question that radio transmission and reception among the states are interstate commerce. To be sure it is a new species of commerce. Nothing visible and tangible is transported. . . . The joint action of the transmitter owned by one person and the receiver owned by another is essential to the result. But that result is the transmission of intelligence, ideas, and entertainment. It is intercourse, and that intercourse is commerce. (31 F 2d 454, 1929)†

■ *Does deleting a license deprive a person of property without due process of law, in violation of the Fifth Amendment?* When this question was asked by a radio preacher who lost his license because of program excesses (§7.1), the appeals court replied:

One who applies for and obtains a grant or permit from a state, or the United States, to make use of a medium of interstate commerce, under the control and subject to the dominant power of the

---

*Telephone and telegraph services are subject either to state or federal jurisdiction, depending on whether or not a given service crosses state lines or national boundaries. States have their own utilities commissions that (for example) approve changes in telephone rates for systems within states. Systems that cross state lines, however, need FCC approval for changes in rates.

†The legal sources most frequently cited in the pages that follow are: USC (*United States Code*) for the Communications Act of 1934 and other federal statutes; CFR (*Code of Federal Regulations*), for FCC rules and regulations; FR (*Federal Register*), for FCC announcements, policy statements, etc.; FCC or FCC 2d (*Federal Communications Commission Reports*, 1st and 2d Series), for FCC decisions; F or F 2d (*Federal Reporter*, 1st and 2d Series), for appeals court opinions; US (*United States Reports*) for Supreme Court opinions. MLR (*Media Law Reporter*) is a useful commercial service that prints the full texts of a variety of legal decisions that affect the media. The full names of the cases mentioned in the text, together with their sources, are given in the citation list at the end of the book.

government, takes such a grant or right subject to the exercise of the power of the government, in the public interest, to withdraw it without compensation. (62 F 2d 854, 1932)

■ *Does deleting a license deprive a person of freedom of speech, in violation of the First Amendment?* In the same case the court, after reviewing the ways in which the preacher had misused his station, said that to take away the license "is neither censorship nor previous restraint, nor is it a whittling away of the rights guaranteed by the First Amendment, or an impairment of their free exercise." He was free to say whatever he liked, said the court, "but he may not, as we think, demand, of right, the continued use of an instrumentality of commerce for such purposes . . . except in subordination to all reasonable rules and regulations Congress, acting through the Commission, may prescribe" (62 F 2d 853, 1932).

The more obvious constitutional questions were laid to rest by such cases as these in the early years of regulation. The underlying constitutionality of the act has thus long since been settled in the courts, but specific interpretations of the act by the FCC continue to provoke litigation.

15.3 Communications Act Basics

Passage The Radio Act of 1927 restored order to broadcasting, but it still left control of some aspects of radio and of all interstate and foreign *wire* communication scattered among several federal agencies. The need for a more centralized approach to these communication resources remained. Efforts to expand the radio act's scope culminated in 1934, when President Franklin D. Roosevelt forwarded an interdepartmental committee's recommendation to Congress with the following comment:

I have long felt that for the sake of clarity and effectiveness, the relationship of the Federal Government to certain services known as utilities should be divided into three fields: Transportation, power, and communications. The problems of transportation are vested in the Interstate Commerce Commission, and the problems of power . . . in the Federal Power Commission. In the field of communications, however, there is today no single Government agency charged with broad authority.

Congress promptly passed the proposed revised statute with a new name, the Communications Act of 1934. As the name implies, it went beyond radio, bringing wire as well as wireless under unified control. Nevertheless, Congress simply reenacted the broadcasting provisions of the 1927 law as part of the 1934 act. This means that the 1980s framework of broadcasting law goes all the way back to the beginnings of radio in the 1920s. Although the act has been amended many times, its underlying concepts remain unchanged.

Organization The Communications Act of 1934 consists of six major chapters, called "titles." They cover roughly the following subjects:

I. Definition of terms, provision for setting up the FCC.
II. Common carriers.
III. Broadcast licensing, general powers of the FCC, equal treatment of candidates for public office, sponsor identification.
IV. Hearings on and appeals from FCC decisions.
V. Penal provisions.
VI. War emergency powers of the president, etc.

Definition of Broadcasting As we have seen, in the early 1920s the telephone company at first tried to treat broadcasting as a *common carrier* (§6.4).

Common carriers supply communication services to all comers without concern for what is communicated over their facilities. Telephone companies are the most familiar example, but the common carrier field has become diversified as more and more uses are found for satellites, computers, and other high-technology devices for getting information from point A to point B. A second characteristic of common carriers is that their rates are usually subject to government approval — by the FCC in the case of interstate operations.

If broadcasting were to be classed as a common carrier, programming would be entirely at the discretion of those who bought time on stations and networks, which would be obliged to charge fixed prices in accordance with an FCC-approved tariff (rate) scale. As we pointed out in §6.4, this concept of broadcasting was rejected in practice in the 1920s. The act formalized the distinction in Section 3:

"Common carrier" or "carrier" means any person engaged as a common carrier for hire, in interstate or foreign communication by wire or radio or in interstate or foreign radio transmission of energy, except where reference is made to common carriers not subject to this Act; but a person engaged in radio broadcasting shall not, insofar as such person is so engaged, be deemed a common carrier.

The act defines *radio communication* in the same section as "transmission by radio of writing, signs, signals, pictures, and sounds of all kinds, including all instrumentalities, facilities, apparatus, and services . . . incidental to such transmission." By giving the word *radio* such a broad definition, Congress made it possible for the radio provisions of the act to be applied without alteration to television when it became a licensed service nearly 15 years after the 1927 act was adopted.

Finally, the same section defines the term *broadcasting* as "the dissemination of radio communications intended to be received by the public, directly or by intermediary of relay stations."

The key phrase "intended to be received by the public" excludes private radio communication services aimed at individuals or specific groups of individuals. Even radio communications not intended for the general public can be *received* by anyone who has the right kind of receiver. People can tune in police, ship-to-shore, space satellite, and other nonbroadcast transmissions for their own entertainment. But these messages are not *intended* for the general public and the communications act's Section 605 on "unauthorized publication or use" forbids the disclosure of nonbroadcast messages to people for whom they are not intended. Nor may people use broadcasting to send private messages not intended for the general public. Thus it is technically illegal for athletes (for example) to greet their families over the air during interviews at sporting events.

More important, the unauthorized disclosure clause of Section 605 gives purveyors of services such as FM's background music and television's over-the-air subscription programming (STV) a means of combatting piracy of their transmissions. In 1981 an appeals court held that STV, because intended for reception *only* by subscribers using special unscrambling devices, is not a form of broadcasting (7 MLR 1399). This ruling enabled STV stations to invoke Section 605 to prevent piracy of their programs by sellers of unauthorized decoding devices.

Piracy of subscription services is a growing

problem. Eventually direct broadcast satellites may greatly expand such services, creating a need for more stringent controls over unauthorized uses. Already hobbyists have begun to install their own satellite earth-station receivers in their back yards to pick up data and programs being relayed to commercial customers via satellite.

Provisions for the FCC The very first paragraph of the 1934 act sets forth the underlying reasons for creating the FCC and for repealing the predecessor 1927 act. They are

for the purpose of regulating interstate and foreign commerce in communication by wire and radio so as to make available, so far as possible, to all the people of the United States a rapid, efficient, National-wide, and world-wide wire and radio communication service with adequate facilities at reasonable charges, for the purpose of the national defense, for the purpose of promoting safety of life and property through the use of wire and radio communication, and for the purpose of securing a more effective execution of this policy by centralizing authority heretofore granted by law to several agencies and by granting additional authority with respect to interstate and foreign commerce in wire and radio communication.

The president appoints the seven FCC members, with the advice and consent of the Senate. Commissioners must be citizens, may not have a financial interest in any type of communications business, and must devote full time to the job. No more than four of the seven commissioners may be of the same political party.

Congress thus sought to minimize economic and political bias on the part of the commission. The term of seven years, contrasted with the presidential term of four years, makes it impossible for an incoming president to change the commissioners all at once (the terms of the commissioners are staggered so that only one expires each year).

On the other hand, the act gives an incoming president a chance to have immediate impact on the commission by allowing him to appoint one of its members as chairman.

Section 4 of the act gives the commission broad power to "perform any and all acts, make such rules and regulations, and issue such orders . . . as may be necessary in the execution of its functions." In few instances did Congress tie the commission's hands with hard-and-fast requirements, such as the original upper limit of three years on the terms of broadcasting licenses and the requirement that licensees must be U.S. citizens. Most provisions of the act give the commission wide latitude in applying its own experience and (presumably) expert judgment to the particular sets of facts presented by each case.

Congress knew, however, that the new law would have met the same fate as the Radio Act of 1912 if the commission were given *unlimited* discretionary latitude. It was just such an undefined grant of licensing power that caused urgent demand for new legislation in the 1920s (§6.7). Needed was a highly flexible yet legally recognized standard by which to limit the commission's discretion every time it made a decision not dictated by specific requirements of the act. Congress chose for this purpose a phrase familiar since the 1850s in the public utility field — "public interest, convenience, and [sometimes "or"] necessity."

Origins of Public Interest Standard The idea that radio communication must of necessity serve the public interest emerged during the earliest days of maritime radio, when it became obvious that selfish interests and commercial profit could not be allowed to stand in the way when lives were at stake in emergencies at sea (§6.7).

When broadcasting emerged it too was recognized as carrying an obligation to serve the public interest. As Secretary of Commerce Hoover said at a congressional hearing in 1924, "Radio communication is not to be considered as merely a business carried on for private gain, for private advertisement, or for entertainment of the curious."

At the Fourth Radio Conference, in 1925, the National Association of Broadcasters presented a resolution recommending that a law should be enacted making "public convenience and necessity" the basis of choice among competing applications. At that conference, Hoover remarked, "We can surely agree that no one can raise a cry of deprivation of free speech if he is compelled to prove that there is something more than naked commercial selfishness in his purpose."

The legislative history of the Radio Act of 1927 shows that Congress adopted essentially the same point of view. In answer to the NAB's later contention that the commission was created merely to regulate technical aspects of broadcasting, Senator Burton K. Wheeler replied, "I went through all those hearings at that time, sat as a member of the committee, and it was not the intention of the committee, nor of the Senate, just to regulate these physical things" (Senate CIC, 1944: 238).

Whenever Congress intended to give the FCC maximum latitude to use its own judgment, it used the "public interest" phrase. It occurs in the key sections of the broadcasting parts of the act. For example, Section 303 begins: "Except as otherwise provided in this Act, the Commission from time to time, as public convenience, interest, or necessity requires shall. . . ." The section goes on to list 19 functions, ranging from the power to classify radio stations to the power to make whatever rules and regulations the FCC needs to carry out the provisions of the act. The public interest phrase similarly occurs in the crucially important sections dealing with granting, renewal, and transfer of licenses.

Definition of Public Interest Most people think of the public interest clause as being aimed directly at broadcasters. In turn broadcasters tend to picture themselves as constantly faced with excruciating dilemmas as to what the public interest requires.

The fact is, nowhere does the act address the public interest phrase directly to licensees. It invariably tells the *commission* to decide what the public interest requires.

Of course the ultimate aim is to ensure that broadcast licensees operate in the public interest, but the act does not leave them adrift in a sea of doubt as to how to interpret the phrase. That is the job of the commission. As an appeals court put it:

The only way that broadcasters can operate in the "public interest" is by broadcasting programs that meet somebody's view of what is in the "public interest." That can scarcely be determined by the broadcaster himself, for he is in an obvious conflict of interest. . . . Since the public cannot through a million stifled yawns convey that their television fare, as a whole, is not in their interest, the Congress has made the F.C.C. the guardian of that public interest. (516 F 2d 536, 1975)

This does not mean that the FCC entirely preempts the obligation of licensees to judge what would be in the public interest for their particular publics. Only the licensee can make informed judgments on local matters. The commission says, for example, that it is in the public interest for stations to carry *some* programs touching on *some* local community needs. It goes so far as to give television licensees detailed guidelines on how to ascertain which local needs should be addressed (radio licensees were excused from this requirement in 1981). But it remains for the licensees to do the ascertaining and then to decide what kinds of programs and how many such programs to devote to this aspect of their public service obligation.

Because the very purpose of the public interest standard was to give the FCC maximum flexibility in meeting unforeseeable new situations, it is unavoidably open to the charge of vagueness. But as an appeals court judge pointed out, "It would be difficult, if not impossible, to formulate a precise and comprehensive definition of the term 'public interest, convenience, or necessity,' and it has been said often and properly by the courts that the facts of each case must be examined and must govern its determination" (153 F 2d 628, 1946).

Enforcement   Congress relied on the threat of license loss as the means of enforcing the communications act, giving the FCC two procedures for taking away a license: refusal to renew and outright revocation.

 Upon applying for a renewal, a licensee has the *burden of proof*. It is up to licensees to convince the FCC that their previous performance as licensees justifies renewal. If the FCC wants to revoke a license before the expiration of its normal term, however, the burden of proof is reversed. The FCC must then prove that the licensee committed one or more of seven transgressions that Section 312 lists as justifying revocation. Of these, the violations most likely to occur in practice are making false statements in license applications and "willful or repeated failure to operate substantially as set forth in the license."

In practice, penalties of such finality seemed too extreme for the types of infractions that most often occur. Accordingly, nearly three decades later Congress amended the act to allow for three milder penalties:

short-term renewals, fines, and cease-and-desist orders.

(1)   *Short-term renewals* can be used as a way of keeping pressure on licensees to demonstrate that they are capable of mending their ways. In practice, such renewals are usually for six-month or one-year periods. [*of revocation*]

(2)   *Fines* (referred to in the act as "forfeitures") may be levied for substantially the same types of violations listed in the revocation section. The amendment to Section 503 authorizes forfeitures of up to $2,000 for each day on which the offense occurs, to a maximum of $20,000.

(3)   *Cease-and-desist orders* impose no penalty beyond whatever it costs to stop doing something. In practice this option has rarely been chosen as an enforcement method.

FCC Appeals and Hearings   A fundamental safeguard of individual liberties under the Constitution is the *due process* clause of the Fifth Amendment. It guarantees that government may not deprive a person of "life, liberty, or property without due process of law." This means, among many other things, that the FCC (in effect "the government") may not use its powers arbitrarily. Fairness, which is the goal of due process, requires that applicants and petitioners have ample opportunities to present their cases under nondiscriminatory conditions; and it requires that people adversely affected by decisions must have the right to appeal for rehearings and for review by higher authorities than the ones that made the first-level decisions.

When an issue arises that requires presentation of opposing arguments, an FCC *hearing* may be held to settle the dispute. Hearings are conducted along the same lines as court cases, with witnesses, testimony, evidence, counsels for each side, and so on. Rule-making proposals, which may come from the public, from any of the three government branches (legislative, executive, or judicial), or from within the FCC itself, are also subject to due process. Notice of proposed new rules must be given in advance so that interested parties have time to prepare arguments for or against them, and they too are subject to reconsideration.

Frivolous interventions and intentional delays are held down by procedural rules that carefully define the circumstances that justify hearings and the qualifications of those entitled to *standing* (the legal right to participate fully in hearings). This means that procedural rules, tedious though they seem, are crucially important to anyone trying to lodge a complaint.

Here are a few examples of procedural rules laid down in the communications act:

■ Section 309 of the act requires the commission to advise license applicants of its reasons for rejecting an application. The applicant may reply, and if the commission still decides against the applicant it must set the matter for hearing, "specifying the particular matters and things at issue."

■ On the other hand, if the commission grants a license application *without* a hearing, for the next 30 days the grant remains open to protest from "any party in interest"; if the protesting parties raise pertinent issues, the commission must then postpone the effective date of the grant and hold a hearing.

■ If the commission wishes to revoke a license, impose a fine, or issue a cease-and-desist order, Sections 312 and 503 require the FCC to invite the licensee to "show cause" why such action should not be taken.

Court Appeals   Even after all the safeguards of FCC hearings and rehearings have been exhausted, the communications act gives people who are adversely affected by FCC actions a further recourse.

Section 402 provides that appeals concerning station licenses must go to the U.S. Court of Appeals for the District of Columbia Circuit in Washington, D.C. This court consists of nine judges, but most cases are heard by panels of only three judges. The court may reverse or confirm commission actions, in part or in whole. It may *remand* a case, meaning that it sends it back to the commission for further consideration in keeping with the court's interpretation of the law. Appeals from FCC decisions in cases not involving licenses may be initiated in any of the eleven other U.S. Courts of Appeal, each serving a specific region called a "circuit" — hence they are called "circuit courts of appeals."

From the federal circuit courts, including the one in Washington, D.C., final appeals may be taken to the Supreme Court of the United States. The request to the Supreme Court, called a *writ of certiorari*, may be turned down ("*cert. den.*"). If that happens, the appeal process has reached the end of the line. Refusal to hear a case does not mean that the Supreme Court has concurred in the lower court's finding; however, the earlier finding stands, so that the Supreme Court's inaction amounts to endorsement for practical purposes.

15.4 Licensing

Regulatory power centers on licensing power. Control over issuance, renewal, and transfer of station licenses means control over broadcasting.*

*The communications act also ensures control by providing for the licensing of various classes of *operators*, the technicians responsible for making sure that transmitters operate in accordance with the engineering rules.

"Ownership" of Channels   It is generally recognized internationally that the electromagnetic spectrum cannot be literally "owned," either by persons or by nations (§1.1). In the early days of radio, however, some broadcasters claimed they had acquired perpetual squatter's rights to the channels they already occupied. Conscious of this potential problem for the success of broadcast regulation, Congress went to special lengths to prevent claims of channel ownership. One of the aims of the communications act, said Congress, in Section 301 of the act is

to maintain the control of the United States over all the channels of interstate and foreign radio transmission; and to provide for the use of such channels, but not the ownership thereof, by persons for limited periods of time, under licenses granted by Federal authority, and no such license shall be construed to create any right beyond the terms, conditions, and periods of the license.

Congress stressed the point still further by requiring in Section 304 that each licensee sign a waiver "of any claim to the use of any particular frequency or of the ether as against the regulatory power of the United States because of the previous use of the same." Furthermore, although the FCC may determine the form of station licenses it issues, Section 309 requires that every license *must* include the condition that it "shall not vest in the licensee any right to operate the station nor any right in the use of the frequencies designated in the license beyond the term thereof nor in any other manner than authorized therein." As we have seen, despite these precautions, denial of prior ownership claims was challenged, but the courts ruled that it was constitutional (§15.2).

Construction Permits   Congress was also concerned that, because of limited engineering experience with broadcasting at the time, licensees might take advantage of the unpredictability of radio propagation patterns. To make sure transmitters behaved exactly as planned and authorized, the act requires would-be licensees to apply first for a *construction permit* (CP). Only after satisfactory transmitter performance tests may the holder of a CP apply for an actual license.

Term of Licenses   Section 307 of the act mandated a maximum broadcast station license term of three years (extended by a 1981 amendment to five years for television, seven for radio), renewable "if the Commission finds that public interest, convenience, and necessity would be served thereby." The FCC has the option of using short-term renewals as a means of putting pressure on licensees if it finds that their performance needs improvement.

Licensee Qualifications   Congress again became specific when it came to enumerating licensee qualifications. According to Section 308 of the act, licenses may be issued only to *U.S. citizens*, a requirement that harks back to the wireless national security considerations that came into evidence after World War I (§6.2). Applicants must also qualify as to *character*, *financial ability*, and *technical ability*. The last does not mean that licensees must be engineers, but they must show that they have employed technically competent persons.

Usually all competing applicants meet these minimum statutory qualifications for licenses. The FCC therefore resorts to its right under the act to specify "other qualifications," such as program plans and the extent to which ownership is localized. These become crucially important when, as usually happens, the FCC has to choose among several competing applicants.

License Fees The communications act makes no provision for any payment of fees for the privilege of using the electromagnetic spectrum, despite the great commercial value of the right to use channels. Congress was concerned, no doubt, that setting a precedent of exacting payments for licenses might favor the rich over the less rich as potential licensees — which is what happened anyway as soon as all the valuable channel assignments had been snapped up by investors.

Granting commercial licensees the use of channels without a rental charge created the paradoxical situation of the taxpayers having to pay $77 million a year (the FCC's 1980 budget) in order to enable commercial investors to mine the spectrum for billions in profit each year.

Prompted by congressional sentiment that federal agencies serving commercial interests should become self-supporting, in 1964 the FCC began collecting *filing fees* on CP, license renewal, and the many other applications it processes. However, the Supreme Court decided that the fee scale adopted by the FCC was not reasonably related to the actual costs of its services (415 US 336, 1974). Refunding of over $50 million in filing fees was still in progress in 1980 and the FCC had not yet put a revised fee schedule into effect.

Assignment of Licenses Stations are sold, but CPs and licenses are *assigned* (because they are not owned they cannot be sold). Applicants for assignment must meet the same qualifications as original licensees.

In the periods following World War II (for radio) and the licensing freeze (for television) a lively business of investing in CPs solely for the purpose of quick turnover and high profit emerged. Alert investors, realizing that the right to use desirable channels would quickly enhance in value, tied up the most promising channels that then remained unoccupied.

Called *trafficking,* this practice completely subverted the communications act, which licenses the use of the spectrum to enable service to the public, not merely to enable trade in licenses as a speculative commodity.* The FCC tried to curb trafficking by asserting control over the choice of assignees when CPs or newly won licenses were put on the market. Congress objected so strongly to this interference with free enterprise that it amended the communications act to prevent such FCC intervention. Under the amendment to Section 310, an assignment must still be in the public interest, but the FCC may not consider whether it "might be served by the transfer, assignment, or disposal of the permit or license to a person other than the proposed transferee or assignee."†

License Renewal In the licensing provisions of the communications act, Congress lumped together applications for licenses and applications for renewals of licenses. It apparently wanted to emphasize the point that renewal is not automatic but depends on the licensee's meeting the same public interest standards as were met in obtaining the original grant. This left to FCC discretion the choice between granting renewal to an incumbent licensee or denying the renewal in favor of a new applicant who promised a better service. Making this choice became one of the most difficult and controversial of all FCC functions, as we shall see in §16.7.

---

*The term "trafficking" is also used in an entirely different sense, referring to the scheduling of commercials by a station's traffic department (§13.3).
†The term "transfer" refers to an internal change in stock ownership rather than a total change in both ownership of physical assets and identity of the licensee, which is what assignment entails.

15.5 Control over Programs

The communications act says surprisingly little *explicitly* about programs, though of course the "public interest" concept implies volumes.

Censorship Disclaimer   Congress had a reason for restraint in mentioning program matters in the act, realizing that the very existence of a federal law governing broadcasting invited challenge on constitutional grounds. After all, the First Amendment says expressly that "Congress shall make no law . . . abridging the freedom of speech, or of the press." Radio broadcasting is certainly "speech," and the Supreme Court had long since agreed that "the press" includes modern media of information. Yet here was Congress passing a law about who could become broadcasters and what broadcasters could and could not say.

Conscious of the need to avoid infringing on First Amendment rights in the field of broadcasting, Congress took care to include a disclaimer in the act, saying in Section 326:

Nothing in this Act shall be understood or construed to give the Commission the power of censorship over the radio communications or signals transmitted by any radio station, and no regulation or condition shall be promulgated or fixed by the Commission which shall interfere with the right of free speech by means of radio communication.

Localism: Station Distribution   As we have seen, Congress, in its statement of purpose prefacing the act, referred to making services available "so far as possible, to all the people of the United States." Later, in Section 307 of the act, the idea of universally available service was again stressed:

In considering applications for licenses, and modifications and renewals thereof, when and insofar as there is demand for the same, the Commission shall make such distribution of licenses, frequencies, hours of operation, and of power among the several States and communities as to provide a fair, efficient, and equitable distribution of radio service to each of the same.

The emphasis on "fair, efficient, and equitable distribution" of stations to each state and community reflects a major congressional concern. In fact in the early years of the 1927 act Congress mandated a quota system to ensure that each region would get an allotted share of the radio channels. But the system broke down when it became apparent that (for example) a station on the border of one state and therefore in that state's quota could extend most of its coverage into a neighboring state whose quota did not reflect the added service. Congress gave up on quotas but retained the "equitable distribution" principle, leaving the FCC to work out practical details in its licensing policies.

An unintended consequence of the policy of localizing station distribution is that people in big cities can choose from 40 or more stations, while people in many rural areas have little or no choice. Localism in station distribution, coupled with commercial free enterprise, inevitably leads to maldistribution — too many stations where the money is, not enough where stations cannot operate at a profit.

A policy of equitable *service*, at the price of equitable local distribution of *stations*, would rely on fewer, larger, more powerful stations, strategically positioned to serve the widest possible areas. Big cities would have fewer choices, but rural areas would have almost the same choices as metropolitan areas. Most countries of the world opted for this kind of nationally oriented service, engineered for maximum efficiency. Their aim is to cover entire populations using the fewest possible transmitters. Thus we have another instance of the price that must be paid for democracy — less efficiency, more freedom.

Localism: Access to Stations

The implications of the localism principle reach farther than the jealous concern of each state for its share of a federal handout. Localism means not only stations but also local *access* to stations. Ideally, it means opportunities for local public service agencies to promote their objectives, for partisans in local controversies to air their points of view, for local governments to inform the electorate, for local educational and cultural institutions to broaden their community service, for local talent to have an outlet, and so on. Ideally, a station thereby serves its area as a means of community self-expression, giving it a broadcast voice as well as a broadcast ear.

Localism in this sense has to do with the deep-rooted American political tradition of community autonomy. Idealists in the earlier days of radio looked to localized broadcasting to revive the fading spirit of the traditional New England town meeting. They confidently hoped that, given local radio voices, communities would find new opportunities for grass-roots citizen participation in local affairs. Radio would bring a new sense of community togetherness.

Such hopes were doomed to failure. The irresistible force of syndication swept away most local production, while much wider and more fundamental social changes weakened grass-roots political institutions, outmoding participatory democracy of the ideal kind symbolized by the New England town meeting.

This does not mean that localism has been entirely abandoned. Licensing and renewal policies continue to hold it up as a goal. For example, local residence is a point in favor of

an applicant as against an absentee-owner applicant. We describe details of the FCC's localism efforts in the next chapter.

"Equal Time" for Political Candidates

The most substantial explicit program requirement of the communications act is the well-known "equal time" provision for political candidates. A cynic might conclude that the politicians who wrote the statute only too naturally took their own welfare as their first concern. The fact is, however, that incumbent members of Congress were sufficiently public-spirited to ensure that their rivals would have equal opportunities to oppose them on the radio in the next election.

Congress correctly foresaw in 1927 that broadcasting would one day exert a major influence on voters. If the party in power could monopolize broadcasting (as of course it now does under authoritarian regimes elsewhere in the world), candidates of opposing parties would stand little if any chance of winning elections. In order to equalize the political benefits of broadcasting as nearly as it could, Congress adopted the "equal time" provision (which actually refers to "equal opportunities"), now Section 315 of the act:

If any licensee shall permit any person who is a legally qualified candidate for any public office to use a broadcasting station, he shall afford equal opportunities to all other such candidates for that office in the use of such broadcasting station: Provided, *That such licensee shall have no power of censorship over the material broadcast under the provisions of this section. No obligation is imposed under this subsection upon any licensee to allow the use of its station by any such candidate.*

Originally, the "no obligation" clause in Section 315 at least gave licensees a chance to avoid being subjected to demands for equal time. This option was summarily removed as far as candidates for *federal* offices were concerned by a series of amendments adopted to bring the communications act in line with the Federal Election Campaign Act of 1971. One of the 1971 amendments mandated letting federal candidates have time by adding to Section 312 a new basis for license revocation:

willful or repeated failure to allow reasonable access to or to permit purchase of reasonable amounts of time for the use of a broadcasting station by a legally qualified candidate for Federal elective office on behalf of his candidacy.

Other changes mandated by the Federal Election Campaign Act of 1971 were incorporated in a new subsection of Section 315 itself, limiting stations to their "lowest unit charge" for candidates (federal and nonfederal) in the weeks just before elections.

Candidates in the News   Section 315's original equal-time mandate had the potential for interfering with news coverage of candidates. The problem lay dormant for over thirty years because, according to the prevailing FCC interpretation, Section 315 left licensees free to make their customary judgments as to newsworthiness, to distinguish between self-promotion and bona fide news in covering candidates' activities.*

In 1959, however, the FCC inexplicably reversed its interpretation, ruling in the *Lar Daly* case that even a bona fide news-related broadcast involving a candidate was a polit-

ical "use" of broadcasting that triggered equal-time obligations (26 FCC 715, 1959).

This unexpected ruling came in response to a petition from a colorful eccentric named Lar Daly. He qualified technically as a legal candidate for the office of mayor of Chicago, opposing the incumbent mayor, the famed political boss Richard Daley, who was running for reelection. Every time Mayor Daley was personally involved in a broadcast news story about the mayor's office, Lar Daly claimed the right to equal time under Section 315.

The irony of the FCC ruling was that Lar Daly, though legally qualified, was never a serious contender. Campaigning in a red-white-and-blue Uncle Sam costume, he was a perpetual candidate, running with absolutely no success for president, governor, senator, and lesser offices.

Lar Daly had, of course, a perfect right to run for office, no matter how eccentric his causes or how hopeless his case. Indeed, Section 315 is predicated on the very principle that all candidates are entitled to equal opportunities, regardless of party or platform. But the ruling in Daly's favor meant, in practical terms, a blackout of in-person news broadcasts involving Chicago's mayor. Broadcasters were not prepared to give Lar Daly equal time to advance his doomed candidacy every time they covered the mayor of the nation's then second largest city opening a new children's playground.

This was indeed a strange subversion of congressional intent. While ensuring equal treatment of all candidates, Section 315 unintentionally also denied the public the right to receive political news of possible consequence. At the same time it prevented licensees from using their right to make responsible judgments as to what qualifies as news. This affront to First Amendment principles caused a furor, galvanizing Congress into action with unaccustomed speed.

---

*That newsworthiness is an acceptable guide in distinguishing self-promotion from news is well recognized. For example, an appeals court pointed out that in situations in which to publish routine information about a lottery would be illegal, it would nevertheless be legal to treat the reactions of a big winner in a lottery as a news story (414 F 2d 990, 1969).

Though he failed to win political office, Daly won a small niche in broadcasting history as the gadfly who drove Congress to amend Section 315 of the communications act. The amendment adopted in 1959 added to the opening of Section 315 the following four exemptions:

Appearance by a legally qualified candidate on any —
(1) bona fide newscast,
(2) bona fide news interview,
(3) bona fide news documentary (if the appearance of the candidate is incidental to the presentation of the subject or subjects covered by the news documentary), or
(4) on-the-spot coverage of bona fide news events (including but not limited to political conventions and activities incidental thereto),
shall not be deemed to be use of a broadcasting station within the meaning of this subsection.

The amendment liberated political news coverage from equal-time harassments by future Lar Daly's, but it also left many knotty problems of interpretation to the FCC and the courts, as we shall see in §16.5.

15.6 Communications Act Issues

Favorable View It can be argued that Congress devised a remarkably sound piece of legislation when it wrote the Radio Act of 1927. Congress found no reason to change the substance of the broadcasting statute in 1934 when it adopted the communications act. The law survived in the 1934 version, though much amended, into the 1980s.

Written at a time when broadcasting consisted of only about 600 AM stations and two networks, the act managed to foster the development of FM radio, VHF and UHF television, use of satellite relay services, and many other innovations. It now presides over a dozen national networks (counting radio and television separately) and scores of regional and ad hoc networks, while the number of stations on the air has increased to more than 10,000.

Amendments Framers of the original 1927 legislation could not have anticipated in detail every new problem that would arise, but as we have seen (§15.3) they ensured flexibility in the law by giving the FCC wide discretionary powers. In addition, subsequent Congresses made many changes in the act by amendment. Not counting amendments to the original 1927 law prior to adoption of the 1934 act, by 1980 the statute had been amended nearly a hundred times. These changes, however, never struck at the underlying philosophy of the act as we have outlined it in preceding sections of this chapter.

Amendments sought (1) to correct unforeseen weaknesses, (2) to adapt to new conditions or to introduce new subjects of regulation, and (3) to curb certain actions that the FCC took under the broad grant of discretionary powers conferred upon it by the act. We have mentioned examples in preceding pages:

■ *Type 1*: The unforeseen effect of the equal-time provision for political candidates on news coverage of candidates led to amendment of Section 315 to exempt bona fide news programs in which candidates appear.
■ *Type 2*: To encourage UHF television, Congress gave the FCC power to force the manufacture of all-channel television receivers.
■ *Type 3*: Objecting to the way the FCC used its discretionary powers to curb trafficking in licenses, Congress adopted an amendment forbidding the FCC from interfering with the selection of station buyers.

It should be added that the broadcasting portion of the act was expanded by the addition of an entire new part dealing with public broadcasting.

Contrary View On the other hand, the act has not lacked critics. For example, historian Erik Barnouw wrote that the act was "based on a premise that had been obsolete in 1927 and by 1934 was totally invalid: that American broadcasting was a local responsibility exercised by independent station licensees" (1968: 33). Barnouw was referring to the fact that national syndication, especially in the form of networks, preempted most local program production, despite the act's emphasis on the localism ideal.

Many First Amendment scholars objected that imposing any limits at all on the licensee's freedom of choice in programming violated a basic constitutional guarantee. Broadcasters themselves complained about these limitations and also about the shortness of the license period and the uncertainty of license renewal.

These and other rumblings of discontent gained strength from a general sense of disillusionment with government overregulation that emerged in the 1970s. For the first time, serious attempts were made in Washington to scrap the 1934 act in favor of entirely new legislation. Although called "rewrites," these legislative proposals went far beyond the kinds of patching-up done by earlier amendments to the act.

Rewrites The House Subcommittee on Communications began working up a major communications act "rewrite" in 1976, proposing a new philosophy of regulation and sweeping changes in the method of administering the statute.

The draft bill (H.R. 13015, "The Communications Act of 1978") received a great deal of publicity, most of it favorable at first. After weeks of hearings, however, it became evident that the necessary votes for passage in the House could not be mustered, and the bill died in committee.

During the next two years three more new bills were introduced — two competing "partial rewrites" in the Senate and a House "rewrite of the rewrite." But with broadcasting, cable television, and common carrier issues competing for attention, no single bill was able simultaneously to resolve all the conflicting industry, consumer, and government interests.

Despite their failure, the 1976–1980 rewrite efforts are worth studying because they bring into focus the chief criticisms of the 1934 act and illustrate the range of policy alternatives under consideration. Examples of major broadcasting issues addressed in the bills follow.

■ *Public Interest Standard.* The first rewrite eliminated the public interest standard. Because the proposed new commission would no longer have the broad mandate of the FCC, there was no need to set limits on its discretionary powers. Instead, market competition was counted on to ensure that licensees would serve the public interest. Regulation was to be used only when market forces proved deficient. Later rewrites restored the public interest standard but reduced somewhat the commission's powers under the 1934 act. Here, as in the items that follow, we see evidence of a move toward a compromise position, closer to the 1934 act's philosophy.

■ *Localism.* The first rewrite eliminated the present FCC's rules for ascertaining local needs and the fairness doctrine as such. Nevertheless, it allowed the commission to require television stations to broadcast "some" news, public affairs, and locally produced programs and to treat controversial issues fairly. It also required channels to be allocated so as to ensure "the maximum" full-time services in every community. Some of the proposed bills encouraged establishment of more local stations by changes in spectrum policies and by encouraging new types of service.

■ *Spectrum Use Fees.* The provision of the first rewrite that drew the most energetic protests from existing commercial broadcasters would have exacted substantial fees for use of the spectrum. These were not mere filing fees, but use-fees, based upon the economic value of each channel, as indicated by station income. Revenue from fees was to be used to pay the expenses of running the commission, to help support public broadcasting, and to encourage minority ownership and development of rural telecommunications. The commercial broadcasters' protests appeared to be effective, for the use-fee concept disappeared as further rewrite bills evolved.

■ *License Term.* As one of many attempted trade-offs, the rewrites assured broadcasters indefinite licensing in place of the renewable three-year licenses of the 1934 act. Consumer groups opposed this provision because it deprived them of the leverage they gained from opposing renewals of broadcasters they thought were not serving them well. Strong support from industry and government witnesses prevailed, however, and most rewrite proposals retained this provision — which would have gone into effect immediately for radio, and after a decade for television.*

*So intense was the pressure for extending the license term that the first communications act amendment passed by the Ninety-seventh Congress in 1981 lengthened licenses to seven years for radio, five for television. Quick adoption was obtained by attaching the amendment as a rider on unrelated budget legislation.

■ *Competing Applications.* The rewrites agreed on the need to eliminate the cumbersome hearing procedures used under the 1934 act to choose among applicants competing for new facilities. Instead they proposed deciding the winner by lot, completely eliminating the commission's discretionary role in choosing among applicants.

It can be seen from these examples that the general thrust of the rewrites was to severely reduce the commission's discretionary powers in setting standards and choosing licensees. The rewrites proposed to make this cutback in two ways: (1) by leaving more room for the play of market forces, and (2) by substituting hard-and-fast statutory requirements for the more flexible, judgmental requirements set up by the FCC under the public interest mandate. These changes, which are described as the substitution of *structural* controls for *behavioral* controls, have their counterpart at the level of administrative law, where they are called *deregulation* (§16.10).

15.7 Other Laws Affecting Broadcasting

The communications act gives to the FCC exclusive right to regulate broadcast licensees. But broadcasters are also subject to many other laws, both federal and state, that affect their operations. Of particular relevance are laws having to do with fair employment (discussed in §12.7), international treaties, copyright, fair trade, the press, obscenity, and lotteries.

International Treaties Agreements between the United States and other nations concerning radio and wire communications have the status of treaties, which means that they must be endorsed by the U.S. Senate and have the force of federal law. Section 303 of the communications act gives the FCC the task of carrying out such treaties.

Separate regional treaties governing AM, FM, and television have been entered into by the United States and its neighbors. AM agreements cover the widest territory because long-distance sky-wave propagation affects the scattered islands of the Caribbean as well as the two common-border nations, Canada and Mexico. Agreements on FM and television have been reached with the last two.

On a broader scale, membership in the International Telecommunication Union (ITU) involves the United States in worldwide agreements (discussed in §1.4).

Copyright Law   We saw how dependence on music embroiled radio in copyright problems from the very birth of broadcasting (§7.7). In those days, creative people relied for protection of their property on a combination of traditional legal precedent (common law) and a copyright statute dating back to 1909. When that law was passed, copyrightable materials consisted basically of published works, and the law prevented only unauthorized use and *live* performance of such works. The act was amended from time to time in an effort to catch up with technology, but mere amendments could not cope effectively with modern forms of recording, duplication, distribution, and reproduction that interest contemporary copyright owners.

Thus Congress was faced with another "rewrite" problem. The problem was to give copyright holders fair protection without at the same time stifling development of new communication technologies and denying the public the benefits of their use. Congress

wrestled with new legislation for some 15 years, finally passing the Copyright Act of 1976, which went into effect in 1978.

The act is administered by the Copyright Office, which is part of the Library of Congress. Relevant key provisions of the new act can be summarized as follows:

■ *Purpose.* The Constitution gives Congress the power to enable authors to make a profit from their works, as we pointed out in §5.5. Copyright holders *license* others to use their works in exchange for payment of *royalties.* "Use" consists of making public by publishing, performing, displaying, and the like.
■ *Copyrightable works.* Such works as sculptures, choreographic notations, and computer programs can be copyrighted as well as works traditionally copyrightable such as books, musical compositions, motion pictures, and broadcast programs. Among the things *not* copyrightable are ideas, slogans, brand names, and titles.
■ *Length of Copyright.* In general, a copyright is good for the life of the creator of the work, plus 50 more years. After that a work enters the *public domain* and can be used without securing permission or paying royalty.
■ *Compulsory Licensing.* In some cases it is expedient to *compel* copyright owners to license their works on a fixed-royalty basis. The 1976 law mandated compulsory licensing to cable systems, for example. Owners of copyrighted material who license television stations to use their works must grant *retransmission rights* to cable systems that pick up such programs off the air and deliver them to subscribers (§11.1).
■ *Fair Use.* Absolutely rigid enforcement of copyright restrictions would not be in the public interest. It would prevent, for example, a student from photocopying a magazine article, or an author from quoting other writers without securing permission. The new act retained the traditional concept of *fair use,*

which gives users of copyrighted material reasonable latitude without risking suits for infringement.

Interpretation of fair use nevertheless remains controversial. For example, a significant broadcasting-related fair use issue arose soon after the new copyright act went into effect. In *Universal City Studios* vs. *Sony*, some Hollywood producers sued to prevent the making of home video recordings of their copyrighted programs without payment of royalty. The court rejected the producers' claims on the grounds that home video recording of broadcast programs was legally a fair use of copyrighted material (480 F Sup 429, 1979).

The court pointed out, however, that this was a legal case of "first impression," one that raised a specific issue never before adjudicated. No evidence of actual harm to the program producers was presented, said the court, but the case nevertheless left "many issues undecided."

Federal Trade Commission Act   Like the communications act, the Federal Trade Commission act created a regulatory agency to oversee an aspect of interstate commerce. Similarity between the two acts stops at about that point. The communications act sets out to regulate a new technology with little legal precedent. The FTC act, however, deals with a field having a long tradition in the common law, which greatly complicates its regulatory activity.

The FTC act as originally conceived in 1914 was intended to protect businesses from unfair competition, not consumers from unfair business practices. Consumers were expected to look out for themselves — the doctrine of *caveat emptor*, "let the buyer beware." Not until the 1930s was it legally recognized

that "the rule of *caveat emptor* should not be relied upon to reward fraud and deception" (302 US 112, 1937).

The act was amended in 1938, making it unlawful to use "unfair methods of competition in commerce, and unfair or deceptive acts or practices in commerce" (15 USC 45). The amendment gave the Federal Trade Commission the basis for attacking deceptive broadcast advertising. This was a needed weapon, in that the communications act gives the FCC no such authority over advertising, except insofar as a licensee's character qualifications may be brought into question as a result of actions by the FTC.

Law of the Press   When broadcasting functions as a news medium it shares with the print media a miscellaneous body of laws, precedents, and privileges known as "the law of the press." Press law relies heavily on common-law traditions and case-law precedents built up over many generations. Broadcasting law, in contrast, is based mostly on statute and has a relatively short history.

Nevertheless, much of press law also affects news broadcasters. Typical areas of common concern are libel, obscenity, fair trial, freedom of access to information, right of privacy, antitrust laws, labor laws, advertising laws, copyright, and reporter's privileges. The last includes the asserted right of news personnel to withhold the identity of news sources and to refuse to surrender personal notes (including audio and video "outtakes" in the case of recorded television news and news documentaries).

Lottery and Obscenity Laws   Statutes directed specifically against broadcasting of lotteries and obscenity are found not in the communications act but in the U.S. Criminal Code. This allows for more severe penalties than the FCC could impose for violations in these areas.

424

(1) *Lotteries.* Broadcast of advertising or information about lotteries is subject to a fine of $1,000 and/or a year's imprisonment for each day's offense (18 USC 1304). This law created a dilemma for broadcasters when individual states began legalizing their own state lottery operations. Congress therefore amended the law to permit licensees to carry lottery information and advertising, but only within their own and adjacent states. The exemption applies only to state-operated lotteries.

The antilottery statute has a wider effect on broadcasters because of the frequent use of *contests* in station promotional campaigns. Care must be taken that such contests do not turn into lotteries in the legal sense. This happens when three elements are present: a *chance* for a *prize* for a *price*. A contest that requires participants to pay any kind of entrance fee ("price" or "consideration") in which the winner is chosen by lot ("chance") and which awards the contestant something of value ("prize") is a lottery and can get a station into serious trouble.

Efforts have been made in Congress to liberalize the antilottery statute, and it seems possible that advertising of charitable and nonprofit lotteries may eventually be permitted.

(2) *Obscenity.* "Whoever utters any obscene, indecent, or profane language by means of radio communication shall be fined not more than $10,000 or imprisoned for not more than two years, or both" (18 USC 1464). The FCC requested Congress to amend this law so as to explicitly broaden it to cover not only "language" but also visual presentations. Cases arising from this potentially significant source of program control are discussed in §17.2.

Equal Employment Opportunities

Broadcasting, once rated as one of the most discriminatory fields of employment, sub-stantially improved its record during the 1970s as a result of the Civil Rights Act of 1964, which prohibits discrimination in employment practices by any firm with 15 or more employees. In 1969 the FCC incorporated federal Equal Employment Opportunities (EEO) requirements in its own rules, becoming the first federal administrative agency to take such action.

State Laws Under the Constitution, federal laws prevail over state laws in areas designated as federal matters. This means that a state law cannot rise above the communications act, but state laws nevertheless govern many activities of broadcasters that are not covered by the act.

The most notable instance of federal/state conflict in broadcasting arose between the laws of *libel* (which are a state matter) and the communications act Section 315 provision forbidding licensees from censoring political candidates. Broadcasters were caught in a dilemma: they could be sued for libel as a result of broadcasting material over which they had no control. The matter was settled by the Supreme Court in 1959 when it ruled that broadcasters were exempt from state libel laws under such circumstances (360 US 525).

A study of state laws that affect broadcasting found that they touch upon no less than 89 different aspects of the medium (Sadowski, 1974). The areas most frequently affected by state laws are: (1) individual rights (libel, for example); (2) advertising (laws controlling advertising of specific products and services, for example); (3) educational broadcasting (many states have commissions to coordinate statewide public broadcasting activities); and (4) business operations (state taxes, for example).

Summary

Constitutionally, broadcasting comes under the control of Congress because of the commerce clause. Through the Communications Act of 1934, Congress delegated supervisory responsibility to the FCC, using the guideline of "public interest, convenience, and necessity" to limit the FCC's discretionary powers.

The commission's central power is that of licensing, which confers only temporary use of channels. Both the First Amendment and a provision of the communications act forbid censorship by the FCC. Nevertheless, the act does authorize some indirect control over programs, for example by mandating a degree of localism, equal time for political candidates, and other constraints imposed by the FCC under the act's requirement that licensees serve the public interest.

Regulation under the act is subject to ample safeguards to ensure due process, including opportunities for hearings, rehearings, and appeals to the federal courts.

The communications act accommodated to the many changes that occurred in broadcasting since passage of the original 1927 radio act. Frequent amendments helped the act cope with new developments, but they never struck at its fundamental philosophy. In the 1970s, however, a strong sentiment for a complete "rewrite" of the statute developed in Washington. Proposed changes would narrow the FCC's discretionary latitude, relying more on marketplace economic competition than on regulation to ensure service in the public interest.

In addition to the controls imposed by the communications act, licensees are affected by a number of other federal as well as by state laws. Notable among these are federal laws on copyrights, fair trade, obscenity, and fair employment. Among state laws, those having to do with libel are especially significant for broadcasters.

and Robert E. Lee (1953–1981, the longest term of any commissioner in a federal agency) led the battle for UHF television for over a quarter-century.

Staff Roles References to "the commission" often signify not only the seven commissioners but also the heads of its various bureaus and divisions. Most of the applications, inquiries, and complaints sent to the FCC are handled by these staff members; thus they do not come to the commissioners' personal attention.

Staff decisions are subject to formally delegated authority and are guided by *processing rules*. The rules spell out which decisions may be settled at the staff level and which need to be put on the agenda for consideration by the commission itself. Even when the staff forwards items for personal attention by the commissioners, such items are accompanied by staff recommendations. The staff thus exerts a pervasive influence, not only on day-to-day operations of the FCC, but even on the longer-term policy decisions. Barry Cole, a communications professor who spent six years at the FCC closely observing its internal operations, noted that

staff members who are accomplished politicians and wily empire builders may find themselves with greater power than any single commission member except, perhaps, the chairman. . . . Unless the chairman or a majority of the commissioners has become distrustful of them, key staff members have the power to decide what information to bring to the commission's attention and in what form. (Cole & Oettinger, 1978:11)*

Paperwork The staff deals with hundreds of thousands of letters from the general public as well as applications and reporting

*We also get an inside view of the FCC from the perspective of a commissioner in Nicholas Johnson's "A Day in the Life of the FCC" (Johnson & Dystel, 1973).

forms. Over thirty forms affect broadcasting, ranging from initial applications for construction permits to annual financial reports, from applications for license renewals to annual employment reports.

The mountains of paperwork generated by FCC operations earned it the dubious honor of a place among the most burdensome federal agencies. In a 1978 report to Congress, the General Accounting Office said the FCC led all federal agencies in the number of hours consumed in meeting its business reporting requirements. This criticism spurred reforms that have since reduced the amount of paperwork by streamlining some forms and eliminating others.

Rule Making Rule making generates the large body of administrative law called FCC *rules and regulations*.† When the commission accepts a petition for rule making it puts out either a *notice of inquiry* (for a subject that needs extensive preliminary research and consideration) or a *notice of proposed rule making* (for a subject on which specific new rules are already formulated). These notices invite further comment from interested parties. Often the parties submit extensive research studies in support of their arguments. Proposed rules of special significance are scheduled for oral argument before the commission.

After digesting the public input and the comments of its own staff, the commission issues a *report and order* announcing the new rule with an explanation of its background and purpose. This decision is subject to petition for reconsideration, which may lead to

†The phrase "rules and regulations" is traditional, though operationally a "rule" does not differ from a "regulation."

further modifications of the rule (Exhibit 16.1.2).

To illustrate the relation between the statute (communications act) and administrative law (FCC rules), the program log rules serve as a good example. Section 303(j) of the act says that the FCC shall, "as public convenience, interest, or necessity requires . . . have authority to make general rules and regula-

Exhibit 16.1.2
Rule making process

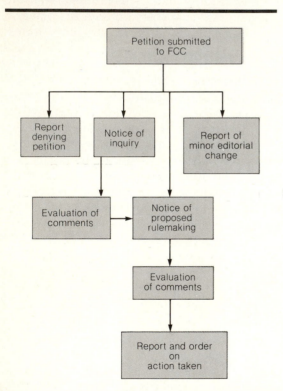

A petition for a new rule or a change of rules can come from the general public, from any branch of the federal government, or from a unit within the FCC itself. A denial or an adoption may be appealed for reconsideration. Each step of the process must be documented in the *Federal Register* so that all interested parties can keep themselves informed of rule-making actions.

tions requiring stations to keep such records of programs, transmissions of energy, communications, or signals as it may deem desirable."

Taking this cue, the FCC has adopted many pages of rules specifying in great detail several kinds of records that stations must keep. The rules governing television *program logs* run to half a dozen densely packed pages. The log, an official minute-by-minute history of a station's program output, gives the FCC a statistical record of how well a station fulfills the promises made in its license application. Formerly required of both radio and television, the log-keeping requirement was lifted for radio in 1981.

In some situations rule making would be too cumbersome, too restrictive, or too difficult to defend. In such cases the FCC can resort to *policy making* instead, laying down general directives instead of hard-and-fast rules. An example is its response to a petition for rule making on children's programs offered by a consumer group, Action for Children's Television. Instead of adopting rules as proposed by ACT, the FCC issued a statement of policy, outlining what it expected of licensees (§9.8).

Adjudication The second major class of FCC decision making on broadcasting matters consists of *adjudication*. This is the procedure for settling disputes, whether between contending outside parties (rival applicants for a channel, for example), or between internal FCC units such as the Broadcast Bureau and outside parties (resistance to imposition of a fine, for instance).

The simplest disputes may be settled summarily at the staff level, but many become the subjects of *hearings*. The right to a hearing is crucially important to an aggrieved party. Anyone denied an opportunity to present evidence in a hearing is effectively cut off from any judicial remedy of a real or imagined wrong.

Especially qualified FCC staff members called *Administrative Law Judges* (ALJs) preside over initial hearings. They conduct the proceedings like courtroom trials, with sworn witnesses, testimony, evidence, counsels for each side, and so on. ALJ initial decisions are reviewed by the FCC Review Board, then by the commissioners themselves.

When opposing sides exploit all the possibilities for reviews and appeals (§15.6), final decisions can take a long time. In extreme cases, years of delay and millions of dollars in costs can occur before settlement. The oldest case in FCC annals, the KOB case, began in 1941. It entailed among other things an argument over nighttime use of the 770-kHz AM radio channel, shared by KOB in Albuquerque and WABC in New York. In 1977 the FCC confirmed WABC's primary status on the channel and KOB's final objections were quashed in 1980 by a summary affirmation of the FCC's ruling by the appeals court, which the Supreme Court refused to review. The next year, however, KOB's irrepressible owner filed a new petition asking the FCC to reclassify the channel, which would give him a new avenue of appeal.

Informal Regulation Not all regulation comes from formal rule making and adjudication. Commissioners also influence licensee conduct through the public statements they make in speeches and articles and through their personal contacts with licensees. Licensees and their lawyers study unofficial pronouncements with all the zeal of bettors analyzing racing forms. Broadcaster organizations eagerly seek commissioners as speakers at their meetings.

Newton Minow, the FCC chairman remembered for his "vast wasteland" speech, believed that the sting of that criticism re-

sulted in better budgets and more air time for many station news departments (Terry, 1976). This indirect, "raised eyebrow" form of regulation hides an implied threat: "If you broadcasters don't take it upon yourselves to put your own house in order the next thing you know the government will have to step in and do it for you."

Carried a step farther, the raised eyebrow technique of regulation turns into *jawboning*. In the mid-seventies, for example, the FCC found itself under intense pressure from Congress and public groups to "do something" quickly about the exposure of children to increasing levels of television sex and violence. Knowing that a direct assault on the problem would certainly collide with the First Amendment, the commission jawboned the networks and the NAB Code Authority into voluntarily adopting *family viewing standards*. The industry representatives agreed in 1975 not to schedule "entertainment programming inappropriate for viewing by a general family audience" until after the first two hours of prime time; or, in cases where postponements were not feasible, to flash "advisories" on the screen to alert viewers that family standards might be violated.*

Network Regulation The family viewing standards jawboning incident is symptomatic of the dominant role played by networks in setting program standards. Yet the communications act is ambiguous about FCC control over networks, merely empowering the commission to regulate "*stations* engaged in chain broadcasting." Accordingly, nearly all controls imposed on networks have been indirect — couched not in terms of what networks may or may not do, but rather in terms of

---

*This instance of jawboning led to a series of lawsuits, reviewed in §17.1.

what licensees may or may not do in making contracts with networks. We noted earlier how the FCC used this indirect route to network control in adopting the chain broadcasting regulations (§7.5) and the prime-time access rule (§12.4).

Such curbs as these grew out of in-depth studies of network operations conducted by the FCC. Its first major study was the landmark *Report on Chain Broadcasting* in 1941. Soon after that the FCC set up a permanent Office of Network Study, which kept the networks under continuous investigation. The most recent of the major investigations undertaken by the FCC's Network Study Special Staff reported on the prospects for new networks (FCC, 1980). Its conclusions are summarized in §16.10.

16.2 License Application

Finding a Channel   A would-be licensee must apply for specific facilities (channel, power, antenna pattern, time of operation, and so on). Because the FCC has allotted all FM and television channels to communities in advance, the applicant consults the allotment tables to find a vacant channel. Alternatively it is possible to petition for a change in the allotment tables. In the case of AM channels, however, there is no such table. Applicants must employ engineering consultants to search out locations where AM channels could be activated without causing interference.

The most desirable commercial channels have long since been licensed, so that the would-be licensee of today nearly always seeks to buy an existing station. Station brokers, of which there are about 75, bring sell-

ers and buyers together. So far the biggest year for ownership changes was 1979, when over 600 stations were sold. Their total cost amounted to over a billion dollars, an average of about $1.7 million per station.

In order to discourage *trafficking* in licenses (§15.4), the FCC expects a licensee to operate a station for a full three-year term before attempting to sell. Earlier sale is subject to FCC hearing unless the seller can give a good reason other than simply the desire to turn the license over for a profit. Assuming that the three-year rule is not invoked, the entire process takes from 30 to 60 days according to the NAB's guide to station buying (NAB, 1978).

Mutually Exclusive Applications   In the days before all the commercially desirable channels had been licensed (and even today when desirable channels become available because of deletions of existing licenses or changes in channel allocation rules), several applicants might compete to obtain a license for the same channel in the same market. Such competitors are called *mutually exclusive* applicants, and the FCC makes a choice among them after conducting *comparative hearings*. These are usually long-drawn-out and costly proceedings.

A notorious example of delay because of such proceedings involved Channel 9 in Orlando, Florida, one of the exceedingly valuable VHF channels released at the end of the television freeze. The original application dates back to 1953, when the FCC granted Channel 9 to an applicant called Mid-Florida TV. Competing applicants challenged this award and three times in succession the appeals court overturned FCC decisions favoring Mid-Florida. In 1969, pending still further hearings, the FCC allowed the five competing applicants to operate the station jointly on an interim basis. After 28 years of uncertainty, Channel 9 in Orlando became a fully licensed operation in 1981 when the FCC allowed the interim joint venture to become permanent.

A different kind of interim operation kept an AM station on the air for 18 years while twenty applicants fought for a license. The FCC took away the license of KRLA in Pasadena, California, in 1962, but allowed a non-profit corporation to operate it pending the outcome of the contest among competing applicants. The nonprofit group ran the station commercially but turned over the net proceeds to public broadcasting in the area. The case was finally settled in 1980 when the FCC awarded the license to a coalition of five remaining applicants.

Application Forms   The basic license application, Form 301, is for a *construction permit* (CP). It asks for FCC permission to construct a new station or to make changes in an existing station. Sales of existing stations require different forms because they involve showings by both an existing licensee and a would-be licensee, but the information is basically the same as for a new station.

Form 301 serves, with some adaptations, for both radio (AM and FM) and television applications. The following description is based on the television version.

Form 301 asks for the personal and financial qualifications of the applicant, program plans, engineering plans, and equal employment opportunities implementation plans. Completing the program section of Form 301 entails the most extensive preparation by the applicant. Briefly summarized, this section requires statements and explanatory exhibits on the following:

■ How local needs and interests will be ascertained and how they will be served by programs.
■ Statement of general program policies, if any.

■ Policy on handling discussions of public issues.
■ Time to be devoted to news, public affairs, and other nonentertainment and nonsports programming, in hours and minutes.
■ Percentage of news time to be devoted to local and regional news, and staff devoted to this purpose.
■ Staff plans in relation to overall program proposals.
■ Identity of key program decision makers.
■ Number of public service announcements planned per week.
■ Methods of keeping abreast of changes in the communications act and FCC rules.

In a comparative hearing, providing detailed plans for these aspects of programming is an exacting business. Opposing applicants can be counted on to sift through rival applications (which become matters of public record) in search of the smallest discrepancies and weaknesses. Such boners as planning more local programming than would be feasible in the proposed studio facilities will be pounced on by the opposition. A favorite angle of attack is to suggest that there are inadequacies in the ascertainment of local needs — segments of the population overlooked, failure to consult representative community leaders, and so on.

Form 301 runs to about 30 pages, but in a hotly contested comparative hearing the accompanying exhibits can run into hundreds, even thousands, of pages and months of hearings. In 1981 a communications act amendment attached to a congressional budget bill adopted a solution proposed by the FCC itself. The FCC would abandon any pretense of choosing the best contender, conducting a lottery instead of a hearing. The luckiest, not necessarily the best qualified, applicant would win the license.

16.3 Applicant Qualifications

As we have noted (§15.4), the communications act requires licensees to qualify as to citizenship, character, finances, and technical ability. The FCC fleshes out these bare requirements and adds others based on its interpretation of public interest obligations.

Finances   Form 301 requires detailed disclosure of financial resources. An applicant must have enough money in the bank or available on loan not only to build the proposed station according to plan but also to operate without depending on station income for 90 days.

This concern for ensuring that applicants have enough money to start up station operations does not extend to concern about future economic injury that might be inflicted by the licensing of more competitors than the market can sustain. An early Supreme Court decision, the *Sanders Brothers* case, established that the FCC's duty is to consider only how increased competition would affect the *public* interest, not the private economic interest of existing licensees (309 US 470, 1940).

Generally, the FCC has avoided trying to weigh the impact of competition on the public interest, leaving stations to survive as best they can. An exception to this rule was the commission's concern at one time for protecting broadcasters from the economic injury that might result from cable and pay television, reviewed in §11.1. The sink-or-swim policy is probably desirable on the whole, given the difficulty of forecasting the effects of competition. But it has had the unfortunate effect of encouraging more stations to go on the air than some markets can support. Oversupply of stations means that some are woefully underfinanced. Such marginal stations tend to erode both industry and FCC standards. The FCC is often over-lenient with marginal stations out of sympathy for licensees struggling to stay afloat, as is shown by its record on license deletions (§16.6).

Technical Qualifications   Most applicants hire engineering consultants to prepare their technical proposals. Such consultants specialize in showing how a proposed station will get maximum physical coverage without causing objectionable interference to existing stations. Engineering plans must also show expertise in meeting FCC engineering standards, and the proposed physical plant must be capable of achieving the amount and types of production proposed in the program section of the application.

Character   Applicants are expected to be free of histories that suggest defects in character of a type that could cast doubt on their ability to operate in the public interest. Criminal records and violations of antitrust laws are examples of such evidence. If the applicant has previous history as a licensee, prior misrepresentations to the FCC would be regarded as fatal defects. In comparative hearings opposing applicants dredge up even the smallest evidence of their rivals' past wrongdoing in order to impugn their character qualifications.

Complications arise when a licensee is a large corporation engaged in several different business enterprises. A nonbroadcast arm of a corporation may have been found guilty of illegal activities in which the broadcasting subsidiary took no part. Should the sins of the parent corporation be visited on its broadcasting offspring?

Few large corporations have survived the commercial wars without blemish. Close scrutiny of corporate character could endanger scores of existing licenses. This became evident in 1980 when the FCC, in a surprise move, refused to renew the licenses of three major television stations licensed to RKO General, Inc. — WNAC in Boston, KHJ in Los Angeles, and WOR in New York. Among the FCC's reasons for denying renewal was the fact that RKO's parent corporation, the General Tire and Rubber Company, had admitted in a Securities Exchange Commission case to illegal contributions and bribery of foreign officials (78 FCC 2d 1, 1980). RKO owns 13 other stations, all of which were later also designated for hearing. The likelihood of anything coming of such threats of nonrenewal based on alleged character defects seemed remote in the deregulatory climate of the 1980s. Moves were afoot in Washington to downplay the character qualification test for licensees. Indeed, in 1981 the FCC started an inquiry looking toward recommending its deletion from the communications act.

1965 Policy Statement: Localism Criteria

Assuming that competing applicants meet the basic statutory citizenship, financial, technical, and character qualifications, the FCC next looks at localism criteria. The commission outlined these criteria in a 1965 policy statement on comparative hearings (1 FCC 2d 393). To the specific statutory criteria for licensing, the commission added:

- *Diversification of media ownership.* An applicant without other media interests is preferred over one already involved in broadcasting or publishing.
- *Participation in station operation.* An applicant proposing to take an active role in day-to-day station operations is preferred to an absentee or inactive owner.
- *Program service.* An applicant whose proposed programming best promises to serve local interests is given preference.

These criteria, said the FCC, would not be applied mechanically. Final decisions would rely on subjective judgments by the FCC as to the relative weights that should be assigned to each merit and demerit of each competing applicant.

Minority Ownership Initially the FCC disregarded the minority status of owners as an aspect of diversification of media control. A series of court reversals in the 1960s and early 1970s, however, caused it to reexamine this position (Meeske, 1976).

Of particular note was a finding of an appeals court at one stage in the long-drawn-out Channel 9 Orlando case mentioned earlier in this section. The FCC had refused to give favorable consideration to the fact that two of the stockholders of one of the competing firms were black, despite the fact that about a quarter of Orlando's population is black. The communications act, said the FCC, is "color blind," but the court rejected this view, pointing out:

It is consistent with the primary objective of maximum diversification of ownership of mass communications media for the commission . . . to afford favorable consideration to an applicant who, not as a mere token, but in good faith as broadening community representation, gives a local minority group media entrepreneurship. (495 F 2d 937, 1973)

As a result of this and other cases, minority applicants began to get more consideration from the FCC in the 1970s. In 1978, spurred on by Carter administration policies on aid to minorities, the FCC took two steps that further enhanced the opportunities for members of minority groups to become licensees.

(1) The FCC, after prodding by the NAB, agreed to issue *tax certificates* to licensees proposing to sell stations to minority applicants.

These certificates encourage such sales by allowing the sellers to defer paying capital gains taxes on their profits if they purchase another station within two years.

(2) The FCC also agreed to consider allowing *distress sales* to minority applicants. Normally the FCC does not permit an owner whose license is under threat of nonrenewal to sell anything other than the station's physical assets. In making exceptions to this rule to encourage sales to minority applicants, the FCC permits the previous licensees to gain some, but not all, of the total value of both tangible and intangible assets. For example, in 1979 the FCC agreed to drop fraudulent billing charges against a small AM station in Windsor, Connecticut, when the incumbent licensee offered to sell the property to a minority group for 75 percent of its appraised value.

Minority applicants receive still more help both from other government agencies and from private agencies such as the NAB. The Small Business Administration, for example, began in 1978 for the first time making loans to would-be broadcasters.

Minority ownership increased markedly during the 1970s. At the end of the decade a *Broadcasting* special report listed a hundred stations controlled by blacks and 17 by Hispanics (15 Oct. 1979). But according to the National Black Media Coalition, ownership of stations by minorities in proportion to their actual numbers would require 1,224 owned by blacks and 436 owned by Hispanics.

16.4 Applicant Program Plans

Public Service Programs   In 1960 the FCC issued a statement of policy on programming, summarizing its views on what should be expected of licensees (44 FCC 2d,

2303). This became a key document on the subject of public service program obligations. It is quoted in the basic station application form and provides the basis for program logging rules. The policy statement singles out specific program types as having special public interest significance:

The major elements usually necessary to meet the public interest, needs and desires of the community in which the station is located as developed by the industry, and recognized by the Commission, have included: (1) Opportunity for Local Self-Expression, (2) The Development and Use of Local Talent, (3) Programs for Children, (4) Religious Programs, (5) Educational Programs, (6) Public Affairs Programs, (7) Editorialization by Licensees, (8) Political Broadcasts, (9) Agricultural Programs, (10) News Programs, (11) Weather and Market Reports, (12) Sports Programs, (13) Service to Minority Groups, (14) Entertainment Programming.

It may come as a surprise to learn that entertainment is only one of *fourteen* major program elements considered important by the FCC for operation in the public interest. However, the policy statement emphasizes that this list of program types is not "a rigid mold or fixed formula."

In practice, commercial broadcasters tend to lump all the program elements other than entertainment, sports, and news, under the catchall heading "public service programming."* It has been their experience that such programs not only fail to draw large audiences but actually tend to drive existing audiences away. Most commercial stations

---

*In an attempt to correct this misleading generalization, some church-related organizations unsuccessfully petitioned the FCC in 1978 to adopt an additional program category, "Community Service," to denote noncommercial programs produced by or in conjunction with nonprofit organizations and government agencies.

therefore schedule as little public service programming as they dare. Even that little is usually "graveyarded," that is, scheduled during hours that have the lowest audience potential, such as the 2–5 A.M. period.

Localism in Programming   The 1960 policy statement linked the listed program elements closely with the doctrine of localism. Some of the categories — local self-expression, local talent, service to minority groups, for example — are in fact local by definition. The FCC went on to say that *"the principal ingredient* of the licensee's obligation to operate in the public interest is the diligent, positive, and continuing effort by the licensee to discover and fulfill the tastes, needs, and desires of his community or service area"* (44 FCC 2316, 1960, emphasis added).

The ideal of localism, always a goal of FCC's rule making and decisions, had been strongly endorsed over the years by the courts. In the early case that confirmed the FCC's right to regulate network contracts, for example, the Supreme Court agreed with the argument that networks should not be allowed to dominate programming to the point of impairing affiliates' ability to provide a localized service (319 US 190, 1943). And a few years later an appeals court upheld the FCC's denial of an application because the applicant proposed to act as a "mere relay station" for network programs (169 F 2d 670, 1948).

Nevertheless, some stations ignore their obligation to localism because they are more interested in the advertising potential of an adjacent big market than in serving the small market that happens to be their community of license. This was the situation in the aptly named *Suburban Broadcasters* case. In applying in 1962 for a radio license in Elizabeth, New Jersey, a dozen miles from the heart of New York City, Suburban Broadcasters made no effort whatever to plan a service to suit the needs of Elizabeth. Pointing out that the applicant simply copied the program schedule used in its proposals for stations in other states, the FCC denied the application (302 F 2d 191). Such cases led the FCC to adopt its *Suburban policy,* which required applicants for stations adjacent to large markets to "rebut a presumption" that their real intent was to serve the adjacent metropolitan market, not the suburban market that their channel was licensed to serve.

The fact is, however, that even in the absence of the "Suburban" motive for ignoring local needs, the economics of broadcasting drives it away from localism and toward syndication, including networking (§7.5). Syndicated material is nearly always cheaper, easier to put on the air, more popular, and thus more profitable than local material.

Ascertainment   Despite FCC urging, many licensees failed, or at best made only a halfhearted effort, to devote any programming toward serving the real needs of their local communities. Resorting to compulsion, during the 1960s the FCC evolved mandatory procedures intended to guarantee a degree of localism in programming. Known collectively as *ascertainment,* the procedures consist of three distinct stages:

(1)   Top station personnel conduct interviews with local community leaders and the station makes a survey of local public opinion, both aimed at identifying the currently most pressing community needs and problems in the station's service area. The FCC spelled out these procedures in minute detail — for example, listing 19 specific types of community leaders that should be consulted.

(2)   From the list of problems so ascertained the station selects a group of priority items that it intends to use as the basis for local programs.

✗(3)   The station produces local programs dealing specifically with the needs and problems enumerated in step 2.

Some broadcasters still professed to have trouble grasping what the FCC was trying to achieve. A common misunderstanding, even today, is that the object of ascertainment is to find out what kinds of *programs* people want. Its real goal, however, is to find out what kinds of *problems* the community faces. The *licensee,* not the public, has the responsibility of devising programs relevant to community needs and problems.

Unfortunately for the goal of relevant localized programming, no amount of FCC-mandated ascertainment can get worthwhile results without willing cooperation from broadcasters. Those already convinced of their obligation to serve their local communities have little need to be told how to do it. Those most in need of being reminded of that obligation tend to go through the ascertainment ritual mechanically, with correspondingly uninspired results. Lacking support from either side, ascertainment has been one of the most unpopular of all the FCC's devices for getting stations to comply with the public interest mandate of the communications act.

The FCC dropped ascertainment as a formal obligation for radio stations in 1981. The obligation to deal with local problems remains, and radio licensees must show evidence of fulfilling it. The evidence consists of a list of five to ten local problems identified by each station, along with descriptions of programs it has produced in the past year that were relevant to those problems. This material must be put in the station's public file, where it is open to inspection by listeners. It may be cited as evidence for or against renewal.

Television stations must still carry out the full ascertainment routine, updating their lists of local problems each year. Their enthusiasm for going through the procedures cannot be much enhanced by the radio deregulation order, in which the FCC said that its own prescribed routine "only obscures the issue of responsiveness and exhausts otherwise valuable resources in meaningless minutiae" (84 FCC 2d 998, 1981).

Quantitative Criteria   In its 1960 statement on programming, the FCC avoided saying how much time or what class of time should be devoted to each of the fourteen "program elements." Nor did it fix the amount of time that should be devoted to programs designed to answer local needs as part of the ascertainment obligation. But it said that incumbent licensees should demonstrate at renewal time that their past programming had been "substantially attuned" to meeting local needs. This statement raised the question: How *much* public service programming constitutes "substantial" in this context?

Without going so far as to adopt explicit rules for measuring substantiality, the FCC requires television applicants to state the minimum amount of time they plan to devote to nonentertainment, nonsports programs. Once on the air, television licensees must submit an annual programming report (Form 303-A). This report, based on programming in a sample week, shows how much news, public affairs, and other nonentertainment the station broadcast during the past year, and how much of each type of program was local.* Resorting to *processing rules* (§16.1) in-

---

*The FCC defines local programs as those "originated or produced by the station, or for the production of which the station is substantially responsible, and employing live talent more than 50 percent of the time." A DJ show, for example, would count as a recorded program unless the DJ or other local live talent filled more than half of the show's time on the air.

stead of going through the regular rule-making process, the FCC instructed its staff to call to the commission's personal attention any stations that failed to meet a minimum level of news, public affairs, and other nonentertainment. It set as the minimum level for these types of programs in combination 10 percent of the station's overall programming — hardly an exacting standard. Each year since 1974, when the FCC began issuing reports on how television stations in each market met the criterion, they have averaged more than twice that much nonentertainment. In 1979, for example, about 26 percent of the average television station's programming consisted of nonentertainment materials (details are given in Exhibit 9.4.1).

16.5 Operating Under License: Contingent Requirements

After an applicant completes construction and finally receives a license, several operational rules come into play. These may be called *contingent* requirements because they arise out of the experience of actual operations and therefore cannot be anticipated in detail during program-planning stages.

Nondelegable Responsibility   It would be pointless, of course, for a licensee to go through the elaborate licensing procedures only to turn over actual operations to someone else who has not met the same tests. To prevent this happening, the FCC places great emphasis on the licensee's *nondelegable responsibility* to maintain control over the station's programming. In its 1960 programming statement, the FCC said that responsibility for programming

is personal to the licensee and may not be delegated. He is obligated to bring his positive responsibility affirmatively to bear upon all who have a hand in providing broadcast matter for transmission through his facilities so as to assure the discharge of his duty to provide an acceptable program schedule consonant with operating in the public interest in his community. (44 FCC 2313, 1960)

Ignorance is no excuse. Licensees cannot plead that a program was in a foreign language, that offensive material was buried in an otherwise inoffensive program, or that a speaker made an unauthorized statement.

Fairness Doctrine Obligations   To serve the public interest, each licensee should devote some time to the discussion of public issues. The CP application form reminds applicants of this expectation by asking for a statement of ''policy with respect to making time available for the discussion of public issues and the methods of selecting subjects and participants.''

Such discussions invoke the *fairness doctrine*, obligating stations both to schedule time for, and to allow time for expression of opposing viewpoints on, issues of public importance (the reasons for this requirement are discussed in §17.4). This obligation means that licensees should continuously monitor their own programming to make sure that, if anyone introduces controversial issues, fair opportunities for reply are offered to opposing interests. If licensees themselves introduce controversial issues in the form of station editorials, they must offer time for the expression of opposing views.

Also part of the fairness obligation is the duty to inform individuals or groups of *per-*

sonal attacks on their "honesty, character, integrity or like personal qualities" that may occur in the course of discussions of public issues. Licensees must inform those attacked within a week of the offending broadcast of the nature of the attack and must offer a chance to reply.

The personal attack rule does not, however, cover any and all attacks. For example, the Polish American Congress claimed a fairness doctrine right to reply to some Polish jokes on *The Dick Cavett Show* on ABC. The FCC said that even though the skit potentially offended ten million Polish-Americans, it did not invoke the fairness doctrine. The appeals court agreed that no violation occurred because nowhere in the complaint was there "a clear statement of the issue which is alleged to be both controversial and of public importance" (520 F 2d 1254, 1975).

Licensees make their own decisions under the fairness doctrine on such questions as:

- Whether or not a subject qualifies as an issue of public importance.
- How much time should be devoted to replies.
- When replies should be scheduled.
- What format replies should employ.
- Who should speak for opposing viewpoints (except, of course, for those replying to personal attack).

The FCC gives licensees wide latitude. For example, a homosexual rights organization alleged that a station was unfair in granting replies to attacks on homosexuals that occurred in the syndicated fundamentalist religious series, *PTL Club*. The attacks occurred during eight hours of the program over a four-month period. The "reasonable opportunity" for reply offered by the station con-sisted of a single program repeated nine times during a four-day period. Despite the discrepancy between attack and reply opportunities the FCC said the licensee had used reasonable discretion (68 FCC 2d 1500, 1978).

Given such latitude, conscientious broadcasters normally have no reason to fear that fairness doctrine obligations will impose undue demands on station time. Not all broadcasters, however, are willing to act in good faith by complying with the fairness doctrine. Some use their stations to promote extreme positions on controversial issues, oblivious of the fact that as licensees they have an obligation to offer opportunities for rebuttal.

One of the most publicized instances of licensee one-sidedness occurred when WXUR, a Media, Pennsylvania, AM/FM radio station, lost its license for defying the fairness doctrine. WXUR was licensed to an organization headed by Carl McIntire, a cantankerous right-wing fundamentalist preacher. Despite opposition from citizen groups in the community, he had acquired WXUR when stations in nearby Philadelphia refused to carry his *Twentieth Century Reformation Hour*, a syndicated radio series noted for its intemperate attacks on opponents of McIntire's ultraconservative philosophy.

From the moment the station went on the air in 1965, citizen groups began bombarding the FCC with complaints about WXUR's "hate clubs of the air." In 1970 the FCC finally refused to renew the license, alleging not only fairness doctrine violations but also failure to fulfill program promises and to ascertain local needs. An appeals court upheld the FCC's action, making WXUR the first station to lose its license because of fairness doctrine violations. The court of appeals used unusually strong language in condemning McIntire's stewardship. "With more bravado than brains," said the court, his station ". . . went on an independent frolic, broadcasting what it chose, abusing those who dared to differ from its viewpoints" (473 F 2d 48, 1972).*

Few fairness complaints have such drastic consequences. Thousands arrive at the FCC each year. They tend to come from zealous partisans with strong views on such emotional issues as gun control, abortion, women's rights, gay liberation, environmental protection, prayers in schools, and nuclear power. Most complaints are dismissed out of hand by the FCC Complaints and Compliance Division. Either complainants cite no legally definable controversial issue or they fail to show that the overall programming of accused stations had in fact denied reasonable opportunities for both sides to be argued.

Political Candidates   Because they both deal with access to station time, the fairness doctrine is often confused with equal opportunities (popularly "equal time") for political candidates. Unlike fairness doctrine speakers, however, candidates have a *personal right* of access, spelled out in Sections 312 and 315 of the communications act. These laws concern specific categories of *persons* (candidates) and afford equal opportunities to other specified persons (candidates for the same office). The fairness doctrine rules, on the other hand, concern *issues* and offer only *reasonable* opportunities to opposing points of view. People speaking on behalf of candidates cannot make Section 315 claims; only candidates in person (Exhibit 16.5).†

*The appeals court was divided on the fairness doctrine issue, basing its opinion mainly on failure to live up to program promises (which did, however, contain fairness elements). McIntire had some success, despite the vigor with which the court condemned his tactics, in recruiting support from some First Amendment experts for his argument that the nonrenewal violated the First Amendment (§17.8).

†In the *Zapple doctrine,* the FCC held that spokespersons for candidates could make fairness doctrine claims to reply to attacks on candidates, but could not expect *free* time for reply, as can other persons making fairness claims (23 FCC 2d 707, 1970).

The equal time rules apply both to candidates for party nomination in the primaries and to nominees of all parties in the final election. Equal opportunities can be claimed only by candidates for each specific office. For example, if the candidate for representative in a specific congressional district receives time, all candidates in the same district are entitled to equal time, but not candidates for other districts or for other offices.

Broadcasting has assumed such an important role in political campaigns that candidates bring tremendous pressures to bear on both the stations and the FCC, especially during presidential elections. Problems of interpretation arise from the amendments to Sections 312 and 315 of the communications act (discussed in §15.5).

The most recent FCC primer on political candidate broadcasts runs to over a hundred pages (FCC 1980). Following are a few examples of the kinds of complications that have arisen:

■ *Are presidential news conferences bona fide news programs?* The FCC answered first no, then yes to this question. In the 1980 presidential campaign, Senator Edward Kennedy claimed a right to reply to an attack by President Jimmy Carter (also a candidate at the time) in a presidential news conference. Another candidate, Governor Jerry Brown, asked for a chance to rebut Carter's comments on a *Meet the Press* interview program. The FCC turned down both claims on the ground that each program qualified as a bona fide news event and therefore was exempt from Section 315 equal time requirements.

■ *Are presidential candidate debates news?* The FCC also at first decided that debates between leading presidential candidates failed to qualify as bona fide broadcast news events under the Section 315 exemptions. The debate between John F. Kennedy and Richard

Exhibit 16.5
Fairness doctrine and equal time law compared

Basis of comparison	Fairness doctrine	Equal time law
Legal status based on . . .	FCC policy Clause in Section 315 Rules for personal attack and political editorials	Section 315, supplemented by Section 312 of communications act
Access for . . .	Controversial *issues* of public importance	Political *candidates* in person
When invoked?	Any time	During political campaigns only
Right of access initiated by . . .	Introduction of an issue	"Use" by another candidate for same office
Speakers chosen by . . .	Licensee	Self — all other candidates automatically eligible
Amount of access time required . . .	"*Reasonable* opportunity" to reply	"Equal" opportunity
Permissible time charges, if any . . .	None if speaker unable to pay (exception: spokespersons for political candidates)	"Lowest unit charge" (but depends on stage of campaign)
Types of programs affected . . .	Any except news (unless evidence of deliberate distortion is presented)	Any except 4 types of bona fide news programs listed in Section 315
Format chosen by . . .	Licensee	Candidate
Licensee editing allowed?	Yes	No (if appearance is based on Section 315 obligation)
Special features . . .	Notification by licensee within specified times in case of personal attacks and political editorials	Candidates must be legally qualified and request time within a week of "use" by rival candidate

Comment: It is called the fairness *doctrine* because most of it takes the form of policy rather than explicit rules. Equal opportunities, on the other hand, are mandated as a matter of law in the communications act.

M. Nixon in 1960 took place only because Congress temporarily suspended Section 315 in that specific case.

In 1975, concluding that its previous view of Section 315 had misinterpreted the intent of Congress, the FCC said that debates between presidential candidates qualified as bona fide news events as long as precautions were taken, such as leaving debate arrangements to third parties with no personal interest in the outcome. Shirley Chisholm, a black member of Congress who ran for president in 1976, and others challenged this decision, but the appeals court upheld the FCC (538 F 2d 349, 1976). Accordingly, in the campaign of 1976 the two leading candidates, Gerald R. Ford and Jimmy Carter, debated under auspices of the nonpartisan League of Women Voters. The same group arranged a debate between Carter and Ronald Reagan in 1980.

■ *How much time provides "reasonable access"?* Certain stations tried to limit candidates to one-minute political spots because of formats (such as all-news radio) that do not lend themselves to extended political speeches. But this limitation violated the reasonable access provision of Section 312, said the FCC. Another station adopted a policy of selling no more than five minutes of time to presidential candidates, but again the FCC ruled this an unreasonable limitation on access.

■ *May "on-the-spot" news appearances by candidates be recorded for later playback?* In 1976 a station asked the FCC whether the "on-the-spot" news exemption of Section 315 allowed for recording of a debate between congressional candidates for later playback. The commission agreed that if broadcast within 24 hours a recorded news event would be considered as on-the-spot coverage. The appeals court upheld this ruling.

■ *Are candidate appearances in magazine and talk shows bona fide news?* Magazine programs such as NBC's *Today* and ABC's *Good Morning*

America qualify for exemptions as bona fide news programs under Section 315. Late in 1980, however, FCC ruled that Phil Donahue's interview programs, which take place in an audience participation setting, did not qualify.

■ *What constitutes a station's "lowest unit charge"?* This phrase in Section 315 defines the maximum rates stations may charge candidates who buy time for political purposes shortly before elections. A commercial advertiser might have to buy several hundred spots to earn the maximum discount; a political candidate, however, gets the benefit of the maximum discount even when buying only a single spot announcement. One station proposed charging a candidate for a five-minute program more than five times its rate for a one-minute spot on the ground that program rates differ from spot rates. The FCC ruled, however, that the lowest-unit charge provision required the station to charge no more than five times its one-minute spot rate.*

Employment Policies and Practices

The CP application form contains a special section on Equal Employment Opportunities (EEO). Applicants proposing, or already having, more than five employees must set up a "positive, continuing program of practices to assure equal employment opportunities." These EEO requirements refer to women in all cases and to minority groups in cases where minorities form 5 percent or more of the work force in the station's service area.

Guidelines in the CP Form 301 show how to set up EEO programs. They call for statements about plans or practices with regard to:

■ General EEO policy.
■ The officer responsible for implementing the EEO policy.

*Late in 1981 the FCC recommended to Congress repeal of the entire equal opportunities law.

- Method of publicizing the policy.
- Methods of recruitment and training.
- An analysis of the racial composition of the population in the station's service area.
- The station's current employee profile.
- How many people were hired for what jobs in the last twelve months.
- Promotion policies.
- Effectiveness of the plan.

Disclosures to Aid Consumers Operating requirements include certain disclosures that help the public understand and enforce the licensee's obligations. The *public file*, for example, consists of a collection of documents that both applicants and licensees must assemble and keep ready to show to any member of the public on request (47 CFR 1.526). The file assists consumers in assessing the station's performance and, if need be, in gathering data to challenge license renewal.

Consumers should be able to find in the public file a copy of the station's program proposals, annual disclosures (ownership, employment, program, and television ascertainment reports), copies of letters received from the public, television program logs, and a copy of the FCC's *Broadcast Procedure Manual,* the primer on how the public can participate in FCC proceedings (39 FR 32288, 1974).

A second type of disclosure consists of announcements that each station must put on the air calling attention of the public to licensees' obligations to serve local needs and making known when the station's renewal application comes due.

Self-Monitoring As the preceding discussion of contingent duties makes amply apparent, application forms are merely the first stages of a continuing flood of paperwork. In addition to daily engineering and (television only) program logs, each station makes several annual reports.

In the meantime, conscientious licensees must be alert to avoid the many hazards that can endanger smooth processing of renewal applications. They must check periodically to ensure that their actual programming reflects with reasonable accuracy their program promises; they must be careful to adhere to fairness doctrine and equal time obligations and to avoid violating obscenity, lottery, copyright, libel, and other statutes. Sales departments need to be watched to make sure they are not tempted into double-billing, excessive commercialization, and other commercial abuses. Public complaints must be dealt with diplomatically and the public file kept in order and readily accessible.

While keeping one eye on the store, the licensee must direct the other toward Washington to keep up with new FCC regulations and new interpretations of old ones. All this would be an overwhelming load of administrative paperwork for a station of any size and stature were it not for the help that comes from the numerous trade organizations and the corps of communications attorneys in Washington.

Lawyers who represent stations in FCC dealings belong to the Federal Communications Bar Association (FCBA), which had about a thousand members in 1981 (including those that handle common carrier as well as broadcasting matters). Most stations of any size keep an FCBA lawyer on retainer as a precautionary measure:

Like dentists, the communications lawyers can tell their clients to come to them before they have trouble — or later when it will hurt worse. Lawyers point out that the FCC lacks clear guidelines on many important policies and procedures, that it sometimes enforces its rules in an arbitrary fashion, and that the FCC has traditionally preferred a "case-by-case" or "let's-wing-it" approach to making decisions. (Cole & Oettinger, 1978: 30)

Because of such ambiguities and because of the FCC's ultimate power to put them out of business, broadcasters tend to have exaggerated fears about confrontations with the commission — fears that communications lawyers at times tend to encourage. Nevertheless, proximity to the commission and personal contacts with FCC staff members enable Washington lawyers to get things done faster than distant licensees unfamiliar with federal bureaucratic labyrinths (*Broadcasting*, 16 June 1980).

Most of the routine work of communications lawyers is simply a matter of keeping their clients alert and properly informed. Very few of all the thousands of applications, petitions, and other matters the FCC handles ever reach the point of being "designated for hearing," when formal legal representation becomes indispensable. Most lawyers mail out information regularly to their clients, reminding them of filing dates, informing them of new regulations, interpreting recent decisions. Legal clinics are a common feature of trade association meetings, such as those of the National Association of Broadcasters. The NAB also publishes special primers on how to handle political candidates, how to comply with EEO guidelines, and how to avoid violating the antilottery law. A particularly valuable NAB publication for current legal information is its frequently updated review called *Broadcasting and Government*, describing the current status of pending broadcast legislation, rule-making procedures, and industry petitions on file with the FCC.

16.6 Appraisal of Licensee Performance

In the course of normal operations, a conscientious broadcaster experiences little official supervision or monitoring. The FCC actively inspects only technical aspects of operation through its engineering field offices. Questions about programming and commercial practices, if they arise at all, are usually brought to FCC attention by the general public, consumer groups, other licensees, and competing applicants at renewal time.

Public Complaints   The FCC's Complaints and Compliance Division receives more public comments than any federal agencies other than those dealing with environmental protection and consumer product safety. The division came into being in 1960 in the aftermath of quiz and payola scandals (§8.8). Originally planned as an active monitoring arm of the FCC, the division settled into the more passive role of disposing of the thousands of cards and letters sent to the FCC each year by the general public (Exhibit 16.6).

Few people seem to realize the FCC's legal limitations. Most letters of complaint have to be discarded simply because they ask the commission to censor material the writers personally dislike. Some writers are troubled by what they themselves read into programs:

A wide range of human pathology is exhibited in letters to the FCC. Each year women complain that Johnny Carson is watching them undress at night, and men complain that certain programs are being broadcast solely to render them impotent. Some people inveigh against Communist propaganda on regularly scheduled news programs, and others suspect that TV characters are "saying things about me." (Cole & Oettinger, 1978: 122)

Exhibit 16.6 shows the pattern of complaint topics for a recent year. The leading topics vary only slightly from year to year, often influenced by organized letter-writing campaigns as well as by program trends. The most persistent letter-writing campaign started in 1975 in reaction to a petition for rule making. The petition came from two somewhat unconventional but deeply committed believers in listener-supported radio, Jeremy Lansman and Lorenzo Milam. The latter is well known for his connection with the Pacifica Foundation stations (§7.9).

The Lansman/Milam petition asked the FCC to stop exempting noncommercial educational FM and television stations from the multiple ownership rules. It also asked for a freeze on licensing of such stations to government and religious groups, pending an investigation of the extent to which they complied with the fairness doctrine and fulfilled the educational purposes of the noncommercial channel allocations. The FCC

turned down the petition in August, 1975, less than a year after it had been submitted.

That should have closed the episode, because Lansman and Milam did not ask for reconsideration. But the dismissal of the petition had no effect whatever on the flood of mail opposing it from letter writers who had been misled into believing the petition asked for a flat ban on religious programs. By 1980 over eight million complaints had been received and they were still coming in at the rate of a thousand a month. There was a double irony in this mindless outpouring: not only had the petition long since been denied, but the writers were even misinformed as to what it would have done if accepted by the FCC.

With so many groundless complaints pouring in, the complaints staff has difficulty in sorting out those that might have substance and merit. A close observer who described the complaints procedures at the FCC in detail, noted that cases clearly needing investigation tended to be thrown out along with the "junk mail." He concluded that the commission had been unable to find "a middle ground on which frivolous public objections would be turned aside politely and serious derelictions of broadcasters' public trusteeship would be investigated and corrected" (Cole & Oettinger, 1978: 120).

Consumer Group Intervention Individual letters and the cumulative effect of many letters on the same topic can, on occasion, call FCC attention to real licensee abuses. More effective public input comes, however, from organized consumer groups consciously taking advantage of the legal machinery by which stations are licensed and renewed.

Such groups systematically collect data on station performance (or nonperformance) to

Exhibit 16.6
Public complaints received by FCC, 1979–1980

Subject of complaint	Complaints received
Criticism of specific programs	19,815
Obscenity, profanity, indecency	14,570
Section 315 (political candidates)	10,440
Fairness doctrine	9,896
Other program complaints	4,961
Total program complaints	59,682
Miscellaneous & non-program	8,627
Advertising	1,879
Grand total	70,188

Comment: The Complaints and Compliance Division also received 24,316 non-complaint items.

Source: Based on data supplied by FCC Complaints and Compliance Division.

present as evidence to the FCC in both adjudicatory and rule-making proceedings. Two key cases of historic significance, involving major consumer groups, will serve to illustrate the process: the *WLBT* case and the *Action for Children's Television* case.

The first of these established the vital principle that citizen groups are entitled to *standing* in FCC hearings that affect their interests. This term refers to the legal right to participate fully and formally as a party at interest in a hearing process (§15.3). In brief, for several years citizens of Jackson, Mississippi, had complained to the FCC about WLBT-TV, a VHF station in that community. They alleged systematic neglect of the needs and interests of black citizens, who formed a large percentage of the population served by WLBT. In a complex series of maneuvers (detailed in §18.3) consumer representatives succeeded in winning the right of citizen groups to legal standing in renewal hearings. Their testimony led to the eventual revocation of WLBT's license and sale of the station to a new licensee.

The second example of consumer intervention was an FCC rule-making hearing that resulted from a petition of Action for Children's Television (ACT).

In 1970 ACT petitioned the FCC to adopt rules aimed at eliminating advertising from children's programs while nevertheless requiring stations to program at least 14 hours of children's programming a week, scheduled in designated time-periods and aimed at well-defined age groups. The FCC declined to adopt the proposed rules, issuing a policy statement instead. Nevertheless, the proceeding set in motion certain reforms in commercial children's programming. As an immediate and tangible gain, the NAB Television Code Board adopted the special rules for children's programs mentioned in §13.4. Later the Federal Trade Commission also became involved in the issue (§13.5).

Composite Week The sources of information about programming mentioned so far are haphazard in nature. The only systematic source of information about the program performance of all licensees comes from the station *program logs*. Formerly required of all commercial stations, but since deregulation only of television, program logs keep a running record of the items actually broadcast — programs, commercials, PSAs and other announcements such as political spots and the required consumer information announcements.

To appraise television station performance, the FCC relies on a sample of logs known as the *composite week*. This consists of the logs for seven days of programming, each day chosen by the FCC from a different week in the three-year license period. This randomizing of sample days is supposed to minimize the effect of untypical programming that might occur on some days. The FCC specifies which days commercial stations must use to make up the composite week, but leaves it to noncommercial stations to choose their own representative days.

Because renewal dates are staggered, only a third of the licensees need apply for renewal each year. Composite logs for any one year therefore fail to give a complete picture of the entire industry's program statistics. This is one reason that the FCC began to require *annual* reports of television local and nonentertainment programming (described in §16.4).

16.7 License Renewal

Renewal Forms Near the end of the three-year license term, stations submit applications for renewal. The forms are not simple. For example, the longest one, the television renewal application, runs to 21 pages plus a variety of attached exhibits. The task of processing some 10,000 renewal applications is formidable, even though the FCC has staggered the expiration dates so that only a third of the stations submit renewal applications each year. In 1980 the FCC adopted a much simplified radio renewal form, reducing the application to a single half-page. The price of this simplification is that some radio licensees have to expect random on-the-spot auditing checks by the Field Operations Bureau (normally confined almost entirely to technical checks). A smaller random sample of licensees must fill in a long renewal form.

Renewal Application Routes The communications act says that licenses should be renewed *if public interest, convenience, and necessity would be served* by renewal. In making this decision, the FCC uses the evidence of the composite week program data (since 1981 available only for television) together with any other information that may have accumulated in a licensee's file as the result of complaints or penalties during the license period. Whether or not renewal decisions make any use of this evidence depends on the route the renewal application takes through the FCC bureaucracy.

Renewal applications take one of three basic routes: (1) the uncontested route, (2) the petition-to-deny route, or (3) the mutually-exclusive-application route. The steps involved in each case are outlined in Exhibit 16.7.

(1) For the great majority of stations, renewals present no problem because they are *uncontested.* No serious complaints against them having been lodged, no major penalties having been inflicted during the preceding license period, and no opposition having

been filed, the FCC staff renews their licenses automatically. In fact, one of the major complaints of consumer advocates is that the FCC Renewal and Transfer Division merely rubber-stamps uncontested applications, no matter how mediocre a station's previous performance may have been.

(2) Petitions to *deny* renewal come primarily from citizen groups that oppose incumbent licensees. They claim incumbents have failed to meet public interest standards and therefore should not be allowed to retain their licenses.

(3) *Mutually exclusive* applications occur when would-be licensees try to displace incumbents, claiming that they can do a better job in serving the public interest.

Uncontested Renewals Barry Cole (§16.1) tried valiantly to get the commission to look critically at uncontested renewal applications. For example, it was his suggestion to adopt processing rules requiring the renewal staff to refer stations with below-par percentages of local and nonentertainment programming to the commissioners. He also persuaded the FCC to revise its renewal forms to give more information on licensee performance. Cole expected these measures to assure that the most glaring instances of weak performance by licensees would be brought to the commission's personal attention. Later, he described the outcome:

None of what Cole hoped for happened. Instead, the commissioners, exposed to some renewal applications that raised problems, responded with no interest. Things soon returned to normal: the staff ground out renewal grants, commissioners remained uninvolved, and the processing rules were ignored. (Cole & Oettinger, 1978: 142)

It remains, then, for outsiders to force the commission to focus attention on the few renewal cases in which interveners have a special interest — the *contested* cases in which petitions to deny renewal or rival applications have been filed. These amount to far less than one percent of the renewals handled each year.

Contested Renewals Contested renewals present the FCC with especially difficult decisions. The commission is torn between two desirable but opposite goals: (1) giving incumbent licensees "legitimate renewal expectations" but (2) ensuring that incumbents will nevertheless feel a "competitive spur" to keep on striving to serve the public interest. On the one hand, incumbent licensees need reasonable assurance of continuity to justify investments in equipment, personnel contracts, and program plans. Without strong assurance of renewal at the end of each li-

Exhibit 16.7
License renewal routes

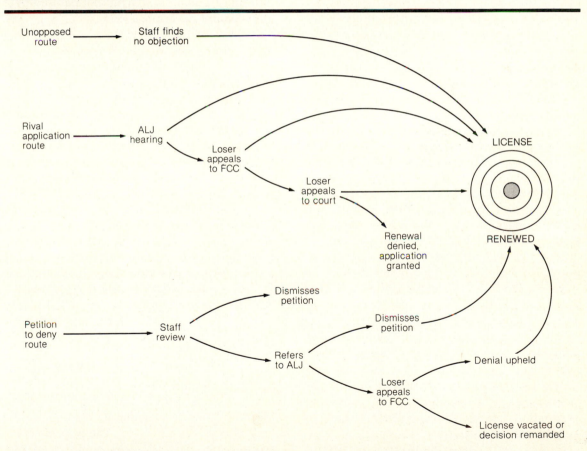

The great majority of renewals travel the unopposed route. Opposed applications, however, sometimes travel a long and rocky road before renewal or denial becomes final.

cense period, no prudent investor (commercial or noncommercial) would be willing to build a station.

On the other hand, if incumbent licensees feel assured of automatic renewal no matter how poor their program performance, they will be tempted to take the low road, wringing maximum personal benefits out of their stations, giving no serious consideration to the public interest. Assured renewal would in effect give existing licensees a monopoly on channels, freezing out competing applicants. The philosophy of the Communications Act of 1934 plainly rejects this solution. Renewals must serve the public interest, not merely the private interest of existing licensees.

Renewal Criteria In deciding between incumbents and competing applicants the FCC is left with the dilemma of comparing apples and oranges — an *actual* past service with a *proposed* future service. What sort of performance by an incumbent licensee should the FCC accept in preference to a would-be licensee's glowing promises to do even better if given a chance? Should just average past performance assure renewal? Better than average? What evidence should the FCC weigh in grading past performance to decide whether an incumbent deserves a superior, passing, or failing grade?

These questions became especially urgent as a result of the loss by their original licensees of two major VHF television stations in 1969. One we alluded to in the preceding section, the case of WLBT in Jackson, Mississippi. Its renewal was canceled by the appeals court after the FCC ignored consumer complaints about the licensee's failure to serve local needs.

The second conspicuous loss of license was the FCC's own doing. It took away the license of WHDH on Boston's Channel 5, owned by a daily newspaper, awarding the license to a competing applicant. Actually WHDH's loss was not a clear-cut renewal decision. Because of a long series of alleged violations of various kinds, the station had never been fully licensed but had operated on interim permissions for all of its 16 years. The FCC therefore assured the industry that WHDH should not be regarded as representative of its renewal policies.

Nevertheless, the *WHDH* case caused shock waves throughout the industry. The unthinkable had happened: a major VHF television station in a metropolitan market was put out of business, its channel handed over to a competing applicant. Furthermore, the industry read the *WHDH* case as a signal that in the future newspaper-owned stations in particular might be vulnerable to renewal challenges.

Hastily the FCC adopted a new renewal policy, calculated to soothe the industry's alarm. The revised renewal policy set up a two-step renewal hearing procedure. In phase one, *only* the question of the incumbent's previous performance could be discussed. Rival candidates could not introduce any evidence about their own plans for bettering the incumbent's performance. A past performance "substantially attuned to the needs and interests of its area" and without any serious operational deficiencies would assure renewal without further argument (22 FCC 2d 424, 1970). Only if the FCC decided that an incumbent's performance had been less than "substantial" or marred by serious deficiencies would rival applicants be allowed to initiate the second step by presenting their own proposals.

A consumer group, the Citizens Communication Center, immediately challenged the new policy. Within a year the appeals court had nullified it. The court pointed out that under the communications act, according to a doctrine long since confirmed by the Supreme Court, the FCC *must* conduct a full comparative hearing when considering mutually exclusive applications. The FCC renewal policy, said the appeals court, gave the incumbent licensee "a virtually insuperable advantage." One of the judges said in a concurring statement that the policy would

effectively prevent a newcomer applicant from being heard on the merits of his application, no matter how superlative his qualifications. It would also, in effect, substitute a standard of substantial *service for the* best possible *service to the public and effectively negate the hearing requirements of the statute. (447 F 2d 1215, 1971, emphasis in original)*

This rebuff forced the FCC to fall back on its 1965 comparative hearing criteria — choices based on diversification of media ownership and localism in management and programming. The inevitable tendency to favor the incumbent licensee over challengers remained. Repeatedly the appeals court reminded the FCC that the communications act implies no such preference. For example, in the *Central Florida* case (WESH-TV) the court reversed an FCC decision in favor of an incumbent in a contested renewal (598 F 2d 37, 1978).

The court pointed out that the history of renewal cases "reveals an ordinarily tacit presumption that the incumbent licensee is to be preferred over competing applicants." It charged the FCC with being inconsistent in applying its own criteria, as outlined in its 1965 statement of policy. "We do not see how performance that is merely average," said the court, ". . . can warrant renewal or, in fact, be of especial relevance without some finding that the challenger's performance would likely be no more satisfactory."

Issue: Renewal Dilemma These conspicuous reversals of FCC decisions in major renewal cases seemed to call for one of two solutions: either (1) the statute should be changed so that the FCC is not put in the position of having to conduct comparative hearings on renewals; or (2) the FCC should set up clear-cut objective criteria for measuring the relative "substantiality" of past performance by incumbent licensees against proposals of challengers.

The FCC preferred the first solution, recommending that Congress consider an amendment to the act enabling it to deal more easily with renewal challenges by rival applicants. Significantly, the communications act rewrite attempts of the 1976–1980 period proposed granting permanent licenses, thus eliminating the need for renewal proceedings.

If the FCC were to opt for evaluating licensee performance more rigorously, it would need to clarify what constitutes superior service. The following have been suggested at various times as possible elements of quantitative tests for measuring licensee performance:

■ The percentages of time devoted to nonentertainment and locally produced programs. The FCC took a tentative step in this direction by adopting the staff processing rules mentioned in §16.4, but then retreated, first by declining to make use of the data, later by deleting the rule altogether for radio.
■ The number, placement, and variety of public service announcements (a proposal specifically rejected by the FCC in 1980).
■ The number, types, and scheduling of children's programs, free of commercial exploitation.
■ The number and intrusiveness of commercials.
■ The extent to which licensees reinvest profits in improved programming services.

Consumer groups advocate *financial disclosure* to enable this kind of analysis. They are frustrated, however, by the fact that the FCC treats individual licensee financial data as confidential. The FCC releases financial data reports such as those quoted in §12.6 only on a market-by-market basis.

But using such data to set up quantitative targets for program performance (not to speak of qualitative evaluations) seems to require a level of government intrusion that would possibly violate the First Amendment of the Constitution, and would certainly be politically unacceptable. Moreover, to make such evaluations the FCC would need increased staff at a time when the existing bureaucratic burden is already under attack. Thus from the consumer perspective, requiring licensees to meet minimum program standards seems only logical and reasonable, but from the political perspective it seems impossible. The dilemma remained.

Exhibit 16.8
Reasons for license deletions, 1934–1978
(N = 142)

Reasons cited by FCC	Frequency cited	Reasons cited by FCC	Frequency cited
Misrepresentations to FCC	58	Fairness doctrine violations (including personal attacks)	5
Unauthorized transfer of control, misrepresentation of ownership	42	Slanted news	4
Abandonment, failure to prosecute renewal	36	Log falsification	4
Technical violations	32	Overcommercialization	2
Character defects of licensees	21	Lottery violations	2
Fraudulence (contests, billing, improper business and advertising practices)	20	Failure to control programming	2
		Equal Employment Opportunities violation	1
Departure from promises	12	Indecent programs	1
Financial qualification defects	7	Miscellaneous	20

Comment: These figures include nonrenewals of license, revocations, and failures to apply for renewal. The number of reasons exceeds the number of stations deleted because in most cases the FCC cited more than one reason. Included are 15 deletions that were still pending in 1978. There is some overlap in the categories of reasons because the FCC does not always use identical language in identifying reasons.

Sources: Based on data in John A. Abel, Charles Clift III, and Frederic A. Weiss, "Station License Revocations and Denials of Renewal, 1934–1969," and Frederic A. Weiss, David Ostroff, and Charles E. Clift III, "Station License Revocations and Denials of Renewal, 1970–1978," *Journal of Broadcasting* 14 (Fall, 1980): 411–21, and 24 (Winter, 1980): 69–77.

16.8 License Deletion

Frequency and Types The same constraints that prevent the FCC from adopting hard-and-fast program performance standards in evaluating renewal applications prevent it from resorting freely to the ultimate penalty of license deletion. In the 45-year period 1934–1978, only 142 stations lost their licenses (Exhibit 16.8). Nonrenewal accounted for 98 deletions, revocation for 40, and voluntary abandonment for 36. The average rate of involuntary deletions amounted to a mere three stations per year. In short, though an ever-present background threat, loss of license hardly ever becomes a reality.

Nonrenewal occurs more frequently than revocation because the burden of proof for showing that renewal would be in the public interest falls on the licensee. *Revocation*, the canceling of a license before its normal term expires, reverses the burden of proof.

Reasons for Deletion Exhibit 16.8 lists reasons given by the FCC for all deletions that occurred in the 1934–1978 period. The frequency with which the various types of violations were cited makes a striking comment on the FCC's regulatory outlook. Program faults such as news slanting, overcommercialization, indecency, and fairness doctrine violations figure only rarely as reasons for putting stations off the air. In the great majority of cases the FCC cited nonprogram violations, such as misrepresentation, concealment of ownership, technical violations, and fraudulent business practices.

This emphasis does not necessarily mean that licensees are less prone to bad programming practices than they are to bad business practices. It merely reflects the fact that the FCC is on much safer constitutional ground when it exacts the maximum penalty for nonprogram violations. The *WXUR* case (§16.5), one of the few deletions based squarely on program violations, illustrates the point. The licensee flagrantly disregarded program promises and was guilty of grossly unfair program practices. Nevertheless, he won sympathy from First Amendment experts who felt that freedom of speech in broadcasting should be defended no matter how extreme the licensee's departure from FCC standards of conduct.

In most cases of revocation or nonrenewal, loss of license climaxed a sorry history of willful misconduct. "Misrepresentation" heads the list of reasons for deletion because the FCC is most severe when licensees compound their violations with lies and evasions. The FCC is often extraordinarily lenient with transgressions as long as licensees are candid in admitting error and contrite enough to promise reform.

Case Histories Most deleted stations have been obscure radio outlets guilty of long lists of misdemeanors and lacking in any redeeming qualities. The more conspicuous cases of deletion, however, receive a great deal of notoriety in the industry. Surviving licensees read FCC militancy into deletions. Any involuntary deletion may be a foot in the door leading to more rigorous regulation in the future.

We have already alluded to some of the key deletions: KFKB and KGEF, the stations deleted for program excesses in the 1930s (§7.1); WXUR, the first deletion for fairness doctrine violations (§16.5); WHDH, the first major television station to be deleted (§16.7); and WLBT, the television station deleted for failing to serve its local constituency (§16.6). We have also mentioned renewal delays caused by the discovery of nonbroadcast violations by the parent corporation of the RKO group of stations (§16.3).

The following additional examples indicate the types of licensee misbehavior that the FCC has found serious enough to warrant the rare penalty of license deletion:

■ *Fraudulent Billing.* The appeals court upheld the FCC's 1978 denial of renewal to a Berlin, New Hampshire, AM radio station charged with double-billing (§13.8). The station collected over $22,000 in overcharges to national advertisers. Claiming that the two other stations and the newspaper in his market did the same thing, the owner pleaded "business necessity" — an interestingly candid acknowledgment that so-called market forces do not always operate in the public interest! The court was especially severe in its condemnation, pointing out that double-billing probably also violates the mail fraud statute. Said the court, "it appears to us that the Commission has not been giving sufficient consideration to the fraudulent conduct implicit in double billing as the serious *criminal* violation it constitutes" (626 F 2d 869). The FCC ultimately refused to renew *all three* of the stations in Berlin.

■ *Failure to Serve Minorities.* In 1970 the FCC refused to renew the licenses of eight stations of the Alabama Educational Television Commission. This case (previously reviewed in §10.4) was unique for the number of stations involved and for the severity of punishment given a noncommercial licensee.

■ *Character Defects.* In denying renewal to five commercial radio outlets licensed to Star Stations of Indiana, the FCC said "the record reflects a reprehensible course of conduct involving the basic character qualities of the licensee" (51 FCC 2d 95, 1975). Don Burden, the owner, claimed the FCC's action cost him $20 million. The long list of transgressions charged against Burden included the use of fake audience research data, fraudulent billing, fraudulent contests, illegal political donations, and slanting of news. Climaxing a

long-drawn-out legal battle, the Supreme Court declined to review the FCC's decision.

■ *Staging of News.* The FCC denied the renewal application of a Tucson, Arizona, AM station in 1980 because of an irresponsible promotional stunt. When a recently employed DJ temporarily left town on personal business, the station management concocted a story that he had been kidnapped. The station broadcast "news" of the kidnapping over a period of five days, even faking a police interview. Listeners taken in by the hoax flooded the Tucson police lines with calls. The deception was finally exposed by a local television station. The FCC would not allow the absentee owner to shift responsibility: "A licensee cannot expect to be insulated from the irresponsible conduct of a vice-president and director" (78 FCC 2d 865, 1980).

Aftermath of Deletion When a station is deleted the licensee is not the only loser. The public loses a broadcasting service. Even if the station's service was substandard, the FCC may question whether it is in the public interest to deprive a community of its only local broadcast service. This consideration may account for some cases of seemingly excessive lenience by the FCC.

In any event, when a station loses its license the FCC gives it a grace period to wind up its affairs. During this interim a new applicant may well arrive upon the scene to pick up the pieces and make a fresh start. When hearings delay renewals, licenses remain in effect until the case is settled. We have mentioned instances in which the FCC allowed stations to continue operating under caretaker arrangements for years, pending the settlement of especially long-drawn-out disputes (§16.2).

Lesser Penalties Not all offenses, of course, warrant capital punishment. For lesser offenses the FCC inflicts the milder sanctions of short-term renewals or forfeitures (fines).

Short-term renewal (usually for only a year instead of the normal time) puts the licensee on probation, so to speak, pending the correction of general deficiencies evident during the preceding license period. *Conditional renewal* is also granted, pending correction of some specific fault.

The FCC can also impose penalties for day-to-day infractions of the rules without waiting for the end of the license period. These take the form of *forfeitures* ranging in amount from $25 to a maximum of $20,000. In the past most forfeitures have been in the low end of that range, but in 1981 the FCC asked Congress to increase the maximum to $100,000.

A study of all forfeitures imposed from 1961 to 1978 revealed an average of only a little more than a hundred fines per year (Clift et al., 1980). Most of them involved violations of technical operating rules. Fines for program violations have been few. The most frequent program-related reasons have been failure to give sponsor identification in commercials and violations of the lottery law.

The low number of forfeitures contrasted with the large number of stations on the air reflects the FCC's generally lenient treatment of licensee wrongdoing, even when the capital punishment of deletion is not involved. Commissioners tend to sympathize with marginal radio stations struggling to survive, which are the ones that commit the great majority of punishable infractions.

16.9 FCC Issues

Over the years the FCC has been among the most frequently analyzed and scathingly criticized of the federal regulatory agencies. Official investigations and private studies of the commission and its methods have reached negative conclusions with monotonous regularity. A few of the recurrent criticisms have been the following:

■ The politically controlled process for choosing commissioners fails to come up with suitably qualified people.
■ As a consequence, the commissioners tend to lack the expertise and sometimes the dedication expected of them by the communications act.
■ Fraternizing by commissioners with the regulated industries, as well as their hopes for future jobs with those industries, undermines sensitive concern for the public interest.
■ Commission policies have had the effect of encouraging, rather than preventing, a quasi-monopoly situation in network television.
■ Taken as a whole, the regulatory process has an air of make-believe, setting up high-sounding goals that neither the industry nor the commission seriously tries to achieve.

Appointment Process Despite the power the FCC wields over vital aspects of national life, appointments to the commission do not rank high in the Washington political pecking order. The president uses regulatory commission appointments primarily to pay off minor political debts. The degree of personal involvement varies with each president, of course, but most are far too busy with higher level appointments to take much interest in the FCC.

A study of FCC and FTC appointments prepared for the Senate Commerce Committee in 1976 reviewed the histories of 48 selections by five successive presidents. The authors concluded:

Partisan political considerations dominate the selection of regulators to an alarming extent . . . other factors — such as competence, experience, and even, on occasion, regulatory philosophy — are only secondary considerations. Most commission appointments are the result of well-stoked campaigns conducted at the right time with the right sponsors, and many selections can be explained in terms of powerful political connections and little else: Commission seats are good consolation prizes for defeated Congressmen; useful runner-up awards for persons who ricochet into the appointment as a result of a strong yet unsuccessful campaign for another position; appropriate resting berths for those who have labored long and hard in the party vineyards; and a convenient dumping ground for people who have performed unsatisfactorily in other, more important Government posts. (Graham & Kramer, 1976: 391)

Despite the fact that the commission's main function is to represent the public interest, few commissioners have been primarily identified with consumer concerns. The majority have come from other government jobs, usually with training as lawyers. Appointees with relevant experience in engineering, professional broadcasting, and academic specialties have been rare. Nor do many stay in office long enough to attain great expertise. The more ambitious and well-qualified appointees soon leave the job to move on to something else, often a much higher-paying job in the communication industries.

Commissioners Many commissioners became apologists for the very industries they were appointed to regulate, advocating a "hands-off" regulatory policy. Often cited as examples of this approach to the job have been commissioners George McConnaughey (1954–1957), Rosel Hyde (1946–1969), Robert E. Lee (1953–1981), and James H. Quello (1974–   ).

Quello, one of the few commissioners with extensive commercial broadcasting experience, faced the longest Senate confirmation hearings of any commissioner. Consumer organizations strongly opposed his nomination, anticipating that he would be exceptionally tolerant of licensee infractions of the rules.

A few commissioners are remembered for opposite tendencies. Chairman James Fly (1939–1944), a liberal consumer advocate, inspired intense hostility among broadcasters and their congressional allies. In fact a Georgia congressman, Eugene Cox, tried to have Fly impeached. Cox called off his vendetta, however, when evidence was found that he had accepted a bribe to help in obtaining a license for a Georgia constituent.

President John F. Kennedy's FCC chairman, Newton Minow (1961–1963), was another public interest advocate, but he resigned after completing less than half a term. Nicholas Johnson (1966–1973) was an outspoken critic of the FCC itself. A colorful consumer advocate, Johnson wrote frequent and pungent dissents to FCC decisions. He was such a thorn in the side of commercial broadcasters that when his term finally expired, the leading trade journal of the industry headed its editorial on his departure "Good Riddance." The editorial charged him with having trained upward of a hundred young people as "guerrillas against the system." It concluded: "We cannot point to a constructive word or deed bearing his imprimatur" (*Broadcasting*, 17 Dec. 1973).

The first woman commissioner, Frieda B. Hennock (1948–1955), was instrumental in ensuring the reservation of noncommercial television channels in 1952 (Exhibit 16.9). After her term expired, women again went unrepresented until the appointment of

Charlotte Reid (1971–1976). Since then it has been taken as a foregone conclusion that at least one of the seven chairs on the commission should be reserved for a woman. Anne P. Jones, whose term began in 1979, is a lawyer with a background in Washington securities regulation.

The first black commissioner was Benjamin Hooks (1972–1977). A Memphis Lawyer, businessman, and county judge, Hooks tended to be a one-issue commissioner. He resigned before completing his term to become head of the National Association for the Advancement of Colored People. He was succeeded in 1977 by Tyrone Brown, who was once law clerk to Supreme Court Chief Justice Earl Warren. In 1981 President Reagan appointed Henry Rivera, the first Hispanic FCC member.

Exhibit 16.9
Representative FCC members, past and present

Frieda B. Hennock (1948–1955), the first woman commissioner, and a current woman commissioner, Anne P. Jones, appointed in 1979.

Newton N. Minow, a Kennedy-appointed chairman, served only three years (1961–1963) but had a strong impact. President Reagan's choice for chairman in 1981 was Mark Fowler.

Benjamin L. Hooks (1972–1977), appointed by President Johnson, was the first black commissioner; he was followed by Tyrone Brown (1977–1981).

Sources: United Press International, Corporation for Public Broadcasting, Federal Communications Commission.

Ex-Commissioners   One reason some commissioners have tended to be more solicitous of business interests than the public interest is the fact that they looked forward to well-paying jobs with the industries they regulate. "Employment by the regulated industries following commission service is a long-established tradition," said the authors of the 1976 Senate Commerce Committee study (Graham & Kramer, 1976: 416).

Of course, it is only natural that ex-commissioners should capitalize on their previous regulatory experience for their own benefit. Some degree of restraint is needed, however. The Senate study, like others before it, recommended that former commissioners should be barred for more than the present one year after leaving the agency before being allowed to represent clients in dealings with the FCC.

In the past, commissioners sometimes reversed their roles with almost indecent haste. Sam Pickard (1927–1929) became a CBS vice president and also part owner of a radio station, the latter a reward for helping the station to obtain CBS affiliation (at the time network affiliation was much coveted by radio stations). The station later lost its license because it concealed Pickard's role in its ownership (Bendiner, 1957: 26). Only weeks after the completion of the post-freeze television allotment plan in 1952, Chairman Wayne Coy resigned to become television consultant for Time, Inc., which was about to acquire a string of television outlets. At the expiration of his term, Commissioner Kenneth Cox (1963–1970) became senior vice president of a large common carrier subject to FCC regulation. These are some of the more glaring transformations from regulator to regulatee. Many more could be cited.

Ex Parte Contacts   Commissioners are also subject to temptations while still in office. They are ardently courted in Washington by industry representatives, attorneys, power brokers, lobbyists, and pressure groups. Commissioners also travel widely, making speeches at trade meetings and attending such functions as dedications of new broadcasting facilities.

In the period of 1971–1975, FCC commissioners and their top aides made 781 trips for appearances before industry groups, but only seven to appear before groups representing the public's stake in broadcasting (Cole & Oettinger, 1978: 84). It must be added, however, that about that time the commission began making efforts to increase its contacts with the general public and consumer groups (§18.3).

The constant personal interaction between commissioners and the people they regulate creates suspicion of *ex parte* contacts. This is the legal term for private meetings between judges (or people acting in a judicial capacity) and individual litigants that may give unfair advantage to one litigant over another. All parties at interest should be present at such meetings, but representatives of the public are usually conspicuously absent when commissioners attend private functions staged by broadcasters.

Many such contacts are legitimate, some only ethically doubtful, some downright illegal. The most scandalous cases of FCC ex parte contacts that have been exposed occurred during the 1950s. Following the television freeze, the FCC was subjected to unusually intense pressures as a result of the frantic competition for the few extremely valuable VHF channels that became available in metropolitan areas. In 1957 the House Subcommittee on Legislative Oversight unraveled the classic ex parte scandal in broadcasting, the award of the hotly contested Channel 10 in Miami (Schwartz, 1959). After prolonged hearings, an FCC Administrative

Law Judge had awarded Channel 10 to a Miami Beach radio station owner who scored high in terms of local ownership, integration of ownership with management, and local broadcasting experience. The commission, however, unaccountably threw out this initial decision, awarding the channel to National Airlines instead.

Investigation revealed that Commissioner Richard A. Mack, a recent appointee from Florida, had received a suspiciously large number of payments and profitable business favors from a Miami lawyer. It turned out that the lawyer had been retained by the airline solely because of his long friendship with Commissioner Mack. These links were only part of a network of questionable business and political relationships stretching between Florida and Washington. Three of the four Channel 10 applicants were later disqualified for maintaining ex parte contacts, and Commissioner Mack was forced to resign in 1958. The commission chairman of that period, John C. Doerfer, was implicated in the same investigation for accepting favors from licensees. He resigned under pressure in 1960.

Regulation as Myth With astonishing unanimity investigators have used such words as "myth," "fiction," "formality," and "ritual" to describe the FCC's enforcement of its own regulations. One investigator said in an official report, "The anonymous opinion writers for the commission pick from a collection of standards those that will support whatsoever decision the commission chooses to make" (Landis, 1960: 53). Contrary to the stated rules of the commission, another study reported, "local ownership, news and public affairs programming, and local program origination all *detract* from the likely success of an application" in FCC hearings (Noll et al., 1973: 113).

Even some of the commissioners themselves joined the chorus of condemnation. Two members of the commission, after making a detailed case study of programming by the television stations of Oklahoma, concluded that "the concept of local service is largely a myth" (14 FCC 2d 12, 1968). One of the two was Nicholas Johnson, who described the FCC's renewal ritual as follows:

At the sound of the bell the licensee jumps in the ring and begins shadowboxing. At the end of three minutes he is proclaimed the winner by the FCC majority, found to have been serving the public interest in his community, and given a three-year license renewal. (Johnson, 1970: 176)

In 1978, Commissioner Tyrone Brown, addressing the Federal Communications Bar Association, took up the familiar theme:

In comparative renewal cases, the FCC has mouthed many myths — deference to diversification, to integration of ownership and management, to past programming, to programming proposals. The result, however, is always the same: heads the incumbent wins; tails, the challenger loses. (Brown, 1978: 9)

In short, many responsible critics both outside and within the FCC have agreed that it has simply failed to practice what it preached. It sets up the elaborate standards to govern renewal, choice among competing applicants, public service programming, ownership diversification, and other matters that we have described in this chapter. But when it comes to deciding actual cases, the commission too often ignores its high-sounding standards.

16.10 Deregulation

Evidently the FCC needs to bring its professed standards into closer harmony with its actual decisions. One way of doing this would be *deregulation* — if the rules cannot, or should not, be enforced, change the rules.

Definition The administrative counterpart of the legislative rewrites discussed in §15.6 is *deregulation.* Deregulation fever, like rewrite fever, struck Washington during the 1970s. It affected not only the FCC but other federal administrative agencies as well. Increasingly people began to feel that government regulation costs too much for the benefits it confers; that competition could better achieve many of the goals of present regulation; and that less administrative regulation would tend to insulate national life from undue control by political parties (by reducing the impact of political appointments on the rule making of federal agencies). As we noted in §15.6, deregulation became part and parcel of national telecommunications policy in the 1970s.

Radio Deregulation In 1981, after an inquiry initiated four years earlier, the FCC deleted four of its longstanding constraints on radio licenses, abandoning (1) the formal *ascertainment* procedures for ensuring localism in programming; (2) the keeping of radio *program logs,* thus eliminating the composite week for assessing program performance; (3) processing rules for setting a minimum level of *nonentertainment programming*; and (4) processing rules for setting a maximum level of *advertising content* in programming (84 FCC 2d 968).

To justify freeing radio from these requirements, the FCC relied on theoretical economics, arguing that the public interest can best be served by curbing government regulations and unleashing competitive forces in their stead:

Producers (providers) of goods and services must be responsive to consumers' desires in order to compete successfully with rival producers. Consumers, by their choice of purchases, determine which producers (providers) will succeed. Moreover, not only does the competition among producers for consumers lead to the production of the goods and services that consumers want most, the same competitive process forces producers continually to seek less costly ways of providing those goods and services. As a result, parties operating freely in a competitive market environment will determine and fulfill consumer wants, and do so efficiently. (73 FCC 2d 492, 1979)

According to deregulatory theory, the FCC should abandon most regulation of *behavior* (requiring licensees to go through the ascertainment procedure to determine local needs, for example). Instead it should rely on *structural* regulation, which affects the number of competitors able to offer services to the public (rules on the number of stations under single ownership, cross-ownership between broadcast stations and other types of media outlets, and the ease with which new competitors can enter a market, as examples). The FCC would pursue a hands-off policy on licensee behavior except in cases of "market failure."

Network Deregulation Radio network rules offered an inviting early target for deregulation because many had become hopelessly archaic as a result of changes in the industry's practices caused by television. In 1977 the FCC canceled most of the chain broadcasting regulations as they applied to radio. These rules, adopted in 1943 (§7.5) at a time when radio networks dominated the industry, had long since lost their point.

The more difficult target, network television deregulation, was the subject of a study by the FCC's Network Inquiry Special Staff, completed in 1980. The study's scope and purpose were suggested by the title of the special staff's final report to the FCC — *New Television Networks: Entry, Jurisdiction, Ownership and Regulation*. After exhaustive research on each of these four topics, the special staff concluded that prior television network regulation had utterly failed to bring about its stated goals of fostering increased competition and diversity of programming.

Chiefly responsible, said the report, was a fundamental error in designing the post-freeze television channel allotment plan. As we pointed out in §8.4, the plan made it impossible for a fourth network to recruit enough affiliates to compete effectively on a national basis. The commission had compounded this mistake, according to the report, by adopting counterproductive rules on network ownership of stations and on their relations with affiliates and program suppliers. These measures virtually guaranteed, said the report, continued monopoly by the three traditional networks.

The special staff saw little hope of breaking the mold except by fostering increased competition from cable, multipoint distribution systems, direct broadcast satellites, and pay television. Past commission policy, as we have seen (§11.1), had aimed at protecting the existing networks from inroads by these same new technologies.

The same economic theories that were used to justify radio deregulation underlay the 1980 network study report. Network regulation, the report concluded, tended to stifle competition rather than promote it. Deregulation, on the other hand, would stimulate competition by making entry into the market easier for new firms. Indeed, "the very appearance of new networks and new broadcast outlets," said the report, "should substantially reduce the concerns which led the Commission to adopt the rules initially" (FCC, 1980: 491).

Not everyone agrees with the FCC's economists, nor do all economic theorists agree with one another. Theory aside, moreover, a variety of interests benefit from the regulatory status quo. Nevertheless, the change-over to a Republican administration in Washington in 1981 gave added impetus to the drive, already started by the previous administrations, both Democratic and Republican, to "get the government off the backs" of the regulated industries.

Summary

FCC regulation is imposed through formally adopted rules, processing standards, adjudicatory decisions, and informal "raised eyebrow" and "jawboning" activities. FCC control is imposed through the licensing power. License applicants must qualify in terms of citizenship, financial and technical ability, character, and program proposals. The FCC treats localism in ownership and programming as pluses in competitive applications. Minimum levels of nonentertainment programming are expected, along with efforts to ascertain local needs and to serve such needs through programs.

In the course of operations a licensee is solely responsible for programming, which must observe the fairness doctrine and treat political candidates equally. There are also equal employment rules to follow and numerous reports to file.

The FCC learns of a licensee's performance from public complaints, from interventions by consumer groups and rival applicants, and (for television) from a composite week of program logs. Most license renewals are uncontested and therefore almost automatic. Contested renewals usually arise because of petitions from consumer groups or rival applications. The latter pose difficulties for the

FCC in striking a balance between reasonable renewal expectancy and giving new applicants a chance to improve the existing service.

In practice few licenses are lost through nonrenewal and still fewer through revocation. Deleted licensees are usually guilty of repeated infractions of rules having to do with technical operations, ownership, and misrepresentations to the commission. The same types of infractions may also draw lesser penalties in the form of short-term renewals and fines.

The FCC has been much criticized in terms both of the quality of individual commissioners and of their collective performance. Presidential appointments to the commission are used as political rewards, and commissioners sometimes use their positions as stepping-stones to jobs within the industries they regulate. Weak and inconsistent enforcement by the FCC of its own rules has led critics to conclude that the supposed goals of regulation are largely mythical.

More realistic rule making and enforcement may come with deregulation. Its purpose is to reduce bureaucratic controls over licensee behavior, relying more on regulating industry structure in ways that will encourage competition. Some deregulation of radio networks and stations has already taken place. Television stations and television networks are probably next in line.

CHAPTER 17

Freedom and Fairness in Broadcasting

We turn now from the FCC's practical day-to-day regulation of broadcasting to the broader question of the constitutional limits on such regulation. The First Amendment prohibits federal regulation of speech — yet the communications act imposes federal regulation.

This paradox is not unique to broadcasting. There are many occasions when the welfare of society seems to call for striking a balance between ideal freedom and practical need to prevent speech that would harm individuals or society as a whole. Defining the point of compromise between these contradictory goals is an enduring First Amendment problem. At one extreme, absolutist interpreters of the amendment deny the right of government to impose any limitations whatever on free expression; at the other extreme, relativists are willing to accept severe limitations on freedom in the name of "fairness," "morality," or "national security."

17.1 First Amendment Basics

Marketplace of Ideas In staking their future on the Bill of Rights as a constitutional shield against government tyranny, the framers of the Constitution knew they were em-

barking on a risky experiment. They counted on the ability of ordinary people to rule themselves, provided only that they could have unhampered access to information, ideas, and opinions needed for the task of self-government. One of the indispensable means of access, they decided, was an uninhibited "marketplace of ideas." They sought to ensure its existence by guaranteeing freedom of speech and press.

Everyone knew, of course, that a free press is not necessarily always a responsible press. But the risk had to be taken. As Thomas Jefferson wrote to a friend:

I have lent myself willingly as the subject of a great experiment, which was to prove that an administration, conducting itself with integrity and common understanding, cannot be battered down, even by the falsehoods of a licentious press. . . . This experiment was wanting for the world to demonstrate the falsehood of the pretext that freedom of the press is incompatible with orderly government. (Padover, 1946: 95)

The eighteenth-century laissez-faire economic doctrine taught that open, unregulated competition automatically and inevitably results in the greatest economic good for the greatest number of people. That economic model led quite naturally to the metaphor of a *marketplace of ideas,* where concepts and opinions from various sources would compete for acceptance.

Even though the rise of business monopolies has long since caused revision of laissez-faire economic theory, the communication marketplace metaphor persists in the present era. As the Supreme Court said in a major broadcasting decision, for example, "it is the purpose of the First Amendment to preserve an uninhibited market place of ideas in which truth will ultimately prevail, rather than to countenance monopolization of the market" (395 US 390, 1969).

Priority of Freedom to Communicate

Freedom of expression occupies only one part of one amendment among the ten constitutional amendments that make up the Bill of Rights. Yet its role is so crucial to the success of the American experiment that it stands out, in the words of the late Supreme Court Justice William O. Douglas, as "the first article of our faith. We have founded our political system on it. It has been the safeguard of every religious, political, philosophical, economic, and racial group amongst us. . . . We have deemed it more costly to liberty to suppress a despised minority than to let them vent their spleen. We have above all else feared the political censor. We have wanted a land where our people can be exposed to all the diverse creeds and cultures of the world" (341 US 584, 1951).

What the Amendment Says

The First Amendment protects four fundamental citizen rights that governments in all ages have had the most reason to fear and the greatest inclination to violate: freedom to believe, to speak, to gather together, and to ask rulers to correct injustices. The amendment ensures these freedoms in only 45 words, of which 14 guarantee freedom of expression:

"Congress shall make no law *respecting an establishment of religion, or prohibiting the free exercise thereof; or* abridging the freedom of speech, or of the press; *or the right of the people peaceably to assemble, and to petition the Government for a redress of grievances.*"

"No Such Thing as a False Idea"

So radical and dangerous an experiment was the First Amendment that to this day many people who benefit from it still cannot fully accept its premises.

The American Constitution has served as a model all over the world. Many governments have adopted the words of the First Amendment, but rarely its spirit. They promise freedom of expression only to take it away with contradictory provisos. Freedom is yours, they say, but only so long as you use it "constructively," "responsibly," or "truthfully." Such provisos subvert the central meaning of the First Amendment, which makes no prior assumptions. "Under the First Amendment," said the Supreme Court, "there is no such thing as a false idea. However pernicious an opinion may seem, we depend for its correction not on the conscience of judges and juries, but on the competition of other ideas" (418 US 339, 1974) — again, the marketplace metaphor.

A fundamental goal of the First Amendment is to *encourage* disagreement. "A function of free speech under our system of government is to invite dispute," wrote Justice William O. Douglas. "It may indeed best serve its highest purpose when it induces a condition of unrest, creates dissatisfaction with conditions as they are, or even stirs people to anger" (337 US 4, 1949).

It may seem unreasonable, for example, to ask survivors of Nazi concentration camps to tolerate the head of the American Nazi Party in their living rooms to argue his racist viewpoint on television. Nevertheless, that is what the First Amendment asks, as was demonstrated by an edition of *Black Perspective on the News,* shown on public television despite protests from some of its own best supporters. The program consisted of a discussion with leaders of the Nazi party and the Ku Klux Klan (*PTR* Nov./Dec. 1977). This was an extreme but not altogether unusual example of the kinds of painful decisions the First Amendment sometimes expects of broadcasters.

Private vs. State Censorship Another misconception is that the First Amendment affords protection from *private* censorship. But the amendment aims at protecting people from *government,* not from themselves. Station and network officials who edit, cut, bleep, delete, revise, and otherwise mangle programs may be guilty of bad judgment, timidity, and other faults, but not the fault of unconstitutionality. They may go so far as to break FCC rules and federal laws without violating the First Amendment. Only if private censorship takes place because of *state action* is it unconstitutional.

State (or government) action refers to acts that licensees undertake on behalf of, or at least at the behest of, the federal government. Only then is a private censor guilty of violating the First Amendment. When the FCC chairman jawboned the networks and the NAB into adopting family viewing standards to protect children from unsuitable programs (§16.1), a lower court called it state action, holding that both the chairman and the industry elements involved had acted unconstitutionally.* Said the court:

Broadcasters daily are forced to make ad hoc subjective decisions as to what should and should not be broadcast. Those excluded from the airwaves call this censorship. Those permitted to participate call it visionary editorial decision making. (423 F Sup 1134, 1976)

In a different state action context, a station manager cut material from the scripts of mayoral candidates appearing on his station, saying the deleted material was "in bad taste." The candidates whose scripts had been edited went to court to sue for damages on the ground that their First Amendment rights had been violated. The licensee countered by arguing in court that his censoring of the candidates' speeches was private, not state, action. Therefore, he said, he could not have violated the First Amendment. The court accepted this defense and dismissed the suit.†

Freedom of Religion A second First Amendment clause of particular interest to broadcasting is the guarantee of religious freedom. In addition to assuring the "free exercise" of religion, the amendment explicitly rules out the elevation of any particular creed as the official state (that is, *established*) religion.

The colonists, belonging to different sects and many of them refugees from religious persecution, knew all too well what happens when the overwhelming power of the state is harnessed to the implacable dogma of religious zealots. They wanted to make it impossible for the historical repressions and incredible cruelties of state-supported religions ever to be repeated in the United States.

Today the likelihood of any religious

---

*A federal appeals court overthrew the lower court decision, but only on jurisdictional grounds (609 F 2d 355, 1979).

†Ironically, one of the proofs that the licensee had indeed been acting in a private rather than government capacity was the fact that the FCC penalized him for violating Section 315 of the communications act, which forbids censoring the scripts of candidates (566 F 2d 384, 1977).

group achieving establishment status is remote, of course, but the Supreme Court has held that even the smallest step in that direction violates the First Amendment. The overt intrusion of television evangelists into the 1980 national election campaign with the aim of electing officials conforming to one particular set of religious convictions disturbed many people sensitive to First Amendment rights. Ironically, though, that same amendment protected the right of the evangelists to have their say.

Doubly protected by the freedom of speech and the freedom of religion clauses, some religious broadcasters have been emboldened to treat FCC regulation with extraordinary highhandedness. Instances already mentioned include the misuse of his station by the Reverend Shuler (§7.1), refusal of the PTL Club to give the FCC information about its activities as a licensee (§9.7), and the failure of WXUR to honor its program promises and fairness doctrine obligations (§16.5).

17.2 Unprotected Speech

Despite the uncompromising command "Congress shall make *no law* . . . ," Congress and other legislative bodies do in fact make laws that punish some forms of speech. These forms include speech (or publication) that is defamatory or obscene, or speech that plagiarizes, invades privacy, or incites insurrection. Such punishable types of speech are called *unprotected* because they are regarded as falling outside the First Amendment's protective shield against government interference.

Chilling Effect　To be sure, laws against defamation and the like do not normally impose *prior* restraint. They punish only after

the event. Nevertheless, the very fact that punishment may follow a given course of action tends to inhibit freedom to take that action.

This threat of future punishment is said to have a *chilling effect.* It cools down argumentative ardor and willingness to make facts and ideas public. Self-censorship can, for all practical purposes, have the same repressive effect as external prior restraint. For this reason government action that *potentially* has a broad and indiscriminate chilling effect can be held to violate the First Amendment, even though aimed only at preventing unprotected speech.

Libel　The law of libel affords the best example of how the chilling effect of prospective punishment can undermine First Amendment goals.*

A crucial test of genuine freedom of expression is its use to criticize those in power. Democratic societies count on tenacious news reporting to uncover official wrongdoing, sloth, or incompetence, even at the highest political levels. Vigorous investigative reporting cannot flourish, however, in a society where harsh, easily invoked libel laws threaten journalists with ruinous fines or imprisonment when they dare to criticize public officials.

Libel laws thus involve conflicting social interests. On the one hand, defamation should be punishable because society has an interest in protecting the welfare and dignity

---

*Libel is defamation by published words tending to bring upon its victim public hatred, shame, and disgrace. Spoken defamation is called *slander,* but because broadcasting spreads spoken words far and wide, broadcast defamation is treated as libel. If defamation can be proved, victims can sue for damages. Juries often award very large sums in libel suits, as happened in the *Faulk* case (§8.8).

of the individual citizen. On the other hand, society also has an interest in exposing official corruption and incompetence. The chilling effect of harassing libel suits can serve as a screen to protect crooked politicians.

The first act of a dictator on seizing power is to suppress the freedom of the media to criticize the new regime — ironically, even when one of the complaints against the old regime was the lack of freedom to criticize. In the United States, however, not only politicians but all public figures must be prepared to face harsh, sometimes even unfair and ill-founded, criticism from the media without being able to retaliate easily with libel suits.

The leading case establishing present-day immunity of the news media from easily won libel suits occurred during the civil rights protests of the 1960s. By chance it involved an instance of "editorial advertising" (§17.6), not investigative reporting.

Supporters of the Montgomery, Alabama, bus boycott protesting segregation bought space in the *New York Times* for a full-page advertisement that criticized Montgomery officials. Some of the statements in the advertisement were false, though apparently not deliberate lies. One of the officials in question, a man named Sullivan, sued for libel in an Alabama court (libel laws are under jurisdiction of the states, so that all libel suits have to be initiated at the state level). The court's award of half a million dollars in damages was affirmed by the Alabama Supreme Court. On appeal to the U.S. Supreme Court, however, the *New York Times* won a reversal. Criticism of public officials, said the Court, had broad First Amendment protection. Even though some of the allegations against Sullivan were untrue, under the circumstances they did not constitute libel.

Argument over public issues, said the Court, should be "uninhibited, robust, and wide-open." It is likely to include "vehement, caustic, and sometimes unpleasantly sharp attacks on government and public officials." Such free-wheeling debate is discouraged if, in the heat of debate, the critic must pause to weigh every unfavorable word.

The constitutional guarantees require, we think, a federal rule that prohibits a public official from recovering damages for a defamatory falsehood relating to his official conduct unless he proves that the statement was made with "actual malice" — that is, with knowledge that it was false or with reckless disregard of whether it was false or not. (376 US 279, 1964)

Subsequent libel cases broadened the term "public officials" to include anyone who, because of notoriety, could be classed as a *public figure.* People so classified had little chance of bringing a successful libel suit against the media. Even if stories about public figures could be proved false, deliberate malice on the part of a news medium was exceedingly difficult to prove.

In 1979, however, a libel case involving broadcasting gave public figures a new weapon in seeking to obtain evidence of malice in libel suits.

A former Army officer, Anthony Herbert, became a public figure in the news because of his charges of Army coverups of atrocities committed by American troops during the Vietnam war. On the basis of investigations of Herbert's claims by producer Barry Lando, Mike Wallace interviewed Herbert on *60 Minutes.* Herbert alleged, among other things, that the videotaped interview depicted him as a liar. He sued Lando for libel on this and other grounds.

In order to find evidence of malice, Herbert sought to explore Lando's "state of mind" during the process of preparing the program. For example, he wanted to know what Lando thought about the veracity of his sources and what Lando and Wallace had said to each other in deciding what to include in the broadcast. Lando refused to answer such questions, claiming that the First Amendment protected him from inquiries into the editorial process.

Lando based this claim on the traditional view that newspeople have the right (known as *journalist's privilege*) to keep news sources and editorial processes confidential. In the past few decades journalists had begun to assert this privilege as a First Amendment right. They argue that to be forced by the courts to reveal the names of news sources or to give up their reporting notes (including sound and video recordings) and internal memoranda would have a chilling effect on their freedom to gather and report the news.

Against this background, it came as a shock to the news media when the Supreme Court upheld Herbert's demand to inquire into Lando's state of mind when preparing the *60 Minutes* segment. But, said the Court, the *New York Times* doctrine "made it essential to proving liability that plaintiffs focus on the conduct and state of mind" of those responsible for the reports that allegedly contain libel.

Rejecting Lando's chilling effect argument, the Court emphasized that "according an absolute privilege to the editorial process of a media defendant in a libel case is not required, authorized or presaged by our prior cases, and would substantially enhance the burden of proving actual malice, contrary to the expectations of *New York Times*" (441 US 169, 1979).

Broadcasters and others involved in news reporting regard the *Herbert* decision as a serious weakening of their First Amendment protection. They believe that to allow libel

complainants to rummage through their tape archives and correspondence files will have a perceptible chilling effect on their work.

Even before the *Herbert* case, libel suits had been on the rise. In a 1980 survey the National Association of Broadcasters found that only about half of its members already carried libel insurance. The association initiated a special insurance plan for its members designed to protect them from losses in libel and invasion of privacy suits and also to assist them in opposing barriers to newsgathering such as denial of access to court proceedings.

Evolution of Obscenity Law   Prior to the 1930s, obscenity in literature and art could be arbitrarily suppressed at the whim of officials and censorship boards. The successful defense in 1933 of James Joyce's literary masterpiece, *Ulysses*, initiated a series of court decisions that have set up complex legal barriers against heavy-handed suppression by zealous moral watchdogs.

Current obscenity law is based on the 1973 *Miller* case, in which the Supreme Court ruled on the constitutionality of a California state obscenity law. The decision emphasized that *community standards* vary from place to place: "It is neither realistic nor constitutionally sound to read the First Amendment as requiring that the people of Maine or Mississippi accept public depiction of conduct found tolerable in Las Vegas or New York City."

Nevertheless, warned the Court, state laws must be carefully defined because of the dangers inherent in government regulation of any type of speech. In summary:

We now confine the permissible scope of such regulation to works which depict or describe sexual conduct. That conduct must be specifically defined by the applicable state law . . . A state offense must also be limited to works which, taken as a whole, appeal to the prurient interest in sex, which portray sexual conduct in a patently offensive way, and which, taken as a whole, do not have serious literary, artistic, political, or scientific value. (413 US 24, 1973)

The practical result of the *Miller* case along with some later cases that added minor modifications was to restrict censorship for obscenity to hard-core pornography. All that remained was for the states to define hard-core pornography, but that is exceedingly difficult to do to everyone's satisfaction. In any event, the law rules out abuses of power that were freely committed by censors in the past. For example, the First Amendment now prevents censors from taking such arbitrary action as:

■ Condemning an entire work because of a few isolated obscene words.
■ Using outdated standards no longer common to the local community.
■ Applying as a standard the opinions of hypersensitive persons who are untypical of the general public.
■ Ignoring serious artistic or scientific purpose in judging a work.

Obscenity in Broadcasting Broadcasting's traditional conservatism delayed its response to the liberalized social climate of the 1960s. Obscenity cases began to emerge in the 1970s as a new phenomenon.

Section 1464 of the criminal code makes punishable utterance of "any obscene, indecent, or profane language by means of radio communication," but the FCC remained in doubt as to its constitutional powers to enforce the law. Broadcasting's role as a home medium and the medium most widely available to all ages and classes of people makes it especially vulnerable to attacks. Material accepted as commonplace in other media would be regarded as patently obscene, indecent, or profane by most of the broadcast audience. Because broadcasting is largely a national medium it must adapt to a great variety of local standards. Publications and films distributed nationally can be confined to "local" circulation within groups having common interests and standards.

The FCC expressed the dilemma of broadcasting in this way:

Radio and TV programs enter the home and are readily available not only to the average normal adult but also to children and to the emotionally immature. . . . Thus, for example, while a nudist magazine may be within the protection of the First Amendment . . . the televising of nudes might well raise a serious question of programming contrary to [the obscenity statute]. . . . Similarly, regardless of whether the "four-letter words" and sexual description, set forth in "Lady Chatterley's Lover," (when considered in the context of the whole book) make the book obscene for mailability purposes, the utterance of such words or the depiction of such sexual activity on radio or TV would raise similar public interest and [obscenity statute] questions. (44 FCC 2307, 1960)

Nevertheless, the liberalization of standards in other media inevitably affected broadcasting. In the early 1970s a "topless radio" fad triggered thousands of complaints to the FCC. Said to have been invented by Bill Balance, a well-known Los Angeles DJ, the format invited women to call in and talk about intimate details of their sex lives on the air. And there was no lack of candid women callers to *Femme Forum*, a midday talk show on WGLD-FM in Illinois.

Responding to complaints, the FCC imposed a $2,000 fine on WGLD for violating the obscenity statute. This was in accordance with the forfeiture clause of the communications act, Section 502, which explicitly authorizes fines for obscenity violations. To the FCC's disappointment, WGLD did not ask for a court test. Instead the licensee wrote a letter claiming innocence — but enclosing a check in payment of the fine.*

After the WGLD fine the topless radio fad collapsed, but since then sexual discussions on radio talk shows have reached almost the same level of explicitness. The difference is that the talk on *Femme Forum* was full of leering sensationalism while sex talk on contemporary phone-in radio usually occurs in the somewhat clinical atmosphere of psychological or medical advice programs.

Channeling Concept Later in 1973, however, the FCC finally initiated a test case. One of the Pacifica group of stations (always a reliable source of program provocation) challenged an indecency ruling. Pacifica's WBAI-FM, New York, included in a discussion of social attitudes about language a recording by George Carlin, a comedian popular on the campus speaker circuit. Called "Filthy Words," the monologue dealt with society's hangups about seven words, mostly four-letter terms, "depicting sexual or excretory organs and activities" — the seven words least likely ever to be heard on the air. This time they were — 106 times in 12 minutes.

This assault on the airwaves produced only one complaint. It came from a man who (it later turned out) was associated with an organization called Morality in Media. He happened to hear the broadcast while driving in his car with his teenage son. The fact that the boy was exposed to Carlin's four-letter words became a key element in the case.

On the rather flimsy basis of that lone complaint, the FCC wrote to Pacifica, advising that the WBAI broadcast was indecent and in violation of the statute. The only pen-

alty was that the notification went into the station's file at the FCC. Nevertheless, Pacifica challenged the ruling as a matter of First Amendment principle.

After an initial setback in the appeals court, the FCC won Supreme Court approval of its reasoning. Focusing its argument on the Carlin monologue as *indecent* rather than obscene (it could hardly have been found obscene according to the Supreme Court's definition), the FCC stressed the fact that the broadcast came at a time when children would normally be in the audience.

Children, said the FCC, are not yet sufficiently developed sexually to be able to respond to the "prurient appeal" of obscenity. They are entitled, however, to be protected from indecency, which the FCC defined as material that fails to conform to "accepted standards of morality." In referring to the court-approved "community standards" test, the commission slipped in a qualifier of its own, making it read "community standards *for broadcast media.*"

Instead of meeting the First Amendment head on by flatly banning such material as the Carlin monologue, however, the FCC said it should be *channeled* to a part of the day when children are least likely to be in the audience.† The channeling concept had a precedent in nuisance law, which recognizes that something acceptable in one setting could be an illegal nuisance in other settings.

The Supreme Court agreed with the nuisance law rationale. Recalling that a judge had

---

*The FCC action was in fact appealed by citizen groups that wanted to test the law. The appeals court upheld the FCC, but the case was not decisive because WGLD did not itself lodge the appeal.

†In assessing the channeling rationale it should be borne in mind that the notion of most children being present in audiences only at certain hours of the day may be an illusion. It appears from ratings research data that nearly as many children watch television in late prime time as on the traditional children's enclave, the Saturday morning hours.

once said that a nuisance "may be merely a right thing in a wrong place — like a pig in the parlor instead of the barnyard," the Court added that if the FCC "finds a pig has entered the parlor, the exercise of regulatory power does not depend on proof that the pig is obscene." The Court also tacitly accepted the FCC's redefinition of community standards by adding the words "for broadcasting," saying, "We have long recognized that each medium of expression presents special First Amendment problems. . . . And of all forms of communication, it is broadcasting that has received the most limited First Amendment protection" (438 US 748, 1978).

Clear and Present Danger

A category of unprotected speech even less often injected into broadcasting than obscenity is inflammatory language that may be said to create a *clear and present danger* to the survival of the government.

The phrase goes back to a World War I attempt to obstruct the military draft. A man named Schenk was accused of circulating a document that incited direct, violent resistance. Schenk's action seems mild in the light of acts of resistance committed during the Vietnam war, but in 1918 emotions against the Germans were running high.

In one of the best-known First Amendment commentaries, Supreme Court Justice Oliver Wendell Holmes wrote in the opinion that found Schenk guilty:

We admit that in many places and in ordinary times the defendants in saying all that was said in the circular would have been within their constitutional rights. But the character of every act depends upon the circumstances in which it is done. . . . The question in every case is whether the words used are used in such circumstances and are of such a nature as to create a clear and present danger that they will bring about the substantive evils that Congress has a right to prevent. It is a question of proximity and degree. (249 US 52, 1919, emphasis added)

In this same opinion Holmes reinforced the concept with his oft-misquoted theater fire analogy. The First Amendment does not require us to tell the truth, he said; however, that does not mean that it gives us the right *falsely* to cry "Fire!" in a crowded theater, causing an unnecessary panic and endangering innocent lives.

In dangerous circumstances, with catastrophe imminent, the clear and present danger test of unprotected speech may be justified. It is less persuasive in ordinary circumstances when the danger is by no means as clear or as immediately present. This point was made by the FCC in rejecting a plea that Section 315's prohibition against censoring political candidate broadcasts should be temporarily suspended. The Atlanta chapter of the National Association for the Advancement of Colored People alleged that outrageous language used on the radio by a Georgia candidate for the U.S. Senate, J. B. Stoner, created a clear and present danger. Stoner proclaimed himself a white racist, making such statements in campaign speeches as, "The main reason why niggers want integration is because the niggers want our white women."

Such inflammatory language, said the NAACP and others, threatened to provoke violence that endangered the safety of the stations that broadcast Stoner's speeches and of the people of Georgia generally. The FCC refused to impose prior restraint. The clear and present danger doctrine would only apply, said the FCC, quoting a Supreme Court opinion, if the speech provokes a reaction that "rises far above public inconvenience, annoyance, or unrest" (36 FCC 2d 637, 1972).

Despite Stoner's gross abuse of the right of free speech, it did not literally endanger survival of the Republic, and so he was still entitled to First Amendment protection.

Free Press vs. Fair Trial   Free speech sometimes loses its First Amendment protection when a counterbalancing constitutional right is involved. The Fifth Amendment guarantees defendants in court *due process of law* (§15.2). At the same time the First Amendment guarantees freedom of the press in covering trials. But press coverage in some cases violates Fifth Amendment rights, subjecting defendants and others to publicity that makes fair trial impossible. This *free press vs. fair trial* issue concerns the print media primarily, but broadcasting becomes deeply involved when it attempts radio or television coverage of actual trials.

In 1937 the American Bar Association adopted a policy recommendation as part of its advisory rules of judicial ethics barring news still cameras and radio from court trials. Later this rule, called *Canon 35*, was extended to television cameras. The rule said that such coverage tended to "detract from the essential dignity of the proceedings, degrade the court and create misconceptions with respect thereto in the mind of the public." Nearly all state judicial systems adopted Canon 35.

One exception for a time was Texas. In the 1960s, however, the conviction of a particularly colorful defendant was overthrown by the Supreme Court because of the distractions caused by television coverage of the trial in a Texas court. Billie Sol Estes, a Texas wheeler and dealer, was convicted for swindling and other crimes. Over his objection the judge had allowed television to cover the trial. Twelve cameras with their attendant lights and crews turned the courtroom into a scene of turmoil and confusion (this was before the development of ENG equipment made it possible to cover events at close quarters far less conspicuously).

Estes appealed, in part because he claimed the presence of television had created a courtroom atmosphere that denied him due process of law. In upholding this claim, the Supreme Court said that the First Amendment rights of the television news teams must be subordinated to the constitutional rights of defendants to a fair trial under the Fifth and other amendments (381 US 582, 1965).

In the 1970s, with improved equipment, changing social standards, and more mature broadcast journalism practices, the ban against live coverage of court trials began to seem less urgent. In 1972 the bar association liberalized Canon 35, giving it a new designation as *Canon 3(A)(7)* and recommending that judges be given wide latitude in allowing still and motion picture coverage of trials.

Since then one state after another has liberalized the rules. As an example of these changes, the Nevada Supreme Court's new rules, adopted in 1980, provide as follows (5 MLR 2609, 1980):

■ The media must get written permission from the judge in charge of the trial and must pool their resources.
■ Radio and television must use a common audio system.
■ Cameras must be located in fixed positions.
■ Cables must be unobtrusive.
■ The jury may not be photographed except incidentally in background shots.

Subject to such safeguards, by 1981 over half the states had either allowed cameras in the courtroom or started allowing experimental coverage. Early that year the Supreme Court virtually assured continuation of this trend by denying an appeal by two Florida policemen who had been convicted of burglary. The defendants complained that television coverage of their trial over their objections in a Florida court had denied them due process, citing the precedent of the *Estes* case in Texas. But the Supreme Court held that the Constitution does not prevent states from allowing such coverage as long as suitable safeguards are maintained (7 MLR 1041, 1981).

17.3 Uniqueness of Broadcast Speech

If it is conceivable that some types of speech lack First Amendment protection it is also possible to conceive of different media of expression having different degrees of protection. In any event, throughout the history of broadcast regulation the courts have developed as a consistent theme the idea that broadcasting has somewhat different First Amendment status than the other public media. Broadcasting has unique features, the argument runs, that justify imposing regulations on it that would be considered violations of the First Amendment if imposed on print media.

The most striking evidence of this distinction was the Supreme Court decision in the *Tornillo* case. This decision overthrew a Florida law that gave political candidates the right to reply to attacks against them printed in newspapers (418 US 241, 1974). Five years previously the same court had taken exactly the opposite view with regard to broadcasting. It upheld the FCC's personal attack rule, entitling persons attacked on broadcast stations a right of reply (§17.4).

Broadcasters as Publishers In the traditional freedom-of-the-press perspective, publishers have the right to print what they choose by virtue of owning the publishing organizations and (usually) the printing facilities. Broadcasters, however, cannot fully own their "publishing" facilities. They are only temporary licensees, borrowing access to segments of the publicly owned electromagnetic spectrum. They accept licenses on the understanding that they will use their spectrum allotments in ways that serve the public interest, under supervision of the FCC.

Moreover, the available space in the publishing medium of broadcasters, the electromagnetic spectrum, is limited. The factor of *spectrum scarcity*, as we pointed out in connection with early constitutional challenges to the communications act (§15.2), had a major impact on broadcasting law. It has been used by the courts as the primary basis for upholding a federal law that regulates broadcasting, despite the First Amendment's warning that "Congress shall make no law" abridging freedom of speech and press. Today the scarcity factor is being reappraised in the light of technological changes that may make spectrum scarcity less cramping; nevertheless, historically it has been treated as a conclusive argument justifying regulation.

"Composition of the Traffic" Government licensing does not, in and of itself, represent a significant loss of freedom. First Amendment theory accepts the practical need for *traffic management* of various forms of communication by government. "Rules to effect this purpose are entirely manageable and, if they are non-discriminatory, either promote, or at least do not seriously impair, the system of free expression" (Emerson, 1972: 168).

When the industry challenged the FCC's right to impose network regulations it asserted that the communications act authorized traffic management, nothing more. This meant, said the networks, that the FCC could legally regulate only technical aspects of broadcasting such as channel allotments and signal strength specifications. Regulating anything else, they said, would violate the First Amendment. But the Supreme Court emphatically rejected this argument, saying:

We are asked to regard the Commission as a kind of traffic officer, policing the wave lengths to prevent stations from interfering with each other. But the Act does not restrict the Commission merely to supervision of the traffic. It puts upon the Commission the burden of determining the composition of that traffic. (319 US 215, 1943)

By "composition of that traffic" the Court meant choice of stations through the licensing process. But a certain amount of influence on programming is also implied, because deciding which licensees will best serve the public interest involves taking program services into account.

Thereafter the courts frequently cited the composition-of-the-traffic rationale of the network decision as a legal precedent for approving such limited control of programming.

Absence of Prior Restraint   Another major legal argument in support of program regulation has been the claim that *no prior restraint* is involved. The classic definition of censorship, that of the noted eighteenth-century British legal commentator William Blackstone, stresses the difference between before-the-fact and after-the-fact government action against speech:

The liberty of the press is indeed essential to the nature of a free state; but this consists in laying no previous restraints upon publications, and not in freedom from censure for criminal matter when published. Every freeman has an undoubted right to lay what sentiments he pleases before the public; to forbid this is to destroy the freedom of the press,

but if he publishes what is improper, mischievous, or illegal, he must take the consequences of his own temerity. (Quoted in Hachten, 1968: 41)

Thus specific program rulings by the FCC prior to broadcast (the equivalent of "publication" in Blackstone's terms) would certainly violate the First Amendment. Broadcasters are free to make their own decisions about programs, but if they violate the rules they must take the consequences.

17.4 Regulated Fairness

Broadcasting's uniqueness is used as a justification for government intrusion into some aspects of the freedom of licensees to use their facilities entirely as they might wish. One of these intrusions seeks to ensure *fair play* in the use of broadcast facilities. If regulated fairness enhances the public good that comes from broadcasting, the government is cast in the role of an ally, rather than an enemy, of First Amendment values.

Access to Means of Expression   In order to realize First Amendment goals, citizens need to be able to listen to diverse voices in the marketplace, but they also need to have voices of their own. The notion of *access* thus has reciprocal meanings — access both to what is expressed and to the means of expression.*

Not every person who wants to express ideas over the air can own a broadcasting

*We have discussed other, more specific meanings of access: (1) admittance of journalists to the sources of news (§9.4); (2) use of broadcasting by political candidates (§15.5); (3) legal standing and other avenues for citizen participation in the regulatory process (§16.6); and (4) access and leased channels on cable television (§11.7).

station; nor is it feasible to give everyone access to broadcasting stations owned by others. The FCC chose to deal with this problem by assuring access to broadcasting for *ideas* rather than for specific *people*. But even access for ideas has to be qualified. It would be impracticable to force stations to give time for literally every idea that might be put forward. The FCC mandates access only for ideas about *issues of public importance,* thus stressing another First Amendment value.

The FCC's solution for the access problem has two advantages: (1) it allows licensees to retain general responsibility for programming, for example leaving to their discretion decisions about which issues have public importance and who should speak for them; and (2) it obligates licensees, though in a relatively unstructured way, to allow access to some ideas other than their own. Thus licensee First Amendment rights are generally preserved along with those of the public at large.

Eventually the FCC elaborated its access concept into a formalized set of procedures, the *fairness doctrine.* We reviewed the practical aspects of implementing the doctrine in the preceding chapter (§16.5). Our concern here is with its development and its rationale in terms of First Amendment goals.

Evolution of Fairness Doctrine   Implicit in broadcast regulation from the outset was the notion that fairness played a central role in the *fiduciary responsibility* of licensees — their role as holders of broadcast channels *in trust* for the benefit of the general public. However, the fairness requirement as a set of formal precepts did not emerge until 1949 with the issuance of an FCC report on editorializing by licensees.

In an earlier ruling, known as the *Mayflower* decision, the FCC had said that licensees took an unfair advantage when they used their facilities for expressing their own

points of view in the form of editorials. The 1949 policy statement reversed that ruling. It would be fairer to all concerned, the FCC concluded, to *encourage* licensees to introduce controversial issues by means of editorials — provided that they also gave outsiders access to their facilities to express opposing points of view. In announcing this fairness concept the FCC said:

It is the right of the public to be informed, rather than any right on the part of the Government, any broadcast licensee or any individual member of the public to broadcast his own particular views on any matter, which is the foundation stone of the American system of broadcasting.

This affirmative responsibility on the part of broadcast licensees to provide a reasonable amount of time for the presentation over their facilities of programs devoted to the discussion and consideration of public issues has been reaffirmed by the commission in a long series of decisions. (13 FCC 1249, 1949)

In effect, the FCC was saying that it is a kind of *unfairness* for a licensee to program nothing but bland entertainment, avoiding all serious or provocative program matter. That policy would deprive the public of an important First Amendment benefit that it had a right to expect from broadcasting.

Thus the fairness doctrine imposes two requirements: licensees should (1) ensure that controversial issues receive some airing on their facilities; and (2) ensure that once an issue has been introduced, speakers for other sides have a chance to be heard.

In practice, however, stations afraid of controversy ignore the first requirement with little risk of FCC objection. Only once has the FCC reprimanded a station for failing to *initiate* a controversy. This occurred in 1976 when a congresswoman and others complained that WHAR, a small AM radio station in West Virginia, refused to air a tape she had sent. The congresswoman had circulated the tape to a number of stations, counteracting arguments against a strip-mining bill that had already been circulated on tape by the U.S. Chamber of Commerce. Having neither aired the chamber tape nor raised the issue of the strip-mining bill locally on its own, WHAR claimed it had no obligation to air a reply. However, the FCC agreed with the congresswoman. It was, said the FCC, a violation of the fairness doctrine to *fail to bring up* an issue of great local importance (59 FCC 2d 987, 1976).

It is no mystery why stations ordinarily ignore with impunity their fairness doctrine obligation to initiate discussion about controversial subjects. As a rule the FCC sits back and waits for third parties to bring station misbehavior to its attention, rather than conducting its own monitoring activities to seek out violations (§16.6). In the nature of things, the most frequent and urgent fairness doctrine complaints are *reactive.* They come from people reacting to ideas that have already been discussed on the air, rather than from those who want to initiate discussions of new issues.

Legislative Affirmation   The fairness doctrine began as an FCC administrative interpretation of the general public interest mandate of the communications act. In 1959, however, Congress appeared to lend statutory endorsement to the concept in an incidental way when it amended Section 315.

"Last week, the management of this station wished our listeners a happy New Year. Here now is Mr. Clyde Wilmer with an opposing view."

Drawing by Dana Fradon, © 1979 *The New Yorker* Magazine, Inc.

This amendment, it will be recalled, exempted bona fide news programs involving political candidates from the equal-time requirements of Section 315 (§16.5). After enumerating four types of exempt news programs (newscasts, interviews, documentaries, on-the-spot coverage) the amendment continued (emphasis added):

Nothing in the foregoing sentence shall be construed as relieving broadcasters, in connection with [the exempt news programs], from the obligation imposed upon them under this Act to operate in the public interest and to afford reasonable opportunity for the discussion of conflicting views on issues of public importance.

The phrase "in connection with" seems to limit such discussions to news-related issues. Nevertheless, the FCC and the courts have treated this statement as congressional endorsement of the fairness doctrine generally.

Judicial Affirmation: Red Lion Doubt still lingered as to whether the FCC could enforce the fairness doctrine without violating the First Amendment. Two additional fairness requirements, adopted in 1967, caused special concern to opponents of FCC interference: the personal attack and the political editorial rules. Both were issued as actual rules and both required that those affected by such broadcasts must be given copies of the relevant material within specified time limits.

Objections to these rules led to a crucial Supreme Court test of the fairness doctrine's constitutionality in 1969. The Court heard two separate appeals simultaneously, issuing a single opinion. The lower courts had ruled favorably to the FCC in one case, unfavorably in the other. Most of the Supreme Court's attention was focused on the first, which was an appeal by a licensee from a personal attack violation ruling by the FCC.*

The case was initiated by the licensee of WGCB, a Pennsylvania AM/FM radio station licensed to a conservative minister of religion under the name Red Lion Broadcasting Company. In 1964 the station had refused to give reply time to a personal attack aired on a syndicated radio series carried by WGCB. The complaint came from a writer named Fred J. Cook, author of an article titled "Hate Clubs of the Air" and a book critical of the recently defeated Republican presidential candidate, Barry Goldwater. The alleged attack occurred in the right-wing syndicated radio series of the Rev. Billy James Hargis, *Christian Crusade* — one of the programs criticized by Cook in his "hate clubs" article.

Hargis charged Cook with having communist affiliations, with attacking the FBI and the CIA, and so on — the usual litany of accusations Hargis routinely made against liberals in his broadcasts. The FCC agreed that Cook was entitled to air time in which to reply to the attack, if necessary without charge, and ordered WGCB to comply. But the licensee refused on First Amendment and other grounds.

In unanimously confirming the FCC five years later, the Supreme Court gave a ringing affirmation of the entire fairness doctrine concept in an opinion written by Justice Byron White (395 US 367, 1969). It was notable for his trenchant commentary on several of broadcasting's recurrent First Amendment issues. Here is a sampler:

■ *On the uniqueness of broadcasting*: "It is idle to posit an unabridgeable First Amendment

---

*The other case challenged the political editorial and the personal attack rules as such. It was initiated by the Radio and Television News Directors Association, which felt that the station's personal attack case might not be strong enough to afford a definitive test of the First Amendment issue.

right to broadcast comparable to the right of every individual to speak, write, or publish."

■ *On the fiduciary principle*: "There is nothing in the First Amendment which prevents the Government from requiring a licensee to share his frequency with others and to conduct himself as a proxy or fiduciary."

■ *On the public interest*: "It is the right of the viewers and listeners, not the right of the broadcasters, which is paramount."

■ *On the scarcity factor*: "Nothing in this record, or in our own researches, convinces us that the [spectrum] resource is no longer one for which there are more immediate and potential uses than can be accommodated, and for which wise planning is essential."

With the *Red Lion* case the fairness doctrine achieved emphatic legal endorsement from the highest court. From then on legal appeals concerned not the doctrine itself, but its applicability in given cases. Not surprisingly, considering the latitude licensees have in responding to fairness doctrine complaints, disputes about its applicability in specific instances continue to arise.

17.5 Fairness and News

Role of Editorial Discretion   News, though it often deals with controversial topics, is not in itself a presentation of "controversial issues of public importance" in the fairness doctrine sense. Therefore bona fide news programs generally enjoy exemption from fairness doctrine constraints similar to their exemption from Section 315 equal time constraints.

This exemption is based on the assumption that reporters and editors use *editorial discretion*, which in itself calls for fair treatment of the events and controversies in the news. No one is so naive as to believe that journalists always use the best possible judgment, or that they are never without bias or prejudice. The First Amendment teaches, however, that it is better to tolerate journalists' mistakes and incompetencies than to set up the government as the arbiter of truth. In reaffirmation of this reliance on journalistic judgment, the Supreme Court said:

For better or for worse, editing is what editors are for; and editing is selection and choice of material. That editors — newspaper or broadcast — can and do abuse this power is beyond doubt, but that is not reason to deny the discretion Congress provided. Calculated risks of abuse are taken in order to preserve higher values. (412 US 124, 1973)

Deliberate Distortion   Reliance on journalistic discretion does not mean that the FCC must ignore *deliberate* slanting, distortion, or withholding of news. But the FCC normally leans over backward to avoid conflict with the First Amendment by giving journalists the benefit of the doubt. As the commission said in its *Fairness Report*, "we do not believe that it would be either useful or appropriate for us to investigate charges of news misrepresentations in the absence of extrinsic evidence or documents that on their face reflect deliberate distortion" (43 FCC 2d 21, 1974).

An example of the kind of face-value "extrinsic" evidence the FCC would consider an adequate basis for intervening would be memoranda from a station licensee explicitly instructing subordinates to doctor news reports to make them conform to the licensee's personal wishes. Such evidence, like evidence of malice in libel cases, is not easy to come by. Therefore few authentic instances of calculated misuse of broadcast news have come to light.

We have mentioned the *Star Stations of Indiana* case, in which five stations were deleted partly because the licensee had ordered news personnel to give favored treatment to political candidates he preferred (§16.8). An example of a different type of news distortion was alleged in the case of WPIX(TV) in New York. Among other things, it was accused by members of its own news staff in 1969 of misrepresentation of the sources of news stories — making them seem more timely and impressive than they really were. A long-drawn-out renewal fight followed, with WPIX finally winning renewal in 1978 by a 4–3 vote (68 FCC 2d 381).

News Bias Critics sometimes accuse broadcasters of a more pervasive kind of journalistic unfairness: overall *news bias*. Typically such charges come from political conservatives, who tend to believe that the news media as a whole have a liberal bias. They argue not so much that specific news stories are false, but that the cumulative effect over time tends to build up one-sided perceptions of certain issues.

For example, an organization called the American Security Council Educational Foundation (ASCEF) made a content analysis of CBS television news stories on national security matters during 1972. The published study claimed that over 60 percent of CBS's statements on the subject were biased in suggesting that "the threat to U.S. national security is less than that on which present policy is based or the government ought *to do less* in response to the lesser threat" (Lefever, 1974: 75, 86).

ASCEF petitioned the FCC to order CBS to allow fairness doctrine time for expression of opposing views. The FCC rejected the complaint, pointing out that the evidence of the ASCEF study failed to single out a specific controversial issue as required by fairness doctrine procedures. The concept "national security" involves many different issues in many different parts of the world, said the FCC.

The Supreme Court agreed with the FCC, calling the ASCEF's claim a "blunderbuss approach to the fairness doctrine." Granting ASCEF's claim, said the Court,

would create a precedent that might well have a serious effect on daily news programming, by inducing broadcasters to forego programming on controversial issues or by disrupting the normal exercise of journalistic judgment in such programming that is aired. . . . In attempting to comply with the fairness doctrine as interpreted by ASCEF, an editor's news judgment would be severely altered. An editor preparing an evening newscast would be required to decide whether any of the day's newsworthy events is tied, even tangentially, to events covered in the past, and whether a report on today's lead story, in some remote way, balances yesterday's, last week's or last year's. (607 F 2d 451, 1979)

News Documentaries Programs that take a point of view on news events such as news documentaries almost inevitably provoke controversy.

In preparing documentaries, producers often resort to techniques that could be regarded as staging or rigging of news events. Producers have been charged with helping to stage an invasion of a foreign country, mislabeling pictures offered as evidence, organizing a pot-smoking party at a university, and using interview replies out of context to give a misleading impression. Such charges triggered both FCC and congressional investigations, but they uncovered no evidence of deliberate dishonesty on the part of broadcast management. Individual employees, however, were sometimes guilty of indiscretion and bad judgment, if not of outright deception.

A 1968 CBS documentary, "Hunger in America," caused intense resentment on the part of agricultural interests. It is said that FBI agents were assigned to track down every scrap of evidence that could be used to discredit the CBS news team. For example, one of the picture sequences depicted babies in a pediatric ward, many suffering from malnutrition. The narration attributed the later death of one of the infants to starvation. A check on the death certificate disclosed that death was attributed to other causes.

It is probably safe to say that *any* documentary that says anything worth saying could be faulted for minor lapses in accuracy if investigated with sufficient intensity. In any event, the FCC sensibly declined to accept such evidence as "misrepresentation" sufficiently gross to deny renewal of CBS station licenses:

We do not intend to defer action on license renewals because of the pendency of complaints of the kind we have investigated here — unless the extrinsic evidence of possible deliberate distortion or staging of the news which is brought to our attention, involves the licensee, including its principals, top management, or news management. (20 FCC 2d 150, 1969)

Another case of alleged misrepresentation in a news documentary caused a dramatic confrontation between a network president and a congressional committee. CBS aired a documentary in 1971 called "The Selling of the Pentagon." It criticized the spending of huge sums by the Pentagon for propaganda directed toward American citizens, aimed at drumming up support for higher military budgets. The issue of military spending was extremely sensitive at the time because the Vietnam war was still going on.

No one could deny the basic fact that the military spends a lot on public relations, but critics attacked details of editing that suggested biased interpretations. For example,

replies of military spokespersons in recorded interviews were taken out of context, allegedly in order to misrepresent what they actually said.

The Pentagon lobby created such a furor that a House Special Committee on Investigations held hearings on the subject. The committee subpoenaed material that had been edited out of the original footage. Appearing as a witness before the committee, CBS President Frank Stanton declined to turn over the film outtakes. To do so, he said, would have an unconstitutional chilling effect on the freedom of broadcasters to do news programs. "There can be no doubt in anyone's mind," Stanton testified, "that the First Amendment would bar this subpena [*sic*] if directed at the editing of a newspaper report, a book, or a magazine article" (House CIFC, 1971: 73).

Angered at this defiance, the committee recommended to the House that Stanton be cited for contempt of Congress. The House failed to act, however, averting perhaps the most serious clash ever threatened between the federal government and the broadcasting industry.

When queried by the congressional committee as to what it proposed to do about the alleged misrepresentations in "The Selling of the Pentagon," the FCC said in effect, "Nothing." The commission replied that it regretted any misrepresentations that might occur in news broadcasts, but steadfastly maintained its position that newscasters, not the FCC, should use editorial judgment. The FCC should not, it said, "dictate the particular response to thousands of journalistic circumstances" (30 FCC 2d 153, 1971).

Editorial Discretion Vindicated The FCC seemed to forget these words two years later when a 1973 NBC documentary, "Pensions: The Broken Promise," caused complaints of unfairness. The program depicted the plight of workers who are left stranded late in life because of the failures of private industrial pension plans.

Accuracy in Media (AIM), an aggressive conservative watchdog organization that frequently makes fairness doctrine complaints, objected that NBC had presented only one side of a controversial issue (Congress was at that time considering legislation to tighten up on laws governing private pension plans). In an apparent departure from its previous rulings, the FCC agreed with AIM. This time the FCC felt impelled to substitute its judgment for that of journalists and ordered NBC to advise how it proposed to make time available for a pro-industry reply. It would have been simple and painless for NBC to give some industry spokesperson a few minutes on one of its regular news shows to satisfy the fairness doctrine claim. But the network felt that a principle was at stake. Accordingly it refused to comply and took the FCC to court.

"Pensions" was widely discussed at the time as a critical test case of broadcast journalism's First Amendment rights. NBC was vindicated when the appeals court agreed that the FCC had been inconsistent in applying its own fairness doctrine principles:

The Commission's error of law is that it failed adequately to apply the message of applicable decisions that the editorial judgments of the licensee must not be disturbed if reasonable and in good faith. The licensee . . . has wide discretion and latitude that must be respected even though, under the same facts, the [FCC] would reach a contrary conclusion. (516 F 2d 1118, 1974)

The three-judge appeals court divided two to one on the decision, with the dissenting judge writing a vigorous contrary opinion. Nevertheless, the Supreme Court refused to review the case. Thus the broadcast journalists' editorial discretion was upheld and the chances of harassment from fairness doctrine

complaints about news programs lessened. However, the court had based its decision on faulty FCC procedures, rather than on First Amendment grounds. Thus the constitutional immunity of broadcast news documentaries from fairness doctrine complaints in the future remains to be definitively confirmed by the Supreme Court.

17.6 Fairness in Advertising

Editorial Advertising   At the time the fairness doctrine emerged, no one thought of advertising as involving "controversial issues of public importance." There had been occasional exceptions in the past, but most commercials dealt with toothpaste, headache remedies, soft drinks, and soap — not with serious discussions of socially significant problems.

Technology and consumer consciousness changed all that in the 1960s. When manufacturers began to find themselves under attack for environmental pollution and other alleged antisocial behavior, they started using their product advertising as a vehicle for arguing their point of view. Consumers wanted to talk back, using the same punchy 30- and 60-second spot announcement format as the advertisers. Thus emerged what came to be called *editorial* (or *issue*) *advertising*.

Counter-Commercials   The pioneer case in the development of editorial advertising came as a result of the Surgeon General's 1964 report linking cigarette smoking with cancer and its follow-up, the Federal Cigarette Labeling and Advertising Act of 1965, which mandated health warnings on packages and printed advertising.

In 1967 a young Washington lawyer, John Banzhaf III, forwarded an unusual complaint to the FCC. WCBS-TV in New York had violated the fairness doctrine, Banzhaf asserted, by refusing to give time for antismoking spot announcements to counteract cigarette commercials on television.

CBS somewhat complacently assured the FCC that it had already more than fulfilled its fairness obligation regarding the issue of cigarette smoking on many programs featuring news and discussion of the Surgeon General's report. To almost everyone's astonishment, the FCC sided with Banzhaf. It agreed that, in view of the Surgeon General's report and the 1965 labeling act, cigarette commercials presented a unique fairness doctrine issue in and of themselves. "We stress," warned the commission, however, "that our holding is limited to this product — cigarettes."

The appeals court upheld the FCC. Rejecting the claim of First Amendment infringement, the court pointed out that the FCC ruling did not in fact ban any speech — indeed antismoking spots would actually add to the information available to the public on the issue. Moreover, the FCC ruling seemed clearly to carry out congressional intent, as expressed in the cigarette labeling act, to inform the public of the dangers of smoking cigarettes (405 F 2d 1082, 1968).*

Despite the FCC's warning (repeated by the court) that the extension of fairness doctrine obligations to commercials applied only to cigarette advertising, claims for the right to reply to other product advertising began pouring in to the FCC. It could not reject these claims out of hand without being accused of inconsistency. When it did turn

down a group called Friends of the Earth, which asked for time to reply to commercials glorifying large, powerful automobiles, the appeals court reversed the FCC. To ignore the cigarette ruling was an arbitrary and capricious application of its own policies, said the court (449 F 2d 1164, 1971).

Caught in a trap, the FCC decided to formally reverse itself, which it did in its 1974 *Fairness Report*:

We do not believe that the underlying purposes of the fairness doctrine would be well served by permitting the cigarette case to stand as a fairness doctrine precedent. . . . Accordingly, in the future we will apply the fairness doctrine only to those "commercials" which are devoted in an obvious and meaningful way to the discussion of public issues. (48 FCC 2d 26, 1974)

Just because a commercial advertises a controversial product does not necessarily mean that the commercial deals "in an obvious and meaningful way" with a controversial issue. This distinction was affirmed when a consumer group tried to invoke the fairness doctrine to combat commercials for snowmobiles. The group asked a Maine station to allow counter-commercials, asserting that snowmobiles caused ecological damage, encouraged vandalism, are dangerous to occupants, and so on.

Turned down by both the station and the FCC, the group also lost a court appeal. The court said the FCC was within its rights to reverse itself on the Banzhaf decision, and that its policy of excluding straight product commercials, no matter how controversial the product, from fairness doctrine claims was reasonable (522 F 2d 1060, 1975).

Editorial Commercials In addition to being asked to give time for unpaid "commercials" under the fairness doctrine, sta-

---

*The surge of antismoking spots that followed subsided after Congress banned cigarette advertising in broadcasting in 1972, thus removing the fairness doctrine obligation to carry the counter-advertising spots.

tions are also sometimes asked to *sell* time for use in making editorial statements. Traditionally, broadcasters have opposed this practice, known as *editorial advertising* or *issue advertising*. We have already mentioned the example of the sale of time for religious proselytizing and fund raising (§9.7).

Some broadcasters argue against selling time for editorial or issue advertising because they claim that (1) serious issues cannot be adequately discussed within the confines of spot announcements; (2) selling larger blocks of time for editorializing by outsiders involves surrender of licensee editorial responsibility. Also in the background is the less high-minded, play-it-safe motive: controversies initiated by outsiders can have all sorts of troublesome repercussions for the licensee.

The legality of the policy against selling time for editorial advertising was challenged by the Business Executives Move for Vietnam Peace (BEM). During the bitter controversy over the Vietnam war, BEM prepared spot announcements arguing against the war and countering Army recruiting spots. Failing to place its antiwar spots as public service announcements, BEM sought to buy commercial time for them. In refusing, a Washington station said that it had a fixed policy against selling announcement time for editorial commercials. BEM appealed.

The controversy over the legality of a policy against accepting editorial advertising took on great significance. If BEM had prevailed it would have meant (1) that licensees were no longer free to use journalistic discretion in controlling controversial discussions on their stations; (2) that a new right of access to the airwaves would be created; and (3) that broadcast stations would take on the character of common carriers, contrary to the def-

inition of broadcasting in the communications act (§15.3).

None of this happened because the Supreme Court upheld the FCC's ruling. Joining BEM with another pending case involving a similar complaint, the Court once again upheld the principle of licensee journalistic discretion. The Court noted that during debate on the original broadcasting statute, the Radio Act of 1927, the prospect of "private censorship" by licensees was discussed. Congress even considered a proposal to make broadcasting a common carrier whenever "any question affecting the public" was discussed on the air, but the proposal was defeated. The Court concluded in the BEM case:

Since it is physically impossible to provide time for all viewpoints . . . the right to exercise editorial judgment was granted to the broadcaster. The broadcaster, therefore, is allowed significant journalistic discretion in deciding how best to fulfill the Fairness Doctrine obligations, although that discretion is bounded by rules designed to assure that the public interest in fairness is furthered. (412 US 111, 1973)

Although the outcome of the *BEM* case allowed broadcasters to continue using their own judgment in accepting advertising, controversy over this immunity from fairness claims continued. In the 1970s, environmental and energy supply issues subjected the oil companies and other large corporations to sharp new criticism. Dissatisfied with broadcast coverage of these issues, they sought to get their side to the public by other means. Here are some examples:

■ Mobil Corporation spent over a quarter of a million dollars to buy full-page ads in major newspapers and journals headlined "How CBS on October 24, 1979, prefabricated the news." The ads charged the network with having misrepresented Mobil's earnings in a news report.

- In 1980 Illinois Power produced a video-taped item-by-item rebuttal of a *60 Minutes* segment that accused the company of bungling construction of a nuclear power plant. The company sent out 1,500 copies of its "60 Minutes: Our Reply" tape for screenings before interested groups.

- Also in 1980, when Mobil syndicated the prime-time mini-series, *Edward and Mrs. Simpson,* the built-in Mobil commercials consisted of editorial advertisements. Calling them "fables for now," Mobil used animated animal stories to get across its editorial message. For example, one fable ended with the moral, "like an elephant, if our energy producers don't earn a profit proportionate to their size, they won't be able to find and produce more energy." A few stations that had scheduled the Mobil series canceled it when they saw the commercials, but the oil company had no difficulty in finding substitute outlets.

A 1980 Television Advertising Bureau survey indicated that about 90 percent of all television stations were willing to at least consider accepting editorial advertising on a case-by-case basis. The networks and their O&O stations remain the principal holdouts against selling time for issue advertising as a matter of fixed policy. But even the networks seemed to be weakening in their resolve, for in 1981 ABC announced the start of an experiment in selling late-night, one-minute segments for "paid commentaries."

17.7 Antimonopoly Regulation

Diversification   First Amendment theory stresses the value of maintaining a marketplace where ideas, information, and opinions from many "diverse and antagonistic sources" can compete for acceptance. Under modern conditions, however, unregulated competition tends to produce monopoly. Government can play a positive First Amendment role by means of regulations intended to prevent media monopolies. *Diversification* of ownership and control therefore becomes a major goal of FCC regulation. This is *structural* regulation, to use the term employed by deregulation theorists (§16.10). It contrasts with the *behavioral* regulation discussed in the preceding sections.

Examples of structural regulation are rules on (1) the number and kind of stations licensed to any one owner; (2) concentration of control over program production and distribution; (3) cross-media ownership (broadcasting stations and other media under common ownership); and (4) equal employment opportunities.

Multiple Station Ownership   Every station is a kind of monopoly, licensed to have exclusive use of a given channel in a given market. The FCC prevents this form of monopoly from getting out of hand by imposing power limitations on each class of stations.

Because of the monopolistic nature of even one station, limits on multiple station ownership are especially necessary. On the national scale, the *rule of seven* limits single owners to seven stations in each service — AM, FM, and television (§12.1). The 21 stations that may be owned according to the rule of seven is reduced somewhat for types of ownership that imply excessive concentration. Only five of the seven television stations may be VHF, and there are special restrictions on ownership by networks and regional concentration of ownership. For the low-power television class of stations proposed by the FCC in 1980, an interim maximum of 15 stations to a single licensee was established.*

*Noncommercial educational stations are exempt from most of the rules limiting commercial station ownership.

On the level of each individual market, the basic limitation is the *duopoly rule*, which prevents ownership of more than one station of the same type in any one market. Originally one owner could have a single-market AM-FM-television combination. The more recent *one-to-a-customer* policy limits new licensees to either television or radio.

Most of these ownership rules are softened by *grandfathering* (exempting present owners) and the right to appeal for the grant of exceptions. Much of the restructuring of ownership will therefore take place over time as grandfathered groups are broken up when sold and as new licenses are issued on a one-to-a-customer basis.

Production-Distribution Controls As the chief producers and procurers of programs as well as the chief distributors, the networks have long been the target of FCC antimonopoly controls. The original radio chain broadcasting regulations (§7.5) prohibited overlapping networks under a single owner. This rule forced NBC to divest itself of one of its networks. The emergence of ABC as an independent competitor brought about a major structural change in the industry.

We reviewed television network regulations in describing network operations (§12.4). In brief, they seek to prevent the networks from completely dominating their affiliates so that stations will also be able to serve local interests, produce local programs, and purchase some of their programming from nonnetwork sources.

The prime-time access rule was intended specifically to increase the ability of nonnet-

work sources of program production to compete for acceptance (§8.7). Associated with the rule are additional restrictions preventing networks from syndicating their own programs and from acquiring ownership of the programs they lease from production companies.

These structural regulations all aim at increasing diversity by stimulating competition among networks, syndication companies, and program producers while at the same time maintaining the independence of network-affiliated stations.

Apparently not satisfied with these FCC attempts at curbing network monopolistic tendencies, the Department of Justice filed a suit against the three major television networks in 1972, charging them with using a variety of monopolistic dodges to control network programming. For example, the Justice Department objected to the networks' practice of demanding a financial interest in programs they bought from outside producers.

NBC settled its part of the suit in 1976 by agreeing to a *consent decree*. This is a legal maneuver that saves all concerned from a long-drawn-out court battle. NBC agreed to alter the practices in question in exchange for withdrawal of the suit, without any admission of guilt. The network promised to refrain, for stipulated periods of time, from practices that allegedly gave NBC undue competitive advantages (449 F Sup 1127, 1978).

Essentially the consent decree reinforced the rules already adopted by the FCC to limit network control over independently produced programs, adding some more details as to permissible relationships between the network and its program suppliers. In 1980 both ABC and CBS signed similar preliminary consent decrees.

Some states have networks of educational stations with more than seven owned and operated affiliates, and in some cases single educational entities operate both a VHF and a UHF television station in the same community.

Interpreting and applying the terms of the decrees should keep lawyers busy for years. The FCC's Network Inquiry Special Staff, after analyzing the Justice Department charges and the consent decrees, concluded that they would present an "enforcement nightmare." In the opinion of the FCC study group, the decrees would probably not have any practical effect on the practices to which the Justice Department objected.

Cross-Media Ownership Every broadcast license granted to a newspaper publisher automatically reduces diversification of media ownership. This reduction in public sources of information is especially undesirable in small communities where the only newspaper might own the only broadcasting stations.

For decades the FCC struggled to find a politically acceptable solution to this problem. It was clearly inconsistent with First Amendment theory and FCC philosophy to allow newspaper interests to dominate broadcasting. Yet at times in the past as many as a third of the stations on the air were commonly owned with newspapers.

The Department of Justice took an interest in the matter and pressed the FCC to take action. Finally, after several false starts, the commission issued a set of rules in 1975. By that time radio-newspaper cross-ownership had declined, but about 27 percent of the television stations on the air were still newspaper owned, though few involved ownership of both media in the same market.

The new rules avoided a confrontation with the most powerful newspaper interests by allowing grandfathering cross-ownerships that already existed. No future combinations would be allowed, and existing combinations would eventually disappear, broken up when changes in ownership oc-

curred. Only a few small-town monopolies that the FCC called "egregious cases" were forced into divestiture.

When the new rules were appealed, the Supreme Court rejected both the industry's plea for less stringent rules and the consumer interests' plea for even tougher rules. The court agreed with the FCC that sweeping divestiture would be too disruptive to serve the public interest, while requiring divestiture of the most serious cases of monopoly was a reasonable measure (436 US 775, 1978).

17.8 First Amendment Issues

Does breaking up ownership concentrations help or hinder achievement of First Amendment goals? Does the eighteenth-century marketplace-of-ideas concept have relevance to business conditions of the twentieth century? Is the fairness doctrine a workable solution to the problem of access to broadcasting? Should First Amendment protections from government intervention be different for broadcasting than for other media? These are some of the current First Amendment–related issues in broadcasting.

Relevance of Marketplace Concept Communicators of the eighteenth century entered the marketplace of ideas as many small traders, competing on relatively equal terms. A *self-righting* process was expected to occur. Given enough time and sufficiently diverse market inputs, people were expected to be able to explore all offerings before drawing their own conclusions.

Now, however, entry into the marketplace is prohibitively costly for most traders. Giant media conglomerates like the television networks distribute ideas throughout the national market, in fact the whole world, with the help of high technology. A few national media can saturate the entire country with an idea overnight, raising questions as to whether the self-righting process has enough time to run its course.

One response to these problems, discussed in §17.7, is enforced ownership diversification. However, research has failed to show conclusively that diversification of broadcast station ownership actually produces the predicted beneficial results. In fact marginal stations are less likely to behave responsibly than large, group-owned stations. The manager of a failing enterprise, worried about meeting next week's payroll, is an easy mark for questionable programming and sales practices that stations in sounder financial condition would refuse to consider. Integrity is a luxury that marginal stations often cannot afford.

Thus diversification of media ownership as a First Amendment value remains somewhat hypothetical. Nevertheless, most First Amendment scholars remain convinced that, even if in specific instances concentration of ownership may further rather than hinder First Amendment values, in the long run freedom is best served if the maximum possible number of voices can get a hearing in the marketplace of ideas.

Access as a Right   Another response to the contemporary distortions of the marketplace is to assert a *right of access* as a new First Amendment right. As we indicated in §1.5, the notion of access as a fundamental human right is part of recent worldwide communication theory speculation.

A leading proponent of enforced access regards it as a necessary next step to correct the inadequacies of the marketplace concept, which he says is now a mere romantic illusion:

Today ideas reach the millions largely to the extent they are permitted entry into the great metropol-

itan dailies, news magazines, and broadcasting networks. The soap box is no longer an adequate forum for public discussion. Only the new media of communication can lay sentiments before the public, and it is they rather than the government who can most effectively abridge expression by nullifying the opportunity for an idea to win acceptance. As a constitutional theory for the communication of ideas, laissez faire is manifestly irrelevant. (Barron, 1967, in Gillmor & Barron, 1979: 595)

Fairness of Fairness Doctrine   One attempt to deal with the problem of access in broadcasting is, as we described it in §17.4, the fairness doctrine. It tries to solve the dilemma of too many potential demands for personal access by shifting the emphasis from persons to issues.

Most broadcasters oppose the fairness doctrine, claiming that it has a chilling effect. It deters treatment of controversial issues, they say, because broadcasters fear being flooded with access claims. Even ill-founded claims can be costly to rebut. As a rather extreme example, KREM-TV spent 21 months defending itself against charges that it had been unfair in treating a controversy about issuance of bonds to finance an international fair in Seattle. Rebuttal, although successful, cost the station $20,000 in legal fees and hundreds of hours of personnel time (Geller, 1973: 42).

By the same token, obtaining fairness doctrine access can also be expensive and time-consuming for petitioners. Fred Cook, the writer whose personal attack claim was finally upheld by the Supreme Court in the *Red Lion* case, had to wait nearly five years for the order forcing WGCB to give him reply time. By then he had lost interest in rectifying a long-ago libel.

The *Red Lion* case also raises the question as to whether the fairness doctrine lends itself to political exploitation. The case as argued in court seemed to involve the valiant fight of a scrappy liberal writer defending his reputation against the politically motivated slanders of a right-wing extremist. But Fred Cook was not exactly as innocent a victim as he seemed. He, too, was politically motivated and to some extent an extremist.

Several years later, Fred W. Friendly, formerly Edward R. Murrow's associate and then professor of journalism at Columbia University in New York, began looking into the background of the *Red Lion* case for material on a book about the fairness doctrine (Friendly, 1976). He discovered that Cook had in fact been a subsidized writer for the Democratic National Committee. His fairness doctrine appeal, if not inspired by, was at least linked to a systematic campaign mounted by the Democratic party organization to discredit right-wing extremists like the Reverend Hargis, in whose syndicated radio commentary the attack on Cook had occurred.

During the 1960s right-wing radio preachers like Hargis inundated radio with syndicated political commentaries. The situation, as described by the Rev. Everett C. Parker of the United Church of Christ (who had himself been attacked by the right-wing preachers) was as follows:

A few very wealthy, powerful and reactionary multimillionaires like H. L. Hunt had established tax-exempt foundations into which huge sums of money were poured to buy radio time to express their views. Typically, their programs were anti-Catholic and anti-Semitic and very hostile to the Bill of Rights. Small stations in one-station markets carried these programs without the licensee even hearing them. In a few years, the airwaves in small towns were virtually taken over by this power of the purse. The stations developed into local political organs for extremists. *

According to Friendly's investigation, the Democratic party organization set out to exploit the fairness doctrine as a means of harassing stations that sold time for the airing of the ultraconservative political programs. Cook mimeographed his complaint against the Hargis program and mailed copies to scores of stations. He received offers of time from some 50 stations, but WGCB (of *Red Lion*) merely sent him a rate card and an invitation to buy time like anyone else.

Friendly concluded that Cook had been part of a campaign to pervert the fairness doctrine into "an instrument of politics and ambition." Cook and others associated with the Democratic National Committee said Friendly had misrepresented their activities. They maintained that Cook had acted as a private individual, not as an agent of the Democrats, in bringing fairness doctrine complaints against the Hargis program.

Whatever the details, it could not be denied that Cook had written political tracts for the Democrats and was closely associated with the party officials who staged the campaign against the right-wing broadcasters. Hargis reported that stations carrying his commentaries shrank from over 300 to 50.

This loss was probably due more to withdrawal of H. L. Hunt's financial support than to fairness doctrine harassment. Nevertheless, a voice in the marketplace had been weakened. First Amendment absolutists would regard this episode as one more ar-

---

*Parker wrote these comments in one of a series of letters from several correspondents, including Cook, that appeared in the *New York Times Magazine*, rebutting Fred Friendly's accusations, which were set forth as an advance chapter of his book in that publication (Friendly, 1975).

gument against FCC intervention in program decisions of licensees.

Presidential TV Another problem of politics and the fairness doctrine arises because of the advantage the President of the United States has in gaining access to broadcasting. No opponent can match the president's unique privilege of speaking to the nation without interruption on all three national television networks simultaneously. In times of intense political confrontation, every utterance of the president tends to take on a partisan flavor, even when he is speaking as president rather than as head of a political party.

This was the situation in the late 1960s, when opposition to President Nixon's Vietnam war policies became extremely intense and emotional. In 1970 the FCC issued rulings settling several thorny fairness doctrine questions that arose out of confrontations with the president. Among them was a decision that five speeches of the president warranted one rebuttal speech under similar favorable conditions. Another was the decision that a Democratic reply speech in time given by CBS in its "loyal opposition" series warranted a Republican reply. This "reply to a reply" was mandated because the original Democratic reply to the president had been devoted mostly to issues not raised in the original presidential address (25 FCC 2d 283, 1970).

These fairness doctrine rulings aroused much adverse criticism. In particular, the arbitrary balancing of five presidential addresses with one lone reply speech caused critics to wonder how the commission arrived at a five-to-one ratio. Why not a four-to-one or even a one-to-one ratio?

The Twentieth Century Fund financed a study to explore the problems involved in "presidential television." The study concluded:

The regulatory law and doctrines that have evolved over the years do not meet the problems created by presidential television. . . . None of this legal machinery makes broadcast time available to party and congressional opposition to balance the president's automatic access to the television audience. (Minow et al., 1973: 89)

First Amendment Parity We have mentioned at various points the unique characteristics of broadcasting that set it apart from other media. Among these are its intrusion into the home, its accessibility to children, its continuous availability, its use of a scarce public resource (the frequency spectrum), and its dependence on consumer investment in receivers.

As we have seen, these characteristics have been cited by the FCC and the courts as justification for treating broadcasting differently from the other media when it comes to First Amendment restraints on government regulation. "The legal status of broadcasting with respect to the First Amendment seems to be clearly established now," wrote a former commissioner, "The First Amendment has simply been rewritten for the Twentieth Century" (Loevinger, 1974: 2).

First Amendment absolutists, however, reject the concept of one law for broadcasting, another for press or motion pictures. They argue for *First Amendment parity*, equal treatment of all media. Absolutists take the words "Congress shall make *no law*" literally, rejecting all infringements on freedom of expression, even those that are supposed to have compensating value, such as libel and obscenity laws. Indeed, some absolutists go so far as to object even to laws that punish false advertising.

If a future Supreme Court majority were to endorse First Amendment parity it could have a revolutionary effect on programming. Despite complaints by moralizers about television indecency, broadcasting still follows much more restrained standards than most other media. The following examples show how broadcasting has adapted only belatedly (though recently with increasing speed) to changing social mores:

■ In 1934 the Surgeon General of the United States was not permitted even to mention the term "venereal disease" on the air in a serious discussion of a genuine national problem (§7.1). By 1972, PBS could broadcast an educational documentary aimed at young people on the same problem (by then far more serious) with lyrics such as "Don't give a dose / To the one you love most." Practically all public broadcasting stations carried the program.

■ In 1978 the Supreme Court said that the "seven dirty words" could be used on the air if "channeled" away from children's listening hours (§17.2).

■ Two documentaries in the 1978–1979 season, "Youth Terror: The View Behind the Gun" (an ABC production for its *Close-Up* series) and "Scared Straight" (independently produced and syndicated to about a hundred stations) for the first time used realistic street language without laundering and with only minor public objections, though about 10 percent of ABC's affiliates turned down the *Close-Up* program.

■ In the prime-time entertainment field, Norman Lear's 1976 *Mary Hartman, Mary Hartman* (§8.7) broke many taboos about sexual content, following up his successful introduction of serious and sometimes controversial subjects into situation comedies with *All in the Family* in 1971 (§9.2).

■ No network would accept *Mary Hartman*, but a year later ABC took a chance on *Soap*, a spoof on the soap-opera genre that pushed the boundaries of sexual freedom still fur-

ther. Strenuous boycott activities by church groups persuaded five percent of ABC's affiliates to refuse the program, which, according to a *Time* review, "became the tardy symbol of a TV sexual revolution that had long since been accomplished" in the real world.

Radical as these changes may have seemed to the more conservative television viewers, they did not appear to mean that broadcasting had abandoned its own fundamental conservatism. Magazines and motion pictures freely use material that is still inconceivable on the air (though cable television is far less reticent). First Amendment parity that would put broadcasting on a par with *Hustler* magazine still seems a long way off.

Summary

The constitutional guarantee of free expression is embodied in the metaphor of a marketplace in which ideas compete for acceptance. The First Amendment protects even inflammatory, hateful, and false ideas from government interference, but does not prevent private censorship unless done on behalf of the government. Also relevant to broadcasting are the First Amendment's protection of freedom of worship and its prohibition against a state-established religion.

Unprotected forms of speech such as libel and obscenity are punishable after the fact, but punishment must not be so easily imposed as to have a chilling effect on freedom of speech generally. Other unprotected types of speech create a clear and present danger to the state and interfere with fair trial in courts of law.

Broadcasting has unique features that have been used to justify treating it differently from other media under the First

Amendment. Regulation of broadcasting is tolerated because licensees have a fiduciary role in the use of a scarce public resource. Moreover, licensees have extensive latitude in making program judgments and are free of prior restraint.

Broadcast regulation can also be justified because it seeks to further First Amendment goals. The fairness doctrine, for example, helps assure that conflicting ideas on important social issues will have access to the airwaves. When it comes to news, however, primary reliance is placed on journalists' editorial discretion rather than on FCC-enforced fairness doctrine restraints. Advertising triggers the fairness doctrine only if commercials deal explicitly with controversial issues of public importance. The right of broadcasters to adopt policies against accepting paid editorial advertising has been affirmed by the FCC and the courts. Nevertheless, some advertisers (especially the large energy-related corporations) argue that it is unfair to prevent them from buying time in which to rebut what they consider to be unfair news treatment.

Another way in which regulation seeks to further First Amendment goals is enforced diversification of ownership, which is intended to help ensure that the marketplace of ideas will not succumb to monopoly controls.

Some critics question whether the marketplace concept is workable under modern conditions, arguing for a right of access to the media. The fairness doctrine is such a means of access but is criticized for having a chilling effect on the initiation of controversial discussions and for perhaps being subject to political exploitation.

First Amendment absolutists argue against treating broadcasting differently under the First Amendment from any other medium. It seems doubtful, however, that the public would accept the same degree of sexual freedom in broadcasting that is common in some other media, despite marked liberalization of broadcasting standards in recent years.

CHAPTER 18

Beyond the FCC: Nonregulatory Influences

Preceding chapters on the social control of broadcasting dealt with formal controls exercised through statutes and regulations. In this chapter we review forces outside the formal regulatory machinery that also influence the conduct of broadcasters.

Some of these forces operate indirectly by influencing the formal regulatory process through lobbying and participation in hearings and court cases. Other forces operate directly on broadcasters, using social and economic pressures to force changes in their conduct.

18.1 Informal Government Controls

We have seen how all three branches of government have an input to the formalized regulatory control system — the legislative branch through statutes, budget review, and ongoing oversight activities; the executive branch through the power of appointment to the commission; and the judicial branch

through its power to rule on appeals from FCC actions.

The FCC's mixed functions and divided allegiances put it under constant and often conflicting pressures — from Congress, the White House, the courts, the industries it regulates, lobbyists representing various special interests, and from the general public as the ultimate consumers of broadcasting services.

Thus a major task of the FCC (and other regulatory agencies) is not only to conform to the letter of the law but, beyond that, to attune its behavior to the requirements imposed by its political environment. To retain some flexibility and freedom of choice in its policy making, the commission must try to gain political support over opposition. (Krasnow & Longley, 1978: 8)

Congressional Intervention Congress gave the FCC a mandate in the Communications Act of 1934 and turned it loose to carry out the mandate on its own. But Congress continually brings the commission up short if it wanders too far afield. Not only does the legislature give advice and consent concerning the president's commissioner nominations; it also keeps control of the purse strings by setting the commission's annual budget.

Moreover, Congress conducts frequent hearings on the commission's performance as a regulatory agency. In fact, it tends to second-guess the FCC on virtually every regulatory issue that arises. This oversight has its effect because the FCC is extremely sensitive to congressional criticism. As one commentator described the relationship, "Much of the effort of the FCC resembles the launching of trial balloons, only to find them punctured by a congressional committee. The common technique of a committee or its chairman who opposes a proposed rule is to say the Commission is exceeding its authority" (Carey, 1967: 45).

As politicians, members of Congress depend on broadcasting not only for electioneering but for keeping themselves before their constituents between elections. Elaborate congressional broadcast production facilities on Capitol Hill are available to members of both houses. Legislators can prepare, at minimum expense and trouble, radio and television programs about their achievements in Washington for distribution to their home-district stations. All this tends to ensure that senators and representatives give a sympathetic hearing to licensees and attentively listen to their advice on upcoming legislation that affects the broadcasting industry.

Executive Branch Intervention From the start of broadcasting the White House had a tendency to use the president's influence to lean on broadcasters who said on the air things that the administration found objectionable. As early as 1924 WEAF summarily canceled H. V. Kaltenborn's commentaries when a member of the president's cabinet complained about a broadcast that questioned a decision he had made.

After the Radio Act of 1927 created a presidentially appointed commission to regulate broadcasters, the White House had an avenue for exerting pressure less directly. Franklin D. Roosevelt, for example, occasionally asked Commission Chairman James L. Fly to pass on to the networks his dissatisfaction with the way they handled news stories.

White House intervention reached an unprecedented level during the presidency of Richard M. Nixon. The Office of Telecommunications Policy (OTP) was set up during his administration. Its function was to advise the president on broad communication policy questions (it was in fact the forerunner of the present National Telecommunications and Information Administration, §15.1). But much of the OTP's energies were devoted to obtaining more sympathetic news treatment of the Nixon administration's activities and goals. The chairman of the House Communications and Power Subcommittee described presidential misuse of the OTP as "the most serious, continuous threat to free broadcasting in this country" (Macdonald, 1972: 5).

OTP's brash young administrator, Clay Whitehead, roamed the country stirring up antagonism against the networks, both commercial and noncommercial. In one of his controversial speeches, Whitehead accused the networks of "ideological plugola" and "elitist gossip." He warned owners of affiliated stations that it was their job to set the record straight. Affiliates who failed to "correct imbalance or consistent bias in the network or who acquiesced by silence can only be considered willing participants, to be held fully responsible at license renewal time." This was a shrewd attempt to drive a wedge between the networks and their affiliates at an especially vulnerable spot (§12.3).

Commenting on this attempt, Fred Friendly wrote in an article on "the campaign to politicize broadcasting":

The most alarming and mischievous weapon in the Administration's strategy is its transparent attempt to exploit the worst of the broadcaster's instincts. . . . The timid station manager, afraid of the local gun lobby or political boss, has an ally to comfort his timidity — the Executive Branch of the government. If the Whitehead plan becomes law it would mean that stations which reject the nightly network news or hard-hitting controversial documentary would get points where they once got demerits. (1973: 18)

After leaving the administration, Whitehead ruefully admitted that he had been used. On a CBS *Face the Nation* broadcast he replied to a reporter's question about Nixon and his lieutenants, "They were lying to me and they were lying to you."

He was referring to attempts to intimidate broadcasters that had been revealed in the Watergate tapes and in the testimony of broadcasting executives who had been threatened by White House representatives. CBS said that a presidential aide had boasted that he would bring the network "to its knees." FCC Chairman Dean Burch had been instructed by the White House to telephone the networks personally, demanding copies of their commentaries on a key Nixon speech on the Vietnam war. The CBS chairman observed that Burch "could have obtained a transcript routinely, but instead he had called top network executives. The meaning was loud and clear: the White House wanted us to know they were watching" (Paley, 1979: 314).

The long-term effectiveness of these and other White House maneuvers to influence broadcasting by nonregulatory means is hard to gauge. Most such efforts take place behind the scenes and are difficult to document. However, the revelations on the White House tapes provided unique documentary confirmation of activities that otherwise might never have been more than rumors.

Additional evidence came from a study of differences between television and newspaper coverage of government activities during the Nixon administration. A content analysis indicated that the attacks on broadcasting did in fact have a chilling effect on its handling of government news. Moreover, the difference between newspapers and television was more evident when the news dealt with the president and the Watergate scandal. As the scandal unfolded, newspapers became progressively more vigorous in their commentary, television less so (Lashner, 1979).

18.2 Direct Citizen Action

Boycotts The crudest route for ordinary citizens to follow in trying to influence the behavior of broadcasters is the *boycott*. Usually it involves the threat of refusing to buy advertised products by means of letter-writing campaigns and demonstrations. Effects of boycotts on network clearance are described in §12.3.

In a pluralistic society it is difficult for boycotters to achieve sufficient consensus and discipline to do substantial economic damage. Were it not for the fact that advertisers and broadcasters often surrender without attempting to call the boycotters' bluff, boycotts would rarely have any discernible success.

Though broadcasting boycotts often have worthwhile goals, the technique is negative and even counterproductive. Boycotts seek to impose by coercive means the values of one group of people on all other groups. Not only do they rarely accomplish anything of permanent value, they also run the risk of alienating prospective supporters who value freedom of expression. Even those who agree philosophically with the objectives of a boycott campaign may well refuse to cooperate because they dislike being told by self-appointed judges what they may see and hear.

Economic boycotts have the regressive tendency of forcing advertisers once more to intrude into the area of program decision making. Direct advertiser control over programs inevitably invites conflicts between commercial expediency and the public interest. In fact advertiser program control is expressly forbidden in the broadcasting laws of most other countries. A vivid example of its potential consequences was afforded by the blacklisting episodes of the 1950s (§8.8).

Boycotts usually arise because programs (or even proposed programs) offend (1) church groups, (2) ethnic groups, (3) single-issue groups. Following are examples of efforts by each type to suppress specific programs.

(1) Church Groups. Stop Immorality on Television was one of several church organizations that opposed the showing of a 1973 two-part episode in the CBS situation comedy series, *Maude,* because it dealt with abortion in a noncondemnatory way. Thirty-five network affiliates yielded to the pressure, refusing to carry the objectionable episode, and the commercial spot openings remained unsold. Ironically, women's organizations staged a counterboycott against advertisers that had withdrawn commercial support.

In 1977 ABC's new, sexually candid series *Soap* (§17.8) spurred opposition from church groups, who formed the Coalition for No Soap. Most of the opposition was generated on the basis of private screenings of the pilot episode, before the series actually had its debut on the air. As often happens in such cases, the actual airing of the series proved anticlimatic. ABC told reporters that it received 22,000 letters protesting *Soap* before its debut, hardly any after people actually saw it on the air.

In 1981 a widely publicized attack on immorality in television emerged, spurred on by the success of fundamentalist religious broadcasters in the 1980 political campaign. The Coalition for Better Television, a joint venture by several fundamentalist groups, threatened to boycott advertisers whose commercials appeared in programs judged to be immoral. It set up a national panel of monitors to evaluate levels of sex, profanity, and violence in television. The coalition kept the identity of its monitors secret and revealed nothing as to the reliability of the methods they used or the validity of their findings.

Unlike the previously mentioned boycott campaigns, this one aimed at programming generally, not just at a few especially provocative programs. The networks vigorously denounced the coalition's goal of forcing its views on the rest of the public, but the advertising community reacted less militantly. Procter and Gamble, the biggest television advertiser of all, announced that it had withdrawn advertising from fifty program episodes found to be morally objectionable; other major advertisers showed concern by consulting with the coalition leaders.

(2) Ethnic Groups. Ethnic awareness and separatism increased markedly during the 1970s, raising the sensitivity of minority groups to the images projected in broadcast fiction. Common stereotypes of American Indians, Chinese, Irish, Italians, Japanese, Jews, Mexicans, and Poles have all come under attack. Old films are now routinely edited for television to remove the gross ethnic slurs they often contained.

In some cities, certain films are not seen on the air at all because of local opposition from ethnic groups. In a rather extreme example, WTEV in Massachusetts agreed to refrain from showing 37 of the 165 episodes in

Indian Derogatories

TV Guide sent a writer to interview the people involved in an agreement with a television station in Massachusetts to ban more than one fifth of the episodes in the syndicated *Daniel Boone* series. The writer, Edith Efron, talked with Princess Necia Hopkins, secretary of an Indian association, about the implications of the ban. In part, the dialogue ran as follows:

TVG: What exactly didn't you like?

PRINCESS: Derogatories. Derogatories against Indians. Indians scalping settlers. Burning. Dragging women. Being called savage, red devils, painted devils, red monsters.

TVG: Didn't these "derogatories" exist, historically?

PRINCESS: Whether this existed or not, it's past history. We want this to be stamped out. . . .

TVG: Would you abolish all villains in dramatic fiction?

PRINCESS: Yes, if they have identifiable racial backgrounds.

TVG: You mean the only villains you'd allow would be whites?

PRINCESS: Yes. But if the whites don't want that, then there shouldn't be any white villains either.

TVG: Do you realize, Princess, that if we followed your prescription, dramatic fiction would cease to exist?

PRINCESS: What?

TVG: Plays are actually stories about the conflict between good and evil. If you knock out all the villains, there's no way to show evil. Wouldn't you just settle for diversity, showing both the good and the bad?

PRINCESS: Well . . . yes, if Indians are portrayed like every other race. We want to be equal. There should be lots of plays where everybody is shown as good. And all bad would be OK too, so long as it's not just Indians.

TVG: Tell me, do writers have any rights, in your opinion? Do they have the right to write as they please?

PRINCESS: No. It depends what they're writing about. If they write derogatories about Indians, I want to stop them.

Source: Edith Efron, "This Time the Indians Won," *TV Guide* 22 Jan. 1972, pp. 44–45.

the syndicated *Daniel Boone* series it had purchased — a considerable financial sacrifice. The Schaghticoke and other Indian tribes of New England objected to episodes in the action/adventure series that in their judgment portray Indians in an unfavorable light (see Box).

(3) *Single-Issue Groups.* Months before CBS showed a 1975 television documentary, "The Guns of Autumn," the National Rifle Association and similar organizations began a boycott. When the 90-minute program about hunting went on the air, 14 of its 16 commercial spots remained unsold. CBS said it received 19,000 letters of complaint — its largest mail count since Edward R. Murrow's famous *See It Now* program on Senator Joseph McCarthy (§8.8).

In view of such high level of interest, CBS followed with a second program, "Echoes of the Guns of Autumn," in which opponents of the program as well as its producers had a chance to argue their case face to face. CBS could find only one advertiser willing to risk being identified with the show. Later a Michigan association of conservation clubs brought an unsuccessful libel suit against CBS, asking for $300 million in damages because an episode in the documentary depicted a bear-shooting incident in their state.

Consumer Movement A distinction can be made between boycotts and consumer activism. The differences are often blurred, but fundamentally consumerism represents a more constructive, positive approach to social control than does the boycott. Consumer goals are usually broader in scope, less wedded to special interests. Even when the basic goals are the same, the methods of consumerism are likely to result in more beneficial and longer lasting results than merely persuading advertisers to withdraw a commercial commitment or a network affiliate to turn down a particular program. Consumerism goals usually prefer to stimulate the production of a new program that portrays ethnic minorities fairly rather than suppress an existing program that treats them unfairly.

Consumerism as an organized movement began in the early 1900s, in part as a response to the exposés of *muckrakers*. The equivalent of present-day investigative reporters and news documentary producers, muckrakers gained access to a large public through mass-circulation magazines. One of their conspicuous successes was reform of the meat-packing industry. Upton Sinclair's 1906 book *The Jungle* described in horrifying detail how rats, poisoned bait, and even human bodies went into the vats in which cooking lard was processed. Such disclosures gave impetus to passage of the Pure Food and Drug Act of 1906,

the first comprehensive consumer-protection legislation.

The centralized mass-production methods of the meat packers were symptomatic of the growth of technology and the distancing of the consumer from the origination points of products. Ordinary consumers, unaided by scientific research, have no way of judging the safety and quality of the goods they buy; nor have they any way of assessing the ways that industrial pollution can poison the environment. Numerous government consumer protection agencies were created to deal with these problems, as were consumer self-help organizations.

During the 1960s several factors converged to strengthen the consumer movement — civil rights activism, government antipoverty programs, legal support for local consumer actions by the Department of Justice, the women's movement, organized opposition to the Vietnam war. Consumer-oriented activities flourished, and among them was heightened interest in broadcast reform.

Broadcasting and Consumerism
Broadcasting posed somewhat different problems from those emphasized by the earlier consumer movement. Traditional consumerism stressed relationships between buyer and seller, tenant and owner, borrower and lender. In this perspective the broadcast receiving set, as an item of consumption, was the focus of interest, rather than the content of programs delivered by the receiver.

In the 1960s, however, the consumer movement began to concern itself more with intangibles such as fair credit reporting, mail frauds, and the readability of consumer contracts. This trend included concern for the quality of broadcast programming. Physical consumer products like toys, drugs, food, and household appliances were not the only products that could be hazardous to health and well-being. Broadcast programs and advertisements could be damaging as well.

The pioneer broadcast consumer organization came into being before this new outlook became popular. The National Association of Better Broadcasting, founded in 1949, had little impact during its first decade of existence. Neither the industry nor the FCC paid much attention to its program monitoring reports. It was easy for complacent broadcasters to brush off such reformers as impractical do-gooders.

This attitude changed during the 1960s. By the end of the decade, *Broadcasting Yearbook* listed broadcast consumerism as a major trend in the industry. Trade association meetings that dealt with broadcasting often featured an address or a panel devoted to the new movement. For example, in 1970 a top advertising agency executive warned his colleagues against "killing the goose that lays the golden eggs," saying:

In the past criticism of television was pretty much the property of the "intellectual" few. Those who carped were reminiscent of the old definition of a critic as "the legless man who teaches running." And about as effective! But not any more. In today's climate where criticism of our institutions has become a way of life, the vociferous new breed of consumer critics of TV is not only getting plenty of exposure, but demonstrating surprising political muscle, too. (Meyer, 1970: 4)

The single most important event that crystallized this changed view of broadcast reform efforts was an unprecedented direct intervention by the federal court of appeals in a television station renewal case. In 1969, exasperated by the FCC's persistent refusal to take adequate account of consumer complaints, the court summarily canceled the license renewal of WLBT-TV, throwing the channel open to new applicants.

18.3 Consumer Standing to Challenge Renewals

WLBT Case   Back in 1955, the dark ages of broadcast consumerism, some citizens of Jackson, Mississippi, made the first of a long series of complaints to the FCC about the conduct of WLBT, a major VHF television station in that market. Forty-five percent of WLBT's potential audience was black; yet the station blatantly discriminated against black viewers. Typical of the extent to which the station went to keep its service white was its suppression of a network appearance by a black official of the National Association for the Advancement of Colored People. When the official was about to speak a slide came up, "Sorry, cable trouble." Deciding that the instances of unfairness alleged by citizens' groups were only "isolated" cases, the FCC renewed the station in 1958.

Charges of unfairness continued as the national civil rights drive accelerated in the early 1960s. Finally, when WLBT's license came up again for renewal in 1964, local groups obtained expert legal assistance from the United Church of Christ. The church's Office of Communication, headquartered in New York, gives legal and advisory support to local groups seeking broadcast reforms. The UCC petitioned the FCC on behalf of the local groups for leave to intervene in the WLBT renewal, but the FCC turned down the petition. Citizens had no legal standing to intervene, said the FCC (§15.3). The commission recognized only signal interferences and economic injury as reasons to give other parties the right to demand a hearing in renewal cases. This meant, in effect, that only other *licensees* had standing to challenge existing licensees. The fact that the 45 percent of the population that was black had made a substantial investment in receivers did not, in the FCC's view, give them an economic stake in the station's operation.

The UCC appealed to the federal court, claiming that the FCC had no right to bar representatives of the viewing public from intervening in renewals, or to award a renewal without a hearing in the face of substantial public opposition. The court agreed, saying "there is nothing unusual or novel in granting the consuming public standing to challenge administrative actions," mentioning several specific cases in which consumers had been given that right in connection with both goods (coal) and services (electric power). Accordingly, the court directed the FCC to hold hearings on WLBT's renewal and to give standing to representatives of the public to participate in the hearings (359 F 2d 994, 1966). Still the FCC dragged its feet. It foresaw what it called "an administrative nightmare" — thousands of petitions to deny from every Tom, Dick, and Harry, swamping the commission's hearing rooms.

Three years went by. Finally, in 1969 the exasperated court reopened the case. By this time 14 years had elapsed since the first recorded complaints against WLBT had begun. The court rebuked the FCC for "scandalous delay." The commission, said the court, had shown "at best a reluctant tolerance of this court's mandate and at worst a profound hostility to the participation of the Public Intervenors and their efforts."

In view of the FCC's sorry record, the court saw no point in once more remanding the case back to the commission for still more procrastination. Instead, it ordered the commission to cancel the license, to consider a plan for an interim operation on the channel, and to invite new applications for the license (425 F 2d 543, 1969). The FCC acted accordingly and the incumbent licensee was eventually removed. Another ten years were to elapse, however, before the channel was finally awarded to a new licensee. Altogether,

the case stretched over a quarter-century of delays.

Fallout from WLBT Decision By establishing once and for all the standing of citizens to intervene in broadcast license renewals, with no more at stake than their inherent right to a satisfactory service, the *WLBT* case had far-reaching effects.

The most immediate effect was, of course, to release a flood of similar petitions all over the country, just as the FCC had feared. In the years just before, only two or three renewal challenges had been filed each year. Following *WLBT* in 1969, however, petitions to deny renewal rose dramatically: 16 stations were affected in 1970; 84 stations in 1971; 108 stations in 1972; 150 stations in 1973. However, this "reign of terror" as a trade magazine once called it, resulted in very few actual hearings, and still fewer denials of renewal. Of the 342 stations challenged in the 1971–1973 period, only 16 ended in denials.

This high failure rate of petitions to deny was due to the exacting standard of evidence set up by the FCC and approved by the court. The first test case occurred almost immediately in 1969, when Chuck Stone and other community leaders in Washington, D.C., challenged the renewal of WMAL-TV, a major newspaper-owned station in the District of Columbia.

The community group alleged that WMAL had made inadequte efforts to ascertain the needs of its audience, had been unresponsive to the needs of blacks, had been discriminatory in employment, and was part of an undue concentration of media (the newspaper-licensee also owned AM and FM radio stations in the same market). But the FCC rejected the petition. The community group failed to support its charges by raising "substantial and material questions of fact" that would, on their face, show that it might be contrary to the public's interest to renew WMAL's television license. The appeals court concurred. The communications act, said the court, called for overwhelmingly convincing evidence that a hearing was needed to decide whether a renewal would be in the public interest. Only then was the FCC obliged to schedule a license renewal application for hearing (466 F 2d 316, 1972).

This meant that challengers opposing license renewals had to gather highly relevant, concrete, and legally convincing evidence to make valid cases. Collecting such evidence can be tedious. In fact, without access to underlying documents such as renewal applications, it could be virtually impossible. To make fact-gathering somewhat easier, in 1971 the FCC (by then considerably more favorably inclined toward public intervenors) mandated the keeping of a station *public file* (described in §16.5). It requires licensees to keep the basic documents about their stations readily available for public inspection.

Evidence Against Renewal Following are examples of the kinds of evidence that can be gathered in building a case to show that license renewal would not be in the public interest:

■ *Past Programming*. Review of a television station's composite-week program logs (§16.6) enables asking such questions as: Has licensee classified programs correctly? Are percentages of program types in line with previous promises? Is the composite week truly representative of the station's general program practices? Did the licensee upgrade programming toward the end of the license period to create a false impression of overall performance? In the case of radio, programming has to be monitored on the air because

radio stations are not required to keep official program logs.

■ *Ascertainment*. For television, questions can be asked about the adequacy of the station's interviews with community leaders and its survey of the general public, as well as about its programs designed to deal with ascertained community problems. For radio, ascertainment documentation is skimpier and less formal, but nevertheless the public file can be checked to see whether the station has identified relevant community problems in the past year and broadcast programs related to those problems.

■ *Proposed Programming*. Does the station plan to produce adequate local programs? To use local talent? Is proposed programming so similar to that of the preceding license period as to suggest lack of progress or improvement?

■ *Equal Employment Opportunities*. Do employment patterns reflect the demographic composition of the station's service area? Are claims of efforts to recruit minority employees verifiable? Have complaints been lodged against the station with local fair employment agencies?

Broadcast Consumer Organizations The success of the United Church of Christ's Office of Communication in the *WLBT* case propelled it into the forefront of national consumer organizations. The UCC provides a broad spectrum of services to local consumer broadcast groups, of which more than 500 had been organized by 1974.

About a dozen national organizations comparable in scope to the UCC Office of Communication operate in the broadcast consumerism field. Other notable examples are:

■ *Action for Children's Television (ACT)*. Founded as a local housewives' organization in Massachusetts in 1968, ACT grew into a formidable national force. It draws wide support because the impact of television on children is of universal concern to responsible parents, and because it uses sophisticated consumer strategies at a high professional level. ACT testifies at congressional hearings, petitions the FCC and FTC, stages international festivals of children's programming, monitors stations and networks, sponsors research studies, prepares demonstration films, books, and pamphlets — in short uses every art of the expert public interest lobbyist (Barthel, 1975). ACT's efforts at persuading the FCC to adopt stringent rules controlling children's programming were described in §9.8.

■ *Citizens Communications Center (CCC).* A general-purpose law firm, CCC has been called upon by most of the broadcast consumer groups for advice and legal counsel. It has participated in over 200 license renewal challenges. CCC's name is linked with the important appeals court decision overturning the FCC's short-lived 1970 renewal policy, which the commission adopted in the hope of reducing the number of renewal challenges (§16.7). In 1981, as an economy measure, CCC merged with an institute at Georgetown University in Washington, D.C.

■ *National Black Media Coalition (NBMC).* The major umbrella organization for black media groups, NBMC has about 80 affiliates. In 1978 the NBMC submitted an elaborate petition for rule making, asking the FCC to take action on 35 proposals. They amounted, in the words of the FCC, to "a comprehensive agenda for regulatory action . . . to enhance the position of Black Americans in all aspects of electronic mass communication."

Among the NBMC's proposals was the imposition of severer penalties for licensee transgressions than the customary fines and short-term renewals; for example, licensees could be required to operate on a nonprofit basis or forced to share their channels with others for stipulated periods. Another imaginative suggestion was that all new channel assignments should be reserved for minority applicants for at least five years. The FCC received the petition with praise for NBMC's accomplishment, granting or putting on its future agenda most of the NBMC's requests. Only ten of the 35 were denied without qualification — an impressive success rate (76 FCC 2d 385, 1980).

■ *National Citizens Committee for Broadcasting (NCCB).* Originally founded to support public broadcasting, NCCB later shifted gears to general broadcast consumerism. It has been active in trying to ensure consumer input to critical communications posts in government. NCCB's name is linked to the Supreme Court case confirming the FCC's rules on ownership of broadcasting stations by newspapers (§17.7).

Consumer Publications Another consequence of the *WLBT* decision was publication of a variety of how-to-do-it books advising consumers on their rights and on ways to obtain them. Commissioner Nicholas Johnson, while still in office, led the way in 1970 with a book called *How to Talk Back to Your Television Set.* The UCC Office of Communication and other consumer assistance groups followed suit.

These publications advocate hard-nosed, professional consumerism, based on *using,* instead of deploring or fighting, the system. As Johnson summarized the process in his book:

In order to get relief from legal institutions (Congress, courts, agencies) one must assert, first, the factual basis for the grievance and the specific parties involved; second, the legal principle that indicates relief is due (constitutional provision, statute, regulation, court or agency decision); and third, the precise remedy sought (new legislation or regulations, license revocation, fines, or an order changing practices). (1970: 202)

FCC Consumer Assistance   During the 1970s the FCC began acknowledging the legitimate role of consumerism in other ways as well. In 1974 FCC Chairman Wiley started a series of regional meetings between the commission and the general public. The sessions were often chaotic; certainly they were diverse:

At the meetings almost all the issues debated in this country found spokespeople — antiabortionists, gun collectors, senior citizens, gay rights advocates, opponents of drug lyrics in songs, and opponents and proponents of Women's Liberation. The Commission was denounced as an instrument of the Rockefeller interests and as part of the Communist conspiracy. (Cole & Oettinger, 1978: 113)

Wiley persisted despite harassment and insults in the meetings, opposition from the FCC staff, and cynicism from some of the other commissioners. Even the FCC, in a conspicuous reversal of its pre-*WLBT* outlook, offered in its 1974 "Broadcast Procedure Manual" precise details on what public intervenors should do to make sound legal cases. The manual explains how the FCC handles complaints and how citizens can participate in its official proceedings (39 FR 32288, 1974).

In 1976 the FCC opened a small Consumer Asssistance Office (CAO) to help citizens get information about the commission's activities. The CAO publishes *Action Alert*, a weekly newsletter summarizing current and upcoming FCC activities of general public interest. In 1978 the CAO began a series of workshops involving broadcasters, FCC staff members, and the general public.

Praiseworthy as these attempts at consumer aid were, they fell short of a prime goal of consumers — substantial legal assistance for citizens within the FCC itself. As it stands, the Broadcast Bureau speaks for the public interest in FCC proceedings, but the bureau cannot assume as strong a partisan role as could a special consumers' representative.

18.4 Negotiated Settlements

Though renewal challenges leading to actual loss of license as in the *WLBT* case are rare, the mere fact that the FCC had to consider such challenges radically changed licensee attitudes toward consumer groups. Even weak challenges could cause a great deal of trouble, obliging licensees to prepare initial responses to argue against the need for renewal hearings. After *WLBT* it was no longer possible to casually brush aside citizen complaints as the work of inconsequential do-gooders. Licensees learned to listen seriously to citizen complaints and to take steps to prevent their growing into full-scale petitions to deny renewal.

KTAL Agreement   A model for settling citizen complaints before they reach the stage of renewal hearings emerged in 1969, the same year the appeals court canceled WLBT's license.

Renewal of KTAL, a VHF television station in Texarkana, Arkansas, came under attack from a coalition of citizen groups. Basic to the dissatisfaction of Texarkana residents with KTAL was the fact that it neglected its community of license in order to serve a more lucrative market beyond its borders. Although licensed to Texarkana, KTAL had moved its main studios to Shreveport, Louisiana — 70 miles distant and in another state.

Before the FCC made a decision on the complaints (most of which the station was in no position to deny), the parties arrived at a mutually satisfactory settlement. With the help of the UCC Office of Communication, they prepared a 13-point policy statement. In it the station agreed to take remedial action, in return for which the citizen groups agreed to withdraw their objection to the renewal. Among other things, KTAL agreed to furnish a toll-free telephone service for sending local Texarkana news to the Shreveport studio and to improve both its production equipment and its news coverage in Texarkana. The station obligated itself to "discuss programming regularly with all segments of the public" and to announce its willingness to do so regularly over the air in prime time.

In accepting the withdrawal of the citizen opposition to renewal, the FCC commented that such voluntary local cooperation was preferable to "imposition of stricter guidelines by the commission." However, the FCC warned KTAL that its performance would be "carefully examined at the end of the license term to determine whether you have made an affirmative and diligent effort to serve the needs and interests of the city to which KTAL-TV is licensed" (19 FCC 2d 110, 1969). The KTAL model for settling disputes between licensees and citizen groups was widely imitated in the years that followed.

Settlement by agreement is particularly effective in situations involving proposed changes of ownership. An offer to buy is good only for a stipulated period of time. Opposition to a sale from citizen groups can make the would-be buyer especially anxious to come to terms before the seller's offer expires.

An example of a negotiated settlement involving a major, multistation change of ownership occurred in 1971. Walter Annenberg, publisher of *TV Guide*, decided to sell over a hundred million dollars worth of broadcasting properties when he accepted appointment as ambassador to Great Britain in 1969. The prospective buyer, Capital Cities Broadcasting Corporation, persuaded groups that opposed the sale in the three cities of license to withdraw their protests in exchange for Capital Cities' promise to devote a million dollars to production of minority programs. The money was to be spent over a three-year period in the three markets involved, Philadelphia, Bakersfield, and New Haven, with concerned minority groups fully involved in the planning and production of the programs. The FCC accepted the agreement and the sale went through.

FCC Policy on Agreements   Not all agreements won enthusiastic FCC approval. In their anxiety to reach a settlement, licensees sometimes surrendered too much to citizen groups, giving up that "nondelegable responsibility" for programs that the FCC considers fundamental to operation in the public interest (§16.5).

For example, the National Association for Better Broadcasting (NABB) and other groups opposed to violence in children's programs persuaded KTTV-TV in Los Angeles to commit itself to extensive and permanent changes in its programming. In what NABB announced as a "spectacular milestone" in broadcast consumerism, KTTV agreed in 1969 to ban from their programming all episodes of the syndicated series *Batman*, *Superman*, and *Aquaman*. The station also promised to broadcast a "caution to parents" notice before showing any of 81 other series if scheduled before 8:30 P.M. The agreement, which ran to fifteen pages, was to be binding even on future licensees should the incumbent owner, Metromedia Incorporated, sell the station.

The FCC balked at approving this agreement. Not only did it infringe on the licensee's duty to maintain responsibility for all programming decisions; FCC approval would have put it in the untenable position of participating in prior censorship of the banned programs.

Shortly after shooting down the NABB/KTTV settlement, the FCC adopted a policy statement setting up guidelines for such agreements (57 FCC 2d 42, 1975). Taking a cautious approach, the FCC said it would neither approve nor disapprove of lawful agreements. The main points of the policy provided that:

1. Licensees must retain ultimate responsibility for all program decisions. (In practice it became customary to insert a "saving clause" in agreements to the effect that, no matter what the agreement said, the licensee would retain ultimate program control.)
2. Written agreements may be submitted as part of a licensee's program promises in renewal application forms.
3. Such written agreements must be placed in the station's public file.
4. An agreement cannot rule out the filing of a petition to deny renewal.
5. Nor does withdrawal of a petition to deny renewal as a result of an agreement necessarily dispose of the issues that may have been raised in the original petition.

Reimbursements to Consumer Advocates

One of the items of agreement in the KTAL case was a promise on the part of the station, subject to FCC approval, to repay the expenses of the UCC Office of Communication. The UCC calculated that it had spent about $15,000 in helping the local citizens to carry out the negotiations. A precedent existed for reimbursement of expenses to those who assist in settling a case: commercial applicants in mutually exclusive hearings sometimes pay the expenses of competitors who expedite matters by withdrawing from such hearings (§16.2).

The FCC refused to give blanket approval, but considers reimbursements to consumer advocates on a case-by-case basis. Amounts have run as high as $310,000, while the costs of litigation to licensees have run as high as $1.5 million (Grundfest, 1976).

Opposition to Format Changes

A special and highly controversial type of citizen involvement in station program policies emerged as a result of opposition to abrupt *changes in format.* Typically opposition arises because of planned shifts from classical to popular music when change of ownership occurs. But changes from other music formats and altered news policies have also been opposed.

Format protest cases have involved only a very few radio stations, but they had a disproportionate impact because they raised a fundamental issue of regulatory policy. Should competition of the marketplace be the sole control over the diversity of broadcast programming? The FCC said yes. That led to an unprecedented confrontation between the appeals court and the FCC, with the FCC defiantly accusing the court, in effect, of failing to understand the communications act.

This breach of deference occurred in an FCC statement of policy on the format issue in 1976. The immediate occasion for the statement was the court's reversal of the FCC's refusal to consider format change in the *WEFM* case. A group owner asked permission to buy a Chicago FM station that had followed a classical-music policy ever since the station went on the air in 1940. The buyer

[handwritten marginalia: "...of prgmg. S. court best determinant of market hands off — says"]

proposed to substitute a rock music format. A citizens group protested the loss of the classical format, asking the FCC to designate WEFM's change of ownership for hearing. When the FCC refused, the citizens group appealed. The court reversed the FCC's decision, forcing it to hold a hearing (506 F 2d 246, 1974).

Reluctantly the FCC followed the court's bidding. However, in its statement of policy on format changes, issued two years after the WEFM reversal,* the FCC argued vehemently against the court's reasoning.

WNCN Listeners Guild (a New York citizens' group that became involved in a format change controversy similar to the one in Chicago) appealed to the court to overturn the FCC's policy on formats. With considerable asperity (courts do not take kindly to being told by an administrative agency that they do not understand the law!), the court ordered the FCC to reconsider its hands-off policy. The court emphasized that it did not by any means discount the value of market forces in achieving diversified programming. But market forces do not always work perfectly. For example, the fact that advertisers want to sell advertising means that "they tend to serve young adults with large discretionary incomes in preference to demographically less desirable groups like children, the elderly, or the poor" (610 F 2d 851, 1979). This, of course, is the classic consumerism argument against unrestrained commercial competition in broadcasting.

The FCC appealed to the Supreme Court, which handed down its decision in 1981, re-

jecting the lower court's proregulation arguments, accepting instead the FCC's contention that decisions about program formats are best left to the interplay of market forces. The decision came as a significant affirmation of the FCC's growing reluctance to regulate.

18.5 Consumerism Issues

Abuses of Consumer Power   The right to intervene in renewals gave consumer groups unaccustomed leverage to exert influence over powerful corporations. Some groups took advantage of their new-found strength. As an FCC chairman once said, "The citizen movement gives a lot of room to the self-starters to create a group that may not represent anything but the individuals involved" (quoted by Zeidenberg, 1971:21).

Not infrequently citizens groups won capitulations from licensees but then failed to make any constructive use of the gains they had won. This was the case with some of the minority groups that shared in the million-dollar windfall from Capital Cities for the production of minority-oriented programs (§18.4). Suddenly given hundreds of thousands of dollars to spend on television production, for which they had no training or preparation, they wasted the opportunity in petty squabbling among themselves.

New Consumer Strategies   These problems were essentially temporary, however, the result of the novelty of the situation. By the late 1970s the raw exercise of consumer power began to give way to more constructive tactics. Consumerism had assumed an acknowledged role as a legitimate element among the forces that exert social control on

---

*Almost lost sight of in the struggle over policy was the fate of classical music on WEFM. The citizens group, beset with funding problems, in the end accepted a compromise. It withdrew its protests in exchange for substantial contributions from the new owner of WEFM to encourage classical-music programming on other Chicago stations.

broadcasting. As Les Brown put in a consumer-oriented book he wrote for the UCC Office of Communication, "citizen groups have become a full-time component of the American broadcasting system. They occupy the void between a reluctant FCC and an essentially amoral broadcasting industry distracted by the ever-blooming opportunity to increase profits" (Brown, 1979: 77).

In 1978 the Citizens Communications Center and others commissioned a study of the past achievements and future prospects of broadcast consumerism. Called "Broadcast Reform at the Crossroads," it surveyed thirteen of the major groups, ranging alphabetically from Accuracy in Media to the UCC Office of Communication.

The report claimed progress in 24 areas of concern, due either in whole or in part to the consumer movement. These included, as examples, the achievement of legal standing for citizens to intervene in license renewals; improved fairness doctrine enforcement; increased diversification of station ownership; growth in minority employment and ownership; increased sensitivity of licensees to public complaints; development of consumer-oriented talk-radio programs; improvements in children's television; and support of public broadcasting development.

With regard to the future, the report concluded:

We believe the major thrust in broadcast reform will be in arenas outside the federal administrative agencies and the courts. These areas would appear to be shareholder pressure on corporate decision making, mobilization of public opinion to influence Congress, the development of rating systems which measure targeted audience responses to particular program content, increased research on the effect of program content on particular audience segments, and the development of production skills which will translate into a more varied and balanced representation of American society on the television scene. (Branscomb & Savage, 1978: 28)

As the 1980s opened, consumerism in general faced the most hostile political climate it had experienced since the 1950s. A reaction had set in against what many voters regarded as excessive government solicitude for consumer interests in such areas as environmental protection, occupational safety, and public health. Consumer-interest activities were among the first to suffer when budget cutbacks forced economies on federal agencies such as the FCC. At the same time, deregulation began to deprive consumers of leverage in using the regulatory machinery to achieve their goals.

18.6 Industry Self-Regulation

Most large industries adopt voluntary codes of conduct. Such codes serve to forestall abuses that might otherwise bring about government regulation; they help cultivate good public relations for the industry; and they enable the more enlightened (or more prosperous) members of an industry to insulate themselves from the proverbial bad apples in the barrel that otherwise tend to corrupt all the rest.

Legal Limitations Self-regulation also has a dark side, however. It can be used as a smoke screen to conceal illegal restraint of trade. A few companies could dominate the market for their product by conspiring to set up codes of conduct that others could not meet, driving competitors out of business under the pretext that they fail to meet industry standards. Even the most well-intentioned industry codes have the potentiality for discriminating unfairly against competitors.

For this reason, enforceable private codes that affect the freedom to compete have been made unlawful by the antitrust statute, the Sherman Act, which rules out all restraining agreements among competitors. The antitrust law prevents the National Association of Broadcasters (NAB) from setting up any method of whipping backsliding member stations into line so that they will live up to the NAB codes. Subscribing to the codes remains entirely voluntary, and the NAB is powerless to punish subscribers who fail to live up to the rules.

Content of NAB Codes The NAB has separate codes for radio and for television. They cover essentially the same ground, but the television version sets somewhat higher standards. For example, commercial time allowances for radio are a good deal more liberal than those for television (§13.4).

The following description of code content is based on the 1980 edition of the Television Code. After a preamble on the responsibilities of broadcasters, advertisers, and viewers, the code's 15 sections cover the following topics (examples of items within sections are given in parentheses):

I. *Principles Governing Program Content.* (Goals of television, responsible use of artistic freedom, family viewing considerations).
II. *Responsibility Toward Children.* (Role of television in social development).
III. *Community Responsibility.* (Localism, public service announcements).
IV. *Special Program Standards.* (Especially sensitive topics, such as violence, crime, drugs, sex, obscenity, lotteries).
V. *Treatment of News and Public Events.* (Avoidance of morbid details, distinction between news and commentary, journalistic ethics).

VI. *Controversial Public Issues.* (Fairness considerations).
VII. *Political Telecasts.* (Separation from other content, equal time considerations).
VIII. *Religious Programs.* (Should be shown, but fairly apportioned among different faiths).
IX-XV. *Advertising Sections,* already discussed in §13.4. Somewhat more than half the space in the entire code is devoted to these sections.

Code language meticulously avoids implying restraint of trade or violation of the First Amendment and the communications act. Most rules leave a good deal to licensee discretion. They are usually expressed in the form of "should" or "should not," rather than in the form of "must" or "must not." Even the latter are often qualified in some way. Unqualified content prohibitions usually relate to specific commercial standards, as shown by the following examples:

■ "Shall not" be broadcast: *material determined by the licensee to be obscene, profane, or indecent.*
■ "Not permissible": *use of violence for its own sake.*
■ "Forbidden": *Hypnosis shown on camera.*
■ "Not acceptable": *Advertising of hard liquor.*
■ "Unacceptable": *Advertising of fireworks.*

Despite the precautions taken to avoid any hint of coercion in the language and administration of the codes, the Department of Justice brought suit against the NAB in 1979. The suit alleged the code time standards "artificially curtailed" television advertising, repressing price competition, and depriving advertisers of "the benefits of free and open competition."

This move was the more surprising because the FCC has in the past tacitly accepted the code's time standards as a reasonable norm, though without adopting them officially.

Code Administration Stations and networks can belong to the NAB without necessarily subscribing to the codes, as shown in Exhibit 13.4. The ultimate penalty for violation of the codes is withdrawal of the right to use the *code seals*, the offical symbols of subscribership.

Separate radio and television boards supervise the form and administration of the codes. They are appointed from code subscribers as standing committees by the NAB president. The boards may amend the codes and suspend the right of members to use the code seals. A Code Authority under a general manager handles the day-to-day work of screening material for compliance and handling complaints. Offices are located in New York and Hollywood as well as Washington, D.C., where the NAB is headquartered.

Advertising agencies use boundless ingenuity to push code restrictions beyond the limits, making it necessary for the Code Authority to issue frequent code interpretations and revised guidelines for specific products and situations. Among the subjects of such fine-tuning have been acne, children's television commercials, personal products, testimonials, and weight-reducing offers. The Code Authority publishes a monthly bulletin to keep subscribers abreast of such changes.

Attitudes Toward Codes The very fact that the FCC looks to the codes as expressions of industry consensus on acceptable controls troubles some broadcasters. The industry fears that adoption of voluntary standards might have the opposite of its intended effect: instead of forestalling government regulation, voluntary codes might actually invite intervention by the FCC. Cases in point were the special advertising standards for children

(§13.4) and the prime-time family viewing hour restraints (§16.1) adopted by the Code Board. The FCC was under pressure to impose such controls itself. Deterred from rule making by the First Amendment, it encouraged self-regulation instead.

In some cases, licensees want (and can afford to meet) higher standards than the industry as a whole is willing or able to accept. In 1969 the president of Westinghouse Broadcasting Company withdrew the five Group W television stations from subscribership. As he explained it:

We felt it hypocritical to support a code we could not proudly defend. We believe the Code has not been tough enough in dealing with crime and violence on TV; we also strongly object to the Code's policy of allowing too many commercials and the advertising of intimately personal products. (McGannon, 1977)

On the other hand, some stations are so marginal economically that conforming strictly to the codes would undoubtedly force them into bankruptcy (§12.6). The NAB itself tacitly recognizes this problem by setting the overall code standards relatively low; it also softens their impact by leaving much to the discretion of the individual station and allowing for many exceptions to the rules.

From the consumer perspective, the codes seem more oriented toward public relations than toward public service, despite their protestations of high responsibility. No consumer representatives speak for the public on the code boards, which consist exclusively of broadcasters. Under their guidance, the codes follow rather than lead.

The pragmatic function of the codes is continually to test the limits of social acceptability, keeping in mind (in the words of the Television Code) "how best to present the complexities of human behavior" while maintaining "exceptional awareness of considerations peculiar to the medium." As one critic expressed it in a general analysis of broadcasting self-regulation, the codes "act as radar guiding the fleet, to help spot storms and trouble ahead, to chart the currents, and to calculate the paths of least turbulence" (Gerbner, 1972: 394).

Over the years (the Radio Code since 1929, the Television Code since 1952), the rules have grown more and more permissive. We noted earlier how the amount of permissible commercial time has increased. Similarly, the acceptability of intimate personal products has broadened and rigid moral rules about fictional programs have grown more flexible. These changes reflect, of course, growing permissiveness in society generally. Broadcasting responds more cautiously than other media to these changes. The role of the code boards and administrators might be said to be that of judging the precise moments at which broadcasting can safely jump on the bandwagon of new permissiveness.

Network Standards   The fact that the major networks are subscribers gives the codes far more pervasive influence than they would have if adopted only by individual stations. Networks also have their own program standards departments. They evaluate network commercials and programs repeatedly at various stages of development. Network officials in charge of standards departments therefore exercise multilayered control over programs made for television, starting with basic program concepts and ending with specific words and scenes in final productions.

When networks show theatrical feature films, however, their standards departments face problems of conforming ready-made products to broadcasting standards. No better evidence of the differences in standards between the two media can be found than

the dilemma this situation creates. As movies became more explicit in language and subject matter, deletions became more drastic. Many film producers now take advantage of an optional provision in Directors Guild contracts giving them the right to consultation before their films are subjected to editing for television. Sometimes the original actors cooperate by recording substitute words that are dubbed onto the television version soundtrack in place of obscenities.

Cable television has much more relaxed standards than broadcast television, and even the major independent stations tend to be more liberal than the networks. This difference in standards puts pressure on the networks to lower their standards. For example, all three networks turned down an acclaimed Vietnam war film, *The Deerhunter*, because it was impossible to edit out the unacceptable violence and profanity without emasculating the film. However, *The Deerhunter* made such a hit on pay television that some of the major independent stations, such as WOR-TV in New York, decided to risk it with only a few dialogue cuts. A Los Angeles independent even opted to run it uncut.

18.7 Other Influences

Professional Self-Regulation   Broadcasting is often referred to as a profession, a term that implies both self-regulation and self-denial. "A rough-and-ready way to decide whether you have a profession," wrote Harold Lasswell, "is to find out if people will turn down jobs" (1952: 160).

By this test, probably not many practicing broadcasters would qualify as professionals. There is not much evidence of broadcast employees (as distinguished from owners and managers) turning down jobs on the grounds that to accept them would violate their own personal codes of ethics or be contrary to the public interest. Aside from engineers, probably the broadcast employees that come closest to meeting the test of professionalism are the ones represented by the Radio Television News Directors Association (RTNDA). Members subscribe to a "Code of Broadcast News Ethics." They agree in the code that accurate and comprehensive presentation of broadcast news takes precedence over all other motives. Article Six of the code appears to mandate refusal to distort the news to suit the whims of owners and managers:

Broadcast journalists shall seek actively to present all news the knowledge of which will serve the public interest, no matter what selfish, uninformed or corrupt efforts attempt to color it, withhold it, or prevent its presentation.

Instances of news personnel denouncing attempts of owners to control the news occasionally surface (§17.5), but not very often. It appears that ethical journalists are more likely to quietly depart from a station where this happens than to make it a public issue.

National News Council An organization to deal with complaints about allegations of unfairness in the treatment of news was founded in 1973 with the help of a grant from the Twentieth Century Fund. The National News Council is an independent watchdog organization at the professional level, somewhat comparable to the National Advertising Review Board at the industry level (§13.5).

The council consists of a mix of distinguished journalists and people from other fields, with journalists in the minority. It considers complaints about news stories in any of the media. After investigation, the council makes its findings public. It has no powers to demand retractions or corrections but depends entirely on the moral weight of its findings and whatever publicity they receive.

Soon after the council began operations it took up President Richard Nixon's charge that network television news had been "outrageous, vicious, and distorted." After three months of fruitless negotiations with members of the White House staff the council gave up trying to obtain evidence on which to judge the truth of the Nixon charge. In the period 1973–1980 the council reviewed some 5,000 other complaints, in most cases getting cooperation from both the media and those making the charges.

Not everyone in the media approves of the National News Council. Although its members and methods are beyond reproach, many news people think it sets a bad First Amendment precedent for any organization to assume the power to say what is right or wrong about news stories. On the other hand, some consumer organizations also object to the news council because they feel it lets wrongdoers off the hook with only a wrist slap when perhaps they deserve more severe penalties from the FCC or the courts.

Although findings of guilt by the National News Council usually get little attention in the news media, the targets of its investigations are nevertheless sensitive to the adverse publicity. As one observer put it, after reviewing the work of the council, "it may be the most controversial unknown organization going. It has no power and wants none, yet it causes the mighty to flinch and the maligned to feel there is some redress of grievance" (Townley, 1980).

Press Critics Theater, book, and movie critics are generally assumed to have some influence on the media they monitor and assess. If the newspaper and magazine columns of broadcasting critics have any influence at all, they probably have more impact on news and public affairs programming than on mass appeal entertainment. Moreover, they influence producers of such programs more than the general audience.

Les Brown, the best interpreter of broadcast industry news for the general reader, asserted that network news departments were significantly influenced by reviews of their work in the *New York Times*. "Its favorable recognition of a network news effort," wrote Brown, "is a source of elation within the company and held up as proof of distinguished achievement, its criticism a cause of anguish" (1971: 223). Writing of Jack Gould, who was the *New York Times* broadcasting critic for a quarter-century, Brown asserted that "he became known as 'the conscience of the industry' because his critical observations frequently influenced those who wielded power in broadcasting" (1977: 177).

When Gould retired in 1972, Fred Friendly wrote an appreciation of his influence:

His comprehensive reaction to the "See It Now" McCarthy broadcast and, later, to "Harvest of Shame," and in 1971 to Peter Davis's "The Selling of the Pentagon" stiffened backs that might easily have bent. His early interest in "Omnibus," "See It Now" and other prime-time documentaries kept them alive long after the destruct button was intended to go off. The number of jobs he saved in those 25 years are legion. . . . His best work was as a reporter, and his interpretive analysis about the life and death of quality programming, the quiz scandals, program practices, the ratings sweepstakes, the FCC, compatible color, satellites, video cassettes and public television were always bright, searching and usually accurate. (Friendly, 1972)

A little-appreciated aspect of press coverage of broadcasting is its influence on the FCC. Barry Cole, one of the few to recognize this influence, was surprised during his years as an academic observer at the FCC to find that people there read "reviews" of their performance as regulators in the trade press as avidly as stage stars devour the notices of Broadway critics.

Summary

Informal influences on the conduct of broadcasting that supplement formal FCC regulation include the following:

1. Congressional and Executive Branch influence on the FCC and on broadcasters directly.
2. Consumer boycotts — essentially a negative way of trying to influence the medium.
3. (Consumer intervention in law-making and rule-making processes — more positive ways of exerting influence. The chief avenues for such intervention are opposition to license renewals and petitions for FCC rule making. Consumers have also tried to intervene in format changes by licensees, but the Supreme Court supported the FCC's contention that format decisions should be left to the marketplace.
4. Agreements between licensees and consumer groups. Licensees agree to make certain changes and consumers in turn agree not to oppose renewal. The FCC encourages such agreements if they do not infringe on licensee responsibility for programs. It permits licensees to reimburse public interest law firms for expenses incurred in helping to negotiate such agreements.
5. Industry self-regulation. The chief influences are the NAB codes and those of individual networks. Their basic goal is to avoid program and advertising content that will cause widespread adverse public reactions without unduly stifling creative and commercial freedom.
6. Other, less influential, sources of informal control are professional self-regulation and the published commentary of broadcasting critics and analysts.

PART VI

Effects of Broadcasting

Up to this point we have sought to answer the question, "What makes broadcasting in America the way it is?" We have treated broadcasting itself as an effect, the end result of many shaping influences — physical, historical, economic, legal, and social. Now we are about to reverse our perspective to look at broadcasting as a cause rather than an effect. The question now becomes, "What role does broadcasting play in making America the way it is?"

The importance of the second question is what gives significance to the first. That is to say, broadcasting merits serious attention only because it has consequences. People buy receivers, advertisers purchase time, donors give to noncommercial broadcasting — all in the expectation of getting something of value in return. Congress passes laws, the FCC makes regulations, other public and private forces seek to exert control over the medium — all on the assumption that it produces results, some good and some bad. Seen in this perspective, everything about broadcasting in America that we have examined up to this point culminates in the study of what we know, and what we guess, about its effects.

CHAPTER 19

Inventory of Effects

In this chapter we examine a selected inventory of effects of broadcasting, kinds that are generally regarded as both significant and relatively verifiable. Broadcasting has such varied and widespread effects that a complete inventory would be virtually endless. It would be complicated, moreover, by the fact that it is often impossible to isolate the contribution of broadcasting from other influences. Most effects have many different contributory causes that interact in complex, often hidden, ways.

19.1 Pervasiveness of Effects

Claims about effects vary from the grand generalizations of the late media theorist Marshall McLuhan to the complaints of union members about how workers are depicted in television plays. The mass media, said McLuhan, "are so pervasive in their personal, political, economic, aesthetic, psychological, moral, and social consequences that they leave no part of us untouched, unaffected, or unaltered" (McLuhan & Fiore, 1967: 26). Virtually everybody has an ax to grind when it comes to controlling the effects of broadcasting, real or imagined. Either they want to prevent effects they believe unfavorable to their interests, or to encourage effects they hope will promote their goals.

Users and Subjects of Media We usually think of effects in terms of what media do to members of *audiences*. A complete inventory, however, has to consider also the effects of media on the people who are the *users* of media and on those who are the *subjects* of media attention.

As an example of how *users* of the medium are affected by the medium, consider the behavior of politicians. No longer do they crisscross the country by train, making speeches at every whistle stop to small crowds of wellwishers. Now they reach the public at distant places primarily by making radio and television appearances. They have changed their ways accordingly. The style of pretelevision politics was too long-winded and boring to make effective use of the medium. Campaigning and political conventions have been adapted to the needs of microphone and camera and the convenience of station and network.

The long debate about whether broadcasting should be allowed to enter the courtroom is an example of concern about the effects of the medium on the *subjects* of coverage. When the legal profession took steps to bar coverage of court trials by microphone and camera (§17.2), its action was based on the belief that their presence would affect the behavior of jurors, witnesses, lawyers, and defendants. Broadcast coverage, the bar association argued, would adversely affect the judicial process.

Hierarchy of Effects

When we think about communication effects, our first image is likely to be of visible outcomes clearly traceable in a direct line to specific causes. The announcer tells about the morning weather, causing the listener to wear a raincoat and carry an umbrella; a commercial mentions a sale, causing the shopper to go to the store and buy; one candidate does better than others in a political debate, causing the voter to choose that candidate on election day.

Seldom, however, are effects as easily identified or as direct as those in the examples. Nor can most effects be traced with any certainty to a single, sufficient cause. To have any effect, a message must at the very least capture attention; thus attention itself is an intermediate, subjective effect. It may lead to various other subjective outcomes, such as formation of an opinion or change in an attitude. Immediate effects of these kinds may lead to other, more remote effects.

Thus we see that effects of messages may be direct or indirect, immediate or delayed, subjective or overt, intended or accidental, single or complex. Such ambiguities need to be mentioned as a reminder that tracing the effects of broadcasting, or of other communication media, is exceedingly difficult. This does not stop people from making assumptions about effects and forming definite opinions about them, but it does warn us that such assumptions and opinions should be treated with skepticism unless backed up by reliable research.

Media Symbiosis

As we have seen, the older media at first regarded broadcasting as an implacable enemy, threatening their very existence. But competitors such as newspapers and movies did not succumb; after a period of uncertainty, they adapted to the new situation and continued to flourish, even if in somewhat altered form. It turns out, in fact, that newer media often end up being supportive of the older media. The relationship can be described in biological terms as a form of *symbiosis*. Animals and plants that have symbiotic relationships are mutually dependent, often to their mutual benefit. Media symbiosis occurs when one medium borrows another's content and talent, invests in another's stocks and corporations, or capitalizes on another's technological advances.

We saw in previous chapters how radio nearly killed the phonograph industry, then revived it, making recordings more popular than ever; and how television took over the role of family entertainer from radio, forcing radio to become more personal and individualized. Other reciprocal media effects can be observed in motion pictures, newspapers, magazines, and books.

Pop Culture vs. High Culture

Reciprocal effects extend to culture generally. Radio and television have been credited with helping to popularize classical music, ballet, art, and museum attendance. Interest in the fine arts has reached new heights; attendance at concerts, recitals, and plays is higher than ever before, and art shows are setting attendance records every year.

On the other hand, some elite critics regard radio and television as nothing less than a disaster for high culture. In the view of these critics, adapting works of art to make them broadcastable inevitably debases them.

Dwight MacDonald, a radical intellectual who was in the forefront in articulating the elitist viewpoint on mass media, described the process as follows:

Mass Culture is a dynamic, revolutionary force, breaking down the old barriers of class, tradition, taste, and dissolving all cultural distinctions. It mixes and scrambles everything together, producing what might be called homogenized culture. . . . It thus destroys all values, since value judgments imply discrimination. . . .

There are theoretical reasons why Mass Culture is not and can never be any good. I take it as axiomatic that culture can only be produced by and for human beings. But in so far as people are organized (more strictly, disorganized) as masses, they lose their human identity and quality. (MacDonald, 1953: 5, 13)

Historically, the upper social classes have always regarded the amusements of the lower classes with condescension or disgust. Gutenberg's contemporaries deplored printing as a vulgar and debasing substitute for fine calligraphy. Traditionalists objected to putting the Metropolitan Opera on radio in the 1920s. In the 1970s the *New York Times* art critic condemned Lord Kenneth Clark for "fictionalizing" fine art by bringing it to television viewers in his highly successful series *Civilisation*.

Never before have entire populations been pampered with such deferential attention as the mass media provide. One result is that poor as well as rich can benefit from high culture designed originally for the elite. As Boorstin expressed it:

Broadcasting is the great leveller, going without discrimination into the homes of rich and poor, white and black, young and old. If you own a set, no admission fee (at least in the USA) is required to enter TV-land and to have a front seat at all its marvels. . . . The Age of Broadcasting, then, is a fitting climax to the history of a nation whose birth-certificate proclaimed that "all men are created equal" and which has aimed to bring everything to everybody. (Boorstin, 1978: 20)

Mass culture differs from both the high culture and the folk culture of the past. The mass media cater to such a mixture of tastes and standards and have such insatiable appetites that their effects on both the higher arts and media audiences are, say the elitist critics, appalling:

The entertainment industry is confronted with gargantuan appetites, and since its wares disappear in consumption, it must constantly offer new commodities. In this predicament, those who produce for the mass media ransack the entire range of past and present culture in the hope of finding suitable material. This material, however, cannot be offered as it is; it must be prepared and altered in order to become entertaining. (Arendt, 1964: 48)

The work of the famed media critic Marshall McLuhan was an outgrowth of the cultural criticism tradition. Although McLuhan at first deplored the popular arts in the usual vein of cultural critics, he later arrived at a unique new way of denigrating them indirectly. McLuhan simply rejected the entire content of the mass media as irrelevant by invoking the formula "the medium is the message." He did not mean by this that the media no longer have effects. Quite the contrary, he ascribed to them more profound and far-reaching effects than any communications scholar before had dared to suggest— nothing less than the transformation of man.

McLuhan also reversed conventional cultural criticism by declaring that the effects of media are good after all. Here was a certified intellectual who, instead of berating the popular media for homogenizing and debasing culture, lavished praise upon them. "This vision of a salutary effect of television—while other people are worrying about the effects of its materialistic and violent content—was more than anything else responsible for McLuhan's vogue" (Schramm, 1973: 129). His vogue has faded, but McLuhan will always be remembered in media annals as a superb phrasemaker and as a stimulator of unconventional thinking about communication.

19.2 Effects of Advertising

Of the many consequences of broadcasting, none is subjected to more continuous measurement and manipulation than the immediate effects of advertising. Advertisers demand results. Ascertaining and reporting those results has therefore become a multimillion dollar business in itself, as we saw in Chapter 14.

We are now concerned, however, with the broader, long-range social consequences of advertising rather than with its immediate effects on sales. What effects does advertising have in terms of the public interest, as distinguished from the private commercial interests of its users?

Advertising as Subsidy   It can be argued, for example, that advertising plays a useful social role in reducing the direct costs of the media to the public. Readers pay only about a third of the cost of metropolitan newspapers and about 40 percent of the cost of general-interest magazines. The rest is defrayed by advertising income. In the case of commercial broadcasting, advertising appears to pay the entire cost of the service. This is only an appearance, however, because, as we have pointed out (§12.6), broadcasting differs from the other media in asking the general public to invest in part of the

system's essential capital equipment by purchasing and maintaining receivers. This public investment, combined with the fact that the medium uses the publicly "owned" frequency spectrum, gives the consumer more of an equity in broadcasting than in other media. Arguably, their investment entitles consumers to be especially critical of broadcast advertising that it judges to have harmful effects.

In any case, consumers eventually pay the full cost of the media because advertising costs are added to the final price of consumer goods and services. But at least the burden of these hidden subsidies is distributed widely and so weighs relatively lightly on each individual purchaser. In this sense advertising is a fairer way of charging the public for a broadcast service than set-use license fees. Many set-users evade paying fees, unfairly increasing the burden of those who do pay because the fewer the licenses the higher the license fees have to be to meet the costs of the service.

Synthesizing Wants   Does advertising impose a penalty on consumers by generating the desire for unnecessary purchases — the *synthesizing of wants,* to use a phrase of the liberal economist John Kenneth Galbraith. Broadcast advertising can stimulate widespread demand for goods and services for which consumers had never recognized any previous need. Almost overnight markets can be generated for novel but essentially uesless products or for "new and improved" versions of old products.

Some thoughtful observers regard this constant synthesizing of unessential wants, accompanied by the expense of elaborate advertising campaigns, as socially undesirable and economically wasteful. One of the most prestigious critics, Arnold Toynbee, the noted historian of world civilizations, voiced this view in an essay about America:

There is a limit, and a narrow one, to the quantity of goods that can be effectively possessed. . . . The true end of Man is not to possess the maximum amount of consumer goods per head. When we are considering the demand for consumer goods, we have to distinguish between three things: our needs, our wants, and the unwanted demand, in excess of our genuine wants, that we allow the advertising trade to bully us into demanding if we are both rich enough and foolish enough to let ourselves be influenced by advertising. (1962: 131, 144)

Power of Advertising   Academics like Toynbee take it for granted that advertising has the power to overcome almost any consumer defenses. Practitioners of advertising often find themselves wishing it were only so. The failure of a high percentage of new consumer products that are planned for the market each year hardly supports the assumption that manufacturers and advertising agencies can synthesize consumer appetites at will.

Failures could be blamed on unskillful marketing rather than on consumer rejection, except that there have been notable examples of promising new products ushered into the market with the most skillful and generous advertising campaigns money can buy, only to fail miserably to win consumer approval. The classic case was the failure of the Edsel automobile, introduced by the Ford Motor Company in 1957 after the most prodigious campaign of research, promotion, and advertising ever staged to introduce a new product. An advertising executive of that era wrote:

Advertising, together with a vast program of publicity . . . brought three million people into showrooms across the country when the drumbeating was loudest and the car was introduced. There,

completely unmoved, they turned thumbs down on it. Why, no one exactly knows. (Cone, 1969: 5)

There have been almost equally stunning, though less publicized, failures, such as that of Corfam, a synthetic leather developed by DuPont, one of the most sophisticated and successful marketers of new high-technology products in the world. Corfam's failure was as mysterious as that of the Edsel.

Not only do many new products fail to catch on, but leading established products often give way to competitors, despite intensive advertising support. The transfer of *brand loyalty,* as it is called, is a well-recognized marketing problem.

Experience thus shows that advertising cannot create consumer wants without the cooperation of consumers. People are not merely passive automatons, responding mechanically to advertising cues. After 40 years and billions of dollars' worth of practical advertising experience, Fairfax Cone summed up his view of the matter:

Most of the viewers who fear advertising as an evil force give it too much credit. About all it can do under the most skillful direction (and by skillful direction I don't mean either hidden or otherwise undue persuasion) is to exploit a given interest, predilection, disposition, prejudice or bias and bring this to bear on a buying decision. (1969: 8)

Advertising to Children   All that we have said and quoted so far about advertising assumes that its targets are rational adults. Commercials in children's programs create special problems of fairness and equity. The advertising assault on children is truly massive, as the following data in a Federal Trade Commission staff report indicate:

The average American child aged 2 through 5 watched 25 hours and 36 minutes of television per week, or just under 3 2/3 hours per day. Older children, aged 6 through 11, watched slightly more, 25 hours and 41 minutes per week, or more than 3 2/3 hours per day. This works out to well over 1,300 hours per year, or more time than the older group spent in the classroom. (FTC, 1978: 51)

Children start watching television below the age of four, when they find commercials just as fascinating as programs. Indeed, one of the major concerns of Action for Children's Television (§9.8) and other such consumer organizations is that commercials take unfair advantage of the fact that young children are not yet able to recognize the purpose of advertising, or indeed that advertisements are not part of the programs themselves.

Another major issue with consumer groups and health authorities is that the overwhelming majority of commercials aimed at children urge them to eat and drink sugared foods. One study quoted by the FTC staff counted 7,515 network food commercials in daytime weekend children's programs during the first nine months of 1976 (excluding ads for fast-food eating places). Of these, half promoted breakfast cereals, a third promoted candy, gum, cookies and crackers.

The FTC staff report recommended that "the present televised advertising of sugared products to children, and the televised advertising of any product to children too young to understand the selling purpose of, or otherwise understand or evaluate advertising, violate the Federal Trade Commission Act" (FTC, 1978). The staff went on to document at length its opinion that the FTC had ample legal authority to ban such advertising. This recommendation galvanized industry lobbyists into action, eventually precipitating a crackdown by Congress on the FTC, which gave up any idea of banning children's television advertising.

In addition to the extensive study of the effects of children's advertising by the FTC staff, other studies have been made by the FCC's Children's Television Task Force (FCC, 1979) and a panel of experts funded by the National Science Foundation (Adler et al., 1978).

The five-volume study by the FCC's task force reported on the industry's response to an earlier FCC policy statement on advertising in children's programming (§9.8). Some progress had been made in implementing the policy, said the report, such as eliminating host selling and cutting back on commercial time in children's programming hours (§13.4). The task force's main recommendation, far less sweeping than that of the FTC staff, emphasized encouraging alternative nonbroadcast sources of entertainment for children. This was in keeping with the emerging regulatory trend of abandoning efforts to force the broadcasting industry to change its practices by regulation, relying more on the pressure of competition to achieve regulatory goals.

Of the three studies, the one financed by the National Science Foundation was the most restrained in its conclusions, in keeping with its nature as a scientific document. Its purpose was to review the existing research literature on the effects of television advertising on children and to make recommendations for future research. The team of experts analyzed 21 existing research studies. Its main conclusion, not surprisingly, was that still more research was needed. Its more specific conclusions were cautiously expressed, as the following examples indicate:

■ "There is evidence that parents tend to overstate the degree of control they exercise over children's TV viewing and, simultaneously, to overestimate their children's understanding of commercials."

■ "While various statistics have been cited by parties concerned with the nutritional health of the U.S. populace, including children, no evidence directly links televised food commercials to these statistics since the appropriate studies have not yet been conducted."

19.3 News and Pseudonews

With most people in the country known to depend primarily on television for news, it seems safe to assume that this category of programming has important effects. Most of us presumably perceive the world beyond our personal neighborhoods pretty much the way broadcasting shows it to us.

Gatekeeping Of the incalculable number of events that occur in the world on any given day, a tiny fraction end up on our plate as the "news of the day." On its way to becoming the neatly packaged tidbits that tell us "the way it is," the raw material of news passes through the hands of many *gatekeepers*. Some are deliberate gatekeepers, deciding which events to cover in which places, and how stories should be written, edited, and positioned in the news presentation. Some gatekeeping is inadvertent, the result of external factors such as the accessibility of news events and the availability of transportation and relay facilities. Some is institutional and some ideological. Network news, for example, has been described as being

shaped and constrained by certain structures imposed from without, such as government regulation of broadcasting and the economic realities of networks; certain uniform procedures for filtering and evaluating information and reaching decisions; and certain practices of recruiting newsmen and producers who hold, or accept, values that are consistent with organizational needs, and reject others. (Epstein, 1973a: 43)

Thus the media profoundly affect the material they transmit, both consciously and inadvertently, in the very process of transmission.

An example of involuntary gatekeeping is the elementary fact that television, as a visual medium, demands pictures. This tends to bias the medium toward covering events that have intrinsic visual content, despite the fact that much of the news is not inherently pictorial. Effects of visual bias that can be readily observed in television news are (1) a preference for stories that make good pictures and (2) a forced effort to illustrate nonvisual stories with essentially irrelevant stock shots, as when scenes of bidding on the floor of the stock exchange are used to illustrate a story on financial trends.

Agenda Setting One result of the filtering and shaping effects of gatekeeping is the exertion of control over which subjects will come to the attention of audiences. Gatekeeping focuses attention temporarily on specific events, persons, and issues that are "in the news." The list changes day by day as old items drop out and new ones claim attention, and as the rank order of importance changes from day to day. This process of selection and ranking, referred to as *agenda setting*, is regarded as one of the primary ways in which the media affect our perceptions of the world around us.

A related effect is *prestige conferral*. The very fact that an event rises to the level of importance of being placed on the current news agenda gives it an aura of importance. Well-known network reporters lend glamor and significance when they cover an event in person. Commenting on how television coverage has exaggerated the importance of the state primary elections that come earliest in national political campaigns, former presidential press secretary Ron Nessen pointed out that "television acts like a giant megaphone in the election campaign, greatly amplifying and magnifying the significance of events. . . . The mere presence of Walter Cronkite and Barbara Walters confers significance. If it weren't important, *they* wouldn't be there, would they?" (Nessen, 1980).

Staging by the Medium The news-shaping effects discussed so far are largely inadvertent, but others result from calculated acts by news personnel. For example, television's need for images creates an ever-present temptation to artificially enhance the pictorial content of news stories. This tendency came to critical public notice during the urban riots of the 1960s. Instances were reported of news crews "coaxing youths to throw rocks and interrupt traffic, and otherwise acting irresponsibly at the incipient stages of a disturbance" (National Advisory Commission on Civil Disorders, 1968: 36).

Even when news crews make no move to provoke reaction, the very presence of cameras in tense situations tends to escalate ongoing action. After experience with the 1960s riots, the networks and many stations adopted written guidelines for their news personnel, aimed at minimizing the effects of cameras at scenes of public unrest. Even so, legitimate exercise of news judgments in the process of editing can raise awkard problems for conscientious broadcasters. News documentaries, as we have seen (§17.5), are prone to charges of bias and of tampering with the facts. Payments for participants' signatures on legally required release forms have been interpreted as bribes; selective editing has been described as deliberate misinterpretation; encouraging people to express opinions has been construed as sensationalism; and selecting specific cases to illustrate a general theme has been called deceptive (F. Smith, 1974).

An amusing illustration of the difficulty of drawing a reasonable line between legitimate editing and fakery was described by Daniel Schorr, formerly a CBS newsman. He told how William Paley, head of CBS, praised him for his unflappability in conducting a tense, dramatic filmed interview with the East German leader, Walter Ulbricht. Schorr modestly disclaimed any special credit, pointing out that the "reverse shots" showing him listening urbanely to the vehement Ulbricht had actually been filmed and inserted later. This is a common trick of the editing trade. To save time and trouble for busy interviewees, news producers often use only one camera, trained the whole time on the interviewee. Shots of the interviewer asking questions and reacting to the answers are photographed and spliced in at a later time. Paley was so shocked at what seemed to him dishonest reporting that he promptly sent down an order that CBS should ban staged reverse shots in the future. After learning that the new rule against reverses would seriously impede the work of news teams, Paley relented, changing the rule to require only that interviewees subjected to the practice be made aware of it (Schorr, 1977: 262).

As a practical matter, a certain amount of artifice is accepted as permissible in news coverage. The FCC recognized this latitude in rejecting claims that the networks had staged fake news stories at the riot-plagued 1968 Democratic convention in Chicago:

In a sense, every television press conference may be said to be "staged" to some extent; depictions of scenes in a television documentary — on how the poor live on a typical day in the ghetto, for example — also necessarily involve camera direction, lights, action instructions, etc. . . . Few would question the professional propriety of asking public officials to smile again or to repeat handshakes, while the cameras are focused upon them. (16 FCC 2d 656, 1969)

Pseudoevents: Staging by News Subjects

Outright staging *by the subjects of news* occurs when press agents and public relations counselors seek to "plant" information in the media or to create happenings designed to attract the attention of reporters. Daniel Boorstin coined the term *pseudoevent* to describe these contrived happenings, analyzing the many forms they take, such as press conferences, trial balloons, news leaks of supposedly confidential information, background briefings (in which information is released anonymously, "not for attribution"). Not all preplanned events such as press conferences deserve to be condemned as pseudoevents. When a newsworthy figure such as a president is involved, a certain amount of ceremonial event-making is expected. The events that deserve the term are deliberate attempts to disguise fabricated nonevents as genuine news events.

Organizations interested in maintaining a favorable public image constantly churn out self-serving material in the guise of news. Government departments no less than private organizations exploit pseudoevents. Military spending on image building was the subject of the controverisal documentary "The Selling of the Pentagon," discussed earlier in connection with First Amendment issues (§17.5).

Conscientious news departments avoid using self-serving handouts. But free *news clips* are a tempting money saver for stations short on photographic material. These short items supplied by business and government public relations departments contain pictorially interesting material in which the real message is unobtrusively buried. For example, a dramatic sequence of helicopter shots depicting offshore oil drilling that could be used to illustrate an energy story might just incidentally name the company engaged in the drilling. Or a film about high school training in auto mechanics might happen to feature students working on a particular make of auto (Kiester, 1974).

Technically speaking, the sponsor identification law (§13.3) requires licensees to inform the audience of the source of free materials of this kind, but the FCC has not invoked the law for material used in newscasts. Some stations superimpose a title at the beginning of such film clips to identify their source, but many do not.

Publicity Crimes

News staging for self-publicization took a vicious turn when criminals and terrorist organizations began kidnapping hostages in order to obtain coverage in the news. Such *publicity crimes*, as they have been called, are paradoxical blends of pseudoevents and real events. The very act of covering a publicity crime turns the media into accomplices in the crime; so does the avidity with which the public awaits the latest news about them.

Publicity crimes reached bizarre new heights with the taking of American Embassy personnel hostage in Iran in 1979. This entire episode, which lasted for 444 days, became an unprecedented international media event. The Iranians exploited television from beginning to end with clumsy but nevertheless attention-getting propaganda tactics.

American broadcasters had never before faced such a tantalizing news dilemma. Every time they showed footage of street rallies in which Iranian marchers burned American flags or of the American hostages paraded before the cameras to mumble words of transparently grudging praise for their captors, the American networks gave the terrorists priceless publicity. Yet the pressure on broadcasters to air every scrap of footage about the hostages was almost irresistible.

The networks were caught in a multiple bind, whipsawed by the terrorists, the U.S. government, the families of hostages, the American public, and the need to compete with each other. Their confusion reached a peak early in the game when the Iranians offered to supply a television interview with a hostage. The Iranians taped the interview, accompanied by a mandatory unedited propaganda speech by their own version of Barbara Walters, a bundle of veils known as ''Mary.''

Two networks turned down the offer, but NBC, after tempering the Iranian terms somewhat through negotiation, ran the interview with the accompanying statement by ''Mary,'' but also with appropriate warnings as to the source. It was said that U.S.-based Iranian accomplices stood by on the telephone to warn their colleagues in Iran to cut the satellite feed if NBC failed to live up to its end of the bargain.

NBC was roundly criticized by members of Congress as well as by many media representatives for giving the terrorists a propaganda platform. The network's Pentagon correspondent, Ford Rowen, resigned in protest because NBC refused to accompany the Iranian material with a counterstatement from the U.S. State Department. Later in 1979, however, NBC joined the other networks in turning down similar Iranian propaganda offers.

Media events on this scale have a way of taking on a life of their own. In the end, the Iranians' strategy backfired when the story took off in an unplanned direction. Many Americans who at first sympathized with

Iran's grievances were turned off by the clumsy attempts at media manipulation. Instead of inducing a sense of American humiliation, the contrived publicity about the hostage-taking generated a sense of righteous indignation. This feeling culminated in an unprecedented television event — the coverage of the hostage homecoming, which turned into a national celebration of patriotism and pride.

Effects on the Subjects of News Coverage

In the course of the national celebration for the returned Iran hostages in 1981, observers began asking what effect the prodigious media coverage of their every move and every word would have on the returnees. Some critics even speculated that the overwhelming barrage of media attention might cause more psychological trauma than the imprisonment itself.

In less unusual situations undoubtedly media coverage does affect its recipients. For example, many people featured as the subjects of investigative reports on *60 Minutes* have paid fines, gone to jail, or been penalized in other ways after being exposed to the probing cameras and the inquisitorial skills of reporters like Mike Wallace (Kowet, 1979). Of course, the previous deeds or misdeeds of the people investigated were the real causes of their downfall, but cameras and reporters called attention to their actions in especially compelling ways.

More widespread but more ambiguous effects may occur when people become the subjects of other types of broadcast coverage. For example, the rule barring cameras and microphones from courts of law, discussed in §17.2, was based on the assumption that (1) broadcast coverage would affect the behavior of witnesses, lawyers, and defendants, and (2) that these effects would be detrimental to the judicial process. Experience has suggested, however, that although people are undoubtedly at first affected by the presence of broadcast equipment, it is by no means certain that their reactions have adverse effects on the judicial process, once the novelty effect wears off.

Three factors may account for this reevaluation. Cameras, microphones, lights, and associated equipment have become less bulky and obtrusive than they were when the rule barring photography and radio in courtrooms was originally adopted back in the 1930s. Moreover, broadcast news crews have become more professional and sensitive to their obligation to avoid causing undue disruptions.

Thirdly, society itself has become more tolerant of broadcast access to official activities, coincidental with (if not actually caused by) the consumerism movement of the 1960s and 1970s (§18.2). Increased public access has been specifically mandated by *sunshine laws* (requiring various official bodies to meet in public) and the *Freedom of Information Act* (mandating access to certain government information formerly withheld from public scrutiny).

These changes do not mean that broadcast coverage is no longer thought to have effects on the people it covers, only that the effects may not be as unfavorable as at first supposed. There is even reason to believe that with long exposure, camera subjects eventually begin to accept the equipment and crew as a normal part of their environment.

19.4 Entertainment Programming

Entertainment as well as news and public affairs programming tends to play an agenda-setting role. It is safe to predict that any big news story that holds the headlines for any length of time will soon turn up as the subject of a special program or miniseries and will influence future episodes of established entertainment series. Docudramas are an especially striking evidence of this tendency. Moreover, to the extent that they change the facts around to suit the needs of drama, they add still more distortions to the version of reality perceived by broadcast audiences.

Stereotypes Fiction influences audience perceptions by reinforcing *stereotypes*, which are versions of reality deliberately oversimplified to fit in with preconceived images. Examples of stereotypes are the stock characters of popular drama — the Italian gangster, the inscrutable Oriental, the mad scientist, the bespectacled librarian.

Even authors capable of more individualized and realistic character portrayals resort to stereotypes when writing for television in order to save time — both their own and that of the medium. Stories must be told with the utmost efficiency to fit them into the confines of half-hour and hour-long formats (minus times out for commercials, of course).

Television dramas have little time to develop situations or characters, necessitating the use of widely accepted notions of good and evil. Since the emphasis is on resolving the conflict or the problem at hand, there is little time to project the complexities of a character's thoughts or feelings or for dialogues which explore human relationships. To move the action along rapidly, the characters must be portrayed in ways which quickly identify them. Thus the character's physical appearance, environment, and behavior conform to widely accepted notions of the types of people they represent. (U.S. Commission on Civil Rights, 1977: 27)

We saw in the case of the "Indian derogatories" (§18.2) how bitterly stereotypes are resented by those who feel demeaned by them. This feeling is based on the assumption that stereotypical images in television help to establish and to perpetuate those same images in the minds of the viewers. As the U.S. Commission on Civil Rights put it, "To the extent that viewers' beliefs, attitudes, and behavior are affected by what they see on television, relations between the races and the sexes may be affected by television's limited and often stereotyped portrayals." The commission was careful not to state flatly that such effects always occur, but it called for research to assess what actually happens.

World of Fiction When researchers take a census of the characters in a body of television plays they find that demographic characteristics of the fictional population invariably differ markedly from the characteristics of people in the real world. Compared to life, the world of fiction has far more men than women, for example. Most of them are young adults, with few very young or elderly persons. Many have no visible means of support, but if they do work they have interesting, exciting, action-filled types of jobs. Fiction therefore contains an unrealistically higher proportion of detectives, criminals, doctors, scientists, business executives, and adventurers than the real world, where most jobs are unglamorous, dull, and repetitive. Most people in the real world solve their personal problems undramatically, even anticlimatically or incompletely, using socially approved methods. Fictional characters are much more likely to solve their problems with decisive, highly visible acts, often entailing violence.

All of this is to be expected, of course. Fact may be stranger than fiction, but fact does not occur in neatly packaged half-hour epi-

sodes, with periodic times out for commercial interruptions.

Socialization Nevertheless, the make-believe world of radio and television serves as a model of reality for countless people, especially for children at the very time when they are eagerly reaching out to learn what the world is all about. Those too young to read, those who never learned to read or acquired the habit of reading, and those who have little access to printed sources of information and entertainment — all depend heavily on radio and television to inform them of the world outside their own immediate surroundings.

Dramatic fare is especially influential because viewers and listeners identify with heroes, participating vicariously in their adventures. Research indicates that young children are especially vulnerable. They tend to believe what they see in television, making no distinction between fact, fiction, and advertising. The proportion of believers is higher among poor children than among those whose real lives are more varied. It is also higher among black children than white.

Given the enormous amount of time most children spend with television, this means that broadcasting has become a major agent of *socialization* — that all-important process which turns a squalling infant into a functioning member of a society. Socialization is enormously complicated in even the most primitive culture. It is a lifelong process, but much of it occurs in the first few years of life when the child first learns language and the meticulously detailed rules of behavior and the value system of its own culture.

In the past, socialization has always been the jealously guarded prerogative of family and religion, formalized by education, and extended by peer group experiences. The intrusion of a new, external agent of socialization represents a profound change. Of course, broadcasting is part of national culture, too, but it comes from beyond the immediate circle of the family and its community-linked supports. It imports ideas, language, images, practices that may be alien to the local culture.

Just what effects the intrusion of broadcasting into socialization has or might have is the subject of much research and much debate. The effects could of course be both good (*prosocial*) or bad (*antisocial*). Such programs as *Sesame Street* and *Fat Albert and the Cosby Kids* were researched and designed with prosocial effects in mind. Follow-up research indicates that such programs do in fact succeed in achieving prosocial results. Much more effort, however, has gone into research to prove the existence of antisocial effects of television program content, most of it focused on the effects of violence.*

19.5 Effects of Violence

Assumptions About Effects Concern about the possible antisocial effects of portraying violence and crime date back to pre-television days. The film industry adopted a motion picture code in 1930 in response to strong public pressure, mobilized by the Catholic Legion of Decency in particular. The code imposed stringent rules on scenes involving crimes, weapons, and sex, and mandated that plots must carry the message that "crime does not pay." The first systematic

*The closely related topic of the effects of pornography has also been studied intensively. This research is not discussed here because pornography, as legally defined, has so far been effectively excluded from broadcasting, though it does have a role in pay cable. The moralistic campaigns against sex in television that erupt periodically are aimed at programs that do not remotely approach legally preventable pornography.

scientific research on the effects of media violence was attempted in the 1930s, when a foundation underwrote a series of studies on the impact of feature films.

The film code was criticized for its dogmatically moralizing tone, its disregard for artistic realism, and for the way it took for granted unproved assumptions that specific items of content had specific bad effects. The industry finally abandoned the code for the present system of rating pictures according to their acceptability for young audiences.

Meanwhile, concern about the effects of violence shifted to television, with a corresponding shift in emphasis. The broadcasting codes, though inspired by the example of the motion picture code, are framed more in secular and legalistic terms than in religious and moralistic terms. There has been a shift, moreover, toward buttressing conclusions about effects with scientific evidence, rather than merely taking effects for granted.

Direct Imitation Real-life cases of violence modeled on similar actions in films and television programs occasionally surface in news reports. A particularly repellent instance of such imitation led to an unprecedented lawsuit. In 1974 NBC broadcast a made-for-television film called "Born Innocent" in which inmates of a detention home for young delinquents "raped" a young girl with a mop handle. Four days later, a nine-year-old California girl was subjected to a similar violation by four older children using a bottle.

Parents of the child sued NBC, asking for $11 million in damages for negligence in showing the scene in the film, which they alleged had directly incited the attack on their daughter. This suit raised a question of great moment for broadcasters: could they be held legally responsible for the reactions of audience members to their programs? NBC's lawyers persuaded the trial judge in preliminary hearings to define the issue as a First Amendment question, rather than as a negligence question. This put upon the opposing counsel the burden of proving that NBC had surrendered its First Amendment protection by *deliberately inciting* the children to attack their victim. Because this was clearly an impossible task, the case collapsed.

Generalized Effects   However, public concern about television violence is based primarily on its possible generalized effects rather than on the risk of occasional direct imitations. Effects are assumed to be far more widespread and pervasive than isolated instances of imitation. This point of view emerged in another much-publicized court case in 1977. A 16-year-old Florida boy, Ronnie Zamora, was charged with murdering an elderly neighbor. The counsel for the boy tried to introduce in his defense the argument that Zamora was a television addict, "intoxicated" by the thousands of murders he had seen enacted on the screen, and therefore not responsible for his violent behavior. The trial judge rejected this defense and the boy was convicted of murder. This attempt to blame television for the crime, though ill-considered, was inspired by the findings of research on the generalized adverse effects of televised violence, which had accumulated rapidly during the 1970s.

In 1968, following the assassinations of Senator Robert Kennedy and Dr. Martin Luther King, President Lyndon Johnson had set up the National Commission on the Causes and Prevention of Violence. The commission reported that it received more "strong and often bitter complaints" about television violence from the general public than about any other issue. One of the many commission-sponsored studies found that three-quarters of a national sample of adults believed it "likely or possible" that violence in television plays a part in making America a violent society (Baker & Ball, 1969: 242).

Much further research has added scientific support to this belief. A large group of studies was supported by the Surgeon General's Scientific Advisory Committee on Television and Social Behavior in 1969. Congress allotted a million dollars to the committee's work, which resulted in five volumes of reports and papers by 38 researchers. The committee's final conclusion was expressed somewhat ambiguously, but the Surgeon General himself, when asked by a Senate committee to comment on the report, said flatly:

The broadcasters should be put on notice. The overwhelming consensus and the unanimous Scientific Advisory Committee's report indicates that televised violence, indeed, does have an adverse effect on certain members of our society.

While the committee report is carefully phrased and qualified in language acceptable to social scientists, it is clear to me that the causal relationship between televised violence and antisocial behavior is sufficient to warrant appropriate and immediate remedial action. (Senate CC, 1972: 26)

The studies made for the Surgeon General were among 2,500 books, articles, and other documents surveyed by George Comstock and his associates for their report, *Television and Human Behavior* (1978). Their comprehensive analysis of the research literature established that, of all the types of television effects that have been studied, television's linkage to aggression has been the effect most intensively analyzed. The fact that every research method available has been employed in the study of television violence makes the cumulative evidence of its effects especially persuasive. They summarized their findings in these words:

The evidence is that television may increase aggression by teaching viewers previously unfamiliar hostile acts, by generally encouraging in various ways the use of aggression, and by triggering aggressive behavior both imitative and different in kind from what has been viewed. Effects are never certain because real-life aggression is strongly influenced by situational factors, and this strong role for situational factors means that the absence of an immediate effect does not rule out a delayed impact when the behavior in question may be more propitious. (Comstock et al., 1978: 13)

In the light of the research evidence, Congress pressed the FCC to take action. As we have seen, the commission passed the pressure on to the industry, persuading it to adopt the ill-fated family viewing policy in 1975 (§16.1). As a result of the policy the level of violence in prime-time television entertainment seemed to fall somewhat in the next few years, but, in apparent compensation, programs began to exploit sex more openly. In a 1979 national survey, 28 percent of the sample criticized television for violence, 21 percent for sex (Callum, 1979).

Violence and Perceptions of Reality

During the 1967–1968 television season, George Gerbner and his associates at the University of Pennsylvania began conducting annual analyses of television violence. From these data they constructed "The Violence Profile," based on a content analysis that enumerated every violent act in a sample week of prime-time and weekend morning network entertainment programs (Exhibit 19.5). In this way they tracked changes in the

Exhibit 19.5
Trends in television violence, 1967–1979

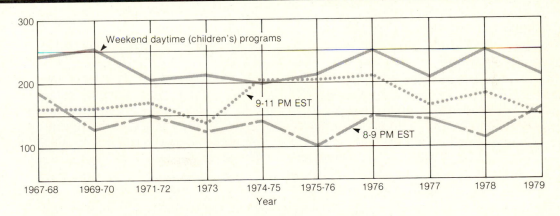

The scale on the left refers to the Gerbner "violence index," a measurement of the level of violence in programs that combines values for three variables: "the extent to which violence occurs at all in the program sampled, the frequency and rate of violent episodes, and the number of roles calling for characterization as violents, victims, or both." The dip in the 8–9 P.M. index in 1975 reflects the introduction of the family viewing hour restraints in that year. Notice that the index level for children's programs is generally much higher than that for adult programs.

Source: George Gerbner et al., "The 'Mainstreaming' of America: Violence Profile No. 11," *Journal of Communication* 30 (Summer, 1980), p. 13.

level of violence from year to year according to network and program type. The Gerbner data indicated, for example, that cartoons depict a higher percentage of violent acts than any other program category (no doubt because the coding system counts comic as well as serious acts of violence).

Gerbner believes that violence in programs creates anxiety in viewers, who tend to perceive the real world in terms of the television world. Viewers identify with victims of violence in fiction who are like themselves. Gerbner found that the elderly, the poor, and blacks have high "risk ratios," or expectations of becoming victims. This anxiety effect he believes may be a more important by-product of violence than the imitation effect.

Desensitization   The Gerbner risk ratio hypothesis reverses an older hypothesis that predicts that people exposed to fictional violence will become *desensitized*. According to this view, when the experience of violence in fiction becomes routine, people grow callous and indifferent to real-life violence. The many instances that can be cited of callousness in the face of urban violence lend color to this hypothesis. For example, in 1979 eleven young people were crushed to death in a scramble to get into an arena to hear a rock concert. Appalled observers reported later that the fans, in their rush to enter the hall, trampled with complete indifference over the bodies of those who had fallen to the floor.

A related hypothesis holds that viewers become indifferent to violence because it is depicted so unrealistically on television, having been deliberately *sanitized*. The consequences of violence are made to seem neat and clean compared to what happens when real people are hurt. The revolting, bloody aftermath, the screams of agony, are never seen or heard. Joe Wambaugh, a one-time

police officer who became a writer of police stories, withdrew from a television series based on his writings because the producers treated violence so unrealistically. He was quoted in the press as saying, "If they had a cop kill someone on TV, you never saw the blood. You never saw the face shot away. And you never saw the cop throwing up afterwards."

Wambaugh put his finger on a seemingly insoluble dilemma: ideally such graphic consequences should perhaps be seen, but the public would never tolerate showing them. The NAB Television Code reflects this dilemma when it says "programs involving violence should present the consequences of it to its victims and perpetrators," while warning in the same section that "the detailed dwelling upon brutality or physical agony, by sight or by sound," is not permissible.

In Defense of Violence   Given the range and depth of research evidence of the antisocial effects of television violence, the broadcasting industry has found it increasingly difficult to defend its use. Yet if television is expected to serve as a medium for serious artistic expression for adult viewers, it is relevant to ask how far the industry should be expected to go in banning violence, which is, after all, integral to all literature. The stage is littered with bodies when the curtain falls on some of Shakespeare's tragedies. And popular entertainment and sports have always featured violence.

Writers would have a hard time inventing enough plays for the needs of television without resorting to clashes between opposing forces involving violence. A study was made of the attitudes and opinions of those responsible for network entertainment — the writers, producers, network executives, and program standards chiefs (Baldwin & Lewis, 1972). The problem as most of them saw it was well expressed by a writer who pointed out that authors of dramas have at their disposal four basic types of conflicts around which to build their plots. Only one of the four is well adapted to the limitations imposed by television, and that happens to be the one most likely to involve personal violence:

1. *Man against nature*: "This is usually too expensive for television."
2. *Man against God*: "Too intellectual for television."
3. *Man against himself*: "Too psychological, and doesn't leave enough room for action."
4. *Man against man*: "This is what you usually end up with."

Defenders of current practice argue that violence in television merely reflects violence in real life. To ignore it or to pretend that it does not exist would restrict writers unreasonably. Curiously enough, however, comparison of American culture with others does not seem to bear out the assumption of a positive correlation between real and fictional violence.

If television were the sole determinant of violent behavior, it would be difficult to explain the disparity in aggravated assault rates (almost 8 to 1) between Boston and Montreal, since these cities are both saturated with the same and similar television programs. This does not mean that there is no relationship between television violence and actual violence; it simply means that such a relationship cannot be defined explicitly at present. (Kutash, 1978: 118)

Japan offers an interesting example in this connection. Crime statistics in Japan indicate a much lower level of social violence than that of the United States. Yet Japanese television regularly imports the most violent of U.S. action dramas, whose violence is mild compared to the ferocity seen in home-grown Japanese television plays (Barnard, 1978).

Another justification of violent content sees it as having a positive role in defusing aggressive instincts. The ancient Greek theory of *catharsis*, as propounded by Aristotle, held that stage tragedy purges the viewer of pity and fear. The analogous modern argument is that television viewers' feelings of aggression will be drained off in harmless fantasies as a result of watching fictional violence. Experimental studies have not always supported this assumption. In fact, most studies suggest that seeing violence in fiction arouses aggressive feelings rather than purging them (Comstock et al., 1978: 237).

19.6 Effects on Political Life

Crisis Management All political systems go through processes of change; free communication improves the chances that change will take place peacefully. If dissident elements can let off steam and argue revolutionary causes openly, they have no need to go underground, possibly to break out later in violent revolution. In times of crisis, open communication allays panic and eases the stress of transition. Broadcasting, with its immediacy and its instant national scope, can play a vital role in managing crisis situations.

The first great test of television's role in such a crisis came in 1963, when President John F. Kennedy was assassinated. The country had not been faced with a similar national emergency since 1901, when President William McKinley was shot. Everyone agreed that broadcasting did its job magnificently. Addressing the House of Representatives at its first session after the Kennedy funeral, Representative Oren Harris declared: "We can say truthfully today that we Americans have felt fused together as one people largely because of the outstanding contribution made by the broadcasting industry." He and many others were quoted in *Broadcasting* magazine's special report on the four-day coverage of the assassination and its aftermath. Canceling commercials and commercial programs for "the most massive and the most concentrated broadcasting coverage in history," the networks won praise for competence, sensitivity, and dignity in handling the crisis (*Broadcasting* 2 Dec. 1963).

Since then broadcasting has risen to the occasion of other national crises with equal distinction. For example, the networks covered the historic House Judiciary Committee's hearings on impeachment charges against President Richard Nixon in full in 1974. For 54 days they rotated the assignment day by day. It was the first time the House had permitted television coverage of any of its committee hearings. People who blamed "the media" for Nixon's downfall predicted that to put the hearings on television would turn them into a circus. Exactly the opposite happened. Again, commentators were unanimous in their praise of broadcasting as a unifying force in a period of national crisis.

Election Campaigns   Almost from its beginning broadcasting exerted a powerful influence on political campaigning. Radio speeches by Calvin Coolidge, whose low-key delivery suited the microphone, were believed to have been a key factor in his reelection in 1924. Radio became especially important to Democratic national candidates because it gave them a chance to appeal directly to the electorate, going over the heads of the newspapers, which were owned mostly by Republicans (Carroll, 1980).

Television brought Madison Avenue sales techniques to the presidential campaign of 1952, when the master of the hard-sell commercial, Rosser Reeves, designed spots used in a saturation campaign for General Dwight Eisenhower. The commercialization of political campaigns culminated in the Nixon elections of 1968 and 1972. Nixon had learned that television could make a vital difference years before when he ran as Eisenhower's vice-presidential candidate in 1952. On the verge of being disowned by Eisenhower in mid-campaign because of alleged misuse of election funds, Nixon rescued his candidacy in one bold stroke. In a do-or-die effort, he paid NBC $75,000 for network time to defend himself in his famous "Checkers" speech (Nixon referred satirically to his dog Checkers as a gift that he dared keep in defiance of his critics). "It was perhaps the most brilliant political use that had ever been made of the mass media," wrote former FCC Chairman Newton Minow. "The speech saved Nixon's political career but also spread his fame far beyond his California political base" (1973: 49)

By 1968, when Nixon won election as president, television had taken over as the most important factor in political campaigning. A young writer, Joe McGinniss, sensing that something profound had happened to American politics, won permission from the Nixon strategists to follow them on the campaign trail as an intimate documentary observer. The resulting book *The Selling of the President, 1968*, was a sensation, a shocking revelation to many readers. They had not realized the extent to which television had become the merchandiser of candidates.

For example, McGinniss told how Nixon's media technicians meticulously organized local television question-and-answer programs at various places around the country. Seemingly spontaneous, they were in fact as carefully calculated as any commercial, with both questions and questioners selected in advance. Up to that time conventional wisdom had said that television's cold, unblinking eye could expose the true nature of a candidate who was trying to fool the public. McGinniss showed this ability to be a myth. With a candidate's own staff controlling the planning, scripting, makeup, and production, television could present a totally misleading picture. McGinniss concluded:

With the coming of television, and the knowledge of how it could be used to seduce voters, the old political values disappeared. Something new, murky, and undefined started to rise from the mists. . . . Style becomes substance. The medium is the massage and the masseur gets the votes. (McGinniss, 1969: 28)

Party presidential nominating conventions have been completely restaged for the sake of making them more effective as television shows. In 1968, the Democratic convention, occurring at the height of the resistance to the Vietnam war, erupted into riots between demonstrators and the Chicago police. Violence spread to the convention floor itself, where it was witnessed on television by the entire nation. Television journalist Sander Vanocur wrote later that the American public "had never seen on their television screens so much sustained dissent in so compressed a period of time, and it came, at least within the convention hall, not from longhairs, not from hippies shouting obscenities, but from outraged members of the middle class" (1972: 146). Some accused television of inciting the violence, but the FCC exonerated the news teams after an investigation (§19.3). Thereafter, the producers of the nominating conventions saw to it that they were as meticulously staged as any beauty pageant.

Aside from the conventions, the television high points of presidential campaigns became the debates between the leading candidates, carried on all networks (Exhibit 19.6). This tradition began with the confrontation between candidates Kennedy and Nixon in 1960, courtesy of a special act of Congress exempting their appearances from the consequences of Section 315 equal-time requirements (§16.5). Often called "Great Debates" (though critics have questioned whether they qualify either as great or as debates), these television bouts have been exhaustively researched. Their effects nevertheless remain uncertain, though it is generally thought that Kennedy benefited more than Nixon from the original debates of 1960 (Rubin, 1967). Political strategists think that if a debate results in a tie it benefits the challenger more than the incumbent. This seems to have been the case in the 1980 debate between President Carter and Candidate Reagan, which was followed by the rare outcome of the incumbent losing the election.

Given the undoubted power of television to influence the outcome of campaigns, it might seem a foregone conclusion that candidates with the most money to buy the most time and the best media consultants would inevitably win elections. Again, however, something elusive in the political process intercedes to prevent such cut-and-dried certainty. Ford lost to Carter in 1976 despite what was described as the costliest campaign in history. In 1980 Governor John Connally's expenditure of some $2 million on media advertising to win the Republican nomination netted him one single delegate at the convention.

Many other such examples could be cited. In the political realm, broadcasting is powerful, but not necessarily all-powerful. One reason may be that broadcasting combines two different sets of forces, those of advertising/public relations and those of news/public affairs. Bona fide news about candidates has credibility that can never be

Exhibit 19.6
The Great Debates, 1960 and 1980

Above, Kennedy debates Nixon in one of the series of four confrontations in 1960.
Howard K. Smith was the moderator (seated, center); a panel of news
correspondents representing the networks (including Mutual) asked questions.
Below, Carter debates Reagan in 1980. The format has changed, but not as much
as one might expect in 20 years.

Sources: CBS News photo; World Wide Photos, Inc.

attained by 30-second advertising spots. Candidates sometimes complain that their best chances of getting in the news come from their bloopers and their boners rather than from their platforms and their policies. If this is true, perhaps it is because the public welcomes evidence of human frailty after being bombarded with paid spots and speeches depicting candidates as inhumanly perfect.

Presidential Television After the campaign is over, an incumbent American president enjoys almost insurmountable advantages over political opponents in exploiting the media. The fairness doctrine seems powerless to give other branches of government or members of opposing parties sufficient access to counterbalance the influences of *presidential television* (§17.8).

Presidents have endless opportunities for manufacturing pseudoevents to support their policies or to divert attention from their failures. No matter how clearly news editors sense that the president is exploiting them, they dare not ignore the head of state, for virtually anything a president says or does has inherent news value.

One familiar presidential tactic is to make a foreign trip to visit other heads of state. President Kennedy is said to have been the first to capitalize on this ploy: "the farther he was from Washington, the less he was seen as a partisan political figure and the more he was viewed as being President of all the people" (Halberstam, 1979: 316). Nixon's frantic foreign tours at a time when investigations of his conduct at home were threatening to drive him from office were regarded with the utmost cynicism by news executives, but they felt obliged to spend millions of dollars to cover these pseudoevents as though they were real news — which of course in a way they were (Minow, 1973: 67).

The single most powerful media weapon of an incumbent chief executive is the option of calling upon all the networks to provide simultaneous national coverage of a presidential address to the nation. Such an event gives a president a gigantic captive audience, a virtual monopoly of access to 90 percent of the potential audience. Moreover, opinion surveys indicate that such heavy exposure usually pays off in terms of increased acceptance of presidential policies (Rutkus, 1976: 18).

Nothing in the law requires the networks to defer to presidential requests for time, and indeed it was not customary until President Johnson's tenure. In the 1966–1975 period, presidents experienced only one refusal in 45 requests for simultaneous television time. Shortly before Nixon's resignation in 1974 the networks turned down some requests for speeches by presidential aides, not the president himself. Thereafter, however, network news divisions began to evaluate such requests more critically. Only ABC carried a 1975 address by President Ford on the economy. Refusal by both CBS and NBC meant that Ford reached only 11 million viewers instead of the 55 million that the combined networks would have reached (a routine presidential speech loses out in competition with mass entertainment if the audience is given a choice). In 1978 CBS turned down live coverage of an address by President Carter on the Panama Canal treaties, which were then awaiting Senate approval.

Such a decision is difficult for a network to make, not only because of the newsworthiness of any presidential appearance, but also because it opens broadcasters to the accusation that they are more interested in making money than in performing a public service. For these reasons, presidents continue to enjoy the unique advantage of simultaneous network coverage almost every time they make a request.

Congressional Television   The failure of Congress to take advantage of television has been explained by David Halberstam in terms of personalities and the generation gap. In the years when television was on the rise, Congress was dominated by old men such as House Speaker Sam Rayburn, "the last towering figure of the House of Representatives." Rayburn had no love for the press. When handed a petition from journalists asking that radio and television be allowed more freedom in covering the House, Rayburn simply uttered an obscenity and tore up the paper.

The decision was to have a profound impact, making the House less able to compete with the executive branch, and diminishing its importance in the eyes of the public. . . . Characteristically, the only time the Congress of the United States appeared on television during this era was when the President of the United States came to the House to deliver his State of the Union speech. Then the congressmen could be seen dutifully applauding, their roles in effect written in by the President's speech writers. (Halberstam, 1979: 250)

The Senate, less adamant than the House, began allowing broadcast coverage of its committee hearings, subject to approval of committee chairpersons, in the early 1950s. The first coverage of a House committee hearing did not come until 1974, when the Judiciary Committee debated the Nixon impeachment resolution.

Some of the most interesting and socially useful public affairs programs have originated from congressional committee hearing rooms. Early examples were the hearings on organized crime in 1951 (chaired by Senator Estes Kefauver, who became a 1952 presiden-

tial candidate on the strength of the television publicity) and the Army-McCarthy hearings in 1954 (§8.8).

Not until 1966, however, did the Congress begin to use its access to television to seriously challenge the president's advantage. In that year, Senator William Fulbright, the prestigious chairman of the Foreign Relations Committee, was bold enough to publicly question White House policy on the Vietnam war in televised hearings before his committee.

Television in the beginning had trivialized both the debate and the forces involved in Vietnam. It had confirmed the legitimacy of the President, made his case seem stronger than it was, and made the opposition appear to be outcasts, frustrated, angry, and rather beyond the pale. The Fulbright hearings gradually changed this balance. Like the Ervin [impeachment] hearings some seven years later, they were the beginning of a slow but massive educational process, a turning of the tide against the President's will and his awesome propaganda machinery. . . . From that time on, dissent was steadily more respectable and centrist. (Halberstam, 1979: 506)

Although the Senate led the House in opening committees to live broadcast coverage, the reverse was true when it came to allowing coverage of actual sessions of Congress. Bills to authorize coverage of House debates had been pending since 1941. Approval finally came in 1979, but the House refused to let outsiders run the show. It set up its own closed-circuit television system, run by House employees, inviting broadcasters to plug into the system at will. Commercial broadcasters, unenthusiastic about coverage they cannot themselves control, use only occasional excerpts of the House debates. Cable subscribers in many communities, however, can see gavel-to-gavel coverage on the C-SPAN cable network. To acquaint viewers with floor procedures and to explain how the television system works, the House published a descriptive pamphlet in 1980.

The effects of television on the conduct of members of Congress on the floor of the House seem to have been slight, disposing of fears that some members would put on a show for the folks back home. The results should encourage the Senate to follow suit. It had already experimented with live radio coverage in 1978, the year before the House system went into operation. National Public Radio carried the entire 300 hours of Senate debate on the Panama Canal treaties. The experiment proved a success (though it was somewhat embarrassing that the Panamanians also received the broadcasts, enabling them to hear themselves roundly condemned by some of the conservative senators as communist-dominated incompetents incapable of running the Panama Canal on their own). It seems inevitable that the day must come when the Senate joins the House in allowing both radio and television to cover its regular sessions.

Television's First War Radio broadcasting played a highly supportive role in helping to build both civilian and military morale in World War II (§7.6). Television's first experience of war came with Vietnam (the Korean War occurred early in the 1950s when television was still in its formative years). The impact of television on history's first "living room war" as it was called by *New Yorker* critic Michael Arlen, was far from being entirely supportive. Its influence on national morale and on government policy was undoubtedly great. Yet, like the impact of broadcasting on party politics, its ultimate dimensions have yet to be clearly defined.

David Halberstam, who won a Pulitzer prize for his work as a war correspondent in Vietnam, supports the thesis that television had a decisive impact on the course of the war.

The camera caught the special quality of this war, magnified the impropriety and brutality of it, emphasized how awesome the American firepower was and that it was being used against civilians. . . . The camera also magnified the length of the war; the beginning of the combat escalation came with the bombing in February 1965, and the Tet offensive, which sealed the doom of the American mission, came three years later, and three years was, in the television age, an infinitely longer time than it used to be. The war played in American homes and it played too long. (Halberstam, 1979: 507)

In total, this longest war in U.S. history played out its tragic course in American living rooms for fifteen years. CBS sent its first combat news team to Vietnam in 1961. News photography of the final evacuation of Saigon, showing desperate pro-American Vietnamese being beaten back as helicopters lifted off the landing pad atop the U.S. embassy building in Saigon, came in 1975. During the height of the war, each network maintained its own news bureau in the field, each sending back two or three photographic stories and eight or ten radio tapes daily. In addition, many individual stations assigned their own reporters to the scene. Altogether, broadcasters spent an estimated $50 million on war coverage, which also cost the lives of 15 news personnel (Zeidenberg, 1975).

During the earlier years, coverage tended to be "sanitized," stressing U.S. military efficiency and might, playing down the gore and suffering of actual combat. No military censorship had been imposed (as it had in all previous wars), but public relations was uppermost in the minds of the generals, who went to great lengths to obtain the kind of optimistic coverage expected by the administration back home.

A new, more violent phase of news coverage came as a result of the 1968 Tet offensive. This was a widespread series of coordinated assaults by the North Vietnamese, extending into the very heart of the southern capital, Saigon. Even the American embassy came under attack. Officially, the U.S. command interpreted Tet as a costly failure for the North Vietnamese. Psychologically, however, it gave the North a tremendous victory. It turned the broadcast news coverage toward the realities of the war, bringing the fighting to the very doors of the Saigon hotels where correspondents were staying. At that point it began to become a real war in American living rooms, not the sanitized war of military public relations. Analyzing the contradictory images of the war projected by television, Edward Epstein wrote in *TV Guide*:

It is no doubt true that television was to a large extent responsible for the disillusionment with the war, as those in the media take relish in pointing out. But it is also true that television must take responsibility for creating — or at least, reinforcing — the illusion of American military omnipotence on which much of the early support of the war was based. (Epstein, 13 Oct. 1973: 54)

During the Tet offensive, several specific television happenings served to polarize U.S. public opinion against the war: Walter Cronkite reported on the war personally after a visit to Vietnam, and two especially vivid photographic images from the battlefields became icons of American disillusionment.

On his return from Vietnam, Cronkite took the unprecedented step of devoting a half-hour news special to a personally written analysis. Up to this point he had essentially reflected the administration's official optimism about the ultimate outcome. In the special broadcast, however, he spoke of a new conviction: the time had come for American withdrawal from the Vietnam morass. As Halberstam put it:

It was the first time in American history a war had been declared over by an anchorman. In Washington [President] Lyndon Johnson watched and told his press secretary . . . if he had lost Walter Cronkite he had lost Mr. Average Citizen. It solidified his decision not to run again. (Halberstam, 1979: 514)

Correspondent Morley Safer was responsible for one of the two memorable photographic reports, a film showing an American marine holding a Zippo lighter to the straw eaves of a Vietnamese hut, starting a fire that leveled 150 homes in the village of Cam Ne. The Cam Ne Zippo scene came as a "total reversal of the American myth . . . a moment that touched the soul," wrote Halberstam (quoted in Zeidenberg, 1975: 29). The second image was that of a South Vietnamese general calmly shooting a suspected Viet Cong sympathizer in the head.

Broadcasting's role in the Vietnam experience left troublesome questions about what might happen should the United States again become involved in warfare overseas. Could the Defense Department afford to let television bring the horror of unsanitized warfare into American living rooms night after night? Alternatively, if the military imposed tight censorship on television coverage, would the country continue blindly supporting a war it was prevented from seeing with its own eyes?

James Michener, applying his novelist's imagination to these questions, speculated on what might have happened in the 1860s if television had been able to bring the reality of the Civil War into living rooms of the North:

Abraham Lincoln would not have been able to prosecute the Civil War to a successful conclusion had television been flooding the contemporary scene with daily pictures of the northern Copper-heads who opposed the war, of the draft riots that rocketed through northern cities, and especially of the stark horror of Vicksburg. Sometime late in 1862 he would have been forced to capitulate, with the probability that slavery would have continued in the southern states till the early years of this century. (1970: 71)

19.7 Gratification Effects

We have talked so far in this chapter about what broadcasting does *to* people — how it informs or misinforms, guides or misguides, helps or hinders them in achieving their individual and social goals. In this final section on effects we change the perspective to look at broadcasting from the point of view of what it does *for* people in subjective terms. These personal satisfactions that people derive from the media are referred to in the research literature as *gratification effects*. Media critics often refer to such gratifications in terms of *escapism* or *passivity*, regarding them as undesirable effects brought about, or at least encouraged, by heavy media consumption.

Significance of Time Spent   One cannot help feeling that any activity that *takes up* as much time as radio and television must have profound effects. At the very least, time spent on broadcasting could have been spent in some other way — perhaps on some useful, constructive activity. Some critics take it for granted that *anything* active would be more beneficial than passive absorption in broadcasting. This criticism seems to imply a moral judgment, the unstated feeling that it is wrong for people to waste their time staring like zombies at the television tube. Long ago one of the pioneers of social research on broadcasting, Paul Lazarsfeld,

noted this tone of moral criticism. He pointed out that intellectuals who had fought for shorter hours and other labor reforms unconsciously resented the fact that the masses failed to take constructive advantage of their hard-won leisure. Instead they wasted it in passive enjoyment of broadcasting (Lazarsfeld & Kendall, 1948: 85). But it has not been demonstrated that listening and watching necessarily displace more useful and active forms of recreation. In the absence of broadcasting, people would do other things with their time, of course, but not necessarily better or more beneficial things.

In any event, all those hours of passive listening and watching may be far less significant than they seem. Subjectively, time is relative, dragging on interminably in some circumstances, passing all too quickly in others. Each clock-hour has exactly the same value; not so each hour of human experience. It follows that the huge amount of time that audiences devote to broadcasting may have far less psychological significance than the sheer number of hours suggests.

Play Theory   Nor can we assume that time spent passively listening and watching has value only if devoted to programs that uplift, educate, and inform. People also have a need simply to pass time as painlessly as possible. That, after all, is what *pastimes* are for, and tuning in to radio and television is the most universal pastime.

Scholars of broadcasting effects usually study them from the point of view of serious, socially significant consequences, such as those discussed earlier in this chapter. They want to know how broadcasting affects buying, wanting, voting, stereotyping, learning, aggression, and so on. A notable exception to this rule is William Stephenson, author of *The Play Theory of Communication* (1967). His thesis is that "at best mass communication allows people to become absorbed in *subjective play.*" Playing is not merely a substitute for some valuable activity, but a valuable activity in itself. It is vital to all human life — "thousands of customs, devices, and occasions are employed to gratify playing in every culture of the world, in all history."

Unfortunately, Stephenson linked this theory to a somewhat idiosyncratic research method that failed of widespread adoption. For that reason, his play concept has not received the attention it deserves. A leading commentator on communication studies said that "if Stephenson's book had been easier to read, and if he, like McLuhan, had been a coiner of phrases, the commercial entertainment media might have chosen to lionize him rather than McLuhan. . . . After once exposing oneself to this brilliantly conceived theory, one can never again ignore the importance of the play-pleasure elements in communication" (Schramm, 1973: 26).

"Glow and Flow" Principle

The play theory helps to explain the widely acknowledged fact that programming seems of secondary importance as long as something fills the screen: "it is the television set and the watching experience that entertains. Viewers seem to be entertained by *the glow and the flow*" (Meyersohn, 1957: 347, emphasis added).

In one of the landmark analyses of audience attitudes, Steiner found that most of the people surveyed said they were more satisfied with *television* (the medium) than they were with television *programs* (the message). Respondents betrayed similar ambivalence when reacting to projective tests designed to probe their subjective feelings about the amount of time they spent watching television. "A large number of respondents . . .

were ready to say television is both relaxing *and* a waste of time" (Steiner, 1963: 411). A similar study of attitudes made a decade later indicated that this ambivalence persisted (Bower, 1973).

The glow and flow principle comes sharply to the fore in situations where broadcasting becomes the only companion people have. When Steiner asked respondents to describe the satisfactions they derived from watching television, he sometimes received moving testimonials such as this:

I'm an old man and all alone, and the TV brings people and music and talk into my life. Maybe without TV I would be ready to die; but this TV gives me life. It gives me what to look forward to — that tomorrow, if I live, I'll watch this and that program. (Steiner, 1963: 26)

At extreme levels of deprivation, in hospitals and similar institutions, television has a recognized therapeutic function as the most valuable nonchemical sedative available. A psychiatrist described its role as

"The following is not a program. It's just TV."
Drawing by Christianson, © 1978 *The New Yorker* Magazine Inc.

centering around the wish for someone to care, to nurse, to give comfort and solace. . . . These infantile longings [in adults] can be satisfied only symbolically, and how readily the television set fills in. Warmth, sound, constancy, availability, a steady giving without ever a demand for return, the encouragement to complete passive surrender and envelopment — all this and active fantasy besides. Watching these adults, one is deeply impressed by their acting out with the television set of their unconscious longings to be infants in mother's lap. (Glynn, 1968: 77)

However, we need not rely on the inmates of hospitals and retirement homes for evidence of the glow and flow principle at work. Broadcasting answers a compelling need of the mass audience simply to kill time painlessly, to fill an otherwise unendurable void. Boredom is neither an exceptional nor an inconsequential state of mind in modern culture. It is a by-product of the economic and social changes that have freed mankind from the bondage of the personal struggle for the bare necessities of life. What to do with surplus time has become a major preoccupation of our culture.

Lewis Mumford, a social philosopher especially concerned with the impact of technology on the quality of human life, expressed the dilemma succinctly:

The emancipated masses now confront precisely the same problem that every privileged minority sooner or later has been forced to face: how to make use of its surplus of goods and its free time without being surfeited by one and corrupted by the other. With the enlargement of the benefits of mass production has come an enlargement of the unexpected penalties: of which perhaps the most deadly is boredom. What Thorsten Veblen ironically called "the performance of leisure" is fast becoming the tedious obligatory substitute for the performance of work. (Mumford, 1970: 326)

Broadcasting gives people a way of *performing leisure*. Those who assail broadcasting for not being more constructive should ponder alternative ways of performing leisure, such as drug abuse and vandalism.

Summary

The fact that broadcasting has practical effects justifies serious study of the medium. Effects are so diverse and pervasive that practically everyone has strong opinions about them and an interest in exerting some form of control over them. Categories of broadcasting effects singled out for comment, in outline form, are as follows:

1. As a medium, on other media: symbiotic relationships between broadcasting and other media and the fine arts.
2. As an advertising medium, on consumers: synthesized wants versus consumer sovereignty.
3. As a source of news, on perceptions of reality: gatekeeping, agenda setting, staging of pseudoevents, influence on news subjects.
4. As a source of entertainment, on perceptions of reality: agenda setting, stereotyping, socialization.
5. As a source of violent images, on aggressive behavior and perceptions of reality: imitation, anxiety, sanitization, catharsis.
6. As a molder of public opinion, on political life: crisis management, election campaigns, power struggle between branches of government, mobilization of public support in wartime.
7. As a medium, on the need for play: primacy of medium over message, relief of boredom.

CHAPTER 20

Research on Effects

20.1 Uses of Research

As the preceding chapter shows, there is no dearth of opinions about the effects of broadcasting. But public policy decisions about regulation of the medium need to be based on more than hunches. Research is needed to test assumptions and to verify conclusions about effects. This chapter concerns the evolution, methods, and present status of such research.

Policy Decisions When Congress wrote the Radio Act of 1927 and the Federal Radio Commission first began writing rules to put the act into effect, neither the legislature nor the commission had the benefit of social and economic research on mass media effects. Necessarily they relied primarily on legal-historical considerations and sheer guesswork. Today, however, any major regulatory decision involving policy questions is certain to be supported by research on its goals, assumptions, and probable outcome.

Among the many examples of research on matters of policy cited in previous chapters, the following may be recalled as typical:

■ In defending its hands-off policy with regard to radio station format changes, the FCC used a study of the formats available in major markets as evidence that competition alone would ensure sufficient variety in formats (§18.4).

■ Congressional concern about the possible adverse effects of violence in programming led to the allocation of a million dollars to the Surgeon General for research studies (§19.6).

■ To justify its radio deregulation proposals the FCC relied on economic theory about the effects of competition, supported by research on current practices of radio stations (§16.10).

As these examples suggest, the emphasis in FCC policy studies has been on *economic* research. Only the Surgeon General's study, the most ambitious of the group, was aimed at the kind of research we are concerned with here, studies of *behavioral effects*.

During the 1970s the FCC came increasingly under the dominance of economic theorists in making policy decisions about the future of broadcasting. This trend was set in motion by the economic challenge, first of cable, then of other new technologies, especially satellites. The FCC's initial reaction was to adopt restrictive rules to protect the financial stability of broadcast television. These rules brought strong attack from many quarters; the commission was severely criticized for holding back the wheels of progress and for pampering the highly profitable broadcast industry. Research on the economics of broadcasting and cable television, along with predictions of their future interrelationships, became a growth industry. Foundations began funding such research, and economists at major universities and research centers undertook numerous projects.

The FCC came to rely increasingly on economic theory and research to make the case for its regulatory policies. Examples are its rationale for deregulation (§16.10) and for refusing to take action on consumer complaints about program format changes (§18.4).

Privately Sponsored Research When Congress holds hearings on proposed new legislation or the FCC convenes to consider proposed new rules, private interests are invited to present their views. Representatives of the broadcasting industry usually buttress their arguments with surveys of prior research on the topic, frequently adding especially commissioned research of their own.

Consumer organizations, too, have learned that good intentions and moral fervor are not enough to ensure serious attention from government and industry. Their claims need to be supported by the kind of hard evidence that research alone can supply. Indeed, research on the effects of broadcasting has been explicitly singled out by the consumer groups as a major concern of their movement for the future (§18.5).

Following are typical examples of research undertaken by private sponsors:

■ Critics of broadcast news have used content analysis research to support their allegations of news bias (§17.5).
■ When educational broadcasters were battling to convince the FCC that some of the about-to-be allocated television channels should be reserved exclusively for noncommercial use, their most convincing argument was a content analysis of commercial programming, demonstrating the lack of educational and cultural material on the commercial stations.
■ Action for Children's Television used research data to support its petition for rule making on advertising in children's programming (§9.8).

20.2 Development of Behavioral Research Concepts

Mass Media Because scientific theories are designed to embrace as wide a field as possible, broadcasting as a subject of research exists in the more general context of mass media research.

The term *mass media* is used to refer to the methods of communicating that enable delivering identical messages approximately simultaneously and at low unit cost to relatively large numbers of undifferentiated people, using high-speed means of reproduction and distribution. Mass media audiences are not merely large audiences; they are also highly variegated (heterogeneous) audiences whose members need have little in common beyond receiving the same messages at about the same time. Broadcasting carries this characteristic of heterogeneity to an extreme, attracting the most varied audiences of all the media.

Mass media have unique properties, not only because of the unique characteristics of their audiences, but also because of the special nature of their own physical and organizational make-up. Thus mass media communication can be distinguished as a special field of communication research. Nevertheless, in the final analysis all audiences are composed of individuals. The study of mass media communication therefore inevitably also involves the study of personal communication, both in terms of the individual (intrapersonal communication) and the individual in relation to others (interpersonal communication). As Wilbur Schramm put it, "There is no meaning in a message except what people put into it. When we study communication, therefore, we study people. . . . To understand human communication we must understand how people relate to one another" (1973: 3).*

There can be few concepts more all-embracing than that of communication when viewed in its broadest sense. Every art, every science, indeed life itself, depends on communication. Scholars from over a score of academic fields contribute to communication research, in addition to those from the field specifically designated as mass media communication. Notable among the contributory fields are anthropology, political science, psychology, social psychology, and sociology. Surveys of research literature have shown that even the definition of "communication" is debated. Over 25 definitions have been formulated, over 50 descriptions of the communication process, and more than 15 graphic models purporting to depict the process (Sereno and Mortensen, 1970: 1).

In sum, mass media research is far from being a neatly packaged discipline with universally accepted theories embracing a well-defined range of phenomena. The following reviews some of the chief concepts and theories, with emphasis on studies that have specific reference to broadcasting.

---

*Wilbur Schramm, one of the elder statesmen of mass media research, has been especially successful in explaining communication theory and research concepts in terms the layman can understand. His introduction to the field, *Men, Messages, and Media: A Look at Human Communication* (1973), is frequently cited in this chapter because of its concise common sense.

Bullet Theory   Mass propaganda was widely used for the first time in the 1914–1918 world war. That war preceded the broadcast era, but nevertheless written and pictorial propaganda succeeded in whipping up mass hysteria on both sides. After the war the extent of deception by propagandists became known. People were shocked to find out how unscrupulously they had been manipulated. It seemed as if a sinister new weapon had been found, capable of almost any excess. The advent in the 1920s of a new propaganda medium, radio broadcasting, as well as the emergence of a potential new political threat, the recently installed communist regime in Russia, made the prospect of propaganda manipulation all the more alarming. This heightened concern with the effects of mass persuasion stimulated funding for research focused on analyzing the social and psychological dynamics of propaganda.

The concept of media effects that developed in the 1920s visualized propaganda messages as so many pellets of information (or misinformation) aimed at passive multitudes. It was hypothesized that the messages would penetrate individuals, causing specific reactions. Accordingly, the concept later became known, somewhat derisively, as the *bullet* or *hypodermic injection* theory of communication effects.

Intervening Variables   By the end of the 1930s and the approach of World War II, researchers had come to realize that the bullet theory of propaganda effects had erred in concentrating entirely on messages and their senders, treating the receivers of messages as mere passive targets. They found that, far from passively absorbing injections of propaganda, audience members *act upon messages as individuals*. The effects of messages therefore depend on a great many variables within and among the individual members of audiences.

These factors, many of which are subjective and therefore not directly observable, were labeled *intervening variables*. They intervene between messages and effects, varying effects according to each individual's previously acquired attitudes, traits, experiences, social situation, and so on. Intervening variables explain why it is possible for an identical message to have different effects on different people.

During the 1940s World War II stimulated renewed interest in propaganda studies. A team of researchers at Yale University received a government grant for a major research effort called the Program on Communication and Attitude Change. The Yale team conducted a wide-ranging series of studies, later summarized in four volumes under the general title *The American Soldier* (Hovland et al., 1949). The immediate task of the researchers was to study the effects of so-called orientation films the Army was using to indoctrinate new recruits. Research was focused on measuring *attitude change*, a type of effect that lent itself readily to laboratory tests. A great variety of personal variables that might be expected to influence the outcome of persuasive communications was studied by the Yale researchers. They asked such questions as: What is the most effective message source for persuasive messages? What order of presentation of an argument works best? Is it better to ignore counterarguments in a campaign of persuasion, or to try to refute them? What difference do people's group affiliations make as to their persuadability? To what extent do group decisions affect the independence of individual decision making?

The Yale studies ushered in a new phase of effects research. According to Schramm's estimate, they laid the groundwork for "a new scientific rhetoric, in which there was an attempt to set forth principles of communication effects in scientific terms backed by scientific evidence" (1973: 221).

Two-Step Flow   One of the most influential discoveries concerning intervening variables called attention to the personal influence of *opinion leaders*, as contrasted with the impersonality of the media. The flow of influence from the mass media, it was found, often passes through leaders to followers rather than affecting all individuals directly.

During the 1940s a team of sociologists at the Columbia University Bureau of Applied Social Research, led by Paul Lazarsfeld, demonstrated the significance of opinion leaders as intervening variables.

Lazarsfeld and his associates developed their theory about personal leadership vis-à-vis media influence from an intensive study of how people in Erie County, Ohio, made up their minds about voting in a national election. Although the media directly influenced the votes of some people, they influenced many more people indirectly. The media acted on most people through intervenors whom the researchers called *opinion leaders* — respected family members or acquaintances whose personal views carry special weight. The researchers called this process the *two-step flow* of influence — step one, from media to opinion leaders; step two, from opinion leaders to others (Lazarsfeld et al., 1944).

A decade later, Lazarsfeld and another associate followed up the Erie study with a more refined and detailed investigation of the two-step flow concept (Katz & Lazarsfeld, 1955). They painstakingly tracked down decisions people had made about movie-going, food buying, dress selection, and public issues, ascertaining whether the media or opinion leaders had been more influential.

Again, for most people personal influence was more instrumental in each type of decision than the influence of radio, newspapers, magazines, and books. Other experiments and field investigations confirmed and refined the hypotheses developed in these well-known studies.

The two-step flow theory had great impact on mass media research in the ensuing 20 years. As one scholar put it, the Lazarsfeld concept "turned the mainstream of media effects thinking away from man as an atom to man as a member of many groups, each providing a context and sometimes a screening mechanism for receiving messages" (Kline, 1972: 22).

Selective Exposure Lazarsfeld and his associates found that the media did not influence even opinion leaders in direct proportion to the amount of persuasive content in the media. Media consumers, it appeared, tend to be *selective* in taking in what they can see and hear in the media. They pay attention to communications that fit their established opinions and attitudes but avoid communications that challenge or contradict their established mind-set. Because of this factor of *selective exposure*, media tend to reinforce people's existing views, failing to convert them to new viewpoints.

Selective Perception A related phenomenon is the effect of existing mind-sets on how people perceive the communications they do select for attention. Several people who select the same communication may interpret it in several different ways. Though the stimulus remains constant, the response varies. This variable, called *selective perception*, is explained by the fact that people react to messages rather than receiving them passively (as the old bullet theory had supposed).

A typical finding of selective perception

research is the *boomerang effect*. Experiments showed that highly prejudiced people tend to misinterpret messages containing evidence against their prejudices. They distort the evidence or sift out those elements that reinforce their existing attitude, rather than allowing the message to reduce their hostile feelings. Thus propaganda can boomerang, producing exactly the opposite of the intended effect (Cooper & Jahoda, 1947). A classic recent example of the boomerang effect is a reaction to the character of Archie Bunker in *All in the Family*. Many viewers misread the antibigotry message of Archie's character, seeing in it an endorsement of the very prejudices that Norman Lear intended to satirize.

Even in the absence of prejudice, people under emotional stress may have difficulty in accepting evidence that contradicts an existing mind-set. Striking examples of this kind of selective perception occurred during the panic caused by the famous Orson Welles Halloween broadcast of an imaginary invasion from Mars. The radio dramatization of an H. G. Wells science-fiction story, *The War of the Worlds*, simulated news reports to create a realistic atmosphere that fooled a number of listeners, despite explicit warnings in the introduction to the drama. A sociological study of the panic revealed how some of the listeners tried to check on the authenticity of the broadcast. When presented with evidence that it was fiction, however, they turned the facts around to support their conviction that the invasion was real:

"I looked out of the window and everything looked the same as usual so I thought it hadn't reached our section yet."

"We looked out of the window and Wyoming Avenue was black with cars. People were rushing away, I figured."

"My husband tried to calm me and said, 'If this were really so, it would be on all stations' and he turned to one of the other stations and there was music. I retorted 'Nero fiddled while Rome burned.'" (Cantril, 1947: 93)

Congruence Theory Such stubborn refusal to forsake an existing mind-set suggests that people have a kind of internal gyroscope that tends to maintain a consistent set of attitudes, opinions, and perceptions. Psychologists developed several versions of a concept known generally as *congruence theory* to account for this tendency, which acts as an intervening variable in determining the effects of communications.

In brief, congruence theories hold that a person's internal state of mind normally has the property of balance or congruence. A message that contradicts established opinions causes dissonance, lack of congruity, or imbalance. An effort to restore balance (conscious or unconscious) follows. It might take the form of rejecting the message (alleging that the source is "unreliable" for example),

distorting the message to make it fit the existing mind-set (the stations playing music are just fiddling while Rome burns), or adjusting the balance by accepting the new idea and incorporating it into the existing mind-set (conversion to a new point of view).

Information Theory The theories and concepts so far reviewed came out of the social sciences. A fresh way of looking at communication came from the engineering field with the publication of a book called *The Mathematical Theory of Communication* (Shannon and Weaver, 1949). This theory looks at information from the point of view of transmission systems and therefore uses such familiar broadcast engineering terms as channel, channel capacity, noise, encoding, decoding, and information bit. The information theory model of the communication process is probably the one most widely known and most easily understood (Exhibit 20.2).

Information theory has contributed valuable insights and concepts to the study of

Exhibit 20.2
Information theory model of communication process

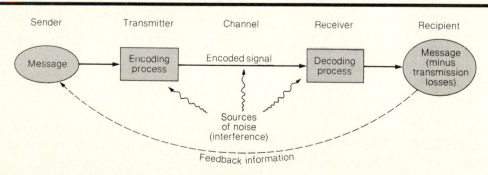

The model can be adapted to describe many modes of communication, from the simplest technology (African talking drums, for example) to the most complex (satellite relays or television broadcasting, for example). It can also be applied to unaided human communication by voice and gesture.

mass communication. For instance, the concept of *feedback* (Wiener, 1950) is one of the most widely used ideas derived from the information theory approach, though it is often misunderstood (§14.1). The usual engineering model for describing feedback is the thermostatic control on a heating or cooling system. As the system delivers air to a room, a thermostat senses changes in room temperature. When critical temperatures are reached (according to the settings on the thermostat) it sends this information to the machine, instructing it to turn itself off or on, as the case may be. This feedback of information and its reinsertion into the system goes on continuously, maintaining temperature within programmed limits.

Analogous to a temperature control system is what occurs when communicators modify their messages in response to information that comes back from audiences. In face-to-face communications, visual and auditory cues continuously tell speakers about audience reactions. Speakers can respond by adjusting what they say and how they say it from moment to moment — heating up or cooling down their rhetoric, so to speak. Lacking this sensitive and immediate give-and-take, mass media operate at a disadvantage. It takes time to obtain feedback and to modify the media product accordingly. The fact that programming is usually frozen on tape or film makes subsequent modification slow and difficult. Yet even recorded material can be modified by editing, explanatory introduction, or cancellation.

20.3 Communication Process

Foci of Research Communication involves a chain of events and so can best be regarded as a *process*, as suggested by the model in Exhibit 20.2. The process is initi-ated by a communicator and culminates in effects as an end result — if indeed definable effects occur. Study of the process can be directed to any one, or any combination of, five different foci in the process: (1) *originators* of messages, (2) *contents* of messages, (3) *channels* through which messages are sent, (4) *audiences* that receive messages, and (5) the *effects* of messages. These five foci were conveniently summarized by a pioneer of communications research, Harold Lasswell, who said that the objects of research could be identified by posing the question:

Who says *what* in which *channel* to *whom* with what *effect?* *

Message Originators We study the ''who'' of communication to find out about the sources of media content. In broadcasting, the sponsor identification law (§13.3) mandates identification of the sources of paid material; otherwise broadcasters have no obligation to reveal the identity of originators (though talent contracts require listing of credits). Message origination in broadcasting is in fact usually a group activity, with many different forces influencing the final shape of the output.

Shapers of content are identified in communication research as *gatekeepers.* The term originated in social psychology but was popularized as a mass communication concept by a study of the role newswire editors play in controlling the flow of syndicated news copy (White, 1950). Some scholars prefer the

---

*Adapted from Smith, Lasswell, & Casey, 1946: 121. It should be understood that this single-sentence paradigm is an intentionally simplified description of the communication process. A later commentator, for example, proposed that a more complete statement would ask the three additional questions: *why?* (policy studies), *how?* (studies of communication techniques), and *who talks back?* (studies of feedback process).

less picturesque but more inclusive term *information control*. Government regulation, industry codes, and network clearance represent types of gatekeeping, as do the selection, placement, and editing of broadcast material.

Gatekeeping studies seek to answer questions about how the controls operate, where the gates in the flow of information occur, and what effects they have on the content by the time it finally reaches its destination. Not only individuals but also institutions play a gatekeeping role in the mass media. The media themselves, as social organizations,

serve as senders and receivers of messages, but they are distinguished from other organizations in that they more often serve as selective relay stations for messages originated elsewhere. One of the principal tasks of mass communication research is to explain why some messages are relayed and others are not; why some information is modified in the relay process, and how this occurs. (Davison & Yu, 1974: 6)

This statement aptly describes the problem posed by the allegation of news bias on the part of television networks. Does "a handful" of biased editors and commentators personally control network television news, as alleged in a famous speech by former vice president Spiro Agnew?* Edward Epstein studied the network news divisions intensively as gatekeeping institutions, concluding that there was no merit in Agnew's allegation. Although key "visible" news staff members doubtless exercise considerable influence, they in turn are constrained by the

traditions of their craft and by institutional gatekeeping forces beyond their control. Such background influences include the economic organization of the networks, the nature of the newsgathering machinery, the technology and budgets available, the role imposed by the network-affiliate relationship, and many other factors not directly controllable by any individual (Epstein, 1973b).

Other areas in which gatekeeping research assists in policy decisions include the effect of cross-media and group ownership on programming decisions; the influence of advertisers on program content; the roles of professional criticism and of industry self-regulation; and the impact of government regulation on programs.

Content The classification of programming into various categories as required by FCC television logging procedures (§16.4) is a simple form of content analysis. The FCC also refers to content analysis data when it asks about the percentages of television news/public affairs and local programming.

Content analysis on a more sophisticated level is a formal research technique for categorizing, enumerating and interpreting items of message content. Broadcasting scholars have used content analysis to study announcers' continuity, censors' comments, cross-national program comparisons, criticism, cross-media news coverage comparisons, television specials, specific types of news content, violent acts in programs, and the portrayal of minorities in television dramas, as examples.

Channel or Medium In the chapters on the physical nature of radio we repeatedly emphasized that the information capacity of channels varies. Thus from a purely physical point of view, channels affect messages.

---

*Agnew said this in a speech attacking the networks for the practice of "instant analysis," the dissecting of presidential speeches by commentators immediately after delivery. Learning from the advance release of Agnew's address that they were to be attacked, the networks canceled regular programs to carry it, "providing the greatest political windfall ever enjoyed by a vice-president" (Lippman, 1972: 192).

Channels also differ in psychological impact because audiences form attitudes and expectations regarding each information medium, interpreting what each sends accordingly.

In the 1940s the NAB commissioned the Columbia University Bureau of Applied Social Research to conduct two studies of public attitudes toward radio (Lazarsfeld & Field, 1946; Lazarsfeld & Kendall, 1948). These national surveys served as models for many subsequent *image studies* of the media. They indicated, among other things, that most people held radio in high esteem. When asked to compare the job radio was doing with other institutions and media, respondents said they believed radio was doing a better job than newspapers, local governments, and schools.

The broadcasting industry employed the Roper Organization to carry forward these image studies to television; Roper conducted eleven national opinion polls between 1959 and 1980. Many of the same questions were used each time so that trends could be monitored. For example, the researchers continued to use the question about comparative performance of social institutions that had been devised for the radio studies in the 1940s. An average of 62 percent of the respondents consistently rated television as doing an "excellent or good" job, whereas the other media, schools, and government declined in esteem during the 1959–1980 period.

Another key question in the Roper series of studies dealt with media credibility. Respondents were asked which of several media they would believe in case of conflicting news reports. Since 1961, they consistently chose television over other media by a wide margin. In 1980, 51 percent chose television, 22 percent newspapers, and 8 percent radio as the most credible medium (Roper, 1981).

CBS sponsored a more in-depth type of study of public attitudes in 1960 (Steiner, 1963), parts of which were repeated, again under CBS auspices, a decade later (Bower, 1973). In the later study, television ranked highest among the major media in terms of a number of specific functions it performed, such as entertaining, giving the most complete news coverage, presenting things most intelligently, and being the most educational. However, it also ranked highest in "getting worse all the time." The author concluded that in the period 1960–1970, "while general attitudes favoring television were declining, more people than before were giving television a high rating as a news medium" (Bower, 1973: 14).

Audience   The research most massively concerned with the "whom" factor of Lasswell's paradigm is the commercial audience research discussed in Chapter 14. Ratings give information on media use, also called *media exposure* or *time-spent* data. Breakdowns of audiences into demographic subcategories give further details about the "whom" of broadcast communication. In §14.6 we discussed some of these subgroupings and their significance to advertisers.

Academic research on media exposure uses more detailed personal and social group indicators to study the composition of broadcasting audiences. In particular, the child audience has been extensively analyzed, using such variables as race, intelligence, social class, home environment, and personality types. These analyses are made for the purpose of relating audience characteristics to effects. Researchers ask such questions as: What types of children will be most likely to believe what they see on television? What types will imitate what they see? What types will learn prosocial behavior from television?

Effects   Only because communication has effects, or is believed to have effects, are the preceding four aspects of the communication process singled out for study. We are interested in communicators, content, channels, and audiences precisely because they are factors in determining the ultimate effects of communicating.

Joseph Klapper summarized the status of effects theories as of 1960 in an influential book called *The Effects of Mass Communication.* After studying more than a thousand research reports, Klapper reached the tentative conclusion that ordinarily communication "does not serve as a necessary and sufficient cause of audience effects, but rather functions among and through a nexus of mediating factors and influences." This circumspect scientific language meant, in practical terms, that up to that time research had failed to support popular beliefs in the efficacy of mass communication. The media could persuade people to buy products that they really wanted, but not to buy Edsel cars or Corfam shoes — and certainly not to change their political allegiances or to adopt a new religion.

The broadcasting industry welcomed this conservative conclusion, known as the *law of minimal effects,* because it gave apparent scientific sanction to the industry's rejection of consumer arguments that programs could be blamed for causing antisocial behavior. In fact, CBS was so pleased that it hired Klapper to conduct social research for the network.

During the 1970s opinion began to shift away from the minimal effects concept, largely because of the intensive research that had been conducted on the effects of violence (§19.6). As the authors of the mass media effects article in the 1981 *Annual Review of Psychology* put it, the 1970s "witnessed a revival of the view that the mass media exert powerful influences on the way people perceive, think about, and ultimately act in their world" (Roberts & Bachen, 1981: 308).

This shift in opinion did not mean a return to the primitive hypodermic injection effects model of the 1920s. Contemporary researchers, in fact, tend to avoid talking about effects as such. The very word "effects" implies an oversimplification of what is now understood to be an extremely complex process. Without denying that specific media content might under specific conditions have specific effects on some specific people, researchers prefer to speak in terms of the *association* of certain inputs with certain outputs. They avoid going so far as to imply a simple, straight-line cause-effect relationship. The following conclusion by an authoritative research team expresses the current view on the effects in typically cautious language:

Science cannot tell us conclusively whether television violence contributes to serious crime because its methods are too imperfect. It can empirically test hypotheses whose confirmation or disconfirmation alters the probability that such a proposition is true and verify the consistency of observed fact with such a proposition. Conclusions of a grander sort depend on judgments about the acceptability of various assumptions and the risk of error that is tolerable. Consequently, the argument that there is no conclusive scientific evidence on this and other broad causal relationships is not impressive. The wrong question is being asked. (Comstock et al., 1978: 3)

Exhibit 20.3 summarizes the stages of research development, from the simplistic cause-effect concept of the early studies to the contemporary interest in looking more deeply into the antecedents of effects.

20.4 Methods of Studying Effects

Research Strategy Options   In designing research projects to study media effects, investigators face the frustrating problem that many effects consist of *subjective responses*, invisible to the eye and therefore beyond the reach of direct observation and measuring instruments. Examples of such submerged effects are attention, understanding, learning, liking and disliking, and opinion formation. Some of these effects do produce observable physical cues — for instance, brain waves and other involuntary signals from the interior can be detected — but they usually reveal little about subjective experiences in human terms.

Even when communications effects emerge as overt, observable responses, a subjective link is nevertheless still involved. In tracing the sequence of events from cause to effect, researchers lose the trail when it disappears into the subjective consciousness of the people being studied. What goes on

Exhibit 20.3
Evolution of research on effects of mass media

Stage	Prevailing viewpoint	Empirical basis
1	Mass media have strong effects	Observation of apparent success of propaganda campaigns
		Experiments demonstrating immediate attitude change after exposure to messages
		Evidence of selective perception — persons ignore message contrary to existing predispositions
2	Mass media largely reinforce existing predispositions, and thus outcomes are likely to be the same in their absence	Evidence of personal influence — persons are more influenced by others than the mass media
		Evidence of negligible influence on voting
		No relationship observed between exposure to mass media violence and delinquent behavior among the young
3	Mass media have effects independent of other influences which would not occur in the absence of the particular mass media stimuli under scrutiny	Evidence that selective perception is only partially operative
		Evidence that media influence by setting the context and identifying the persons, events, and issues toward which existing predispositions affect attitudes and behavior
		Evidence that television violence increases aggressiveness among the young
4	Processes behind effects so far studied may be more general, suggesting new areas for research	New research is finding that under some circumstances television may influence behavior and attitudes other than those related to aggressiveness

Source: George Comstock et al., *Television and Human Behavior*. New York: Columbia University Press, 1978, p. 392.

inside the human brain certainly influences the final outcome, but it cannot yet be directly studied by the researcher.

For these reasons, most research on effects relies in whole or in part on people's introspective testimony. It is much easier for researchers simply to ask questions of people about their subjective experiences than to devise ways of observing their reactions, assuming that observable reactions even occur. Self-reporting of subjective effects, however, is not altogether reliable. Those reporting may be unwilling or unable to tell the truth about their inner experiences. Or they may be willing but forgetful, or even unaware of their own subsconscious motivations.

Furthermore, the consumption of broadcasting is usually a private act, occurring in all sorts of situations where the intrusion of an outside observer would be out of the question. Consequently, data gathering, whether based on self-reporting or direct observations, almost always introduces an element of artificiality, referred to in the research literature as *intrusiveness*.

Taking account of these problems in varying ways, four major research strategies have evolved: sample surveys, content analysis, laboratory experiments, and field studies. There are many variations on these four as well as several less frequently used strategies. Some projects employ two or more strategies. The relative frequency with which each major strategy is used in original research is indicated by an analysis of a sample of studies published in major communications journals (Lowry, 1979). *Sample surveys* were used in 55 percent of the studies; *content analysis* in 13 percent; *laboratory experiments* in 10 percent; and *field studies* or *field experiments* in 10 percent.

Each of the four strategies has its own characteristics in terms of the extent of its reliance on subjective data, its intrusion on the spontaneity of respondents, and — most

important for researchers hard pressed to finance their projects — its level of cost. Comparisons are shown in Exhibit 20.4.

Sample Surveys   The research strategy most familiar to the general public is no doubt the sample survey. The results of such surveys are published in summary form in Gallup opinion polls and audience ratings reports, for example. We discussed earlier how such surveys can be used to estimate the characteristics of entire populations through the use of very small, randomly selected samples (§14.5). Another advantage of the survey research strategy as exemplified by ratings services is that the data are gathered in the natural settings in which listening or viewing normally takes place.

The diary and telephone methods of gathering broadcast audience data rely on self-reporting by sample members. Recording meters attached to sets afford observational data, albeit indirectly. As we pointed out in §14.5, the commercial ratings services measure behavioral effects of the most elementary and objective kind — simply set-tuning, without reference to the effects of actual listening or watching that may ensue after the set is turned on. Sample surveys thus reveal an overt effect, namely set-tuning, but tell us nothing about *causes* of tuning. This is a major weakness of the survey strategy generally — the fact that "causal inferences typically are not permitted" (Comstock et al., 1978: 493).

A subcategory of survey research (also sometimes regarded as a subclass of experimental research) is the *judgment task* strategy. It sacrifices the advantages of random sampling and the use of real-life settings for the sake of the opportunity to probe more intensively into the subjective reactions of respondents. Groups of people referred to as *focus groups* are brought together at a place where the investigator can administer longer and more complex lists of questions (or "tasks") than is feasible with such self-administered instruments as the set-use diary. Its higher degree of experimenter control makes the judgment task more intrusive than the sample survey.

Content Analysis Content analysis examines and summarizes the content of bodies of communication materials (programs, commercials, films, books, etc.), describing and quantifying whatever features interest the researcher.

The program output of broadcasting is so bewilderingly massive and varied that the mind boggles at even talking about it without the help of summarizing categories. When we speak of public affairs programming, news programming, local programming, soap operas, situation comedies, and so on we are using content analysis categories as

descriptive shorthand. We also have reasons to be interested in the details of content that reveal what broadcasting is saying or implying about various subjects. Is broadcast news biased? Are members of minorities portrayed in predominantly inferior roles? How much and what kinds of violence occur in entertainment programs? What instruments are used in killings? Who are the victims, who the aggressors? Are such content dimensions as these changing significantly over the course of time? All such questions contain implicit assumptions about effects. We are concerned about these items of content precisely because we believe or at least suspect that their presence in broadcasting has consequences.

It may seem easy to conduct a content analysis — a matter of carefully defining the content items to be enumerated, drawing a representative sample of the body of programs to be analyzed, and then counting the occurrences of the designated items of con-

Exhibit 20.4
Characteristics of main research strategies

Strategy	Typical level of		
	Subjectivity	Intrusiveness	Cost
Sample survey	high	moderate	variable[a]
Content analysis	moderate[b]	nil	moderate
Laboratory experiment	variable	high	low[c]
Field study	low	low	high
Field experiment	low	moderate	high

[a]Costs of a simple local telephone survey can be low, but national telephone surveys employing sophisticated sampling and data gathering procedures (such as the commercial ratings services use) can be very high.
[b]Subjective in that coders make judgments in classifying content items.
[c]Cost can be high if sophisticated testing equipment or elaborate simulations are employed.

tent in the sample. In practice, however, it is by no means easy to agree on how to define the relevant content items and how to draw a representative sample from the endless stream of programs. Even more controversial is the interpretation of results.

The well-known "Violence Profile" developed by George Gerbner and his associates affords a practical example. The profile, it will be recalled, is based upon annual analyses of violent content in samples of network entertainment (§19.5). David Blank, CBS's chief economist, challenged the Gerbner data on several grounds (Blank, 1977). For example, in enumerating acts of violence, Gerbner counts comic violence, accidents, and natural disasters. CBS objected to putting these acts in the same basket with intentional human violence done in a serious context. But comedy can be used to convey serious lessons, replied the Gerbner team, and there are no "natural" disasters in fiction (Gerbner et al., 1977). In any event, you have to add apples and oranges to find out about fruit. CBS came back with the rejoinder that one can add rabbits and elephants to find out about animals, but that does not mean one rabbit equals one elephant. CBS also objected to Gerbner's reliance on only one week's programming as the sample representing an entire television season. Because prime-time schedules have been subject to rapid changes in recent years, CBS thought sampling should continue throughout the season. And so the disagreement went on, touching virtually every aspect of the Gerbner content analysis, with neither side convincing the other.

Another example of profound disagreement over method occurred in response to an analysis by Edith Efron, a conservative journalist, of a network news sample during the Nixon-Humphrey presidential campaign in 1968. In a book titled *The News Twisters* (1971) Efron presented a series of bar-graphs representing the number of words in the

news sample contained in statements for and against the candidates, U.S. policies on Vietnam, black militants, demonstrators, etc. The graphs depict far more words against Nixon and his policies than against his opponents and their policies. This analysis was presented as empirical evidence of liberal bias in network news coverage.

Social scientists questioned Efron's method, pointing out several ways in which it tended to exaggerate the prominence of pro and con statements. For example, Efron excluded from analysis all *neutral* statements in the news, although they made up the majority of news content. More important, she neglected to check on *coder reliability*. This is an elementary precaution normally taken in content analyses to ensure that the people employed in enumerating the content items are not themselves biased in classifying them into the various content categories.

A subsequent, more rigorous analysis of part of the same content employed lines of news reader's copy instead of words as the units of analysis and included neutral as well as pro and con statements. It also used standard procedures for checking on coder reliability. This study indicated that, contrary to Efron's findings, the networks treated the candidates with remarkable evenhandedness (Stevenson et al., 1973).

Of course the Efron study was intended more as a polemical tract than as an example of scientific research. Nevertheless, it serves as a cautionary example of the pitfalls of content analysis strategy, especially when it is used to prove a point rather than to search objectively for truth.*

*President Nixon's aides bought a thousand copies of *The News Twisters,* allegedly in an effort to turn it into a best seller (*Broadcasting,* 16 July 1973).

Laboratory Experiments Regarded as the classic strategy for conducting behavioral research, laboratory experiments enable investigators to control the various experimental factors precisely, excluding extraneous events and influences. Both subjectively reported data and objectively observed data can be derived from such experiments.

For decades the most popular experimental variable used in studying communication effects was *attitude change.* It will be recalled that this was the focus of the watershed Yale studies of the 1940s. In bare outlines, the method works as follows: members of a group of test subjects are tested for their current attitudes on a given subject. The experimenter then exposes them to a persuasive message on that subject. It may be presented in several different forms, for example as a face-to-face talk, a radio talk, and a filmed talk. After the test subjects have been exposed to the message, a second test finds out whether any change of attitude has occurred. In research terms, the message serves as an *independent variable* — the element the experimenter can manipulate to stimulate responses. Attitude change, as measured by questionnaires or other instruments, serves as the *dependent variable* — the response whose variations can be regarded as an effect of communication.

One trouble with this neat design is that attitudes measured in the laboratory do not always govern real-life actions. People often *say* one thing but *do* another. This discrepancy has often been noted in differences between expressed television program preferences and actual television viewing. Moreover, laboratory experiments put people in artificial situations that bear little resemblance to the complex real-life situations in which people receive messages from mass media.

Laboratory experiments involving observations of *overt* behavior came into wide use with the development of research on television's effects on children. An experiment famous in the annals of violence research was conducted by Albert Bandura at Stanford University. It furnished convincing evidence that young children are prone to imitate violence seen on the screen, even after only one impression (Bandura et al., 1963). Such imitation is referred to as a *modeling effect.*

In brief, Bandura and his associates showed to three groups of preschool children some enacted scenes in which an actor fiercely attacked a "Bobo the Clown" plastic doll. One group saw the scene live, another on film, a third in cartoon form. A fourth group saw no version of the attack.* All four groups were later turned loose to play in a room containing a variety of toys, including a Bobo doll like the one the actor had abused. The fourth group, which had not seen the staged attacks, took no special notice of the Bobo doll, but members of the three experimental groups attacked the doll with both actions and epithets that were clearly modeled on the violence they had previously seen and heard acted out.

Another example of an ingenious experimental design in a laboratory setting is one used to test whether entertainment programs could have a *prosocial* effect on young children. Groups of first-graders were shown three television programs, a *Lassie* episode that depicted a small boy risking his life to save the life of a puppy, a different "pro-dog" *Lassie* episode, and a *Brady Bunch* episode. To test whether the children were in-

*This was the *control group,* which is used by experimenters to isolate the effects of the experimental stimulus (the independent variable). The control group, along with the experimental groups, is tested after the experiment to make sure that some irrelevant outside stimulus has not caused the change instead of the experimental stimulus.

spired to be helpful by the dog-saving story, all three groups were asked after seeing the episodes to listen on earphones for barks from a distressed puppy and to press a button to summon help if they heard barks. But to do so the children had to sacrifice points in a game they were playing, so that help could be given only at some cost to the child. The children who saw the dog-saving *Lassie* episode pressed the buttons much longer (that is, sacrificed more) than those who saw the other *Lassie* and the *Brady Bunch* programs (Rubinstein et al., 1974).

Field Studies   Research done in more naturalistic settings, known as *field studies,* attempts to observe behavior in the real world without intruding into the situation or influencing the subjects of observation. In studying effects of violent programming, for example, researchers will observe children in their normal home or school play environment rather than putting them into a laboratory playroom; or children will see programs at home as usual rather than going to a laboratory viewing facility.

One of the pioneer field studies of television effects compared the way on-the-spot observers saw a civic parade from various locations along its route with the way watchers perceived the same parade on live television. The researchers chose the 1951 "MacArthur Day" parade in Chicago for their study. General Douglas MacArthur had become a great popular hero because of his aggressive conduct of the Korean War. However, his refusal to accept policy guidance from Washington led to his abrupt dismissal by President Harry Truman. MacArthur came back to the United States in an atmosphere of tension. His appearance in Chicago, according to advance news reports, promised to be a moment of high drama that could possibly erupt into violence because popular sympathy was with MacArthur.

Viewed on television by a group of observers, the parade fulfilled the expectation of an event highly charged with excitement. The 31 observers posted along the parade route, however, perceived the event as far less dramatic. The crowds were smaller and less emotional than they appeared to be on television. The contrast between the on-the-spot version of the event and the television-mediated version showed how television affects the apparent nature of reality, an inevitable result of the production process. Each spectator on the scene caught only small fragments of the total event; television conveyed a more comprehensive, unified version laden with added meanings. "The selectivity of the camera and the emphases of the commentary gave the televised event a *personal* dimension, nonexistent for the participant in the crowd" (Lang & Lang, 1968: 60).

Field Experiments   A compromise between the tight controls of the laboratory experiment and the unstructured naturalism of the field study can be achieved in *field experiments*. However, they cost a great deal in time, trouble, and money to arrange and therefore are comparatively rare. An example illustrating these problems was an unusual attempt, funded by CBS, to study television effects.

CBS produced, at the request of the researchers, three different endings for an episode in its popular prime-time dramatic series *Medical Center*. One version showed the theft of money from a charity donation box, followed by punishment of the offender; one showed the same criminal behavior without ensuing punishment; the third (control) version showed no criminal behavior. The audience in each of three test cities saw one of the three versions at the series' regularly scheduled time.

To test whether the versions showing criminal behavior had any effect in terms of causing similar behavior, some audience members in each test city were put into a situation in which they were tempted to steal money from a charity donation box, just as the thief had done in one of the episodes. People were recruited for the test by means of an offer of a free radio in a "contest." Informed that they had won, contestants were asked to come to a certain address to pick up their radios. The attendant left each one alone in a room for a time, providing an opportunity to steal from the conspicuously full donation box.

Test groups were small, because though many thousands saw the test programs, only a few responded to the contest offer and came to pick up their radios. Some of the respondents in each group stole money, but the researchers found no significant differences between groups. About as many thefts were committed by those who had not seen the crime on television as those who had. It cost CBS an estimated half a million dollars to pay for the experiment, the message of which seemed to be that there are so many people already disposed to commit crimes that the stimulus of showing crime on television has little perceptible effect.

20.5 Status of Effects Research

Lack of Unifying Theory   Ideally a science develops general laws that support an overarching theory of the phenomena in its field. Such, for example, is the wave theory of electromagnetic energy, which explains (and therefore leads to predicting and controlling) a vast range of phenomena, including of course the technology of broadcasting.

No such unifying theory of mass communication has emerged to account for the effects the mass media have on individuals and society. Research on these phenomena goes on at an accelerating pace but without the benefit of a universally recognized theory to give systematic coordination to the investigations. In a recent issue of an annual communication yearbook, the author of an article on contemporary mass media research confesses:

I am impressed by the tremendous amount of research that has been done in recent years. Paradoxically, I find I am also impressed by how little we seem to have learned. We have a multitude of individual fragments of information, each of which is interesting in itself. However, most of these fragments are isolated; they do not fit together to make a united whole. . . . Thus far we have discovered little that even remotely approaches the foundation of law and theory, which has been the framework for so much of the development of the physical sciences. (Foley, 1979: 263, 264)

Research Perspectives   The best that can be said about media theory is that research tends to cluster around certain common *perspectives*, or ways of looking at the process of communicating. Looking back over the types of effects mentioned in Chapter 19 and the methods for studying them reviewed in this chapter, we can discern at least five research perspectives that have attracted scholarly interest.*

1. Scholars with backgrounds in psychology have tended to focus on *individual differences* among recipients of communication as determinants of effects. This perspective empha-

*The typology used here is based on that of Melvin DeFleur (with Sandra Ball-Rokeach), *Theories of Mass Communication*, 1975.

sizes the role of personal intervening variables and the phenomena of perception.

2. Another group of researchers has tended to focus their study on the way audiences react to communications in terms of *social categories*. This perspective looks at how social class and other demographic characteristics cause variations in effects. This, of course, is a perspective of particular interest to advertisers, as we saw in §14.6.

3. The watershed study of voting behavior and media by Lazarsfeld and his colleagues in the 1940s (§20.2) pointed up the role of *social relationship* in determining communication effects. This perspective led to the identification of opinion leaders and the concept of a two-step flow from medium to recipients.

4. Researchers studying media from the perspective of *cultural norms* are preoccupied with such phenomena as ways in which mass communication intrudes into the process of socialization.

5. Those with a *functional* perspective emphasize what the media do *for* people, as exemplified by the "glow and flow" principle and the play theory (§19.7).

Broadcasting as Research Subject

The perspective of the earlier researchers failed to give adequate attention to the role of entertainment, the major element in broadcasting content. "Ironically, the concept of entertainment and its functions seems to have no place in empirical media research and was relegated to the critics and analysts of popular culture" (Katz et al., 1974: 13). When the earlier media researchers did refer to entertainment it was usually in derogatory terms. They dismissed it as merely "escapist" and thus hardly worthy of serious scholarly attention, which was preoccupied with the effects of informational programs.

One reason for this failure to recognize the full importance of the entertainment function

of the media (and hence to seriously underestimate the role of broadcasting) was the influence of government funding. Government sponsors wanted to learn how the media influenced opinion formation in the political realm. This goal meant focusing attention on news and information programming almost exclusively.

A second reason early researchers neglected the full range of broadcasting functions was the predisposition of those who conducted the research. Most regarded mass communication, in the words of a leading theorist, as

little more than a kind of intellectual way station — a kind of unclaimed territory where people from all kinds of disciplinary backgrounds have come in, picked up research problems, worked through them for a while, and then dropped them in favor of more pressing interests or pursued their implications back into the mainstream of their own discipline. (DeFleur & Ball-Rokeach, 1975: 216)

Intercommunication between these specialists was often slow and imperfect. Few scholars adopted the stance of media scientists as such, with an interest in the entire range of media content and media effects. Later, when advanced degrees finally began to be offered specifically in the media field, they at first came mainly from journalism departments and schools that looked at broadcasting primarily as a news medium. "We should be particularly on guard," warned a team of scholarly commentators, "against a natural tendency of journalistic researchers to overemphasize the informational functions of the media: the evidence points to various types of entertainment functions as being predominant in the media use patterns of most persons" (McLeod & O'Keefe, 1972: 134).

This neglect of the major part of broadcasting's content has been rectified somewhat in recent years, especially because of heightened interest in the effects of violence, stereotyping, and children's advertising. Study of these subjects necessitates focusing on entertainment programming. Nevertheless, in the 1981 *Annual Review of Psychology*, the authors of an article on media effects still found that "the relative absence of research on this central function of mass communication is disconcerting to say the least."

As to the issue of media studies as an independent discipline, the same writers detected some signs of progress, but achievement of the goal was still far in the future:

Our sense at the end of the search conducted for this review is that mass communication research has entered its adolescence. On the one hand the field is experiencing a period of rapid growth marked by a tremendous outpouring of empirical studies. Many of these have attempted to use new techniques and to adopt new perspectives. We also found conscious — indeed, self-conscious — efforts to assert independence from such parent disciplines as psychology and sociology.

On the other hand, a kind of consolidation of what has gone before is also beginning to emerge. The optimism of the early years and the pessimism of the 1950s have given way to recognition that mass communication plays an important role in our social system, but that it is just one element in that system. (Roberts & Bachen, 1981: 346)

Summary

Economic theory and research are used by government agencies in arriving at policy decisions. Private sponsors also use social and behavioral research, especially for the study of audiences. Scientific mass media research started after World War I, stimulated by fear of propaganda. It progressed from the simplistic concept of audiences responding passively to messages to the concept of audiences interacting with messages, thus making effects far less predictable. Among the factors identified in this interaction process were intervening variables, the two-step flow of influence, selective exposure, and selective perception.

Research can focus upon one or more aspects in the communication process: message originators, message content, channel, audience, and effects. The four principal strategies used in studying these processes are survey research, content analysis, laboratory experiments, field studies or experiments.

Mass communication research lacks an overall, unifying theory. Instead one can speak of various research perspectives that stress individual differences of audience members, social categories, social relationships, cultural norms, and functional roles of the media. The entertainment function of broadcasting has been neglected by researchers. Sponsors of research projects and the predispositions of researchers have pushed research more in the direction of studying news and information because of their relevance to opinion formation. Recent interest in violence and other antisocial content, however, has stimulated increased research on entertainment. An independent science of mass communication research, separate from such disciplines as psychology and sociology, has not yet emerged, although there seems to be a trend in that direction.

EPILOGUE

Future of Broadcasting

Having completed our survey of broadcasting in America we are left with a final question: what of the future? Broadcasting today faces challenges to its most fundamental assumptions. Those challenges will inevitably change the system as we have described it in previous chapters. How far, how fast, and in what directions the changes will go are urgent questions for today's broadcasters.

CHAPTER 21

Challenge and Change

In this concluding chapter we look at some of the present challenges to broadcasting and try to imagine what changes they are likely to bring about in the 1980s. Only the most audacious futurists venture to guess what may occur in the longer term.

21.1 Two Views of the Future

Radical View The new technologies inspire enthusiasts for radical change who predict the end of traditional broadcasting in the near future. They foresee the established broadcasting networks and the system they represent shrivelling away, along with their affiliated stations. In their place, say the enthusiasts, will come a rich variety of providers, using computers, satellites, and fiber optics to store and deliver unlimited varieties of information, entertainment, and services. Instead of passive viewers looking at conventional receivers, there will be active subscribers using communications centers equipped with two-way channels for sending as well as receiving. More than conventional news, entertainment, and education will be involved; subscribers will use their centers to plug into services not previously associated with broadcasting, such as shopping, bank-

ing, mail delivery, utility meter reading, and security surveillance. If broadcasting in its traditional form survives at all, we are told, it will be as just one (and probably a rather minor one) among a wide range of optional services.

True believers among social planners and research and development innovators envision the day when all the many bits and pieces of communications technology now on the market or projected for the near future will coalesce into a single, multipurpose home communications center. In contrast to the earlier trend toward miniaturized, personalized, highly portable units, the home center would be an elaborate and permanent installation. It would probably require setting aside an entire room primarily for the reception, recording, storage, playback, and initiation of communications. There the television screen, like a queen bee glowing in the center of an electronic hive, would be fed by an army of working inputs — disc and tape recorders and players, cable and over-the-air program suppliers, teletext reception capable of making hard-copy printouts as required, direct broadcast satellite relays picked up by rooftop dish antennas, two-way communication circuits, and so on.

A More Modest Scenario   Undeniably the technical resources exist to make all these predicted wonders come true. Less certain is the existence of the economic support, institutional framework, mass consumer participation, and creative reserves for filling all the prospective new channels. Although change in traditional broadcasting patterns must inevitably occur, we suspect that it will neither come as fast nor go as far as enthusiasts for the new technologies predict.

It is true that when radio came upon the scene in the 1920s and modern television in the late 1940s they swept the country, and indeed the world. With unprecedented speed they became household necessities, more prized than refrigerators, bathtubs, or indoor toilets. But we must recall that they offered unique new services that stimulated virtually immediate and universal demand. The newer technologies promise no such fundamentally new services, only variations on existing themes. They offer more varied, better integrated, more efficient versions of established services. So far their success has been in terms of novel methods of delivery, with little novelty in the material they deliver.

The unanswered question is whether the mass of consumers (as distinguished from the trendy minority eager to keep abreast of the latest fashions) will soon regard these improved delivery methods and their content as downright domestic necessities, no matter what the cost. And in calculating costs it is essential to remember that the new technologies rely on consumers to undertake the initial investment and the ongoing expense of operating television receivers. The costs of cable television subscription programs, videorecorders, and the rest are piled on top of that basic consumer investment, originally motivated solely by the desire to receive broadcast stations directly off the air.

In the comments that follow, frankly speculative in nature, we propose a scenario in which broadcasting still plays the major role, with cable television and other alternative modes of delivery playing important, but secondary, roles. To an extent we play the devil's advocate, adopting a skeptical view to counteract what we suspect may be unrealistic promises — some the outcome of legitimate scholarship and research, some the product of opportunism.

21.2 Technological Challenges

Cable Television   The most remarkable physical fact about broadcasting is its wirelessness. This unique ability of radio to reach through space and to link up with any point where anyone chooses to turn on a receiver was once highly prized as an invaluable achievement. Now, by a strange twist of fate, many experts and laypersons alike dismiss wireless as an old-fashioned technology, preferring instead improved forms of the prime communication mode of the nineteenth century — wire communication. In the late twentieth century transmission by coaxial cable and optical fibers has taken the lead away from transmission by radio.

Undeniably cable offers a great advantage in creating an enclosed, interference-free environment within which to manipulate the spectrum; it enables using many more television channels within a single community than is at present possible in the open, interference-prone environment of natural space. But this advantage exacts a penalty of added costs. Stringing cables about the landscape on poles, or burying them under the pavement in utility tunnels, is very costly. A separate cable link has to be installed to every individual delivery point. In sharp contrast, wireless reaches unlimited numbers of additional destinations within a transmitter's service area at no additional cost whatever. Cable ties down the receivers to fixed locations; wireless receivers can travel from place to place with ease.

All in all, cable has the appearance of an expensive clumsy stopgap method compared to the elegant simplicity of wireless. There surely must be a better way than cable to solve the problem of providing multiple two-way channels.

Satellites Direct broadcast satellites (DBS) might offer a wireless alternative to cable. Even before DBS services were authorized in the United States, a reader of *Popular Electronics* could find out how to build a backyard earth station able to pick up dozens of programs from existing relay satellites — not intended as yet for direct reception by consumers, of course, but nevertheless receivable. In theory, if everyone starts using DBS services in the future, programming organizations could bypass not only broadcasting networks and their affiliated stations, but also cable systems. The program supplier that now relays materials to cable systems for delivery to home receivers could deliver the material directly.

There is little prospect of DBS becoming universal, however. Even mass-produced antennas capable of detecting and down-converting satellite signals will continue to be more costly than most outdoor antennas for receiving ground-based broadcasting stations. In fact many viewers can pick up their local broadcast stations with no more than the simple indoor antennas that come at no extra cost as accessories to receivers. Moreover, DBS services will presumably be offered, like cable, on a subscription basis, which means that consumers will have to rent or buy decoders to unscramble DBS signals as well as having to pay monthly fees.

More of a threat to broadcast networks, perhaps, will be the widespread installation of receive-only earth stations by their affiliates for the purpose of receiving relays from satellites. The network affiliate equipped with an earth station is in a position, like the *Popular Electronics* reader previously mentioned, to pick up programs from a variety of sources, thereby becoming less dependent on its network for programs. We explore the implications of this prospect in §21.4.

High-Definition TV Some observers think that direct broadcast satellites should be reserved for relaying high-definition television (HDTV) signals, in view of the fact that conventional relaying methods would have to be redesigned to handle such wide-band requirements. Japanese manufacturers have demonstrated HDTV with over a thousand lines a frame, a two-fold increase in picture detail over the present U.S. standard.

High-definition pictures would be far more satisfactory than the present system for the projected images used in theater television for showing occasional celebrity events such as major prize fights. Flat home-receiver screens covering an entire wall will no doubt soon become possible. It is unlikely that there would be much demand for large-screen television in the ordinary home, however. Optimum screen size is related to the viewer's distance from the screen. According to present knowledge on optimum viewing angles, wall-size screens would not be comfortable for ordinary watching in viewing rooms of the size found in most homes and apartments.

Digital Signal Processing Of all the new technologies, one of the least talked about (except in technical and trade journals) may in the long run have the most universal visible effect. Digital signal processing (described in §4.4) affects the actual appearance and sound of programs and therefore will become evident to every viewer and listener.

So far, because digital processing is expensive both in terms of dollars and frequencies, its use has been confined to studio and relay transmission facilities. Eventually, however, digital techniques should be extended to all aspects of sound and picture transmission and recording. Within a decade, perhaps, digital receivers and recorders will have substantially raised the quality standards of all sound and picture systems, including mass-produced consumer products such as receivers and recorders. Production of digital audio disc players for home use has already started.

21.3 Challenge to Massification

Audience Segmentation The ability of broadcasting to reach a simultaneous audience from coast to coast with identical programs was once considered a highly praiseworthy feat. Ironically this ability has come in recent years to be regarded as a crippling weakness. In developing countries, plagued as they are with divisive tribalism, the potentiality of broadcasting to help unify a nation is still regarded as one of its chief virtues. In the United States, however, the kind of national unity symbolized by the melting pot has fallen into disrepute. The newer goal is maintenance of ethnic and regional identities, in public as well as at home and in private gatherings. Traditional broadcasting, with its *massification* of people into undifferentiated national audiences, overrides local and group differences. It favors cultural uniformity, not cultural pluralism. Its target is the majority, not the many separate minorities that make up the majority.

Cable television is acclaimed as a wonderful corrective to this massification tendency. Its many channels enable segmenting the audience into specialized groups, serving each with appropriately specialized programs. With channels to spare, cable can give even the smallest, most untypical groups access to the system to express themselves and their cultures. Typical of the endorsers of this mission of cable is the widely read futurist Alvin Toffler. In his book *The Third Wave* he celebrates what he calls "de-massification" of the media. After summarizing the alternative technologies he concludes: "All these different developments have one thing in common: they slice the mass television public into segments, and each slice not only increases our cultural diversity, it cuts deeply into the power of the networks that have until now so completely dominated our imagery" (1980: 180).

The failure of cable access channels to give everyone a chance to use the system (recounted in §11.2) undermined one of the arguments in favor of cable television. Audience segmentation survives, however, in the notion of *dedicated channels* — more or less continuous program services of less than general interest, dedicated to specific target groups such as children, women, hobbyists, or culture buffs.

In theory, audience segmentation and corresponding specialization in programming become economically viable because satellites make it possible to aggregate many very small local cable audiences into a large national audience, big enough to justify the cost of specialized programming. There is no guarantee, however, that commercial venturers who succeed in this sort of enterprise will not in the long run behave as commercial venturers usually do — that is, to try making even more money out of a good thing. They will be tempted to broaden the appeal of dedicated channels so as to attract more and more viewers, eventually bringing us back to the situation from which cable was supposed to rescue us — mass appeal programs aimed at the largest possible audiences. We already see this trend at work in the multiple system operations, which combine scores of local cable systems under one owner; in the massive size of the top program syndicators such as HBO, which supply identical programs from coast to coast; and in the increasing intrusion of advertising into cable services, which encourages choosing programs that will attract the largest possible audience.

Future Audience of Cable TV Cable television may eventually settle into a pattern of serving a very large, relatively affluent elite *minority*. The growth of cable subscribership was so spectacular in the 1970s (Exhibit 11.1) that its enthusiasts can be forgiven for thinking that soon the entire nation would be cabled. But cable subscribership may level off while still reaching considerably less than half of all U.S. homes — still a huge audience, but hardly comparable to the 98 percent penetration of broadcasting. The subscribers will, according to this scenario, consist mainly of the kinds of people who follow a certain contemporary lifestyle, people so anxious to keep up with the latest fads and celebrity events that they are willing to pay generously for the privilege of being in the know and ahead of the crowd. In several instances, actual program distribution patterns seem to support this hypothesis.

For example, recent feature films, the most popular items in cable program schedules, tend to go through the following distribution sequence: (1) movie theaters; (2) pay cable and subscription television; (3) network broadcasting; (4) syndication to broadcast stations. The "insiders" will be the first to see the talked-about new releases, either in theaters or on pay cable; later the mass audience will see the same films (at least the ones that are not too explicit about sex and violence) as before, on regular television.

Celebrity sports events such as highly publicized boxing matches furnish another example. Media income for promoters of the much touted match between Sugar Ray Leonard and Roberto Duran in 1980 came mainly from theater television (for which viewers paid a hundred dollars and more a ticket in many cases). Rights were also sold to some of the pay cable services, costing the distributors $2 million. Finally, a month later, the mass public saw the fight on ABC at a cost to the network of half a million dollars for the delayed showing. Again, the "in" crowd paid handsomely to see and be seen in the arena or the television theaters; pay-television subscribers handed over considerably less to see it live via cable on their own sets; but in the end, the mass of viewers saw the fight free on regular network television.

A third example of the apparent emerging distribution pattern may be found in the public television network plan to produce a cultural program service for sale as a pay-cable or subscription television feature (§10.9). After the elite few have had a first look at the programs on pay systems, the regular public television audience will be able to see the same programs at no charge on their regular public broadcasting outlets.

Cable subscribers thus pay for the privilege of seeing certain programs before the mass public. They also benefit from the convenience of being able to see a desired program at their convenience (because of cable's practice of scheduling repeated shows of the same program throughout the month's schedule) and the option of seeing programs that are too "adult" for broadcasting's family-oriented standards. But most of what subscribers pay for on cable systems eventually turns up on regular television at no extra cost. The main exceptions are certain routine sporting events of limited general interest and specialized dedicated-channel program services.

The cross-flow of programs among competing delivery systems occurs because cable programming is just as subject as broadcast programming to the parsimony principle and the consequent irresistible urge toward syndication. Cable and the other newer systems will be neither able nor willing to produce an entirely separate genre of programming, denying themselves the profits from sales to broadcasting networks and stations. Thus the patient viewer can count on eventually receiving at no cost most of the programming that cable subscribers originally paid to see.

Subscribership vs. Viewership Traditional broadcasting relies on the fact that once a home-owner installs a receiving set, the appeal of the medium and the absence of restraints on its use usually guarantees its regular and frequent tuning-in. Broadcast listenership and viewership therefore have proved to be quite stable and predictable. A certain amount of audience flow occurs, pushing first one and then another program, network, or station into the lead; but the sets-in-use ratings vary primarily according to time of day and season rather than programming strategies.

Cable subscribership is more volatile than broadcast viewership because it introduces a new variable — the ability and willingness to pay for the service. Subscribers are constantly dropping out either voluntarily or involuntarily because of failure to pay their monthly fees. At the same time most cable companies carry on vigorous recruiting campaigns to replace drop-outs and, if possible, to increase the percentage of subscribing homes among the houses their cables pass. Thus a certain percentage of the subscribership is always moving in and out of the cable audience, not merely flowing from one channel to another. The cable industry is secretive about the extent of this turnover. It is believed to be considerable, especially in newly cabled areas where many subscribers may try out the service for its novelty only to find the expense greater than the reward.

Estimates of viewing levels must also take into account the fact that at any one time a cable system's audience is divided among many channels. A cable system claiming 3,000 subscribers (about average size) cannot of course claim 3,000 actual viewers at any one time or for any one channel. During prime time the average number of viewing homes per channel for a 12-channel cable system of that size would be about 150.

A further complication in measuring cable audiences is that not all subscribers have equal access to all channels. Many companies offer one or more pay-channels that are sold separately from the basic cable service. Research indicates that at best an average of about 60 percent of a cable company's subscribers are likely also to buy the extra-pay services.

Of course, broadcast audiences, too, are divided among competing stations. But the average number of homes per station is still relatively large, for two reasons: (1) the potential audience is larger to start with (usually about 98 percent of all homes in the market); and (2) the number of competing over-the-air television channels is usually far less than the number of competing cable channels.

Local Programming Not being under the regulatory pressures to serve their local communities that broadcasters experience, most cable company operators have had no incentive to develop expertise in local programming. Even when they do offer such programs, their commitment is very different from that of broadcasters. The cable operator who offers a dull, ineffectual local program is secure in the knowledge that subscribers who may tune it out will simply tune to another channel of the same cable system. The broadcaster who drives audience members away sends them to competitors. Most broadcasters therefore tend to have a somewhat stronger sense of commitment to their local program efforts.

Most broadcast stations have a head start on local programming because of their experience with news and public affairs production. These types of programs make up the bulk of most stations' local efforts. The marked increase during the 1970s in the amounts of news and news-related programming at both the station and network levels may have been a foretaste of a major programming trend in the 1980s. Some industry forecasters go so far as to predict that the television networks will follow the example of the radio networks, eventually confining their output almost exclusively to news and news-related features.

In the past, most broadcasters concentrated their local efforts on news because that was the one type of local programming that proved highly salable. In the future, they may well find it essential to extend local production to other types of programs. With survival at stake, broadcasters may invest a larger share of their income in diversified programming — not as a pro forma gesture to please the FCC, but as a realistic competitive stratagem. Boston's WCVB, as we have related (§12.5), has shown what can be accomplished when the will is there, at least in a lucrative major market. Members of the National Association of Television Program Executives listened with special attention when the president of WCVB gave the keynote address at their 1981 national convention. He said that most stations should *double* their present level of local programming. More money and effort should be spent, he urged, not only on news but also on other formats suited to various times of the day and night. Survival itself, he declared, depended on the ability of broadcast stations to seize this opportunity to function as something more than mere delivery systems for other people's programs (Bennett, 1981). In 1981 WCVB was sold to Metromedia for $220 million, a record price, suggesting that local service programming can pay off.

21.4 Economic Challenges

TV Network Audience Share By the dawn of the 1980s the traditional audience share of commercial network television, 90-plus percent of the prime-time audience, had begun to shrink slightly. Industry experts expected it to drop to 85 percent by the end of the decade (few serious industry forecasters tried to look any further ahead). The decline could, of course, be due to several reasons, not cable competition alone. Public television and independent (nonnetwork) commercial stations had begun to attract slightly larger shares than previously, and the sameness of programming shaped by the frantic network ratings wars was blamed for driving some viewers away.

A reduction to 85 percent of the prime-time television audience would hardly put the networks out of business. Nevertheless, taking no chances, each network company began investing in cable-related enterprises. CBS led the way, capitalizing on its experience and resources as a programmer to plan a complete "channel" of entertainment programming to be distributed by satellite to cable companies as a pay-cable offering. CBS was even prepared to compete against itself as an advertising medium by offering time for commercials in its cable programming service.

Network-Affiliate Relations As we pointed out in discussing the network-affiliate relationship (§12.3), the contractual ties that bind affiliates to their television networks can be easily loosened if affiliates see more profit in obtaining programs from other sources. In practice, shopping around for programs to fill time periods normally scheduled by networks occurs infrequently because (1) networks provide their affiliates with the most attractive programming that is available on a day-to-day basis, and (2) affiliates benefit from the instantaneous delivery of timely program material made possible by the permanent, full-time interconnecting facilities arranged and paid for by their networks.*

Satellite interconnection is far more cost-efficient than terrestrial microwave relays. Satellites are "distance insensitive," so that when used as relay stations they cost no more to reach 200 affiliates than to reach one, no more to connect points a thousand miles apart than points a hundred miles apart. The public broadcasting network has long since proved the feasibility and advantages of satellite interconnection. Nevertheless, the commercial networks have been reluctant to adopt this method, saying it would be more costly than their present arrangements for

microwave interconnection with AT&T. Observers suspect that the real reason has to do with network-affiliate relations. Once an affiliate has installed its own satellite receiving antenna, it can easily and cheaply pick up program feeds from suppliers other than its network. It might well be tempted to refuse to accept low-rated network programs in order to substitute more popular programs from other program suppliers. If affiliates could conveniently shop around for program materials from a variety of sources, it would be difficult for networks to maintain stable schedules. The effects could be devastating to important but commercially unattractive public service programming. The mass audience is notoriously unreceptive to even the most significant and engrossing public affairs programs that are not prepackaged for entertainment values. How many affiliates would be willing to devote hours to the coverage of an important congressional hearing, for example, if they could easily substitute popular entertainment programming, more attractive to advertisers and audiences alike?

With radio it is a different matter. Radio networks have everything to gain from making their limited schedules available to affiliates more cheaply and flexibly. Both the Mutual and the ABC networks announced plans to convert to satellite relays in the early 1980s.

Advertising One of the advantages of cable for subscribers should be lack of advertising clutter. If the customer is paying subscription fees for the program service, to exact a second payment in the form of interruptions in the service for the insertion of advertising seems unjustified. Nevertheless, cable systems and most pay-cable program suppliers seek additional income from the sale of time to advertisers. Even the special-

*Affiliates can, and sometimes do, order their own interconnection facilities from AT&T for special occasions. But interconnection is expensive for only occasional use by a few stations. By leasing full-time, permanent facilities, the major networks reduce the per-hour, per-station cost to a reasonable level.

ized cultural program services count on advertising income.

Television's earning power as an advertising medium began to be fully realized once 30 percent of the homes had television receivers. Some industry observers predict that cable, too, will reach "critical mass" and explode into a major medium of advertising at the 30 percent level of penetration, which is expected to be reached by 1985. The parallel is somewhat shaky, however: early television had no direct competition and stations were few in number at the start. Cable competes not only with a well-established television industry and other newer means of program delivery, but also with itself. Not only is a cable system's subscribership divided among the several channels of the system, a number of those channels consist of broadcast programming already loaded with commercials (when cable companies pick up television stations for delivery to their subscribers they may not delete or substitute commercials).

Nearly half the top hundred broadcast advertisers had begun experimenting with cable advertising by 1981 and over a dozen advertising-supported cable program services were competing for national advertising accounts. For advertising to flourish, however, audience research is essential, and cable offers special measurement problems. Its audiences are still relatively small and, because of cable's many channels, are usually more fragmented than broadcast television audiences (§21.3). The ratings services are experimenting with ways of solving these problems. But ratings services of the kind advertisers have come to expect in broadcasting cost a great deal and therefore can only be undertaken when the volume of advertising reaches a sufficiently high level — again the question of reaching critical mass.

There is small likelihood that cable will cause a stampede of advertisers away from television of the kind that occurred in the early 1950s when television devastated radio. Cable should appeal to advertisers interested in reaching well-defined audience segments, while broadcasting continues to dominate national advertising aimed at the mass audience.

21.5 Regulatory Challenges

Deregulation of Cable   When cable television began to show signs of becoming more than simply an extender of television station coverage, the FCC adopted protectionist rules to control its growth (detailed in §11.1). The FCC reasoned that it had a duty to protect the viewing public, which had invested huge amounts in television receivers on the understanding that television reception would entail no cost other than buying and maintaining receivers. Should cable television (and for that matter over-the-air subscription television) succeed in buying up most of the best available programs and performer contracts, the entire broadcast audience could be forced to buy from cable and pay-television companies what it formerly received at no charge from networks and stations.

Later came deregulation of cable, the result originally of court decisions ruling against the FCC, then of a deliberate shift in FCC policy. Current regulatory theory recognizes no special obligation to protect investors in receivers from loss of free, over-the-air programming. Broadcast television must sink or swim on its own, taking its chances in the marketplace. If it sinks, its fate will be ascribed to the free choice of consumers.

Broadcasters argue, however, that the deregulation of cable results in a double standard that is unfair to broadcasting. As the president of the CBS television network put it, the new technologies with no history to give evidence of their ultimate impact are treated as "neutral and harmless" and therefore entitled to go unregulated; in the meantime, broadcasting is still governed by the FCC. Some examples: cable companies have no legal obligation at the federal level to provide local programming as does broadcasting; they may combine into massive MSOs (multiple system operators) while broadcast companies are limited to owning only a few stations; cable companies usually enjoy monopolies in their franchised areas, while broadcast stations have to compete with other stations as well as with cable.

Deregulation of Broadcasting Cable's escape from federal regulation occurred because of the ruling that cable television is not a form of broadcasting; therefore it cannot be subjected to the broadcasting provisions of the communications act.* The FCC's scope in deregulating broadcasting is limited by the terms of the communications act. The commission can relieve broadcasters of a certain amount of red tape and simplify its own administrative procedures and requirements, but it cannot alter the statute.

The FCC confined its first broadcasting deregulatory moves to radio, eliminating a good deal of meaningless paper shuffling by both licensees and the commission with regard to program logging, ascertainment of local problems, guidelines for minimum nonentertainment programming, and guidelines for maximum time devoted to commercial announcements. Deletion of these items had little substantive effect on radio regulation;

their significance lay more in their symbolic role, signaling the culmination of a long-term trend in FCC thinking about its regulatory function. The deregulation order served as a convenient forum for the public expression of a detailed rationale, based on laissez-faire economic theory, justifying the move away from government-mandated regulation in the direction of self-regulation through market competition. This return to a laissez-faire economic philosophy reflected the widespread national trend that had been gaining strength during the 1970s, culminating in the election of a Republican administration in 1980.

Not all the commissioners were comfortable with the FCC's growing reliance on doctrinaire economic theory for the solution of regulatory issues. For example, commenting on the economic theorists' arguments in the radio deregulation proposal, Commissioner Joseph Fogarty wrote:

While I do agree [with the theorists] that the economic concepts of competition and "consumer well-being" are essential elements of the "public interest" standard established by the Act, they are but component parts of the public interest and not its whole. Other values in addition to "economic" satisfaction are implicated. . . . there is a pervasive and troubling circularity in much, if not all, of the proffered economic justification for complete deregulation: i.e., the marketplace will best serve the public interest because the public interest is best served by the marketplace; or otherwise stated, whatever programming is produced by the marketplace is by definition in the public interest. (73 FCC 2d 611, 1979)

Nevertheless, when the FCC voted final approval of the radio deregulation plan in 1981, Commissioner Fogarty concurred, characterizing the plan as a worthwhile "experiment." Clearly, by that time economic theorists were

---

*However, cable companies are still held responsible for observing the equal opportunities law for candidates for public office, the fairness doctrine, and the criminal code sanctions against obscenity, lotteries, and fraud by wire.

in the ascendant at the FCC, as indeed they were in Washington generally. The only holdout was Commissioner Tyrone Brown, the one black commissioner, who said he reluctantly dissented because the order placed too little emphasis on the "bedrock principle" of the licensee's obligation to serve the local community.

Further deregulatory moves can be expected. The fairness doctrine is often mentioned as a prime target for deletion. In television, the prime-time access rule and some of the other restraints on the networks' freedom of action are examples of likely subjects for deregulatory proposals.

Attack on Scarcity Principle Central to the regulatory philosophy outlined in the radio deregulation order is the argument that the *scarcity principle* no longer has any relevance. We saw in Chapter 15 how heavily the courts have relied in the past on the factor of spectrum scarcity to justify federal regulation of broadcasting, even though it might mean denying certain First Amendment freedoms to broadcasters that are enjoyed by the owners and operators of other media. The FCC, with considerable congressional support, now declares that channel scarcity is a thing of the past. The growth in the number of broadcasting stations on the air from under 600 to over 10,000 during the history of regulation is one argument that scarcity is no longer a factor. Even more persuasive, perhaps, is the argument that scarcity has been relieved by the abundant availability of alternative channels for delivering programs, notably those of cable television.

These arguments seem less convincing when one looks beyond the simple numbers. Scarcity refers not merely to the total number of available channels or stations, but also to the fact that adjacent and cochannel interference imposes limits on the number of channels usable in any one locality. Demand for over-the-air channels still exceeds supply in heavily populated areas. Striking evidence of the continued relevance of the scarcity factor emerged when the FCC began processing applications for the new class of low-power television (LPTV) stations. Upon reviewing the nearly 6,000 applications, the FCC found that virtually all of them were mutually exclusive — that is, because of spectrum scarcity, choices had to be made among competing applicants for the same channels or for channels that would cause interference.

Nor is it true that cable channels are fully equivalent to over-the-air channels. Cable channels do not and indeed cannot (unless subsidized in some way) reach all the areas where people live that can be reached by broadcasting. Cable channels become available to consumers only at a price over and above the price of owning and operating a television receiver. Even direct-broadcast satellites, though a possible solution to local channel scarcity, will exact additional costs from consumers.

Effects of Scarcity on Public Access Scarcity of channels must also be viewed in terms of the medium's accessibility to users. Cable television has not eliminated this consequence of channel scarcity, nor has the citizen's band (CB) radio as is sometimes asserted (it gives access to other individual CB operators, not to the general public as does broadcasting). Each broadcast licensee is awarded a temporary monopoly on the use of a designated portion of the spectrum in the locality of license. Licensees have obligations to allow access to the channels they control by people other than themselves only in the specific cases of political candidates and proponents of controversial issues and even then only under limited circumstances.

Thus the public is denied access to the broadcast part of the spectrum, even though the spectrum belongs to all as a common national resource. The FCC's device for ameliorating this exclusion, it will be recalled (§17.4), was the fairness doctrine, which gives access to ideas, though not to specific proponents of ideas.

The spectrum scarcity that imposes limitations on public access is not shared equally by other media of expression. The medium of print, for example, is accessible to the general public in a variety of forms. The appeals court made this point in the famous *Banzhaf* case in which it upheld the FCC's right to require licensees to broadcast antismoking spots as a fairness doctrine obligation. The court, when asked by opponents of the FCC to rule that channel scarcity no longer justified such an encroachment on licensee freedom, replied:

It may well be that some venerable FCC policies cannot withstand constitutional scrutiny in the light of contemporary understanding of the First Amendment and the modern proliferation of broadcasting outlets.

On the other hand, we cannot solve such complex questions by replacing one set of shibboleths with another. The First Amendment is unmistakably hostile to governmental controls over the content of the press, but that is not to say that it necessarily bars every regulation which in any way affects what the newspapers publish. Even if it does, there may still be a meaningful distinction between the two media justifying different treatment under the First Amendment. Unlike broadcasting, the written press includes a rich variety of outlets for expression and persuasion, including journals, pamphlets, leaflets, and circular letters, which are available to those without technical skills or deep pockets. (405 F 2d 1100, 1968)

Future of Regulation In arguing that channel scarcity continues to justify regulation of broadcasting we do not mean to en-

dorse the way it has been regulated in the past. Ineffectual, time-wasting rules and bureaucratic red tape should, of course, be condemned and if possible eliminated. As we noted in assessing the FCC's performance (§16.9), to a remarkable degree past commissions allowed regulation to become a sham. They erected an elaborate regulatory framework and buttressed it with high-minded theories about the public interest taking precedence over private gain. In practice, the framework turned out to be little more than a facade behind which ideals were cynically disregarded in all but the most blatantly unregenerate cases. For example, the commission collected mountains of data by which to judge licensee performance, only to ignore the evidence when it came to making most renewal decisions.

The radio deregulation order was amply justified, in our opinion, but not entirely for the reasons given; it was justified primarily by the fact that the deleted rules were either too permissive to be meaningful, or if meaningful too loosely enforced to be effective. Deregulation thus meant abandoning meaningless and unenforced (if not actually unenforceable) rules.

In theory, the force of economic competition will fill the regulatory vacuum. In theory, listeners themselves will penalize stations that abuse deregulation by tuning to competing stations. As a hypothetical example, a station that takes advantage of the removal of the ceiling on commercials by devoting 90 percent of its time to advertising will presumably find that this excess drives listeners away. The licensee will therefore cut back on commercial time in order to recapture listeners. But what if the opposite happens? Suppose all stations in the market start using 90 percent of their time for commercials in order to compete with the maverick station? This "rotten-apple-in-the-barrel" effect has not been unknown in broadcasting. Unless listeners actually want that much advertising, the FCC's economic theorists would call this result a "failure of the market place." Too many such failures could, according to the theory, justify corrective action by the FCC.

Deregulation is indeed an experiment, as Commissioner Fogarty said. It will be interesting to watch its outcome. Will it work as predicted most of the time? Or will frequent marketplace failures require resumption of government regulation? If regulation has to be resumed, one can only hope that it will be both enforceable and enforced.

Future of Broadcast Pluralism An implied corollary of laissez-faire economic theory is opposition to federal tax subsidies for public broadcasting. If people want noncommercial services, says the theory, in effect, they should be willing to pay for them voluntarily rather than involuntarily through taxes. This reasoning runs counter to the notion of pluralism as an ideal goal for national systems of broadcasting as outlined in §1.3. World experience suggests that, in order to be fully responsive to national needs, a broadcasting system should be energized by more than a single motivating force. There is nothing inherently objectionable in either the motive of commercial gain or the motive of public service. Either one working in isolation, however, tends to result in a lopsided service. Competition is needed not only between rival commercial firms, but also between commercial interests and noncommercial interests.

Pluralism requires adequate financing of both alternatives. As we saw in Chapter 10, in the absence of assured revenue from receiver license fees, stable tax-based subsidies are essential to give noncommercial broadcasting the strength to compete effectively as an alternative service.

Some argue that cable television and other innovations eliminate the need for a public broadcasting alternative. Do not these new systems open up a vista of unprecedented pluralism? This argument misconstrues the meaning of pluralism. The goal is not alternative sources or providers, desirable though such options may be; the goal is alternative *motivations*. If all providers share the single motive of making money, pluralism in the sense we have used the term does not exist. There is not much question that the new providers of optional program services will be profit-oriented. Indeed, even nonprofit organizations such as symphony orchestras, opera companies, and public broadcasting itself are hoping to make money from cultural programming they produce for sale on a subscription basis.

Thus the new regulatory atmosphere, with its narrow focus on economic competition as the sole motivator of program suppliers, raises questions not only about the future quality of commercial broadcasting but of noncommercial broadcasting as well.

21.6 Conclusion

We have attempted in this book to describe at some length and in a factual way the many attributes of broadcasting that make it unique as a medium of public communication. To review some of its main attributes, broadcasting:

■ Uses a scarce public resource, the electromagnetic spectrum.
■ Is expected to operate in the public interest in view of its dependence on that public resource.

■ Is a wireless form of communication, able to reach recipients without physical interconnection to their receivers and for that reason able to reach few or many within a service area at the same cost.

■ Is subject to self-interference and therefore must be controlled by technical regulations.

■ Is regulated on a national rather than local basis because its attribute of wirelessness makes it impossible to confine its effects within fixed geographic boundaries.

■ Has special advantages over other media, along with reciprocal special obligations, because it enters the home and adapts itself to audience members' activities throughout the day, week, and year.

■ Can instantaneously shift focus from that of a local to that of a regional or national medium.

■ Has a special responsibility to its audiences because they invest in the technology of the medium by voluntarily buying, maintaining, and operating receivers.

■ Depends for its effectiveness on various forms of syndication, of which networks are the most characteristic type.

Some of these attributes are shared by other media, but no single rival medium achieves the combination of attributes that makes broadcasting unique.

In this concluding chapter, taking a more subjective point of view, we argue that broadcasting's unique status should be preserved. It would not be in the public interest, we think, to allow cable television and other subscription media so to dominate the market for programming that audiences would be forced to pay subscription fees merely to obtain the same kinds of program services they formerly enjoyed from broadcasting networks and stations without having to pay fees. Nor would it be in the public interest, we think, to abandon the goal of pluralism, leaving broadcasting entirely to the control of economic forces of the marketplace, without regard to aspects of the public interest that may not be measurable entirely in terms of commercial profit and loss.

Summary

This final chapter ventures to express opinions about the probable effect on broadcasting of the new technologies and the new regulatory atmosphere, both of which challenge earlier assumptions about the older medium.

1. Cable television, in some ways a throwback to earlier technology, is unlikely to replace broadcasting as the most efficient means for delivering mass entertainment, information, and education.

2. Nor will newer technologies such as direct broadcast satellites and high-definition television displace traditional broadcasting. The technology most likely to have perceptible effects on broadcasting is digital processing.

3. Cable television and other innovative means of delivering services will provide specialized programming for particular audience segments making up a large minority audience; but television broadcasting will continue as the primary medium of national advertising.

4. Local programming will become increasingly important in broadcast station schedules, as will news and news features in network schedules.

5. National broadcast networks will attract a somewhat smaller audience share, but will still offer national advertisers their best access to mass consumers.

6. The development most threatening to the continued success of traditional broadcast networks is satellite relays. They will make it easier for affiliates to shop around for programs to substitute for the lower-rated network offerings, perhaps counteracting the network trend mentioned in item 4 above.

7. Spectrum scarcity is still real, justifying continued governmental supervision to ensure operation in the public interest, notwithstanding claims that the abundance of cable channels and increase in broadcast stations has eliminated scarcity as a consideration.

8. Deregulation is desirable insofar as it removes ineffectual and unenforceable rules, but reliance primarily on economic competition to ensure operation in the public interest is an experiment that may produce the opposite of its intended results.

Further Reading

A Selective Guide to the Literature of Broadcasting

Christopher H. Sterling

The following guide, organized according to chapter and section headings in the text, gives suggestions for further reading on each topic. Space allows for only representative selections from the rapidly growing literature of the field. The guide includes examples of the most significant book-length publications that are readily available and of current interest (some of the rare but important documents have been reprinted in recent years, as noted in the bibliography that follows the guide). The cut-off date for inclusion was mid-1981. Following the chapter-by-chapter guide to readings will be found a short list of bibliographies about media publications and an annotated selection of relevant periodical titles.

Many of the books mentioned in the guide are cited, and in some cases quoted, in the text. However, the reading guide represents an independent assessment of each title. All books cited both here and within the text are listed with full bibliographical details in the table of citations that follows the guide.

Chapter 1: National Contrasts

1.1 Broadcasting and National Character

Broad-based philosophical discussions of broadcasting's role in different societies are not common. Probably the best is Smith, *The Shadow in the Cave: The Broadcaster, His Audience, and the State* (1973), which contrasts the U.S. with Britain, Japan, Canada, and several European countries. Two earlier views, both dealing only with television but surveying many countries, are Green, *The Universal Eye* (1972), and Dizard, *Television: A World View* (1966), which include discussion of Third World applications. Emery, *National and International Systems of Broadcasting* (1969), includes both foreign and national material while stressing European developments. Variance among European countries is detailed in Namurois, *Structures and Organization of Broadcasting in the Framework of Radiocommunications* (1972). Finally, two multivolume series of paperbacks provide detailed material on selected countries from all regions of the world. The IIC, *Broadcasting in . . .*, and UNESCO *Communication Policies in . . .*, discuss history, organization, financing, pro-

gramming, and audience research in specific countries. The UNESCO series includes all media, but concentrates on print and broadcasting.

1.2 Influence of Political Philosophy

Material on U.S. broadcasting is detailed under later chapters. The development of British radio and television is most completely told in Briggs, *The History of Broadcasting in the United Kingdom* (1961–1978, four volumes), written from BBC archival sources. The *BBC Handbook* (1928–date) provides an interesting annual overview of developments in the U.K. and to some degree around the world. The battle for commercial broadcasting in Britain is related in Wilson, *Pressure Group: The Campaign for Commercial Television* (1961). Broad surveys of the organization, funding, and programming of radio-TV in Europe are found in Paulu, *Radio and Television Broadcasting on the European Continent* (1967), dealing with Western Europe, and Paulu, *Radio and Television Broadcasting in Eastern Europe* (1974), which includes the USSR. Two useful studies of the changing role of Soviet domestic media including broadcasting are Hopkins, *Mass Media in the Soviet Union* (1970), and Mickiewicz, *Media and the Russian Public* (1981). The literature on broadcasting (and other media) in the Third World has expanded greatly in the past few years. The best overview is Katz and Wedell, *Broadcasting in the Third World* (1977), based on examples from Asia, Latin America, and Africa and showing the varied applications of radio and television. Two collections of original articles covering each country in the region, plus material on international broadcasting, are Head, *Broadcasting in Africa* (1974), and Lent, *Broadcasting in Asia and the Pacific* (1978). Rogers and Shoemaker, *Communication of Innovations* (1971), is a summary of research on the diffusion of innovations, based mainly on agricultural studies done in Latin America. Finally, Arnove, *Educational Television: A Policy Critique and Guide for Developing Countries* (1976) is just that!

1.3 Pluralism in Broadcasting

Discussion of works on American broadcasting appear later. For current overviews of British pluralism, see Great Britain, Committee on the Future of Broadcasting,

Report (1977), and compare it to its predecessor, Great Britain, Committee on Broadcasting, *Report* (1962). The BBC in a competitive world is best discussed in Burns, *The BBC* (1977), while the commercial companies are analyzed in the reports above plus the Independent Broadcasting Authority, *Guide to Independent Broadcasting* (annual). Historical material on British broadcasting is discussed under §1.2.

1.4 Legal Foundations
For material on American broadcast law, see notes under Chapters 15–17. British material is found under §1.2 and §1.3 above. Standard histories of the ITU are found in Codding, *The International Telecommunication Union* (1952), and Leive, *International Telecommunications and International Law* (1970). A dated but still useful view is in Smythe, *Structure and Policy of Electrical Communications* (1957). The official record of WARC 1979 is found in ITU, *Final Acts* (1980). Material on the U.S. position at that conference, and the implementation of its results here can be obtained by writing to the FCC (1919 M St. NW, Washington, DC 20554).

1.5 Access to Broadcasting
The best comparative analysis is found in Berrigan, *Access: Some Western Models of Community Media* (1978).

1.6 Economic Influences
The standard annual of information on broadcast systems and programming is Frost, *World Radio-TV Handbook*. The standard handbook of information on all of the media in most countries of the world is UNESCO, *World Communications* (1975), which is revised every decade. Specific facility and programming comparative statistics are found in UNESCO, *Statistics on Radio and Television, 1960–1976* (1979), partially updated in UNESCO, *Statistical Yearbook* annually. An interesting analysis of the development of three conflicting systems of color TV standards is found in Crane, *The Politics of International Standards* (1979). The many European and British "pirate" broadcast operations are detailed in Harris, *Broadcasting from the High Seas* (1977).

1.7 Influence of Geography and History
The oldest union of broadcasting systems is traced in Brack, *The Evolution of the EBU through Its Statutes from 1950 to 1976* (1976). For broadcasting in Germany see Paulu (1967), Sandford, *The Mass Media of the German-Speaking Countries* (1976), and Williams, *Broadcasting and Democracy in West Germany* (1976), which concentrate on post-World War II developments. Canadian Broadcasting is discussed in Ellis, *Evolution of the Canadian Broad-*

casting System (1980), and is placed in context with other Canadian media in Hindley, *The Tangled Net: Basic Issues in Canadian Communications* (1977). See also the Canada, Radio-Television and Telecommunications Commission, *Annual Report*. For developments elsewhere, see IIC (§1.1), Head, and Lent (§1.2) and Nippon Hoso Kyokai, *50 Years of Japanese Broadcasting* (1977), which, as with the German case, shows the impact of World War II.

1.8 Programs and Schedules
On current schedules, see Frost and the UNESCO citations under §1.6. For the impact of trade, see citations under §1.10. An example of research interests abroad is found in Katz, *Social Research in Broadcasting: Proposals for Further Development* (1977), done for the BBC, but in large part applicable in the U.S. and elsewhere.

1.9 Broadcasting to Other Countries
The *BBC Handbook* annually includes a table and short discussion comparing international broadcast efforts. Hale, *Radio Power: Propaganda and International Broadcasting* (1975), reviews the modern role of short-wave international radio, while Lindahl, *Broadcasting across Borders* (1978), provides a content analysis of both Western and Communist radio propaganda as received in Sweden. Abshire, *International Broadcasting* (1976), suggests policy for Western broadcasting, while the Board for International Broadcasting *Annual Report* reviews RFE and RL developments. For the USSR and Eastern Europe, see Paulu (1974).

1.10 "Free Flow" or "New Order"
A sizable polemical literature is building on this cross-cultural debate. An early and influential statement of the media imperialism idea is Schiller, *Mass Communications and American Empire* (1971), while one update of many is Nordenstreng and Schiller, *National Sovereignty and International Communication* (1979). A less shrill argument for the same view is Smith, *The Geopolitics of Information: How Western Culture Dominates the World* (1980). UNESCO's McBride Commission, *Many Voices, One World* (1980), sums up the official UNESCO position, essentially that of the Third World. While arguing a point of view disagreeing with that of many Western nations, the report is a landmark effort with much valuable data. Western points of view are found in Tunstall, *The Media Are American* (1977), addressed to Schiller's arguments; Righter, *Whose News?* (1978), providing a British analysis, and 20th Century Fund Task Force on the International Flow of News, *A Free and Balanced Flow* (1979), which reflects the Western reporter's point of view.

Chapter 2 Nature of Radio Energy

A good technical dictionary or dictionary of electronics may prove useful in this and the following two chapters. Two broadcast-specific titles are Diamant, *The Broadcast Communications Dictionary* (1978), and Ellmore, *The Illustrated Dictionary of Broadcast-CATV-Telecommunications* (1977). See also Appendix B in Sterling and Kittross, *Stay Tuned* (1978).

2.1 and 2.7 Spectrum and Its Management

Levin, *The Invisible Resource: Use and Regulation of the Radio Spectrum* (1971), is the definitive study, dealing equally with technical, economic, and political issues involved in allocation. Regularly updated is the National Telecommunications and Information Administration (NTIA), *The Radio Frequency Spectrum: United States Use and Management* (annual), which reviews current policy issues, government spectrum uses and users, and international agreements. The official detailed record of frequency use in the United States is in NTIA, *Manual of Regulations and Procedures for Federal Radio Frequency Management* (1979). Two presidential advisory commissions have issued seminal studies, which include much discussion of spectrum problems: President's Communications Policy Board, *Telecommunications* (1951), and President's Task Force on Communications Policy, *Final Report* (1968). The interrelationship of politics and technology in spectrum and related issues is analyzed in text and diagrams in McGillam and McLauchlan, *Hermes Bound: The Policy and Technology of Telecommunications* (1978).

2.2–2.6 Waves, Modulation, Propagation, Antennas

A fascinating discussion of the kinds and impact of sounds is found in Schaefer, *The Tuning of the World* (1977). For a good discussion, with diagrams, of sound modulation, see Beck, *Words and Waves* (1967). Of value here and in the next two chapters is the often quite technical Bartlett, *NAB Engineering Handbook* (1975), designed to aid broadcast station engineers.

Chapter 3 Broadcast Channels

3.1 Basic Concepts

See first of all, the sources noted for Chapter 2. A number of general electronics textbooks focus on the communications process, one of which, Lapatine's *Electronics in Communications* (1978), provides details on much that is discussed in this chapter. For contemporary developments, readers should check on the latest available works from such publishers as John Wiley, Prentice-Hall, McGraw-Hill, and Hayden, all of which publish extensively in the electronics field. Also useful for the broader telecommunications context are Martin, *Future Developments in Telecommunications* (1977), and Lewin, *Telecommunications* (1979).

3.3–3.4 AM and FM Broadcasting

The standard reference is Bartlett (see §2.2) which covers the entire technical side of radio including antennas, transmitters, station operations, etc. For works on the development of these services, see notes for Chapters 5 and 6.

3.5 Short-Wave Broadcasting

The standard, annually revised source book for radio "hams" is the American Radio Relay League, *The Radio Amateur's Handbook*. In addition to Frost (see §1.6), Fallon, *Shortwave Listener's Handbook* (1976), and Wood, *Shortwave Voices of the World* (1969), detail the hows, whens, and wheres of SW listening.

3.6–3.10 Television

There is substantial technical literature on all aspects of television. One of the best introductions remains Fink and Lutyens, *The Physics of Television* (1960), which is directed at the layperson. Kiver and Kaufman, *Television Simplified* (1973), is directed at engineers and is a good basic regularly revised overview. See also Bartlett (§2.2). Providing further details, often with diagrams, of the film and television picture terms and processes discussed is Spottiswoode, *The Focal Encyclopedia of Film and Television Techniques* (1969). For more on film, the best source is Happé, *Basic Motion Picture Technology* (1975). An excellent and clearly diagrammed introduction to the technical side of television is Marsh, *Independent Video* (1974). A recent analysis of the problems of UHF is found in FCC, *Staff Report on Comparability for UHF Television: Final Report* (1980). For the technical history of television, see Chapter 8.

3.11 TV Technical Innovations

Periodical articles will provide the most useful and up-to-date material here. For background, see Costigan, *Electronic Delivery of Documents and Graphics* (1978), which deals with facsimile and related technologies. A number of books deal with teletext and videotex, among them Sigel, *Videotext* (1980).

Chapter 4 Storage, Distribution, and Delivery Systems

4.1 Basic Concepts

A useful approach to topics considered in this chapter is found in Bretz, *A Taxonomy of Communication Media* (1970), which compares the interrelationship of transmission and recorded technologies and their applications.

4.2–4.3 Sound and Picture Recording Technology

A basic diagram-illustrated introduction to this topic is Overman, *Understanding Sound, Video & Film Recording* (1978), which includes some historical information. A detailed guide to modern disc and tape methods is in Lowman, *Magnetic Recording* (1972). For film and video recording, see books by Happé, Marsh, and Spottiswoode discussed at §3.6. Most books on these topics are either highly technical or have a how-to orientation. One of the best recent how-to guides is Alten's *Audio in Media* (1981).

4.4 Digital Recording

There is substantial literature on digital methods of recording, but virtually all of it is highly technical and mathematical in nature. Contact the publishers listed at §3.1 as well as the Institute of Electrical and Electronic Engineers (New York) for the latest.

4.5 Terrestrial Relays in Networking

For booklets and the latest status of cable and microwave relays, write to Broadcast Industry Coordinator, American Telephone & Telegraph Co., 195 Broadway, New York, NY 10007.

4.6 Space Relays

Though a bit dated, a good diagram- and photo-illustrated introduction to the subject is Polcyn, *An Educator's Guide to Communication Satellite Technology* (1973). For a free packet of the latest data on international satellites, write to Communications Satellite Corporation, 950 L'Enfant Plaza, SW, Washington, DC 20024. See also notes under §11.4.

4.7–4.8 Hybrid Delivery/Relay Systems

For basic data on broadcast applications, see Bartlett (§2.2). The technology of translators is discussed in FCC, *Staff Report and Recommendations in the Low Power Television Inquiry* (1980). The ITFS technology is the subject of NEA, *ITFS: Instructional Television Fixed Service* (1967). For cable television, see Martin (§3.1). Fiber optic com-munication is another of those subjects with a huge technical literature available, but little of a general nature. See Martin and contact the publishers listed at §3.1.

Chapter 5 Preconditions: The Stage is Set

5.1 Development of Mass Media Consumption

DeFleur and Ball-Rokeach, *Theories of Mass Communication* (1975), provides brief histories of print, film, and broadcast media along with useful overviews of basic media theory. Good one-volume histories stressing print media include Tebbel, *The Media in America* (1975), and Nye, *The Unembarrassed Muse: The Popular Arts in America* (1970). The rise and role of advertising is related in Presbrey, *The History and Development of Advertising* (1929), and Wood, *The Story of Advertising* (1958). Csida and Csida, *American Entertainment* (1978), provides a text and picture scrapbook approach to popular culture taken from *Billboard*. Standard short histories of single media include Jowett, *Film* (1976), Gelatt, *The Fabulous Phonograph* (1977), or the more detailed Read and Welsh, *From Tin Foil to Stereo* (1976), and Emery and Emery, *The Press and America* (1978), which covers newspapers and magazines. Sterling and Haight, *The Mass Media* (1978), provides an historical statistical abstract of the development of all U.S. media in some 300 tables and analytic text.

5.2 Wire Communication

An old but still useful overview of electrical communication history is in Harlow, *Old Wires and New Waves* (1936), including telegraph, telephone, and radio. Marland, *Early Electrical Communication* (1964), deals with competing telegraph systems and the early telephone. Thompson, *Wiring a Continent* (1947), relates the development of the telegraph to 1866, while Coates and Finn, *A Retrospective Technology Assessment: Submarine Telegraphy* (1979), discusses the impact of the 1866 trans-Atlantic cable. Dugan, *The Great Iron Ship* (1953), is a prize-winning novel-like history of *The Great Eastern*, which laid most early cables. Brooks, *Telephone: The First Hundred Years* (1976) is an informal history of AT&T, while Pool, *The Social Impact of the Telephone* (1977), shows how that impact has changed over time. A recent corporate review of AT&T is Kleinfield, *The Biggest Company on Earth* (1981). The economic, technical, and policy development of both wire and wireless as telecommunications systems is surveyed from 1830 to the present by Brock in *The Telecommunications Industry* (1981).

5.3 Invention of Wireless

Context for the coming of radio is found in Dummer, *Electronic Inventions: 1745–1976* (1977), an annotated listing with useful tables and diagrams covering all fields. Reference biographical data on the inventors discussed in the text is found in Dunlap, *Radio's 100 Men of Science* (1944). Aitken, *Syntony and Spark: The Origins of Radio* (1976), is a fascinating analysis of the work of Hertz and Marconi. Fahie, *A History of Wireless Telegraphy* (1901), is a key source for early theorizing and experiments. Biographical material on Marconi abounds: the latest is Jolly, *Marconi* (1972), which can be supplemented with the detail found in Dunlap, *Marconi: The Man and His Wireless* (1938), and his daughter's viewpoint in Marconi, *My Father, Marconi* (1962). One of the few really good company histories in this field is Baker, *A History of the Marconi Company* (1972), a balanced though undocumented account written with cooperation of the firm.

5.4 Technological Progress

A massive and detailed anthology of articles tracing the first half century of radio electronics development is found in *Proceedings of the IRE: Fiftieth Anniversary* (1962), a commemorative issue of the technical monthly. The best overall analysis of this period is found in Maclaurin (see §5.5), but see also McNicol, *Radio's Conquest of Space* (1946), and Blake, *History of Radio Telegraphy and Telephony* (1928), the latter providing detailed information in a chronological fashion. Definitive treatment in vast detail is found in Tyne, *Saga of the Vacuum Tube* (1977), which takes the story to about 1930. Lacking modesty but providing human interest detail is de Forest, *Father of Radio* (1950). Compare with the views found in Lessing (see §7.3) and Maclaurin (§5.5).

5.5 Business Developments

The premier study of the role of patents in radio is Maclaurin, *Invention and Innovation in the Radio Industry* (1949), which begins with the nineteenth-century electrical industry and ends with early television. The detailed investigation by the FTC, *Report on the Radio Industry* (1924), focuses on the role of patents in the rise of RCA.

5.6 Development of Wireless Services

Because of the predominant role of the U.S. Navy in the period, Howeth's *History of Communications-Electronics in the United States Navy* (1963) is essential to an understanding of nonmilitary events and international and domestic regulation, as well as the cover topic. For the general role of shipboard radio, two good sources are Hancock, *Wireless at Sea* (1950), a Marconi company history of technical applications, and Baarslag, *SOS to the Rescue* (1935), a popular history of wireless in maritime

disasters. The role of radio in the *Titanic* disaster is brought out in Marcus, *The Maiden Voyage* (1969). De Soto relates the early development of amateur radio in *Two Hundred Meters and Down* (1936), while the longer story is told in American Radio Relay League, *Fifty Years of the A.R.R.L.* (1965).

5.7 Experiments with Radiotelephony

Fessenden, *Fessenden* (1940), is a good biography of the inventor by his wife. See also de Forest's autobiography (§5.4 above).

5.8 Wireless and World War I

For coverage of naval radio, Howeth (see §5.6) is unexcelled. The second part of Schubert, *The Electric Word* (1928), gives a popular account of radio at war on land and at sea. The U.S. Army Chief Signal Officer, *Report* (1919), details the use of wire and wireless communication in Europe during the war.

Chapter 6 Emergence of Broadcasting

The major histories of broadcasting include Barnouw, *A History of Broadcasting in the United States* (1966–1970, three volumes), Sterling and Kittross, *Stay Tuned: A Concise History of American Broadcasting* (1978), and the anthology of articles and data assembled by Lichty and Topping, *American Broadcasting* (1975). All three cover both radio and television, begin with technical developments and carry through to the 1970s, though each is arranged differently. For a year-by-year retrospective, see Broadcasting Publications, *The First 50 Years of Broadcasting* (1981).

6.1 The Broadcasting Concept

There are two biographies of Sarnoff, neither fully adequate, though both give a sense of his professional role and the rise of RCA. Dreher, *Sarnoff* (1977), is shorter and less fawning in tone than Lyons, *David Sarnoff* (1966). The music box memo is reprinted in Sarnoff, *Looking Ahead* (1968), a collection of his papers.

6.2 Government Monopoly: The Road Not Taken

That government control was not a new idea is evident in Postmaster General, *Government Ownership of Electrical Means of Communication* (1914), which relates earlier efforts back before the Civil War. Most other records of early government action are found in congressional hearings (especially House CMMF, 1919). The role of the Navy in pushing such action is detailed in Howeth (see

§5.6). See also the FTC report (§5.5), and the Archer histories (§6.4).

6.3 The "First" Broadcast Station
The best analysis of this question is Baudino and Kittross, "Broadcasting's Oldest Station: An Analysis of Four Claimants" (1977).

6.4 Radio Broadcasting vs. Radiotelephony
Ponderous and not clearly organized, but important for its detailed view of the "radio group" side of the debate is the two-volume history by Archer, *History of Radio to 1926* (1938), and *Big Business and Radio* (1939). Both are strongly biased in RCA's favor. A balancing view, from the stance of the telephone group, is Banning, *Commercial Broadcasting Pioneer* (1946), which relates the story of WEAF to 1926. The most objective telling of these events is in Schubert (see §5.8). Day-to-day operations at WEAF are the subject of McNamee, *You're on the Air* (1926), which may be the first on-air-personality autobiography. Husing covers some of the same events in *Ten Years before the Mike* (1935).

6.5 National Networks Begin
See the discussions of the early years of NBC and CBS in the Archer histories (§6.4), and also Bergreen, *Look Now, Pay Later: The Rise of Network Broadcasting* (1980).

6.6 Triumph of Commercialism
The best analysis of the development of radio commercialism is Hettinger, *A Decade of Radio Advertising* (1933), which contains data found nowhere else and documents early network advertising growth. Earlier contemporary views include Jome, *Economics of the Radio Industry* (1925), said to be the first published Ph.D. dissertation on broadcasting; Felix, *Using Radio in Sales Promotion* (1927), the first book-length analysis of how to do radio advertising; and Dunlap, *Radio in Advertising* (1931), which demonstrates how the coming of networks rapidly standardized industry practice. An anticommercial government view is FRC, *Commercial Radio Advertising* (1932), which includes discussion of radio practice in other countries.

6.7 Government Regulation
An overview of the period is in Rosen, *The Modern Stentors: Radio Broadcasters and the Federal Government 1920–1934* (1980). Of the four Department of Commerce National Radio Conferences, only those of 1924 and 1925 published reports. The international context of regulation is covered in the history of ITU by Codding (see §1.4), and Howeth's history of naval radio (§5.6). For the background of the congressional debates leading to

the 1927 act, see Volume 3 of Schwartz, *The Economic Regulation of Business and Industry* (1973), which includes the full congressional debate, the act itself, and a commentary. Covering the same ground with more analysis is House CIFC, *Regulation of Broadcasting* (1958). The best book on the 1927 act is Davis, *The Law of Communication* (1927), which deals with each section of the legislation individually.

Chapter 7   Radio After 1928

For general histories, see titles noted in first paragraph of notes for Chapter 6. See also: MacDonald, *Don't Touch That Dial!* (1979), a narrative overview of radio history with good analysis of network radio programming through the 1950s; Chase, *Sound and Fury* (1942), a useful contemporary view of early radio programs; Settel, *A Pictorial History of Radio* (1967), dealing with network and some local station programs and stars; and the second Archer volume (see §6.4) for network radio in the 1930s. Shurick, *The First Quarter-Century of American Broadcasting* (1946), offers a series of topical chronologies, mainly on programming.

7.1 Radio in the Great Depression
An official statistical analysis, the first in-depth government survey of the business, is in the U.S. Bureau of the Census, *Radio Broadcasting* (1935). Codel, *Radio and its Future* (1930), is an anthology suggesting the likely post-1930 development of radio. A highly critical analysis of the radio industry is in Frost, *Is American Radio Democratic?* (1937), which argues for several major improvements. By the late 1930s, a whole literature critical of radio was appearing, for example Brindze, *Not To Be Broadcast: The Truth about Radio* (1937). Dygert, *Radio as an Advertising Medium* (1939), reflects radio organization and practice in the 1930s. See also Hettinger (§6.6). The structure and development of the FRC is best related in Schmeckebier, *The Federal Radio Commission* (1932), and in the FRC, *Annual Report*. Gross, *I Looked and I Listened* (1970), is the memoir of a pioneer newspaper commentator on the subject of radio.

7.2 From World War II to the Present
Rose, *National Policy for Radio Broadcasting* (1940), is an excellent early analysis of structural and other regulatory problems — many still evident today. White, *The American Radio* (1947), is a compact critical analysis of industry development pleading for more public service and educational applications, while Landry, *This Fascinating Radio Business* (1946), is a description of network radio development and peak years. Of the pretelevision analysis of radio broadcasting, Siepmann, *Radio's Second*

Chance (1946), shows how the public service role of radio could have been improved through the new FM service. The same author's *Radio, Television and Society* (1950), was an early college text focusing on the social impact of broadcasting prior to television. Waller, *Radio: The Fifth Estate* (1950), is a broad description of radio and early television. Wolfe, *Modern Radio Advertising* (1949), provides a long collection of articles assessing the radio business at its peak, while Midgley, *The Advertising and Business Side of Radio* (1948), covering the same period, deals more with structure and organization. Pusateri, *Enterprise in Radio* (1980), is an example of a published history of a single station (WWL in New Orleans) shedding light on this period. The most famous single radio broadcast is discussed in Koch, *The Panic Broadcast* (1970), and Cantril, *The Invasion from Mars* (1940), both of which include the complete Orson Welles script.

7.3 The Fall and Rise of FM Radio

While emotionally biased in the inventor's favor, the best book on the development of FM remains Lessing, *Man of High Fidelity* (1956). See also Siepmann (§7.2), and the sources noted for Chapter 12.

7.5 Radio Networks

The basic references for network radio programming include: Summers, *A Thirty-Year History of Programs* (1958), which is a chronologically arranged listing; and Dunning, *Tune In Yesterday* (1976), an alphabetically arranged narrative of major programs. Definitive treatment of the serial genre in film and radio is in Stedman, *The Serials* (1977), while drama programs for children are discussed in Harmon, *The Great Radio Heroes* (1967). Radio comedy forms are excerpted and analyzed in both Wertheim, *Radio Comedy* (1979), and Harmon, *The Great Radio Comedians* (1970). For musical formats, see §7.7.

The definitive analyses of prewar radio networks are the official view found in FCC, *Report on Chain Broadcasting* (1941), and Robinson, *Radio Networks and the Federal Government* (1943), providing a dispassionate analysis of changing trends. Both give details on affiliations, owned-and-operated stations, subsidiaries, etc. Some of the economic data of early networking is found in Eoyang, *An Economic Study of the Radio Industry* (1936). See also the early chapters of Bergreen (§6.5). Information on historical materials on early radio broadcasting can be found in Adams and Schreibman (1978), Pitts (1976), Schwartz (1973), and Weber (1976).

7.6 Radio News and Public Affairs

A fascinating and scholarly analysis of the impact of early news and comment on the radio networks is found in Culbert, *News for Everyman* (1976), with chapters on Kaltenborn, Carter, Swing, Davis, Lewis, and Murrow.

A more popular treatment of these and other news personalities is Fang, *Those Radio Commentators!* (1977). Individual biographies of newspeople abound — perhaps the best of the lot is Kendrick, *Prime Time: The Life of Edward R. Murrow* (1969). For the role of radio in presidential election campaigns, see Chester, *Radio, Television, and American Politics* (1969).

7.7 Broadcast Music

Two general histories of music in radio are Delong, *The Mighty Music Box* (1980), and Passman, *The Deejays* (1971), both informal narratives dealing with personalities and the music played. MacFarland, *The Development of the Top 40 Radio Format* (1979), is a scholarly analysis of the revolution in radio of the 1950s. Belz, *The Story of Rock* (1972), is dated, but remains one of the best discussions of the genre in both radio and recordings. See the phonograph sources in §5.1 for related developments in the record industry. The most detailed and documented narrative of radio's problems with both ASCAP and AFM is found in Chapters 12–14 of Warner, *Radio and Television Rights* (1953).

7.8–7.9 Radio's Renaissance and Specialty Formats

A useful study of the change brought about by television is Stuart, *The Effects of Television on the Motion Picture and Radio Industries* (1976). Development of music formats and their role is discussed in the works listed under §7.7. Routt et al., *The Radio Format Conundrum* (1978), and Eastman et al., *Broadcast Programming* (1981), Part Four, deal with current radio program types and strategies.

7.10 Fate of Network Radio

See Bergreen (§6.5), House CIFC, *Network Broadcasting* (1958), Chapter 13, and FCC (Network Inquiry Special Staff), *New Television Networks* (1980b), for data on the dramatic changes in network radio.

Chapter 8 Development of Commercial Television

8.1 Overview: The Contrast with Radio

The only good general history of television published to date is Barnouw, *Tube of Plenty* (1975), a one-volume version of the television material taken from his three-volume history (see 6). Books that stress programming trends (for which see Chapter 9), but deal in other aspects of TV as well include Greenfield, *Television: The First Fifty Years* (1977), a coffee-table illustrated history with an intelligently critical text; Shulman and Youman, *How Sweet It Was* (1966), detailing the first 15 years of network television; and Harris, *TV Guide: The First 25 Years* (1978), consisting of reprints of articles from the popular weekly program guide.

8.2 Quest for High Resolution

The only good history of TV technology is Abramson, *Electronic Motion Pictures* (1955). The most complete discussion of early mechanical television systems is Dinsdale, *First Principles of Television* (1932). For the important British work of the early years, see the excellent Pawley, *BBC Engineering: 1922–1972* (1972). Two works focusing on American practice in the late 1930s include Everson, *The Story of Television: The Life of Philo T. Farnsworth* (1949), and Waldrop and Borkin, *Television: A Struggle for Power* (1938), which relates the patent and business organization moves of the period. A summary of the papers and reports leading to the FCC's 1941 approval of television standards is in Fink, *Television Standards and Practice* (1943). Shiers, *Technical Development of Television* (1977), contains key articles on the development of video to the 1960s.

8.3 TV Freeze

A solid analysis of television allocation to the late 1950s is found in House CIFC, *Network Broadcasting* (1958), often referred to as the "Barrow Report." The famous "Sixth Report and Order" which ended the freeze is found in its entirety in *FCC Reports*, Volume 41. That entire volume is devoted to television allocation matters, including the two color-system decisions: one in 1950 favoring CBS, and one in 1953 favoring RCA (the current standard). Two published dissertations shedding light on this complicated period are Kittross, *Television Frequency Allocation Policy in the United States* (1979), and Stern, *The Federal Communications Commission and Television* (1979).

8.4 Implementation of Post-Freeze Allotment Plan

In addition to the House CIFC, *Network Broadcasting* (1958) report, and Kittross (§8.3), see Plotkin, *Television Network Regulation and the UHF Problem* (1955), and Jones, *Investigation of Television Networks and the UHF-VHF Problem* (1955), all of which describe the "deintermixture" debate of the 1950s.

8.5 TV Network Rivalries

The best source for the first decade of network development is House CIFC, *Network Broadcasting* (1958), the final report of the second FCC network investigation. It was continued by FCC (Network Inquiry Special Staff),

New Television Networks (1980a and 1980b), which exhaustively explores the changes of the 1960s and 1970s. See the reports by Plotkin and Jones (§8.4), and Cox, *Television Network Practices* (1957) for early concerns about the network role. Bergreen (§6.5) provides a readable overview of the rise of TV networks. Long, *The Development of the Television Network Oligopoly* (1979), is a scholarly analysis of the crucial years (to 1956) when the network pattern of centralized control was established. For specific networks, see Paley, *As it Happened* (1979), and Metz, *CBS* (1975), for the development of CBS; Quinlan, *Inside ABC* (1979); Hess, *An Historical Study of the DuMont Television Network* (1979); and Campbell, *The Golden Years of Broadcasting* (1976), for NBC's development. Bedell (1981), *Up the Tube: Prime-Time TV and the Silverman Years*, views program developments in all three networks through the career of one key executive. For studies of the economics of the network business, see Chapter 12.

8.6–8.7 Changes in Programming

For historical material, see the titles under §8.1 and §8.5 as well as Chapter 9. The development and impact of VTR is discussed in Abramson, "A Short History of Television Recording" (1954 and 1973).

8.8 Ethical Crises

Definitive treatment of the quiz scandals is in Anderson, *Television Fraud* (1978), which includes transcripts of several programs. An earlier contemporary critique is Weinberg, *TV and America* (1962), which shows the pressure of sponsor funding. Blacklisting is discussed more widely, perhaps the best overview being Vaughan, *Only Victims: A Study of Show Business Blacklisting* (1972). Contemporary works include the original broadcast published blacklist, *Counterattack, Red Channels* (1950), and two subsequent critiques of the blacklisters: Miller's *The Judges and the Judged* (1952), done for the ACLU, and Cogley's *Report on Blacklisting II* (1956). See also the suspenseful narrative in Faulk, *Fear on Trial* (1964).

Chapter 9 Commercial TV Programming

Of general reference value in this chapter are Brown, *The New York Times Encyclopedia of Television* (1977), which is a unique reference work, and Cole, *Television Today* (1981), an anthology of articles from *TV Guide*, mainly in the late 1970s. For historical material, see listings under §8.1, §8.5; for the business of television and its impact on programming, see Chapter 12. Reference works on network television programs include McNeal, *Total Television* (1980), an alphabetical narrative listing; Terrace, *The Complete Encyclopedia of Television Programs* (1979), which includes key credits; and David, *TV Season* (annual), which since 1973 has provided a directory of commercial, public TV, and syndicated programs and credits. See also §9.2.

9.1 Scheduling Strategies

The definitive treatment to date is Eastman et al., *Broadcast Programming* (1981), which details different types of station and network needs as seen by actual program executives. A useful supplement is Clift and Greer, *Broadcast Programming* (annual), a collection of trade press reprints showing trends in recent years.

9.2 Prime-Time Network Entertainment

Directories of prime-time network television content include Brooks and Marsh, *The Complete Directory to Prime Time Network TV Shows* (1979), which covers all types, and the very detailed directory of episodes (not just series) found in the two volumes of Gianakos, *Television Drama Series Programming* (1978, 1980). Views of what goes on in the prime-time program production process are contained in Levinson and Link, *Stay Tuned* (1981), where two highly successful producers detail what happens and how; and two books by Cantor, *The Hollywood TV Producer* (1972), and *Prime-Time Television* (1980), a broader introduction to the process and content trends. Analyses of specific programs in any depth are usually restricted to fan books of a popular nature. The science-fiction program *Star Trek*, while only marginally successful in its network run, has continued to attract big syndicated audiences. Two excellent books detail what goes into the making of such a complicated show: Gerrold, *The World of Star Trek* (1973), and Whitfield and Roddenberry, *The Making of Star Trek* (1968). Gerrold wrote for the series, and Roddenberry was series producer. Three insightful books on television comedy include Adler, *All in the Family* (1979), an anthology of scripts and critical articles on the 1971–1979 series; Miller and Rhodes, *Only You, Dick Daring* (1965), a tongue-in-cheek account of a real attempt to get a new comedy series on the air; and Allen, *The Funny Men* (1956), a review of the factors in the radio-TV success of a number of stars. Two recent scholarly analyses of television as entertainment are Tannenbaum, *The Entertainment Functions of Television* (1980), an anthology of studies, and Greenberg, *Life on Television: Content Analysis of U.S. TV Drama* (1980), reviewing the portrayal of different images and societal groups.

9.3 Non-Prime-Time Network Entertainment

There is a huge fan literature on daytime serial and quiz shows but it is both ephemeral in nature and shallow in approach. Of value for their historical and analytical content are Fabe, *TV Game Shows* (1979), and Stedman on serials (see §7.5).

9.4 Television News

The book-length literature, much of it highly critical, on television network journalism, is sizable, but much is of short-term interest, focusing as it does on specific events or personalities. Halberstam, *The Powers That Be* (1979), details the rise of CBS news against a context of postwar development of two major newspapers and a news magazine. Johnstone et al., *The News People* (1976), offers a survey of demographics and working views of broadcast and print journalists. LeRoy and Sterling, *Mass News: Practices, Controversies and Alternatives* (1973), includes television and newspaper journalism. The standard review of broadcast journalism on both network and station level since 1968 has been Barrett, *The Alfred I. DuPont-Columbia University Survey of Broadcast Journalism*, issued in connection with annual awards for quality programs. Behind-the-scenes views of network news division operation are found in Epstein, *News from Nowhere* (1973), Fred Friendly's *Due to Circumstances beyond Our Control* (1967), which details the Murrow years at CBS, Kendrick's biography of Murrow (§7.6), and Gates, *Air Time: The Inside Story of CBS News* (1978), providing biographical information on key reporters. See also §19.7.

9.5 Public Affairs Programming

See first of all, all the sources noted under §9.4. The classic study of the early television documentary, Bluem, *Documentary in American Television* (1965), is updated to cover the 1965–1975 period in Hammond, *The Image Decade* (1981). The life and work of an important documentary producer is related in Yellin, *Special: Fred Freed and the Television Documentary* (1973). Mamber, *Cinema Vérité in America* (1974) reviews the relation between the film and television versions of this genre. See also §19.7.

9.6 Sports Programming

Discussing the rise of television impact on sports is Johnson, *Super Spectator and the Electronic Lilliputians* (1971). Sugar's *"The Thrill of Victory:" The Inside Story of ABC Sports* (1978), details the development of the most successful network sports effort.

9.7 The Electronic Church

Most of the literature on religious broadcasting is of the "how-to" variety. Broadly descriptive of religious broadcasting within many different denominations is Duke, *Religious Publishing and Communications* (1981), which profiles several major broadcast organizations. Armstrong, *Religious Broadcasting: Sourcebook* (1978), and NRB, *Annual Directory of Religious Broadcasting*, represent the religious broadcasters' own view of their role and work. Hadden and Swann, *Prime Time Preachers* (1981), and Morris, *The Preachers* (1973), are strong attacks on the conservative users of the TV pulpit.

9.8 Children's Programming

The published research and argument on children's television is huge — aside from listings here, see §10.7, §13.4, and §19.5. An overview of what TV provides for children and of the "kidvid" issues is found in FCC, *Television Programming for Children* (1979), the most intensive investigation of the subject by the commission to date. Part of the research for that study appears in expanded form in Turow, *Entertainment, Education and the Hard Sell: Three Decades of Network Children's Television* (1981), with tables and descriptive/critical discussion. Another useful content analysis of commercial TV station fare, based on a sample of network and independent stations, is Barcus and Wolkin, *Children's Television* (1977). A general advisory guide for parents is Kaye, *The ACT Guide to Children's Television* (1979). The economics driving commercial television is criticized in Melody, *Children's Television* (1973). A nostalgia-filled review of early children's programs is in Glut and Harmon, *The Great Television Heroes* (1975).

9.9 Appraising the TV Program Service

For the literature on and by TV's critics, see §18.7.

Chapter 10 The Noncommercial Alternative

10.1 Why "Public" Broadcasting?

The broadest survey of educational and public broadcasting is Wood and Wylie, *Educational Telecommunications* (1977). While a number of books, noted below, speak favorably of public broadcasting, as yet there is no book-length study critical of the idea. See CPB, *Status Report on Public Broadcasting* (1981), for a statistical overview of stations, networks, employment, programming, and finance.

10.2 Rise of Educational Broadcasting

For overall histories of public broadcasting, see Blakely, *To Serve the Public Interest* (1979), and Gibson, *Public Broadcasting: The Role of the Federal Government, 1912–1976* (1977), both focusing on institutions and such critical moments as the 1952 Freeze and the 1967 Carnegie I report. For a more specific history of the first decade of public television, see Powell, *Channels of Learning* (1962). The early educational/instructional role of radio is discussed in Saettler, *A History of Instructional Technology* (1968), which gets into television and relates both media to wider instructional technology developments. The Carnegie I report is CCET, *Public Television* (1967), while the legislation it fostered is discussed in Burke, *The Public Broadcasting Act of 1967* (1972). The most detailed view of pre-NPR public radio is found in Land, *The Hidden Medium* (1967).

10.3 National Organization

For the best detailing of the problems between CPB and PBS, including the Nixon intervention, see Avery and Pepper, *The Politics of Interconnection* (1979). A history of the period, and argument for one view of public broadcasting, is found in Macy, *To Irrigate a Wasteland* (1974). Best up-to-date information on the Corporation, its research and financial statistics, is in CPB, *Annual Report*. Carnegie II is CCFPB, *A Public Trust* (1979).

10.4 Types of Public Stations

For data on number and types of stations, employment, finance, and the like, see the annual reports from CPB, *Summary Statistical Report of Public Television Licensees*, and the parallel *Summary Statistical Report of CPB-Qualified Public Radio Stations*, the latter covering about 200 of the 1,000 noncommercial stations on the air. See also PTR, "Public Radio" (1979).

10.5 The Search for Funding

Ford Foundation, *Ford Foundation Activities in Noncommercial Broadcasting, 1951–1976* (1976), and Blakely (see §10.2) tell the story of foundation support, especially in the pre-1967 period. For other aspects, see Carnegie I and II reports, Avery-Pepper (§10.3) for the long-range funding battle, the CPB *Annual Report*, and the CPB statistical publications noted under §10.1 and §10.4. State support is detailed in National Public Radio, *Public Radio and State Governments* (1981).

10.6 Programming

The basic statistical information on what public stations program, when, and from whence it comes, is found in the biennial reports from CPB, *Public Television Program Content* (1979), and *Public Radio Programming Content*

(1979). One discussion of what public television should be programming is in Blakely, *The People's Instrument* (1971), while a more recent view is Katzman, *Program Decisions in Public Television* (1976), detailing the process.

10.7 Children and Classrooms

The development of Children's Television Workshop is told in Polsky, *Getting to Sesame Street* (1974), while summaries of what the programs accomplished are in the sympathetic Lesser, *Children and Television: Lessons from Sesame Street* (1974), and the more critical Cook et al., *Sesame Street Revisited* (1975). The use of media in education is annually reviewed in the directory edited by Brown, *Educational Media Yearbook*. CPB, *Uses of Television for Instruction* (1979), is a detailed survey of educational broadcasting across the country.

10.8 Impact of Public Broadcasting

The classic study of PTV audiences is Schramm et al., *The People Look at Educational Television* (1963), based on a survey of six pioneer stations. The standard review of research findings on the instructional role of TV is in Chu and Schramm, *Learning from Television* (1967), while an assessment of recent efforts in both method and substance is in CPB, *Review of 1980 CPB Communication Research Findings* (1981).

10.9 The Outlook

Details on long-range financing are found in *Public Telecommunications Financing Act of 1978*, and in *Public Broadcasting Amendments Act of 1981*. For the future, see CPB, *Five Year Plan for Public Telecommunications 1981–1985* (1981), and also Gunn, *Window on the Future* (1979).

Chapter 11 Cable and Newer Technologies

11.1 Evolution of Cable

Legal and business matters have changed so rapidly in recent years that any book on cable prior to 1979 is of value primarily as history. A good overview of cable and other media, with several sections on federal and state regulation, is Hollowell, *The Cable/Broadband Communications Book, Volume 2, 1980–81* (1980). Dealing with legalities past and present is Hamburg, *All About Cable* (1979). The development of FCC cable policies is described in Le Duc, *Cable Television and the FCC* (1973), up to the 1972 definitive rules. The degree of unraveling of those rules in a short time is evident in Rivkin, *A New Guide to Federal Cable Television Regulations* (1978). Information on state cable franchising and local franchise developments moves too quickly for book discussion

— inquire of the National Cable Television Association (1725 Massachusetts Ave., NW, Washington, DC 20036), the main cable trade association, or the Cable Television Information Center (2100 M St. NW, Washington, DC 20036), an independent advisory service. For background on the copyright question, see Johnston, *Copyright Handbook* (1978), and U.S. Library of Congress, Copyright Office, *General Guide to the Copyright Act of 1976* (1977).

11.2 Cable Economics

Here again, the most important material is in such trade periodicals as the weekly *Cablevision*. Summary statistics on number of systems, ownership, economics, and programming appear in the annual *TV Factbook* (services volume) while historical trend data is in Sterling and Haight (§5.1). Latest financial results for the industry appear in FCC, *Cable Television Industry Revenues*. For survey results of local origination and other material provided by cable systems, see National Cable Television Association, *Cable Services Report: Local Programming* (annual). The public service options available to cable are analyzed in National Science Foundation, *Social Services and Cable TV* (1976). Access channels are discussed in Gillespie, *Public Access Cable Television in the United States and Canada* (1975), while the early New York City experience with access is reviewed in Othmer, *The Wired Island* (1973). To learn more about cable as an advertising medium, see National Cable Television Association, *Cable Advertising Directory* (annual).

11.3 Interactive Cable

The only book on the subject to date is Veith, *Talk-Back TV: Two-Way Cable Television* (1976). The expansion of Qube and other systems is discussed in the trade press regularly. For a packet of information on Qube, write to Warner-Amex, 75 Rockefeller Plaza, New York, NY 10019.

11.4 Satellite Interconnection

For the technical basics, see §4.6. A good historical overview, showing the role of military and international considerations in development of communications satellites is in Smith, *Communication via Satellite* (1977). A good review of the nontechnical issues is Pelton and Snow, *Economic and Policy Problems in Satellite Communications* (1977). The important FCC policy decisions surrounding domestic communication satellites are related in Magnant, *Domestic Satellite* (1977). Directories of satellite services to cable, whether subscription- or advertiser-supported, appear regularly in trade weeklies, especially *Broadcasting* and *Cablevision*. For direct broadcast satellites, see Belendiuk and Robb, *Broadcasting via Satellite*

(1979), FCC (Office of Plans and Policy), *Staff Report on Policies for Regulation of Direct Broadcast Satellites* (1980), and Taylor, *Direct-to-Home Satellite Broadcasting* (1980). All are already somewhat dated as this field moves rapidly. *Television/Radio Age* continues to provide Taylor's good DBS articles. See also the Summer 1981 issue of *Federal Communication Law Journal*, which is largely devoted to DBS policy options and issues.

11.5 Pay Cable

Again, there is little of a book-length nature on this topic. For useful background, see Scott, *Bringing Premium Entertainment into the Home via Pay-Cable TV* (1977), and Mahoney et al., *Keeping Pace with the New Television* (1980), the latter a pilot study for a new cultural pay-cable service, with good chapters on subscription TV and home video as well as pay cable. The most exhaustive analysis is in Technology & Economics Inc., *The Emergence of Pay Cable Television* (1980), with details on operating systems, programs, economics, and vanishing regulation.

11.6 Subscription TV

A good integrative discussion of background and current development, economics, and regulation is Howard and Carroll, *Subscription Television* (1980). There is a rapidly growing literature on teletext and videotex systems and applications. Sigel, *Videotext* (1980), is a basic introduction, while Woolfe, *Videotex* (1980), is more detailed and includes color examples from competing systems.

11.7 Home Video

The EIA, *Consumer Electronics* (annual), is a free collection of statistics and text showing the growth in sale of broadcast and video components, one indicator of the growth in this area. There are a score of consumer guides on purchase of the ever-larger number and variety of consumer electronics components, but aside from expensive industry weekly or monthly newsletters in this field, the best source of information is industry trade periodicals including *Broadcasting*, *Cablevision*, and *Variety*.

Chapter 12 Administrative and Financial Organization

12.1 The Station

Books on broadcast station operations tend to date quickly. Quaal and Brown, *Broadcast Management* (1975), is the most substantial single-volume approach. For radio, Johnson and Jones, *Modern Radio Station Practices* (1978), gives a balanced analysis of different aspects of running a station, along with more than a dozen detailed profiles of actual stations. Dessart, *Television in the Real*

World (1978), is a case study of placing a commercial TV station on the air with related regulatory, economic, and programming questions. For citations on ownership concentration, see §17.7. For the role of programming, see Eastman et al. (§9.1).

12.2–12.5 Networks and Affiliates

The definitive and exhaustive work on this topic is FCC's Network Inquiry Special Staff, *New Television Networks* (1980). Included are documents and analysis of network-affiliate contracts (including copies), compensation schemes, network ownership of stations, program procurement, etc. An excellent anthology of research articles is in Botein and Rice, *Network Television and the Public Interest* (1981). Specific discussions of the network program process are noted at §8.5 and §9.2, but in addition see the dated but still insightful Brown, *Televi$ion: The Business behind the Box* (1971), and the economic analysis in Owen et al., *Television Economics* (1974), which concentrates on the programming process.

12.6 Financial Framework of Broadcasting

The FCC publishes official data on the financial status of commercial networks and stations in FCC, *AM-FM Financial Data* (annual), and *Television Broadcast Financial Data* (annual). Most of this material is incorporated later into the FCC *Annual Report*. While individual station data are not revealed, the reports give much specific market information. It is interesting to compare the FCC data with those of the National Association of Broadcasters, *Radio Financial Report* (annual), and *Television Financial Report* (annual), based on analyses of sample stations and providing data for typical stations in each of about a dozen market sizes as well as for different types of stations. See also notes for Chapter 13.

12.7 Employment in Broadcasting

The FCC financial reports noted just above include official data on employment patterns in radio and television. The role of minority employment (as well as minority content in programming) is detailed in U.S. Commission on Civil Rights, *Window Dressing on the Set* (1977, 1979). The only book on unions in broadcasting is Koenig, *Broadcasting and Bargaining* (1970).

Chapter 13 Broadcast Advertising

Readers may find one of the several available general advertising texts a useful background to this chapter. History of advertising is covered under §5.1. A useful systems approach to this whole subject is DeLozier, *The Marketing Communications Process* (1976), with many unique diagrams. There are several glossaries of advertising terms available, one of the better ones being N. W. Ayer Co.'s *The Ayer Glossary of Advertising and Related Terms* (1977), which is often updated. Turning specifically to broadcasting, a critical essay/history on the development of the advertiser's role first in radio and then in television, and the issues raised by that role, is Barnouw, *The Sponsor* (1978).

13.1–13.3 Advantages, Flexibility, Integration

There are two good general texts on broadcast advertising that touch on most matters in this chapter. See Heighton and Cunningham, *Advertising in the Broadcast Media* (1976), and Ziegler and Howard, *Broadcast Advertising* (1978). More specialized works on radio abound, though they are of considerably less value as most are badly dated — an exception being Murphy, *Handbook of Radio Advertising* (1980). The only book on PSAs is Paletz et al., *Politics in Public Service Advertising on Television* (1977), which contends that PSAs air only establishment views. For the role of promotion in radio and television, increasingly important as local image competition increases, see Eastman and Klein's *Strategies for Broadcast and Cable Promotion* (1982).

13.4 Time and Taste Standards

For the industry standard, see the NAB, *The Radio Code* (1980), and *The Television Code* (1980), now revised almost annually. See also §18.6. There is a good deal on children's TV advertising; see especially, Federal Trade Commission, *Staff Report on Television Advertising to Children* (1978), which, even though nothing came of it, makes a strong case for government-as-parent, and Adler, *The Effects of Television Advertising on Children* (1980).

13.5, 13.8 Deceptive Advertising and Unethical Practices

There is a growing literature on the Federal Trade Commission. Compare the views in Cox et al., *The Nader Report on the Federal Trade Commission* (1969), with the more scholarly and measured analysis in Stone, *Economic Regulation and the Public Interest: The Federal Trade Commission in Theory and Practice* (1978). For the increase in FTC activism after 1970, which eventually got the agency into trouble with Congress, see Clarkson and Muris, *The FTC since 1970* (1981). The standard work on the subject is Rosden and Rosden, *The Law of Advertising* (1974).

13.7 Selling Broadcast Advertising

See the titles noted under §13.1–13.3 for the overall process. Useful books delving behind the scenes are

Diamant, *The Anatomy of a Television Commercial* (1970), a detailed step-by-step narrative of the planning and making of one TV ad and Busch and Landeck, *The Making of a Television Commercial* (1981), which in more generic fashion deals with the same topic. Diamant, *Television's Classic Commercials* (1971), provides storyboards for many of network TV's first decade of ads. Price, *The Best Thing on TV: Commercials* (1978), reviews the making and impact of a number of famous TV spots from the 1970s, treating commercials as a creative art. An interesting study of the well-known "reach out and touch someone" commercial campaign of AT&T is Arlen, *Thirty Seconds* (1980).

Chapter 14 Audience Measurement and Testing

14.1 Feedback in Broadcasting

The first book on audience research in radio dealt mainly with analysis of audience feedback whether solicited by the station or not — Lumley, *Measurement in Radio* (1934). A decade later, the increasing sophistication of research methods, especially use of the telephone, is evident in Chappell and Hooper, *Radio Audience Measurement* (1944). Good background for this chapter as well as Chapters 19 and 20 is NAB, *Standard Definitions of Broadcast Research Terms* (1973).

14.2–14.3, 14.7 Ratings Business, Concepts, Issues

While dated, the most intensive examination of broadcast ratings practice and theory remains Madow et al., *Evaluation of Statistical Methods Used in Obtaining Broadcast Ratings* (1961). The best short description of the current ratings system is a booklet by Beville, head of the Broadcast Rating Council, "Understanding Broadcast Ratings" (1981).

14.4–14.5 Collecting Data and Sampling

NAB, *A Broadcast Research Primer* (1974), gives instructions for conducting elementary local audience surveys as does Fletcher, *Handbook of Radio and TV Broadcasting: Research Procedures in Audience, Program and Revenues* (1981). See also notes for §20.4.

14.6 Broadcast Audiences

The increase in knowledge about characteristics of the radio audience can be traced in several publicatons. One of the first scholarly analyses is Beville, *Social Stratification of the Radio Audience* (1939) — the author still being active in ratings research four decades later (see §14.2).

After World War II, two similar volumes appeared, which detailed national radio listening patterns just before the introduction of television: Lazarsfeld and Field, *The People Look at Radio* (1946), and the more complete report, Lazarsfeld and Kendall, *Radio Listening in America* (1948). The first similar report for television, based on a 1960 survey, was Steiner, *The People Look at Television* (1963). A summary of earlier television studies is found in Bogart (1972). The Steiner study is being updated on a decade basis — Bower, *Television and the Public* (1973), contains data for 1970, and Bower will author the 1980 update as well, to appear in 1982. The definitive study of the television audience, summarizing the now vast research and trade literature on all aspects of the subject, is Comstock et al., *Television and Human Behavior* (1978). Another study seeking to find various types of television viewers as defined by both their viewing habits and broader life styles is Frank and Greenberg, *The Public's Use of Television* (1980). Reissued every year or so with updated national survey information is The Roper Organization, *Evolving Public Attitudes toward Television and other Mass Media* (1981), with comparable information back to 1959. For data on national and market demographics, the prime source is the latest official U.S. Census, volumes of which are held in most public libraries. Easier to use is the annual Department of Commerce, *Statistical Abstract of the United States*. The ratings firms (see §14.2) provide pamphlets on the major markets with population and other demographic information, regularly updated.

14.8 Nonrating Research

Perhaps the first book based on field research in radio and suggesting other studies was Cantril and Allport, *The Psychology of Radio* (1935). Lazarsfeld, *Radio and the Printed Page* (1940), reviewed the impact of the newer medium on the older, and comparative audience use patterns prior to World War II. It led directly to a series of volumes edited by Lazarsfeld and Stanton, *Radio Research* (1942, 1944), and *Communications Research* (1949), which demonstrate the growing academic and radio business interest in serious studies of media impact. Merton, *Mass Persuasion* (1946), is a case study of radio's use to sell war bonds in 1944. For the more modern studies, see Katz (§1.8) and Chapters 19 and 20.

Chapter 15   Law of Broadcasting

Note A: General References

There are a number of books that are of value for material discussed in Chapters 15–18 of *BIA*. For the historical development of broadcast regulation, see notes for §6.7

and §15.3. Socolow, *The Law of Radio Broadcasting* (1939), is the first lengthy treatise on the subject; and used with Warner, *Radio and Television Law* (1948), and *Radio and Television Rights* (1953), will provide the most complete analysis of FCC regulation up to the early decisions on television. A chronological collection of the most important legal cases and other documents is in Kahn, *Documents of American Broadcasting* (1978). A collection of law journal articles on the increasing complexity of broadcast regulation from 1959 to 1978 is in Ferrall, *Yearbook of Broadcasting Articles* (1980). There are two current casebooks on regulation of broadcasting that include excerpts from FCC and court decisions as well as congressional actions: Ginsburg, *Regulation of Broadcasting* (1979), and Jones, *Cases and Materials on Electronic Mass Media* (1979), both covering essentially the same material, though organized differently. An excellent primer to the subjects discussed in these chapters is Krasnow et al., *The Politics of Broadcast Regulation* (1982). Two economic critiques of regulatory decisions and trends are Noll et al., *Economic Aspects of Television Regulation* (1973), and Levin, *Fact and Fancy in Television Regulation* (1980), both of which are quite wide-ranging. The NAB regularly updates industry views of regulatory issues in *Broadcasting and Government*; *Broadcasting* magazine's "Where Things Stand," in the first issue of every month, briefly summarizes the status of outstanding issues.

Note B: Finding the Law

While the documentation of administrative agencies, the courts, and Congress can seem forbidding to the uninitiated, here are some tips on keeping current. On the broadest level, there are a number of legal research texts, two of the more useful being Cohen, *How to Find the Law* (1976), and the shorter, Jacobstein and Mersky, *Legal Research Illustrated* (1977), both regularly updated. A good introduction to specific research on broadcasting topics is Le Duc, "Broadcast Legal Documentation" (1973). See also Foley, "Broadcast Regulation Research" (1973). A composite current source of broadcast regulation materials from the FCC, courts, and Congress is Pike and Fischer, *Radio Regulation*, a loose-leaf reporter system completely indexed and updated weekly. Court decisions of the Court of Appeals for any circuit are printed in the *Federal Reporter*, while Supreme Court decisions are officially reported in *United States Reports* as well as several commercial sources discussed in Le Duc's article noted above. See notes for §16.1 for further FCC document sources.

15.1 National Communication Policy

An excellent general overview of institutions, issues, and trends is found in the "Telecommunications in the

United States" special issue of *Telecommunication Journal* (1980). For some of the development of those agencies, see Will, *Telecommunications Structure and Management in the Executive Branch of Government* (1978). More technical discussions of spectrum issues are found in the two studies by JTAC, *Radio Spectrum Conservation* (1952), and *Radio Spectrum Utilization* (1965). See also the sources noted under §2.1 and 2.7.

15.2 Constitutional Context
See notes for §15.7 and 17.1.

15.3 Communications Act Basics
The official compilation, in chronological order, of all U.S. laws on radio and telecommunications from 1910 to date is U.S. Congress, House of Representatives, *Radio Laws of the United States* (1978), frequently revised. For a printing of the Act as currently used, see FCC, *The Communications Act of 1934* (1978), issued in loose-leaf form with an index; it includes the COMSAT Act of 1962, other additions to the original act, and relevant parts of the Administrative Procedures Act. Of considerable historic interest is a book written by the senator most responsible for the 1934 act, Dill, *Radio Law* (1938).

15.4–15.5 Licensing and Programming
See notes for §16.2–16.4 for licensing, and Chapter 17 for program matters.

15.6 Communications Act Issues
The official transcripts of the hearings on the various rewrite attempts, though voluminous, are very useful for a broad view of issues on telecommunications and broadcasting. The process began with publication by its staff of House CIFC, *Options Papers* (1977), a very broad survey of possible courses of action for the Congress and FCC. This led to seemingly endless hearings over the next several years, valuable for their detailed record of opinions and research on all aspects of telecommunications, thus providing a context for broadcasting. See House CIFC, *The Communications Act of 1978: Hearings on H.R. 13015* (1979), House CIFC, *The Communications Act of 1979: Hearings on H.R. 3333* (1980), for the first "rewrite of the rewrite"; Senate CCST, *Amendments to the Communications Act of 1934* (1980), which marked the first serious interest in that side of Congress; and House JC, *Telecommunications Act of 1980* (1980), where one committee of the House disagreed with another and held up the third complete rewrite attempt.

15.7 Other Laws Affecting Broadcasting
For the international side, see Bobroff, *United States Trea-*

ties and Other International Agreements Pertaining to Telecommunications (1974), as well as the sources noted at §1.4. Copyright sources are noted under §11.1. For the role of the FTC, see §13.5. There are a number of useful books on the media and regulation. DeVol, *Mass Media and the Supreme Court: The Legacy of the Warren Years* (1976), includes most of the important recent cases. Of the many available media regulation texts, see Pember, *Mass Media Law* (1981), for the most journalistic and least "legal" treatment, François, *Mass Media Law and Regulation* (1978), for a more inclusive journalist approach, and for a case book, try either Gillmor and Barron, *Mass Communication Law* (1979), or Franklin, *The First Amendment and the Fourth Estate* (1981). A good annual review of the latest trends and cases is Practising Law Institute, *Communications Law*. For minority employment, see §12.7. A practical approach to current equal employment opportunity rules of the FCC is found in Aird, *A Broadcaster's Guide to Designing and Implementing an Effective EEO Program* (1980). State telecommunications regulation is covered in Sadowski, *An Analysis of Statutory Laws Governing Commercial and Educational Broadcasting in the Fifty States* (1979), and Hochberg, *The States Regulate Cable* (1978).

Chapter 16 Administration of the Law: FCC at Work

16.1 FCC Basics
One of the most extensive and intensive analyses of administrative agencies is found in Senate CGO, *Study on Federal Regulation* (1977), which analyzes all aspects with suggestions for improvement, including many references to the FCC. Noted throughout are citations on the substantial literature dealing with administrative agencies, regulation, and policymaking. A good collection of case studies, three dealing with electronic media, is Owen and Braeutigam, *The Regulation Game* (1978). Kittross, *Administration of American Telecommunications Policy* (1980), provides a collection of documents on the development of and criticism of the FCC. Obviously a key document for study is the FCC *Annual Report*, with text and tables on both the agency and the industries regulated. More recently, the agency has produced a detailed annual guide to ongoing "dockets" and rulemakings: FCC, *Major Matters Before the Federal Communications Commission*. A unique guide to nearly a half century of FCC decision-making with regard to the 1934 Act is found in Rubin et al., *FCC Decisions Interpreting the Communications Act of 1934: An Index* (1978). The FCC's rules and regulations are published in CFR (*Code*

of *Federal Regulations*), *Title 47: Telecommunications* (annual). Of the four volumes, the first deals with the FCC itself (organization and procedures) while the third is devoted to broadcasting matters and runs to 600 pages. FCC-proposed and final rules first appear in the daily issues of the FR (*Federal Register*), and are gathered chronologically in FCC and FCC 2d (*Federal Communications Commission Reports*, 1st and 2d series), now accumulating at the rate of four to six fat volumes annually. See also Pike and Fischer under Note 15-B. Two useful books critical of the FCC are Cole and Oettinger, *Reluctant Regulators* (1978), reporting on the FCC's impact on broadcasting (and vice versa) in the early 1970s, and GAO, *Organizing the Federal Communications Commission for Greater Management and Regulatory Effectiveness* (1979).

16.2–16.8 Broadcast Licensing

All of the sources mentioned under Note 15-A include material on the all-important licensing process. Though dated, Emery, *Broadcasting and Government: Responsibilities and Regulations* (1971), contains detail on the licensing process found nowhere else. For the development of the process, see especially Edelman, *The Licensing of Radio Services in the United States, 1927–1947* (1950), and Jones, *Licensing of Major Broadcast Facilities by the Federal Communications Commission* (1966). Two more of the detailed GAO reports on the Commission, GAO, *Selected FCC Regulatory Policies* (1979), and the same agency's earlier *The Role of Field Operations in the Federal Communications Commission's Regulatory Structure* (1978) shed considerable light on the licensing process. Heavily devoted to the initial application process as well as subsequent renewals is NAB *Legal Guide to FCC Broadcast Rules, Regulations and Policies* (1977). For the WHDH case, see §17.7, while for licensee appraisal by citizen's groups, see §18.2.

16.9 FCC Issues

A fascinating and yet chilling report is Graham and Kramer's report to the Senate Committee on Commerce, *Appointments to the Regulatory Agencies* (1976), which uses the FCC as one example and deals with all members of that body from 1949 through 1974. One criticism of the FCC has been its handling of innovations, which is discussed in Mosco, *Broadcasting in the United States: Innovative Challenge and Organizational Control* (1979).

16.10 Deregulation

For network regulation trends, see §12.2. Two good additional examples of the role of economics in deregulatory moves at the FCC are FCC, *Deregulation of Radio* (1981), and *Cable Television Syndicated Program Exclusivity Rules* (1980).

Chapter 17 Freedom and Fairness in Broadcasting

17.1, 17.3 First Amendment and Broadcast Speech

Recent text overviews are Barron and Dienes, *Handbook of Free Speech and Free Press* (1979), and Cullen, *Mass Media and the First Amendment* (1981). Two earlier classics, both done for the postwar Commission on the Freedom of the Press or Hutchins Commission (after its chair) are Hocking, *Freedom of the Press: A Framework of Principle* (1947), and Chafee, *Government and Mass Communications* (1947). See also the general texts under Note 15-A and §15.7.

17.2 Unprotected Speech

These topics are covered in the books in Note 15-A and §15.7, but in addition a number of specialty volumes are of value. Lawhorne, *Defamation and Public Officials* (1971), details the development of libel law. Still a standard work is the Commission on Obscenity and Pornography, *Report* (1970). For censorship in film, see Randall, *Censorship of the Movies* (1967). For the question of reporter privilege, see van Gerpen, *Privileged Communication and the Press* (1979). The ever-larger concern about privacy in an age of increasing technology is well analyzed in Privacy Protection Study Commission, *Personal Privacy in an Information Society* (1977).

17.4–17.6, 17.8 Fairness

The standard work promoting a right of access to the media is Barron, *Freedom of the Press for Whom?* (1973), based on the author's path-breaking 1967 law journal article. A solid history of the Fairness Doctrine is found in Simmons, *The Fairness Doctrine and the Media* (1978). Kittross and Harwood, *Free and Fair* (1970), reprints *Journal of Broadcasting* articles on free press vs. fair trial and the early years of the Fairness Doctrine. While sometimes difficult to read, Schmidt, *Freedom of the Press vs. Public Access* (1976), provides an excellent comparison of the legal status of print compared to that of the electronic media. Written almost like a novel, and relating the entire story of the Red Lion Case, is Friendly, *The Good Guys, The Bad Guys, and the First Amendment* (1976). One topic of considerable controversy is covered in Prakash, *Advocacy Advertising and Large Corporations* (1977).

17.7 Antimonopoly Regulation

A good overview relating structure to content and examining the conflicting pressures in various media is Owen, *Economics and Freedom of Expression* (1975). The best analyses of ownership specifically, relating regulatory and business trends and current status is Compaine,

Who Owns the Media? (1979). FTC, *Proceedings of the Symposium on Media Concentration* (1979), provides a wealth of text and tabular detail in a series of scholarly papers reviewing press and broadcasting control. Baer et al., *Concentration of Mass Media Ownership* (1974), is an earlier but still useful review of existing literature, especially with its concern for the impact of ownership patterns on media content. Quinlan, *The Hundred Million Dollar Lunch* (1974), tells the tortured tale of Boston's WHDH television case. For a strong attack on established patterns of television control, including network and newspaper ownership, see Bunce, *Television in the Corporate Interest* (1976). On the other hand, Cherington et al., *Television Station Ownership* (1971), is more descriptive and supportive of existing trends, while Seiden, *Who Controls the Media?* (1974), attempts to debunk the thesis that concentration is always bad.

Chapter 18 Beyond the FCC: Nonregulatory Influences

18.1 Informal Government Controls

A critical but valuable overview of how the congressional system works can be obtained from two works that touch on communication matters: Price et al., *The Commerce Committees: A Study of the House and Senate Commerce Committees* (1975), done for the Ralph Nader organization, and Peabody et al., *To Enact a Law* (1972), which traces a proposed congressional campaign financing measure from inception to final passage. The literature on Congress is immense, but much is dated or of only tangential concern. See the annual oversight hearings by both the Senate and House Commerce committees over the FCC, NTIA, CPB, and similar agencies to get a flavor of the indirect oversight/intervention process. The classic example of government (presidential) intervention into the media is the Nixon administration (1969–1974), though of course somewhat similar moves were taken in earlier administrations. See Porter, *Assault on the Media: The Nixon Years* (1976), for a dispassionate overview.

18.2–18.5 Citizens and Consumerism

A good general analysis is Guimary, *Citizen's Groups and Broadcasting* (1975). For more specific information, though it dates fast as groups decline and re-form is Draves, *Citizen's Media Directory* (1977), supplemented by NCCB, "Citizen's Media Directory Update" (1979). One of the more active organizations, the Office of Communication of the United Church of Christ, has helped other groups with a series of publications. While deregulatory moves by the FCC and Congress have changed some of the ground rules, the following are still of some value: Jennings and Richard, *How to Protect Your Rights in Television and Radio* (1974), and Bennett, *A Lawyer's Sourcebook: Representing the Audience in Broadcast Proceedings* (1974). A review of the situation in the 1970s is found in Grundfest, *Citizen Participation in Broadcast Licensing before the FCC* (1976). Providing a guide for the general public, though also somewhat dated by deregulatory actions since it was written, is Shapiro, *Media Access: Your Rights To Express Your Views on Radio and Television* (1976). Of interest historically because its author then was a member of the FCC is Johnson, *How to Talk Back to Your Television Set* (1970). Though its title is merely an attention-getter, Milam, *Sex and Broadcasting: A Handbook on Starting Community Radio Stations* (1975), provides much detailed valuable advice on starting and running a noncommercial or only semicommercial small radio station.

18.6 Industry Self-Regulation

A basic reference is NAB, *Broadcast Self-Regulation: Manual of the National Association of Broadcasters' Code Authority*, a loose-leaf publication with the latest edition of the NAB codes (see §13.4), along with the frequently issued guidelines and interpretations. A number of other codes, including those of the RTNDA and the ABA are found in Kittross and Harwood (§17.4) among other sources. For a case study of self-regulation via the so-called "family viewing" hour, see Cowan, *See No Evil* (1979). Of the many books and anthologies on media ethics and self-regulation, the oldest yet most recently revised offers the best overview: Rivers et al., *Responsibility in Mass Communication* (1980).

18.7 Other Influences

From time to time, the National News Council issues cumulative reports of its activities. See National News Council, *In the Public Interest — II* (1979), which covers decisions in the 1975–1978 period. There is an increasing library of books on television criticism. The best introduction is Smith, *Beyond the Wasteland: The Criticism of Broadcasting* (1980). Dealing with the work of several specific critics is Himmelstein, *On the Small Screen: New Approaches in Television and Video Criticism* (1981), while Newcomb, *Television: The Critical View* (1979), is a thoughtful anthology of both program and longer-range critical writing. Shayon, *Open to Criticism* (1971), is unique in that a critic takes his own columns for a number of years and self-criticizes them. Thought by many in recent years to be the best critic of television is *The New Yorker* columnist Michael Arlen. Much of his work has been gathered into book form, worth looking at both for what he says on a medium in transition (he began writing in the late 1960s) and for his graceful prose. See Arlen, *Living-Room War* (1969), *The View from Highway 1*

(1976), and *The Camera Age* (1981). Based on two summer workshops in Aspen, is Adler, *Understanding Television: Essays on Television as a Social and Cultural Force* (1981), offering original essays on different types of programs on and role for television. Adler (1979, see §9.2) is a useful anthology on a popular television comedy. For an extremely negative view see Mander, *Four Arguments for the Elimination of Television* (1978).

Chapter 19 Effects of Broadcasting

19.1 Pervasiveness of Effects

Three classics, all somewhat dated but still of value, provide good background for this chapter. Klapper, *The Effects of Mass Communication* (1960), is especially good on the persuasive role of media. Berelson and Steiner, *Human Behavior* (1964), was a monumental attempt to combine in a single volume what researchers had discovered — including a chapter on mass communications. Schramm and Roberts, *The Process and Effects of Mass Communication* (1971), is an anthology of articles that is only marginally dated even a decade later. See also the titles under §20.5.

19.2 Effects of Advertising

The classic study is Borden, *The Economic Effects of Advertising* (1942). A short review of recent research is Ramond, *Advertising Research: The State of the Art* (1976). For children's advertising impact, see Adler and FTC noted at §13.4.

19.3 News and Pseudonews

The famous study here is Boorstin, *The Image: A Guide to Pseudo-Events in America* (1964). The agenda-setting function of media is analyzed in McCombs and Shaw, *The Emergence of American Political Issues* (1977).

19.4 Entertainment Programming

An early analysis of types of viewers categorized by what and how much they watch is Glick and Levy, *Living with Television* (1962). A scholarly argument in favor of the entertainment role of media is Mendelsohn, *Mass Entertainment* (1966). The literature on children and media is extensive (see §9.8, §10.7, §13.4, and also §19.5 for others). Dealing heavily with media socialization are the first two scholarly studies of the subject: Himmelweit et al., *Television and the Child* (1961), based on a British study, and Schramm et al., *Television in the Lives of Our Children* (1961), using American examples. One of the best of the later reviews is Liebert et al., *The Early Window: The Effects of Television on Children and Youth* (1973).

Later anthologies include the British work edited by Brown, *Children and Television* (1976), Wartella, *Children Communicating: Media and Development of Thought, Speech, Understanding* (1979), and the broader work dealing with all audiences, Withey and Abeles, *Television and Social Behavior* (1980).

19.5 Effects of Violence

The benchmark American study is Surgeon General, *Television and Growing Up* (1972), a summary of a year-long analysis mandated by Congress. The fascinating background of how the report was developed is told in Cater and Strickland, *TV Violence and the Child* (1975). Five years later the Canadians mounted their own intensive examination, with much data on other countries. See Canada, Royal Commission on Violence in the Communications Industry, *Report* (1977). Polar positions on violence can be found in Feshbach and Singer, *Television and Aggression* (1971), the definitive research study promoting the catharsis thesis; and Eyesenck and Nias, *Sex, Violence and the Media* (1978), which calls for government action to control content excesses. See also Comstock (§14.6) and Liebert et al. (§19.4), for more measured approaches.

19.6 Effects on Political Life

For a good example of media in a crisis, see Greenberg and Parker, *The Kennedy Assassination and the American Public* (1965), detailing how newspapers and broadcasting covered the death of John F. Kennedy. The best review of research on the subject is Kraus and Davis, *The Effects of Mass Communication on Political Behavior* (1976). Histories of media impact on presidents and their elections are Barbour, *The Pulse of Politics* (1980), and Chester, *Radio, Television, and American Politics* (1969), the latter dealing more with media than politicians. The pioneer research study on radio's election impact dates to the third term race of FDR: Lazarsfeld et al., *The People's Choice* (1944). Its results were updated in an age of television, but generally supported a decade later in Berelson et al., *Voting* (1954). Other early election media applications along with a study of television coverage of nonelection political events appear in Lang and Lang, *Politics and Television* (1968). One of the more widely read attacks on political use of media is McGinniss, *The Selling of the President 1968* (1969), with revealing insights into the Nixon campaign. MacNeil, *The People Machine* (1968), contended television's impact had grown almost unnoticed, while Gilbert, *Television and Presidential Politics* (1972), noted how that impact had grown since 1948. The so-called "great" debates of 1960 are exhaustively reviewed in Kraus, *The Great Debates* (1962), while those between Carter and Ford in 1976 are dealt with in Kraus,

The Great Debates (1979). Two books with broader analysis, covering earlier debates and projecting to the future are Bishop et al., *The Presidential Debates* (1979), and Ranney, *The Past and Future of Presidential Debates* (1979). Nonelection impact on the White House is discussed in Minow et al., *Presidential Television* (1973), contending television has given the president too much visibility and power. Bernstein and Woodward, *All the President's Men* (1974), demonstrated how the press and television could take it all away! Blanchard, *Congress and the News Media* (1974), reviews problems in covering the "Hill" and use of the media by congressmen. Role of the media in Vietnam is dissected in Braestrup, *Big Story: How the American Press and Television Reported and Interpreted the Crisis of Tet 1968 in Vietnam and Washington* (1977).

19.7 Gratification Effects

The standard book on play theory is Stephenson, *The Play Theory of Mass Communication* (1967), which is difficult going because of the arcane methodology used. See also Tannenbaum and Greenberg (§9.2) and Mendelsohn (§19.4).

Chapter 20 Research on Effects

20.1–20.3 Development of Research and Theory

A basic reference for those lacking any background in these subjects is Blake and Haroldson, *A Taxonomy of Concepts in Communication* (1975). Severin and Tankard, *Communication Theories* (1979), reviews their origins and development, methods of application, and specific uses. McCombs and Becker, *Using Mass Communication Theory* (1979), does the same with a journalism bias. The latest overview is Tan, *Mass Communication Theories and Research* (1981). See also DeFleur and Ball-Rokeach, (§5.1). Basis of much thinking in electronic communications is Shannon and Weaver, *The Mathematical Theory of Communication* (1949), in which Weaver explains in layman's terms the mathematical ideas of Shannon. The classic statement on the two-step flow idea, now somewhat debunked, is Katz and Lazarsfeld, *Personal Influence* (1955). While difficult to read in many places, one of the most influential thinkers of the 1960s best expresses his theories in McLuhan, *Understanding Media* (1964), and is, in turn, best explained in Theall, *The Medium is the Rear-View Mirror* (1971). More recent theoretical work is evident in Clarke, *New Models for Mass Communication Research* (1973), and Blumler and Katz, *The Uses of Mass Communications* (1975), the latter focusing on "uses and gratifications" approaches. For related material, see §14.1, §14.6, §19.1, and §19.6.

20.4 Methods of Studying Effects

The methodological literature is huge and rapidly growing. One good entry is Miller, *Handbook of Research Design and Social Measurement* (1977), a combination "cookbook" and reference source. Long standard as a text of methodology in quantitative field and laboratory research is Kerlinger, *Foundations of Behavioral Research* (1973). Somewhat less forbidding for the lay reader is Simon, *Basic Research Methods in Social Science* (1977). A very handy anthology written with a strong journalism bias by many respected authors is Stempel and Westley, *Research Methods in Mass Communication* (1981). For the more advanced worker, see Hirsch et al., *Strategies for Communication Research* (1977). On specific methods of research see the following: Dillman, *Mail and Telephone Surveys* (1978), Krippendorff, *Content Analysis* (1981), Cochran, *Sampling Techniques* (1963), and Osgood et al., *The Measurement of Meaning* (1957), the last dealing with the semantic differential method of research.

20.5 Status of Effects Research

Given the size and scope of the field, it is hard to get a comprehensive picture. Good attempts are Kline and Tichenor, *Current Perspectives in Mass Communications Research* (1972), and Davison and Yu, *Mass Communication Research: Major Issues and Future Directions* (1974). See also the mass media reviews which appear every three or four years in Rosenzweig and Porter, *Annual Review of Psychology*, for both integrative reviews and bibliographies. See also Nimmo, *Communication Yearbook* (1977–date), though much does not deal directly with mass communications. A newer annual (begun in 1980) is Wilhoit and de Bock, *Mass Communication Review Yearbook*.

Chapter 21 Challenge and Change

Book material on the future of broadcasting or other media is not yet common. What there is tends to mush across subject lines covered in this chapter, so rather than dividing along chapter sections, the reading suggestions are presented in a single essay. Certainly the most well-known popularizer of futuristic thinking is Toffler, *Future Shock* (1970), and *The Third Wave* (1980). Both touch on many fields but include, especially the latter, some communications comment. Looking into the future is increasingly a scientific process. One of the better serious studies of methods of future predictions is Armstrong, *Long-Range Forecasting* (1978), which is also a key to much other writing on the subject. Taking a broad view of communication's future is Haigh et al.,

Communications in the Twenty-First Century (1981), and University of Missouri, *Communications 1990* (1980), both of which provide many viewpoints on the probable roles of different media over the long-term future. Smith in *Goodbye Gutenberg* (1980), though dealing mainly with the impact of electronic techniques on the print media, devotes attention to television-related technology as well. Edelstein et al., *Information Societies* (1979), draws comparisons between the U.S. and Japan in suggesting likely future trends. Hiltz and Turoff, *The Network Nation: Human Communication via Computer* (1978), combines discussion of technology, economics, sociology, and politics to suggest quite specific scenarios for specific times in the future, a time when communications will play a larger role in daily life. Several earlier studies are interesting in that one can see to an extent how much of what they predict has already come true. Works in this category include "Communications and Electronics 2012 AD" (1962), in which a panel of technical experts made predictions for a period already now half gone. Widely read on publication was Bagdikian, *The Information Machines* (1971), which focused on technology's impact on news reporting in print and broadcasting, and included results of surveys of predictions for the rest of the twentieth century. Maddox, *Beyond Babel* (1972), reviewed the future of the telephone, satellites, and cable television. More recent works focusing on likely technological changes forthcoming include Lighthill et al., *Telecommunications in the 1980s and After* (1978); a British anthology, Elton et al., *Evaluating New Telecommunications Services* (1979), a massive compilation of original papers on the process of integrating new technologies with existing structures; Henderson and MacNaughton, *Electronic Communication: Technology and Impacts* (1980), reviewing the social and other effects of technological change; and Martin, *Future Developments in Telecommunications* (1977), a fascinating, readable, and clearly illustrated guide to the technology of today with predictions from an expert of likely change to the year 2000. Dealing specifically with broadcasting, and mainly with its probable economic performance against new competitors, are *Radio in 1985* (1977), and NBC Corporate Planning, *Broadcasting: The Next Ten Years* (1977), both of which see a rosy future for radio and television, despite all the changes. Finally, Robinson, *Communications for Tomorrow: Policy Perspectives for the 1980s* (1978), is a combination technology tutorial with policy implications for the decade — a useful inventory of changes in thinking and structure that have to be considered.

Bibliographies

This short selected list includes the most useful media bibliographies for research or further reading on American broadcasting. Libraries should have most of them.

Avery et al. *Research Index for NAEB Journals, 1957–1979* (1980). Chronological abstract of all articles in three successive journals over a period of tremendous change in educational/public broadcasting.

Blum *Basic Books in the Mass Media: An Annotated, Selected Booklist* (1980). The standard overall guide, includes a long section on broadcasting, both foreign and domestic, as well as other media.

Brightbill *Communications and the United States Congress: A Selectively Annotated Bibliography of Committee Hearings, 1870–1976* (1978). The unique guide to Senate and House hearings on all matters dealing with media and common carrier communications.

Brown and Brown (eds.) *Educational Media Yearbook* (annual). Includes the most complete and current listing of print and nonprint references, books, periodicals, etc., on all aspects of public and educational media.

Chin *Cable Television: A Comprehensive Bibliography* (1978). Though not as complete as it should be, is the latest available.

Comstock et al. *Television and Human Behavior* (1975). Not to be confused with same author's 1978 book surveying TV research; this is a three-volume bibliography: *Vol I: A Guide to the Pertinent Scientific Literature* (the main list) *Vol II: The Key Studies* (50 of them, detailed annotations) *Vol III: The Research Horizon, Future and Present* (ongoing projects). Each contains citations and annotations, along with some integrative review of the massive literature.

Cooper *Bibliography on Educational Broadcasting* (1942, repr. Arno Press 1971). Far more inclusive than the title suggests, this annotated listing is the best key to pre-World War II AM broadcasting developments of all kinds.

Friedman *Sex Role Stereotyping in the Mass Media: An Annotated Bibliography* (1977). The definitive guide to this question, with a great deal on television programming.

Gordon and Verna *Mass Communication Effects and Processes: A Comprehensive Bibliography, 1950–1975* (1978). While not annotated, provides a good overview of broadcast-related research within a larger context.

Johnson *TV Guide 25 Year Index: By Author and Subject* (1979). Covers the 1953–1977 period inclusively.

Kaid et al. *Political Campaign Communication: A Bibliography and Guide to the Literature* (1974). Great deal of material on the rising impact of television, especially on presidential campaigns.

Kittross (ed.) *A Bibliography of Theses and Dissertations in Broadcasting, 1920–1973* (1978). The only complete listing and guide to often very useful academic research.

"Mass Communication" (title varies) in Rosenzweig and Porter (eds.) *Annual Review of Psychology*. A series of review articles with appended bibliographies that appear every five or six years, detailing the current research literature. See: Vol. 13 (1962): 251–284 for writings up to 1960; Vol. 19 (1968): 351–386 for research in 1961–1966; Vol. 22 (1971): 309–336 for 1967–1970 work; Vol. 28 (1977): 141–173 for 1970–1976 research; Vol. 32 (1981): 307–356 for 1976–1979 period.

Matlon *Index to Journals in Communication Studies through 1979* (1980). Includes chronological contents listing and subject/author index for 15 journals, such as those of the Speech Communication Association, *Journalism Quarterly*, and *Journal of Broadcasting*.

McCavitt (comp.) *Radio and Television: A Selected, Annotated Bibliography* (1978). Not at all complete, but a good indication of book-length material available, divided by subject.

McCoy *Freedom of the Press: An Annotated Bibliography* (1968) and *Freedom of the Press: A Bibliocyclopedia Ten-Year Supplement (1967–1977)* (1979). Broad bibliography with second volume including a good deal of broadcast material. Excellent annotations in both.

Meringoff *Children and Advertising: An Annotated Bibliography* (1980). One of the more complete bibliographies of media impact on children.

Rivers et al. (eds.) *Aspen Handbook on the Media, 1977–1979 Edition: A Selective Guide to Research, Organizations, and Publications in Communications* (1977). Still an invaluable guide to periodicals, to 125 media bibliographies, and to books, films, organizations, research fund sources, law programs, and other aspects of media and telecommunications.

Shiers and Shiers *Bibliography of the History of Electronics* (1972). Detailed annotated guide to the history of radio, telegraph, telephone, television, and related communications applications.

Broadcast-Related Periodicals

The following short list includes the more important and/or useful broadcast-related periodicals, most of which should be in any good library. Given the rate of change in this field, these are the best sources for tracking the latest developments.

Advertising Age (1929, weekly). The main trade paper for the industry with details of new accounts and agency doings and periodical statistical summaries.

Broadcasting (1931, weekly). The single most important broadcasting trade periodical; although it usually takes a strong proindustry editorial stance, it is indispensable for understanding current events, especially those concerning broadcast management and government relations. Issues annually the basic reference *Broadcasting Yearbook* (1935), which provides details on all stations (and cable systems), plus overall statistical reviews.

Cablevision (1975, weekly). The standard weekly trade journal of cable television field, with articles on economics, programming, technology, and regulation.

Channels of Communications (1981, bimonthly). Journal of television criticism and comment, including broadcast and related means of delivery.

Columbia Journalism Review (1962, bimonthly). National critical review of journalistic media (print and broadcast) performance.

Federal Communications Law Journal (1946, triannual). Detailed, documented articles on law and regulation of broadcasting and on the roles of the FCC and the court system.

Intermedia (1970, bimonthly). Review of worldwide communications issues done by the Institute for International Communication in London. Individual issues often built around specific topics, and help to relate broadcasting to newer technologies and U.S. developments to other systems.

Journalism Quarterly (1924, quarterly). Academic research on all aspects of American and foreign media journalism with excellent large book and journal review sections.

Journal of Broadcasting (1956, quarterly). Research studies on all aspects of broadcasting, cable and allied areas, plus reviews and bibliographies. Includes American and foreign/international systems.

Journal of Communication (1951, quarterly). Especially since 1974 editorial revision has published heavily in mass communications field, with research and opinion material as well as reviews.

Public Broadcasting Report (1978, biweekly). Trade report on activities of CPB, PBS, NPR, Congress, other funding sources, the FCC, and public stations.

Public Opinion Quarterly (1937, quarterly). Key research journal in polls, media, opinion measurement, etc., with frequent reference to the role of the media.

Public Telecommunications Review (1973, bimonthly). Educational and public broadcast developments and fiscal/programming policy dealt with in research and descriptive articles. Successor to *Educational Broadcasting Review* (1967–1973, bimonthly), which was more research oriented, and *NAEB Journal* (1941–1967). Suspended publication in 1980.

Satellite Communications (1976, monthly). Trade journal with material on broadcast and cable signal distribution by satellite, technical information, profiles of satellite carrier firms, regulation.

Telecommunications Policy (1976, quarterly). Scholarly analysis of domestic and international policy developments, especially useful for role of newer media, and broader context for broadcasting and cable.

Television Digest (1945, weekly). Newsletter format report of the previous week in the fields of broadcasting and consumer electronics with a wealth of statistics and in-depth reporting. Issues annual *Television Factbook* (1945) with directories and statistics and *CATV and Station Coverage Atlas* with weekly addenda to keep data current.

Television News Index and Abstracts (1972, monthly). Detailed content listing of ABC, CBS, and NBC television network newscasts, indexed by topic with annual overall index.

Television/Radio Age (1953, weekly) Trade journal stressing advertising topics; special issues on news, FCC affairs, foreign television, etc.

Topicator (1965, monthly with annual index volume). Index to periodical literature of broadcasting and advertising, covering many periodicals in this list.

TV Guide (1953, weekly). Each issue of the well-known viewing guide contains one or more articles on programs, people, or trends in television, often written by outstanding specialists or scholars (indexed for first 25 years — see Johnson's bibliography list.)

Variety (1905, weekly). The major trade paper for show business; besides coverage of stage and screen, offers detailed reviews of television programs, analyses of trends, and critical comments on the industry.

Bibliography

The following lists both textual citations and the works annotated by Sterling in the guide to further reading. The fact that hard-to-find items have been reprinted in recent years by Arno Press is indicated where appropriate, together with the year of the reprint.

Abel, John A., et al. 1970. "Station License Revocations and Denials of Renewal 1934–1969," *Journal of Broadcasting* 14 (Fall): 411–421.

Abramson, Albert. 1955, 1973. "A Short History of Television Recording," *Journal of the SMPTE* 64 (February): 72–76; and 82 (March): 188–195. (Repr. Arno Press, 1976).

Abshire, David M. 1976. *International Broadcasting: A New Dimension of Western Diplomacy*. Washington Policy Papers No. 35. Sage Publications, Beverly Hills, CA.

AD (Appellate Division, New York Supreme Court). 1963. *John H. Faulk v. AWARE, Inc., et al.* 19 AD 2d 464.

Adams, William, & Schreibman, Fay. 1978. *Television Network News: Issues in Content Research*. George Washington U., Washington, DC.

Adler, Richard P., ed. 1979. *All in the Family: A Critical Appraisal*. Praeger, New York.

———. 1980. *The Effects of Television Advertising on Children: Review and Recommendations*. Lexington Books, Lexington, MA.

———. 1981. *Understanding Television: Essays on Television as a Social and Cultural Force*. Praeger, New York.

Agostino, Don. 1980. "New Technologies: Problem or Solution," *Journal of Communication* 30 (Summer): 198–206.

Aird, Enola. 1980. *A Broadcaster's Guide to Designing and Implementing an Effective EEO Program*. National Association of Broadcasters, Washington, DC.

Aitken, Hugh G. 1976. *Syntony and Spark: The Origins of Radio*. Wiley, New York.

Allen, Steve. 1956. *The Funny Men*. Simon & Schuster, New York.

Alten, Stanley R. 1981. *Audio in Media*. Wadsworth, Belmont, CA.

American Radio Relay League. Annual. *The Radio Amateur's Handbook*. A.R.R.L., Newington, CT.

American University School of Communications. Dec. 1979. "Broadcast News Doctors: The Patient Is Buying the Cure." AUSC, Washington, DC.

Anderson, Kent. 1978. *Television Fraud: The History and Implications of the Quiz Show Scandals*. Greenwood Press, Westport, CT.

Archer, Gleason, L. 1938. *History of Radio to 1926*. American Historical Society, New York. (Repr. Arno Press, 1971).

———. 1939. *Big Business and Radio*. American Historical Company, New York. (Repr. Arno Press, 1971.)

Arendt, Hannah. 1964. "Society and Culture," in Jacobs, 1964: 43–52.

Arlen, Michael J. 1969. *Living-Room War*. Viking, New York.

———. 1976. *The View from Highway 1: Essays on Television*. Farrar, Straus & Giroux, New York.

———. 1977. "Getting the Goods on President Monckton," *The New Yorker* (Oct. 3): 115–125.

———. 1980. *Thirty Seconds*. Farrar, Straus & Giroux, New York.

———. 1981. *The Camera Age*. Farrar, Straus & Giroux, New York.

ARMS (All-Radio Methodological Study). 1966. *ARMS: What It Shows, How It Has Changed Radio Measurement*. National Association of Broadcasters, Washington, DC.

Armstrong, Ben, ed. 1978. *Religious Broadcasting: Sourcebook*. Rev. ed. National Religious Broadcasters, Morristown, NJ.

Armstrong, J. Scott. 1978. *Long-Range Forecasting from Crystal Ball to Computer*. Wiley-Interscience, New York.

Arnove, Robert F., ed. 1976. *Educational Television: A Policy Critique and Guide for Developing Countries*. Praeger, New York.

Astrachan, Anthony. 1975. "Life Can Be Beautiful/Relevant," *New York Times Magazine* (March 23): 12.

Aurthur, Robert A. 1973. "52 Plays a Year, All Original, All Live," *TV Guide* (March 17): 6.

Avery, Robert K., & Pepper, Robert. 1979. *The Politics of Interconnection: A History of Public Television at the National Level*. National Association of Educational Broadcasters, Washington, DC.

Avery, Robert K., et al. 1980. *Research Index for NAEB Journals, 1957–1979*. NAEB, Washington, DC.

Ayer, N. W., Co. 1977. *The Ayer Glossary of Advertising and Related Terms*. 2d ed. Ayer, Philadelphia, PA.

Baarslag, Karl. 1935. *SOS to the Rescue*. Oxford U. Press, New York.

Baer, Walter S. 1973. *Cable Television: A Handbook for Decision Making*. Rand Corporation, Santa Monica, CA.

————, et al. 1974. *Concentration of Mass Media Ownership: Assessing the State of Current Knowledge.* Rand Corporation, Santa Monica, CA.

Bagdikian, Ben H. 1971. *The Information Machines: Their Impact on Men and Media.* Harper & Row, New York.

————. 1973. "Out of the Can and into the Bank," *New York Times Magazine* (Oct. 21): 31.

Baker, Robert K., & Ball, Sandra J. 1969. *Mass Media and Violence.* Staff Report No. 9 to National Commission on the Causes and Prevention of Violence. Government Printing Office, Washington, DC.

Baker, W. J. 1971. *A History of the Marconi Company.* St. Martin's, New York.

Baldwin, Thomas F., & Lewis, Colby. 1972. "Violence in Television: The Industry Looks at Itself," in Comstock & Rubinstein, eds., 1972: 290–365.

Bandura, A. D., et al. 1963. "Imitation of Film-Mediated Aggressive Models," *Journal of Abnormal and Social Psychology* 66: 3–11.

Banning, William P. 1946. *Commercial Broadcasting Pioneer: The WEAF Experiment, 1922–1926.* Harvard U. Press, Cambridge, MA.

Barber, James D. 1980. *The Pulse of Politics: Electing Presidents in the Media Age.* Norton, New York.

Barcus, F. Earle, & Wolkin, Rachel. 1977. *Children's Television: An Analysis of Programming and Advertising.* Praeger, New York.

Barnard, Charles N. 1978. "An Oriental Mystery," *TV Guide* (Jan. 28): 2.

Barnouw, Erik. 1966. *A Tower in Babel: A History of Broadcasting in the United States to 1933.* Oxford U. Press, New York.

————. 1968. *The Golden Web: A History of Broadcasting in the United States, 1933–1953.* Oxford U. Press, New York.

————. 1970. *The Image Empire: A History of Broadcasting in the United States since 1953.* Oxford U. Press, New York.

————. 1975. *Tube of Plenty: The Development of American Television.* Oxford U. Press, New York.

————. 1978. *The Sponsor: Notes on a Modern Potentate.* Oxford U. Press, New York.

Barrett, Marvin, ed. 1969. *The Alfred I. duPont-Columbia University Survey of Broadcast Journalism, 1968–1969.* Grosset & Dunlap, New York.

————. 1970. *Year of Challenge, Year of Crisis: The Alfred I. duPont-Columbia University Survey of Broadcast Journalism, 1969–1970.* Grosset & Dunlap, New York.

————. 1971. *A State of Siege: The Alfred I. duPont-Columbia University Survey of Broadcast Journalism, 1970–1971.* Grosset & Dunlap, New York.

————. 1973. *The Politics of Broadcasting: The Alfred I. duPont-Columbia University Survey of Broadcast Journalism, 1971–1972.* Thomas Y. Crowell, New York.

————. 1975. *Moments of Truth?: The Alfred I. duPont-Columbia University Survey of Broadcast Journalism, 1973–1974.* Thomas Y. Crowell, New York.

————. 1978. *Rich News, Poor News: The Sixth Alfred I. duPont-Columbia University Survey of Broadcast Journalism.* Thomas Y. Crowell, New York.

————, & Sklar, Zachary. 1980. *The Eye of the Storm: The Seventh Alfred I. duPont-Columbia University Survey of Broadcast Journalism.* Lippincott & Crowell, New York.

Barrington, John R. 1980. "Pay TV: Now a Staple on the Cable 'Menu,'" in Hollowell, 1980: 135–148.

Barron, Jerome A. 1973. *Freedom of the Press for Whom? The Right of Access to Mass Media.* Indiana U. Press, Bloomington.

———— & Dienes, C. Thomas. 1979. *Handbook of Free Speech and Free Press.* Little, Brown, Boston.

Barthel, Joan. 1975. "Boston Mothers Against Kidvid," *New York Times Magazine* (Jan. 5): 15.

Bartlett, George W., ed. 1975. *NAB Engineering Handbook.* 6th ed. National Association of Broadcasters, Washington, DC.

Baudino, Joseph E., & Kittross, John M. 1977. "Broadcasting's Oldest Station: An Examination of Four Claimants," *Journal of Broadcasting* 21 (Winter): 61–83.

BBC (British Broadcasting Corporation). Annual. *BBC Handbook* (title varies). BBC, London.

————. External Broadcasting Audience Research. 1980. "World Radio and Television Receivers." BBC, London.

BBDO (Batten, Barton, Durstine & Osborn). Annual. *BBDO Audience Coverage and Cost Guide.* BBDO, New York.

Beck, A. H. 1967. *Words and Waves: An Introduction to Electrical Communication.* McGraw-Hill, New York.

Bedell, Sally. 1979. "Where the Money Is," *TV Guide* (Mar. 3): 39.

————. 1981. *Up the Tube: Prime-Time TV and the Silverman Years.* Viking, New York.

Belendiuk, Arthur, & Robb, Scott. 1979. *Broadcasting via Satellite: Legal and Business Considerations.* Communication Research Institute, New York.

Belz, Carl. 1972. *The Story of Rock.* 2d ed. Oxford U. Press, New York.

Bendiner, Robert. 1957. "FCC: Who Will Regulate the Regulators?" *The Reporter* (Sept.): 26.

Bennett, Robert M. 1981. "The Television Station's Future Identity." Keynote Address to National Association of Television Program Executives Annual Convention, March 16, New York.

Bennett, Robert W. 1974. *A Lawyer's Sourcebook: Representing the Audience in Broadcast Proceedings.* United Church of Christ, New York.

Berelson, Bernard, et al. 1954. *Voting: A Study of Opinion Formation in a Presidential Campaign.* U. of Chicago Press, Chicago.

——, & Steiner, Gary A. 1964. *Human Behavior: An Inventory of Scientific Findings.* Harcourt, Brace & World, New York.

Bergreen, Laurence. 1979. "What's Edward VII Doing in 'The Incredible Hulk's' Time Slot," *TV Guide* (Feb. 24): 25.

——. 1980. *Look Now, Pay Later: The Rise of Network Broadcasting.* Doubleday, New York.

Bernstein, Carl, & Woodward, Bob. 1974. *All the President's Men.* Simon & Schuster, New York.

Berrigan, Frances J., ed. 1978. *Access: Some Western Models of Community Media.* UNESCO, Paris.

Besen, S. M. 1973. "The Value of Television Time and the Prospects for New Stations." Rand Corporation, Santa Monica, CA.

Beville, H. M., Jr. 1939. *Social Stratification of the Radio Audience.* Princeton U. Office of Radio Research, Princeton, NJ.

——. 1981. "Understanding Broadcast Ratings," 3d ed. Broadcast Rating Council, New York.

Bishop, George F., et al., eds. 1979. *The Presidential Debates: Media, Electoral, and Policy Perspectives.* Praeger, New York.

Bitting, Robert C., Jr. 1965. "Creating an Industry," *Journal of the SMPTE* (November): 1015–1023.

Black, David. 1975. "How the Gosh-darn Networks Edit the Heck out of Movies," *New York Times* (Jan. 26): II-1.

Blair Company. 1979. *1979 Statistical Trends in Broadcasting.* 15th ed. John Blair Co., New York.

Blake, George. 1928. *History of Radio Telegraphy and Telephony.* Chapman & Hall, London. (Repr. Arno Press, 1974).

Blake, Reed H., & Haroldson, Edwin O. 1975. *A Taxonomy of Concepts in Communication.* Hastings House, New York.

Blakely, Robert J. 1971. *The People's Instrument: A Philosophy of Programming for Public Television.* Public Affairs Press, Washington, DC.

——. 1979. *To Serve the Public Interest: Educational Broadcasting in the United States.* Syracuse U. Press, Syracuse, NY.

Blanchard, Robert O., ed. 1974. *Congress and the News Media,* Hastings House, New York.

Blank, David M. 1977. "The Gerbner Violence Profile," *Journal of Broadcasting* 21 (Summer): 273–279.

Bluem, A. William. 1965. *Documentary in American Television: Form, Function, Method.* Hastings House, New York.

Blum, Eleanor. 1980. *Basic Books in the Mass Media: An Annotated, Selected Booklist.* 2d ed. U. of Illinois Press, Urbana.

Blumler, Jay G., & Katz, Elihu. 1975. *The Uses of Mass Communications: Current Perspectives on Gratification Research.* Sage Publications, Beverly Hills, CA.

Board for International Broadcasting. Annual. *Annual Report.* Government Printing Office, Washington, DC.

Bobroff, Sara A. 1974. *United States Treaties and Other International Agreements Pertaining to Telecommunications.* O.T. Report 74-26. Government Printing Office, Washington, DC.

Bogart, Leo. 1972. *The Age of Television.* 3d ed. Ungar, New York.

Boorstin, Daniel J. 1964. *The Image: A Guide to Pseudo-Events in America.* Harper & Row, New York.

——. 1978. "The Significance of Broadcasting in Human History," in Hoso-Bunka Foundation: 9–23.

Booz, Allen & Hamilton, Inc. 1978. *Feasibility of a New Local Television Audience Measurement Service: Phase I Final Report.* Television Bureau of Advertising, New York.

Borden, Neil H. 1942. *The Economic Effects of Advertising.* Irwin, Chicago.

Botein, Michael, & Rice, David M., eds. 1981. *Network Television and the Public Interest: A Preliminary Inquiry.* Lexington Books, Lexington, MA.

Bower, Robert T. 1973. *Television and the Public.* Holt, Rinehart & Winston, New York.

Brack, Hans. 1976. *The Evolution of the EBU through Its Statutes from 1950 to 1976.* Monograph No. 11. European Broadcasting Union, Geneva.

Braestrup, Peter. 1977. *Big Story: How the American Press and Television Reported and Interpreted the Crisis of Tet 1968 in Vietnam and Washington.* 2 vols. Westview Press, Boulder, CO.

Branscomb, Anne W., & Savage, Maria. June 1978. "Broadcast Reform at the Crossroads." Kalba Bowen Associates, Cambridge, MA.

Bretz, Rudy. 1970. *A Taxonomy of Communication Media.* Educational Technology, Englewood Cliffs, NJ.

Briggs, Asa A. 1961. *The Birth of Broadcasting: The History of Broadcasting in the United Kingdom.* Vol. 1. Oxford U. Press, London.

——. 1965. *The Golden Age of Wireless: The History of Broadcasting in the United Kingdom.* Vol. 2. Oxford U. Press, London.

——. 1970. *The War of Words: The History of Broadcasting in the United Kingdom.* Vol. 3. Oxford U. Press, London.

——. 1979. *Sound and Vision: The History of Broadcasting in the United Kingdom.* Vol. 4. Oxford U. Press, London.

Brightbill, George D. 1978. *Communications and the United States Congress: A Selectively Annotated Bibliography of Committee Hearings, 1870–1976.* Broadcast Education Association, Washington, DC.

Brindze, Ruth. 1937. *Not To Be Broadcast: The Truth about Radio.* Vanguard, New York. (Repr. DaCapo, 1974).

Broadcasting. 1963. "A World Listened and Watched." Special Report. (Dec. 2): 36.

———. 1970. "A Play-by-Play Retrospective." Special Report. (Nov. 2): 74.

———. 1973. "The Rites of Passage Are all over for FM Radio." (Sept. 24): 31.

———. 1973. "Good Riddance." Editorial. (Dec. 17): 74.

———. 1975. "Contraceptives Get on Two TV's." (Aug. 14): 28.

———. 1975. "There's a Floating Scrabble Game at the FCC." (Oct. 6): 378.

———. 1977. "CBS: The First Five Decades." (Sept. 19): 45.

———. 1978. "Singlehanded Victory." (July 3): 23.

———. 1978. "Preventive Maintenance in D.C." (Sept. 11): 50.

———. 1978. "Listeners Are a Faithful Lot." (Oct. 9): 47.

———. 1979. "Minorities in Broadcasting: The Exception Is No Longer the Rule." Special Report. (Oct. 15): 27.

———. 1979. "Children's Programming." Special Report. (Oct. 29): 39.

———. 1980. "The Top 100 Companies in Electronic Communications." (Jan. 7): 35.

———. 1980. "Arbitron Recalling Orlando Book over Diary Irregularities." (Apr. 2): 92.

———. 1980. "The Washington Lawyer: Power Behind the Powers That Be." Special Report. (June 16): 32.

———. 1980. "Another Piece of the Legend." (Sept. 8): 20.

———. 1980. "New Oklahoma City Outlet to Program News and STV." (Nov. 3): 43.

———. 1981. "Faint Victory." Editorial. (Jan. 12): 106.

———. 1981. "Broadcasting's Top 50 Agencies and Their 1980 Radio-TV Billings." (Jan. 26): 30.

———. 1981. "Cable Advertising: Growing Blip on Media Radar." (Feb. 16): 37.

Broadcasting Publications, Inc. Annual. *Broadcasting/Cable Yearbook.* Broadcasting Publications, Washington, DC.

———. 1981. *The First 50 Years of Broadcasting.* Broadcasting Publications, Washington, DC.

Brock, Gerald W. 1981. *The Telecommunications Industry: The Dynamics of Market Structure.* Harvard U. Press, Cambridge, MA.

Broder, Mitch. 1976. "The Late Show Clocks 25 Years," *New York Times* (Feb. 22): D-29.

Brooks, John. 1976. *Telephone: The First Hundred Years.* Harper & Row, New York.

Brooks, Tim, & Marsh, Earle. 1979. *The Complete Directory to Prime Time Network TV Shows: 1946–Present.* Ballatine Books, New York.

Brown, James A. 1980. "Selling Air Time for Controversy: NAB Self-Regulation and Father Coughlin," *Journal of Broadcasting* 24 (Spring): 199–224.

Brown, James W., with Shirley Brown, eds. Annual. *Educational Media Yearbook.* Libraries Unlimited, Littleton, CO.

Brown, Les. 1971. *Televi$ion: The Business behind the Box.* Harcourt Brace, Jovanovich, New York.

———. 1977. *New York Times Encyclopedia of Television.* Times Books, New York.

———. 1979. *Keeping Your Eye on Television.* Pilgrim Press, New York.

Brown, Ray, ed. 1976. *Children and Television.* Sage Publications, Beverly Hills, CA.

Brown, Tyrone. 1978. "Remarks Before the Federal Communications Bar Association," Oct. 12.

Buckley, Tom. 1978. "Popularity of '60 Minutes' Based on Wide-Ranging Reports," *New York Times* (Dec. 17): 99.

———. 1979. "Game Shows — TV's Glittering Gold Mine," *New York Times Magazine* (Nov. 18): 49.

Bunce, Richard. 1976. *Television in the Corporate Interest.* Praeger, New York.

Burke, John E. 1972. *The Public Broadcasting Act of 1967.* National Association of Educational Broadcasters, Washington, DC.

Burns, Tom. 1977. *The BBC: Public Institution and Private World.* Macmillan, London.

Busch, H. Ted, & Landeck, Terry. 1981. *The Making of a Television Commercial.* Macmillan, New York

Cable Television Information Center. 1973. "Technology of Cable Television." Urban Institute, Washington, DC.

Callum, Myles. 1979. "What Viewers Love/Hate About Television," *TV Guide* (May 12): 6.

Campbell, Robert. 1976. *The Golden Years of Broadcasting: A Celebration of the First 50 Years of Radio and Television on NBC.* Scribners, New York.

Canada. Radio-Television and Telecommunications Commission. Annual. *Annual Report.* Queen's Printer, Ottawa.

Canada, Royal Commission on Violence in the Communications Industry, 1977. *Report.* 7 vols. Publications Centre, Toronto.

Cantor, Muriel G. 1972. *The Hollywood TV Producer: His Work and His Audience.* Basic Books, New York.

———. 1980. *Prime-Time Television: Content and Control.* Sage Publications, Beverly Hills, CA.

Cantril, Hadley, & Allport, Gordon. 1935. *The Psychology of Radio.* Harper, New York. (Repr. Arno Press, 1971.)

Carey, William L. 1967. *Politics and the Regulatory Agencies.* McGraw-Hill, New York.

CCET (Carnegie Commission on Educational Television). 1967. *Public Television: A Program for Action.* Harper & Row, New York.

CCFPB (Carnegie Commission on the Future of Public Broadcasting). 1979. *A Public Trust.* Bantam Books, New York.

Carroll, Raymond L. 1980. "The 1948 Truman Campaign: The Threshold of the Modern Era," *Journal of Broadcasting* (Spring): 173–188.

Cater, Douglass, & Nyhan, M. 1976. *The Future of Public Broadcasting.* Praeger, New York.

Cater, Douglass, & Strickland, Stephen. 1975. *TV Violence and the Child: The Evolution and Fate of the Surgeon General's Report.* Russell Sage, New York.

CFR (*Code of Federal Regulations*). Annual. 47 CFR 0.1 ff. Telecommunication. 4 Vols. Government Printing Office, Washington, DC.

Chafee, Zechariah, Jr. 1947. *Government and Mass Communications.* U. of Chicago Press, Chicago.

Chagall, David. 1977. "The Child Probers," *TV Guide* (Oct. 8): 8.

———. 1978. "Can You Believe the Ratings?" *TV Guide* (June 24): 2; (July 1): 20.

Chappell, Matthew N., & Hooper, C. E. 1944. *Radio Audience Measurement.* Stephen Daye, New York.

Chase, Francis. 1942. *Sound and Fury: An Informal History of Broadcasting.* Harper, New York.

Chaseman, Joel. 1979. Keynote address to National Association of Television Program Executives Annual Convention, Las Vegas, Nevada, March 12.

Chester, Edward. 1969. *Radio, Television, and American Politics.* Sheed & Ward, New York.

Chin, Felix, 1978. *Cable Television: A Comprehensive Bibliography.* Plenum Publishing, New York.

Clancy, Thomas H. 1979. "Nine and a Half Theses on Religious Broadcasting," *America* (Apr. 7): 271–275.

Clark, David G. 1965. "H. V. Kaltenborn's First Year on the Air," *Journalism Quarterly* (Summer): 373–381.

Cherington, Paul W., et al. 1971. *Television Station Ownership: A Case Study of Federal Agency Regulation.* Hastings House, New York.

Chu, Goodwin, & Schramm, Wilbur. 1967. *Learning from Television: What the Research Says.* National Association of Educational Broadcasters, Washington, DC.

Clarke, Peter, ed. 1973. *New Models for Mass Communication Research.* Sage Publications, Beverly Hills, CA.

Clarkson, Kenneth W., & Muris, Timothy J., eds. 1981. *The FTC since 1970: Economic Regulation and Consumer Welfare.* Cambridge U. Press, New York.

Clift, Charles, III, et al. 1980. "Forfeitures and the Federal Communications Commission: An Update," *Journal of Broadcasting* 24 (Summer): 301–310.

Coates, Vary T., & Finn, Bernard. 1979. *A Retrospective Technology Assessment: Submarine Telegraphy — The Transatlantic Cable of 1866.* San Francisco Press, San Francisco.

Cochran, W. G. 1963. *Sampling Techniques.* Wiley, New York.

Codding, George. 1952. *The International Telecommunication Union: An Experiment in International Cooperation.* Brill, Leiden. (Repr. Arno Press, 1972).

Codel, Martin, ed. 1930. *Radio and Its Future.* Harper, New York. (Repr. Arno Press, 1971).

Cogley, John. 1956. *Report on Blacklisting II: Radio-Television.* Fund for the Republic, New York. (Repr. Arno Press, 1971.)

Cohen, Morris L., ed. 1976. *How to Find the Law.* 7th ed. West Publishing Co., St. Paul, MN.

Cole, Barry, & Oettinger, Mal. 1978. *Reluctant Regulators: The FCC and the Broadcast Audience.* Addison-Wesley, Reading, MA.

Cole, Barry, ed. 1981. *Television Today: A Close-Up View, Readings from TV Guide.* Oxford U. Press, New York.

Commission on Obscenity and Pornography. 1970. *Report.* Bantam, New York.

Compaine, Benjamin M., ed. 1979. *Who Owns the Media? Concentration of Ownership in the Mass Communications Industry.* Crown, New York. [rev. ed. forthcoming, 1982].

Comstock, George, & Rubinstein, E., eds. 1972. *Television and Social Behavior: Media Content and Control, I.* Government Printing Office, Washington, DC.

Comstock, George, et al. 1975. *Television and Human Behavior.* 3 vols. Rand Corporation, Santa Monica, CA.

———. 1978. *Television and Human Behavior.* Columbia U. Press, New York.

Cone, Fairfax M. 1969. *With All Its Faults: A Candid Account of Forty Years in Advertising.* Little, Brown, Boston.

Connor, Michael J. 1973. "It's Not as Cushy as It Sounds," *TV Guide* (Nov. 24): 16.

CONTAM (Committee on Nationwide Television Audience Measurement). 1969. "How Good Are Television Ratings? (Continued)," Television Information Office, New York.

Cook, Anthony. 1980. "The Peculiar Economics of Television," *TV Guide* (June 14): 4.

Cook, Thomas D., et al. 1975. *"Sesame Street" Revisited.* Russell Sage Foundation, New York.

Coolidge, Calvin. 1926. *Message to Congress, 68 Congressional Record* 32.

Cooper, Eunice, & Jahoda, Marie. 1947. "The Evasion of Propaganda: How Prejudicial People Respond to Anti-Prejudice Propaganda," *Journal of Psychology* 23 (January): 15–25.

Cooper, Isabella. 1942. *Bibliography on Educational Broadcasting*. U. of Chicago Press, Chicago. (Repr. Arno Press, 1971).

CPB (Corporation for Public Broadcasting). Annual. *Annual Report*. CPB, Washington, DC.

———. Annual. *Summary Statistical Report of CPB Qualified Public Radio Stations*. (Title varies). CPB, Washington, DC.

———. Annual. *Summary Statistical Report of Public Television Licensees*. (Title varies). CPB, Washington, DC.

———. 1979. *Uses of Television for Instruction 1976–77*. CPB, Washington, DC.

———. 1979. *Public Radio Programming Content by Category, Fiscal Year 1978*. CPB, Washington, DC.

———. 1979. *Public Television Programming Content By Category, Fiscal Year 1978*. CPB, Washington, DC.

———. 1981. *Five Year Plan For Public Telecommunications, 1981–1985*. CPB, Washington, DC.

———. 1981. *Review of 1980 CPB Communication Research Findings*. CPB, Washington, DC.

———. 1981. *Status Report on Public Broadcasting*. CPB, Washington, DC.

Costigan, Daniel M. 1978. *Electronic Delivery of Documents and Graphics*. Van Nostrand Reinhold, New York.

Counterattack. 1950. *Red Channels: The Report of Communists in Radio and Television*. Counterattack, New York.

Cowan, Geoffrey. 1979. *See No Evil: The Backstage Battle Over Sex and Violence on Television*. Simon & Schuster, New York.

Cox, Edward F., et al. 1969. *The Nader Report on the Federal Trade Commission*. Richard W. Baron, New York.

Cox, Kenneth. 1957. *Television Network Practices*. Staff Report for Senate Committee on Interstate and Foreign Commerce, Television Inquiry. 85th Cong., 1st Sess. Government Printing Office, Washington, DC.

Crane, Rhonda J. 1979. *The Politics of International Standards: France and the Color TV War*. Ablex Publishing, Norwood, NJ.

Csida, Joseph, & Csida, June Bundy. 1978. *American Entertainment: A Unique History of Popular Show Business*. Billboard Books, New York.

Culbert, David H. 1976. *News for Everyman: Radio and Foreign Affairs in Thirties America*. Greenwood Press, Westport, CT.

Cullen, Maurice R., Jr. 1981. *Mass Media and the First Amendment: An Introduction to the Issues, Problems, and Practices*. Wm. C. Brown, Dubuque, IA.

Curtis, John A., & Blatecky, Alan R. 1978. "The Economics of ITFS Use," *Educational and Instructional Television* (April): 47–58.

Danielian, N. R. 1939. *AT&T: The Story of Industrial Conquest*. Vanguard, New York. (Repr. Arno Press, 1974).

David, Nina. Annual. *TV Season*. Oryx Press, Phoenix, AZ.

Davidovitz, Paul. 1972. *Communication*. Holt, Rinehart & Winston, New York.

Davis, Robert E. 1976. *Response to Innovation: A Study of Popular Argument About New Mass Media*. Arno Press, New York.

Davis, Stephen. 1927. *The Law of Communication*. McGraw-Hill, New York.

Davison, W. Phillips, & Yu, Frederick T. C., eds. 1974. *Mass Communication Research: Major Issues and Future Directions*. Praeger Special Studies, New York.

DeFleur, Melvin L., & Ball-Rokeach, Sandra. 1975. *Theories of Mass Communication*. 3d ed. Longman, New York.

de Forest, Lee. 1950. *Father of Radio*. Wilcox & Follett, Chicago.

Delong, Thomas A. 1980. *The Mighty Music Box: The Golden Age of Musical Radio*. Amber Crest Books, Los Angeles.

DeLozier, M. Wayne. 1976. *The Marketing Communications Process*. McGraw-Hill, New York.

Department of Commerce. Annual. *Statistical Abstract of the United States*. Government Printing Office, Washington, DC.

———. 1922. "Minutes of Open Meeting of Department of Commerce on Radio Telephony." Mimeo. [1st Conference]

———. 1923. "Recommendations of the National Radio Committee as Reproduced in *Radio Service Bulletin No. 72*," [2d Conf.] Bureau of Navigation, Department of Commerce. Government Printing Office, Washington, DC. (Repr. Arno Press, 1977).

———. 1924. *Recommendations for Regulation of Radio*. [3d Conf.] Government Printing Office, Washington, DC. (Repr. Arno Press, 1977).

———. 1926. *Proceedings of the Fourth National Radio Conference and Recommendations for Regulation of Radio . . . .* Department of Commerce, Washington, DC. (Repr. Arno Press, 1977).

De Soto, Clinton. 1936. *Two Hundred Meters and Down: The Story of Amateur Radio*. A.R.R.L., West Hartford, CT.

Dessart, George. 1978. *Television in the Real World: A Case Study Course in Broadcast Management*. Hastings House, New York.

DeVol, Kenneth, ed. 1976. *Mass Media and the Supreme Court: The Legacy of the Warren Years.* 2d ed. Hastings House, New York.

Diamant, Lincoln. 1970. *The Anatomy of a Television Commercial.* Hastings House, New York.

———. 1971. *Television's Classic Commercials: The Golden Years, 1948–1958.* Hastings House, New York.

———. 1978. *The Broadcast Communications Dictionary.* 2d ed. Hastings House, New York.

Dill, Clarence C. 1938. *Radio Law: Practice and Procedure.* National Law Book Co., Washington, DC.

Dillman, Don A. 1978. *Mail and Telephone Surveys.* Wiley/Interscience, New York.

Dinsdale, A. A. 1932. *First Principles of Television.* Wiley, New York. (Repr. Arno Press, 1971).

Dizard, Wilson P. 1966. *Television: A World View.* Syracuse U. Press, Syracuse, NY.

Doan, Richard K. 1973. "We Pause Briefly," *TV Guide* (May 12): 28.

Dominick, Joseph R., & Pearce, Millard C. 1976. "Trends in Network Prime-Time Programming, 1953–74," *Journal of Communication* 26 (Winter): 70–80.

Dort, Dennis. 1980. *Program Distribution, Scheduling, and Production Support in the Public Television System: A Study Prepared for the Network Inquiry at the Federal Communications Commission.* FCC, Washington, DC.

Drake-Chenault Enterprises, Inc. 1978. "History of Rock and Roll." Drake-Chenault, Canoga Park, CA.

Draves, Pamela, ed. 1977. *Citizen's Media Directory.* National Citizen's Committee for Broadcasting, Washington, DC.

Dreher, Carl. 1977. *Sarnoff: An American Success.* Quadrangle/New York Times Book Co., New York.

Droesch, Paul. "Stalking Bigfoot, Meeting Mystics and Marinating Beef," *TV Guide* (Mar. 1): 37.

Dugan, James. 1953. *The Great Iron Ship.* Harper, New York.

Duke, Judith S. 1981. *Religious Publishing and Communications.* Knowledge Industry Publications, White Plains, NY.

Dummer, G. W. A. 1977. *Electronic Inventions: 1745–1976.* Pergamon, Press, NY.

Dunlap, Orrin E., Jr. 1931. *Radio in Advertising.* Harper New York.

———. 1938. *Marconi: The Man and His Wireless.* Rev. ed. Macmillan, New York. (Repr. Arno Press, 1971).

———. 1944. *Radio's 100 Men of Science.* Harper, New York.

Dunning, John. 1976. *Tune in Yesterday: The Ultimate Encyclopedia of Old-Time Radio, 1925–1976.* Prentice-Hall, Englewood Cliffs, NJ.

Dygert, Warren. 1939. *Radio as an Advertising Medium.* McGraw-Hill, New York.

Eastman, Susan Tyler, & Klein, Robert. 1982. *Strategies for Broadcast and Cable Promotion.* Wadsworth, Belmont, CA.

Eastman, Susan Tyler, et al. 1981. *Broadcast Programming: Strategies for Winning Television and Radio Audiences.* Wadsworth, Belmont, CA.

Edelman, Murray. 1950. *The Licensing of Radio Services in the United States, 1927–1947.* Illinois Studies in the Social Sciences, Vol. 31. U. of Illinois Press, Urbana. (Repr. Arno Press, 1980).

Edelstein, Alex S., et al. 1979. *Information Societies: Comparing the Japanese and American Experiences.* U. of Washington Press, Seattle.

Efron, Edith. 1971. *The News Twisters.* Nash, Los Angeles.

———. 1972. "This Time the Indians Won," *TV Guide* (Jan. 22): 42.

EIA (Electronic Industries Association). Annual. *Consumer Electronics.* EIA, Washington, DC.

Elliot, William. 1956. *Television's Impact on American Culture.* Michigan State U. Press, East Lansing.

Ellis, David. 1980. *Evolution of the Canadian Broadcasting System: Objectives and Realities, 1928–1968.* Canadian Government Printing Office, Ottawa.

Ellmore, R. Terry. 1977. *The Illustrated Dictionary of Broadcast-CATV-Telecommunications.* Tab Books, Blue Ridge Summit, PA.

Elton, Martin C. J., et al., eds. 1979. *Evaluating New Telecommunications Services.* Plenum, NY.

Emerson, Thomas I. 1972. "Communication and Freedom of Expression," *Scientific American* (September): 163–172.

Emery, Edwin, & Emery, Michael. 1978. *The Press and America: An Interpretive History of the Mass Media.* 4th ed. Prentice-Hall, Englewood Cliffs, NJ.

Emery, Walter B. 1969. *National and International Systems of Broadcasting: Their History, Operation and Control.* Michigan State U. Press, East Lansing.

———. 1971. *Broadcasting and Government: Responsibilities and Regulations.* 2d ed. Michigan State U. Press, East Lansing.

Ennes, Harold E. 1953. *Principles and Practices of Telecasting Operations.* Howard W. Sams, Indianapolis.

Eoyang, Thomas T. 1936. *An Economic Study of the Radio Industry in the United States of America.* Columbia U. Press, New York. (Repr. Arno Press, 1974).

Epstein, Edward J. 1973a. *News From Nowhere: Television and the News.* Random House, New York.

———. 1973b. "What Happened vs. What We Saw," *TV Guide* (Sept 29, Oct. 6, Oct. 13): 7, 20, 49.

Everson, George. 1949. *The Story of Television: The Life of Philo T. Farnsworth.* Norton, New York. (Repr. Arno Press, 1974).

Eyesenck, H. J., & Nias, D. K. B. 1978. *Sex, Violence and the Media.* Harper & Row, New York.

F (*Federal Reporter,* 1st and 2d Series)
    1926 *U.S.* v. *Zenith Radio Corp.,* 12 F 2d 614.
    1929 *U.S.* v. *American Bond & Mortgage,* 31 F 2d 448.
    1931 *KFKB* v. *FRC,* 47 F 2d 670.
    1932 *Trinity Methodist Church, South* v. *FRC,* 62 F 2d 850.
    1946 *WOKO* v. *FCC* 153 F 2d 623.
    1948 *Simmons* v. *FCC* 169 F 2d 670.
    1962 *Suburban Broadcasters* v. *FCC* 302 F 2d 191.
    1966 *Office of Communication* v. *FCC* 359 F 2d 994.
    1968 *Banzhaf* v. *FCC* 405 F 2d 1082.
    1969 *New York State Broadcasters Association* v. *U.S.* 414 F 2d 990.
    1969 *National Association of Theater Owners* v. *FCC* 420 F 2d 194.
    1969 *Office of Communication* v. *FCC* 425 F 2d 543.
    1971 *Citizens Communications Center* v. *FCC* 447 F 2d 1201.
    1971 *Friends of the Earth* v. *FCC* 449 F 2d 1164.
    1972 *Stone et al.* v. *FCC* 466 F 2d 316.
    1972 *Brandywine-Main Line Radio* v. *FCC* 473 F 2d 16.
    1973 *TV 9* v. *FCC* 495 F 2d 929.
    1974 *Citizens Committee to Save WEFM* v. *FCC* 506 F 2d 246.
    1974 *NBC* v. *FCC* 516 F 2d 1101.
    1975 *National Assocation of Independent Television Distributors* v. *FCC* 516 F 2d 526.
    1975 *Polish American Congress* v. *FCC* 520 F 2d 1248.
    1975 *Public Interest Research Group* v. *FCC* 522 F 2d 1060.
    1976 *Chisholm et al.* v. *FCC* 538 F 2d 349.
    1977 *Warner-Lambert Co.* v. *FTC* 562 F 2d 749.
    1977 *ACT* v. *FCC* 564 F 2d 458.
    1977 *Kuczo* v. *Western Connecticut Broadcasting Co.* 566 F 2d 384.
    1977 *Home Box Office* v. *FCC* 567 F 2d 9.
    1978 *Office of Communication* v. *FCC* 590 F 2d 1062.
    1978 *Central Florida Enterprises* v. *FCC* 598 F 2d 37.
    1979 *American Security Council Education Foundation* v. *FCC* 607 F 2d 438.
    1979 *Writers Guild* v. *ABC* 609 F 2d 355.
    1979 *WNCN Listeners Guild* v. *FCC* 610 F 2d 838.
    1979 *Berlin Communications* v. *FCC* 626 F 2d 875.
    1980 *CBS, Inc.* v. *ASCAP* 620 F 2d 930.
Fabe, Maxine. 1979. *TV Game Shows.* Doubleday, New York.
Fahie, J. J. 1901. *A History of Wireless Telegraphy.* Dodd, Mead, New York. (Repr. Arno Press, 1974).
Fallon, Norman. 1976. *Shortwave Listeners Handbook.* 2d ed. Hayden, Rochelle Park, NJ.

Fang, Irving E. 1977. *Those Radio Commentators!* Iowa State U. Press, Ames.
Faulk, John H. 1964. *Fear on Trial.* Simon & Schuster, New York.
FCC (Federal Communications Commission)
    Annual. *AM-FM Financial Data.* FCC, Washington, DC.
    Annual. *Annual Report.* Government Printing Office, Washington, DC. (1935–1955 vols. repr. Arno Press, 1971).
    Annual. *Major Matters before the Federal Communications Commission.* Government Printing Office, Washington, DC.
    Annual. *Television Broadcast Financial Data.* FCC, Washington, DC.
    Annual. *Television Broadcast Programming Data.* (Title varies). FCC, Washington, DC.
    1939. *Investigation of the Telephone Industry in the United States.* Government Printing Office, Washington, DC. (Repr. Arno Press, 1974).
    1941. *Report on Chain Broadcasting.* Government Printing Office, Washington, DC. (Repr. Arno Press, 1974).
    1978. *The Communications Act of 1934 with Amendments and Index Thereto, as Amended through Nov. 2.* Government Printing Office, Washington, DC.
    1979. (Network Inquiry Special Staff). *An Analysis of the Network-Affiliate Relationship in Television.* Preliminary Report. (October) FCC, Washington, DC.
    1979. (Children's Television Task Force). *Television Programming for Children.* 5 vols. (October) FCC, Washington, DC.
    1980. *Cable Television Industry Revenues.* FCC, Washington, DC.
    1980. *The Law of Political Broadcasting and Cable Casting: A Political Primer.* Government Printing Office, Washington, DC.
    1980. (Network Inquiry Special Staff). *The Market for Television Advertising: The Determinants of Television Station Profitability.* Preliminary Report. (June). FCC, Washington, DC.
    1980. (Network Inquiry Special Staff). *New Television Networks: Entry, Jurisdiction, Ownership and Regulation. Final Report,* Vol. 1. *Background Reports,* Vol. 2. Government Printing Office, Washington, DC.
    1980. *Staff Report and Recommendations in the Low Power Television Inquiry.* FCC, Washington, DC.
    1980. *Staff Report on Comparability for UHF Television: Final Report.* FCC, Washington, DC.

1980. (Office of Plans & Policy). *Staff Report on Policies for Regulation of Direct Broadcast Satellites*. FCC, Washington, DC.

1980. "Television Channel Utilization," Mimeo #35899. (Oct. 30). FCC, Washington, DC.

FCC (*FCC Reports*, 1st and 2d Series)

1949 *Editorializing by Broadcast Licensees*. Report. 13 FCC 1246.

1952 *Amendment of Sec. 3.606 [adopting new television rules]* . . . Sixth Report and order. 41 FCC 148.

1959 *Columbia Broadcasting System*. An Interpretive Opinion. 26 FCC 715.

1960 *En Banc Programming Inquiry*. Report and Statement of Policy. 44 FCC 2303.

1965 *Comparative Broadcast Hearings*. Policy Statement. 1 FCC 2d 393.

1966 *Contests and Promotions Which Adversely Affect the Public Interest*. Public Notice. 2 FCC 2d 464.

1968 *Broadcasting in America and the FCC's License Renewal Process: An Oklahoma Case Study*. 14 FCC 2d 1.

1969 *Network Coverage of the Democratic National Convention*. Letter. 16 FCC 2d 650.

1969 *Application . . . for Renewal of License of Station KTAL-TV, Texarkana, Tex*. Letter. 19 FCC 2d 109.

1969 *Complaints Covering CBS Program "Hunger in America."* Memorandum Opinion. 20 FCC 2d 143.

1970 *Comparative Hearings Involving Regular Renewal Applicants*. Policy Statement. 22 FCC 2d 424.

1970 *Nicholas Zapple*. Letter. 23 FCC 2d 707.

1970 *Complaint of the Committee for the Fair Broadcasting of Controversial Issues, Against Columbia Broadcasting System . . .* Memorandum Opinion and Order. 25 FCC 2d 283.

1970 *Amendment of Part 73 of the Commission's Rules and Regulations with Respect to Competition and Responsibility in Network Television Broadcasting*. Memorandum Opinion and Order. 25 FCC 2d 318.

1971 *Licensee Responsibility to Review Records Before Their Broadcast*. Public Notice. 28 FCC 2d 409.

1971 *Complaint Concerning the CBS Program, "The Selling of the Pentagon."* Letter. 30 FCC 2d 150.

1972 *Request by Walt Disney Productions for Declaratory Ruling with Respect to Political Broadcast Equal Opportunities*. Letter. 33 FCC 2d 297.

1972 *Cable Television*. Report and Order. 36 FCC 2d 143.

1972 *Complaint by Atlanta NAACP*. Letter. 36 FCC 2d 635.

1974 *Handling of Public Issues Under the Fairness Doctrine and the Public Interest Standard of the Communications Act*. Fairness Report. 48 FCC 2d 1.

1974 *Practices of Licensees and Networks in Connection with Broadcasts of Sports Events*. Report and Order. 48 FCC 2d 235.

1974 *Children's Television*. Report and Policy Statement. 50 FCC 2d 1.

1975 *Applications for Renewal of Star Stations of Indiana*. Decision. 51 FCC 2d 95.

1975 *Inquiry into Subscription Agreements Between Radio Broadcasting Stations and Music Format Service Companies*. Report and Policy Statement. 56 FCC 2d 805.

1975 *Agreements Between Broadcast Licensees and the Public*. Report and Order. 57 FCC 2d 42.

1976 *Representative Patsy Mink, The Environmental Policy Center and O. D. Hagedorn re Radio Station WHAR, Clarksburg, West Virginia*. Memorandum Opinion and Order. 59 FCC 2d 987.

1976 *Development of Policy Re: Changes in the Entertainment Formats of Broadcast Stations*. Memorandum Opinion and Order. 60 FCC 2d 858.

1977 *Review of Commission's Rules and Regulating Policies Concerning Network Broadcasting by Standard (AM) and FM Broadcast Stations*. Report, Statement of Policy and Order. 63 FCC 2d 674.

1977 *Application of Sponsorship Identification Rules to Political Broadcasts, Teaser Announcements, Government Entities, and Other Organizations*. Public Notice. 66 FCC 2d 302.

1978 *Application for License Renewal by WPIX, Inc., and Construction Permit by Forum Communications*. Decision. 68 FCC 2d 381.

1978 *Commission Policy in Enforcing Section 312 (a) (7) of the Communications Act*. Report and Order. 68 FCC 2d 1079.

1978 *Complaints Against Station KVOF-TV by Council on Religion and the Homosexual, Inc*. Memorandum Opinion and Order. 68 FCC 2d 1500.

1979 *PTL of Heritage Village Church (WJAN-TV)*. Memorandum Opinion and Order. 71 FCC 2d 324.

1979 *Objectionable Loudness of Commercial Announcements . . . .* Notice of Inquiry. 72 FCC 2d 677.

1979 *Deregulation of Radio*. Notice of Inquiry and Proposed Rule Making. 73 FCC 2d 457.

1979 *Children's Television Programming and Advertising Practices*. Notice of Proposed Rule Making. 75 FCC 2d 138.

1980 *Rules and Policies to Further the Advancement of Black Americans in Mass Communications*. Memorandum Opinion and Order. 76 FCC 2d 385.

1980 *Application of RKO General, Inc. (WNAC-TV), Boston, Mass., for Renewal of Broadcasting License*. Decision. 78 FCC 2d 1.

1980 *Application of Walton Broadcasting, Inc. (KIKX), Tucson, Arizona, for Renewal of License.* Decision. 78 FCC 2d 857.

1980 *Cable Television Syndicated Program Exclusivity Rules [and] Inquiry into the Economic Relationship Between Television Broadcasting and Cable Television.* Report and Order. 79 FCC 2d 663.

1981 *Application of Faith Center, Inc., Station KHOF-TV, San Bernardino, Calif.* Memorandum Opinion and Order. 84 FCC 2d 542.

1981 *Deregulation of Radio.* Report and Order. (Proceeding Terminated). 84 FCC 2d 968.

Federal Communication Law Journal. 1981. Special issue on Direct Broadcast Satellites.

Federal Radio Commission. Annual. *Annual Report,* 1927–1933. Government Printing Office, Washington, DC. (Repr. Arno Press, 1971).

——. 1932. *Commercial Radio Advertising.* Government Printing Office, Washington, DC. (Repr. Arno Press, 1974).

Felix, Edgar. 1927. *Using Radio in Sales Promotion.* McGraw-Hill, New York.

Ferrall, Victor E., ed. 1980. *Yearbook of Broadcasting Articles: Anthology Edition, Vol. I, 1959–1978.* Federal Publications, Inc., Washington, DC.

Feshbach, Seymour, & Singer, Robert D. 1971. *Television and Aggression: An Experimental Field Study.* Jossey-Bass, San Francisco.

Fessenden, Helen. 1940. *Fessenden: Builder of Tomorrow.* Coward-McCann, New York. (Repr. Arno Press, 1974).

Fink, Donald G., ed. 1943. *Television Standards and Practice: Selected Papers from the Proceedings of the National Television System Committee and Its Panels.* McGraw-Hill, New York.

Fink, Donald G., & Lutyens, David M. 1960. *The Physics of Television.* Anchor Books, Garden City, New York.

Fireman, Judy, ed. 1977. *TV Book: The Ultimate Television Book.* Workman Publishing Co., New York.

Fiske, Edward B. 1973. "The Oral Roberts Empire," *New York Times Magazine* (Apr. 22): 14.

Fletcher, James, ed. 1981. *Handbook of Radio-TV Broadcasting: Research Procedures in Audience, Program, and Revenues.* Van Nostrand-Reinhold, New York.

Foley, Joseph M. 1973. "Broadcast Regulation Research: A Primer for Non-Lawyers," *Journal of Broadcasting* 17 (Spring): 147–158.

——. 1979. "Mass Communication Theory and Research: An Overview," in Nimmo, 1979: 263–270.

Ford Foundaton. 1976. *Ford Foundation Activities in Noncommercial Broadcasting, 1951–1976.* Ford, New York.

FR (*Federal Register*)
1974 *Program Length Commercials.* 39 FR 4042.

1974 *The Public and Broadcasting: A Procedure Manual.* Rev. ed. 39 FR 32288.

F Sup (*Federal Supplement*)
1976 *Writers Guild et al.* v. *FCC* 423 F Sup 1064.
1977 *CBS* v. *Stokely-Van Camp* 456 F Sup 539.
1978 *U.S.* v. *NBC* 449 F Sup 1127.
1979 *Universal City Studios* v. *Sony* 480 F Sup 429.

François, William E. 1978. *Mass Media Law and Regulation.* 2d ed. Grid, Inc., Columbus, OH.

Frank, Ronald E., & Greenberg, Marshall G. 1980. *The Public's Use of Television.* Sage Publications, Beverly Hills, CA.

Franklin, Marc A. 1981. *The First Amendment and the Fourth Estate: Communications Law for Undergraduates.* 2d ed. Foundation Press, Mineola, NY.

Freed, Fred. 1972. "The Rise and Fall of the Television Documentary," *Television Quarterly* 10 (Fall): 55–62.

Friedman, Leslie J. 1977. *Sex Role Stereotyping in the Mass Media: An Annotated Bibliography.* Garland Publishing, New York.

Friendly, Fred W. 1967. *Due to Circumstances beyond our Control . . . .* Random House, New York.

——. 1972. "Dear Jack Gould, They Say You've Retired," *New York Times* (Feb. 27): 17.

——. 1973. "The Campaign to Politicize Broadcasting," *Columbia Journalism Review* (March/April): 9–18.

——. 1975. "What's Fair on the Air," *New York Times Magazine* (Mar. 30): 11–12, 37–48.

——. 1976. *The Good Guys, the Bad Guys, and the First Amendment: Free Speech vs. Fairness in Broadcasting.* Random House, New York.

Frost, J. M., ed. Annual. *World Radio-TV Handbook.* Billboard, New York.

Frost, S. E., Jr. 1937. *Is American Radio Democratic?* U. of Chicago Press, Chicago.

FTC (Federal Trade Commission).

Annual. *Annual Report.* Government Printing Office, Washington, DC.

1924. *Report on the Radio Industry.* In response to H. Res. 548, 67th Cong., 4th Sess. Government Printing Office, Washington, DC. (Repr. Arno Press, 1974).

1978. *Staff Report on Television Advertising to Children.* Government Printing Office, Washington DC.

1979. *Proceedings of the Symposium on Media Concentration.* (2 Vols) Government Printing Office, Washington, DC.

Funt, Peter. 1974. "How TV Producers Sneak in a Few Extra Commercials," *New York Times* (Aug. 11): 1B.

——. 1980. "What's Allowed on TV — Pressures for Change Are Mounting," *New York Times* (Nov. 2): 2.

GAO (General Accounting Office)
    1978 *The Role of Field Operations in the Federal Communications Commission's Regulatory Structure.* Government Printing Office, Washington, DC.
    1979 *Organizing the Federal Communications Commission for Greater Management and Regulatory Effectiveness.* Government Printing Office, Washington, DC.
    1979 *Selected FCC Regulatory Policies: Their Purpose and Consequences for Commercial Radio & TV.* Government Printing Office, Washington, DC.

Gates, Gary P. 1978. *Air Time: The Inside Story of CBS News.* Harper & Row, New York.

——. "If You Can't Beat 'Em, Raid 'Em," *TV Guide* (Feb. 9): 4.

Gelatt, Roland. 1977. *The Fabulous Phonograph: 1877–1977.* 2d rev. ed. Macmillan, New York.

Geller, Henry. 1973. *The Fairness Doctrine in Broadcasting: Problems and Suggested Courses of Action.* Rand Corporation, Santa Monica, CA.

Gelman, Morris. 1971. "Yesterday's Yarns, Tomorrow's Legends," *Broadcasting* (Oct. 18): 29.

Gerbner, George. 1972. "Communications and Social Environment," *Scientific American* (September): 153–160.

Gerbner, George, et al. 1977. "'The Gerbner Violence Profile': An Analysis of the CBS Report," *Journal of Broadcasting* 21 (Summer): 280–286.

——. 1980. "The 'Mainstreaming' of America: Violence Profile No. 11," *Journal of Communication* 30 (Summer): 10–29.

Gerrold, David. 1973. *The World of Star Trek.* Ballantine, New York.

Gianakos, Larry J. 1978. *Television Drama Series Programming: A Comprehensive Chronicle, 1959–1975.* Scarecrow Press, Metuchen, NJ.

——. 1980. *Television Drama Series Programming: A Comprehensive Chronicle, 1947–1959.* Scarecrow Press, Metuchen, N.J.

Gibson, George H. 1977. *Public Broadcasting: The Role of the Federal Government, 1912–76.* Praeger, New York.

Gilbert, Robert E. 1972. *Television and Presidential Politics.* Christopher Publishing House, North Quincy, MA.

Gillespie, Gilbert. 1975. *Public Access Cable Television in the United States and Canada.* Praeger, New York.

Gillmor, Donald M., & Barron, Jerome A. 1979. *Mass Communication Law: Cases and Comment.* 3d ed. West, St. Paul, MN.

Ginsburg, Douglas H. 1979. *Regulation of Broadcasting: Law and Policy Towards Radio, Television and Cable Communications.* West, St. Paul, MN.

Glick, Ira O., & Levy, Sidney J. 1962. *Living with Television.* Aldine, Chicago.

Glut, Donald, & Harmon, Jim. 1975. *The Great Television Heroes.* Doubleday, New York.

Glynn, Eugene D. 1956. "Television and the American Character — A Psychiatrist Looks at Television," in Elliott: 177–182.

Goldenson, Leonard H. 1978. Address to the Academy of Television Arts and Sciences, Los Angeles, Nov. 16.

Goldmark, Peter C., & Edson, Lee. 1973. *Maverick Inventor: My Turbulent Years at CBS.* Saturday Review Press, New York.

Goodson, Mark. 1976. "TV Shows Are Hoodwinking Viewers Again," *New York Times* (May 9): II-1.

Gordon, Thomas F., and Verna, Mary E. 1978. *Mass Communication Effects and Processes: A Comprehensive Bibliography, 1950–1975.* Sage Publications, Beverly Hills, CA.

Graf, Richard. 1972. "How National News Gets to Local Stations," *TV Guide* (July 8): 16.

Graham, James M., & Kramer, Victor. 1976. *Appointments to the Regulatory Agencies: The Federal Communications Commission and the Federal Trade Commission (1949–1974).* Report to Senate Committee on Commerce. Government Printing Office, Washington, DC.

Great Britain. Committee on Broadcasting. 1962. *Report, 1960,* Cmnd. 1753. ["Pilkington Report"]. Her Majesty's Stationery Office, London.

——. Committee on the Future of Broadcasting. 1977. *Report.* Cmnd. 6753. ["Annan Report"]. Her Majesty's Stationery Office, London.

Green, Timothy. 1972. *The Universal Eye: The World of Television.* Stein and Day, New York.

Greenberg, Bradley S. 1980. *Life on Television: Content Analysis of U.S. TV Drama.* Ablex, Norwood, NJ.

——, & Parker, Edwin B., eds. 1965. *The Kennedy Assassination and the American Public: Social Communication in Crisis.* Stanford U. Press, Stanford, CA.

Greenfield, Jeff. 1977. *Television: The First Fifty Years.* Abrams, New York.

Gross, Ben. 1954. *I Looked and I Listened.* Rev. 1970. Random House, New York.

Gruenstein, Peter. 1978. "Is the TV Sports Fan Getting Shortchanged?" *TV Guide* (Nov. 25): 26.

Grundfest, Joseph A. 1976. *Citizen Participation in Broadcast Licensing before the FCC.* Rand Corporation, Santa Monica, CA.

Guimary, Donald L. 1975. *Citizen's Groups and Broadcasting.* Praeger, New York.

Gunn, Hartford. 1979. *Window on the Future: Planning for Public Television in the Telecommunications Era.* NAEB, Washington, DC.

Gunther, John. 1960. *Taken at the Flood: The Story of Albert J. Lasker.* Harper & Bros., New York.

Gunther, Max. 1978. "Commercials," *TV Guide* (Dec. 2): 4.

Hachten, William A. 1968. *The Supreme Court on Freedom of the Press: Decisions and Dissents.* Iowa State U. Press, Ames.

Hadden, Jeffrey K., & Swann, Charles E. 1981. *Prime Time Preachers: The Rising Power of Televangelism.* Addison-Wesley, Reading, MA.

Haigh, Robert W., et al., eds. 1981. *Communications in the Twenty-First Century.* Wiley-Interscience, New York.

Halberstam, David. 1979. *The Powers That Be.* Knopf, New York.

Hale, Julian. 1975. *Radio Power: Propaganda and International Broadcasting.* Temple U. Press, Philadelphia.

Hamburg, Morton I. 1979. *All About Cable: Legal and Business Aspects of Cable and Pay Television.* Law Journal Press, New York.

Hammond, Charles M. 1981. *The Image Decade: Television Documentary: 1965–1975.* Hastings House, New York.

Hancock, Harry. 1950. *Wireless at Sea: The First 50 Years.* Marconi International Marine Communication Co., Chelmsford, England. (Repr. Arno Press, 1974).

Happé, Bernard. 1975. *Basic Motion Picture Technology.* Hastings House, New York.

Harlow, Alvin. 1936. *Old Wires and New Waves: The History of the Telegraph, Telephone and Wireless.* Century, New York. (Repr. Arno Press, 1971).

Harmon, Jim. 1967. *The Great Radio Heroes.* Doubleday, New York.

———. 1970. *The Great Radio Comedians.* Doubleday, New York.

Harris, Jay S. 1978. *TV Guide: The First 25 Years.* Simon & Schuster, New York.

Harris, Paul. 1977. *Broadcasting from the High Seas: The History of Offshore Radio in Europe, 1958–1976.* Paul Harris Publishing, Edinburgh.

Hassinger, William. 1978. "Evaluating Loud Commercials: An Experimental Approach." FCC/FOB 78-01. FCC, Washington, DC.

Head, Sydney W. 1974. *Broadcasting in Africa: A Continental Survey of Radio and Television.* Temple U. Press, Philadelphia.

Heighton, Elizabeth J., & Cunningham, Don R. 1976. *Advertising in the Broadcast Media.* Wadsworth, Belmont, CA.

Henderson, Bruce. 1979. "How Residuals Checks Surprise Actors," *TV Guide* (Dec. 22): 3.

Henderson, Madeline M., & MacNaughton, Marcia J., eds. 1980. *Electronic Communication: Technology and Impacts.* Westview Press, Boulder, CO.

Hess, Gary Newton. 1979. *An Historical Study of the Dumont Television Network.* Arno Press, New York.

Hettinger, Herman S. 1933. *A Decade of Radio Advertising,* U. of Chicago Press, Chicago. (Repr. Arno Press, 1971).

Hickey, Neil. 1976. "The Case of the Missing Viewers," *TV Guide* (May 8): 4.

Hiltz, Starr Roxanne, & Turoff, Murray. 1978. *The Network Nation: Human Communication via Computer.* Addison-Wesley, Reading, MA.

Himmelstein, Hal. 1981. *On the Small Screen: New Approaches in Television and Video Criticism.* Praeger, New York.

Himmelweit, Hilde, et al. 1961. *Television and the Child: An Empirical Study of the Effect of Television on the Young.* Oxford U. Press, London.

Hindley, Patricia, et al. 1977. *The Tangled Net: Basic Issues in Canadian Communications.* J. J. Douglas, Ltd., Vancouver, BC.

Hirsch, Paul M., et al., eds. 1977. *Strategies for Communication Research.* Sage, Beverly Hills, CA.

Hochberg, Philip R. 1978. *The States Regulate Cable: A Legislative Analysis of Substantive Provisions.* Kalba Bowen Assoc., Cambridge, MA.

Hocking, William E. 1947. *Freedom of the Press: A Framework of Principle.* U. of Chicago Press, Chicago.

Hofer, Stephen F. 1979. "Philo Farnsworth: Television's Pioneer," *Journal of Broadcasting* 23 (Spring): 153–165.

Hoffer, Tom W., & Nelson, Richard A. 1978. "Documdrama on American Television," *Journal of the University Film Association* 30 (Spring): 21–27.

Hollowell, Mary Louise, ed. 1980. *The Cable/Broadband Communications Book, Volume 2, 1980–81.* Communications Press, Washington, DC.

Hoover, Herbert. 1952. *Memoirs.* 3 vols. Macmillan, New York.

Hopkins, Mark W. 1970. *Mass Media in the Soviet Union.* Pegasus, New York.

Hoso-Bunka Foundation. 1978. *Symposium on the Cultural Role of Broadcasting, October 3–5, 1978.* Summary Report. Hoso-Bunka Foundation, Tokyo, Japan.

House CIFC (U.S. Congress. House of Representatives. Committee on Interstate and Foreign Commerce).

1958. *Network Broadcasting.* Report of the FCC Network Study Staff, House Report 1297. 85th Cong., 1st Sess.

1958. *Regulation of Broadcasting: Half a Century of Government Regulation of Broadcasting and the Need for Further Legislative Action.* 85th Cong., 2d Sess.

1960. *Responsibilities of Broadcast Licensees and Station Personnel (Payola and Other Deceptive Practices in the Broadcast Field)*. Hearings in 2 parts. 86th Cong., 2d Sess.

1963. *Broadcast Advertisements*. Hearings on H.R. 8316, etc. 88th Cong., 1st Sess.

1963, 1964, and 1965. *Broadcast Ratings: The Methodology, Accuracy, and Use of Ratings in Broadcasting*. Hearings, Parts 1–3, 88th Cong., 1st Sess; Part 4, 88th Cong., 1st & 2d Sess.

1971. *Subpenaed Material re Certain TV News Documentary Programs*. Serial No. 92-16. Hearings. 92nd Cong., 1st Sess.

1977. *Network Sports Practices*. Hearings. Serial No. 95-98. 95th Cong., 1st Sess.

1977. *Options Papers*. 95th Cong., 1st Sess.

1979. *The Communications Act of 1978: Hearings on H.R. 13015*. 5 vols. in 7 parts. 95th Cong., 2d Sess.

1980. *The Communications Act of 1979: Hearings on H.R. 3333*. 5 vols. in 8 parts. 96th Cong., 1st Sess.

House CMMF (U.S. Congress. House of Representatives. Committee on Merchant Marine and Fisheries).

1919. *Government Control of Radio Communication*. Hearings on H.R. 13159. 65th Cong., 3rd Sess.

1924. *To Regulate Radio Communication*. Hearings on H.R. 7357. 68th Cong., 1st Sess.

House JC (U.S. Congress. House of Representatives Committee on the Judiciary). 1980. *Telecommunications Act of 1980*. Hearings on H.R. 6121. 96th Cong., 1st Sess.

Hoveland, C. I., et al. 1949. *Experiments on Mass Communication*. Princeton U. Press, Princeton, NJ.

Howard, H. H., & Carroll, S. L. 1980. *Subscription Television: History, Current Status, and Economic Projections*. National Association of Broadcasters, Washington, DC.

Hower, Ralph M. 1949. *The History of an Advertising Agency: N. W. Ayer & Son at Work, 1869–1949*. Rev. ed. Harvard U. Press, Cambridge, MA.

Howeth, L. S. 1963. *History of Communications-Electronics in the United States Navy*. Government Printing Office, Washington, DC.

Husing, Ted. 1935. *Ten Years Before the Mike*. Farrar & Rinehart, New York.

ICA (International Communication Association). Annual. *Communication Yearbook: An Annual Review Published by the International Communication Association*. Transaction Books, New Brunswick, NJ.

ICB (International Christian Broadcasters). 1973. *World Directory of Religious Radio and Television Broadcasting*. Wm. Carey Library, South Pasadena, CA.

IIC (International Institute of Communication). 1976 ff. *Broadcasting in . . .* [various countries, by various authors]. Routledge & Kegan Paul, London.

Independent Broadcasting Authority. Annual. *Guide to Independent Broadcasting*. (Title varies.) IBA, London.

IRE (Institute of Radio Engineers). 1962. "Communications and Electronics — 2012 A.D.," *Proceedings of the IRE* 50 (May): 562–656.

———. 1962. *Proceedings of the IRE* 50 (May): entire issue, 50th anniversary, 1912–1962.

ITU (International Telecommunication Union). 1980. *Final Acts of the World Administrative Radio Conference, Geneva, 1979*. ITU, Geneva.

Jacobs, Norman. 1964. *Culture for the Millions? Mass Media in Modern Society*. Beacon Press, Boston.

Jacobstein, J. Myron, & Mersky, Roy M. 1977. *Legal Research Illustrated*. Foundation Press, Mineola, NY.

Jennings, Ralph M., & Richard, Pamela. 1974. *How to Protect Your Rights in Television and Radio*. Rev. ed. United Church of Christ, New York.

Johnson, Catherine E. *TV Guide 25 Year Index: By Author and Subject*. 1979. Triangle Publications, Radnor, PA.

Johnson, Joseph S., & Jones, Kenneth K. 1978. *Modern Radio Station Practices*. 2d ed. Wadsworth, Belmont, CA.

Johnson, Nicholas. 1970. *How to Talk Back to Your Television Set*. Little, Brown, Boston.

———, & Dystel, John. 1973. "A Day in the Life: The Federal Communications Commission," *Yale Law Journal* 82: 1575–1634.

Johnson, William O., Jr. 1971. *Super Spectator and the Electronic Lilliputians*. Little, Brown, Boston.

Johnston, Donald F. 1978. *Copyright Handbook*. R. R. Bowker, New York.

Johnstone, John W. C., et al. 1976. *The News People: A Sociological Portrait of American Journalists and Their Work*. U. of Illinois Press, Urbana, IL.

Jolly, W. P. 1972. *Marconi*. Stein and Day, New York.

Jome, Hiram L. 1925. *Economics of the Radio Industry*. A. W. Shaw, Chicago. (Repr. Arno Press, 1971).

Jones, Robert A. 1979. "FCC Docket Puts Squeeze on Clear Channel Service," *Broadcast Communications* (April): 54–59.

Jones, Robert F. 1955. *Investigation of Television Networks and the UHF–VHF Problem*. Progress Report prepared for Senate Committee on Interstate and Foreign Commerce. 84th Cong., 1st Sess. Government Printing Office, Washington, DC.

Jones, William K. 1966. *Licensing of Major Broadcast Facilities by the Federal Communications Commission*, in U.S. Congress, House of Representatives Select Committee on Small Business. *Activities of Regulatory Agencies Relating to Small Business*. Hearings. Part 1, A-87-A178. 89th Cong., 2d Sess. (Repr. Arno Press, 1980).

———. 1979. *Cases and Materials on Electronic Mass Media: Radio, Television and Cable*. 2d ed. Foundation Press, Mineola, NY.

Jowett, Garth. 1976. *Film: The Democratic Art*. Little, Brown, Boston.

JTAC (Joint Technical Advisory Committee). 1952. *Radio Spectrum Conservation*. McGraw-Hill, New York.

———. 1965. *Radio Spectrum Utilization*. Institute of Electronic and Electrical Engineers, New York.

Kahn, Frank J., ed. 1978. *Documents of American Broadcasting*. 3d ed. Prentice-Hall, Englewood Cliffs, NJ.

Kaid, Linda L., et al. 1974. *Political Campaign Communication: A Bibliography and Guide to the Literature*. Scarecrow Press, Metuchen, NJ.

Kaltenborn, H. V. 1938. *I Broadcast the Crisis*. Random House, New York.

Katz, Elihu. 1977. *Social Research in Broadcasting: Proposals for Further Development*. BBC, London.

———, & Lazarsfeld, Paul F. 1955. *Personal Influence: The Part Played by People in the Flow of Mass Communications*. Free Press, Glencoe, IL.

———, & Wedell, George. 1977. *Broadcasting in the Third World: Promise and Performance*. Harvard U. Press, Cambridge, MA.

———, et al. 1974. "Uses of Mass Communication by the Individual," in Davison & Yu, 1974: 11–35.

Katzman, Nathan, 1976. *Program Decisions in Public Television*. NAEB, Washington, DC.

Kaufman, David. 1969. *TV 70*. Signet Books, New York.

Kaye, Evelyn. 1979. *The ACT Guide to Children's Television, or How to Treat TV with TLC*. Beacon Press, Boston.

Kendrick, Alexander. 1969. *Prime Time: The Life of Edward R. Murrow*. Little, Brown, Boston.

Kerlinger, Fred H. 1973. *Foundations of Behavioral Research*. 2d ed. Holt, Rinehart & Winston, New York.

Kiester, Edwin, Jr. 1974. "That 'News' Item May Be a Commercial," *TV Guide* (Oct. 5): 10.

———. 1977. "The Great International Ratings War," *TV Guide* (Jan. 29): 34.

Kittross, John M. 1979. *Television Frequency Allocation Policy in the United States*. Arno Press, New York.

———, ed. 1978. *A Bibliography of Theses and Dissertations in Broadcasting, 1920–1973*. Broadcast Education Association, Washington, DC.

———, ed. 1980. *Administration of American Telecommunications Policy*. 2 Vols. Arno Press, New York.

———, & Harwood, Kenneth, eds. 1970. *Free and Fair: Courtroom Access and the Fairness Doctrine*. Association for Professional Broadcast Education, Philadelphia.

Kiver, Milton, & Kaufman, Milton. 1973. *Television Simplified*. 7th ed. Van Nostrand-Reinhold, New York.

Klapper, Joseph T. 1960. *The Effects of Mass Communication*. Free Press, New York.

Klein, Paul. 1971. "The Men Who Run TV Aren't That Stupid . . . They Know Us Better Than You Think," *New York* (Jan. 25): 20.

Kleinfeld, Sonny. 1981. *The Biggest Company on Earth: A Profile of AT&T*. Holt, Rinehart & Winston, New York.

Kline, F. Gerald. 1972. "Theory in Mass Communication Research," in Kline & Tichenor, 1972: 17–40.

Kline, F. Gerald, & Tichenor, Phillip J. 1972. *Current Perspectives in Mass Communication Research*. Sage, Beverly Hills, CA.

Koch, Howard. 1970. *The Panic Broadcast: Portrait of an Event*. Little, Brown, Boston.

Koenig, Allen E., ed. 1970. *Broadcasting and Bargaining: Labor Relations in Radio and Television*. U. of Wisconsin Press, Madison.

Kowet, Don. 1978. "TV Sports: America Speaks Out," *TV Guide* (Aug. 19): 2.

———. 1979. "Do Those '60 Minutes' Crusades Pay Off?" *TV Guide* (Mar. 10): 18.

———. 1979. "Whose 'Truth' Can You Believe?" *TV Guide* (Sept. 22): 6.

———. 1980. "TV Cameras Can Pursue News Only So Far," *TV Guide* (May 3): 4.

Krasnow, Erwin G., & Longley, Laurence. 1978. *The Politics of Broadcast Regulation*. 2d ed. St. Martin's Press, New York. (3d ed. 1982.)

Kraus, Sidney, ed. 1962. *The Great Debates: Background, Perspective, Effects*. Indiana U. Press, Bloomington.

———. 1979. *The Great Debates: Carter vs. Ford, 1976*. Indiana U. Press, Bloomington.

——— & Davis, Dennis. 1976. *The Effects of Mass Communication on Political Behavior*. Penn State U. Press, University Park.

Krippendorff, Klaus. 1981. *Content Analysis*. Sage, Beverly Hills, CA.

Kushner, James M. 1972. "KADS(FM): Want-Ad Radio in Los Angeles," *Journal of Broadcasting* (Summer): 267–276.

Kutash, Irwin L., et al. 1978. *Violence: Perspectives on Murder and Aggression*. Jossey-Bass, San Francisco.

Lachenbruch, David. 1971. "They Called It Radio-movies," *TV Guide* (July 3): 5.

Land, Herman W., Associates. 1967. *The Hidden Medium: A Status Report on Educational Radio in the United States.* NAEB, Washington, DC.

Landis, James M. 1960. *Report on Regulatory Agencies to the President-Elect.* United States Senate Committee on the Judiciary, Subcommittee on Administrative Practice and Procedure. 86th Cong., 2d Sess. Government Printing Office, Washington, DC.

Landry, Robert. 1946. *This Fascinating Radio Business.* Bobbs-Merrill, Indianapolis.

Landsburg, Alan. 1979. "The Independent Producer," in Morgenstern, ed., 1979: 38–67.

Lang, Kurt, & Lang, Gladys. 1968. *Politics and Television.* Quadrangle Books, Chicago.

Lapatine, Sol. 1978. *Electronics in Communications.* John Wiley, New York.

Lashner, Marilyn A. 1979. "The Chilling Effect of a White House Anti-Media Assault on Political Commentary in Network Television News Programs: Comparison of Newspaper and Television Vigorousness During the Nixon Administration." Unpublished doctoral dissertation. Temple University.

Lasswell, Harold D. 1952. "Educational Broadcasters as Social Scientists," *Quarterly of Film, Radio, and Television* 7: 150–162.

Lawhorne, Clifton O. 1971. *Defamation and Public Officials: The Evolving Law of Libel.* Southern Illinois U. Press, Carbondale.

Lazarsfeld, Paul F. 1940. *Radio and the Printed Page.* Duell, Sloan & Pearce, New York. (Repr. Arno Press 1971).

———— & Field, Harry N. 1946. *People Look at Radio.* U. of North Carolina Press, Chapel Hill.

———— & Kendall, Patricia L. 1948. *Radio Listening in America.* Prentice-Hall, New York.

———— & Stanton, Frank N., eds. 1942. *Radio Research, 1941.* Duell, Sloan & Pearce, New York.

————. 1944. *Radio Research, 1942–1943.* Duell, Sloan & Pearce, New York.

————.1949. *Communications Research, 1948–1949.* Harper, New York.

————, et al. 1944. *The People's Choice: How the Voter Makes Up His Mind in a Presidential Campaign.* Duell, Sloan & Pearce, New York.

Le Duc, Don R. 1973. "Broadcast Legal Documentation: A Four-Dimensional Guide," *Journal of Broadcasting* 17 (Spring): 131–146.

————. 1973. *Cable Television and the FCC: A Crisis in Media Control.* Temple U. Press, Philadelphia.

————, ed. 1974. *Issues in Broadcast Regulation.* Broadcast Education Association Monograph No. 1. BEA/NAB, Washington, DC.

Lefever, Ernest W. 1974. *TV and National Defense: An Analysis of CBS News, 1972–1973.* Institute for American Strategy, Boston, MA.

Leinwoll, Stanley. 1979. *From Spark to Satellite: A History of Radio Communication.* Charles Scribner's Sons, New York.

Leive, David. 1970. *International Telecommunications and International Law: The Regulation of the Radio Spectrum.* Oceana Publications, Dobbs Ferry, NY.

Lent, John A., ed. 1978. *Broadcasting in Asia and the Pacific: A Continental Survey of Radio and Television.* Temple U. Press, Philadelphia.

LeRoy, David, & Sterling, Christopher, eds. 1973. *Mass News: Practices, Controversies and Alternatives.* Prentice-Hall, Englewood Cliffs, NJ.

Lesser, Gerald S. 1974. *Children and Television: Lessons from Sesame Street.* Random House, New York.

Lessing, Lawrence. 1956. *Man of High Fidelity: Edwin Howard Armstrong.* J. P. Lippincott, New York. (Repr. Bantam Books, 1969).

Levin, Eric. 1975. "Reginald Bryant of *Black Perspective on the News,*" *TV Guide* (Feb. 8): 36.

Levin, Harvey J. 1971. *The Invisible Resource: Use and Regulation of the Radio Spectrum.* Johns Hopkins Press, Baltimore.

————. 1980. *Fact and Fancy in Television Regulation: An Economic Study of Policy Alternatives.* Russell Sage Foundation, New York.

Levine, Irving R. 1973. "Thirty Minutes on That Show Can Age You 10 Years," *TV Guide* (Feb. 17): 73.

Levinson, Richard, & Link, William. 1981. *Stay Tuned: An Inside Look at the Making of Prime-Time Television.* St. Martin's Press, New York.

Lewin, L. 1979. *Telecommunications: An Interdisciplinary Survey.* Artech House, Dedham, MA.

Lichty, Lawrence, & Topping, Malachi, eds. 1975. *American Broadcasting: A Source Book on the History of Radio and Television.* Hastings House, New York.

Liebert, Robert M., et al. 1973. *The Early Window: The Effects of Television on Children and Youth.* Pergamon, New York.

Lighthill, Sir James, et al. 1978. *Telecommunications in the 1980s and After.* The Royal Society, London.

Lindahl, Rutger. 1978. *Broadcasting across Borders: A Study on the Role of Propaganda in External Broadcasts.* LiberLäromedel, Göteborg, Sweden.

Lippman, Theo, Jr. 1972. *Spiro Agnew's America.* W. W. Norton, New York.

Lipton, Mike. 1978. "That $700 Million Hype," *TV Guide* (Aug. 26): 12.

Little, Arthur D., Inc. 1969. *Television Program Production, Procurement, Distribution and Scheduling.* Arthur D. Little, Cambridge, MA.

Loevinger, Lee. 1974. "The FCC and Content Control," in Le Duc, 1974: 60–72.

Long, Stewart Louis. 1979. *The Development of the Television Network Oligopoly*. Arno Press, New York.

Lowman, Charles E. 1972. *Magnetic Recording*. McGraw-Hill, New York.

Lowry, Dennis. 1979. "An Evaluation of Empirical Studies Reported in Seven Journals in the '70s," *Journalism Quarterly* 56 (Summer): 262–68, 282.

Lumley, Frederick. 1934. *Measurement in Radio*. Ohio State U. Press, Columbus. (Repr. Arno Press, 1971).

Lyons, Eugene. 1966. *David Sarnoff: A Biography*. Harper & Row, New York.

McCavitt, William E., comp. 1978. *Radio and Television: A Selected, Annotated Bibliography*. Scarecrow Press, Metuchen, NJ.

McCombs, Maxwell E., & Shaw, Donald L. 1977. *The Emergence of American Political Issues: The Agenda-Setting Function of the Press*. West Publishing Co., St. Paul, MN.

McCombs, Maxwell E., & Becker, Lee. 1979. *Using Mass Communication Theory*. Prentice-Hall, Englewood Cliffs, NJ.

McCoy, Ralph E. 1968. *Freedom of the Press: An Annotated Bibliography*. Southern Illinois U. Press, Carbondale, IL.

———. 1979. *Freedom of the Press: A Bibliocyclopedia Ten-Year Supplement (1967–1977)*. Southern Illinois U. Press, Carbondale, IL.

MacDonald, Dwight. 1953. "Theory of Mass Culture," *Diogenes* 3 (Summer): 5, 13–14.

MacDonald, J. Fred. 1979. *Don't Touch That Dial! Radio Programming in American Life, 1920–1960*. Nelson-Hall, Chicago.

Macdonald, Torbert H. 1972. Remarks at Massachusetts Broadcasters Association meeting, South Egremont, MA. Sept. 30.

McDowell, Edwin. 1979. "Texaco and the Met: A Long Marriage," *New York Times* (Mar. 10): 25.

MacFarland, David R. 1979. *The Development of the Top 40 Radio Format*. Arno Press, New York.

McGannon, Donald H. 1977. "Is the TV Code a Fraud?" *TV Guide* (Jan. 22): 11.

McGillam, Clare D., & McLauchlan, William P. 1978. *Hermes Bound: The Policy and Technology of Telecommunications*. Purdue U. Office of Publications, West Lafayette, IN.

McGinniss, Joe. 1969. *The Selling of the President, 1968*. Trident, New York.

McGuire, Bernadette, & LeRoy, David J. 1977. "Audience Mail: Letters to the Broadcaster," *Journal of Broadcasting* 27 (Summer): 79–85.

McKay, R. Bruce. 1976. "Financing: Problem or Symptom?" in Cater & Nyhan: 141–161.

Maclaurin, W. Rupert. 1949. *Invention and Innovation in the Radio Industry*. Macmillan, New York. (Repr. Arno, 1971.)

McLeod, Jack M., & O'Keefe, Garrett J. 1972. "The Socialization Perspective and Communication Behavior," in Kline & Tichenor, 1972: 121–168.

McLuhan, Marshall. 1964. *Understanding Media: The Extensions of Man*. McGraw-Hill, New York.

———, & Fiore, Quentin. 1967. *The Medium is the Massage: An Inventory of Effects*. Bantam Books, New York.

McNamee, Graham. 1926. *You're on the Air*. Harper, New York.

McNicol, Donald. 1946. *Radio's Conquest of Space*. Murray Hill Books, New York. (Repr. Arno Press, 1974).

McNeal, Alex. 1980. *Total Television: A Comprehensive Guide to Programming from 1948 to 1980*. Penguin Books, New York.

MacNeil, Robert. 1968. *The People Machine: The Influence of Television on American Politics*. Harper & Row, New York.

Macy, John, Jr. 1974. *To Irrigate a Wasteland: The Struggle to Shape a Public Television System in the United States*. U. of California Press, Berkeley.

Maddox, Brenda. 1972. *Beyond Babel: New Directions in Communications*. Simon & Schuster, New York.

Madison Avenue. 1981. "Interactive Television: Close Look at a Brave New World." (January).

Madow, William G., et al. 1961. *Evaluation of Statistical Methods Used in Obtaining Broadcast Ratings*. House Report 193, 87th Cong., 1st Sess. Government Printing Office, Washington, DC.

Magnant, Robert S. 1977. *Domestic Satellite: An FCC Giant Step Toward Competitive Telecommunications Policy*. Westview Press, Boulder, CO.

Mahoney, Sheila, et al. 1980. *Keeping Pace with the New Television*. NAEB, Washington, DC.

Mamber, Stephen. 1974. *Cinema Vérité in America: Studies in Uncontrolled Documentary*. MIT Press, Cambridge, MA.

Mander, Jerry. 1978. *Four Arguments for the Elimination of Television*. William Morrow, New York.

Marconi, Degna. 1962. *My Father, Marconi*. McGraw-Hill, New York.

Marcus, Geoffrey. 1969. *The Maiden Voyage*. Viking, New York.

Mariani, John. 1979. "Can Advertisers Read — and Control — Our Emotions?" *TV Guide* (Mar. 31): 4.

Marland, E. A. 1964. *Early Electrical Communication*. Abelard-Schuman, London.

Marsh, C. S., ed. 1937. *Educational Broadcasting 1936*. U. of Chicago Press, Chicago.

Marsh, Ken. 1974. *Independent Video: A Complete Guide to the Physics, Operation, and Application of the New Television for the Student, the Artist and for Community TV*. Straight Arrow Books, San Francisco.

Martin, James. 1977. *Future Developments in Telecommunications*. 2d ed. Prentice-Hall, Englewood Cliffs, NJ.

Matlon, Ronald. 1980. *Index to Journals in Communication Studies through 1979*. Speech Communication Association, Annandale, VA.

Mead, Margaret. 1973. "'As Significant as the Invention of Drama or the Novel,'" *TV Guide* (Jan. 6): 21.

Meeske, Milam D. 1976. "Black Ownership of Broadcast Stations: An FCC Licensing Problem," *Journal of Broadcasting* 20 (Spring): 261–271.

Melody, William. 1973. *Children's Television: The Economics of Exploitation*. Yale U. Press, New Haven, CT.

Mendelsohn, Harold. 1966. *Mass Entertainment*. College & University Press, New Haven, CT.

Meringoff, Laurene. 1980. *Children and Advertising: An Annotated Bibliography*. Council of Better Business Bureaus, New York.

Merton, Robert K. 1946. *Mass Persuasion: The Social Psychology of a War Bond Drive*. Harper, New York.

Metz, Robert. 1975. *CBS: Reflections in a Bloodshot Eye*. Playboy Press, Chicago.

———. 1977. *The Today Show: An Inside Look . . .* Playboy Press, Chicago.

Meyer, Edward H. 1970. "Is the Golden Goose Beginning to Lay Leaden Eggs?" Mimeo. Grey Advertising, Inc., New York.

Meyersohn, Rolf B. 1957. "Social Research in Television," in Rosenberg & White: 345–357.

Michener, James A. 1970. *The Quality of Life*. J. B. Lippincott, Philadelphia.

Mickiewicz, Ellen P. 1981. *Media and the Russian Public*. Praeger, New York.

Midgley, Ned. 1948. *The Advertising and Business Side of Radio*. Prentice-Hall, New York.

Milam, Lorenzo W. 1975. *Sex and Broadcasting: A Handbook on Starting Community Radio Stations*. 3d ed. Dildo Press, Saratoga, CA.

Miller, Delbert C. 1977. *Handbook of Research Design and Social Measurement*. 3d ed. Longmans, New York.

Miller, Merle. 1952. *The Judges and the Judged*. Doubleday, Garden City, NY. (Repr. Arno Press, 1971.)

———, & Rhodes, Evan. 1965. *Only You, Dick Darling*. Bantam, New York.

Minow, Newton N. 1964. *Equal Time: The Private Broadcaster and the Public Interest*. Atheneum, New York.

———, et al. 1973. *Presidential Television: A Twentieth Century Fund Report*. Basic Books, New York.

MLR (*Media Law Reporter*).

1980. *In Re Cannon 3 (A)* (Nevada Supreme Court) 5 MLR 2609.

1981. *Chandler v. Florida* (U.S. Supreme Court) 7 MLR 1041.

1981. *National Subscription Television* v. *S&H TV* (U.S. Court of Appeals, 9th Circuit) 7 MLR 1399.

Morgenstern, Steve, ed. 1979. *Inside the TV Business*. Sterling Publishing Co., New York.

Morris, James. 1973. *The Preachers*. St. Martin's, New York.

Morrow, Lance. 1978. "Television and the Holocaust," *Time* (May 1): 52.

Mosco, Vincent. 1979. *Broadcasting in the United States: Innovative Challenge and Organizational Control*. Ablex Publishing, Norwood, NJ.

Mumford, Lewis. 1970. *Myth of the Machine: The Pentagon of Power*. Harcourt Brace, Jovanovich, New York.

Murphy, Jonne. 1980. *Handbook of Radio Advertising*. Chilton, Radnor, PA.

Murphy, Mary. 1980. "The Day Christ Died: Has Television Gone Too Far?" *TV Guide* (Mar. 22): 4.

Murrow, Edward R. 1958. Address to Radio Television News Directors Association, Oct. 5, 1958, in Kahn, 1978: 253–261.

Myers, Kenneth H., Jr. 1968. *SRDS: The National Authority Serving the Media-Buying Function*. Northwestern U. Press, Evanston, IL.

NAB (National Association of Broadcasters). Semiannual. *Broadcasting and Government*. NAB, Washington, DC.

———. Annual. *Radio Financial Report*. NAB, Washington, DC.

———. Annual. *Television Financial Report*. NAB, Washington, DC.

———. 1973. *Standard Definitions of Broadcast Research Terms*. NAB, Washington, DC.

———. 1974. *A Broadcast Research Primer*. NAB, Washington, DC.

———. 1977. *Legal Guide to FCC Broadcast Rules, Regulations and Policies*. [Looseleaf, updated periodically.] NAB, Washington, DC.

———. 1978. "Purchasing a Broadcast Station: A Buyer's Guide." NAB, Washington, DC.

———. 1980. *The Radio Code*. 22d ed. NAB, Washington, DC.

———. 1980. *The Television Code*. 21st ed. NAB, Washington, DC.

Nadel, Gerry. 1977. "One from Column A, One from Column B . . .," *TV Guide* (Oct. 1): 14.

Namurois, Albert. 1972. *Structures and Organization of Broadcasting in the Framework of Radiocommunications*. Rev. ed. EBU Legal Monographs No. 8. European Broadcasting Union, Geneva.

National Advisory Commission on Civil Disorders. 1968. *Report*. Bantam Books, New York.

National Cable Television Association. Annual. *Cable Advertising Directory*. NCTA, Washington, DC.

———. Annual. *Cable Services Report: Local Programming*. NCTA, Washington, DC.

National Citizen's Committee on Broadcasting. 1979. "Citizen's Media Directory Update." NCCB, Washington, DC.

National News Council. 1979. *In the Public Interest — II: A Report by the National News Council, 1975–1978*. The Council, New York.

National Public Radio. 1981. *Public Radio and State Governments*. 2 Vols. NPR, Washington, DC.

National Science Foundation. 1976. *Social Services and Cable TV*. Government Printing Office, Washington, DC.

National Telecommunications and Information Administration. Annual. *The Radio Frequency Spectrum: United States Use and Management*. NTIA, Washington, DC.

———. 1979. *Manual of Regulations and Procedures for Federal Radio Frequency Management*. Government Printing Office, Washington, DC.

Navasky, Victor S. 1975. "A CBS Documentary About a CBS Blacklist," *New York Times* (Sept. 28): II-1.

NBC Corporate Planning. 1977. *Broadcasting: The Next Ten Years*. National Broadcasting Co., New York.

NEA (National Education Association). 1967. *ITFS: Instructional Television Fixed Service: What It Is, How to Plan*. NEA, Washington, DC.

Nessen, Ron. 1980. "Now Television's the Kingmaker," *TV Guide* (May 10): 4.

Newcomb, Horace. 1979. *Television: The Critical View*. Rev. ed. Oxford U. Press, New York.

Newsweek. 1963. "As 175 Million Americans Watched," (Dec. 9): 52.

Nielsen Company, A. C. 1978. *The Television Audience, 1978*. 19th ed. A. C. Nielsen Company, Media Research Group, Northbrook, IL.

———. 1979. *Television Audience: Special Studies*. 2 Vols. Nielsen Co., Northbrook, IL.

Nimmo, Dan, ed. 1979. *Communication Yearbook 3*. Transaction Books, New Brunswick, NJ.

Nippon Hoso Kyokai. 1977. *50 Years of Japanese Broadcasting*. NHK, Tokyo.

Nizer, Louis. 1966. *The Jury Returns*. Doubleday, Garden City, NY.

Noll, Roger G., et al. 1973. *Economic Aspects of Television Regulation*. Brookings Institution, Washington, DC.

Nordenstreng, Kaarle, & Schiller, Herbert I., eds. 1979. *National Sovereignty and International Communication*. Ablex Publishing, Norwood, NJ.

NRB (National Religious Broadcasters). Annual. *Annual Directory of Religious Broadcasting*. NRB, Morristown, NJ.

Nye, Russell B. 1970. *The Unembarrassed Muse: The Popular Arts in America*. Dial, New York.

Osborn, J. Wes, et al. 1979. "Prime Time Network Television Programming Preemptions," *Journal of Broadcasting* 23 (Fall): 427–436.

Osgood, Charles, et al. 1957. *The Measurement of Meaning*. U. of Illinois Press, Urbana.

Othmer, David. 1973. *The Wired Island: The First Two Years of Public Access to Cable Television in Manhattan*. Fund for the City of New York, New York.

OTP (Office of Telecommunication Policy). 1975. *The Radio Frequency Spectrum: United States Use and Management*. OTP, Washington, DC.

Owen, Bruce M. 1975. *Economics and Freedom of Expression: Media Structure and the First Amendment*. Ballinger, Cambridge, MA.

———, & Braeutigam, Ronald. 1978. *The Regulation Game: Strategic Use of the Administrative Process*. Ballinger, Cambridge, MA.

———, et al. 1974. *Television Economics*. Lexington Books, Lexington, MA.

Padover, Saul K., ed. 1946. *Thomas Jefferson on Democracy*. New American Library, New York.

Paletz, David L., et al. 1977. *Politics in Public Service Advertising in Television*. Praeger, New York.

Paley, William S. 1979. *As It Happened: A Memoir*. Doubleday, Garden City, NY.

Passman, Arnold. 1971. *The Deejays*. Macmillan, New York.

Paulu, Burton. 1967. *Radio and Television Broadcasting on the European Continent*. U. of Minnesota Press, Minneapolis.

———. 1974. *Radio and Television Broadcasting in Eastern Europe*. U. of Minnesota Press, Minneapolis.

Pawley, Edward. 1972. *BBC Engineering: 1922–1972*. BBC, London.

Peabody, Robert L., et al. 1972. *To Enact a Law: Congress and Campaign Financing*. Praeger, New York.

Pearce, Alan. 1980. "How the Networks Have Turned News into Dollars," *TV Guide* (Aug. 23): 6.

Pekurney, Robert G., & Bart, Leonard D. 1975. "'Sticks and Bones': A Survey of Network Affiliate Decision Making," *Journal of Broadcasting* 19 (Fall): 427–437.

Pelton, Joseph N., & Snow, Marcellus S., eds. 1977. *Economic and Policy Problems in Satellite Communications*. Praeger, New York.

Pember, Don R. 1981. *Mass Media Law*. 2d ed. William C. Brown, Dubuque, IA.

Pichaske, David. 1979. *A Generation in Motion: Popular Music and Culture of the Sixties.* Schirmer Books, New York.

Pitts, Michael R. 1976. *Radio Soundtracks: A Reference Guide.* Scarecrow Press, Metuchen, NJ.

Plotkin, Harry M. 1955. *Television Network Regulation and the UHF Problem.* Memorandum prepared for Senate Committee on Interstate and Foreign Commerce. 84th Cong., 1st Sess. Government Printing Office, Washington, DC.

Polcyn, Kenneth A. 1973. *An Educator's Guide to Communication Satellite Technology.* Academy for Educational Development, Washington, DC.

Polsky, Richard M. 1974. *Getting to Sesame Street: Origins of the Children's Television Workshop.* Praeger, New York.

Pool, Ithiel de Sola, ed. 1977. *The Social Impact of the Telephone.* MIT Press, Cambridge, MA.

Porter, William E. 1976. *Assault on the Media: The Nixon Years.* U. of Michigan Press, Ann Arbor.

Post, Steve. 1974. *Playing in the FM Band.* Viking Press, New York.

Postmaster General. 1914. *Government Ownership of Electrical Means of Communication.* Senate Document 399, 63d Cong., 2d Sess. Government Printing Office, Washington, DC. (Repr. Arno Press, 1977).

Powell, John W. 1962. *Channels of Learning: The Story of Educational Television.* Public Affairs Press, Washington, DC.

Powers, Ron. 1977. *The Newscasters.* St. Martin's Press, New York.

Practicing Law Institute. Annual. *Communications Law.* Practicing Law Institute, New York.

Presbrey, Frank. 1929. *The History and Development of Advertising.* Doubleday, New York.

President's Communications Policy Board. 1951. *Telecommunications: A Program for Progress.* Government Printing Office, Washington, DC. (Repr. Arno Press, 1977.)

President's Study Commission on International Broadcasting ("Stanton Commission"). 1973. *The Right to Know.* Government Printing Office, Washington, DC.

President's Task Force on Communications Policy. 1968. *Final Report.* Government Printing Office, Washington, DC.

Price, David E., et al. 1975. *The Commerce Committees: A Study of the House and Senate Commerce Committees.* Grossman, New York.

Price, Jonathan. 1978. *The Best Thing on TV: Commercials.* Viking Press, New York.

Privacy Protection Study Commission. 1977. *Personal Privacy in an Information Society.* Government Printing Office, Washington, DC.

PTR (*Public Telecommunications Review*). 1977. "Black Perspective on the News: Controversy and Comment," 5 (Nov./Dec.): 64–69.

———. 1979. "Public Radio: Where It's Been, Where It's Going," 7 (Mar./Apr.): entire issue.

Pusateri, C. Joseph. 1980. *Enterprise in Radio: WWL and the Business of Broadcasting in America.* University Press of America, Washington, DC.

Quaal, Ward, & Brown, James. 1975. *Broadcast Management.* 2d ed. Hastings House, New York.

Quinlan, Sterling. 1974. *The Hundred Million Dollar Lunch.* O'Hara, Chicago.

———. 1979. *Inside ABC: American Broadcasting Company's Rise to Power.* Hastings House, New York.

Radio in 1985. 1977. National Association of Broadcasters, Washington, DC.

Ramond, Charles. 1976. *Advertising Research: The State of the Art.* Association of National Advertisers, New York.

Randall, R. S. 1967. *Censorship of the Movies: The Social and Political Control of a Mass Medium.* U. of Wisconsin Press, Madison.

Ranney, Austin, ed. 1979. *The Past and Future of Presidential Debates.* American Enterprise Institute, Washington, DC.

Ray, Michael L., & Webb, Peter H. 1978. "Advertising Effectiveness in a Crowded Environment." Preliminary Research Report 78-113. Marketing Research Institute, Cambridge, MA.

Read, Oliver, & Welsh, Walter. 1976. *From Tin Foil to Stereo: Evolution of the Phonograph.* 2d ed. Sams, Indianapolis.

Read, William H. 1976. *America's Mass Media Merchants.* Johns Hopkins U. Press, Baltimore.

Reel, Frank. 1979. *The Networks: How They Stole the Show.* Scribner's, New York.

Reeves, Michael G., & Hoffer, Tom W. 1976. "The Safe, Cheap and Known: A Content Analysis of the First (1974) PBS Program Cooperative," *Journal of Broadcasting* 20 (Fall): 546–566.

Reith, John. 1949. *Into the Wind.* Hodder & Stoughton, London.

Rich, Frank. 1979. "A Super Sequel to Haley's Comet," *Time* (Feb. 19): 84.

Righter, Rosemary. 1978. *Whose News? Politics, the Press and the Third World.* Times Books, New York.

Rivers, William L., et al., eds. 1977. *Aspen Handbook on the Media, 1977–79 Edition: A Selective Guide to Research, Organizations and Publications in Communications.* Praeger, New York.

Rivers, William L., et al. 1980. *Responsibility in Mass Communication.* 3d ed. Harper & Row, New York.

Rivkin, Steven R. 1978. *A New Guide to Federal Cable Television Regulations.* MIT Press, Cambridge, MA.

Roberts, Donald F., & Bachen, Christine M. 1981. "Mass Communication Effects," in Rosenzweig & Porter: 307-356.

Robertson, James, & Yokom, Gerald C. 1973. "Educational Radio: The Fifty-Year-Old Adolescent," *Educational Broadcasting Review* 7 (April): 107–115.

Robinson, Glen O., ed. 1978. *Communications for Tomorrow: Policy Perspectives for the 1980s.* Praeger, New York.

Robinson, Thomas P. 1943. *Radio Networks and the Federal Government.* Columbia U. Press, New York. (Repr. Arno Press, 1979).

Rockwell, John. 1979. "Is Rock the Music of Violence?" *New York Times* (Dec. 16): II-1.

Rogers, Everett M., & Shoemaker, F. Floyd. 1971. *Communication of Innovations: A Cross-Cultural Approach.* 2d ed. Free Press, New York.

Roizen, Joe. 1976. "The History of Videotape Recording," *Television* (London) 16 (Feb. 1976): 15–21.

Roosevelt, Franklin D. 1934. "Proposed Federal Communications Commission." S. Doc. No. 144. 78 *Cong. Rec.* 3181 (Feb. 26).

Roper Organization. 1981. "Evolving Public Attitudes toward Television and Other Mass Media, 1959–1980." Television Information Office, New York.

Rosden, George, & Rosden, Peter. 1974. *The Law of Advertising.* 2 Vols. (Regular supplements.) Matthew Bender, New York.

Rose, C. B., Jr. 1940. *National Policy for Radio Broadcasting.* Harper, New York. (Repr. Arno Press, 1971).

Rosen, Philip T. 1980. *The Modern Stentors: Radio Broadcasters and the Federal Government 1920–1934.* Greenwood Press, Westport, CT.

Rosenberg, Bernard, & White, David M. 1957. *Mass Culture: The Popular Arts in America.* Free Press, Glencoe, IL.

Rosenzweig, Mark R., & Porter, Lyman W., eds. Annual. *Annual Review of Psychology.* Annual Reviews, Inc., Palo Alto, CA.

Routt, Edd, et al. 1978. *The Radio Format Conundrum.* Hastings House, New York.

Rubin, Bernard. 1967. *Political Television.* Wadsworth, Belmont, CA.

Rubin, Michael R., et al. 1978. *FCC Decisions Interpreting the Communications Act of 1934: An Index.* OT Special Publication 78-18. Government Printing Office, Washington, DC.

Rubinstein, E. A., et al. 1974. *Assessing Television's Influence on Children's Prosocial Behavior.* Occasional Paper No. 74-11. Brookdale International Institute, Stonybrook, NY.

Russell, Dick. 1979. "The Return of a TV Outcast," *TV Guide* (Dec. 1): 21.

Rutkus, Denis S. 1976. "A Report on Simultaneous Television Network Coverage of Presidential Addresses to the Nation." (Jan. 12). Congressional Research Service, Washington, DC.

Sabine, Gordon A. 1980. "Broadcasting in Virginia: Benchmark '79." Department of Communications, Virginia Polytechnic Institute & State U., Blacksburg, VA.

Sadowski, Robert P. 1974. "Broadcasting and State Statutory Laws," *Journal of Broadcasting* (Fall): 433-450.

————. 1979. *An Analysis of Statutory Laws Governing Commercial and Educational Broadcasting in the Fifty States.* Arno Press, New York.

Saettler, Paul. 1968. *A History of Instructional Technology.* McGraw-Hill, New York.

Safran, Claire. 1980. "Children's Television: What Are the Best — and Worst — Shows?" *TV Guide* (Aug. 9): 2.

Sampson, Anthony. 1973. *The Sovereign State of ITT.* Stein & Day, New York.

Sandford, John. 1976. *The Mass Media of the German-Speaking Countries.* Iowa State U. Press, Ames.

Sanno, Al. 1980. "The Games Advertisers Can Play on Television," *Broadcasting* (Apr. 7): 16.

Sarnoff, David. 1968. *Looking Ahead: The Papers of David Sarnoff.* McGraw-Hill, New York.

Saudek, Robert. 1973. "Omnibus Was Like Running Five Broadway Openings Every Week," *TV Guide* (Aug. 11): 22.

Schaefer, R. Murray. 1977. *The Tuning of the World.* Knopf, New York.

Schiller, Herbert I. 1971. *Mass Communications and American Empire.* Beacon Press, Boston.

Schmeckebier, Laurence F. 1932. *The Federal Radio Commission: Its History, Activities and Organization.* Brookings, Washington, DC (Repr. Arno Press, 1976).

Schmidt, Benno C. 1976. *Freedom of the Press vs. Public Access.* Praeger, New York.

Schofield, Lemuel B. 1979. "Don't Look for the Hometown Touch," *TV Guide* (Apr. 14): 39.

Schorr, Daniel. 1977. *Clearing the Air.* Houghton Mifflin Co., Boston.

Schramm, Wilbur. 1973. *Men, Messages, and Media: A Look at Human Communication.* Harper & Row, New York.

———— & Roberts, D. F., eds. 1971. *The Process and Effects of Mass Communication.* Rev. ed. U. of Illinois Press, Urbana.

————, et al. 1963. *The People Look at Educational Television.* Stanford U. Press, Stanford, CA.

————, et al. 1961. *Television in the Lives of Our Children.* Stanford U. Press, Stanford, CA.

Schubert, Paul. 1928. *The Electric Word: The Rise of Radio.* Macmillan, New York. (Repr. Arno Press, 1971).

Schwartz, Bernard. 1959. *The Professor and the Commissions.* Knopf, New York.

————, ed. 1973. *The Economic Regulation of Business and Industry.* (5 vols.) Chelsea House, New York.

Schwartz, Ruth. 1973. "Preserving TV Programs: Here Today — Gone Tomorrow," *Journal of Broadcasting* 17 (Summer): 287–300.

Schwartz, Tony. 1981. "Some Say This Is America's Best TV Station," *New York Times* (Feb. 15): II-1.

Scott, James D. 1977. *Bringing Premium Entertainment into the Home via Pay-Cable TV.* U. of Michigan Graduate School of Business Administration, Ann Arbor.

Seiden, Martin H. 1974. *Who Controls the Media? Popular Myths and Economic Realities.* Basic Books, New York.

Senate CC (U.S. Congress. Senate Committee on Commerce), 1972. *Surgeon General's Report by Scientific Advisory Committee on Television and Social Behavior.* Hearings, 92d Cong., 2d Sess.

Senate CCST (U.S. Congress. Senate Committee on Commerce, Science, and Transportation). 1980. *Amendments to the Communications Act of 1934.* Hearings on S. 611 and S. 622. 4 Vols. 96th Cong., 1st Sess.

Senate CGO (US. Congress. Senate Committee on Government Operations). 1977. *Study on Federal Regulation Prepared Pursuant to S. Res. 71.* 7 Vols. 95th Cong., 1st Sess.

Senate CIC (U.S. Congress. Senate Committee on Interstate Commerce). 1930. *Commission on Communications.* Hearings on S. 6. 71st Cong., 2d Sess.

————. 1944. *To Amend the Communications Act of 1934.* Hearings on S. 814. 78th Cong., 1st Sess.

Senate CIFC (U.S. Congress. Senate Committee on Interstate and Foreign Commerce). 1948. *Progress of FM Radio: Certain Charges Involving Development of FM Radio and RCA Patent Policies.* Hearings. 80th Cong., 2d Sess.

Sereno, Kenneth K., & Mortensen, D. David. 1970. *Foundations of Communication Theory.* Harper & Row, New York.

Sethi, S. Prakash. 1977. *Advocacy Advertising and Large Corporations.* Lexington Books, Lexington, MA.

Settel, Irving. 1967. *A Pictorial History of Radio.* 2d ed. Grosset & Dunlap, New York.

Severin, Warner, & Tankard, James, Jr. 1979. *Communication Theories: Origins, Methods, Uses.* Hastings House, New York.

Shannon, Claude E., & Weaver, W. 1949. *The Mathematical Theory of Communication.* U. of Illinois Press, Urbana.

Shapiro, Andrew O. 1976. *Media Access: Your Rights to Express Your Views on Radio and Television.* Little, Brown, Boston.

Shapiro, George H. 1980. "Up the Hill and Down: Perspectives on Federal Regulation of Cable TV," in Hollowell: 20–34.

Shaw, David. 1979. "And That's the Way It Is," *TV Guide* (Apr. 21): 32.

Shayon, Robert L. 1971. *Open to Criticism.* Beacon Press, Boston.

Shiers, George, and Shiers, May. 1972. *Bibliography of the History of Electronics.* Scarecrow Press, Metuchen, NJ.

Shiers, George, ed. 1977. *Technical Development of Television.* Arno Press, New York.

Shulman, Arthur, & Youman, Roger. 1966. *How Sweet It Was: Television — A Pictorial Commentary.* Shorecrest, New York.

Shurick, E. P. J. 1946. *The First Quarter-Century of American Broadcasting.* Midland, Kansas City.

Siepmann, Charles. 1946. *Radio's Second Chance.* Atlantic-Little, Brown, Boston.

————. 1950. *Radio, Television and American Society.* Oxford U. Press, New York.

Sigel, Efrem, ed. 1980. *Videotext: The Coming Revolution in Home/Office Information Retrieval.* Knowledge Industry Publications, White Plains, NY.

Sikes, Rhea G. 1980. "Programs for Children: Public Television in the 1970s," *Public Telecommunications Review* 8 (Sept/Oct): 7–26.

Silvey, Robert. 1974. *Who's Listening? The Story of BBC Audience Research.* George Allen & Unwin, London.

Simmons, Steven J. 1978. *The Fairness Doctrine and the Media.* U. of California Press, Berkeley.

Simon, Julian. 1977. *Basic Research Methods in Social Science.* 2d ed. Random House, New York.

Smith, Anthony. 1973. *The Shadow in the Cave: The Broadcaster, His Audience, and the State.* U. of Illinois Press, Urbana.

————. 1980. *The Geopolitics of Information: How Western Culture Dominates the World.* Oxford U. Press, New York.

————. 1980. *Goodbye Gutenberg: The Newspaper Revolution of the 1980's.* Oxford U. Press, New York.

Smith, Bruce L., et al. 1946. *Propaganda, Communication and Public Opinion.* Princeton U. Press, Princeton, NJ.

Smith, Delbert D. 1977. *Communication via Satellite: A Vision in Retrospect.* Sijthoff International, Reading, MA.

Smith, F. Leslie. 1974. "Hunger in America Controversy: Another View," *Journal of Broadcasting* 18 (Winter): 79–83.

Smith, Leon C. 1970/71. "Local Station Liability for Deceptive Advertising," *Journal of Broadcasting* 15 (Winter): 107–112.

Smith, Richard A. 1958. "TV: The Light That Failed," *Fortune* (Dec.): 78.

Smith, Robert R. 1965. "The Origins of Radio Network News Commentary," *Journal of Broadcasting* 9 (Spring): 113–122.

———. 1980. *Beyond the Wasteland: The Criticism of Broadcasting.* Rev. ed. Speech Communication Association, Annandale, VA.

Smothers, Tom. 1969. "The Whole World Is Watching," in Kaufman: 6–9.

Smythe, Dallas. 1957. *Structure and Policy of Electrical Communications.* U. of Illinois Press, Urbana. (Repr. Arno Press, 1977).

Socolow, A. Walter. 1939. *The Law of Radio Broadcasting.* 2 Vols. Baker, Voorhis, New York.

Spalding, John W. 1964. "1928: Radio Becomes a Mass Advertising Medium," *Journal of Broadcasting* 8 (Winter): 31–34.

Spongberg, Robert C. 1975. *Ancillary Signals for Television: Innovations and Implications.* Final Report. Prepared for U.S. Department of Commerce Office of Telecommunications. Denver Research Institute, Denver.

Spottiswoode, Raymond, ed. 1969. *The Focal Encyclopedia of Film and Television Techniques.* Hastings House, New York.

SRDS (Standard Rate & Data Service). Monthly. *Spot Radio Rates and Data.* SRDS, Skokie, IL.

———. Monthly. *Spot Television Rates and Data.* SRDS, Skokie, IL.

Stabiner, Karen. 1980. "Willie Stargell, You're Hot; Shelley Hack, You're Not," *TV Guide* (Mar. 1): 15.

Statistical Research, Inc., 1972. *A Study of Television Usage in Four Local Markets.* NAB, Washington, DC.

Stedman, Raymond W. 1977. *The Serials: Suspense and Drama by Installment.* 2d ed. U. of Oklahoma Press, Norman.

Stein, Harry. 1979. "How '60 Minutes' Makes News," *New York Times Magazine* (May 6): 28.

Stein, Robert. 1972. *Media Power: Who Is Shaping Your Picture of the World?* Houghton Mifflin, Boston.

Steiner, Gary A. 1963. *The People Look at Television: A Study of Audience Attitudes.* Knopf, New York.

Stempel, Guido H., & Westley, Bruce H., eds. 1981. *Research Methods in Mass Communication.* Prentice-Hall, Englewood Cliffs, NJ.

Stephenson, William. 1967. *The Play Theory of Mass Communication.* U. of Chicago Press, Chicago.

Sterling, Christopher H. 1979. "Television and Radio Broadcasting," in Compaine, ed.: 61–125.

———, & Haight, Timothy. 1978. *The Mass Media: Aspen Institute Guide to Communication Industry Trends.* Praeger, New York.

———, & Kittross, John M. 1978. *Stay Tuned: A Concise History of American Broadcasting.* Wadsworth, Belmont, CA.

Stern, Bill. 1959. *The Taste of Ashes: An Autobiography.* Henry Holt, New York.

Stern, Robert H. 1979. *The Federal Communications Commission and Television.* Arno Press, New York.

Stevenson, Robert L., et al. 1973. "Untwisting *The News Twisters*: A Replication of Efron's Study," *Journalism Quarterly* 50 (Summer): 211–219.

Stone, Alan. 1978. *Economic Regulation and the Public Interest: The Federal Trade Commission in Theory and Practice.* Cornell U. Press, Ithaca, NY.

Stone, Vernon A. 1978. "News Staff Size, Turnover and Sources Surveyed," *RTNDA Communicator* 32 (August): 8.

———. 1980. "ENG Growth Documented in 1979 RTNDA Survey," *RTNDA Communicator* 34 (January): 5.

———. 1980. "Women's Share of New Jobs Kept on Growing in 1970s," *RTNDA Communicator* 34 (March): 6–7.

Stuart, Fredric. 1976. *The Effects of Television on the Motion Picture and Radio Industries.* Arno Press, New York.

Sugar, Bert Randolph. 1978. *"The Thrill of Victory": The Inside Story of ABC Sports.* Hawthorn Books, New York.

Summers, Harrison B. 1958. *A Thirty-Year History of Programs Carried on National Radio Networks in the United States: 1926–1956.* Ohio State U. Speech Department, Columbus. (Repr. Arno Press, 1971).

Surgeon General. Scientific Advisory Committee on Television and Social Behavior. 1972. *Television and Growing Up: The Impact of Televised Violence.* Report of the Committee to the Surgeon General. Government Printing Office, Washington, DC.

Tan, Alexis S. 1981. *Mass Communication Theories and Research.* Grid, Inc., Columbus, OH.

Tannenbaum, Percy H., ed. 1980. *The Entertainment Functions of Television.* Lawrence Erlbaum Assoc., Hillsdale, NJ.

Taylor, John P. 1980. "Direct-to-Home Satellite Broadcasting." *Television/Radio Age*, New York.

Tebbel, John. 1975. *The Media in America.* Crowell, New York.

Technology & Economics, Inc. 1980. *The Emergence of Pay Cable Television.* 4 Vols. National Telecommunications & Information Administration, Washington, DC.

Telecommunication Journal. 1980. "Telecommunications in the United States," 47 (June): 307–412.

Television Advertising Bureau. N.D. "Top 100 National Advertisers." Television Advertising Bureau, New York.

Television/Radio Age. 1981. "Industry Experts See 1981 as Turning Point for Videocassette Recorder, Videodisc Market," (Jan. 12): 56.

Terrace, Vincent. 1979. *The Complete Encyclopedia of Television Programs: 1947–1979.* 2d ed. A. S. Barnes, Cranbury, NJ.

Terry, Clifford. 1976. "Vast Wasteland Revisited," *TV Guide* (Oct. 16): 4.

Theall, Donald F. 1971. *The Medium is the Rear-View Mirror: Understanding McLuhan.* McGill-Queen's U. Press, Montreal.

Thompson, Robert L. 1947. *Wiring a Continent: The History of the Telegraph Industry in the United States, 1832–66.* Princeton U. Press, Princeton, NJ. (Repr. Arno Press, 1972).

Time. 1957. "The $60 Million Question," (Apr. 22): 78.

———. 1971. "The Fellow on the Bridge," (Dec. 27): 57.

———. 1977. "The Man With the Golden Gut: Programmer Fred Silverman Has Made ABC No. 1," (Sept. 5): 46.

———. 1979. "'The Microphone of God': Archbishop Fulton J. Sheen, 1895–1979," Obituary (Dec. 24): 84.

Toffler, Alvin. 1970. *Future Shock.* Random House, New York.

———. 1980. *The Third Wave.* William Morrow, New York.

Townley, Rod. 1980. "They Watch the News — For Mistakes," *TV Guide* (Nov. 29): 8.

Toynbee, Arnold. 1962. *America and the World Revolution and Other Lectures.* Oxford U. Press, New York.

Traviesas, Herminio. 1980. "They Never Told Me about 'Laugh-In,'" *Broadcasting* (July 21): 52.

Trufelman, Lloyd. 1979. "The Missing Chapter: Pacifica Radio," *Public Telecommunications Review* 7 (Sept./Oct.): 27–33.

Tunstall, Jeremy. 1977. *The Media Are American: Anglo-American Media in the World.* Columbia U. Press, New York.

Turnage, Howard C. 1979. "Highway Advisory Radio." Paper presented at International Symposium on Traffic Control Systems, Berkeley, CA Aug. 6.

Turow, Joseph. 1981. *Entertainment, Education and the Hard Sell: Three Decades of Network Children's Television.* Praeger, New York.

Twentieth Century Fund Task Force on the International Flow of News. 1979. *A Free and Balanced Flow.* Lexington Books, Lexington, MA.

Tynan, Kenneth. 1979. *Show People: Profiles in Entertainment.* Simon & Schuster, New York.

Tyne, Gerald F. J. 1977. *Saga of the Vacuum Tube.* Howard W. Sams, Indianapolis.

UNESCO (United Nations Educational, Scientific and Cultural Organization). Various Dates. *Communication Policies in . . .* [Various countries by various authors]. UNESCO, Paris.

———. Annual. *Statistical Yearbook.* UNESCO, Paris.

———. 1975. *World Communications: A 200 Country Survey of Press, Radio, Television, Film.* 5th ed. UNESCO, Paris.

———. 1979. *Statistics on Radio and Television, 1960–1976.* UNESCO, Paris.

———. 1980. *Many Voices, One World: Communications and Society Today and Tomorrow.* ["McBride Commission Report"]. UNESCO, Paris.

US (*United States Reports*)

1919. *Schenck v. US* 249 US 47.

1937. *FTC v. Standard Education Society.* 302 US 112.

1940. *FCC v. Sanders Bros.* 309 US 470.

1942. *Marconi Wireless Telegraph Company of America v. U.S.* 320 US 1.

1943. *NBC v. U.S.* 319 US 190.

1949. *Terminiello v. Chicago* 337 US 1.

1951. *Dennis v. U.S.* 341 US 494.

1959. *Farmers Educational Cooperative v. WDAY,* 360 US 525.

1964. *New York Times v. Sullivan.* 376 US 254.

1965. *FTC v. Colgate-Palmolive.* 380 US 374.

1965. *Estes v. Texas.* 381 US 532.

1968. *U.S. v. Southwestern Cable.* 392 US 157.

1968. *Fortnightly Corp. v. United Artists Television.* 392 US 390.

1969. *Red Lion v. FCC.* 395 US 367.

1973. *CBS v. Democratic National Committee.* 412 US 94.

1973. *Miller v. California.* 413 US 15.

1974. *National Cable Television Association v. U.S. and FCC.* 415 US 336.

1974. *Miami Herald v. Tornillo.* 418 US 241.

1974. *Gertz v. Welch.* 418 US 323.

1978. *FCC v. National Citizens Committee for Broadcasting.* 436 US 775.

1978. *FCC v. Pacifica Foundation.* 438 US 726.

1979. *Herbert v. Lando.* 441 US 153.

University of Missouri. 1980. *Communications 1990: A Report of the Future Committee.* School of Journalism, University of Missouri, Columbia, MO.

U.S. Army, Chief Signal Officer. 1919. *Report to the Secretary of War.* Government Printing Office, Washington, DC. (Repr. Arno Press, 1974).

U.S. Bureau of the Census. 1935. "Radio Broadcasting," part of the *Census of Business 1935.* Government Printing Office, Washington, DC.

U.S. Commission on Civil Rights. 1977, 1979. *Window Dressing on the Set: Women and Minorities in Television.* Government Printing Office, Washington, DC.

U.S. Congress. House of Representatives. 1978. *Radio Laws of the United States.* Government Printing Office, Washington, DC.

U.S. Library of Congress. Copyright Office. 1977. *General Guide to the Copyright Act of 1976.* Government Printing Office, Washington, DC.

Van Gerpen, Maurice. 1979. *Privileged Communication and the Press: The Citizen's Right to Know Versus the Law's Right to Confidential News Source Evidence.* Greenwood Press, Westport, CT.

Vanocur, Sander. 1972. "How the Media Massaged Me: My Fifteen Years of Conditioning in Network News," *Esquire* (January): 82.

Vaughn, Robert. 1972. *Only Victims: A Study of Show Business Blacklisting.* Putnam, New York.

Veith, Richard. 1976. *Talk-Back TV: Two-Way Cable Television.* Tab Books, Blue Ridge Summit, PA.

Waldrop, Frank C., & Borkin, Joseph. 1938. *Television: A Struggle for Power.* Morrow, New York. (Repr. Arno Press, 1971).

Waller, Judith. 1950. *Radio: The Fifth Estate.* 2d ed. Houghton Mifflin, Boston.

Wanamaker, John. 1913. *Golden Book of the Wanamaker Stores.* 2 Vols. John Wanamaker, Philadelphia.

Warner, Harry P. 1948. *Radio and Television Law.* Matthew Bender, Albany, NY.

———. 1953. *Radio and Television Rights.* Matthew Bender, Albany, NY.

Wartella, Ellen, ed. 1979. *Children Communicating: Media and Development of Thought, Speech, Understanding.* Sage, Beverly Hills, CA.

Weaver, Sylvester L. 1955. "The Form of the Future," *Broadcasting-Telecasting* (May 30): 56.

Weber, Olga S., ed. 1976. *North American Film and Video Directory: A Guide to Media Collections and Services.* Bowker, New York.

Weinberg, Meyer. 1962. *TV and America: The Morality of Hard Cash.* Ballantine Books, New York.

Weiss, Frederic A., et al. 1980. "Station License Revocations and Denials of Renewal, 1970–78," *Journal of Broadcasting* 24 (Winter): 69–77.

Wertheim, Frank. 1979. *Radio Comedy.* Oxford U. Press, New York.

West, Donald. 1971. "On the Leading Edge of Broadcasting," Special Report, *Broadcasting* (June 21): 41.

White, David M. 1950. "The 'Gate Keeper': A Case Study in the Selection of News," *Journalism Quarterly* 27 (Fall): 383–390.

White, Llewellyn. 1947. *The American Radio.* U. of Chicago Press, Chicago. (Repr. Arno Press, 1971).

Whitfield, Stephen, & Roddenberry, Gene. 1968. *The Making of Star Trek.* Ballantine, New York.

Whitman, Alden. 1973. "William Benton Dies Here at 73, Leader in Politics and Education," Obituary, *New York Times* (Mar. 3): 1.

Whitney, Dwight. 1974. "Cinema's Stepchild Grows Up," *TV Guide* (July 20): 21.

———. 1976. "'Music Changes, But I Don't'", *TV Guide* (July 17): 25.

Wiener, Norbert. 1950. *The Human Use of Human Beings.* Houghton Mifflin, Boston.

Wilhoit, Cleveland, & de Bock, Harold, eds. Annual. *Mass Communication Review Yearbook.* Sage, Beverly Hills, CA.

Will, Thomas E. 1978. *Telecommunications Structure and Management in the Executive Branch of Government, 1900–1970.* Westview Press, Boulder, CO.

Williams, Arthur. 1976. *Broadcasting and Democracy in West Germany.* Temple U. Press, Philadelphia.

Wilson, H. H. 1961. *Pressure Group: The Campaign for Commercial Television.* Rutgers U. Press, New Brunswick, NJ.

Winkler, Allan M. 1978. *The Politics of Propaganda: The Office of War Information, 1942–1945.* Yale U. Press, New Haven, CT.

Withey, Stephen, & Abeles, Ronald P. 1980. *Television and Social Behavior: Beyond Violence and Children.* Lawrence Erlbaum Assoc., Hillsdale, NJ.

Wolfe, Charles H., ed. 1949. *Modern Radio Advertising.* Funk & Wagnalls, New York.

Wood, Donald N., & Wylie, Donald G. 1977. *Educational Telecommunications.* Wadsworth, Belmont, CA.

Wood, James P. 1958. *The Story of Advertising.* Ronald, New York.

Wood, Richard. 1969. *Shortwave Voices of the World.* Gilfer Assoc., Park Ridge, NJ.

Woolfe, Roger. 1980. *Videotex: The New Television/Telephone Information Services.* Heyden, Philadelphia.

Wurtzel, Alan. 1979. *Television Production.* McGraw-Hill, New York.

Yellin, David G. 1973. *Special: Fred Freed and the Television Documentary.* Macmillan, New York.

Zeidenberg, Leonard. 1971. "The Struggle Over Broadcast Access," Special Report, *Broadcasting* (Sept. 20 & 27): 32–43, 24–29.

———. 1975. "Vietnam and Electronic Journalism: Lessons of the Living Room War," *Broadcasting* (May 19): 23.

Ziegler, Sharilyn K., and Howard, Herbert H. 1978. *Broadcast Advertising.* Grid, Inc., Columbus, OH.

Index

Note: page numbers in italics call attention to main entries for subjects mentioned more than once. Stations identified by call letters are listed collectively under "Stations, by call letters."

Absolutism, First Amendment, 488–89
Absorption, wave, 41, *47–48*
AC (electric power), 69, 112
Access: cable TV channels, 298, *304–05*, 568; for issues, 475–84; to means of expression, 15–17, 417, 474; to news sources 228–30; political, *417–18*, 473, 535–36; prime time, 206–07; as a right, *15–16*, 483, 487, 576. *See also* Equal time law; Fairness doctrine
Accessory signals, TV, 69
Account servicing, 371
Accuracy in Media (AIM), 481, 507
Acoustics, 41
Action for Children's Television (ACT), *245–56*, 363, 447, *501–02*, 520
Action News, 236
Actualities, 239
Administrative functions, station, 238
Administrative Law Judge (ALJ), 428 (fig.), 431
Advertising: advantages of broadcast, 351–54; & blacklisting, *214*, 496; on cable TV, 572–73; to children, *245–46*, 363, 398, 509, *519–21*; clutter, 463-64; complaints about, 446 (table); cooperative, 159, *354*, 369, 376; deceptive, 364–65, 423; deregulation of, 460; as economic base for broadcasting, 19–20; editorial, 356, 467, *481–88*; effects of, 518–21; expenditures, 352 (fig.), 372 (table); in Great Britain, 10–12; & fairness doctrine, 481–84; integration in program schedule, 356–58; local, 352–54; loudness of, 362; major users, 372 (table); national spot, 353 (fig.), 355; network, 353–55; on noncommercial stations, 269–70, *276–77*; origins of broadcast, 130–31, *136–37*, 145–46; rates,

366–71; religious, 174, 240–43; research on, 397–98; sale of, 371–76; as subsidy, 518; taste standards, 362–63; time standards, 358–62; *See also* Advertising agencies; Commercials; Sponsorship
Advertising agencies, 136–37, 145–46, *372–75*
Affiliates, network, 134–35, 175, *198*, *330–31*, 335
Affiliation, network, 331, 334–35, 338, 366
Agence France Presse (AFP), 103
Agency for Instructional Television, 288
Agenda-setting, 521
Agnew, Vice President Spiro, 550
Agreements, citizens-licensee, 503–05
Agricultural programs, 436
Alabama Educational Television Commission (AETC), *267*, 454
Alexanderson. *See* Alternator
All-channel receivers, 154, 190, 419
All in the Family, 197, 203, 219, 223–24, 225, 490, 547
All-news radio, 172
All-news TV, 233
All Things Considered, 285
Allocation, frequency, *52–53*, 57, 139, 152, 188
Allotment of channels, *57–58*, *188–91*
Alternating-current (AC), *44*, 69, 72, 106, 112
Alternator, Alexanderson, 106, 108, 115, 116, 119, *122–23*
AM radio: antennas, 48, 51 (photo); band, 14, *59*, 73; carrier current, 61–62; channels, 59, 62 (table), 73 (table); comedy, 159–60; coverage, 59–60; documentaries, 164; drama, 148; editorializing by licensee, 164; educational, 138, *254–55*; in Great Depression, 143–44; music, 164–67; news & public affairs, 160–64; nostalgia for, 149 (box); origins, 125–36; post World War II history, 150–51; program excesses, 146–47; station classes, 60–62; station numbers, 144 (fig.); soap operas, 155; stereophonic, 151; in World War II, 147–48. *See also* Formula radio; Networks

Amateur radio, 53 (table), 115, 125, 127
Amendments to communications act: all-channel receivers, 190; amendments generally, *419–20*; fairness doctrine, 476–77; license term, 414; mutually exclusive applicants, 433; payola, 376; political candidates, 418–19; public broadcasting, 259; trafficking in licenses, 415; unions, 167
American Bond & Mortgage case, 407
American Broadcasting Company (ABC): breaks recording ban, 167; corporate character, 198–200; O&O stations, 199 (table); & cultural pay TV, 317; radio network, 176; TV network, 169, *197–98*, 202; news, 231; sports, 239; origins of, 157, *159*
American Federation of Musicians (AFM), 166–67, 347
American Federation of Television & Radio Artists (AFTRA), 213, 347
American Forces Radio and Television Service (AFRTS), 28–29
American Marconi Company, 106, 113, 117, *122–23*
American Security Council Educational Foundation case, 479
American Society of Composers, Authors, & Publishers (ASCAP), 165
American Telephone & Telegraph Company: audion use by, 109, 119; as broadcaster, *130–33*, 163–64; & cross-licensing, 106, 118–19, *133*; network interconnection facilities, 87–88, 131–32, *180*, 187; origin of, *87–88*, 103; patent strategies, 110–113; & RCA, 123; satellite use, 308
Amos 'n' Andy, 160, 175
Ampex Corporation, 81–82, 202
Amplification, signal, *108–110*, 111
Amplitude, wave, 39–40
Amplitude modulation (AM), 44–46, 69n. *See also* AM radio
Analog vs. digital signal processing, 82, 85

Ancillary signals, TV, 77
Annenberg, Walter, 288, 504
Announcements, 359–60, 361, 362. *See also* Commercials
Announcers, 145, 347. *See also* Disc jockey
Antenna, 48–52, 65, 74–75, 88 (photo), 94, 191. *See also* Earth station
Antitrust suits: AT&T, 112; motion pictures, 159; NAB TV code, 508; networks, 485–86; pay cable, 316; RCA ownership, 123
Appeals court, 413, 608
Applications, license, 192, *432–33*, 447–50, 448
Arbitron Company, 379–80, 385, 387
Arc (as signal generator), 106
Area of Dominant Influence (ADI), 380
Arledge, Roone, 197
ARMS (All-Radio Methodology Study), 393
Armstrong, Edwin, 113, 151–53
Army-McCarthy hearings, broadcast of, 215, 536
ASCAP. *See* American Society of Composers, Authors & Publishers
Ascertainment, 411, *437–38*, 460, 501
Assignment (sale) of stations, 415
Associated Press, 103, 160–61, *229*
Association of Independent Television Stations (INTV), 331
Association for Public Television, 263
Attenuation: in cable, 87, 94; as propagation factor, 46; of sound, 40 (fig.), 41; of satellite signals, 67–68, 91; of UHF signals, 52, 75, 87
Attitude change (as an effect), 546,· 557
Attitudes, market research on, 396
Audience(s): cable TV vs. broadcast, 391, 570; characteristics of, 390–92; complaints to FCC, 446 (table); first radio, 127; flow, *217–18*, 220-21, 391, 570; gratification effects, 539–41; heterogeneity, 544; mail from, *377–78*, 445; of public broadcasting, 289; as research focus, 551; segmentation, 150, 151, *170*, 176, *568*; size of, 381, *390–91*; time spent, *391–92*, 519–20, 539, 551. *See also* Demographics; Effects; Ratings

Audimeter, 385
Audion, 108–11, 117
Audit Bureau of Circulation, 378
Augmentation of cable TV services, 296–97
Authoritarianism, 7–8, 8–9
Aurthur, Robert Alan, 201
Authorizations, broadcast, 54 (table)
Automation, 171–73
Auxiliary stations, 54 (table)
Availabilities, commercial, 329
AWARE, Inc., 213
Ayer, N. W. & Son, 137

Baird, John Logie, 181–83
Bakker, Jim, 242
Balance, Bill, 469
Ball, Lucille, 202
Band(s), frequency: definition, 53; guard, 71; short wave, 64 (table); summary of, 43 (table), 50 (table), 73 (table). *See also* Allocation; Sideband
Bandura, Albert, 557
Banzhaf case, 482
Barry, Jack, 210, 211
Barter syndication, *208*, 355n, 370
Batman, 245, 504
Behavioral vs. structural regulation. *See* Regulation, structural
Bell, Alexander Graham, 85, *103*, 111
BEM case, 483
Benny, Jack, 158, 175
Benton, William, 145–46
Bergen, Edgar, 145, 158
Berle, Milton, 163, 187
Berlin Convention of 1906, 138–39
Beta (VTR format), 82
Betamax, 322
Bias: news, *479*, 550; research, 378, 389; TV visual, 236, 521
Bicycle network, 205, 259
Billboard music charts, 169
Billboards, commercial, 137, 359
Billing, fraudulent, 376, 453–54
Bimodality, *225*
Binary code, 85
Bit (information unit), 85, 584
Black Entertainment Network (BET), 312–13
Black Perspective on the News, 284, 465
Blacker-than-black (TV signal component), 69–70
Blacklisting, 212
Blacks. *See* Minorities

Blanket licensing: cable TV, 301; music, 166
Blanking (TV signal), 69
Block, Martin, 156
Block programming, 218
Blue Bird (cable TV), 293, 317
Blue Network, 134, 157, *159*
BMI. *See* Broadcast Music, Inc.
Board for International Broadcasting, 28
Boomerang effect, 547
Boredom & broadcasting effects, 541
"Born Innocent," 527
Boycotts, 337, 490, *495*
Brain wave research, 397–98
Branly, Edouard, 103, 108
Bridge on the River Kwai, 197, 204
Brightness (color signal), 70
Brinkley, J. R., 146
British Broadcasting Corporation (BBC): audience research, 25, 395; Broadcasting House, 7 (photo), 163; external service, 26–27, 29; historical influence, 22; vs. IBA, 10–12; legal controls, 13; as paternalistic model, 5–6; political broadcasts, 15; program exports to U.S., 21, 278, *281–83*, 293, 317; receiver license fees, 19; schedules, 25; TV system, 183
Broadcast Advertising Reports (BAR), 374
Broadcast Bureau, FCC, 428 (fig.), 430, 503
Broadcast Music, Inc. (BMI), 165–66
Broadcast Rating Council (BRC), 393
Broadcasting: as advertising medium, 351–55, 518–21; audience characteristics, 390–92; clandestine, 30–31; conservatism of, 136–37, *145–47*, 211–12, 490; & culture, 24–25, 246–47, 516–18; & consumerism, 498–507; continuousness of, 217; definition of, 80, 121–22, *129–33*, *409*; economics of, 17–21, 341–43; employment in, 343–48; ethical issues, 211–12, 214–15, 374–76, 392–95; future of, 565–77; & national character, 3–4; obscenity in, 469–71; ownership of, 9 (table), 327–30; & politics (domestic), 4–9, 531–37; & politics (international), 26–33, 147; vs. publishing, 473; & socialization, 526–27; term, 121; Third World, *8–9*, 17–18, 31–33;

voracity of, 154–55, 204–205. *See also* AM radio; FM radio; Public broadcasting; Public radio; Public TV; Uniqueness of broadcasting

Brokerage, time, 319, *371*

Brokers, station, 432

Brown, Les, 507, 512

Brown, Commissioner Tyrone, 457

Budget: advertising, 372 (fig.); FCC, 427

Bullet theory (media effects), 545

Bumper (announcement), 360, 363

Burch, Commissioner Dean, 495

Burden of proof, 412, 453

Burns & Allen, 142, 158

Cable News Network (CNN), 229, *311*, 313 (fig.), 332

Cable TV: access channels, 298, *304–05*, 568: advertising, *305*, 569, 572–73; audiences for, 296 (table), 319 (table), 391, 569–70; augmentation, 296; vs. broadcast TV, *566–67*, *575*; channels, 93 (fig.), 296 (fig.), 304; & copyright, *301–302*, 332–33, 422; definition of, 295; diversity role of, 10, 568; economics, 302–05; franchises, 299–300; & home video center, 322–23, 565; interactive, *305–07*, 315, 397; interconnection, 95 (fig.), *307–13*, 332; leapfrogging, 297; leased channels, 305; local origination, 296, 299, *304*, 570–71, 574; origins & growth, 295–97; ownership, 302–03, 574; pay cable, 299, 301, *315–17*; & piracy, 301–02; program services, 296–97, *304–05*, 569–71; program standards, 510, 569–70; & public broadcasting, 292–93; regulation of 297–301, 573–74; as relay/delivery hybrid, 92; as research tool, 397; subscriber turnover, 297, *570*; system plan, 95 (fig.); technology, 93–96, 566–67. See also Coaxial cable

Cam Ne incident, 538

Campus radio, 61–62

Camera, TV, 67, 73–74, 233

Canada, 22, 60, 422, 531

Candidates for political office. *See* Equal time

Canon 3(A)(7), 228, 472–73, 524–25

Capital Cities Communications, Inc., 330, 504, 506

Carlin, George, 470

Carnegie Commission on Educational Television, *258–61*, *262–63*, 273, 291–92

Carriage rules, cable TV, 298

Carrier current radio, 61–62

Carrier waves, *43–46*, 48, 59, 62, 71 (fig.), 93

Carson, Johnny, 227

Carter, President Jimmy, 151, 441, 443, 533–35

Cartridge, tape, 81, 173 (photo)

Cassettes, tape, 81–82

Catharsis, 531

Caveat emptor, 423

CBS Incorporated: antitrust suit, 485; color TV systems, 192–93; corporate character, 198–99; Electronic Video Recording (EVR), 322; *Faulk* case, 213; & LP recordings, 167; news, 161–64, 231; Nixon administration pressure, 495; O&O stations, 199 (table); pay TV venture, 317; radio network, 134–36, 158; talent raid, 158; TV network, 196–97. *See also* Paley

Cease-and-desist orders, 365, 412–13

Censorship: disclaimer in communications act, 416; vs. editing, 223, 465, 478–81; under First Amendment, 466–73; military, 147, 537–38; of news, 478–81; of political candidates, 424, 465, 471; as prior restraint, 474, 505; by public broadcasters, 267–68

Chain broadcasting regulations, 157, *338–39*, 485

Channel(s) [as frequency band(s)]: activation of, 432–39; allocation, *52–53*, 57, 90, 152–53, 188; allotment of, *57–58*, *188–91*; broadcast, 59–62, *71–73*, *188–92*; cable TV, *93–94*, 309; definition, 46; ownership of, *414*; picture, 44–47; reserved, 10, 188–90, *255–56*; sale of, 415; satellite, 90, 308; telephone, 58; width, 72 (table)

Channel (as medium), 548 (fig.), 550–51

Channel (as program service), *304–306*, 315, 568

Channel 9 (Orlando) case, 435

Channel 10 (Miami) case, 458–59

Channeling, *470*, 490

Character (of licensee), 414, *434–35*, 452 (table), 454

Charlie's Angels, 198

Checkerboarding, 206

Children & broadcasting: & advertising, *363*, 398, 509, *519–*

21; FCC policy on, 245; imitation effects, 527–28; indecency, 469–71; programming, 244, *286–89*, 436, 529 (fig.); socialization of, 526–27. *See also* Action for Children's Television

Children's Television Workshop (CTW), 277, 280 (fig.), *286–87*

Chilling effect, *466–68*, 480, 487, 495

China, 8, 26 (table), 33

Chisholm case, 443

Christian Broadcasting Network (CBN), 200, *241–42*, 313 (table), 333

"Christmas in Korea," 237

Cigarette advertising, 481–82

Cinéma vérité, 237–38

Citizen's Band Radio, 53 (table), 115, 192, 575

Citizens Communication Center (CCC), *502*, 507, 450

Citizenship (of licensees), 414

Civilisation, 278, 283, 517

Clear channels, 60–62

Clear and present danger, 471

Clearance, network, *335–39*, 494

Clipping of commercial content, 376

Closed captioning, 77, 321 (fig.)

Clutter, commercial, 363–64

Coalition for Better Television, 496

Coaxial cable: description, 87, 96 (fig.); as relay/delivery hybrid, 92–95; as TV network interconnection, 180, *187*

Code: binary, 85; Morse, *102*, 117, 127. *See also* NAB code

Coherer, 103, *108*

Coincidental telephone (research method), *385–86*, 393

Cole, Barry, 429, *448*, 512

Colgate-Palmolive case, 364

Color TV, 69n, *70–71*, 76 (fig.), 186, *192–93*

Columbia Broadcasting System. See CBS Inc.

Commentary, paid, 484

Commentary, radio, *161–64*, 494

Commerce, interstate (broadcasting as), 405–07

Commercials: in children's programs, 363; clutter, 363–64; corrective, 365; deceptive, 364–66; editorial, 482–84; evolution of, 128, 137, 146; in foreign systems, 25; identification of, 356; integration into programs, 356–

Commercials, *cont.*
  58; loudness of, 362; political, 532–33; quality of, *362–63*, 510; quantity of, *359–62*, 451, 452 (table), 460, 510; religious, 242; scheduling of, 25, *356–58*, 361 (box), 367–68; taste standards, 362–63, 510; testing effectiveness of, 397–98; trafficking of, 356. *See also* Advertising; NAB codes

Commercialism in broadcasting: in foreign countries, 19–20; ethical issues, *211–12, 214–15*; origins, 130–31, *136–38*; & pluralism, 10; public broadcasting, 253–54

Common carrier(s): vs. broadcasting, *129–33, 409*, 483; definition, 79; number of, 53 (table); services, 259, 308, 319, 320

Communication: concept, 545; process, 549–52. *See also* Research, mass media

Communications Act of 1934: basics, 408–13; constitutional basis, 405–08; licensing provisions of, 413–15; program controls of, 416–19; rewrites, 262, *420–21*; vs. state laws, 424. *See also* Amendments to communications act

Communication policy, national, 4, *403–04*

Community needs. *See* Ascertainment

Community standards (obscenity test), 468–71

Community stations, 174–75, 266, 268

Comparative hearings, 432, *435*, 451

Compatibility, technical: FM, 153; generally, *57–58*; TV, 70, 82, *179*, 193, 322

Compensation, network, *334–35*, 353 (table)

Competition, role of in broadcasting: in consumer perspective, 506; diversification, 300, 461; pluralism, *10–12*, 573, 577; public broadcasting, 292–93; standards, 358. *See also* Regulation, structural

Complaints to FCC, public, 13, 428, 444, *445–46*

Composite week, 447

"Composition of the traffic" doctrine, *473–74*

Comsat (Communications Satellite Corporation), *308*, 312

Congress & broadcasting: constitutional role, 405–06; vs. executive branch, 536–37; FCC monitoring, *407*, 431, 480; intervention in regulation, 493–94. *See also* Amendments to communications act

Congruence theory, 548

Conrad, Frank, 125–27

Consent decree, 485

Consent order, FTC, 365

Constitution, U.S.: & broadcast regulation, 12, 140, *405–08*; on patents, 110; as world model, 464. *See also* First Amendment; Fifth Amendment

Construction Permit (CP), 414, *433*

Consultants, 235–36, 328

Consumers: boycotts by, 337, 490, *495–98*; disclosures to, 444; FCC assistance to, 503; & format change, 505–06; & FTC, 423; in general, *498–99, 506–07*, 525; & negotiated settlements, 503–05; organizations of, 501–02; publications for, 502–03; standing (legal) of, 499–501

Content analysis (research method), 479, *550*, 555–56

Contests, promotional, *170*, 424, 454

Contours, coverage, 46–47

Contraceptive advertising, 363

Contract, network affiliation, *334–35*, 338–39

Conventions, political, 515, 522, *533*

Cook, Fred, 477, *487–88*

Coolidge, President Calvin, 140, 532

Cooperative advertising: local, 354, 376; network, 159, 354, 369, 376

Co-production, *21*, 281 (fig.), 282

Copyright: cable TV, *301–02, 332–33*; law, 422–23; music, 165

Corporation for Public Broadcasting (CPB), *259–63*, 269, 271 (fig.), 273–76

Corrective advertising, 365

Corwin, Norman, 148

Cosell, Howard, 197, 396

Cost per thousand (CPM), 367, 392

Coughlin, Rev. Charles E., *146*, 240

Counter-commercials, 481–82

Counter programming, *218, 220*, 317

Counterattack, 212–13

Courts: appeals to 413; broadcasts from: *see* Canon 3(A)(7)

Coverage area, broadcast, *46–47*, 60, 352. *See also* Markets

Cox, Commissioner Kenneth, 458

Coy, Commissioner Wayne, 458

Credibility, media, 551

Criminal Code, broadcasting clauses, 469

Criticism of broadcasting, *246–47*, 511–12

Cronkite, Walter, *231–32*, 538

Crosby, Bing, 158, 159, *167*, 175

Cross-licensing, *125, 132–33*

Cross-media ownership: cable, 303 (table); newspapers, 330, *486*

Crystal: detector, 108; receiver, 127

C-SPAN (Cable Satellite Public Affairs Network), *312–13*, 536

Cuba, *21, 26*, 60

Cultural imperialism, 24–25

Culture, broadcasting and, 24–25, *246–47, 516–17*

Cume measurement, 382, *384*

Cycle (wave motion), 41

Dallas, 24, *382*

Daly case, 418–19

DATE (Digital Audio for Television), 77

Davis, Elmer, 147

Day part, 217–18

Day parting, 172

Daytime-only (Class II) stations, 60

Death of a Princess, 267–68

Dedicated channel, 568

Deerhunter, 510

Defamation. *See* Libel

Deficit financing, 340

Definition (resolution), picture, 65, 69, *181–84*, 567

De Forest, Lee: audion invention, 109–10; on commercialism, 137–38; broadcast experiments, 117–21; patent suit, 112–13

Deintermixture (VHF/UHF TV), 190

Delayed broadcasts, *79*, 202, 261, 265, 336

Deletion, license, 146–47, 407–08, *452–54*. *See also* Revocation

Delivery system, broadcasting as, *80*, 91

Demassification, 568

Democratic Convention of 1968, 522, 533

Demographics: & program preferences, 170, *392*; in ratings reports, 384; & sales efficiency, 243, *392*, 506

Department of Justice: consumer aid, 498; & newspaper cross-ownership, 486; opposition to ABC-ITT merger, 198. *See also* Antitrust suits

Deregulation: of cable TV, 299–300; & children's TV, 246; & consumer movement, 507; critique of, *574, 576*; definition of 459–60; of radio, 151, 339, 438, *460–61,* 506

Desensitization (to violence), 530

Designated market area (DMA), 382

Detection, signal, 108

Dial (program guide), 277

Diaries (in audience research), *384–85,* 389

Digital signal processing, 77, *82–87,* 153, 567–68

Diode, 109

Direct waves, 47, *50* (table), 62

Disc jockey (DJ), *155–56,* 169, 172

Disc recording: sound, 80–81; TV, 82

Disclosure, financial (licensee), 452

Disclosure of radio messages (law against), 409

Disco radio formula, 170–71

Disney, Walt, 197

Distress sale (station), 436

Distribution systems: "bicycle" network, 205, 259; vs. delivery, 80; hybrid, 91–96; space relays, 88–91; terrestrial relays, 87–88

Diversification (First Amendment goal), 484, 487. *See also* Cable TV; Ownership; Programs

Divestiture: motion picture, 159; newspaper, 486; network syndication, 205

Docudrama, 224–25

Documentaries: radio, 164, 285 (fig.); TV *236–38,* 479–81

Doerfer, Commissioner John C., 459

Domsat (domestic satellite), 90 (fig.), *308–09*

Double billing, *376,* 444

Douglas Edwards with the News, 202, 231

Down-frequency converter, 92, 312, 314 (fig.)

Downlink, satellite, 91

Drake-Chenault Enterprises, 171

Drive-time, 154

Drop-in channels, 188n

Drug lyrics case, 168

Ducting, wave, 47

Due process (of law), 407, *412,* 472

Dumont Television Network, *200,* 205, 215n

Duopoly rule, 485

DX listening, 128, 136

Dynamic range (FM radio), 63

Earth station, satellite, *90–91,* 264–66, 308–309, 314 (fig.), 567

East Germany, 22–23, 26 (table)

Economic injury (to licensee), 434

Economics of broadcasting: commercial, 341–43; noncommercial, 269–78; world, 17–21

Edison, Thomas A., *100–01,* 109

Editorial (issue) advertising, 208n, 240n, 356, 467, *481–88*

Editorial discretion (judgment), *478–81,* 483

Editorial process, 468

Editorializing (by licensee), 436

Edsel fiasco, *519,* 552

Educational programs: commercial stations, 436; noncommercial stations, 288–89

Educational radio. *See* Public radio

Educational television (ETV). *See* Public TV

Educational Television Facilities Act of 1962, 273

Edward & Mrs. Simpson, 208, 484

Effects of broadcasting: advertising, 518–21; on culture, 24–25, 246–47, *516–18;* gratifications, 539–41; law of minimal, 552; on perception of reality, *521–27, 529–30;* pervasiveness of, 515–16; on political life, 515, *531–37;* prosocial, 527; public broadcasting, 289; as research focus, 551–52; on socialization, 526–27; stereotyping, 525–26; on subjects of programs, 524–25; symbiotic, 516; theories about, *544–49, 559–60;* on Vietnam war, 537–38; violent behavior, 527–31

Efron, Edith, 556

EHF band, 43 (table), *50* (table), 87

Eisenhower, President Dwight D., *228,* 532

Elections, effect of broadcasting on. *See* Effects of broadcasting; Equal time law

Electrical transcription (ET), 149 (box), 166, *167*

Electromagnetic energy, 37–38

Electron beam, *67,* 76 (fig.), 84 (fig.)

Electronic church, 240–44

Emergency Broadcasting System (EBS), 147n

Employment in broadcasting, 343–48

Employment, fair. *See* Equal Employment Opportunities

En banc (FCC proceeding), 428

Encoding-decoding process, 85, 317, 548 (fig.)

Enforcement of FCC rules: statute, 412; in practice, 452–55

ENG (Electronic news gathering), *76,* 233–34

Entertainment as media function, *539–41,* 560–61

Epstein, Edward, 538, 550

Equal Employment Opportunities (EEO), 345, 424, 443, 445, 452, 501

Equal time (opportunities) law: censorship clause, 424, 465, 471; complaints, 446 (table); FCC rules, 441–43; in foreign countries, 14–15; in NAB codes, 508; statutory basis, 417–19; & uniqueness of broadcasting, 473

Equitability of service, 416–17

Escapism, *539,* 560

Estes case, 472–73

European Broadcasting Union (EBU), 21, 229

Evangelism in broadcasting, 174, *241–44,* 466

Exclusivity (program rights): network, 338; syndication, 205, *332*

Ex parte contacts, 458–59

Executive branch & broadcasting, 406 (fig.), *410, 455, 494–95. See also* Nixon administration

External broadcasting, *26–31,* 64–65

Face the Nation, 238, 495

Facsimile, 78

Fair use (of copyrighted material), 422

Fairness doctrine: & advertising, 481–84; complaints concerning, 446 (table); & deregulation, 575; vs. equal time law, 442 (table); evolution of, 474–76; First Amendment justification, *477–78,* 487–88; licensee obligation under, 439–41; & loss of license, 452 (table); & news, 478–81; personal attack rule, *440,* 473, 477; & spectrum scarcity, 575–76; statutory basis, 476–77

Fairness Report (FCC), 478, 482

Family viewing standards, *431,* 509, 529

Farnsworth, Philo, 183

Faulk case, *213–14,* 466n

Feature films, *203–04*, 316, 357, 510, 569

Federal Communications Bar Association (FCBA), 444

Federal Communications Commission (FCC): adjudicatory role, 430–31; assessment of, 455–59; budget, 427; cable TV regulation, 297–301; complaints to, 445–46; & Congress, *405–407*, 427, 493–94; & consumers, 444, 446, 456, *503*; decisions of, 608–9; deregulation theory of, *460–61*, 544, 576–77; discretionary powers of, *407*, *410-12*; and EEO, 443–44; enforcement powers, *412*, 452–55; & executive branch, 406 (fig.), *410*, 455, *494–95*; & industry self-regulation, *431*, 509; informal regulation by, 431; jurisdiction of, *406*, 410; leniency of, 453, 455, *459*, 475–76; licensing power, *413–16*, 432–35, 447–52; organization of, 427–28; paper work, 429; program policies (1960), 244, *436–39*; rules & regulations, 406–07, *429–30*; spectrum management role, 403–04; staff role, 429; statutory basis for, 410

Federal Radio Commission, *140–41*, 143, 255

Federal Trade Commission (FTC), *364–65*, 393, 395, *423*, 455, 520

Feedback: circuit, 112–13; research concept, *377–78*, 548–49

Fees: filing, 415; music copyright, 165–66; set use, 19; spectrum use, 274, *415*, 421

Femme Forum, 469–70

Fessenden, Reginald, 106–107, *116–17*, 121n

Fiber, optical, 94

Fiction: content analysis of, 526–27; role of violence in, 530–31

Fiduciary responsibility of licensee, *475*, 478

Field, Cyrus W., 102

Field experiments (research method), 555 (table), 558–59

Field frequency, 66, *69*, 72

Field studies, 555 (table), 558

Fifth Amendment, 407, 472

Film: sound, 101; technology, 65–66; vs. videotape, 202–03. *See also* Feature films

Financial data, broadcast industry, 341–44, 353 (table), 372 (table)

Financial disclosure (licensee), 452

Financial qualifications of licenses, *414*, 434

Financial support options: advertising, 9 (table), 19–20; foundations, 270–74; government, 9 (table), 18–19, 273–77; license fees, *19*, 518; underwriting, 276–77

Fines (FCC penalty), 412–13

"Fireside chats," 145

First Amendment: absolutism, 441n, *488–89*; & access to broadcasting, *474–78*, 487; & broadcast advertising, 481–84; & communications act, 408, *416*, 473–74; constitutional role, 464; diversity of voices, 12, 484–86; & equal time rule, 417–19; vs. Fifth Amendment, 472–73; & libel, 466–68; marketplace of ideas, 12, *463–64*, 484–87; & national security, *471–72*, 479; vs. negligence law, 528; & news broadcasts, 418, *478–81*; & obscenity law, 468–71; parity (media), *488–89*; & private censorship, 465; & religious freedom, 465–66; & spectrum scarcity, *405*, 473, 575–76; wording, 464

First-run syndication, *205–06*, 337

Flicker, 66, 69

Flow, audience, *217–18*, 220, 391

Fly, Commissioner James L., *456*, 494

FM radio: channels, *62*, 255; development of, 153–54; free form, 174–75; origins, 151–53; rebroadcasting of, 91; station numbers, 144 (fig.); SCA, *64*, 409; technology, 62–64. *See also* Public radio

Focus groups, 396, 555

Fogarty, Commissioner Joseph, 574

Ford Foundation, 258, *270–75*

Ford, President Gerald R., 443, 533, *535*

Forfeitures (fines), 455

Formats, radio: all-news, 172; audiences of, 392; & automation, 171, 173 (photo); classified advertising, 353n; opposition to change in, 505–06; religious, 173–74; syndication of, 171; talk, 172; Top-40, 169–71

Forms, FCC application, 433

Formula radio, 169–76

Fortune telling, 146, 363

Fourth network (TV), *200*, 275 (box), 461

Fowler, Commissioner Mark, 457 (photo)

Frame frequency, *66*, 181–83

Frame, sampling (research), 388

Franchise, cable TV, 299–300

Fraudulence, 452 (table), 453–54

Free flow controversy, 31–33

Free form programming: radio, 174–75; TV, 192

Freed, Alan, 168

Freedom of expression. *See* First Amendment

Freeze, television, *187*, 226

Frequency: distress (SOS), 139; of radio waves, 43 (table); & propagation range, 48, 50 (table); of sound waves, 39–40, *42*; spectrum 38 (table)

Frequency modulation: *45* (fig.), 69, 71 (fig.). *See also* FM radio

Frequency division multiplex (cable TV), 93 (fig.)

Friendly, Fred, 164, 215, *488*

Friends of the Earth case, 482

Fringe time, 217–18

Frost, David, 230

Functional FM, 64, 153

Fund for Adult Education, 271–73

Future: of broadcast networks, 571–77; of cable TV, 568–70; of local programming, 570–71; of pluralism, 577; of public broadcasting, 291–93; of regulation, 573–76; of technology, 566–68

Gain, antenna, 52

Galbraith, John Kenneth, 283, 518

Game shows, *155*, *226*, 209–12, 362, 361 (box)

Garroway, Dave, 194–95

Gatekeeping, *521*, 549–50

General Electric, 106, 119, *112–13*, 123, 129–30, 183

Generator, sync, 69, 74 (fig.), 76

Geostationary (geosynchronous) orbit, *90* (fig.), 308

Gerbner, George, 529–30, 556

German Democratic Republic, *22–23*, 26 (table)

German Federal Republic,15, 18, *22–23*, 26 (table), 27, 28, 29

Ghosts, TV, *41*, 51, 297

Gigahertz, 43 (table)

"Glow and flow" principle, 540–41

Goldmark, Peter, *167*, 193

Gone With the Wind, 204

Good Morning, America, 227, 443

Goodson, Mark, *211, 227*
Gould, Jack, 512
Government ownership of broadcasting, 7, 9 (table), *122–23*
Graham, Rev. Billy, 241
Grandfathering, 485
Gratification effects, 539–41
Graveyarding (schedule strategy), 437
Great Britain: program exports to U.S., 281–83. *See also* British Broadcasting Corporation; Independent Broadcasting Authority
Great Debates, 441, 442, *532–34*
Grid (rate card), 369
Grossman, Lawrence, 263, 284
Ground station. *See* Earth station
Ground waves, *47–48,* 50 (table), 59–60
Group ownership, *329–31,* 453, *484–85,* 487
Group W, *112,* 330
Guard bands, 71
Guiding Light, 155, 226
Guns of Autumn, 497

Haley, Alex, 224–25
Hammock (scheduling strategy), 218
Happy Talk (news style), 235
Hargis, Rev. Billy James, *477,* 488
Harmonics (in sound), 41–42
Hear It Now, 164
Hearings: broadcast of congressional, 536–37; comparative, *432–33, 450–51;* communications act provisions for, 412–13; renewal, 500–501
Helical recording format, 82–83
Hennock, Commissioner Frieda, 428, *456–57*
Herbert case, 467
Hertz (Hz), *42–43,* 104
Hertz, Heinrich, 104–5
Heterogeneity, audience, 544
Hewitt, Don, 238
HF band, 14, 43, *50,* 64 (table)
High definition TV (HDTV), 567
High fidelity sound, 41, *167*
Hill, Lew, 174
Hollywood, 197, *202–03*
Holocaust, 225
Home Box Office (HBO), 308, 309, 313, *315–16,* 318
Home Box Office case, 299
Home Video (Communications) Center, *322–23, 565*
Home video recording, 82, 84 (fig.)

Hooks, Commissioner Benjamin, 428, *456*
Hoover, Herbert: as commerce secretary, 132, 136, 139–40; as president, 143–45, 411
Household(s): as sampling unit, 382; using TV (HUT), 220, *383–84*
Hughes TV Network, 200, 333
"Hunger in America" case, 479–80
Hunt, H. L., 488
Huntley, Chet, 214
Hybrids, relay-delivery, 91–96
Hyde, Commissioner Rosel, 456
Hypodermic injection theory (effects research), *545,* 552
Hyping of ratings, 394–95
Hz, 42–43

IATSE, 348
Iconoscope, 68 (photo), *183–84*
ID (station identification), 358
I Love Lucy, 202, 205
Image studies, media, 551
Image orthicon, 68 (photo), 184, *187*
Imitation effect, 527–29
Impeachment hearings, Nixon, 284, *532,* 536
Imported signals, cable TV, *296–97,* 299
Income of broadcasting, 342–43
Indecency in broadcasting, 446 (table), *452, 470–71*
Independent Broadcasting Authority (Great Britain), *10–12,* 15, 20
Independent producers, *230,* 279, 280 (fig.)
Independent (nonnetwork) station(s), 191, 239, *331,* 375 (fig.)
Indians, American, *497,* 525
Information: capacity, 58; color, 70; control, 550; motion as, 66; synchronizing, 69; theory, 548–49
Innovation vs. invention, 106
Instant analysis, 550n
Instant replay, 197
Instructional Television Fixed Services (ITFS), *92,* 289
Intelsat (International Telecommunications Satellite Organization), 308
Interactive cable TV, 93, *305–07,* 397
Interconnection, 87. *See also* Cable TV; Networks
Interdepartmental Radio Advisory Committee (IRAC), *403–04,* 428 (fig.)

Interference: adjacent channel, 59; cochannel, *58–59,* 140, 187; coverage, 47; cross-national, 4, *21;* in 1920s, 139–40; static, 63; zone, *58,* 406
Interlace scanning, 69
International broadcasting. *See* External broadcasting
International Brotherhood of Electrical Workers (IBEW), 348
International commercial stations, 20
International Communication Agency (ICA), 27
International News Service (INS), 160–61
International Radio & Television Organization (OIRT), 21
International Telecommunication Union (ITU), *13–14,* 59n, 422
International Telephone & Telegraph (ITT), 198
Interstate commerce, broadcasting as, 405–07
Interstate Commerce Commission, 427
Interval, blanking, *69–70,* 77, 321 (fig.)
Intervening variables, 545–46
Interviews, personal (research), 386
Invasion from Mars, 148, 362, 547
Investigative reporting, 466
Investment in broadcasting: by public, *342,* 499, 518; by industry, 343 (fig.)
Ionosphere, *48–49,* 64
Iran, 27, 30, 233, 523
Issue advertising. *See* Editorial advertising
Issues of public importance, 433, *439–40,* 442 (table), 475, 477

Jamming, 30
Japan, 13, 531
Jawboning by FCC, 357n, 431, *465*
Jenkins, Charles F., 181–82
Johnson, President Lyndon, 535
Johnson, Commissioner Nicholas, 456, 459, 502
Joint Committee on Educational Television (JCET), 256
Jones, Commissioner Anne P., 456–57
Journalism schools, research focus of, 560
Journalistic discretion. *See* Editorial discretion
Judgment task research, 554
Judicial branch of government, role of, 406 (fig.), *413,* 427

Kaltenborn, H. V., *162*, 163–64, 494
Kefauver, Senator Estes, 536
Kennedy, Senator Edward, 441
Kennedy, President John F., 239,
    533–34, 441, *531*
KFKB case, 146, 453
KGEF case, 407–08, 453
Kilohertz, 43
Kinescope: tube, 76 (fig.);
    recording, *81*, 181, *201*
Klapper, Joseph, 552
Klein, Paul, 391
KOB case, 431
Korean War, 193
KPIX case, 330
KRLA case, 433
KTAL case, 503–05
KTTV case, 504–05
KUHT case, 267–68
Ku Klux Klan, 284, 465

Laboratory experiments, 555 (table),
    557–58
Laissez faire (economic theory),
    463–64, 487, 574, 577
Lamp Unto My Feet, 240
Lando, Barry, 467
Lansman-Milam case, 446
Large-screen TV, 77, 567
Larry King Show, 176
Laser, 84 (fig.), 94, 322
Lasker, Albert, 137
Lasswell, Harold, 549
Late Show, 203
Laugh-In, 223
Law of broadcasting: federal, 12,
    408–24; foreign countries, 13–14;
    international, *13–14*, 422; state,
    424. *See also* Communications act
Law of minimal effects, 552
Law of the press, 423
Lawrence Welk Show, 208
Lawyers, communications, 444
Lazarsfeld, Paul, 539, 546
Lea Act, 167
Lead-in, 218
League of Women Voters, 443
Leapfrogging (cable TV), 297
Lear, Norman, 223, *243–44*
Lee, Commissioner Robert E., 429,
    456
Legion of Decency, 527
Legislative branch of government,
    role of, 405–07
Leisure time, & broadcasting, 541
LF band, 43 (table), *50* (table)
Libel, 213, 424, 444, *466–68*, 498
Licensees, broadcast: appraisal of
    performance by, 438–39, *445–47*,
    452 (table); as fiduciaries, 475,

478; financial disclosure by, 452;
    promises vs. performance of,
    444, 451–52, *501*; qualifications
    of, 414, *434–36*, 454;
    responsibilities of, *439–45*, 505
Licenses, broadcast: applications
    for, 432–33; deletion of, 146, 412,
    452–54; earliest, 129n, 139; fees
    for, *415*, 421; interim, 432–33;
    legal basis, 413–16; renewal of,
    412, 415, *447–52*; term of, 141,
    414, 421; transfer of, 415
Licenses, set-use, *19*, 518
Light (as electromagnetic energy),
    37–38
Likeability rating (performers), 396
Line-of-sight propagation, 47
Lines, TV picture, *69*, 72 (table),
    181–84
Liquor advertising, *362*, 508
Live programming, 150, 162, 164–
    65, 167, *201–203*
Lobbying, 485, 593
Local advertising, 352 (fig.), *353–54*,
    375 (fig.)
Local production: amount of, 220,
    230 (table); cable TV, 296;
    employment in, 344; FCC
    definition of, 438n; future of,
    570–71; public TV, 258, 279–80;
    TV, *206–7*, *229–30*, *340*, 571. *See
    also* Ascertainment; Live
    programming
Localism: & cable TV, 298–99; FCC
    rules on, 433, *435–39*; in foreign
    countries, 12, *16–17*; myth of,
    459; as policy goal, 12, *416*; in
    public broadcasting, 261; in
    rewrites, 420–21. *See also* Access;
    Ascertainment
Logs, program, 476, *430*, 447, 452
    (table), 460
Lone Ranger, 158
Long-play (LP) recordings, 167
Loomis, Mahlon, 103
LOP (Least Objectionable Program)
    theory, 391
Lotteries, 170, 210, 424, 452 (table),
    508
Loudness: as amplitude, 39; of
    commercials, 362
Loudspeakers, low fidelity of AM,
    59, 151
LF band, 43 (table), *50* (table)
Low-power TV (LPTV), *192*, 318,
    320, 484
Low noise amplifier (LNA), 91, 314
    (fig.)

Lowest unit charge (candidates),
    418, 442 (table), *443*
Luminance (color signal), 70

McBride Commission (UNESCO),
    32
McCarthy, Joseph R., 214–15
McConnaughey, Commissioner
    George, 456
McGinniss, Joe, 532
McHugh-Hoffman, Inc., 235
McIntire, Rev. Carl, 440
Mack, Commissioner Richard A.,
    458
McLendon, Gordon, 169
McLuhan, Marshall, 391, *517*, 540
MacNeil/Lehrer Report, 284
McPherson, Aimée Semple, 139
Magazine format, *194*, 443
Magazines, 352 (fig.), *356*, 378
Magid, Frank M. Associates, 235
Magnavox VDR, 322
Magnetic recording. *See* Tape
    recording
Mail, audience, 377–78. *See also*
    Complaints to FCC
Make Believe Ballroom, 156
Makegoods, commercial, *329*, 374
Malice (in libel suits), 467–68
Management: of broadcast stations,
    328; of radio energy, 36; of
    spectrum, 52–54, 404 (fig.)
Mankiewicz, Frank, 264
March of Time, 164
Marconi, Guglielmo, *104–06*, 107–
    08, 113. *See also* American
    Marconi
Marginal stations, 341, *434*, 455,
    487, 509
Maritime wireless, 113–15
Market: delineation of, 332, *380–82*;
    failure of (economic theory), 460;
    size, vs. broadcast income, 341–
    42; size, vs. station rates, 370
    (table); test, 398
Marketplace of ideas, *463–64*, 486–
    87
Mary Hartman, Mary Hartman, 208,
    490
Mass culture. *See* Popular vs. elite
    art
Mass media: origin, 101–03;
    definition, *544–45*; credibility of,
    551. *See also* Research, mass
    media
Massification, 568
Master antenna system, 295
Masterpiece Theatre, 224, 276, 278,
    281–82

Maude, 223n, *337*, 496
Maxwell, James C., 103–104
Mayflower decision, 475
Measurement, audience. *See* Research, marketing
Media exposure (time spent), *391*–*92*, 519–20, *539*, 551
Media imperialism, 31–33
Media parity (First Amendment), 488–89
Medium: as message, 391, *517*, *540*; as research focus, 550–51
Meet the Press, 238–39, 441
Megahertz, 43
Message originators (as research focus), 549–50
Meters (set-use recorders), *385*, 389
Metropolitan Opera, 117, *165*, 187, 517
Mexico, 60, 422
MF band, 43 (table), 50 (table), *73* (table)
Microprocessors, *76*, 172
Microwave relays, *87*–*88*, 132, 233, 297
Middle of the road (MOR) formula, 170
Mid-Florida, case, 432
Milam, Lorenzo, 174–75
Miller case, 468–69
Miniaturization, *76*, 237
Miniseries, 224–25
Minorities: employment of, 347; ownership by, 435–36; portrayal of, 201, 454, *496*–*97*, 499, *525*–*26*; programs for, 150, 394, *436*, 568; and ratings, 394
Minow, Commissioner Newton, *246*, 431, *456*–*457*
Mobil Corporation, 208, 276, 278, *483*–*84*
Modeling effect (imitation), 557
Modulation, carrier wave, *44*–*46*, 102, 103
Monday Night Football, 197, 239
Monopoly: in broadcasting, 484–86; government, *7*, *122*; political, 14, 417; regulated, 111–12. *See also* Antitrust suits
Morality in Media, 470
Morse code, *102*, 117, 127
Motion, illusion of, 66
Motion pictures: made-for-television, 204; origin of, 101; technology of, 65–67
MSO (multiple system operator), cable TV, *302*–*03*, 316
Muckrakers, 498
Muir, Jean, 212
Multipoint Distribution System

(MDS), *92*, 293, 304, 319 (fig.)
Multiplexing: generally, 53–54; FM radio, 63; TV, 70–71; cable TV, 93
Mumford, Lewis, 541
Muppet Show, 209
Murrow, Edward R., *161*–*64*, 180–81, 210, 215, *234*–*35*, 236
Museum of Broadcasting, 149 (box)
Music: background (SCA), 153; ban on recorded, 167; copyright, 165; DJ format, 155–56; drug lyrics, 168; formulas, 169–75; license fees, *166*, 340; live era, 164–65; mass market for, 101; on public radio, 284–86; rock & roll, 168–69; syndicated formats, 171; union, *166*–*67*, 347
"Music box" memo, *121*–*22*, 134
Mutual Broadcasting System (MBS), 157, *158*–*59*, 176, 200
Mutually exclusive applications, 192, 405, *432*–*33*, 448

NAB Codes: advertising standards of, 145, *359*–*64*; & children, *244*–*45*, 447; critique of, 509–10; family viewing standards, 431; re misleading demonstrations, 366; re news flash, 148n; program standards, 508–09; re religion, 174n, 241; subscribership, 360 (table); re violence, 530
Narrowcasting, 319
National Advertising Review Board, 366
National Aeronautics & Space Administration (NASA), 308, 312
National Association for the Advancement of Colored People (NAACP), 160, 457, *471*, 499
National Association for Better Broadcasting (NABB), 499, *504*
National Association of Broadcast Engineers and Technicians (NABET), 348
National Association of Broadcasters (NAB): & industrial self-regulation, 508; membership in, 360 (table); origins, 165; services to members, 329, 445, 468. *See also* NAB Codes
National Association of Educational Broadcasters (NAEB), 256, 258, 260
National Association of Television Program Executives, (NATPE), 205
National Black Media Coalition (NBMC), 502

National Broadcasting Company (NBC): antitrust suit, 485; Blue Network, *134*, 157, 159, 160–61, 338; O&O stations, 199 (table); organization of, 333–34; origins of, 134–35; "Pensions" case, 480–81; Red Network, *134*, 157, 159, 338; TV network, *193*–*96*, 227
National character, & broadcasting, 3
National Citizens Committee for Broadcasting (NCCB), 502
National Educational Television (NET), 258–60
National News Council, 511
National Public Radio (NPR), *263*–*64*, 266, 269, 284, 291, 537
National radio conferences of 1922–1925, 132, *139*–*40*
National Religious Broadcasters (NRB), 174
National Rifle Association, 497
National Science Foundation, 520
National security, *471*–*72*, 479
National spot advertising, 355, 375 (fig.)
National spot sales, 353 (table)
National Telecommunications & Information Administration (NTIA), *403*–*404*, 428 (fig.)
National Television Systems Committee (NTSC), *184*, 193, 18, 187
Navy, U.S., 115, 117–20, *122*–*23*
NBC Symphony Orchestra, 165
NET (National Educational Television), *258*, 260, 282
Network(s), broadcast: ad hoc, 200, 572n; advertising, 352 (fig.), *354*–*56*, 369–70, 371–72, 375 (fig.); affiliate numbers, 175, 198 (table); affiliate relations, *335*–*38*, 494, 572; affiliation contracts, 134–35, *334*–*35*, 437; audiences, 220, 390–91; benefits of, *156*, 331, 335; cable TV ownership, 303; clearance, 335–38; clipping, 376; control over news production, 230; control over programs, 194, 485–86; corporate character, 198–99; definition, 79, 175, *333*, 339; deregulation of, *460*, 575; as distribution system, 80; & editorial advertising, 484; employment by, 345 (table); FM, 91; in foreign countries, 5–6, 10–11, 17; fourth, 200; future of, *565*–*66*, *571*–*72*; income of, 344 (table); interconnection of, 87–91,

Network(s), *cont.*
180–81, 187, 572; as monopolies,
485–86; news, 228–34, 521;
organization of, 323–24; origins,
131–32; owned & operated
stations (O&Os), 199 (table, 330;
preemption, 335–38; preview of
programs by affiliates, 326; &
prime-time access rule, 339;
program procurement, 194, *221,*
340; programs (radio), 159–60;
programs (TV), 220–40, 244–45;
radio, 131–32, *134–36,* 150, 169,
175–77; ratings reports on, *380–
81,* 385, 387, 388, 390; regional,
200, 279, 333; regulations, 338–
39, *431–32,* 455, 485, *473–74,* 485;
scheduling, 219–20; self-
regulation, *366,* 510; as
syndication method, 156;
syndication by, 205, 339; TV,
192–201. *See also* PBS network
Networks, cable TV, 309–12
Network Inquiry Special Staff,
FCC, 432, *460,* 486
New world information order, 32–
33
New York Sun (penny press), 100
New York Times case, 467
News: access to, *228,* 472–73, 525;
agenda setting role, 521–22; all-
news stations, 172, 233; amount
of, *231–33,* 433; bias in, *479,* 550;
on cable TV, 311, 313 (table);
consultants, 235–36; effects of on
subjects of coverage, 524–25;
electronic newsgathering, *76,
233–34;* & equal time law, *418–
19, 441–43;* & fairness doctrine,
478–81; flashes (false), 148n;
gatekeeping, 521; importance in
broadcasting, *160, 228,* 436; jobs,
344, 346 (box); & libel, 466–68;
19th century, 100; prestige
conferral by, 521; public
broadcasting, 275 (box), 281
(fig.), *283–85;* & publicity crimes,
523–24; radio, 160–64; slanting of,
452 (table), *478–79,* 483, 511;
sports, 239; staging of, 454, 479–
80, *522–25;* in station
organization, 328–29; syndication
of, 102–03; in television, 228–36;
& Vietnam war, 537–39; in World
War II, 147–48, *161–63*
News agencies, 102–03, 160–61, 229
Newspapers: analogy with cable
TV, 299; cross-ownership, 486; as
mass medium, *100,* 352–53;

opposition to broadcasting, 20,
160–61
Nickelodeon, 101, 312
Nielsen, A. C., 218, 290, *379–82,*
385, 387–90
Nightline, 233
9 kHz channels, 59n, 151
Nipkow, Paul, 181
Nixon, President Richard M.:
"Checkers" speech, 532; Frost
interview, 230; impeachment
hearings, *532,* 536; Kennedy
debates, 533–34; 1968 campaign,
532–33, 556; & presidential TV,
489, 535; tapes, 174, 285, *495*
Nixon administration: & networks,
337, 494–95, 511; & public
broadcasting, 275 (box), 283
Noise, 22
Noncommercial vs. nonprofit
operation, 269
Noncommercial broadcasting. *See*
Public Broadcasting
Nondelegable responsibility
(licensee), *439,* 454, 505
Nonduplication rule, AM-FM, 153–
54
Nonentertainment programs, 230
(table), 433, *438–39,* 460
NTSC. *See* National TV Systems
Committee
Nuisance law (re indecency), 470

Oboler, Arch, 148
Obscenity: complaints about, 446
(table); definition, 468–69; vs.
indecency, 470–71; law of, 424,
468; Mae West incident, 145; in
public broadcasting, 268; in
realistic programs, *490,* 510
Off-network syndication, 205–206
Office of Communication case, 450
Office of Network Study, FCC, 432
Office of Telecommunications
Policy (OTP), 494
Office of War Information (OWI),
147
Offset scanning, 69
Old Time Gospel Hour, 243 (box)
Omnibus, 201
"On a Note of Triumph," 148
On-the-spot news, 443
One-to-a-customer policy (FCC),
485
$128,000 Question, 211
O&O stations. *See* Networks
Open University, 11, 268
Operation Prime Time, 208
Operator licensing, 413n
Opinion leaders, 546

Optical fiber cable, 94
Orbit, satellite, 90 (fig.), 308
Oscillation, 37, *39,* 106, 108
Overnights, 380
Overtones, in sound, 41–42
Ownership: of cable TV systems,
303 (table); of channels, 4, *414;*
cross-media, 486; diversity goal,
435, 484, 487; by government, 7,
9 (table), *122–23;* group, *329–31,
484–85;* limitations on, 327, *484–
85;* by minorities, 435–36; by
networks, 338; transfer of, *415,*
504; of world broadcasting
facilities, 9 (table). *See also*
Licensees

Pacifica case, 470–71
Pacifica Foundation, *174,* 470–71
Package plans, advertising, 357,
367, *369*
PAL (color TV system), 18
Paley, William: CBS origins, 134–
36; & radio news, 162; talent raid
by, 158; & TV news staging, 522;
as TV programmer, 222–23; in
World War II, 148
Panama Canal Treaties, 285, 535,
537
Panic ("War of the Worlds"
broadcast), 547
Paramount Theaters, 159, *197*
Parasitism, 295
Parker, Rev. Everett C., 488
Parsimony principle, *154–56,* 340,
570
Participation advertising, 354, *357*
Passivity, audience, 539
Patents, *110–13,* 119, 152, 183
Paternalism in broadcasting, 5–6
Path, wave. *See* Propagation
Pay cable, 301, *315–17,* 319, 569
Payola, 156n, 375
PBS Cable (pay cable service), 292
PBS (Public Broadcasting Service)
network: vs. CPB, 259–62; as
fourth network, 200n; funding,
273–76; program sources, 278–81;
restructuring of, 262–63; satellite
interconnection, *264–65,* 308;
Station Program Cooperative, 279
Penalties (in communications act),
412
Penetration, set, 390
Penny press, 100
People for the American Way, 243–
44
"Pensions: The Broken Promise" case,
480–81

Per inquiry (PI) advertising, 371
Performer Q, 396
Performing rights, music, 165
Permissiveness in broadcasting, *5,* 458, 490, 510
Persistence of vision, 66
Person to Person, 210
Personal attack rule, *440,* 473, 477
Personal influence vs. media influence, 546–47
Personal products, advertising of, 362–63
Personnel, broadcast, 343–48
Petrillo, James C., 166
Phase (of waves), *40–41,* 70
Phil Donahue Show, 443
Philco TV Playhouse, 194n, 201
Philips company, 82, 84 (fig.), 322
Phillips, Irna, 155
Phone-in radio talk shows, *172,* 269–70
Phonograph: origins, 100–101; development, *167–689*
Physiological testing, 397
Pickard, Commissioner Sam, 458
Pickup tube, TV, 67–68, 70 (fig.)
Picture: definition (resolution), 65, *69;* fidelity, 71–72; motion, 66; projection of, 77; processing, 67–69
Pilot program, 219–21
Pioneer (VDR System), 322
Piracy, signal, 301–02, *409*
Pirate stations, 16, *20*
Pitch, sound, 39
Pitch advertising, 362
Play function of media, 539–40
Playlist (formula radio), 169
Plowback of profits, 451–52
Plug, commercial, *227,* 360, 362, 370
Plugola, 375
Plumbicon tube, 68 (photo)
Pluralism, *9–12,* 253–54, 577
PM Magazine, 330, 340
Point-to-point communication: relays as, 79; satellite, 308; wire, 101
Polarization, signal, *51–52,* 154
Policy, communications, 403–05
Policy making vs. rule making, FCC, 430, 442 (table)
Polish-American Congress case, 440
Political philosophy, broadcasting systems & 4–10, 18
Political broadcasting: access to, 14–15, *417–19, 441–43;* effects of, 531–39; fairness in, 441n; as FCC approved type, 436
Popoff, Alexander, 103

Popular vs. elite art, 246–47
Pornography: in broadcasting, 527n, *469–70;* definition of, 468–69; & First Amendment parity, 490; vs. indecency, 470–71
Portable receivers, *150,* 193
Poulsen arc, 106
Power, transmitter: AM radio, 60, 62 (table); antenna gain, *52,* 87; ERP, 74; FM radio, 63; short wave radio, 54; satellites, 91; TV, 75
Preemption: of commercials, 369; of network programs, 335
Prefreeze TV stations, 187
Premiere (cable service), 316
Premium channels, 305, 315
Presidential TV, 441, *489,* 535–36
Presley, Elvis, 168
Press associations, *102–103,* 160–61
Press law, 424
Press-Radio Bureau, 161
Prestige conferral by media, 352, 521
Previous (prior) restraint, 474
Prime time, *206,* 217–18, 220
Prime-time access rule (PTAR), *206–07,* 330, 331, 339, 381 (fig.), 485
Prime-time syndication, 208
Privilege, journalist's, 468
Probability theory (role in sampling), 387
Processing rules, FCC, *429,* 438–39, 448
Procter & Gamble, 372 (table), 496
Production: budgets, 340–41; monopoly control, 485; move to Hollywood, 202–03; of pilots, 219–20; in station organization, 329. *See also* Local production
Professionalism in broadcasting, 510–11
Professor Quiz, 155
Profitability of broadcasting, 341–42
Program analyzer, 397
Program departments: station, *328–29,* 339–40; network, 340–41
Program-length commercials, 242, *359*
Program log. *See* Logs
Programming: consultants on, 235–36, 328; excesses in, 146–47; functions, 327 (fig.), 329; generic, 12; strategies, 217–20
Programs, broadcast: in access-time, *206–07,* 220; advertiser influence on, *20, 194,* 277, 357–58, 496; annual report on, 438;

cable TV, *304–05;* 313 (table), 316–17; cancellation of, 196–97; complaints about (to FCC), 446 (table); cost of, 20–21, *154–55,* 204–05, *339–41;* criticism of, *246–47,* 511–12; diversity of, *221–22,* 485, 506; duplication of (AM-FM), 153; export & import of, *20–21, 24–25, 31–33,* 282–83, 287, 289, 339; FCC 1960 policy on, 436; in foreign countries, 8, *23–25;* highest rated, 220–21, 224, *382;* legal controls over, 245–46, *416–19, 472–73, 473–74, 474–78, 478–81;* licensee responsibility for, 439, 454, 505; local TV, 206–207, *229–30, 340,* 438, 570–71; preemption of, 339, *336–38;* provocative, 475; quest for novelty, 222–23; relevance of, 223–24; sources of, 171, 194, 203–05, 208, *221,* 242; sustaining, 357–58; TV live decade, 201. *See also* Networks; Program types by name
Promises, program. *See* Licensees
Promotion, *170,* 367, 424, 454
Promotional announcements (promos), *358,* 360
Proof of performance (advertising), 374
Propaganda, 523–24, 545–46. *See also* External broadcasting
Propagation, wave, *46–52,* 75, 90–91
Proporz, 15
Pseudoevents, 523–25
PTL Club, 242–43, *440, 466*
PTL network, 200
Public affairs programs, 163–64, 230 (table), *236–39,* 436
Public broadcasting: audience of, 254, 289–91; audience research, 395; & cable TV, *297,* 569; channel reservations, 62, 188–89, *255–56;* in communications act, *259,* 420; criticism of, 254; & executive branch, 275 (box); funding of, *269–78,* 291; future of, 291–93; national organizations, 259–64; network interconnection, 258–59, *264–66,* 292; origins, 188, 254–58; pluralism role, 10; regulation of, 484n; revenue, 274 (fig.); station numbers, 182 (table); station types, 266–69; term, 259. *See also* PBS network; Public radio; Public TV

Public Broadcasting Act of 1967, 259
Public Broadcasting Financing Act of 1975, 275
Public Broadcasting Laboratory, 260
Public interest standard, *410–12*, 420, 478
Public domain (copyright), 422
Public figure (libel law), 467
Public file, *444*, 501, 505
Public investment in broadcasting, *342*, 499, 518
Public radio: audience of, 291; channels, 255–56; CPB-qualified stations, 257 (table), *269*; local production, 284; networks, 256, *263–64*, 266; origins, 137–38, *254–55*; programs, 284–85; station numbers, 144 (table), 255–56, *257* (table); 10-watt FM, 63n, *256*, 269. *See also* Public broadcasting
Public service announcements (PSAs), *358*, 360, 433, 451, 508
Public Telecommunications Financing Act of 1978, 276
Public TV: & cable, 292; Carnegie I, 258–59; Carnegie II, 266, *291–92*; children's programs, 286–87; college stations, 267–68; contrast with commercial TV, 284; entertainment & culture, 281–83; federal funding, 273–76; instructional programs, 281 (table), 288–89; local production, 253, 258, *279–80*; news & public affairs, 281 (table), 283–84; program distribution, 280 (fig.); program guide, 277; programming sources, 278–80; program types, 281 (table); revenue sources, 274 (table); satellite terminals of, 265 (table); school stations, 268; state & municipal stations, 266–67; station numbers, 257 (table); underwriting, 266–67. *See also* PBS network
Publicity crimes, 523–24
Pure Food & Drug Act of 1906, 498

''Q'' score, 396
Quadraphonic FM, 63n
Quadraplex VTR, *81–83*, 202
Qualitative ratings, 25, *395–96*
Quality, sound, 41
Quasioptical waves, 47, *50* (table)
Qube, *306–07*, 315, 397
Quello, Commissioner James H., 456
Quiz show scandals, 209–12

RADAR (Radio's All-Dimension Audience Research), *380*, 386, 387
Radiation, electromagnetic, 37. *See also* Propagation
Radio Act of 1912, 139–40
Radio Act of 1927, *140–41*, 408, 411, 416, 483
Radio Advertising Bureau, 329, 371
Radio Conferences of 1922–1925, *139–40*, 411
Radio Corporation of America. *See* RCA Corporation
Radio energy: definition of, 37n; management of, 36, *52–55*; modulation of, 44–46; place in electromagnetic spectrum, 37–38; propagation of, 46–52; wave-like character of, 41–44
Radio Free Europe (RFE), 26 (table), 28, 30–31
Radio Group, 129–30
Radio Liberty (RL), 28, 26 (table), *30–31*
Radio Luxembourg, 6, *20*
Radio networks. *See* Network(s)
Radiotelegraphy, 107 (photo), 115, *116*
Radiotelephony, *116–17*, 119–20
Radio-Television News Directors Association (RTNDA), 347, 477n, *511*
Raised eyebrow, regulation by, 431
Random digit dialing, 386, *388*, 393
Rates, advertising, *366–71*, 339
Rather, Dan, 231, *238*
Ratings: cable TV, 573; collection of data for, 384–86; concepts, 380–84; investigation of, 392–93; local market, 379–80; methodological studies of, 393; misuse of, 394–95; network, *380–81*, 387; qualitative, 25, *395–96*, 507; radio, 380, *384*, 386; reliability of, 393–94; as sales tool, 371; sampling methods, 386–90; validity of, 394
RCA Corporation: as conglomerate, 199–200; & cross-licensing, 125, 132–33; & FM, 152; & NBC, 133–34, *157*; origins of, 123–25; & phonograph industry, *100–02*, 168; satellite (Satcom I), 90 (fig.), 309, 310 (fig.); & TV development, *183–86*, 192; & VDR, 82, *84* (fig.), 322; & VTR, 202
Reach (audience measurement), 384

Reagan, President Ronald, 443, *533–34*
Real time (vs. recordings), 79
Reasonable access (for candidates), 443
Reasoner, Harry, 238
Rebroadcasting, 91–92
Receive-only earth station. *See* Earth station
Receivers: adaptation of to cable TV, 94; all-channel, *154*, 190, 419; in foreign countries, 17–18; penetration of, 390; portable, *150*, 193; TV, 75–77, 258, 567
Recordimeter, 385
Recordings: music union opposition to, 166–67; network ban on, 167; picture, *81–84*, 86, 202, 322; sound, 80–81, *167–68*; syndication role of, 79, 202
Red Channels, 212
Red Lion case, *477–78*, 487–88
Red Network (NBC), 134, *157*, 159, 338
Reeves, Rosser, 532
Reflection, wave, *41*, 47
Refraction, wave, 47
Regenerative radio circuit, 152
Regulation: cable TV, 297–301; fair employment, 443–44; future of, 576–77; of licensing, *413–15*, 433–36; myths of, *459*, 576; of network-affiliate contracts, 338; origins of, 138–41; of programs, *416–19*, *436–43*; of station operations, 439–44; structural vs. behavioral, 421, *460*, 505, 520, 484–85, *576*. *See also* Communications Act of 1934; Deregulation; Federal Communications Commission; Self-regulation
Reid, Commissioner Charlotte, 456
Reinvestment of profit (licensee), 451–52
Reith, John, 5–6
Relay(s): in hybrid distribution-delivery systems, 91–96; international, 28; network dependence on, 18, *80*, 87, 131–32, 133; satellite, *88–91*, 264–66, 308–313, 332; terrestrial, *87–88*, 180, 187
Religion in broadcasting: & boycotts, 337, 490; as FCC-approved program type, 436; & First Amendment, 465–66; international stations, 64; NAB codes on, 174, 241, 508; origins,

240–42; & politics, 146, 243–44; radio formats, 173–74; sale of time for, 174, *242*, 483; stations & networks, 139, 146–47, 174, *241–42*, 446

Remote vehicles, 76

Remote pickup transmitters, 54 (table)

Renewal, license: burden of proof, 412; in communications act, 415; conditional, 454; dilemma of FCC, 551–52; FCC policy, *450–52*, 500–01; myths of, 459; negotiated settlement, 503–05, 506n; routes, 448–49; short-term, 412, *454*; standing to oppose, 499–500

Repeater amplifiers, *87–88*, 94, 109

Report on Chain Broadcasting, 432

Representatives, national sales, 339, *355–56*, 371, 375 (fig.)

Reruns, 205–06

Research, marketing: on children's advertising, 398; costs of, 379; firms, *378–80*, 396; nonrating, 396–98; physiological, 397; public broadcasting, 290–91. *See also* Ratings

Research, mass media: costs, 555 (table); evolution of, 544–49, 553 (table); foci of, 549–52; methods, 552–59; policy role, 543–44; status of, 559–61; on violence, *528–31*, 557–59. *See also* Research, marketing

Reservation of noncommercial channels, 62, *189–90*, 255–56

Residuals (reuse compensation), 348

Resolution: photographic, 54; TV, 69

Response rate (in sampling), 389

Retrace interval (TV signal). *See* Interval, blanking

Retransmission rights, *332*, 422

Revocation of licenses, 412–13, 418, *452–53*

Rewrites, communications act, 262, *420–21*

Rich Man, Poor Man, 224

Rigging: of documentaries, 479–80; of quiz contests, 210–11. *See also* Staging, news

Right-wing fundamentalists: radio, 243, 488; TV, 243

Risk ratios (re violence), 530

Rivera, Commissioner Henry, 457

RKO General case, 435

Roadside radio (travelers' advisory), 62

Roberts, Oral, 241

Robertson, M. G. "Pat," 241

Rock music, 156, 171, *188*, 354

Rockefeller Center, *157*, 317

Roosevelt, President Franklin D., 144, *145*, 184, 408, 494

Roots, 224–25

Roper Organization polls, 551

Royalties, copyright, *165–66*, *301*, 422

Rule making, FCC, 245, *429–30*

Rules, FCC processing, *429*, 438–39, 448

Rule of Seven (station ownership), 327, 330, *484*

Run-of-schedule (ROS) spots, 367

Russia. *See* U.S.S.R.

Sales function, *328–29*, 333, 345–46, 353–54

Sale of stations. *See* Ownership transfer

Samizdat, 28

Sample: convenience, 386; probability, 387; projection of, 383; size, 307–08; stratified, 390; turnover, 388; weighting, 390. *See also* Sampling

Sample surveys, 555–56

Sampling: in digital processing, 85; error, 388–89, *394*; frame, 388; in non-ratings research, 396; in ratings research, 386–90; response rate, 389; units, 382

Sanders Brothers case, 434

Sanitized violence, 530

Sarnoff, David: & American Marconi, 119–22; & color TV, 193; Music Box memo, 121–22; & network development, *133–34*, 136, 211; as radio telegrapher, 114 (photo); & RCA, 124–25; in World War II, 148; & TV development, 186 (photo)

Satcom I satellite, 90 (fig.), 309–10

Satellators, 92

Satellite(s), space: advantages of, 88, 90; for broadcast interconnection, 192, 200, 263–65, 308, 313 (table), 572; for cable TV interconnection, 95 (fig.), 205n, 309–13; as common carriers, 308; coverage of, 89 (fig.); development of 307–08; direct broadcast (DBS), 312, *314* (fig.), 410, *567*; domestic, 308–09; earth stations, *90–91*, 264, 266, *308–09*, 314 (fig.); frequencies used, 14, *90*; international, 308; Mariner,

46; orbital positions, *90* (fig.), 309; piracy of signals, 302; transponders, *91*, 309–10, 364–65; VOA use, 28

Satellite Television Corp. (DBS proposal), 312

Satellites, terrestrial, 92

Saturation, set, 150, *390*

Scarcity principle (spectrum), 4, *405*, 473, 478, *575–76*

SCA, *64*, 153

Scansion, TV picture, *67–69*, 84 (fig.), 179, 181–87

"Scared Straight," 490

Scatter buying (spots), 354

Scheduling, program: local, 220; network, 219 (table), 225–26, public broadcasting, 256, 258, *266*, 269, 284–85; of satellite-distributed services, 313 (table); sports, 239; strategies, 191, *217–220*, 205; world comparisons, 25

Schenk case, 471

Schiller, Herbert, 31, 33

Schlockmeister, 227

Schorr, Daniel, 522

Schramm, Wilbur, 545n

Schulke Radio Productions (SRP), 171

Scrambled signals, 302, 315, 317, 567

Screen Actors' Guild (SAG), 347

Season, broadcast, 219

SECAM (color TV system), 18

Section 315. *See* Equal time

See It Now, *180–81*, 215, *236–37*

Segmentation, audience, 150–51, 170, 176, *568*

Segmented sponsorship, 194

Selectavision (RCA VDR), 82, 84 (fig.)

Self-regulation: industrial, 366, 393, *507–10*; professional, 510–11. *See also* NAB codes

Selective exposure, 547

Selective perception, 547

Self-monitoring by licensee, 444–45

Self-righting process, 486–87

"Selling of the Pentagon," 480, 523

Selling of the President, 1968, 532

Senate, broadcasts from, 536–37

Sesame Street, 277, *286–87*, 290

Set-use: as test of audience membership, 386–87; collection of data on, 384–86; as behavioral effect, 554

700 Club, 241–42

Share, audience, 220, *383–84*

Sheen, Bishop Fulton J., 240

Sherman Act, 508
SHF band, 43 (table), 50 (table), 87
Shirer, Willliam, 162
Short-term renewal, 412, 414, *454*
Short-wave (HF) broadcasting, 14, *26–31*, 64–65
Showtime (pay-cable), 313 (fig.), 316
Shuler case, 407–08, 466
Sideband, 45, 59, 71 (fig.)
Silicon chips, *76*, 110
Silverman, Fred, 196–98
Simulcast, AM-FM, 153
Single-sideband (SSB) transmission, 46
Siphoning, 292, 318
Situation comedy, 221
16 mm film, 65, 233
Sixth Report and Order (FCC), *188*, 256
60 Minutes, 207 (box), *238*, 467–68, 484, 524
$64,000 Question, 209, 211
Sky waves, *48–50*, 64
Slander, 466n
Slant track (VTR), 82, 83 (fig.)
Slow-scan TV, 64
Smothers Brothers Comedy Hour, 223
Soap, 490, *496*
Soap operas, 155, 226
Socialization, TV role in, 526–27
Soil conductivity, *48*, 50
Solid state devices, 76
Sony company, 82, 150, 322, *423*
SOS (emergency signal), 121, *139*
Song lyrics, 168
Sound: AM radio, 59; digital, 77, *86*; film, *66*, 101; FM radio, 63; recording, 80–81, *167–68*; TV, *69–70*, 71 (fig.), waves, *39*, 42
Southwestern Cable case, 298
Space relays. *See* Satellites
Spanish International Network (SIN), 200, 311–12, 313 (fig.), 333
Spark signal generator, 104–06
Special (program), 194, 218
Spectacular (program), 194
Spectrum, electromagnetic: description, 37–38; management of, *3–4*, *52–54*, 403–05, 414; use-fees, 274, 415, 421
Spillover (coverage), *21–22*, 29
Spin-offs, 223
Sponsor control over programs, 194, 496
Sponsor identification law, *356*, 366, 375, 523
Sponsorship, program, 137, *159–160*, 194, *354*, 357

Sports programs, *239–40*, 392, 436, 569, 570
Spot announcements, *357*, 367
Spot beams, satellite, 89 (fig.)
Staging, news: by medium, 454, 479–80; by subjects of medium, 522–24
Standard broadcasting. *See* AM radio
Standard Rate & Data Service, 242, *357*, *367–69*
Standing (in legal proceedings), *413*, 474n, 499
Stanton, Frank, 210, *480*
Star Stations of Indiana case, *454*, 478
State action, 465
State law: broadcasting, 424; cable TV, 300–301
State of mind (in libel law), 467–68
Static (interference), 63
Station break commercials, 358
Station identification (ID), 358
Station Program Cooperative, PBS, 279
Station(s), broadcast: cost of, *343* (table), 432; definition, 327; equitable distribution of, 416; marginal, 341, *434*, 455, 487, 509; organization of, 327–29; number of, 53 (table), *54* (table), 129, 139–40, 144 (fig.), 182 (fig.), 257 (fig.); sale of, *415*, 504; sales function of, 371. *See also* Licensees
Stations (by call letters): 8MK, 129; 9XK, 125–27; KABL, 368 (fig.); KCET, 268; KDKA, 112, 117, 126 (photo), *127–29*; KFKB, *146*, 453; KFPA, 174; KGB, 171; KGEF, *407–408*, 453; KHJ, 435; KPIX, 330; KPTV, 190n; KQED, 268, 277; KQW, 129; KREM-TV, 487; KTAL, 503–05; KTLA, 331; KTTV, 504–05; KUHT, 258, *267*; 9XM, 254; WABC, *159*, 431; WBAI, 470; WCAU, 136; WCBS, 203; WCFL, 159; WCVB, 340, *571*; WEAF, 129–34; WEFM, 105–06; WESH, 432; WETA, 268, *278*; WGBH, 268, 278, 283; WGCB, 477, *487–88*; WGLD, 469–70; WGN, 158, *331*; WGY, 112; WGFM, 112; WGRV, 112; WHAR, 475; WHDH, *450*, 453; WHYY, 284; WJAZ, 140; WJZ, *129–34*, 159; WLBT, 201n, 447, 450, 453, *499*; WMAF, 131; WMAL, 500; WNAC, 435; WNCN, 506; WNET, *190*, 260, 268, 277, 278, 282, 284; WNEW, 156; WNYC, 267; WOI, 245;

WOR, 158, 331, *435*, 510; WPIX, 479; WQED, 268; WQTV, 52 (photo); WRC, 132 (fig.); WTBS, *309–11*; 313 (table), *332*; WTEV, 496; WTVJ, 235; W2XMN, 152; WVDR, 154; WWJ, 129; WXPN, 268; WXUR, *440*, 453, 466; WXYZ, 158; WYAH, 242
Stephenson, William. 539
Stereophony, *63*, 151, 285–86
Stereotypes, 496, *525–26*
Stern, Bill, 212
Sticks and Bones, 337
Stoner case, 471
Stop Immorality on Television, 496
Storage function (syndication technology), 79
Storz, Todd, 169
Stripping (scheduling strategy), *206*, 217
Structural vs. behavioral regulation. *See* Regulation
Studio One, 203
Stunting (scheduling strategy), 219–20
Stylus (recording/pickup), 80, 84 (fig.)
STV. *See* Subscription TV
Subliminal perception, 362
Subcarrier, *63*, 70
Subscription TV (STV), 192, 312, *317–20*, 409, 569
Subsidiary Communications Authorization (SCA), *64*, 153
Substantiality (of local programming), 438–39
Suburban Broadcasters case, 437
Sullivan, Ed, 187
Superstation, *309–11*, 331–33
Supreme Court of U.S., 413, 623
Surgeon General of U.S., 145, 237, *481–82*, 490, *528*
Sustaining programs, 357–58
Sweeps, ratings, 170, 204, *379*
Symbiosis, media, 516
Synchronization: in motion pictures, 101; in TV, *69–70*, 74, 76
Syndication: in access time, 206–08; barter, 208; in cable TV, 304; economics of, 201, *204–05*, 340, 437; first run, 337; to foreign markets, 24, 31–33, 339; of formats, *171*, 245; vs. localism, 417; & market exclusivity, 205, *332*; networks as, 156, 420; by networks, *339*, 485; of news, 85, *102–03*, 549; off-network, 205–06; in prime time, 200; program

consultants as, 156; ratings reports on, 380; of religious programs, 242–43; technology of, 58–59, *80*

Synthesizing of wants, 518

Talent raids, 158, 231
Talk radio, 172–73
Talk shows, TV, *227*, 443
Tape recording, *81–83*, 167, 202
Tass, 103
Taste in advertising, 362–63
Tax certificates (re minority ownership), 435
Tax support of broadcasting: in foreign countries, 18–19; in U.S., *273–77*, 292
Technical qualifications of licensees, 414, 434
Technology, influence of: on documentary style, 237–38; on industry patterns, 202–03
Telegraphy, 102–03
Tele-movies, 204
Telephone (in audience research), *385–87*, 389
Telephone-talk programs, 172–73
Telephone Group, 129–33
Telephone, 58, *103*, 109
Teleprompter (cable TV), 302
Teletext, *77*, *320–21*
Television broadcasting: advertising rates, 368; ancillary signals, 77–78; antennas, 52 (photo), *75–75*; audience, *390–91*, 571–72; channels, 71–73, *188–92*; closed captioning *77*, 321 (fig.); color, 69n, *70–71*; 76 (fig.), 186, *192–93*; economics of, 341–43; emergence as mass medium, 187; employment in, 343–48; freeze of 1948–1952, 187–88; future of, 365–72; high-definition, 567–68; live decade, 201; low power (LPTV), 192; networks, 192–201; origins, 179–187; public image of, 551; ratings, *380–81*, 384; station numbers, 181–82, 187; station power, 190; UHF problem, 190–92; world technical standards, 72 (table); in World War II, 183–84. *See also* Broadcasting; Networks; Programs; Public TV
Television Bureau of Advertising (TvB), 329, *371*, 484
10-watt FM stations, 63n, 269
Texaco Star Theater, 187, 194n
Theater television, 567
Therapy, television as, 540–41

Third World broadcasting, *8–9*, 13–14, 16–19, 24–26, *31–33*, 568
Theories of communication, 545–61
35 mm film, *65*, 237
30-second commercials, *361*, 363
30 Minutes, 245
Thomas, Lowell, 161
Time-bank syndication, 208
Time base corrector, *76*, 86, 233
Time classes, advertising, 367
Time spent (audience effect) *391–92*, 519–20, *539*, 551
Time standards, commercial, 358–62
Timeliness (broadcasting attribute), 351
Time zones (re scheduling), 79, 202
Titanic disaster, *113–15*, 121, 139
Today, 194–95, 210, 227, 334, 354, 381 (fig.), 392
Toll broadcasting, 130–31
Tonight, 194, 208, 227
Top-40 formula, 169–171
Topless radio, 469–70
Tornillo case, 473
Toscanini, Arturo, 165
Toynbee, Arnold, 518
Trade deals, 370
Trade press, 512
Traffic function (in station organization), 328–29
Trafficking: of commercials, 356; in licenses, *415*, 419
Training for broadcasting, 346 (box)
Transatlantic: cable, 102; wireless, 115
Transduction, *44–45*, 102
Transfer of ownership, 415
Transistor, *110*, 150
Translators, 54 (table), *92*, 192
Transmission of radio energy, 46–52
Transmitter, radio, *44*, 46, 73–74
Transponder, *91*, *264*, 309
Transponder Allocation Committee (TAC), 264
Travellers Information Service (TIS), 62
Treaties, telecommunication, 138–39, *421–22*
Trials, court (broadcast coverage), 228, *472–73*; 524–25
Trinity Methodist Church case, 146
Triode, 109
Truman, President Harry, 558
Tubes, vacuum: Audion, 108–10, 119; kinescope, 76 (fig.); TV pickup, *67–68*, 70 (fig.)
Tuning: behavior, 386, 391; technology, 108

Turner, Ted, 309, 311, 332
TVRO. *See* Earth station
Twentieth Century Fund, 489, 511
Twentieth Century Reformation Hour, 440
Twenty-One, 209–11
Two-step flow, 546–47
Two-way cable TV, 305–07

UHF band, 14, 43 (table), 50 (table), 87
UHF television, 73 (table), 75, *188–.92*, 297, 429
U-Matic (VCR), 322
Unauthorized publication or use (of nonbroadcast radio), 409
Underground radio, 174
Underwriting, program, 270, 276–77
Unions: broadcasting administrations, 21; trade, 166–67, 347–48
Uniqueness of broadcasting: as advertising medium, 351–52; continuousness, *217*, 379; re critical standards, 246–247; re First Amendment, 469–71, 473–74, *477–90*; public investment in, *342*, 499, 518; responsibility to children, *469*, *526–27*; summary, 577–78; voracity, 154–56; wirelessness, *37*, 566. *See also* Scarcity principle
United Church of Christ, 488, 499, *501*, 505
UNESCO (U.N. Educational, Scientific & Cultural Organization), 32–33
United Nations, 31
United Press (UP), 160–61
United Press International (UPI), 103, 229
United Press International-Independent Television News (UPTIN), 229
Universal City Studios case, 423
University of Mid-America, 288
Uplinks, satellite, *91*, 264–65, 310 (fig.)
Upstairs, Downstairs, 282
USA Network (cable TV), 313 (fig.)
U.S. Commission on Civil Rights, 346–47, 526
USSR broadcasting, *7–8*, 22–23, 25–26, *29–30*

Van Doren, Charles, 210
Vanocur, Sander, 275, 533

Variables, research, *545–47*, 557
"Vast wasteland," *246*, 352, 431
Velocity, wave, 37, 40 (fig.), 42
Vertical blanking interval, *77*, 321 (fig.)
Vestigial sideband (VSB), 46
VHF band, 43 (table), *50* (table), 73 (table), 187–88
VHS (VTR format), 82, 322
Viacom Enterprises, 173, 316
Videocassette tape recorder (VCR), 82, 322
Video discs, 82, *84* (fig.), 322
Videotape recording (VTR), *81–83, 202–03*
Videotex, 320–21
Vidicon, 68 (photo)
Vietnam war, 273, 337, 480, 483, 498, 510, *536–38*
Violence in broadcasting: consumer opposition to, 504–05; defense of, 530–31; effects of, 527–30; in NAB code, 508; & network program policies, 197; research on, 553 (table), 556–57, 561
VLF band, 43 (table), *50* (table)
Voice of America, *26–28, 64–65,* 147, 403

Wald, Richard, 284
Wallace, Mike, *238,* 467, 524
Walters, Barbara, 194, *231*
Want ads, broadcast, 353n
Wants vs. needs, consumer, 518–19
War of the Worlds, 148, *547*
WARC '79, *13–14,* 151
Warner-Amex, 307, 317
Warner Cable, 302, 306
Warner-Lambert case, 365

Watergate: *See* Nixon; Nixon administration
Wave(s): amplification, 108–09; carrier, 43–44; detection, 108; generation, 106–07; light, 37–38; modulation, 44–46; motion concepts, 39–42; propagation, 46–52. *See also* Interference; Spectrum
Wavelength, *39–40,* 42–43
Weaver, Sylvester, *193,* 227
WEFM case, 505–506
Weighting (in ratings research), 390
Welk, Lawrence, 208
Welles, Orson, 148, 547
WESH case, 451
West, Mae, 145
West Germany, *See* German Federal Republic
Westar I satellite, 90 (fig.), 308, *264–65*
Western Electric, 111–12
Western Union, 102, *132,* 308
Westinghouse: & broadcasting, *125–29,* 330, 509; & cable TV, 302; origins, *112,* 119; & RCA, *123,* 125, 183
WGCB case, 477, *487–88*
WGLD case, 469–70
WHAR case, 475
WHDH case, *450,* 453
White House tapes, 174, 285, 495
Whitehead, Clay, 275 (box), *494*
"Who Says What" formula, 549
WHYY case, 284
Wide World of Sports, 197, *239*
Wild, Wild World of Animals, 208
Wilson, President Woodrow, 119, 123

Wire communication, *101–03,* 407
Wired radio, 8
Wireless, *103–06,* 113–16
Wirelessness (broadcasting attribute), *37,* 566
Wiseman, Frederick, 237
WLBT case, 201n, 447, 450, 453, *449*
WMAL-TV case, 500–01
WNCN Listeners Guild case, 506
Women in broadcasting, 345–47. *See also* Equal Employment Opportunities
World Administrative Radio Conference (WARC) of 1979, *13–14,* 59n, 151
World Premiere, 204
World TV standards, 72 (table)
World War I, *117–20,* 122–23, 254, 471, 545
World War II, 147–50, *161–64,* 546
World's Fair of 1939, 152, 186 (photo)
WPIX case, 479
Writ of certiorari, 413
Writers' Guild of America, 347
WXPN case, 268
WXUR case, *440,* 453, 466

X-rays, 37–38

Yale University Program on Communication & Attitude Change, 546
Young, Owen D., 123–25
"Youth Terror: The View Behind the Gun," 490

Zworykin, Vladimir, 183–84